THE BROTHERS
REUTHER

THE BROTHERS REUTHER

AND THE STORY OF THE **UAW**

A MEMOIR BY
VICTOR G. REUTHER

Illustrated with Photographs

Houghton Mifflin Company Boston 1979

Copyright © 1976 by Victor G. Reuther

Library of Congress Cataloging in Publication Data
Reuther, Victor G   1912–
The brothers Reuther and the story of the UAW.
Includes index.
1. Reuther, Victor G   1912–   2. Reuther,
Walter Philip, 1907–1970. 3. International Union,
United Automobile, Aircraft and Agricultural Imple-
ment Workers of America. 4. Trade-unions—Auto-
mobile industry workers—United States—History.
I. Title.
HD6509.R39A33   331.88'12'920924 [B]   76-840
ISBN 0-395-24304-1   ISBN 0-395-27515-6 pbk.

Printed in the United States of America

v 10 9 8 7 6 5 4 3 2 1

In Memory of our parents,
Valentine and Anna Stocker Reuther

Foreword

MY LAST CONVERSATION with Walter, only several days before his untimely death in May 1970, dealt in part with his often expressed intent to collaborate with me in the writing of this book. It was never our intention to attempt a history of the United Automobile Workers' Union, to whose organization, growth, and development we had dedicated our entire adult lives. Rather, we spoke of a very personal book that would relate the experiences of three brothers and a family bound together by common hopes and aspirations and tempered by common suffering and tragedy. In the preparation of this book, I have tried to hold to that commitment.

This is the story of social activists, not onlookers. Great controversies constantly swirled about our heads. In reporting on these, I have made no pretense of "objectivity," which is a luxury reserved for historians. At its best, a personal memoir offers only a partial and limited view. I have sought, however, to set forth with utmost candor and accuracy the events as we lived and experienced them. My own recall has been reinforced by frequent reference to voluminous personal papers and even more extensive documentation from personal files of both Walter and Roy, now at the Labor Archives at Wayne State University, Detroit. Fortunately, Walter was frequently able to dictate his recollections of events a few hours after they had taken place. I have quite naturally been under fewer restraints, political or personal, in relating conversations or incidents that involve people who are alive than I would have if each of us was still actively carrying public responsibilities. But this in no sense diminishes my awareness of an obligation not to substitute my views for those of anyone else, including my brothers. I have endeavored to present any differences among us with the same forthrightness with which they were customarily debated by us.

I wish to acknowledge my deep appreciation to Arthur M. Schlesinger, Jr., not only for having given me encouragement to move ahead with the book but for having provided the initial contacts with my publisher. I owe Joseph Rauh and Oscar Cohen, close friends and coworkers in so many civil rights and political battles, a particular debt for persuading me to stay with the project despite the many attractions that retirement offered. I am also in debt to vice-presidents Irving Bluestone and Doug Fraser of the UAW, whose warmth and friendship brought them into a unique relationship with each of the brothers Reuther. To all the members of my family, and especially to my wife, Sophie, who suffered through the long months of my obsession with completing this project, I wish to express my thanks for their indulgence and their patience.

Additional thanks go also to Dr. Philip Mason of the Labor Archives of Wayne State University for his genial and able assistance in helping me locate historical material. For the initial assistance in typing the manuscript I thank my former secretary, Hilda Frutig; for the much longer and more tedious help in typing each draft, an undertaking that extended well beyond a year, I am in debt to Mrs. Julie Allen, my neighbor and friend. For the tedious and painstaking review of this lengthy manuscript, for corrections of factual errors, and for substantive suggestions, I am in debt to my brother Ted, Fania (Mrs. Roy Reuther), and her son Alan, my sister, Chris (Mrs. Eugene Richey), Joseph L. Rauh, Jr., Irving and Zelda Bluestone, Ken Morris, Ben Stephansky, and, of course, my wife, Sophie and our sons, Eric and John.

In the arduous task of final checking of page proofs I pressed into service the expertise of two good friends, Ita and Bob Kanter, who in their own right contributed much to that part of history with which this book deals.

Because speaking was always easier than writing for the Reuthers, I yielded to the temptation to dictate the first draft of this book. Outwitting my efforts to trim and cut, it grew in length beyond all bounds. But I was rescued by the skillful editorial assistance of Gerta Prosser, who convinced me that in writing (in contrast to my accustomed soapbox speaking style) it was not really necessary to make the same point six different times for emphasis.

Reconstructing is always difficult, if not impossible; reliving parts of my life, especially the years of organized terror against us, when we were beaten and shot at, was harrowing! But to recall, at the same time, the many family reunions on the hill at Bethlehem; to savor the victories over private entrenched greed and arrogance; to reflect on progress against centuries of inbred bigotry and racial hatred — this has been therapeutic in healing the pain and loss of brothers in arms who are no longer at our side.

It has been said that history is prologue. Perhaps, then, our lives may provide a more sure path for those who will pick up the torch and run the next heat.

Washington, D.C.   V.G.R.
January 10, 1976

Contents

Illustrations

My turn came next. Here I am with Roy and Walter in May 1949, my first public appearance after being gunned down by a would-be assassin.

Walter, a lifelong abstainer, pledged to have a smoke and take a drink if he was elected President of the CIO. He was — and he kept his promise.

George Meany and Walter shake hands and hold aloft a gavel, marking the merger of the AFL and CIO in 1955. But their cordial relations proved short-lived.

At the summer home of Swedish Prime Minister Tage Erlander, Walter rows while Hubert Humphrey, Willy Brandt, and Erlander enjoy the ride.

Sophie and I are received by coal miners at Asansol in India, 1965.

"You are still the best cook," Walter tells our mother in the Reuther family kitchen, as our father looks on. The year is 1950.

The Reuther family, 1954: Gathered around our parents at their 50th Anniversary celebration in Bethlehem, West Virginia, are Ted, our sister, Christine, Roy, myself, and Walter.

My mother and Eleanor Roosevelt at the 1956 UAW convention in Atlantic City.

At the same convention, Walter introduces an "old soapboxer" — Valentine Reuther.

Leonard Woodcock, the new president of the UAW, presents me with the union's "Social Justice Award" on my retirement in 1972.

"He was the only friend I had": Alexander Cardozo, retired auto worker, breaks down in front of Walter's coffin.

THE BROTHERS REUTHER

CHAPTER 1

In Search of Freedom

"People will not look forward to posterity who never look backward to
their ancestors."

— EDMUND BURKE,
Reflections on the Revolution in France

MY FATHER, Valentine Reuther, was born August 26, 1881, in the
German village of Edigheim on the Rhine, not far from the French
border. When he was eleven, his parents, Jacob and Christine
(Fuchs) Reuther, emigrated with their three children to the United
States, settling in another small farming town, Effingham, Illinois.

Europe had been consumed for centuries by wars both political
and religious, and thousands had already fled from starvation of
body and repression of soul. By the end of the nineteenth century,
a conviction was deepening in many minds that the church — Protestant, Catholic, or Lutheran — was paying too much attention to
the afterlife of its parishioners and too little to their plights and miseries on earth. I heard that view expressed many times, when I was
a child, by my grandfather Jacob, and it was often echoed by my father. But only recently did I discover that members of my family
have been struggling with the doctrinaire authoritarianism of the
powers that be for at least three hundred years. The careers of the
Reuther brothers in twentieth-century America merely reaffirmed
convictions rooted deep in the inherited family consciousness.

According to Karl Otto Braun's excellent history of the area, the
inhabitants of Edigheim and its sister village, Oppau, were noted
from early days for their tendency to rebel. (I found to my surprise
that Copernicus had a grandmother born in Oppau.) They took up
the banner of the Reformation in 1556 and gave wide support to the
"new character of religious belief." The tide turned, however, when

Catholic Prince Johann Wilhelm came to power in 1690. In 1705 "he
ordered the church of Edigheim to embrace the traditional Catholic
views despite the fact that there was only a handful of Catholics in
the community. There followed many years of actual physical repression of the reformists by arbitrary removal of ministers, by use
of the public church press to attack the reformists as heretics . . ."
One item of special interest to me concerned a "protest against the
treatment given Dean Reuther because improper financial costs were
punitively leveled against Reuther's parishioners."

Jacob Reuther was about twenty years old when Bismarck began
his unification of the German states. After years of resisting domination by local princes, the Rhinelanders faced a new form of oppression, this time by Bismarck's great national campaign. Prussian
troops opened offices in nearby Ludwigshafen, and began to force
the residents of Edigheim and Oppau to join up. The Prussians
created more local resistance by collecting arms from private households, and it was apparently only the outbreak of fighting with
France that persuaded the Rhineland to back Bismarck.

Johannes Berry, an enthusiastic volunteer from Oppau, is reported to have said, as he took leave of a widow by the name of
Reuther, whose four sons had already been taken off to the front,
"Don't worry, mother [sic], we will beat the enemy until you are sick
of it." The Edigheim records show that forty-six of the town's con-
scripts died in France, among them Christopher Reuther II. The
village of Oppau contributed eighty-one young men, among them
George, Johann, Leonard, and Valentine Reuther III, all brothers.
The widow Reuther obviously did not have much to celebrate when
the victorious Peace of Versailles was signed.

There was no celebration in my grandfather's house, either.
Jacob, left behind to tend the farm during the war, found life difficult indeed. He had little to eat but potatoes and *schmir* — cottage
cheese. But Jacob had deep religious convictions against war, and at
least he had not been forced to take the life of another human
being: he regarded the killing of any living thing as a sin. Although
my grandfather was a farmer and spent his whole life on a farm, he
could never bring himself to slaughter animals, even to feed his family. His bitterness against war and the military was so intense and so
articulate that some of my most vivid memories are of long discussions with him, as well as with my own father, on that subject.

On March 20, 1872, Jacob married Christina Fuchs. Ten years

later, when there were already three children and the youngest, my father, was only a year old, a terrifying catastrophe struck: dams on the canals suddenly burst and an enormous wall of flood water ravished the two villages. For Jacob, who already found life in the Rhineland unacceptable for religious and political reasons, the long-term economic consequences of this tragedy were probably decisive. He decided to join his brother in America, and late in 1892 the family took passage on the steamer *Hermann,* bound for New York. There they boarded a train for the long ride to Effingham, Illinois, where Jacob's brother Christian had lived for some years. My father, Valentine Reuther, was then eleven years old.

His memories of childhood in Germany were mostly of hard work on the dairy farm; of a Lutheran church school where the teacher used the rod even when students were good; of sparse but adequate food; and of pranks that were not unlike our own. He was quite a marksman with his slingshot, and in the early mornings, after the hausfraus had brought the chamber pots out, rinsed them, and hung them up in the sun on the backyard posts, he would pick them off one by one. Later in life he found better targets.

Another memory is of a political event. Shortly before the family came to America, Edigheim and Oppau were considerably industrialized; there were cigar-making plants, textile mills, brick factories, and the like. A big employer in the district, a Dr. Gross, had managed to get himself elected to the Reichstag, and represented, naturally, the most conservative faction of the district. The workers had by this time become vaguely aware that they were being exploited by long hours, often extending into nights and Sundays, and extremely low wages, which sometimes went even lower when there was a surplus of available labor. Trade unions were off in the future, but an opposition political movement began to emerge. A local harnessmaker ran against the mill owner and incumbent, Dr. Gross, in what was a heated election. At one point Dr. Gross became so infuriated by the ingratitude of his employees, who were supporting a labor candidate against him, that he had an enormous banner placed across the factory entrance. It read:

> *Wer nicht wählt den Dr. Gross*
> *Seit am Morgen arbeitslos.*

> He who does not vote for Dr. Gross
> will find himself on the day after out of work.

This incident apparently led to intense family discussions both before and after the Reuther emigration, for the story had remained fresh in my father's mind. Grandfather Jacob passionately resented all injustice — he considered it immoral — and would certainly have favored political initiative on the part of Dr. Gross's workers. If Jacob were to be given a political label, it would be Christian Socialist; he was devoutly nonconformist in many areas. He took issue with the established church in Germany, and, quite naturally, in little Effingham he also had difficulty finding a Lutheran church that interpreted the word and will of God according to his lights. The orthodox fire-and-brimstone approach was not for him, and he refused to accept the idea that it was all right for our earthly life to be miserable so long as we could hope for a future in heaven. I remember whole notebooks filled with his articles interpreting religious concepts and their application to everyday realities and decisions. He felt it was an important responsibility of the church to promote social and economic conditions that would make it possible for people to live with one another on a brotherly basis. His opposition to war was a deep part of this conviction; his resistance to the growing pressure of the Prussian military, which was training young men to kill and to become cannon fodder themselves, was one of the prime factors in his decision to leave Europe.

According to my father, it was high adventure to emigrate to America at the age of eleven, to see New York City, and to discover, when he arrived in Illinois, that there were still Indians pitching their tents on the banks of the Wabash. Romance must certainly have been dimmed by hard work; there was the English language to learn and a dairy farm that demanded the toil of every member of the family. Grandfather Jacob had made a down payment on a farm on the outskirts of Effingham — a town even smaller then than it is now — and built a log cabin home no bigger than hard necessity required. Not only the children but Christina worked on the farm around the clock. Short, taciturn, serious, my grandmother knew what tough decisions had to be made merely to survive. When Jacob's religious sensibilities would not allow him to take life, it was Christina who killed the chicken and got the food on the table.

I remember the house well: no electricity even in my time because Jacob insisted on using the old lamp and lanterns; the only heat from the kitchen stove; the bedroom close by containing its old bed with six little steps leading up to it, bringing you near enough to the ceiling to enjoy what meager heat there was. I was reminded of it years later, when I traveled through eastern Europe and saw beds actually built on top of ovens.

Even without the Lutheran church school, my father would have had more than a normal share of religious indoctrination. Jacob Reuther lived out his beliefs, and when he could find no church in the area that espoused God in a manner he could accept, he chose to conduct church services every Sunday morning in his own house, inviting the neighbors to come and join my grandmother and their three children, Jacob, Christina, and Valentine, in singing the hymns. The sermons were his own. Small wonder that the local Lutheran church found Valentine so well versed in the Bible (and sufficiently at home in two languages) that they promoted him for a church training school, with the ministry in mind. But Grandfather, nonconformist, Christian Socialist, was not sure that the proposed training was the sort he wanted one of his children to receive. Valentine went on farming, and for many summers contracted to work for other farmers in the district to increase the family's cash income. His older brother, Jacob, had gone to live and work in Wheeling, where the mushrooming Ohio Valley steel industries promised more jobs than did farm country.

Those were hard summers; my father has admitted that there were times when he swiped eggs from his employer and sucked them raw in order to get enough strength to grow on. But grow he did, in both physical and intellectual stature.

My mother's father was also named Jacob, and her mother's first name was also Christina, though she was always called by her second name, Agatha. Grandfather Stocker, unlike most of his neighbors in Scharnhausen, a village not far from Stuttgart, tucked into a high fertile valley within view of the Swabian Alps, was not a farmer. He was a skilled craftsman — a wagonmaker — and a quiet, sensitive man who took pride in turning out the simple but charming V-shaped wagons so typical of Swabia. When my brother Walter and I on our *Wanderjahr* had the pleasure of several visits to Scharnhausen, we were always referred to by the villagers as "Wagonmaker Stocker's Anna's Victor and Walter." The allusion gave us a satisfying link with our dead grandfather, because we were already beginning to be involved in wagonmaking of our own — the automobile business.

My mother, Wagonmaker Stocker's Anna, was born on February

21, 1882. The person who exerted the strongest influence on her early life was her mother, Agatha, who had been brought up in the simple hard life of Scharnhausen, learning only to worship God and work hard in the fields and the home. She bore Jacob Stocker fourteen children; two died as infants and twelve were reared to adulthood. My mother was the eleventh in that long line.

Their home, still standing when Walter and I went to Germany in the thirties, was a two-story farmhouse with an attic, characteristic of the locale. The second floor served as the living area, and the ground floor housed the cattle and livestock. A section of their first floor had been turned into Jacob's workshop; as the family grew, the attic was finished off to provide additional sleeping quarters.

Each farm family in the village had several plots of land, usually widely scattered: one was best for growing grains, one for the famous pointed cabbage of the region, another for fruit trees and berry bushes. There was also communal land set aside for grazing; here cattle and geese were taken every day and, for a small fee, were watched over by certain members of the community before being led home each night to their own houses.

There were, of course, no newspapers, and all important tidings, whether of a birth or death or sale of cattle or land, were made known by a hired town crier, who, at set hours early in the morning and late in the evening, stood at a designated spot and called out the news.

The true center of village life was the Lutheran church. Its ancient structure dated back to the days of the Crusades; its bell tower rose high above the town and looked out over the entire valley. Here my mother and all her brothers and sisters were baptized; here she was confirmed when she was fourteen; and here she received her religious training, which was taken very seriously in the village. In Agatha's household there was probably little questioning of the church or social conditions, though it must have been to escape something unacceptable about life in the village that caused most of the sons, and daughters too, to emigrate to the Americas.

Agatha was a strong and dominating character, as, indeed, she had to be, since her husband, busy with his trade, had little time for farm work and she bore the full responsibility of managing the land as well as feeding and clothing twelve children. They, in turn, were expected to do chores at home and to carry a good share of the farm work under their mother's stern direction. Their education was equally important to Agatha. My mother could recall as a child going right from school, still carrying her books, into the fields, where she was required to review what she had studied during the day and discuss the homework while she worked together with her mother at that day's chore.

The army took each of Agatha's sons into the service and a heavy burden fell on the girls. Jacob, the oldest son, became a teacher after his army duty and left for Buenos Aires when my mother was only six. (He was soon married and launched on a business career as owner and manager of a large printing equipment firm.) Two years after he left home he wrote to his parents, asking that Anna be allowed to join him in South America, but Agatha refused — she needed Anna's labor in the fields. Soon after that another son and two daughters found their way to Wheeling, West Virginia, and Milwaukee. The Stocker family was dwindling. But the worst blow was the death by cancer of my grandfather Jacob Stocker when my mother was only fifteen.

Agatha, now a widow with young children still to raise, became even more demanding. There are stories about the neighbors warning, "Agatha, you are going to kill this girl Anna, you are working her so hard." But Agatha, whose life had always been difficult, believed in stoicism and courage. She needed the girls once her sons went off, some to the army and some later to America, the latter probably never to be seen by her again. When Theodore, the brother nearest to Anna in both age and companionship, finished his military service in Stuttgart and then followed his older brother Karl and two sisters to Wheeling, it was a distressing time for both Anna and her mother. Agatha was later to undergo the most severe anguish any mother could know: in the First World War she would know that her sons were pitted against each other.

When inflation and hunger struck, as they did many times in her long life, Agatha took care of her own. She had the Swabian thrift, which is more stringent than even the well-known Scottish variety, and she was ingenious in a crisis. I especially like the story of her outwitting a state inspector who, at a time of food scarcity, had come to the village to commandeer a certain percentage of the harvest and the livestock. Anticipating a visit from him, Agatha took some of her chickens and geese and fed them with bread that had been soaked in hard cider. When they became sufficiently drunk and quiet, she covered them with loose straw and hid them from the inspector. Her children first; the state could wait!

Every coin has its other side; perhaps Agatha's strength was the kind that defeats itself. When Anna was in her teens there was only one brother, Adolf, left to help with the farming, and he married young and took on his own family obligations, leaving only a few girls to carry the full load of maintaining the wheat fields, the cabbage plots, and the orchard. The sale of farm products did not bring in enough cash and Anna had to hire herself out to help harvest the vineyards in the Necker Valley. The experience proved to be a stimulating one; it allowed her to enter for the first time what was, so to speak, a new world. A still more exciting event occurred soon after: Anna fell in love.

Agatha turned thumbs down on the young man.

In the village of Scharnhausen, social status was closely related to the size of the manure pile that stood just in front of the house. While widow Agatha Stocker had modest means compared to many in the area, she was extremely proud of the Stocker cattle and the resulting manure pile. She was also adamant about not permitting any of her daughters to marry beneath their social standing. Anna had fallen in love with Fritz Glohr, whose family operated a general store and owned no farm land. What made Fritz even less acceptable was that he had worked in Esslingen, a semi-industrialized area, where he had come in contact with the wage system, a highly corrupting influence in the view of the conservative Scharnhausen farmer. Even worse, this young man had apparently embraced, at a very tender age, the concepts of social democracy and had become known in the community as a "radical." Agatha, whenever she spotted Fritz, used to remark, "There he comes again, wearing his red tie."

Anna, nevertheless, was in love with Fritz and met him in secret on every possible occasion. They managed to sneak off many a Sunday afternoon to meet at the foot of the great linden tree on the road to Nellingen.

When Anna was seventeen and of marriageable age, she and Fritz began to speak of a wedding. Agatha would not hear of it. Stony and implacable, she set about not to lose one more child; she would never allow Fritz to enter the house. Anna poured her heart into letters to her favorite brother, Theodore, in America. But no one in the family dared intercede on such a delicate issue with the strong-willed Agatha.

One day in desperation Anna said to her mother, "If you won't let me marry Fritz, then I'll go to America!" As she told us the story later, this was said more as a threat and an assertion of independence than as a true intention, but Agatha angrily responded, "All right. I'd rather have you go to America than marry him!" Having made the threat, my mother, herself no weakling, felt obliged to carry it through, but she suffered great conflict and strong misgivings; there were numerous tearful sessions with Fritz, who swore to his love for her and promised to follow her across the ocean. After many letters back and forth between Scharnhausen and Wheeling, West Virginia, Theodore and sister Katie finally invited Anna to join them in America.

There is no way of knowing whether Agatha had regrets. My mother recounted that she herself was more sad than excited; she was leaving not only her village, but her first love. Agatha relented to the point of letting Fritz come to the farewell party. Anna sailed on the steamer *Vaterland,* arrived in New York on September 27, 1902, and took a train to West Virginia — ten years after my father had arrived and taken his train to Illinois. Fritz Glohr, "the radical," did not follow Anna to America, in spite of good intentions, and she married Valentine Reuther, as fate decided.

CHAPTER 2

Farm Hand to Industrial Unionist

MY FATHER made his second and perhaps more important migration when he was eighteen; he moved from a farming to an industrial society. Seven American years of church schooling, taking care of cattle, cleaning barns, sucking eggs to get enough nourishment was not really a new world. Europeans did not come to the United States for a change of scene, but for a change in opportunity, for political freedom and economic security. Val Reuther, like thousands of young immigrants, chose the industrial revolution as the means to win freedom and security. In the fall of 1899, when the crops were in and he felt that Grandfather Jacob would be able to take care of the cattle over the winter, my father made his leap.

The distance to Wheeling was not far in miles, but it was indeed a move into a wholly different era. Ideally situated on the Ohio River, a busy route for commerce, Wheeling at the turn of the century was bursting with expansion. Local industries had started as far back as 1812, when an embargo was placed on European products. A wealth of coal energy in the hills and magnificent water transport to the Mississippi and the South made it a natural industrial center. In addition, Wheeling was a major stop on the first national highway, based on the old pike from Cumberland, Maryland, which in its turn had followed the path of an ancient Indian trail.

Although the Civil War divided Wheeling in two, most of the factories supplied the needs of the North. Nonetheless, some Wheeling entrepreneurs were sufficiently avaricious to send cannons, balls, and armor plate to the Confederacy. The Virginia-based owners of the Benwood iron works were among them.

During a much later controversy — a diminutive civil war of another sort — Senator Joseph McCarthy gave Wheeling plenty of un-

solicited publicity when he chose the city for the political scalping
and beheading of many high State Department officials. I doubt he
was aware of a macabre historical coincidence: the name Wheeling
comes from the Delaware Indian word that sounds like "wealin" and
means, quite literally, "the place of the head." Early fur traders and
mapmakers were told by the Delawares that a white trader had been
scalped and his head affixed to a pole at the mouth of what later was
known as Wheeling Creek. George Washington noted the site of
"Wealin or Scalp Creek" in his journal.

The land beside Wheeling Creek — a wild and primitive terrain —
was a popular place for our family picnics, and we used to wander
about the farms in the creek valley looking for bare areas where the
cabbage or corn was not growing properly; this was a sign that the
Indians had once built fires there, and we would find arrowheads
and other artifacts beneath the soil. The Indian civilization around
Wheeling went as far back as 3500 B.C. Polished stones and some
magnificent tools and weapons had been found by others before us.
In Moundsville, just south of Wheeling in the Ohio Valley, sits the
gigantic Great Mound, the most notable pyramid among many left
by a culture that lived in the Ohio Valley between 100 and 500 B.C.

Wheeling had its own Daniel Boone, a man by the name of Lewis
Wetzel. Captured by the Indians when he was fourteen, he escaped
some time later, vowing vengeance on them all, and doing quite well
at keeping his word until a general truce was called between the government and the Indians. Under the new dispensation Wetzel was
jailed for the murder of an Indian, although before the truce such
an act had been considered a patriotic sport, not a crime. We lived
for many years on a street named after this famous Indian fighter.

The fertile Ohio Valley proved to be fortunate hunting ground
for all kinds of pioneers in the nineteenth century, especially craftsmen and businessmen: cigar makers, glass blowers, shipbuilders, mill
owners, big brewery men, and the first steel capitalists. As early as
1840, Wheeling began turning out the famous long, thin Virginia-
style cigars known as stogies. Mr. Mefflin M. Marsh started it all by
selling his handmade cigars to the debonair river-boat men and the
drivers and longshoremen on the wharves of Wheeling. My father
took to stogies as readily as he took to Wheeling and was never
without one to the end of his life.

It was the cigar makers who built up one of the strongest and most democratic unions in the country, one with excellent educational and cultural activities. It is interesting to remember that Samuel Gompers, the founder of the American Federation of Labor, at one point in his life was employed by this union as a "reader." In those days, when the labor force was composed mostly of immigrants, a reader was hired by the union to read to the workers not only the news of the day but the great classics, too, as they busily cut and rolled the tobacco. Val Reuther was deeply impressed with the emphasis the cigar makers' union placed on education; it influenced him to continue his own education, even after his marriage, and had a lasting effect on his concept of what a union should be.

Around 1851, glassmaking became a very important industry in the area, beginning with crude windowpanes, then branching into very fancy crystals, some of which became museum pieces. When my brothers Ted and Walter were boys, they worked in the Northwood Glass Factory, just around the corner from our first house in South Wheeling.

Paddle-wheel river boats were launched from Wheeling shipyards to go down the length of the Mississippi. Calico with the "boot" trademark was made by J. L. Stifel and Sons and shipped away to far countries. In 1884 the first steel was made at Bellaire and the Benwood Bessemer plant, signaling the next round of the industrial revolution. Last but not least, at the end of the century, just about the time Val Reuther was seeking his fortune in Wheeling, beer was pouring into bottles at the rate of eight hundred thousand gallons a year, and the breweries were employing around 150 men, a sizable number for that period.

Val Reuther had no idea what the brewing business would eventually mean to him when, tired but wide-eyed with anticipation, he got off the train that morning in 1899, to be met by his brother Jake and taken to a very proletarian boarding house jammed with immigrants. Dusty South Wheeling was known as Ritchie Town and was full of Germans, Poles, Scandinavians, Yugoslavs, and Irishmen, making about fifteen cents an hour in America instead of twenty-five cents a day in Europe. With Jake's help, Val wangled a job as a laborer in the Riverside Ironworks in Benwood, where he worked seventy-two hours a week, six days' worth of twelve-hour shifts, for $1.50 a shift. The pay looked pretty good to the farm boy from Effingham, but he was not sure he could stay in Wheeling permanently; he felt responsible for his parents and the family farm. He had borrowed the train fare from Jake; he had that to repay, and his return fare to save up. He saw immediately that he must get a more skilled job than that of mill hand. If a man became a "heater" in the rolling mill, he was really in the big money, earning ten to twelve dollars for that same twelve-hour shift.

Such jobs were not easy to come by. Val, as he later told us, began by establishing personal relations with the foreman, and expressing interest in the job. Then he began to go to work at four in the morning, an hour earlier than his own job required, to observe the heater at work on the furnace, and to pick up the tricks of the trade. He waited anxiously for an opening. Finally there was a break; one of the men was ill and Val was there, ready and willing. He charged the furnace well and was soon working as a relief heater.

This new job put him in the aristocracy of labor, eligible to join the Amalgamated Association of Iron, Steel, and Tin Workers. In those days, trade unions were not interested in organizing the unskilled workers. Val attended the meetings regularly and was stimulated by the discussions of social issues, in which he evidently took an active part. Because he was bilingual, he easily established rapport with many of the immigrant workers. He was disturbed by the prejudice against the recent arrivals, the "foreigners," as his father had been distressed by the discrimination against the workers imported into Edigheim, merely from another part of Germany, to build canals. He could not understand why these men should not join the union; he felt that the combined interests of skilled and unskilled workers would strengthen the organization. How could a small, elite group possibly stand up against the powerful employer? It was bad enough, he insisted, that the employers exploited the so-called Hunkies, Micks, Wops, Polacks, and others, why should workers scorn one another merely because of differences in birthplace and way of life?

There was growing dissatisfaction in the Riverside Ironworks. The hours were intolerable: for some it was a seven-day week with perhaps a whole month of work without a day off, and for the bulk of the men the wages were pitifully low. They lived cramped together in shabby rooming houses, many of them unable even to hope that they could save enough money to send for their families back in Europe. When the pressure of discontent caused a strike to be called by the trade union, made up of the craft elite, whose wages were far higher than those of the majority, Val knew the strike would fail unless the unskilled workers, who had a much greater stake in winning, could be involved enough to give their solid support. He walked the picket line, spoke at many rallies, and tried to bridge the gap between the craft union men and the unorganized mill hands. This put him in a crossfire between two camps: his employer had already marked him as a troublemaker, and his own craft colleagues disdained him for trying to water down the quality of their union with ignorant, common laborers.

The strike failed. The mill closed, never to be reopened under its old management. The workers were bitter and disaffected, and the cause of trade unionism at that mill was set back for years. In fact, the working conditions in the steel industry were to remain substandard for most of my father's life. It was not until the Congress of Industrial Organizations held its great drive in the thirties, when mill hands and skilled workers were at last organized into one industrial union, that the vicious twelve-hour shift was changed into the eight-hour day and wages and conditions were significantly improved.

Val was now out of work. He still had not repaid his brother; he had rent and food to pay for; his clothes were becoming threadbare. He searched the entire city for work — docks, glass factories, calico plants where girls received only $2.50 a week and the men's wages were almost as low and everyone worked from twelve to sixteen hours a day with ten-minute breaks for meals. At last one of the men in the German singing society (the Beethoven Gesangverein), of which my father was an active member, suggested he might get a job at the Schmulbach Brewing Company as helper to the driver of a team of horses delivering enormous kegs of beer to outlying areas around Wheeling. He applied and got the job. The pay was low but my father enjoyed being out of doors, and he found nostalgic pleasure in working again with horses. Six months later Val Reuther was driving his own team of four horses.

Out of his small pay he managed periodically to send some money to his parents in Effingham, and in later years, especially after we came along, there were some visits back and forth, although Grandfather came to Wheeling only after Grandmother's death at the age of eighty-five.

The Schmulbach Brewing Company turned out to be fate's accomplice in bringing my mother and father together. When Anna Stocker first came to Wheeling, she lived with her married brother Karl and older sister Katie. Karl ran a small dairy farm out near the Run, a stream that flowed down from the Wheeling hills and passed quite near the brewery. Katie was already employed as housekeeper for the Hofreuters, who lived across from the Schmulbach brewery. Mr. Hofreuter operated a large saloon nearby. By good chance, he needed a cook to prepare the lunches that were served free with the beer, and Anna, too independent and too accustomed to hard work to sit idle and be supported by her brother, took the job. On the side, she was required to help take care of the four small Hofreuter children. This was hardly the work she had expected to find in the New World, where "the streets were paved with gold," and she was too embarrassed to write home to Agatha — much less to Fritz — that she was only a cook in a saloon.

Val and his fellow workers often had lunch there, and he soon noticed the attractive, red-haired Swabian girl. He was also delighted by the improvement in the menu; he liked her cooking from the start. Anna, who spoke no English, must have enjoyed talking in her own tongue to someone her own age. Val began to spend more and more time hanging around the saloon, and eventually was escorting her on Wednesday nights to the singing society, where she met more young German immigrants. Val had already met Karl Stocker at meetings of the society, and he was soon a frequent visitor at the dairy farm. But Anna herself was still thinking of Fritz, and it was eighteen months before she gave up that dream and allowed the casual friendship with Val to turn into courtship.

They were married at Karl's house on June 9, 1904, in a German Lutheran ceremony. They had rented a very modest furnished flat on Wood Street, which Anna had spent part of her wedding day cleaning and preparing. But since the festivities lasted into the early morning hours and Val, who could get only the one day off, had to report for work at the brewery at 4:00 A.M., poor Anna had to spend her first married night alone, still in her brother's home.

The Hofreuters were fond of Anna (they had offered to hold her wedding at their house) and urged her to go on working for them at least until she had children. Val objected at first because of masculine pride, but in the end he conceded. Anna did not work for long,

however; Theodore, my oldest brother, was born in 1905, Walter in
1907, Roy in 1909, and I in 1912. There was a gap of eleven years
before my only sister, Christine, was born. My parents found slightly
larger quarters, a three-room second-floor apartment on Jacob Street,
within easy walking distance of the brewery, in the center of the
working-class district of South Wheeling. For the next few years,
the family was to remain in this grimy, soot-laden section of town,
sandwiched in between the Baltimore and Ohio Railroad tracks on
one side, factories and coal mines on the other.

The house had no electricity when we were young; kerosene
lamps were succeeded by natural gas ones with wicks. Water had to
be carried into the house from a municipal hydrant, and of course
there was no indoor toilet. Walter often recalled his childhood terror at the privy, which was built onto the back of a stable. He would
be comfortably seated when a horse tethered in the stable would
decide to kick the back wall, nearly knocking the small boy down
through the hole. (This may explain Walter's lifelong aversion to
horses.)

Our mother had her full share of Agatha's Swabian thrift. She
saved all the flour sacks, bleached them for pillowcases, or sewed
them together for sheets. She made our clothes, and she made soap
out of fat drippings, lye, and other ingredients. I was already in my
teens before I realized there was any soap other than the homemade
kind.

Many other customs from the Old World persisted in South
Wheeling on Jacob Street, not all of them associated with thrift and
hard work. There was the prayer before every meal; there was the
music that goes wherever Germans go. Mother loved to sing Swabian folk songs and my father enjoyed both his Rhineland songs and
the classical music he had learned in the formal male chorus of the
Beethoven Gesangverein. He had bought a small bowl-backed Italian
mandolin and played it by ear. According to my mother, some of
their pleasantest hours in those early days were spent sitting on the
stoop, making music while the neighbors either joined in or expressed their appreciation.

Wheeling had four legitimate theaters then and one cinema. It
was one of the first four cities in the United States to build an electric street-car system, and Anna could easily get downtown to buy
some calico or a pair of shoes. During a Saturday shopping trip, a

hungry baby could be nursed right on the street car, and if any one of the women left a parcel, it would be returned to her later by the conductor; he knew the names of all the residents of South Wheeling.

Best of all for entertainment were the great outings at Mozart Park, high on one of the hills overlooking the town. Here not only Germans, but Poles too gathered in the outdoor theaters or in the beer gardens for singing festivals and picnics and general gaiety.

In conjunction with the Beethoven Gesangverein, a turnverein, or German gymnastics society, had been organized. Though Val was never much taken with gymnastics, he got to know a second cousin there, a young man who was to have a great influence on his life and career. Philip Reuther was also from Edigheim and Dad had helped bring him to the U.S. at the request of other members of the family. It was he who introduced my father to the Socialist movement in this country. Though Val had been active in the steel mill union, and even before his marriage had helped organize a union in the Schmulbach Brewing Company, he had never, before his friendship with Philip, come in contact with the Socialist literature from the Debs organization and from the Kansas Socialist publishing houses. Soon he was reading not only Debs and other union leaders, but also Plato and Aristotle, the famous Lincoln-Douglas debates, and other Kansas paperbacks, including the lectures of the agnostic Robert Ingersoll. He frequently referred to all of these works during our family discussions.

My father's union work was the major interest of his life. There was no union when he first went to work for the brewery, and after his disillusioning experience in the steel mill, he was determined that the brewery should not be organized on a strictly craft basis but should embrace all the workers, including the teamsters. He secured a charter from the International Brewery Workers' Federation, and this, of course, soon led to conflict with the International Brotherhood of Teamsters, who claimed jurisdiction over the drivers of the wagons. This attempt to fragment the working force was bitterly resisted by my father, who claimed that the principle of industrial unionism was essential to the workers' interests. He fought against the artificial separation of the skilled and more highly paid from the menial laborers, and he was successful in that effort. I remember that he spoke with some pride about the relationship he had established (he was the union spokesman from the beginning) with the owners of the brewery, which was one of mutual respect based on the strength and security held by each side. He believed that direct negotiations should always be conducted with courtesy and consideration for the other party's views. He never lost his faith that when men of reason deliberate together, disputes can be settled, amicably and without violent conflict, across the bargaining table.

Wheeling at that time had a total union movement of roughly four thousand members, organized into some forty-two separate trade or craft unions, and united into a central labor body known as the Ohio Valley Trades and Labor Assembly. When the Schmulbach brewery was organized, Val Reuther was elected its delegate to the Ohio Valley Assembly, where he came into contact with many other trade union representatives. He became deeply involved in the office to which he had been elected, and his skill as a speaker and negotiator were soon well known. But the more he was required to speak at meetings, to contribute to labor journals, and to testify before state legislative committees, the more painfully aware he became that his formal education had been limited. He therefore began to augment it, making an arrangement, in 1909, with the Wheeling branch of the International Correspondence Schools. He enrolled in courses in spelling, grammar, public speaking, and a host of other subjects. He loved words, both spoken and written, and worked hard to improve his comprehension of a language that not long before had been foreign to him. He also continued to expand his working knowledge of German, and read extensively in the works of Goethe, Schiller, and other writers of the classics. I remember many an evening when we would be sitting around the kitchen table doing our homework and my father would ensconce himself in the living room, where he had his desk and small collection of books, to study for many uninterrupted hours.

Val Reuther was often called to distant parts of West Virginia to help the coal miners, who were beginning to organize against tremendous odds in communities, completely controlled by the mine operators, where they were subject to brutal oppression by local police and state troops. He was also asked frequently to journey to Charleston, the state capital, to give testimony before the legislative committees that were considering the banning of child labor, an issue that was burning hotly in many parts of the country. My father remembered with some passion that dramatic period. When we gathered for his eighty-fourth birthday in Walter's house, I recorded some of his words:

It had been the practice of the coal mine employers in West Virginia to work the children of the miners who worked for them. If a man had a son of eleven or twelve years, they would frequently lay off the father so that the family would be compelled to make the child work in the mines or else do without bread, because they never had any cash money. They were required to buy at the company store, where prices were from twenty-five to thirty percent higher than in any other stores. And these children, naturally, if they met with an accident, they perished.

For six years we had attended the sessions of the West Virginia legislature, pleading with them to pass a law prohibiting the employment of men under eighteen. But it was always defeated because those members of the legislature who did not willingly, out of their conviction, vote in support of the bill, they bribed them. And so, each session, the bill was defeated. At the fourth session I appeared before the committee that had the bill under consideration and I told them . . . that if this bill is not passed and you read an account in the daily papers where children of that tender age had again been killed in the mine, then ask your conscience who the guilty party is. I say it's members of the legislature who have refused year after year to pass this law protecting these children and give to them that God-given right that every child has, to go to school and develop the talent which God created there, to the end that, when they have completed their education, they can make their full contribution to a fuller and richer life. I walked through one of the little towns in southern West Virginia at the early hour of four in the morning and I saw a child twelve years old leading a mule into the mine. I saw them bring that child out, his body crushed and mutilated from falling stone. They brought him out on a truck and I saw the mother taking that crushed and mutilated body in her arms and trying with kisses to bring those cold and unresponsive lips to life. Tears came to my eyes and I vowed to the heavens that I would fight that greedy system of child exploitation as long as I had a breath of life in me.

And I again appearing before that committee, they finally passed the law prohibiting the employment of children under eighteen, and I said to the delegates in the congregation, I said, "This indicates that if the men and women in West Virginia that have to work for a living would go to the polls and vote for the right kind of men, this law would have been passed years and years ago and the lives of hundreds of children that were killed in the mines would be here today." I tried to impress upon them that the ballot was the strongest weapon that working men and women had if they just exercise it and use it in the right way. "Don't vote for men because they're a member of your party. Examine

their records. Vote for working men and they will pass laws for the
benefit of the working man. If you elect lawyers or men of industry,
they will pass laws denying working men their God-given rights in order
to make more profit for themselves." And I say that today, that the
ballot is the best weapon we have if we only use it intelligently . . . I did
as my conscience dictated. I believed that with all my heart and I
believe that today. I have never missed a primary. I've talked to
hundreds of people . . . "Oh, it's a primary," and I've said, "Yes, it's a
primary and it's very important. If you don't nominate the right man,
how the heck are you going to vote for him?"

Val Reuther had great success in establishing good and stable
labor relations in the Schmulbach Brewing Company, but he observed during his travels that the arrangement at the brewery was
the exception rather than the rule. He saw the arrogance with
which most employers treated their workers in the steel, glass, and
other industries, and knew that these same industrial princes dominated the influential politicians in both major parties. A degree of
class-consciousness inevitably developed in Val and his fellow delegates to the Ohio Valley Trades and Labor Assembly. It was obvious to them that working men could not look for any real help from
the political party of their employer, be it Republican or Democrat.
My father, therefore, became more and more active in support of
the Socialist Party and especially the candidacy of Eugene V. Debs,
whom he had known of long before the presidential campaign of
1904. Debs's extraordinary efforts in support of the railway workers
in the great national strike that provoked the injunction, followed by
the government's use of troops, and, finally, his imprisonment had
given Debs the stature of a martyred hero in the trade union movement. It was only natural that my father found himself working beside Debs, sometimes traveling on the famous "Red Special," but
more frequently going to workers' rallies and to meetings of ethnic
groups to make speeches and elicit their support for Debs as President on the Socialist ticket. Three times — in 1904, 1908, and
1912 — he campaigned all over the state in Debs's behalf.

His relationship with Debs became ever more intimate when Debs
faced the largest challenge of his life — his open opposition to the
U.S. entry into World War I. He was, as all know, convicted of a
violation of the Espionage Act and sentenced to ten years in jail.
There was such an outcry over the harshness of this sentence and

such a widespread undercurrent of feeling against the war, that the Socialist Party decided to run Debs for President in 1920, even while he was in prison. In the fall of 1919, when Debs was still in the Moundsville penitentiary just south of Wheeling, my father and Walter Hinton, editor of the labor newspaper, *The Majority*, frequently visited the prison, and on one occasion Walter and I were taken along. As I recall, it was the last visit my father had with Debs before he was transferred to the Atlanta penitentiary.

Val literally worshiped the man for his integrity of principle, his compassion, and his burning zeal for justice. But my personal recollection is of an enormous tenderness, and I shall never forget the way Debs greeted Walter and me and patted us on the head and shoulders; I had the feeling we were in the presence of an extraordinarily warm and affectionate person. Nor can I forget the moment when we said goodbye. Debs, dressed in prison garb and looking quite gaunt, maintained the characteristic twinkle in his eyes, and my father was obviously hard-pressed to find words — which was most unusual, because he was a man who never lacked words to express his strong feelings. When the heavy iron gate slammed shut with a clang, I saw tears running down my father's cheeks. I had never seen him weep before. On the way back to Wheeling there was no conversation, until my father broke the silence, shaking his head and saying over and over again, "How can they imprison so kind and gentle a man!"

More than any other individual, Eugene Debs taught my father the lesson he so often repeated to us: there is a relation between the bread box and the ballot box. What we want to achieve must be won not only in the work place but in the political arena as well. Val's application of this principle is described in a history of the West Virginia State Federation of Labor from 1903 to 1957 by Evelyn L. Harris and Frank J. Krebs, entitled *From Humble Beginnings*. The following passage refers to a moment in 1912 when would-be presidential candidates were jostling for position, and the struggle for control of the major political parties was taking place:

> The State Federation had refused to identify itself with one political party on numerous occasions. Yet here in Wheeling the delegates almost openly endorsed the Socialist ticket, both State and National . . .
> One reason why the West Virginia Labor Body had listened to "the thunder on the left" was the influence of certain delegates upon the

Wheeling Convention. The manifesto calling on all workers to unite was introduced by Valentine Reuther, a delegate from the Wheeling Beer Drivers' local, and two other brewery workers, one from Wheeling and the other from Huntington.

The resolution expressed Val Reuther's belief that "politics without economics has no orientation and economics without politics has no engine to propel and guide it toward the welfare of the working man."

Harris and Krebs went on to summarize my father's career:

Valentine Reuther, whose son Walter P. Reuther became president of the United Automobile Workers and vice-president of the AFL-CIO, was a leader of the labor movement in Wheeling. He was an active delegate to the 1911 and 1912 conventions of the State Federation working diligently to strengthen the state labor organization. Val Reuther worked for $1.50 a day and brought up four sons and a daughter to lead distinguished lives. He ran the Wheeling Local Brewers' Union so effectively that his workers never had to strike. At the age of 23, he became President of the Ohio Valley Trades and Labor Assembly, the central labor organization of Wheeling. Val Reuther lived in the days when it took courage to act publicly as a labor leader. It took double courage in Valentine's case because in politics he was linked with Debs and the Socialists. Val Reuther had run unsuccessfully for the State Legislature, from the Wheeling district, on the Socialist ticket. "Socialism in American politics has been most thoroughly under German influence," according to one writer. Wheeling had a strong German element. This German influence reached back to the founding of the state of West Virginia . . . Sixteen delegates at the 1912 State Federation had German names, including the three delegates Reuther, Reiber and Seidler, who introduced the "unity of workers" resolution.

Val Reuther's sons were to pick up the gauntlet in the thirties and challenge the conservative AFL national leadership.

As in other parts of the country, the German community in Wheeling suffered from the First World War in both subtle and open ways. As patriotic protestations reached an almost ridiculous crescendo and war bond rallies were staged in the main streets of Wheeling, one technique used for selling bonds was to hang the Kaiser in effigy on a scaffold and, with each additional thousand dollars' worth of bonds sold, hoist the figure up one more inch. During a parade down Market Street, one of the oldest music houses in town threw all of its recordings of German classics and German folk songs out into the street as the crowd marched by.

With very few exceptions the German immigrants loved their new citizenship and were working hard to prove their loyalty. For Val and for all the Reuthers there was no question of divided allegiance. Val's love of America was as deep as his religious faith, and like his father before him he had no reason to be attached to the Kaiser or to any potentate. "Too often kings are highwaymen who by superior physical force have robbed merchants and plundered," Grandfather Jacob said many times in my memory. As for the divine right of kings, he declared that his God "never has been in partnership with bandits or outlaws."

Both Jacob and his son Valentine were emotionally and intellectually committed to democracy. Neither of them believed that war solved any problems or ensured the well-being and rights of the people. The jingoist slogan, "Make the world safe for democracy," was never accepted by my father. When Debs was imprisoned for his opposition to our entering the war, Val stood by him, sharing Debs's view that democracy in Germany would certainly not be established by the weight of American arms. Indeed, they felt that the development of a war economy and the strengthening of the military and its conservative political allies would weaken democracy in the United States. How prescient they were! For following quickly on the heels of World War I came the greatest single threat to American liberalism and civil rights: the Palmer raids, and the attempt to destroy both unionism and any political opposition in the country.

The enemies of labor in Wheeling as elsewhere sought to identify the opponents of war as pro-German and pro-Kaiser, and my father became the butt of ugly personal and political attacks. Vigilantes painted our front door yellow and sent anonymous diatribes through the mail. While the hysteria lasted, the Board of Education in Wheeling discontinued the teaching of German in the schools. The Beethoven Gesangverein, other German organizations, and German newspapers published in the area had to operate under a thickening smog of suspicion.

CHAPTER 3

Winning and Losing

MY FATHER'S battles were not all fought on a statewide stage. His energies and passions were fired by several controversies right in Wheeling, some to be won and some lost. One of the most colorful was the Carnegie Library affair, which came to a head as far back as 1904, the year of his marriage.

In the early eighties a group of citizens had built a small library in Wheeling that was soon after taken over and maintained by the Board of Education and paid for by means of a special real estate tax. Then in 1899, Andrew Carnegie, steel monarch and intransigent foe of the trade union movement, entered the picture with an offer to erect a new public library in Wheeling, provided the city would contribute to the tune of at least 10 percent of his capital gift. The city was led to believe that the donation would be in the neighborhood of $50,000 to $70,000. Carnegie at that time was busy disposing of the excess millions he had made by shrewdly investing his U.S. Steel profits (some $250 million). Carnegie Hall in New York and various other institutes and foundations had sopped up a good deal of the excess, but not enough, and he hit upon the idea of engraving his name in over two thousand communities throughout the country by making cash grants for local libraries.

The Wheeling public authorities do not appear to have been in any great rush to take advantage of this proposal, and about five years went by without their taking action on it. Finally, at the end of 1903, the city fathers began to feel considerable pressure from the Carnegie interests, and arranged for a favorable recommendation from the Board of Education. Acceptance of the library proposal would obligate the city to raise extra funds for maintenance, so a referendum on a special bond issue was set for January 16, 1904.

The *Daily Intelligencer* was busy urging the public to support the bond issue: "The gentlemen who have so earnestly championed the acceptance of Mr. Carnegie's munificent offer are entitled to the thanks of the go-ahead citizens of this community." Those go-ahead citizens were the Board of Trade, all Wheeling newspapers, the Mayor, the Council, and the Board of Education. But they had reckoned without the Ohio Valley Trades and Labor Assembly and Val Reuther.

The name "Carnegie" evoked bitter memories in the minds of all workers and trade unionists in the Ohio Valley. According to Horace B. Davis's account in *Labor and Steel,* when a strike was called, in 1892, against a steel mill in Homestead, Pennsylvania, to protest a series of wage cuts, Carnegie's response was to import from the East and Midwest 312 Pinkerton agents armed with 250 rifles, 300 pistols, and a big supply of ammunition, in addition to hundreds of strike-breaking thugs called "watchmen." They came up the Monongahela River on barges from Youngstown, Ohio, late in the night of July 5, 1892. Steelworker scouts spotted them, and at dawn virtually the entire population of Homestead — some twelve thousand men, women, and children — lined the banks of the river as the barges tried to land. Many lost their lives in the fighting. The strike was broken and the plant resumed operation by October, but Carnegie now had blood on his hands. The central Ohio Valley Assembly, under my father's leadership, drafted a resolution to the City Council proposing that the donation of $50,000 to the city of Wheeling "for the purpose of erecting a library with conditions attached . . . to perpetuate the name of Andrew Carnegie at the expense of the taxpayers" be rejected and that the money go "to the widows and orphans created by him on the banks of the Monongahela River on the morning of July 5, 1892."

On Christmas Eve, 1903, the *Daily Intelligencer* pulled out all the stops: "Mr. Carnegie is so situated that any affront to him at this time might in the end prove very disastrous to the physical welfare of Wheeling." The editor then cited all the steel mills in the vicinity of Wheeling as evidence of the city's dependence on the man. "We desire Mr. Carnegie's good will. He deserves our good will."

The Trades and Labor Assembly had by that time met in emergency session to organize what they knew would be a tough battle with the city fathers. They covered the city, precinct by precinct, with leaflets and handbills, and held meetings on street corners and in public halls. Mounted on a soapbox at Fourteenth and Market Place, my father warned that a Carnegie-built library would undoubtedly contain mostly books with an antilabor bias. Other spokesmen compared the library money to the "thirty pieces of silver." They called it blood money.

By this time the city fathers were shaken by the force of the opposition. The Board of Trade tried in vain to woo the Carpenters' and Joiners' Local to support the library. These craft workers declared that they wanted a library that would be Wheeling's own, "not a Carnegie monument where a large portion of our citizens could only enter with repugnance and servility."

The bond issue was defeated by a slim 201 votes, but the labor movement had come of age in Wheeling. The city eventually built its own public library, in a district convenient for the workers and their children. For me, and I am sure for countless others, the course of life was changed by this library's accessibility.

In another, later controversy, Val and his labor committee succeeded, after careful planning and thoughtfully laid groundwork, in convincing the Board of Education that the new Wheeling High School should be built by union labor. Knowing that he faced an actively antiunion contractor, my father realized that he had to prevent some of the hotheads in the Central Labor Council from provoking unnecessary strife. He cautioned them to be reasonable and polite at the hearing and not to allow the contractor or his attorneys to goad them into statements they might later regret. Before the formal hearing of the Board of Education, he decided to visit each member of the board, some of whom he had known in other capacities, and explain in detail the fundamental issues involved. At the hearing itself, after the contractor and lawyers had presented their case, emphasizing the "featherbedding" delays and extra costs that, they insisted, union labor would entail (they were willing to compromise where skilled craftsmen were involved), my father made his speech in behalf of the general construction unions. A few excerpts illustrate his strategy:

> . . . We want the finest plan. We are pleased with the excellence of the architect whom you have suggested. We believe that it is wise to have, and the specifications call for, the very finest of building materials that can go into it, in terms of plumbing and fixtures and the quality of the

desks and blackboards, and the texture of the seasoned wood that shall go into the building and even the type of stone. Surely if the architect feels that it is so important to the quality of the building to specify in such detail precisely what kind of material shall go into the building, he had in mind that the finest of labor would also be used . . . This Board would consider it a breach of contract if the contractor used his own judgment in substituting an inferior type of wood or a type of plumbing less than that specified in terms of quality . . . Why then does anyone have the right to assume that . . . the contracting firm has the freedom to substitute a less skilled and less competent worker when the contract provides for union or the highest of skilled labor?

The case had been methodically prepared and was presented in a courteous and orderly manner. There had been no interruption when counsel for the contractor presented his case; but soon after my father began his presentation there was a steady stream of emotional interruptions from the other side, which did not sit well with the board. At that point Val knew he had won his case. As he told us later, it was another example of lawyers being too smart for their own and their client's good.

Unfortunately, all the expertise and energy of the trade union movement in West Virginia could not stem the tide of Prohibition. The early adoption by the state of the law against manufacture and sale of alcoholic beverages was to have a drastic effect on our own and many other families. It was not passed without a long, hard battle on the part of Val Reuther and a coalition called the Trades Union Liberty League, coordinated by the International Brewery Workers' general secretary. They had against them, of course, the Anti-Saloon League and the Women's Christian Temperance Union, along with many church groups; and the massive campaign that started in 1910 resulted eventually in unemployment for brewery workers, keg and cask builders, wagonmakers, blacksmiths, glass workers, restaurant people, and even agricultural workers involved in growing malt and hops. But more than employment was at stake. There was a serious apprehension that, even though many sincere, well-meaning groups were promoting the cause of Prohibition, there were sinister elements waiting in the wings to make a big profit from the illegal manufacture of liquor. This turned out to be the case. We became a nation of moonshiners and lawbreakers.

The Trades Union Liberty League undertook a campaign of its own to defeat the Prohibition lobby in West Virginia by means of ed-

ucation and eloquence. My father spoke all over the state — he was
given a three-month leave of absence for this activity by the Schmulbach Brewing Company, whose owners knew well his talent for powerful and fluent public speaking. The only thing he regretted about
the assignment was that it entailed his leaving my mother alone with
three small children.

In spite of his enormous personal effort and all the literature put
out by the trade unions, in 1912 the State of West Virginia voted for
Prohibition — to take effect in 1914. In that two-year interim Val
was urged by the Brewery Workers' International to campaign in
Ohio, where they were being more successful in staving off the
feared legislation. When the law finally went into effect, the
Schmulbach brewery, of course, had to shut down, and my father,
with four children now, was out of work. And to add to their economic problems, my mother and father had just built a new house
on Wetzel Street in South Wheeling, so there was the mortgage to
keep up as well as the need to provide food and clothing. For many
weeks my father made the rounds of various industries, but to no
avail. His reputation as an active union man did not help, nor did
the prevailing prejudice against German-Americans. Each day he
became more restless and depressed. He had no specialized trade;
the breweries were gone; and the labor movement, which had been
his real career, was not able to offer him full-time employment at a
salary adequate for supporting a family. I am sure it was at this
moment of crisis and self-examination that he vowed that each of his
boys would, without fail, acquire some trade skill that would enable
him to earn financial security all his life. In very large measure, he
carried out that commitment.

The house on Wetzel Street, for all its unpromising site — so close
to the hill that heavy rains often washed away the garden and half of
the street — turned out to be a much-needed financial aid. Very
wisely, my parents had the second floor renovated as an apartment
with its own entrance, and the modest rent from our first tenants
and dear friends, the Wollenbergers, helped defray the mortgage.
The grocer gave credit until Val could get a new job, and Mother's
sister Katie lent some of her savings to tide us over. My mother
decided to take some steps herself, and persuaded her reluctant husband to let her open a small restaurant, where she would cook and
he would serve the soft drinks. They rented a small basement in a

working-class area, but most of the business was at noon, which was hard on Mother, who had small children to look after. And the venture was no great success from the beginning, because Prohibition had changed the scene: no beer and free lunch; no rush of customers.

The project ended in catastrophe. Several cases of ginger ale had been delivered and evidently one of them had been sitting in a warm place for some time. When father began to move bottles to the icebox, one of them exploded right in his hand. Thousands of tiny glass splinters penetrated one of his eyes. He began to bleed heavily. Mother dropped everything and ran for help, and Val was carried to the nearest doctor's office. He was in terrible pain but refused an anesthetic, fearing the doctor would remove his eye while he was unconscious. Though he usually drank nothing except beer, he asked for a shot of whiskey and, as three men held him, the doctor pulled slivers from his eye with a pair of tweezers. Naturally, infection set in — there were no antibiotics then — and vision in the injured eye was totally destroyed. He refused to let a surgeon remove it. In those days prosthetic eyes were gruesomely obvious. It wasn't until 1930 that my father took advantage of new eye surgery techniques and had an artificial eye put in the socket, in the hope of regaining some movement in the muscles.

For some months after the accident my father had a very disfigured face; in many respects the psychological trauma was much harder for him to bear than was the loss of vision. According to my mother, he became very despondent, nearly suicidal. Even I can remember that he would reach for a glass of milk or try to pour something into a glass, and would overshoot the mark, which made him so furious and depressed that the whole family suffered from the strain.

Mother tried to console him by saying there were many men who had lost an eye at work and yet managed to continue their jobs, and that he should prepare himself for an occupation that did not need perfect vision. My father's stamina began to return and he embarked with considerable courage on the correspondence course mentioned in the preceding chapter, realizing that further education was the key to a suitable job. Meantime a possibility turned up through his cousin Philip. Philip, whom we children called Uncle, had also been laid off by the brewery but had found work in the Tri-

State Beverage Company in Bridgeport, Ohio. Ohio as yet had no law prohibiting the manufacture of beer. Also there were no restrictions against bringing it across the bridge, and after Dad took the job he was able to supplement the meager pay with modest transactions in bootleg beer. I can imagine how gratifying it must have been for his former colleagues and fellow workers to drop in at Wetzel Street and enjoy a taste they could no longer satisfy in a Wheeling bar. But the job at the bottling plant was an unattractive one and of short duration.

My oldest brother, Ted, who had turned eleven, found sporadic work, during the summer months of these lean years, in the Northwood Glass Factory, just a block away from our house. There were no child labor laws at this time, and the plant used to employ children for a half-shift, or one "turn" of five hours. Ted sometimes worked two turns in a day in order to earn eighty cents a day instead of forty. Our need of cash was so severe that his wages were a real supplement to the family income. Ironically, another bad accident befell the family through this job of Ted's. Neighborhood children used to wander at will through the glass factory — the lack of regulations was appalling — and I can actually remember seeing them walk in during working hours on stilts! Walter was nine then and often wandered in, especially when Ted was there. On one such escapade Walter was struck near the eye, on the side of his nose, with a hot blowpipe that had molten glass at its tip. The pipe cut a very large gash, and we thought for a while that he, too, would have to live with only one eye. Fortunately he escaped that loss, but he bore the scar on the side of his nose for the rest of his life.

Later, during a flu epidemic that caused much absenteeism among the glass workers and resulted in many deaths as well, Ted was hired on a steady basis and became even more of a support to the family. After this work experience, and with the worst of the money crisis over, he finished eighth grade and went on to the Elliot Business School for an intensive course in bookkeeping. It was this training that equipped him to work in Ohio at the same Tri-State Beverage Company where Dad was employed for a brief period.

Bad luck pursued Val Reuther for some time. After a long bout of unemployment, in desperation he took a job working for the county on the roads. He did not mind the hard labor, but shortly after he began the job, a chip from a stone flew against his good eye;

it swelled up and he lost all vision for some weeks. The trauma of total blindness, even though it was temporary, drove my father to make a drastic change in his way of life. After his eye healed, he concentrated with fresh intensity on the correspondence schooling, completed it, and then applied for a position as agent with the Metropolitan Life Insurance Company, asking for assignment to South Wheeling, where he had many personal contacts among the workers.

He was a success as an insurance salesman since he knew how to talk in terms of the life problems and insecurities that were familiar to most working people. He had his own tragic experience to draw upon. It was not necessary for him to "back the hearse up" and frighten people into buying insurance. He knew what slim means could and could not finance, and he suggested those policies that gave the maximum protection for the least expensive premium. For the first time in his life, he had a decent and steadily rising income.

CHAPTER 4

Wetzel Street to Bethlehem Hill

MODERN URBAN COMFORTS did not appeal to my farm-reared father. When the house on Wetzel Street was being built, he could not accept the idea of being able to walk directly from the living quarters to the bathroom. The result was that one had to go out on the back porch to find the bathroom door. He had really wanted the whole facility to be completely separate from the house, but my mother had a few private talks with the builder and they worked out the porch compromise. Eventually, with four small children to keep track of and the restaurant to manage as well, she sacrificed the limited cupboard space in the kitchen and had a door cut through to the bathroom.

The house was built against a hillside in old Ritchie Town, beside a derelict mine shaft, a short block from the railroad tracks that divided the hills from the river front of South Wheeling. Hardship and tragedy were common to us and to all of our working-class neighbors; people helped each other out as a matter of course. My mother has often recalled taking in a baby to nurse when its mother became ill, which meant that Walter had to share his mother's milk. It seemed that his combative spirit showed itself at once. Later, when he had to be weaned, he put up such a fight that Mother resorted to the Old World technique of darkening her breasts with shoe polish to frighten him off.

The mine, the hills, and the river made a fascinating setting for exploring boys. Calliope organs resounding from the river drew us to the banks to watch the steamers go by, creating great waves with their side or rear paddle wheels. We fished and swam; it was a rite of adolescence for each boy to make it all the way to the other side of the water. Fortunately Dad had insisted on swimming lessons at the

Y. Sometimes we took bad risks, swimming so close to the stern paddle wheels that we could catch the drops of water. There were tragic incidents; some of our friends were sucked down by the wake of the river boats and drowned.

The nearby abandoned mine also attracted us. Perfect exploring country, it was visited for practical reasons too; we brought out the old roof-supporting timbers for firewood or fences or for terracing the eroding garden. But one never knew when there might be a fall-in.

We had no bicycles and for mobility had to rely on the thrill of climbing up hills and down ravines on stilts, or jumping off boxcars at the glass factory into the soft puttylike clay that is used in the glass-making process. We joined the neighborhood gang to pick off the windows of a section of that factory no longer in use. Word got back to our parents through the police, and one day when I got home from school, Mother warned me that we were going to get a good beating from Dad. I ran out of the house and found Roy, still several blocks from home. I told him about the impending punishment, and we delayed our return as long as we could. Roy then used his favorite strategy: he started weeping and bawling as hard as possible, putting on such a display of self-castigation and repentance that Dad could hardly be severe on him.

It was a pity I could not use that technique when I brought home a Hearst paper one Sunday morning by mistake. Dad naturally considered Hearst the archfiend among all of labor's enemies, and would not tolerate one of his publications in the house. Unaware of my transgression, I was sprawled out on the sofa with the funnies. When Dad discovered what the paper was, he became so angry that he seemed to lose all sense of proportion, and gave me such a thrashing that Mother had to intervene. I was out of school for several days recovering from the whipping, and it was some time before Mother could speak civilly to Dad. He realized he had been unjust and in his remorse became extremely gentle to me and the whole family.

Those were the hard years for him, lean years for all of us, full of troubles, tragedy, and painful thrift, but the family itself was close and warm, and the kitchen a happy boisterous place, lively with conversation and the smell of delicious cooking. During a bad crisis, we ate nothing but potatoes with their jackets on and maybe a can of salmon. The rest of the time, Mother cooked tasty and nourishing meals, with a Swabian flavor, and rarely without the *Spaetzle,* dropped dough noodles, and *Kuchen,* coffee cakes filled with whatever fruit was in season or made with cheese dough in winter. At Christmas, Mother made her hard *Springerle* cookies well ahead of time, put them in a flour sack, and stored them in a potato barrel to be softened by the moisture from the potatoes in time for the celebration.

Ted was the only boy to have new clothes in those years; the rest of us made do with hand-me-downs. Our underclothes, like the sheets and pillowcases, were made from flour or sugar sacks. Walter loved to tell a story about a shirt that Mother made for him:

> I was nine or ten and rather small and light for my age. At county fairs, men would jump with parachutes from captive balloons. I thought it was very exciting and wanted to try it myself. Our mother had bought a great big black cotton umbrella, large enough so that the whole family could get under it, and one day I borrowed that new umbrella and climbed up on a water tower near our home, and opened the umbrella and took off. The tank was thirty-five or forty feet above the ground, the umbrella sustained my weight about two thirds of the way down — and then, disaster. It turned inside out and the umbrella and I landed on the ground with a terrific thump. Believe it or not, I wasn't badly hurt — just a few bruises here and there. But the umbrella was a complete wreck. When I got home, my mother was of course annoyed and gave me a good scolding, although I don't recall that she punished me physically except in a very unique sort of way. She was determined to salvage something from the wreck. And though the frame was completely destroyed, she managed to make a shirt out of the heavy waterproofed material that had covered it. For a long time my brothers and other kids in the neighborhood used to tease me about the umbrella shirt. I'd say to them back: "I bet you haven't got a shirt that sheds water!"

Once Walter, when he was very small, stuffed the gas cooking stove full of the family shoes; the flame was snuffed out, gas accumulated, and at some point the stove exploded. Shoes and stove were ruined, but Walter was not hurt. And one year, when we had no money to buy firecrackers for the Fourth of July, we tried making some with the gunpowder Dad kept in the cellar for an occasional hunting foray. Frustrated and impatient, Roy and I decided to make a "fountain" with a pile of straight gunpowder, and I almost lost my arm that day. Later, I nearly burned us all up on Christmas Eve. Our tree was decorated in the German way, with fruit, strung popcorn, some ornaments, and, best of all, the tiny candles that were lit only for short periods. Something new had been added this year to the nativity scene beneath the tree: a beautiful angel above a candle that, when lit, created enough heat to make the angel twirl. This was so beautiful that, after the family retired, I crept into the living room and relit the candle beneath the angel. Suddenly I heard a noise from the bedroom above and, fearing discovery, I moved too quickly and knocked over the candle. Immediately, the dry lower branches of the tree burst into flame. I must have been blessed either by a real angel or by luck, because Ted, who had evidently heard something, came bounding into the room and with great presence of mind threw open the window, picked up the entire blazing tree, and hurled it out. That's a Christmas I shall never forget. For years thereafter, at family gatherings, reference to my "making the angel fly" always provoked laughter.

Religion had a good deal to do with the shaping of our family life. Mother, a very devout person, believed quite simply that the teachings of Christ should be applied every day and not merely repeated once a week in church. She lived out what she believed. Dad had almost entered the ministry in his youth, and though he had become somewhat of an agnostic and was attracted by the philosophy of Robert Ingersoll, he was not an atheist. He used the Bible constantly to support his social concepts. I remember the thunder of his indignation, when he quoted from James 5:1–4: "Go to now, ye rich men, weep and howl for your miseries that shall come upon you. Your riches are corrupted, and your garments are motheaten . . . Behold, the hire of the labourers who have reaped down your fields which is of you kept back by fraud . . ."

Once the evening meal was over, Dad would discuss with us what had happened that day and what we had learned. Then he would comment on his own day and on world events, drawing on the Bible to underscore his feelings about the exploitation of mine workers, for instance, or the blindness of the powerful to their social responsibilities, or, sometimes, his rejection of the fanaticism of the older branch of the Lutheran church. "God says that you should forgive your enemies. How then could a loving God send erring humans into a life of perpetual damnation and hell?" He looked upon faith as a humanistic commitment.

He went with us to the Zion Lutheran Church and saw to it that we attended Sunday school, until that Labor Day when a new pastor gave his first sermon. Unfortunately, the newcomer was not aware that many members of his congregation were working men and active union members. There was a steel strike going on, and efforts were being made to unionize the mines. The young pastor used the sermon as a means to attack the trade union movement. I was sitting next to Dad and I saw the flush rise in his cheeks. About halfway through the hour, he rose from his pew and, in a loud firm voice, sounding like Moses calling out from the mountain top, he took issue with the preacher. I expected lightning to strike my father dead, and when he survived his deed, and the rest of us survived it, I had a new degree of respect for Valentine Reuther.

Obviously the matter didn't rest with Dad's walking out of church; it became grist for regrinding in the family mill for a long time. It could have been a crisis for Mother, as Dad refused to go to that church again, but when she insisted that we go, he did not object. From then on, every Sunday after dinner he would ask us, "Well, on what subject did the preacher preach today?" After we had told him the general theme, he would review it with us, sometimes agreeing, sometimes opposing, but invariably throwing new light on the topic. The family pattern was reasserting itself: Grandfather Jacob, dissatisfied with Lutheranism in Illinois, had conducted services in his own home, and now Dad in his own way was making sure his sons were not being brainwashed by an overdogmatic or reactionary influence.

Because his sharp criticism of certain Lutheran doctrines often drove Mother to tears, the Sunday sessions were adjourned to our parents' bedroom. They turned into animated debates: Dad would assign a subject that was considered controversial, such as child labor, Prohibition, the yellow press, or women's suffrage, and we would do research, either in our small home library or in the public library, and prepare our cases according to the side of the debate we were told to support. Often we had to defend the side that was contrary to what we believed. "You cannot effectively argue your own view on an issue unless you understand the viewpoint of those who oppose you," Dad often told us. He kept time and made notes on each presentation, and at the end summarized our styles, order and logic, and quality of research.

Ted was very much the orderly accountant, able to construct a fine column of facts; Walter was contentious and pugnacious; Roy tried to emulate the silver-tongued orators of Dad's generation. I am told that in my presentations I relied less on logic than on emotional exploitation of the material. Frequently our voices rose to such a pitch that our baby sister, Christine, would start crying, certain that we were fighting with each other, and would have to be reassured.

All in all this was a remarkable kind of home schooling. It taught us to organize our ideas and to maintain poise in the face of a group. It undoubtedly prepared us for the rough-and-tumble soapboxing that lay ahead of us when we embarked on our union careers.

"Debating is in the Reuther family blood," wrote the Detroit *Free Press* on April 5, 1942.

When Walter, one of the three UAW-CIO officials, took on G.M. president, C. E. Wilson, his mannerisms, which greatly impressed journalistic observers, were a throwback to his youth . . . The Reuthers' father was a union official who set out early to prepare his sons to carry on in his footsteps . . . Contrasting personality traits resulted. Walter, now union G.M. chief, and Roy, a union international representative, found that a little bombast would sink Victor, now a leader in the union war work conversion effort. Victor compensated by becoming precise. No Supreme Court jurist can read a nationally important decision with more finality than Victor can summon to back up a routine report on union finances . . . Working together, the three are deadly . . .

Walter, Roy, and I sometimes tried to enhance our forensic skills by making speeches in the open air. This was after we had moved to the farm on Bethlehem Hill. We had found a secluded area on the old Snedeker farm near our own place, where, within a stand of virgin timber, there was a small clearing and a big stump, maybe six feet across. On this natural platform, we practiced our speeches for the benefit of a grazing goat or cow.

The move to Bethlehem Hill, when I was about fourteen, gave us another sort of education — on a down-to-earth level. Christine's birth, three years before, had been difficult for my mother, and she was hospitalized for some time. Dad was worried about her health and wanted her to live in a place with cleaner air. Wetzel Street had been paved, automobiles had come into wide use, and Dad was concerned about Christine's safety. The neighborhood had become tougher as well as dirtier. I imagine that nostalgia for country and farm life may have grown too strong for Dad to resist.

Ted and Walter probably found the Fisher farm during their

hikes over the hills in search of blackberries, which the farm had in plenty on its back slope overlooking the Wheeling Valley westward and Elmgrove Valley to the east. The house, once the center of a farm of several hundred acres, was in very bad shape. A typical Southern plantation house, it had rambling additions, a separate brick smokehouse, and a double-deck porch running the length and width of the inner court. The whole place had taken on, during its abandonment, a bleak and desolate air, and Mother did not really want to move out there, away from her comfortable house, her friends, the nearby school, the familiar church. But to her husband and her sons it presented an irresistible challenge, and after much argument and soul-searching, she was won over. The resulting improvement in her health eventually removed all her doubts and qualms.

The windows were ill-fitting and needed panes. The wide floorboards were uneven and rough and hard to clean. There was no running water, no electricity. We learned that the eighty-five-foot stone-lined well we had counted on for drinking water had been polluted with refuse, which meant we would have to resort to cisterns. We became plumbers, carpenters, and electricians. Every day after school or work, the whole family worked on the old house until late at night, and sometimes in the hours before dawn, on projects like cementing the inner court, sealing off the old well, or converting the smokehouse into a laundry room-workshop-garage with a cistern beneath it. Before we installed an indoor bathroom, we enlarged the privy into a palatial shack. In time, we made several cisterns to catch rain water, and a pumping and filter system to purify the water for drinking. We constructed an enormous henhouse to accommodate, at the peak of its occupancy, five thousand chickens for selective breeding.

Life now was much rougher than it had been on Wetzel Street; the long trek to school in South Wheeling was grueling in winter, when the wind blew snow into enormous drifts. But the summers rewarded us with a handsome landscape, clean air, and good food. Fresh fruit and vegetables came from orchard and garden. Mother pitted the blackheart cherries one by one and put them into her delicious pancakes; we had our own mill for making apple cider in the fall; pumpkin pies were so popular that one evening Mother greeted us with thirteen of them: "That's all for dinner," she said, "and now I hope you have your fill of pumpkin pie!"

The do-it-yourself project — remodeling the farm — was a part of our education that could not have been traded for gold. We finished our growing-up on Bethlehem Hill, and learned how to work as a unit. Ted, of course, was already twenty when we moved, and was employed at the Wheeling Corrugating Company, first as production clerk and timekeeper, then, after thirteen months, as a member of the staff of the General Accounting Office. (He was to spend forty-eight years with this firm, which later became the Wheeling Steel Corporation.) Walter had, of his own choice, left high school at sixteen. What had absorbed him there was the industrial arts program, especially the machine shop, supervised by Frank A. Schneider, who recognized in this sixteen-year-old a fine mechanical talent. Walter had given up all extracurricular activities, including the sports he excelled in, to spend all his spare time in the shop. This characteristic intensity paid off, for when Walter learned through Ted of an opening for an apprentice in the tool room at the Wheeling Corrugating, he was encouraged by Mr. Schneider to try it and was given an excellent recommendation by his teacher. It was in line with my father's dream that each of his boys should pursue a trade. He never forgot his days of insecurity when the brewery closed down and he had had no skill to fall back on.

Walter's first pay was eleven cents an hour. The skilled toolmakers themselves were making only seventy-five cents. But because the tool room was on the small side, it meant that an apprentice had an opportunity to become a good all-around toolmaker; the experience included months of work on the machines and then considerable time on the bench. Harry Grubler, one of the die leaders at Corrugating, remembers Walter as a very quick learner. His reminiscences reveal how much cooperation and general good will existed between the master mechanics and the apprentices. Walter came in for his share of both assistance and teasing. One day he borrowed a level from Slim Culverson, which he dropped and broke. "What do I do now?" he asked Slim. "Well, you go down to Reed Robert Ryan wholesale drugstore and you ask them for a new bubble for the level." Walter came back the next day and reported, "Well, I went there and they sent me down to the Ohio Valley Drugstore, but they said they didn't have any either. Said they were out of them."

Three years later, when Walter left for Detroit, he was getting forty-two cents an hour. Most of his pay during those years had gone to supplement the family income. What with his contribution and Ted's help, which, of course, was considerably larger, Roy and I were able to have a fuller high school life, without feeling any pressure to take after-school jobs.

Roy was a great success on the basketball team and later on the track squad. But he also had a consuming technical interest: the electrical trade. He was excited by the new field of radio, and his talents helped relieve our long winter evenings, when he put together one of the early Atwater Kent receiving sets with earphones, on which we got good reception from KDKA in Pittsburgh. (I was infected by his enthusiasm and built a little cat's whisker receiving set in a cigar box and picked up local stations.) Roy had already begun working as an electrician by drilling through the sturdy beams of our farm and installing the wiring. So instead of finishing at Wheeling High School, he apprenticed himself to a local electrical firm — for long hours and almost no pay.

Roy joined the Brotherhood of Electrical Workers and took his oath in the same union hall where Dad had presided as president at the age of twenty-three. One of the old-timers came up to him and said, "What's the name again?" and when Roy answered, "Reuther," he asked, "Any relation to Val?" "Yes, I'm his son," Roy replied. "Well, we'll put you on a committee. We have a lot of work to do!" That very night Roy started his service for the trade union movement.

In high school, I had no passion for sports and was not drawn toward any technical trade. Reading and debating were my loves, and in my senior year I was president of two debating clubs. Our speech instructor, A. Dale Riley, was a very imaginative teacher, and undoubtedly spurred my natural inclinations to read and to orate. He had traveled widely and was able to transmit to his students all the excitement of discovering foreign places and peoples, and to make us aware of the social problems that crop up all over the world. I was stimulated to do some exploring on my own, and in the hours between the closing of school and the time when I could hitch a ride home with Ted and Walter in the old Model T, I pored over book after book in the public library: travel books, books on Gandhi, on the ancient Aztecs, on capital punishment, child labor, or on some issue assigned by my father for a family debate.

At that time the tools of *my* trade were obviously words, and as the youngest boy I had soaked up a goodly amount of family eloquence and Dad's ideology. I remember one day when I was pressed for time to find material for a five-minute talk in Mr. Riley's class, I chose a subject from one of our Sunday debates, "Is There a Hell?" I drew more heavily than I realized on a famous speech by Robert Ingersoll. Mr. Riley was greatly amused by my efforts and complimented me on the delivery and on my courage in picking such a controversial subject. I don't know if he or one of my classmates talked about it among the faculty, but the next thing I knew I was summoned to the principal's office.

"What's this I hear about you having made an antireligious speech in class?" he started off. I told him quite frankly the substance of my talk. "Where did you ever get such wild and outlandish ideas?" was the next question, whereupon I mistakenly told him I had got them from a library book. He immediately checked and found there was no volume by Ingersoll in the library. I said, "Well, sir, I think I still have it in my locker," and went to get it. On the flyleaf I found my father's great sprawling signature. When the principal saw the name "Valentine Reuther," he closed the book quickly and said, "Take it home and don't bring it to school again." No further mention was made of the incident. My father was not unknown to the Board of Education and the principal was not about to tangle with him.

I have the impression I was very much of a stuffed shirt in high school. In the class book, one can see a serious face looking out over the caption "I think the needs of humanity are more important." At graduation, I was one of the four speakers; my speech was entitled "The Blessings of Citizenship." As I look over the quotes in the review printed in the high school magazine, I suspect I was again plagiarizing Colonel Ingersoll more freely than I would have admitted. My ego was certainly fortified by compliments on my performances. During my freshman year at West Virginia University, a former high school classmate, Fred Baening, wrote to me, "I hope your Patrick Henry tendencies are still keeping you in your work."

The first break in the family circle came in 1927, when I was still a sophomore in high school: Walter moved to Detroit. He had been getting very restless in the Wheeling Corrugating tool room, where he had heard much talk about Detroit. The company had already lost a number of mechanics to the new automobile kingdom. One of the attractions for Walter was that, since he was now determined to finish his education without letting the family down financially, he could work at Ford and go to school at the same time. So, after three years of apprenticeship, on February 27, 1927, he gave his week's notice and drove to Detroit with Leo Hores, also from Wheeling Corrugating and also in search of a more lucrative job. Hores, a journeyman of four years' standing, was still getting only sixty cents an hour; Walter was earning forty-two.

Ted, Roy, and I were living at home and kept Dad company when Mother had an opportunity to visit her relatives in Germany in the summer of 1928. Before she left, accompanied by Christine, she gave me a course in cooking and housekeeping that was to come in very handy two years later, when I found myself earning my keep by cooking and washing for a houseful of Ford workers in Detroit. The following summer we had a lively addition to our household in the person of Grandfather Jacob Reuther, who kept himself busy replacing some of the sewers, planting hedges on the side road, and spading in the orchard around the younger trees. He had a hard time getting used to the comfortable bathroom, which ran against his living habits. He was in deadly fear of electricity, and wouldn't touch a switch. I found him many a night sitting up late and writing out his interpretations of the Scriptures by candlelight.

When I went to West Virginia University in the fall of 1929, I knew it would not have been possible without the help of my brothers. Ted was a faithful source of support and Walter sent money home from Detroit for several years. I was unusually sensitive about the situation and even more embarrassed when my marks for the first semester were not as high as I wished. They were in the eighties but nothing to boast about in our family of achievers. Dad's letters egged me on benignly: "Most of us get out of life what we put into it . . . Remember that weeds grow of themselves. Choice flowers are carefully cultivated and trained, and so it is with people . . . But let me add to this that success in life should not be measured in terms of fortunes made, wealth accumulated, nor dollars saved, but rather in service rendered, in good deeds done, in friends made . . ."

When, in April 1930, I needed some clothes that I knew would be costly, I must have written to him that I felt like a parasite, because he wrote back:

We were all glad to hear from you, especially since you have been able to improve your percentage in studies . . . and as long as you show you are really interested in your work and prove it by good grades, just so long we will see you along, and right here I want to register my protest against the word you used, *parasite* . . . The profession for which you are training [I was in a prelaw program] has done much in shaping the destinies and policies of this our beloved country and it is my fondest hope that some day you will take your place among these men. If when the time comes you will contribute as best you can to the comfort and happiness of our people, I will be amply compensated for anything I have done to help you along your chosen pathway.

With love,
Your Dad.

CHAPTER 5

Awakening

WALTER AND LEO HORES reached Detroit on the last Saturday in February 1927 and put up with family friends. On Sunday they found a rooming house, and on Monday began making the rounds, looking for work. They went to Fisher Body, Dodge, Ford Highland Park, Hudson, and finally, at three in the afternoon, they were hired by Briggs Body Works in Highland Park. They began work at five-thirty the same day, Leo as a full-fledged journeyman die maker, and Walter as a drill press operator, for eighty-five and sixty cents an hour respectively. Their shift was usually ten but sometimes twelve hours a night. As Leo said to me later, "We were eating a lot of emery dust." In those days, Briggs was called "the slaughter-house." The wages were lower and the conditions worse than at Ford or General Motors. Because the plant was dependent on sub-contracting arrangements with the larger auto producers, the speed-up could be killing.

Walter's own words give the best picture of those first weeks:

"I was employed at the Waterloo Plant at the Briggs Manufac-turing Company, which was the company that made bodies for Ford, where they had a new tooling program that began to relate to the Model A, and I worked there nights — from five-thirty in the eve-ning to seven in the morning. I worked thirteen hours a night with a half-hour lunch period and I worked twenty-one nights in a row, but since this job with Briggs was a night job, and since I preferred to work in the small die division where the tolerances were much more precise, more skilled and more to my liking, I discussed with the other men . . . and they told me I should try to get a job at the

Burroughs Adding Machine where they had a lot of very skilled small tool and die work . . .

"So I went over to the Burroughs Company. The employment manager was rather intrigued with me. I was still a boy. I really looked like I had just fallen off a green apple tree in West Virginia, and he said to me they weren't employing anyone, but he heard that the Ford Motor Company was employing Die Leaders, and he said, 'You obviously won't qualify as a Die Leader but you might go up and just by chance they might be hiring some tool and die makers who are not Die Leaders.'

"A Die Leader is a man who has fifteen or twenty-five years of experience, who is in charge of a group. He is not a foreman, he is a group leader who would be responsible for coordinating a project. Ford was beginning to build up a bigger core of highly skilled personnel to get ready to do the tooling for their Model A. This was the first model change the Ford Motor Company had ever made . . . So I went back and told the men I worked with and they said, 'Well, you got all this stuff. Why don't you go up to Ford. They can't do any more than say no.' I decided that I would do this. So I worked all night, thirteen hours at Briggs, and then I went home to the boarding house where I was living with a family and I had something to eat and I changed clothes and then I went out looking for the Highland Park Plant and Labelle Avenue where the employment office was. I went up to the door there and there was a big tall service man standing there and I said to him, 'I understand that you're hiring Die Leaders.' And he said, 'That's right.' And I said, 'That's why I'm here.' And he said, 'Well, get on your way, you're just a kid.' And I said, 'No, I'm not just a kid, I'm a Die Leader and I'd like to be interviewed.'

"He didn't believe me and I asked him, 'Are you a Die Maker or are you a Die Leader?' I knew he wasn't either. I said 'How can you look at me and tell what qualifications I have? If you really can look at a man and tell what skills he has or doesn't, you really ought to be inside because you ought to have a much more important job than you have. You really can't. Now I admit I'm young. But how can you tell what skills I have, when you aren't even familiar with this particular area of activity?'

"He said he knew Die Leaders had fifteen or twenty years of experience and he wished I'd get on my way. I said, 'Well I really don't

want to make trouble for you. On the other hand, I'm not willing to
have you deny me the right to be interviewed. I want the man who's
competent to make judgments on whether I have these skills or not
. . .' 'If I let you in, I'll lose my job because they'll say why you just
let any kid that comes down the road in here . . .'

"And so back and forth for three hours and I finally told him,
'You may as well let me in because I'm not going to quit easily. I'm
determined to get in there.' 'I'll probably catch a lot of hell because
of this,' he finally said, 'but I can't get rid of you. I have no choice.'
And he told me to go on in.

"When the employment manager looked up at me, he said, 'How
did you get in?'

"'Please,' I said, 'it took me three hours and I prefer not to go
through this whole thing again . . . The man outside said I was too
young and that I obviously couldn't have the skills and I hope I
don't have to go through that again and I hope I can talk to the person who can really find out whether I have any skills.'

"He shook his head. 'I don't know,' he said, 'I never had one like
this.'

"'Look,' I said, 'Who interviews your people who are applying to
be tool and die makers?' 'Mr. George Gardham,' he said. 'Well,' I
asked, 'would I be asking too much to take a half hour of his time?'

"After a lot of conversation about how he would lose his job if he
called, he was finally persuaded to get on the telephone and I sat
down. Where I was sitting I could look up the main highway of the
plant which was a good half a block long, and all of a sudden I saw a
big, tall, white-haired man with a roll of blueprints under his arm
coming down and at first I thought it was Henry Ford himself. It
turned out to be Mr. Gardham who was the chief master mechanic
in charge of all mechanics for the whole company and he came into
the Employment Office and said to the manager, 'Where is the Tool
and Die Leader that I am to interview?'

"The manager said, 'This is the young man,' and Mr. Gardham
looked at the employment manager and said, 'Why did you call me
down here?'

"I spoke then. 'Look, this has been my problem all day. Now
you're here. Maybe you wouldn't have come if you had known I was
waiting. But you're here. You've got the blueprints under your
arm. It will only take a few minutes to find out how competent or
incompetent I am. You've got nothing to lose.'

"He said, 'Well, okay. Let's see what you know!' So he unrolled blueprints of some very complicated dies and asked me some very involved technical questions which I answered to his satisfaction. 'You know much more about this than one would believe, looking at you,' he said. 'That's been my problem all day,' I answered. 'I don't deny I look like a farmer boy but I do believe that if you give me a job I can prove I know a great deal more than you would think. Why don't you give me a job and if I can't do it you won't have any arguments with me. I'll leave quietly.'

" 'I'll make you a sporting proposition,' he said. 'I've never done this with anyone that I've ever employed in my life. If you are willing to go to work without knowing what you're going to get paid for two days and for two days we will watch you carefully and at the end of the two days we'll decide whether we are going to keep you and what we are willing to pay you.' I told him he had got himself an agreement, because if he paid me based on what I looked like I wouldn't get much, but after I had a chance to demonstrate what I could do, I thought I would get the better of the bargain. So I said, 'I agree. When do I start to work?' 'Seven o'clock tomorrow morning,' he said.

"By this time it was about two o'clock in the afternoon. I went straight home to get something to eat and then went in to the Briggs Company half an hour earlier than starting time, which was 5:30, and as soon as my foreman came in — he was a very decent fellow — I told him I had got another job, a better job, in a small tool and die shop where it would be the kind of small, precise work I preferred. He said he didn't blame me, and I said I'd like to get my tool clearance to get by the watchman and the guard at the gate. Otherwise you couldn't get your tools out. And I couldn't go to work for Ford without my tool box.

"But the foreman couldn't give me tool clearance. I had to get it from the superintendent whose name was Knox and he was a real tough character, with a very bad reputation. So when he came around during the shift, I walked into his office and told him I had secured this other job and would appreciate it if he would give me my tool clearance so I could get my tool box out and go to work next morning. I didn't tell him where it was, and he was very antagonistic and said, 'Why are you leaving?' 'I think this other job is a better job,' I told him. 'You mean you're going to get more money?' 'I think so,' I said.

"He offered me a five cents an hour increase and he offered me day work since I said I preferred it. I told him I appreciated his offers but I still would like my tool clearance so that I could get my tool box out because I had promised to report to this other job at seven o'clock in the morning.

"Oh, you're hard to get along with, aren't you? he said, and I said I didn't think so, I just wanted my tool box, and he said, 'If you can be stubborn, I can be stubborn too. I won't give you your tool clearance and maybe you'll change your mind before the night is over.'

" 'I don't know why we should have a difficulty about this,' I said. 'I'm only asking that I be given the right to take my own personal tools out of the plant . . .'

" 'I'm not going to give you your tool clearance and without it you can't take your tool box out and without your tool box you can't start your new job!' Then he walked away.

"I stayed in that plant till five the next morning. I would contact him every time he came through the department. He kept on saying no and I kept on approaching him. Finally at the last minute he realized I was not going to change my mind. He then gave me the tool clearance.

"I rushed home, had a bite of breakfast, then took a taxi in order to get to the Ford plant before seven. And that was the longest day I ever worked. I hadn't been to sleep for two days, and I was on trial and they were watching me. When that day was over, I was totally exhausted. I got some sleep and went back for the second day and at the end of it, Mr. Gardham, and the two foremen who had been watching me, came over together and they said, 'Well, we've been watching you,' which was no news, and Mr. Gardham said, 'You surprised all of us, because we didn't think you had these skills, and you can stay. We're happy to have you and your rate will be a dollar five cents per hour.'

"A dollar five in 1927 was very good money. Back in Wheeling only a month or so before this, I had been getting forty-two cents an hour . . . When I was finally discharged from Ford for trying to organize, I was getting a dollar forty-five cents an hour which made me in that period one of the top handful of highest paid mechanics in the company."

That almost incredible persistence served Walter well when he later took on the giants of the automotive industry.

Detroit in the twenties was expanding as the new industry grew. Hundreds of thousands of immigrants from Poland, Italy, Germany, Scandinavia, Britain, and Ireland were attracted to it by the beckoning light of higher-paying jobs. What few of them anticipated was the new assembly-line system, which all too soon began to take its human toll. The pace was so swift and the hours so long that workers were apt to fall asleep the minute they boarded the crowded street cars and would have to be awakened by the conductor. Then they would get off and make their way home in a daze. There was no time and no energy for anything but the robot life in the factory.

As early as 1913, the Industrial Workers of the World (the IWW) had begun some organizing of Ford workers to demand an eight-hour day, and in the same year the Detroit Studebaker plant went on strike for shorter hours. There was a march down East Grand Boulevard to the Packard plant, and leaflets were distributed at the Highland Park Ford plant, where the pay was twenty-five cents an hour. James Cousins, at that time business manager of Ford, was determined to resist unionization, and conceived an ingenious and cynical gimmick. On January 5, 1914, Henry Ford startled the world with his public announcement that he would pay a flat five dollars a day — come one, come all. The next morning, ten thousand job hunters jammed into Manchester Street in Highland Park, and by the end of the week the crowd was fifteen thousand strong, with many waiting, hungry and cold, for whole days and nights. Such a sight was unnerving to the Ford officials: they called for police help. The Detroit *Journal* of January 9 carried the following item:

ICY FIREHOSE DELUGE STOPS TWELVE THOUSAND IN RIOTOUS PUSH FOR FORD JOBS.

Three thousand soaked with temperatures hovering close to zero. They were an unenviable lot. Their clothes froze the moment they encountered the business end of a hose.

Henry Ford later admitted that the payment of five dollars for an eight-hour day was one of the finest cost-cutting moves his company ever made. A July 1916 financial statement shows that two years after the startling humanitarian announcement fourteen thousand workers at Ford were getting less than five dollars a day. This was accomplished by calling seven thousand or more of them "probationary" and paying them $2.55. After six months a probationary worker would be discharged and another probationary hired in his place. Furthermore, women were not considered eligible for the five dollars a day, nor were unmarried men under twenty-two, nor married men who were engaged in a divorce action. For the final weeding out, a corps of Ford "social workers" was created; its job was to determine whether the conduct of a worker's family justified his receiving the five dollars a day!

It is only fair to say that some of the Detroit workers made more money than they could have made in any other area of the economy. There were no deductions for Social Security, Unemployment Compensation, or pensions. There were no union dues — Detroit was an open-shop town and unions were looked on by all employers as accursed things. (William Green, the president of the AFL, and still a lay preacher in the Baptist church, was considered in Detroit too much of a revolutionary to be allowed to speak in the YMCA.)

When Walter shifted to a daytime job at Ford and no longer had to put in the excessive overtime demanded by Briggs, he was able to indulge in a little recreation, such as swimming at the Y and pursuing his great interest in flying. He and a group of other young men pooled their cash and bought an old World War I Jenny and learned to fly on weekends. The flying club did not last long after an emergency crash-landing in a snowstorm, but Walter kept up his interest and thought for a while of becoming an aeronautical engineer.

He was encouraged in this intention by the supervisors at the River Rouge Ford plant in Dearborn, where he had been taken on because of the gradual phasing out of the tool room at Highland Park. In his new job, he worked on one of the first wind tunnels for Ford's famous trimotor "Tin Goose."

In Dearborn, he found good lodgings in the house of a young machinist, named Emil Schnier, and his wife, Ernestine. They were a hard-working, frugal, and ambitious pair, and provided for Walter a warm atmosphere in a familiar cultural setting. Emil was a German immigrant and later became a professor at a California university. Walter's hourly wage at the River Rouge plant was $1.40, putting him in the aristocracy of labor. He spent little and was able to send 50 percent of his earnings home to help the family. But in September of 1928 he became twenty-one, and Dad wrote him that he would accept no more money from him: "You are now twenty-one. You must think in terms of your own future and your own life. You should begin to bank these extra reserves and invest them well so that you will have security for the future." He thanked Walter for the help he had given, and from then on, all financial assistance was over, except for a few loans, which were fully repaid. Walter took Dad's advice and invested in one commercial lot in Dearborn, assessed at $1600, and two in the Hazelcrest subdivision, valued at $400 each.

Walter at this point was not sure just which engineering field he would enter, but one thing was clear to him: he was going to finish his formal education. He therefore enrolled at the Fordson High School and took on an unusually heavy schedule: classes in the morning, followed by the three-thirty-to-midnight shift at the plant, then the full load of homework. Truly a midnight-oil existence, made more burdensome by overtime at the plant. Excerpts from an essay that Walter wrote in October 1929 for a high school English course give a graphic picture of that hectic life:

Time

"What is Time? Time like space is without beginning and without end. For anything to be without beginning or end is almost beyond human conception; yet if there was a beginning, what existed before the beginning; and if there will be an end, what will exist after the end?

". . . After hours of concentration we arrive at the conclusion that Time, like Space, is one of the elements of Nature that cannot be defined, but there is one thing we discover about Time; it is the most limited, most valuable factor in our lives.

". . . I am awakened by the horrible clamoring of Time's representative, my alarm clock. Sleepily, half conscious, I reach to strangle, to choke off the horrible noise . . . Momentarily I am relieved, but through half closed eyes I see the twelve eyes of time staring at me, challenging me. I collect all my reserve power, count three, and jump out of bed.

"The race is on. First a few hurried calisthenics; the dash to the bathroom, before someone else beats me there . . . I finish breakfast, dash back to my room; the clock says, 'Four minutes till your Geometry class starts.' I grab my hat and books, and start down Horger Avenue on a run. Down the hall, to my locker, and to my Geometry class. Hot and out of breath, I enter the room as the bell rings to end the first lap.

"I no more than get seated when I hear Miss Bartlett say, 'We will have to hurry this morning as I have a lot of work planned.' Hurry! Hurry! Hurry! Gee! If I could only find a teacher whose vocabulary did not include the word hurry. For fifty minutes we juggle angles and triangles. The bell rings . . . German is next. On entering my German class, Miss Horney says, 'Let us hurry and conjugate these verbs, so we will have time to go over our parts for the German play.' . . . To East Hall for a study period. I finish my Algebra, and start on my Geometry. The bell stops me with a triangle standing on one point . . . I enter my English class mostly unprepared . . .

"On entering my Algebra class . . . I find Miss Arnold erect, smiling, ready to get down to work . . . 'We will have to hurry and finish linear equations today, as I want to explain radicals tomorrow.' We spend the hour trying to prove x equals y, or finding out how many days it will take A and B to do a certain job. Poor A and B, they too are racing with that unconquerable opponent Time. The bell rings with A and B still hard at their jobs.

"With the seventh lap over . . . I rush to my locker, get my hat, and rush back to my rooming house, change clothes, and off to the restaurant. . . . With one eye on the clock, the other on my meal, disregarding all health rules, I finish my meal in record time. Two minutes to catch my bus. With a compressed feeling around my abdomen, my coat tail flying, I hurry down Michigan Avenue. I shall miss the bus. No! I get a break! Time in the form of a red light delays the bus long enough for me to get in. I drop my dime in the box and settle down in the only remaining seat.

"A feeling of envy comes over me as I sit there and notice the fleecy white clouds drift lazily in the sky . . . My imaginary journey into the upper hemisphere is suddenly ended by the screeching of brakes and the sudden stopping of the bus. Time has beaten us again. All eyes are on the red light, now it is yellow; gears grind, the light turns green, the clutch grips, we swing the corner, and head down Miller Road . . . We near the Michigan Central tracks. The gates are down, the bus comes to a stop, the New York Express flashes by, with its human cargo . . . The gates go up, I have six minutes till starting time. The bus lunges forward, gate five is reached, the bus stops, half of the men try to get through the narrow door at one time. The last is off, we are off, gate four is reached. Three minutes to go. I am off the bus before it comes to a dead stop — up those steel steps, polished by hurrying feet, over the bridge, down the other side.

"Pushing, tugging, using all the football tactics I know of to get through the milling mob of Ford men, some coming in, others going out . . . I get in the clear, the goal post does not lie before me, but the time clock does. Thirty seconds to go, panting I hit the clock, the bell rings. No cheering crowds, just the roar of machines to acclaim my spectacular dash.

"I open my tool box, get a hurried line from the day man . . . The foreman comes rushing up to me with a set of blueprints, saying, 'Here is a rush experimental job for the Dearborn Engineering Laboratory. It is promised for next week.' I spend the next three hours analyzing and checking the various blueprints, getting castings machined, having forgings heat-treated and normalized.

"The foreman inquires how the job is progressing. I reply, fine, only I could use a few more men in order to keep all the details working. I am given more men. The bell ends the first four hours, and everyone rushes to the lunch wagon.

"The way the men line up you would think it was a soup line during a panic, and that they hadn't had anything to eat for days, but the reason they rush is because they have only twenty minutes in which to eat. I stand in line five minutes to get my lunch, only fifteen minutes in which to eat it. As I sit there and eat, I hear and see the high speed production machines running, in the building across the way. Those poor fellows on production do not get as long to eat as I do, no wonder five percent suffer with indigestion . . .

"The bell ends the lunch period, hurriedly I finish my lunch, and get back to work. I spend the next few hours instructing machine men and keeping all the details working, so as to make the best time possible in getting the jobs finished on the day promised . . .

"With renewed interest I continue my work. Time passes quickly; the midnight shift comes in; one hour to go. I line up the midnight man who is to lead my job. This consumes about forty-five minutes, in the last fifteen minutes I put my tools away, and the bell rings: a rush for the washing room! I grab my hat and coat, and head for the streetcar. All the seats are taken but the men jam in like cattle . . .

"Two blocks from Michigan Avenue, I start working my way toward the door. The car stops, I get off, and head for my room.

The house is dark . . . Swiftly but silently I enter. Inside, my roommate, who is working days, is fast asleep.

"I finish my toilet, look at a few school books, and hit the hay . . .

"In our lives, the thing that really counts is not how long we live, nor how hard we work, but what we accomplish. Time is one of the greatest factors in our efforts to accomplish our aims; therefore

> By the wasting of your Time,
> You do yourself the greatest crime.

> *Walter P. Reuther*
> *Fordson High School*
> *Oct. 24, 1929*

I still find it unbelievable that, with such a schedule, Walter had the energy to organize the 4C Club, a group of students who were also working their way through high school. The four C's stood for cooperation, confidence, comradeship, and citizenship. The club's charter, which set forth the organization's goals and values, sounds like something the local Chamber of Commerce or Jaycees would have happily endorsed. Yet though its vague objectives were in no way unique, the club was a remarkable cross section of the first- and second-generation immigrant work force. The names reveal the sweep of nationalities: Emil Schnier, Walter's landlord; Joseph Ruzyski, Polish-German from Warsaw, who hoped to be a civil engineer; Nicholas Mares, Mexican, an electrician; Sam Creighton, an English die sinker at Ford, finishing high school so that he would not spend his life in a tool shop; John Vitalari from Hungary; Harold Landgarf, with an American father and a German mother; Jerry Fabirowski from Poland; James Tucich from Yugoslavia, a tool maker who planned to remain one; Harold Moore, English; Cecil McCoy, Scottish; Joe Lakomski from Austria; Fred Brierley of British stock, aiming at a medical career. Finally there was Merlin Bishop, of American parentage, a crane operator and later a machinist at Ford, who was supporting his family while he went back to school to improve his chances. Merlin and his brother Melvin would be associated with the Reuther brothers for many years in various ways. But now Merlin was secretary of the 4C Club and Walter was president.

The high-sounding principles of the club were embodied in such mundane projects as selling candy and drinks at games in order to raise money for disadvantaged students, renting films and showing them in the school auditorium, and the like. But the club, indeed, was composed of out-of-the-ordinary young people, virtually all of whom were helping to support their families, and at the same time lifting themselves up by a mutual bootstrap operation. Merlin Bishop recalled later that he and Walter "were paraded before the Rotary Club and Kiwanis Club as the officers of this dynamic organization." On Walter's 4C application blank, he wrote that he had gone back to school because "I realize that to do something constructive in life, one must have an education. I seek knowledge that I may serve mankind."

Walter's natural buoyancy and optimism suffered a severe shock during the Great Depression that began in the fall of 1929 and by 1932 had idled 25 percent of the country's work force. He did not personally suffer any immediate effects. But as he saw the nervous strain among the workers, who never knew when their cards would be pulled out of the rack, and observed the company's increasing pressure on the foremen to step up the pace of the work and get the most out of the last man, his awareness of the social and economic realities became more keen. His essays in English class began to bear a closer resemblance to our early family debates; among the titles were "Educational Opportunities for All" and "The Vices of Prohibition." Later in the year he wrote on Thomas Paine. His composition, "The Misunderstood Hero," began with the famous quotation "The world is my country and to do good is my religion," which became one of the tenets of Walter's philosophy. In the essay he pointed out that, while Paine supported the French Revolution and was elected a deputy to the National Assembly, he attempted to save the life of King Louis XVI. "Picture a leader for democracy pleading to save the life of an enemy of democracy. This proves his heart was bursting with love for all men. He hated no man, no king, he only hated the system under which they governed."

To the end of his life, Walter never forgot that important distinction between individuals and institutions. He said over and over again during his struggles with opposition groups within the union: "One must be careful never to destroy one's opposition. You may defeat them, but your goal should always be to convert them, never to destroy them."

Meanwhile in Morgantown, West Virginia, I was undergoing my

own brand of disillusionment. I became more and more disturbed by the compulsory military training with the ROTC, and by the general reactionary atmosphere of campus life, with its fraternity and sorority status-seeking, and the ridiculous hazing affairs, which often endangered the health, if not the lives, of some students. Most of all I was shocked and depressed by visits to Scotts Run, the mining camp on the outskirts of town. I began to write more frequently to Walter about the pitiful, sordid conditions, the shacks beside polluted streams, the undernourished children, the lack of school and health services, and the miners' dependence on the company stores, which charged them exorbitant prices. We had to do something, I wrote Walter, in our lifetime to correct those cancers on our social system, which our father had pointed out to us so often and which were growing worse and worse as the Depression swept in with all its fury.

During one of the holidays when we were both home, Walter and I talked at great length and finally decided that the most sensible thing would be to study law, which would serve us both as education and as a political base for initiating the appropriate legislation on unemployment, child labor, and other problems that were coming to a head all over the country. "Why don't you come to Detroit and we'll work and study together?" Walter suggested. This idea germinated, and after my freshman year I said goodbye to West Virginia University.

But before my second semester was over, Ted, Walter, Roy, and I were able to schedule a two-week vacation together. I think it was the last time that it was ever possible. Using Ted's Model T sedan, we made our way to Washington and back, camping in state parks and sometimes by the side of the road. We went over the mountains to Virginia, and took in Richmond, the Luray Caverns, and other sights, and at last reached the highpoint of our journey, the Lincoln Memorial. That trip cemented our genuine brotherhood into a solidarity that never failed us from then on.

CHAPTER 6

Gathering Forces

I DOUBT if I could have picked a worse time to go to Detroit than the fall of 1930. It was hard enough for a worker with high skills to find a job in that dire period.

Detroit still had its prosperous façade: the Fine Arts Institute, the marble public library, the Detroit Symphony, and Jessie Bonstelle's repertory playhouse; there was Briggs Stadium, and Ann Corio, with her comic star "Scurvy," at the Cadillac Burlesque.

As the Depression deepened and automobile production was cut back further, the all-night movie houses harbored thousands of homeless workers. Anger and bitterness deepened as the banks foreclosed more and more home mortgages. Then the banks themselves went into crisis and closed down. The city had to pay its teachers and other employees with scrip instead of legal tender. The great downtown stores, which accepted this strange money, managed to pay their taxes with it.

At first I made daily rounds of the employment offices, joining the multitude that moved from factory gate to factory gate. There was not even a chance of getting a waiter's job. But there was one mitigating circumstance: I was not alone. With my brother, I was part of a group that felt as I did: this economic holocaust was not ordained by God in heaven but was manmade, and men could keep it from happening again.

Walter suggested that we organize a housing cooperative with a group of working students, so that we could share the rent and cut down on food expenses by buying in bulk. We began in a small basement apartment. Walter lent me the sixty dollars needed for my fall tuition, and we all went to classes in the morning; then, while the four Ford workers were at their jobs, I earned my keep by shopping for food, cooking, packing lunches, and doing the laundry and necessary housekeeping. In modern terms this might be called a commune — though a very "square" one, confined, as it was, to members of one sex who kept no alcohol on the premises.

Since I had some spare time, I not only visited the library and museum, but did a lot of wandering through the center of the city, where large areas had degenerated into atrocious slums, and through the outskirts, where the homeless had built their Hoovervilles near the city dumps. On weekends, I would take the others on similar "realism" tours. One weekend, deciding to undergo what we knew to be the degrading experience of so many, we spent one unforgettable night in the Salvation Army flophouse. We wore our oldest clothes and gave ourselves fictitious names. We were indeed made to feel less than human as we went through the delousing process, and the whole scene of hungry and humiliated people receiving aggressively impersonal charity was horrifying. We shared this revelation as broadly as we could, beginning in economics and sociology classes, encouraged by both Professor Jandy and Dr. Levin of the College of the City of Detroit. Even though most of the students were from the working class, few had ever realized fully what is inflicted on the really down-and-out in the city.

I also visited the Socialist Party headquarters on Erskine Street, where I found many friends who shared my concern about an economy that couldn't provide the jobs and healthful living that its own technology certainly made possible. It was here that I first met Norman Thomas and heard a lecture by Scott Nearing.

Among Detroit Socialists active in the early thirties I remember John Panzner, a "Wobbly" (a member of the IWW), who was to become a prominent rank-and-file builder of the United Automobile Workers; Mannie Seidler from the Jewish Bund section of the party; Frank Wolfman, father of May, who became Mrs. Walter Reuther; Kathleen Jones, later to marry August Scholle, Michigan State president of the AFL-CIO. Francis King, who became an official of the Civil Service Commission of Detroit, was another participant in the discussion groups that Walter and I were lucky enough to attend. Our closest friends were the Lowries. Dr. William Lowrie was on the staff of the Henry Ford Hospital. Soft-spoken but firm, he was even in those early days an advocate of socialized medicine. His wife, Kathleen, had been secretary to Jane Addams at Hull House, and later served in the Women's Bureau of the Department of Labor.

"When Vic came to Detroit," Merlin Bishop once reminisced, "he got Walter all steamed up about the Socialist movement. I think Walter had pretty well forgotten about it up to that point. He was a very frugal fellow and invested his money, so I think at that point he was more interested in making money. His mind hadn't got onto social problems until Vic came and got him stimulated." This observation is only partly true, considering the essays Walter wrote in his high school classes before I came to Detroit. It is a fact that at the College of the City of Detroit Walter and I organized a club vastly different from his 4C Club; it was not one to gladden the hearts of the Chamber of Commerce. It was called the Social Problems Club and its aims were to discuss prime issues of the day and to stimulate some student and community action around them. We sought and obtained affiliation with the League for Industrial Democracy, which actually had roots as a campus service organization as far back as 1905, when it was called the Intercollegiate Society of Socialists. The name was changed in 1921 because of American antipathy to the Russian revolution. Charter members had included Upton Sinclair, Clarence Darrow, Jack London, Walter Lippmann, and Ralph Bunche. We wanted to become a local chapter so that we could have access to the league's literature and get help bringing national leaders to Detroit to speak in our lecture series.

Most of the planning and paperwork of the club was done in our small basement apartment. A mimeograph machine was beyond our means, so I bought some cookie tins and concocted a mixture of gelatin, glycerin, and water to make my own hectograph. The first product was a list of recommended books for our club members and other interested students. One member of our housing cooperative was a young Indian, Mukerji, who naturally got us stirred up about the problems of India and weighted our reading list considerably. Here is an exact replica of that 1930 list:

Worthwhile Books to Read
1. *Twilight of Empire* — Scott Nearing
2. *Black America* — Scott Nearing
3. *Poverty and Riches* — Scott Nearing
4. *The Rise and Fall of Civilization* — Scott Nearing
5. *Russia* — Scott Nearing

6. *The Tragedy of Waste* — Stuart Chase
7. *You Can't Win* — J. Black
8. *Criminology* — Edwin Sutherland
9. *Crucible of Crimes* — Joseph F. Fishman
10. *A Son of Mother India Answers* — D. G. Mukerji
11. *India in Bondage* — Jabez T. Sunderland
12. *India* — D. G. Mukerji
13. *India* — Annie Besant
14. *India* — M. K. Gandhi
15. *Poems* — Rabindranath Tagore
16. *The Case for India* — Will Durant
17. *The Story of Philosophy* — Will Durant
18. *Transition* — Will Durant
19. *The Brass Check* — Upton Sinclair
20. *The Jungle* — Upton Sinclair
21. *Oil* — Upton Sinclair
22. *The Cry for Justice* — Upton Sinclair
23. *History of Great American Fortunes* — Gustavus Meyers
24. *America's Way Out* — Norman Thomas
25. *As I See It* — Norman Thomas
26. *History of Socialist Thought* — Harry Laidler
27. *Debs* — David Karsner
28. *Debs* — McAlister Coleman
29. Ameringer's books
30. *Outline of History* — H. G. Wells
31. *The Story of Mankind* — Hendrik van Loon
32. *Why We Behave like Human Beings* — George A. Dorsey
33. *Socialism and the Family* — H. G. Wells
34. *The Material Conception of History* — Charles A. Beard
35. *Les Miserables* — Victor Hugo
36. *The Life of Pasteur* — R. Vallery-Radot

The Social Problems Club did not lack for issues. One of our first efforts was to block the advent of the ROTC in City College. I had my own unhappy memories of compulsory military training, and was gratified to find that the Detroit students, most of whom were working their way through school, were less than interested in military games. We were lucky to have a strong ally — Professor Walter Bergman, a veteran of World War I, who himself had organized a pacifist chapter of the American Legion in Detroit. He spoke for us at a student meeting — and was promptly fired by the Board of Education. His defense became our cause célèbre; we sent delegations to the Board of Education and enlisted the support of that great leader of the American Federation of Teachers in Chicago, Miss

Lillian Herstein. She journeyed to Detroit to defend her friend Walter Bergman. I remember her dramatic speech to the Board of Education. Walter and I also spoke, in behalf of C.C.D. students. I remember how pleased Lillian was when Walter identified himself not only as a student, but as a Ford worker and a property owner. (One of his Dearborn lots was to help us later in another campaign.)

Bergman was reinstated. Our strength grew, and the administration began to grant us more permits to use lecture halls and, occasionally, the main auditorium, when we were able to bring Norman Thomas or Dr. Harry Laidler or Scott Nearing or some other prominent so-called radical to the campus. We won a battle with the administration over the race issue when we succeeded in desegregating the swimming facilities of Webster Hall.

Our tightly knit group soon became something of a campus phenomenon. The creative core of the club was the basement housing cooperative, where we talked and planned and worked together. Merlin Bishop once said, again not too accurately, that Walter and I had a twinlike relationship. "Their minds were like one. Walter would start a college paper and then say, 'Vic, you finish it up, I've got to go to work.'" He even suggested that we had a "unique arrangement" with the professors that permitted us to submit a single paper. There was no such "arrangement." All I know is that, despite his heavy schedule at Ford, Walter averaged B+ in college and I averaged a B. I may have short-changed myself along the line somewhere, but if so, it was not important. Walter and I shared the same childhood experience, and we were both fighting for the same social reforms. The cooperation was both practical and satisfying.

Professor Jandy's sociology class provoked discussions about crime and prostitution, and Merlin Bishop, Walter, and I were inspired to take a "whoreology tour." After midnight, we would wander into the red-light district and talk with the streetwalkers, who spoke quite freely once they were convinced we weren't detectives. We spoke in class about their stories, which went beyond tear-jerking drama into the reality of poverty, pimps, helplessness.

The most terrible horror stories, of course, were unfolding in the Hoovervilles. Walter and I did a lot of photographing and eventually made up a small brochure, juxtaposing pictures of the hovels and photographs of the mansions of corporation members and auto industry executives, who lived in Grosse Pointe.

Our frontispiece included a small parody of the opening of the Gettysburg Address:

> Fourscore and seven years ago our forefathers brought forth on this continent a new economic system, conceived of the policies of "laissez faire" and dedicated to the proposition that private profit is the sole incentive to progress. Now we are engaged in a great economic struggle, testing whether this nation or any nation so deceived and so dedicated to rugged individualism can long endure.

Next to our pictures contrasting tin-and-tarpaper shacks with Grosse Pointe mansions, under a caption from Goldsmith — "Where wealth accumulates and men decay" — we commented on the "homes that a dying social order is providing for its unemployed workers . . ."

These unemployed workers had made dugouts along the railroad tracks in the Detroit city dump, using discarded dump truck bodies for shelter, lard cans for stoves, rags and newspapers for beds. We put pictures of these "houses" next to pictures of the Dodge estate under construction. "This beautiful mansion surrounded by private gardens and parks and overlooking the waters of Lake St. Clair illustrates what is possible if one belongs to the exclusive family of American capitalists."

We quoted Jessie Thomas, an unemployed Ford worker, who described the shack he had constructed and the people who lived as he did: "Like hibernating groundhogs, these people crawl into their winter holes."

But, alas, cruel nature had biologically incapacitated them for hibernation — they must eat. "A nearby city garbage disposal plant is a source of food and here by digging around in the garbage trucks as they come, they eagerly search for enough food to keep alive the spark of life within them . . ."

We contrasted the hovels against the neat brick building with large windows where the stray dogs and cats of the city were housed and fed.

Pictures of the barrackslike shacks provided for the miners in West Virginia had this caption:

> The American coal fields have been the scene of capitalism's most vicious exploitation. The coal barons own the shacks the miners live in. The barons own the schools their children attend. They own the church they worship in, the store they must buy from, the roads and railroads over which they must travel. The barons own the judge, the

sheriff and the courtroom where the miners seek justice, and last of all the coal barons own the miners because they own the only jobs upon which the miners depend for their existence. The miners and their families are forged to these hovels and the exploitation they symbolize. They cannot leave because the company pays them in scrip. That is only good at the company store and the company always sees to it that the grocery bill and the rent are higher than the paycheck . . ."

After referring to the irony of the state slogan of West Virginia, "Mountaineers Shall Always Be Free," we quoted the poem "Caliban in the Coal Mines," by Louis Untermeyer, which ends:

> God, if You had but the moon
> Stuck in Your cap for a lamp,
> Even you'd tire of it soon,
> Down in the dark and the damp.
>
> Nothing but blackness above
> And nothing that moves but the cars.
> God, if You wish for our love,
> Fling us a handful of stars!

The public meetings organized by our Social Problems Club were not free from hecklers, usually extreme leftists. On one occasion, Nydia Barker and some of her young Communist friends disrupted a meeting so thoroughly that it was impossible to carry on.

We were not deterred, however, and continued our soapboxing every weekend. At work, Walter became more open about his convictions. He told me it was easier to discuss politics with his deaf-mute coworkers, who had taught him to communicate in sign language, than with the unimaginative and uninterested toolmakers, who considered themselves the aristocracy of the plant. When the shots were fired during the tragic Ford Hunger March — some workers were killed and many wounded in the line of march — the story spread quickly through the plant. Walter was on his shift; the deaf-mutes sent him a message with their hands — "Give the signal for the revolution!" But Walter had no belief in revolution and no desire for it.

When that march of the unemployed to the River Rouge plant occurred, several hundred Soviet technicians were being trained as part of Ford's technical assistance to Russia. They would later go back to teach others in the Gorky plant, where Walter and I were employed some years later. They occupied the second floor of the building, and when the marchers were confronted by the Dearborn police and the Ford service men, and the rocks began to fly, Harry Bennett is said to have wisecracked, "They are stoning their own fellows up there!" It must have puzzled those Soviet technicians to observe, from the windows of that citadel of capitalism, the American proletariat throwing stones and epithets at Henry Ford, the hero of the technology-starved Russian people.

Walter had built into the rumble-seat section of his Model A a small platform that could be unfolded for speechmaking. We were supposed to get a permit for soapboxing from the Dearborn authorities, but they were completely under the thumb of Ford and made it difficult for us to carry out our activities. One day we drew up over the curb into a vacant lot and Walter began speaking; the police arrived and tried to arrest him, whereupon he dramatically drew from his pocket the deed to that particular piece of land. Chagrined, the police left, but soon returned to drive stakes at the corners of the lot, stretch ropes across, and insist that no one in the audience could stand outside Walter's property.

The summer of 1932 saw us campaigning at full steam as the presidential race shifted into high gear. Walter and Merlin stumped for Norman Thomas in Grand Rapids, Lansing, Muskegon, and other parts of southern Michigan, while I went north with several young trade unionists and Socialists on an extensive swing through upper Michigan. When I wrote Dad about what we were doing, we received the following letter:

My Dear Boys:
    Your decision to join and work for the establishment of the socialist society does not surprise me. On the contrary, unless all of you boys would at least by the time you reach maturity recognize the existence of a class struggle and take your place on the side of labor politically, I should be keenly disappointed. To me Socialism is the star of hope that lights the way, leading the workers from wage slavery to social justice, and to know that you boys have joined the movement, and are doing all in your power to spread a doctrine of equal opportunities for all mankind, only tends to increase my love . . ."

For Dad, as for his sons, Socialism was the expression of human idealism, and he was never brainwashed into believing that it was a sinister form of government, to be equated with totalitarianism. In his mind it was the true form of democracy, a proper alternative to military dictatorship or to a government dominated by large financial interests.

We were under no illusion that Norman Thomas could be elected. Campaigning was essentially a chance to do some educational work among factory workers, farmers, students; and it was also a training experience for us, so that we might be prepared for trade union and political battles lying ahead. As it turned out, Norman Thomas received a mere 39,205 votes in Michigan. But Dad lived to see Franklin D. Roosevelt and succeeding Presidents carry through many of the specific reforms that Norman Thomas stood for in 1932; Social Security and Unemployment Compensation, to name two. We haven't achieved an economic system that guarantees jobs for all, or even come as close to it as some European countries, but under Truman, Congress did commit itself to the principle of full employment.

During that election summer, Roy was laid off from his job in Wheeling, and the prospects in the Ohio Valley looked bleak. God knows the Michigan situation was equally depressing, but there would at least be the consolation of joining his brothers if he came to Detroit. We had room for him because we were now living in a larger apartment on Merrick Street and South Boulevard. The original cooperative group had drifted apart, and Walter and I now shared quarters with two toolmakers from Walter's shop, who were also studying at the College of the City of Detroit: Frank X. Braun, a German immigrant who was later to become head of the German Department at the University of Michigan, and Cecil Halbert, a friend from Walter's 4C days, who in later years was to own his own tool and die shop. Life had picked up socially, too, and there were more picnics on Belle Isle or in the Irish Hills.

Roy joined us late in the summer. An ardent trade unionist, he was also interested in the presidential campaign and in what our Social Problems Club had been doing. He, too, made the rounds at the factory gates with no success, and by late fall, with his savings gone, he was one of the first to take advantage of the New Deal's emergency programs. At the same time, he enrolled in the college to continue his education.

Only a few days after the election, the foreman in the River Rouge tool room announced a ten-cents-an-hour pay cut. The workers grumbled but there still was little talk of the need for a union, except

for one master mechanic named John Rushton. Older than many of
the workers, but with very young ideas, he could, I think, be described as a humanitarian Communist. He knew the Ford workers
needed a union, and spoke openly about it and about his admiration
for the Soviet system. Walter admired him personally and liked to
get into discussions with him at lunch time or when they leaned over
a blueprint together.

It is not surprising that, a few weeks later, a pink slip appeared in
the Reuther time-clock rack in place of the time card. Neither the
foreman nor the superintendent could give Walter any clear explanation; his work had always been very satisfactory. Obviously Walter's open campaigning for Norman Thomas had convinced the
Ford Service Department that he was a dangerous radical. Yet,
paradoxically, in the same tool room where Walter worked, Russian
engineers were being trained to set up the first automobile plant in
the Soviet Union and increase the technical power of the leading
Communist state!

Walter came home smiling. "Guess what happened to me today!
I feel like a liberated man. As if a great load had been lifted off my
shoulders." And then he looked at me and said, "Hey, Vic. Why
don't we take that trip we've been talking about so long?"

For many months we had been dreaming about a tour of Europe.
Like all young people, we wanted to see the world, and also had a
great curiosity about Germany, where our parents had been born
and where the Hitler situation was becoming ominous. I was delighted with the idea of leaving as soon as possible. Fate, in the form
of Ford, Rushton, and the Soviet automotive plant, gave us the necessary push.

The Ford Motor Company had made a deal with the Amtorg
Trading Company, the Soviet business arm, to sell it all the tools,
dies, jigs, and fixtures necessary for the manufacture of the Model
A, which was being discontinued in this country. The equipment
was capable of producing many more thousands of cars. Although
Ford, and Harry Bennett especially, were hysterically suspicious of
union organizers, all of whom they considered Communists, they
were quite willing to deal with real Bolsheviks — for cash on the line.
They even went so far as to lend Ford technicians to the Gorky Auto
Works.

John Rushton had already been recruited by the Soviet auto people in Dearborn to go to the Gorky plant and help with the tooling. He had sold his home and taken his family to Russia a short while before Walter was fired. When Walter wrote him about what had happened, Rushton wrote back urging him to come to Gorky. He had already convinced Amtorg of the danger of some of the precision dies breaking down and needing replacement. The Model A head gasket die would be particularly difficult to make because it involved cutting soft brass to the fifteen-thousandth of an inch. Walter had worked on that die, and with Rushton's prompting, Amtorg decided they needed him badly — badly enough to allow him to take me, a completely unskilled worker, along too.

We were thus able to plan our trip around the promise of salaried work at the end of it, and before we left Dearborn we went to the pawnshops and bought two sets of die-maker's tools, including micrometers and height gauges. We also bought secondhand heavy sheepskin coats and warm boots and gloves, since we intended to tour Europe on bicycles. Walter converted $800, a sizable chunk of his savings, into American Express checks, some in my name. We said goodbye to our college professors, Jandy, McFarland, and Bergman, who highly approved of our venture, even though we were leaving school just short a few credits needed for our degrees.

The labor scene that we left behind in Detroit was a stormy one, since the Auto Workers' Union, a small group of scattered auto workers, had called a strike in the Briggs plant. Walter and I had both joined that union as an act of solidarity, so it turned out that our last days in Michigan were spent on the picket line. It was there that we first met the energetic young Emil Mazey, who would play a historic role, at Walter's side, in the transformation of the Auto Workers' Union.

There were two hard farewells: one for me from a beautiful young girl I shall refer to only as Elsie, with whom I was deeply in love, and the other for both Walter and me from our brother Roy. We embraced him and left him on the street corner at an entrance to the Briggs plant, where we had all three been picketing. Within a month, as that ill-fated strike went on, the Detroit police were to smash through the picket line, shoving Roy against a sharp spike in an iron fence, thus causing a wound that would leave him scarred for the rest of his life.

On the long ride to Wheeling and our parents' house, we decided that Walter would teach me the rudiments of shop work during the holiday season at the Wheeling High School, with the permission of his former teacher, Mr. Schneider. Though Rushton expected me to be unskilled, Walter thought it would be unwise for me to go over there completely raw. The shop training would provide a good time-filler, too, since I had to wait until my twenty-first birthday on the first of January to apply for a passport in case parental consent was withheld. We planned to soft-pedal our idea of spending from two to three years abroad, and emphasize instead the visits to our German relatives.

Mother and Dad were more understanding than we had expected; they were pleased that we were going to Germany, certain that the whole trip would broaden and benefit us. Mr. Schneider let us use the shop and we spent long hours there. Squeezing a three-year apprenticeship into a few weeks was Walter's aim, and even with a pupil as eager as I, and a teacher as wildly stubborn as Walter, it was a herculean task that even he found difficult.

The Wheeling newspaper carried an item on February 12 about a farewell party in our honor, and quoted a characteristic Reuther comment, made by Walter: "We are going to study the economic and social conditions of the world, not the bright lights."

We got to New York on February 13, after a long, sleepless bus ride, and headed immediately for the League for Industrial Democracy, once we had checked in at the YMCA. There we renewed some friendships; we had met Joseph Lash, Mary Hillyer, Mary Fox, Paul Porter, and others in connection with our Social Problems Club. During the three days before our ship sailed, Walter and I collaborated on an article for the league's *Student Outlook* magazine and also paid visits to Tucker Smith, a prominent member of the peace movement, and Jay B. Matthews of the Fellowship of Reconciliation, little anticipating that the latter would become a close collaborator of the infamous Joseph McCarthy.

The first evening, we dined with Norman Thomas, Mrs. Thomas, and their daughter Frankie at Mrs. Thomas's little tearoom. After dinner we spoke before two different branch meetings of the Socialist Party, later returning to the Thomases' home, where we ended up spending the night. I am afraid we exploited Norman Thomas that evening with typical youthful thoughtlessness, keeping him up late into the night, talking.

I have never met another candidate who sought public office so many times, never once expecting to win, never once depressed by failure. Even more impressive to us than Thomas's insight into world problems was his basic concept that one cannot separate politics and economics from morality. For sons of Val Reuther this emphasis was irrefutable.

On our final day in New York we visited the National Student League and then had dinner with a group of young Socialist militants. Around nine o'clock that evening they escorted us to the Hamburg American Line to board the S.S. *Deutschland*. We were off at last, and though we traveled third class, the days on board ship seemed a pleasure and a luxury beyond believing.

CHAPTER 7

Into the Nazi Whirlpool

WALTER AND I arrived in Germany only three days before the Reichstag was set on fire and Hitler's campaign to take over Germany became an acknowledged fact. We were in Berlin by March 1 and saw the smoldering remains of the old parliament, surrounded by armed guards, the whole center section gutted and the great glass dome collapsed. Brown-shirted storm troopers were everywhere, hawking special editions of the Nazi-controlled newspapers, which were promoting Goebbels's fabrications about a Communist-Socialist plot to start a civil war, of which this fire was the first signal.

The circus atmosphere around the ruined building — swastika flags flying in the smoke, barkers shouting to the crowd to buy the Nazi papers — would have been ludicrous if it had not been so tragic. We were among the first allowed to go inside, and were taken by a brown-shirted guide into what he said was a former office of the Communist deputies. He dramatically took several books from a shelf and opened them up to show revolvers inserted where the pages had been cut away. This was the Nazis' conclusive evidence of a planned, armed uprising.

With the aid of credentials supplied us by Norman Thomas, we had found a place to live among Socialist university students in a housing cooperative on the top floors of a large warehouse. They took us to one of their last political meetings, held in the rear of a small wine establishment. Voices were kept low. All were disenchanted with the Socialists, Communists, and trade union leaders of the Social Democratic Party, who had failed to patch up their quarrels and unite against Hitler. With the terror on the streets and Goering in charge of an auxiliary force of fifty thousand SA and SS troops, the election of Hitler was a foregone conclusion. The chairman, after cordially acknowledging Walter and me, broke up the meeting early, admonishing everyone not to go home alone but in groups, and to take detours around Nazi strongholds in the city.

The day before the election, March 4, Walter and I mingled with the crowd of twenty-five thousand jammed into the Franz Josef Platz to hear the frenetic voice of Hitler coming over the radio from Koenigsberg. Martial music and church bells fired the crowd, which began to sing, with obviously rehearsed precision, the old national anthem, "Deutschland Über Alles." The message came through loud and clear: "We are ourselves again — we are all Germans — and we want the world to know it!"

Returning to our friends in the student cooperative, we found them barring the windows and doors with furniture. A night watch was assigned, to be changed every two hours; we all slept in our clothes. A back window was left unlocked with a rope ladder near it. We could hear the police marching back and forth on the bridge beneath the front windows. But that night passed without a raid.

Election day was quieter than expected. Walter and I listened to a bulletin from the U.S. announcing that Franklin D. Roosevelt had taken his oath of office and the banks had been closed for three days. Then we toured the polling places with some of the students and watched an enormous parade organized by the veterans' organization. It looked more like a demonstration of preparedness than a political march, as it came through the Brandenburg Gate and up the center of Unter den Linden to be reviewed by von Papen and General Ludendorff. This nationalist and conservative faction would soon become one of Hitler's strong supports, turning his 44 percent of the total popular vote into a sixteen-vote margin in the new parliament.

There was nothing but gloom in our quarters that evening. Our young friends began to prepare for underground activity and were burning papers that might be used against them when the police came, as they, if not the storm troopers, inevitably would. Some were packing and planning to go into exile in Switzerland or Holland. Our lights did not go out until about 2:00 A.M. Soon after 3:00 A.M., we heard the main door broken through and from the windows on the top floor could see brown-shirted troopers gathered below. Our greatest concern was to get the most well-known activists safely out the back window. I remember an emotional farewell to Emil Gross, a marked man in the Nazi book. He was the first we saw down the rope ladder and away into the darkness through a neighboring building. It was clear that the troopers were after Emil; when they couldn't find him, they took only a token few of the students. They looked at our American passports and warned us that we should find other lodgings. That night we faced the reality: political and civil rights were dead in Germany.

The following day we saw the trade union and Social Democrat headquarters surrounded by storm troopers and police carrying off papers and records. The building would soon be turned into a so-called Labor Front center and the vast amount of printing equipment — twenty-four linotype machines and many huge presses — that had put out the trade union publications of a free Germany would be dishing out the propaganda of Herr Goebbels, via Dr. Ley, head of the Nazi Labor Front.

Almost stunned by events, we left Berlin and pushed on to Dresden, where the same process was taking place: the workers' relief organization building, union and democratic headquarters, and Volkhaus all were turned into military barracks. Another show was staged to prove the treason and degeneracy of both Communists and Socialists: a guide unearthed hidden weapons and spicy literature in the modest rooms where visiting functionaries used to stay; he pointed out women's slips that had been draped over beds, and Parisian hatboxes and whiskey bottles that had been thrown around the rooms. "Such is the high life that your comrades enjoyed at your expense!" went the refrain. Such charades were repeated in every city and town of Germany, each one a prelude to arrests and imprisonments.

The very name that Hitler and Goebbels gave to their party symbolized the deception on which they relied to gain popular support. They called it the National Socialist German Workers Party. The words *National* and *German* (Hitler, of course, was an Austrian) were an appeal to the chauvinistic conservatives. The use of the words *Socialist* and *Workers* was, however, the most cynical, evil stroke of all. It was clear from the start that a Nazi government would be the antithesis of everything implied in the Socialist movement, which has always had deep democratic and parliamentary roots. As for the workers, Hitler had made a definite commitment to "put labor in its place." He stripped the trade unions of their property, and then took away the basic rights of the workers, all under the pretense of protecting them. Dr. Ley spouted on the first Hitlerian May Day (no longer called International Labor Day now, but the Day of National Labor):

> Workers, your institutions are sacred to us National Socialists. I myself am a poor peasant's son and understand poverty . . . Workers, I swear to you, we will not only keep everything that exists, we will build upon the protection and rights of the workers still further . . .

Only three weeks later, Hitler was reassuring the employers of Germany that the Labor Front was created to "restore absolute leadership to the natural leader of a factory — that is, the employer." He then decreed an end to collective bargaining, and banned all strikes. He selected his own "labor trustees" to enforce these repressions and also began to exploit and brainwash the German youth: hundreds of thousands, under the guise of what was called a Voluntary Labor Force, were turned into an army of young criminals, soon substituting guns for shovels, and giving their energies to vile acts of persecution. Hitler could not have carried through his pogroms without them.

After looking at the swastika flags flying over the ancient ramparts of Nuremberg, we decided to hurry on ahead of schedule to see our relations in Swabia: Uncle Ernest in Ruit and Uncle Adolph in Scharnhausen, neighboring villages several miles out of Stuttgart.

We had seen many photographs and it was not difficult to recognize our uncles though at first it was hard to understand the Swabian dialect, which might be described as German hillbilly. We became acquainted over beer in a Stuttgart *gasthaus* until it was time to board the infrequent tramway and ride to the top of the hill near Sillenbuch, where Uncle Ernst had left his small handcart. We put our footlockers and suitcases into the cart and pulled it two miles to the village of Ruit. Our Aunt Karolina and two girl cousins, Erna and Julia, who were a little older than we, welcomed us warmly into a home that would serve as our base and mailing address for many months to come.

Uncle Ernst was a typographical worker who earned his living in the city of Esslingen. He was, quite naturally, a Social Democrat; he had long been active in the Typographical Union. Uncle Adolph, however, was something very different: a typical village farmer, con-

servative to the core. In Chapter 1, I have described my mother's
birthplace, Scharnhausen, with its two-and-a-half-story houses, manure piles, rural ideology. Uncle Adolph was proud that he was not
sullied by industry or commerce, proud that during his youthful military service he had been in charge of the stables of the local prince.
He was also Deputy Mayor of the village and officiated in parades.
He could not afford a full Nazi uniform; he wore instead the swastika armband and Nazi hat. He presented his American nephews
with a photograph of himself astride his plowhorse, giving the Nazi
salute. We took this back to our cousins in Ruit, who laughingly
agreed that the appropriate place for that particular photo was the
privy.

It was, however, no laughing matter. I remember a heated clash
between our uncles, when Ernst expressed some real concern about
Hitler, and Adolph flushed red and exploded, "When we march on
Moscow, I hope I shall have the privilege of shooting you down if
you oppose me!"

Even in the remotest village of Germany it had become dangerous
to express any criticism; mayors and other officials were pressured
to take oaths of allegiance to the regime. In the neighboring town
of Neumagen, the Mayor and five members of his council had been
beaten and imprisoned; at Nellingen, where we also had relatives,
members of the age-old Workers' Singing Society were arrested for
singing their traditional freedom song; in Scharnhausen, the Workers' Singing Society was forced to change its name but, even after
complying, was forbidden to meet and rehearse.

The German Memorial Day on March 23, supposedly a day to
honor the war dead, was converted by the Nazis into an occasion for
fascist rallies. In Scharnhausen every house had put out a swastika
flag — it was tantamount to suicide not to display it — and in the
evening the villagers turned out to march to the war memorial,
where a group of uniformed Hitler youth stood around as an honor
guard, periodically chanting, "Heil Hitler." There was a bonfire; a
band played; the children carried torches or lanterns. The spirit
was festive until the Mayor was moved (or had been instructed) to
launch into an ultrapatriotic speech calling for support of Hitler. A
young Volunteer Labor enthusiast did likewise; then, with a dramatic flourish, threw a Communist hammer-and-sickle flag into the
bonfire, shouting, "Let this be a symbol of the complete collapse of
Bolshevism in Germany and of the dawn of a new era!" When the

banner hit the fire, a voice called out from the crowd, *"Das hast du gestohlen!"* ("You stole that!") Needless to say, the speaker was pounced on by the Brown Shirts, beaten up, and arrested, along with his brother, who had come to his defense. The two victims were workers from a factory in Esslingen and known to the villagers, who seemed embarrassed that such brutality had been witnessed by foreigners, but soon shrugged it off: "The fool should have kept his big mouth shut."

Walter and I had expected to receive our work visas for the Soviet Union while we were visiting in Swabia, but they did not arrive and we decided to see something of the rest of Europe. We bought bicycles in Ruit and equipped them with metal packs, of our own making, that fitted neatly over the rear wheels. The best thing about these packs was their concave six-inch telescopic soldered lids, which allowed us to increase or decrease the size of the containers. These waterproof deep lids served as washbasins, as well as basins for testing a punctured tube, among other purposes.

There was no tearful departure from relatives and friends in Swabia; we knew this would be a "home base" to which we would return after each visit to another part of Europe.

After the shocking disillusionment of the preceding weeks, we felt a positive euphoria as we started off in the mountain country and headed through the Black Forest in the direction of France. It was not quite spring; we found snow on the upper hills as, perspiring, we pushed our bikes up and then swooped down through the cool valleys. It took us a while to get our muscles in shape. Fortunately, we had learned about an extensive low-cost chain of excellent youth hostels, where we could eat and sleep and warm ourselves among people of our own age and, for a while at least, of our own political persuasion.

Through the valley of the Rhone, Lyon, Avignon, Orange, we pedaled to Marseilles and then along the Riviera into Italy. The hotels, cars, yachts, and general finery of Cannes and Nice and Monte Carlo made a surrealist contrast to the grimy Marseilles landscape. The Mediterranean coast at the French-Italian border overwhelmed us completely — one continuous rock garden, the scent of azaleas, the brilliant bougainvillea, the blue of the sea. We crossed into Italy early one afternoon and that evening stayed at the Albergo Milan, built literally on the rocky banks of the Mediterranean.

We were snapped back into the reality of the era even before we got to Rome. Exhausted by the trip to Pisa — made on a day of unending rain — we checked our bicycles in a little town called Volaborterro north of Rome and bought train tickets. In spite of Mussolini's publicized good housekeeping, our train was inordinately delayed, and we finally learned that it had to make way for a fast express (we saw it go by, bedecked with banners) bearing Der Führer to Il Duce to a celebration of the tenth anniversary of the Italian fascist revolution.

You might call us gluttons for punishment for choosing this moment to see Rome, but we were as interested in comparing the disaster areas of Europe as we were in seeing its monuments of art and taste. There was a chilling similarity between the German and Italian propaganda; the same familiar nonsense in museum displays of giant photographs, drawings, sculptures showing how Mussolini had saved Italy from a Communist takeover and from the perils of Socialism; the same rallies full of boys and girls formed into paramilitary groups, wearing black uniforms and carrying small replicas of guns. In the evening there was the same hysterical crowd, jammed into the Piazza Venezia, cheering and yelling, "Duce, Duce, Duce."

But Italy has its layers on layers. Historical associations came to me in a flood as we walked along the Appian Way, saw the marks left on the cobblestones by the chariots, and felt the hair-raising shiver in the Colosseum, where slave labor had planted the huge stones, and where many martyrs came to a bloody end rather than deny their faith at the command of an arbitrary state.

The impact of Rome, especially of St. Peter's and the Vatican, was so overpowering that even fascism paled beside it. I had never realized the measure of the gift the church made to the world by safeguarding the art of many centuries. The scale of the architecture alone is soul-stretching. The Italians of the sixteenth century must surely have been overcome with emotion when, after walking great distances from their primitive villages, they approached St. Peter's towering above them, or, once inside, saw the alcove shrines with the candles burning, or craned their necks to stare at the incredible work of Michelangelo on the Sistine Chapel ceiling. Not even modern travelers have been prepared, through reading, reproductions, museums, for the emotions that Rome can evoke.

We made the customary tour of the rest of Italy, a tour highlighted by Florence and Venice. Years later Walter and I went back to Florence, which both of us had loved, and were invited by the

Mayor to call upon him in his office in City Hall overlooking the little square where the statue of David presides. We were having a cup of cappuccino at an outdoor table in the early morning, waiting for our appointment and admiring the city all over again, when the morning traffic began roaring through the square — Renaults, Fiats, Topolinos, and the rasping Vespas, choking us with their gases. We fought our way across and went directly to the Mayor's office, where Walter greeted the dignitary with a small explosion: "Mr. Mayor, why don't you do something about that terrible traffic — it's destroying the whole character of this lovely city!" The Mayor, the famous La Piera, was at first taken aback by the brashness of this American, telling him how to run his city. Then, realizing he was talking to the president of the World Automobile Section of the International Metalworkers' Federation, he leaned back and roared with laughter: "How can *you* make this kind of suggestion?" Walter answered that automobiles were fine, but limits should be set to keep them from debasing the quality of life, especially in a city as stunning as Florence.

In Austria we were conscious of the shadow of approaching disaster. Vienna had just had its May Day celebration and even in that year before the Dollfuss crackdown, the traditional parade had been banned by a government that was beginning to capitulate to Nazi pressure. Most of the people had turned out anyway, locked arms, and circled the entire city by marching down the Ringstrasse. We could sense the emotion that had provoked that act of defiance when we arrived and called for our mail at the headquarters of the Social Democratic Party, which we had given to Uncle Ernst as our forwarding address.

Socialists were still regularly winning about 68 to 70 percent of the Vienna vote, and no wonder, considering the cooperative housing programs, health centers, libraries, laundries, kindergartens, day care centers, all scaled to a worker's wage. We had a good look at the impressive George Washington Hof, where the largest apartment was only about forty schillings a month, 5 percent of the average monthly wage. Parents were charged only one schilling a day per child for the kindergarten. The quality of the housing and the excellent child care provided then is something we should all be proud of in the United States if we could duplicate it in our inner cities today.

We met students, went to one of their political rallies, picnicked with them, and sang with them in the Vienna woods; and we even managed to get to the opera, Austrian-student-style, which meant standing in line at an early hour and hoping that space would become available at the last moment.

Though the Nazi Party was weak in Austria, the Communist Party was still weaker, and foolishly followed its usual practice there, as it did elsewhere, of competing with the Social Democrats instead of uniting with them against the encroachment of fascism. "Divide and conquer" was to be the successful strategy once more. As we cycled on toward Salzburg, we saw more and more evidence of growing Nazi strength among the Austrian peasantry. The large cities were at yet strongly democratic, but in the villages swastikas had cropped up all over, like measles. As we left Austria behind us at the Swiss border, both Walter and I admitted to premonitions of evil.

To shake off some of the burden of our "social study" tour, which our romantic American natures could find rather heavy, and perhaps to avoid returning immediately to what had become a disagreeable grandfatherland, Germany, we decided to try some mountain climbing. Poring over maps, we imagined ourselves on at least the middle slopes of the Jungfrau, drinking in a panorama of snow-clad Alps, far from the troubling injustices of society.

We had had no previous experience and were, of course, being very foolhardy, but bright and early on May 23, armed with alpenstocks and a small length of rope, we began the "practice" ascent of Mount Pilatus. The fact that schoolchildren in the area found the mountain easy to master bolstered our self-confidence, and we were soon at the tree line, admiring the splendid view, which seemed more than sufficient reward for our work. Soon we came upon rocks that were covered with fresh snow. We walked along a ridge where the sun was melting the snow and the path was narrow. Walter stepped too close to a soft edge, lost his balance, and began sliding over. By happy chance, there was a small shrub on the side of the slope, and he hung on to it with determination as we watched his alpenstock turning and tumbling down the thousand-foot drop. I inched myself over and held my staff down to where Walter could grab it, and gradually I helped him back over the edge. We sat in complete silence and a cold sweat for a while, leaning against the mountain with our hearts pounding.

CHAPTER 8

Crisscrossing

THERE WAS STILL no sign of our Russian visas when we went back to touch base at Uncle Ernst's house in Ruit. With our cousins Erna and Julia, and Julia's boy friend, Alfred, a staunch Social Democrat, we recklessly went to Stuttgart one night to take in a Goebbel propaganda movie, all about a mother-loving Nazi boy in the clutches of drunk, criminal, and prostituted Communists. At the end of the picture, an enormous swastika across the screen and the strains of the Horst Wessel song persuaded the audience to rise, with arms outstretched in the Nazi salute, and sing along with the organ. The four of us remained seated, and escaped harm only because Walter and I started speaking English in loud voices to drown out the shouts directed at us: "Communist pigs! Swine! Throw them out!" In order to help, our cousins also started speaking the few English words they knew, and we eased ourselves out of the hall and a very tight situation. Back in Ruit, we all concluded that Germany was *erwacht;* that is, "awakened" as Hitler had called for. After a week of essential repairs to our bicycles and clothes, we hit the open road again, headed for Paris and England, taking a route through the Rhineland to find the village where our father had been born. Unfortunately, we had only the names, not the addresses, of our relatives in Edigheim. We went to the police station there and asked about a Peter Reuther. The officer on duty was unfriendly and uncooperative; he asked us why we wanted to see Peter Reuther. We explained that we were relatives from America. "It would be better if you had no truck with him. He's a no-good Communist," replied the policeman, whose name was Massar.

By coincidence, our old Uncle Peter, looking like a German version of Rip van Winkle, clothes hanging loosely on his haggard frame, came walking down the street on his way home from the fields. Massar hailed him in a harsh, brusque manner, and the expression on our uncle's face clearly asked, as he came toward the police station, "What the hell have *I* done?"

"Well, how are things in Moscow?" was Massar's opening gambit, and this was enough to trigger Peter's anger. He retorted, with fire in his eyes, "I'd rather rot on a manure pile than turn tail and become a Nazi like you and the other weak-willed rats!" Then he crossed his thin wrists, stretched out his arms, and challenged Massar to arrest him. "At least you'd have to feed me, and that's more than you do now for the unemployed."

These were not the most favorable circumstances in which to meet an uncle; indeed, Uncle Peter seemed quite uninterested in a couple of American tourists, even if they were related to him. But we saw him later that evening, together with two cousins, sisters of Philip Reuther of Wheeling, and talked in a calmer atmosphere. Both Walter and I were proud of his fighting courage. Sadly, and feeling some guilt, we learned later that he was arrested soon after we left Edigheim, primarily for embarrassing the new regime in front of Americans.

We stayed in Paris ten days so that we could attend the Second International Socialist Conference on August 21 and 22. We made a visit to the Citroën plant, where the mass-production conveyor belt was similar to that at Ford, though only forty cars were produced in an hour. Walter's reaction was that, in terms of working conditions, the plant was as much a hell hole as River Rouge. About 20 percent of the workers were women, many of them spraying paint without goggles on. Safety equipment of any kind was in short supply: grinders were operated without air pumps; exposed gears and presses had no protective devices; and the air was so thick one could scarcely breathe. Though the workers belonged to a general metal workers' union, they averaged only twenty-five to forty francs a day, the equivalent of $1.25 to $2.00 at that time.

What I remember most vividly about the conference is the tragic figure of Otto Wels, who had been the great leader of the Social Democrats when they held power under the Weimar Republic. He nearly broke down and wept as he sought to explain the circumstances leading to the collapse of German democracy. The leading Socialists from at least thirty countries were there, including many men of fame and stature. The conference was disappointing to us because it did not develop any realistic program to counteract the insistent ideological drumbeat of the expanding Nazi movement. When Walter and I stood in the Père Lachaise cemetery at the graves of great Frenchmen who had strengthened the cause of freedom, brotherhood, and equality all over the world — Rousseau, Victor Hugo, Jaurès, and others — we spoke to each other of our belief that the cause of human freedom had never been in greater jeopardy than at that very moment.

After months on the continent, it was a pleasure to cross the British Channel and see signs and advertisements in English on the highway from Dover, by way of Canterbury Cathedral, to London.

We had an introduction to Fenner Brockway, a leading spokesman for the Independent Labor Party and a member of Parliament, who very kindly gave us the names of useful contacts all over Britain and expedited our research into industrial working conditions, wages, trade unions, and housing. It was he who really ended the delay in our journey to the Soviet Union by putting us in touch with the Soviet Consul General in London, through whom we hoped to pry loose our work visas. We learned that, in spite of all the correspondence with Rushton at the Gorky plant, and contrary to what we had been told in Detroit, there were still more formal applications to be filled out and passport photos to be taken. We set about to unravel the new roll of red tape and kept hoping.

Brockway also suggested that we attend the British trade union conference to be held soon in Brighton. There he introduced us to the charming, brilliant Jennie Lee, and this was the start of a friendship that included her future husband, Aneurin Bevan, equally brilliant and vibrant. Later, she too became a member of Parliament. This warm friendship has stretched a lifetime, ever since that first lunch in Brighton, when Jennie drew Walter and me out about our experiences in Germany, and shared our dismay over events and our fears about the future of Europe.

We saw the magnificent sights of London; then we started on our tour. The big Morris auto works in the outskirts of Oxford, with some seven thousand workers, was turning out 400 cars a day at less than peak capacity. It was a modern and well-lighted factory, and the general pace seemed somewhat slower than in our auto plants, except for the upholstering department, where the "tack spitters," many of them boys no more than fourteen years old, were working furiously on eight-and-a-half-hour shifts. As in the Citroën plant, most of the paint sprayers wore no masks. The average wage was about sixteen shillings a day, or approximately $3.50, plus a small group bonus. We were told by the company guide that the firm could not increase wages for fear the raise "would lead to dissipation on the part of the workers, and the men would tend to drink too much." It was an open-shop plant and most of the workers belonged to no union, even though Britain at that time was much more unionized than the United States.

We had developed a bad trick of taking advantage of the air vacuum behind a big van or truck to make pedaling easier, and as we bicycled toward Stratford-on-Avon, we were indulging in this dangerous game. The truck we were following this day, had two irresistible, long, bent bars sticking out behind it, and we grabbed on for a free ride. But our pleasure was short-lived: the truck made a sudden, sharp swerve; Walter's front wheel turned at a right angle, ripping off the tire; the tube buckled up between mudguard and frame, power-braking the bicycle and throwing Walter, with great force, to the highway, the handle of his front brake jammed deep into his right arm.

As the saying goes, there's nobody like the English in a crisis. The people in the car behind us stopped and gave first aid to Walter while I hailed the first car coming in the other direction. The driver stopped immediately and took us back to Woodstock and a good doctor who, incidentally, was a Socialist. Walter's clothes were in shreds, and he was in acute pain. The doctor put six stitches in the arm, and absolutely refused to take any fee. Walter rested in his office and I found quarters in the village.

I was able to fix Walter's bike myself in a friendly garage, but was not so successful in finding new clothes. Both the motherly landlady and I did some frantic patching, enough so that we could get to Birmingham without Walter's looking indecent.

That night we had a long talk and did some stock-taking. So far we had covered some six thousand kilometers and this was the first time we had ever unethically, and probably illegally, hitched a ride. We had come close to disaster, and resolved that we would either go under our own steam from then on, or stay put.

The pain in his arm notwithstanding, Walter, characteristically, refused to stay put. He looked ragged and exhausted and his arms and legs were so stiff that I literally had to help him onto his bike, hold him as he got seated, and give him a push so that he could steer with his one good arm and hand. I biked right beside him and when we got to a hill and he was unable to pedal, I would grab his handlebars and help him dismount. We traveled in this fashion for weeks, finding doctors, where we could, to dress the wound.

At the Austin automobile plant south of Birmingham, the manager looked askance at us and immediately turned us over to a young apprentice, who took us through the works. Of the fourteen thousand workers, two thousand were women, many of them in the foundry, making molds, which seemed to us quite extraordinary. The atmosphere in a foundry is always noxious, but it was especially bad in the Austin plant: drop hammer machines were set very close together, and the smoke, fumes, and noise were nearly intolerable. The plant was making about two thousand cars a week, and the weekly pay for the very skilled ranged from two pounds sterling to as much as five pounds, or from $8.00 to $20.00 at that time. In contrast to the prevailing practice in the U.S., retired workers over sixty-five were given a pension of three pounds ten shillings per week.

The "Black Country," the area around Stoke-on-Trent, lived up to its name. Soot and slag, black smoke and cinders belching from the chimneys made it difficult for a person to breathe. Our eyes were soon red and swollen from the chemicals in the air. In this blighted region of pottery factories surrounded by scattered workers' houses, the Industrial Revolution seems to have had its beginnings — and to have undergone no improvement. The ancient factory buildings were in disrepair; there was little or no grass, almost no sight of a tree. (I was reminded of Scotts Run in West Virginia.) Only one chimney in three showed signs of activity, and the unemployed filled the streets, many of them occupied in picking up cigarette butts. Obviously, very little effort was being made to initiate decent housing, which would have meant jobs for the unemployed. It was not just the physical degeneration that depressed us; it was the sight of a population too apathetic — except in the case of a few potters — to try to solve its harrowing problems. From huge billboards in Stoke-on-Trent, the Prince of Wales told us: "This nation cannot tolerate slums. Let it be said of our generation that we swept away the slums."

The five little Black Country towns could be described only as one

continuous slum. It was particularly sad to see several of the unemployed potters building small kilns in their own houses and engaging
in sweatshop labor to try to make a living. One can imagine what it
does to the lungs to have the vapors and heat of a pottery right in
the home.

Leaving the Black Country behind us, we felt the wind of the Irish
Sea blowing our faces clean and lifting our spirits. From Birkenhead
the ferry carried us to Liverpool and a hostel located in the birthplace of Gladstone on Rodney Road. An Independent Labor Party
man named Collins said that the shipyards were having one of their
worst sieges of layoffs, and the party was trying to organize the unemployed into special groups to combat evictions from their homes.
The docks were a disheartening sight: vast empty warehouses, ships
at anchor, the cranes silent and motionless. Hordes of workers
hung around in bunches on the wharves. The houses were back to
back — a typical slum-housing setup — with dank inner courts and
filthy entrances. I would have expected the workers of Liverpool to
be much more militant in trade union and political activity, in view
of wage exploitation and miserable housing. But apparently most of
their enthusiasm was saved for sports events.

It was encouraging, however, to see that they did not fall into the
trap of the Black Shirt fascist leader, Oswald Moseley, who sought to
turn their discontent to his own sinister purposes. A renegade Socialist, like Mussolini, he was trying to recruit young radical Liverpool workers into his movement by offering them substantial salaries, but the people in that area were not interested. We were told
that a Nazi propaganda film brought over to Liverpool was heavily
boycotted and had to be canceled.

It was already late fall when we left England, feeling not a little
apprehensive that we might never get our work visas for the USSR.
Determined to return to Stuttgart as fast as we could, we hurried
across northern France and Belgium toward Amsterdam, where
there were important contacts to look up — especially "Der Kleine,"
Emil Gross, whom we had helped escape from the storm troopers in
Berlin earlier that year. We knew he was engaged in underground
opposition to the Nazis.

On October 21 we called at the AJVA (the Socialist youth organization) and were met by a man named Alexander, who escorted us
to the offices of the newspaper *Het Volk,* where we had an emotional

reunion with Der Kleine. We helped him move his belongings, personal and organizational, to what was to be a new home and underground center — identified as a "dancing studio." That night we attended a huge anti-Nazi rally, where most of the speakers were young and very militant, then talked into the small hours of the morning in the Café Centrale with Der Kleine and some of his co-workers about their clandestine work inside Germany. We were asked to make contact for them with seven specific individuals in Germany, each of whom had responsibility for some crucial aspect of the resistance campaign. After hearing about the arrests of some of their comrades, we shed any vestige of a romantic attitude toward the activities we were undertaking. We were, we knew, engaged in extremely serious business. Before going to bed that night, Walter and I removed from our persons and luggage all papers containing names or addresses that might in any way incriminate us or our friends in case we were arrested by the Nazis when we re-entered Germany. Over and over again we repeated the names of important contacts, and the procedures for reaching them, until we were certain they were engraved on our minds. Then all the information was burned. We mailed our diaries and other personal records back to West Virginia.

We knew by then that in the German underground real names were seldom used, and that our key contact was called Fritz and lived in Gelsenkirchen in the Ruhr. We had no address for him, but had been supplied with the names of several bookshops in Dortmund, where we were to inquire about a very rare book. The clerk at the first bookshop we went to said he did not have such a book. We asked if he could suggest where we could find it and he gave us the names of other shops. It was at the third bookshop, where we were quite persistent about purchasing the book, that a young man came from the back room and said, "I do not have it in my shop but perhaps I can lead you to where you can find it." He said he was too busy during the day to help us but suggested that we meet him at the end of the afternoon. So at five-thirty we returned to the store and he escorted us to a house where we met "Fritz." We gave him and two others news of Der Kleine and his work, and his instructions for them. Then we left, wondering whether our paths would ever cross again. We heard later that Der Kleine himself made several trips back into Germany, using false passports and, of course, an assumed name. On one such mission, he was arrested by the Gestapo and sent to a concentration camp. We heard no more, and assumed that he, too, had become a victim of the Nazi holocaust.

Many years later, during the winter of 1958, I was seated in my Washington office — I was director of the UAW's Department of International Affairs — when an official of the State Department phoned me to say that a very distinguished German publisher was there. He was making a tour of the United States under the department's auspices, and had expressed a wish to see me. I asked his name, and when the caller said Mr. Emil Gross, I could not believe he meant the man I had known. But when the visitor walked into my office I saw that he was indeed Der Kleine. I would have recognized him anywhere. He was still his short ebullient self, full of humor and vitality. I embraced him, tears streaming down my cheeks, and exclaimed, "My God, I thought you had been lost!" A flood of questions followed; then I picked up the phone and called Walter in Detroit. "You'll never believe who's in my office!" Walter said he was eager to see him and I made arrangements for Emil and me to fly to Detroit. We had a magnificent reunion, and after we had talked ourselves out, Walter took Emil to lunch at Solidarity House and invited his staff members to meet this long-lost friend and to hear the story of how we had first met him in Berlin during those fateful days.

It was difficult for us, after all that had happened, to maintain what would appear to be a normal schedule. We did, however, visit the Ford works in Cologne and indulge in a bit more tourism than usual so as not to arouse suspicion. In front of the beautiful cathedral, the Minister of Propaganda had erected a huge mock-up of a bomb. Sadly we set off once more for Stuttgart, our home base.

We found it unbelievable that Germany had so rapidly gone from bad to worse. The road to Stuttgart was jammed with storm troopers converging on the city for some great demonstration. The beautiful glockenspiel in the old Rathaus, or City Hall, no longer played its ancient tunes; now the chimes continuously rang out the Horst Wessel song. Our relatives and friends told us that the workers in all the factories were being strong-armed into joining the Luftschutz Bund, the civilian air defense organization. Every fourth Sunday had been designated by the Nazis as a one-meal, one-dish day. By chance we were invited to Sunday dinner with some dear friends on one of these thrift days, and because we were guests from abroad, the lady of the house had prepared several dishes for the dinner. When a storm trooper suddenly appeared at the door, peddling some Nazi literature, she grabbed the serving dishes and rushed into the bedroom to hide them under the bed.

Our last visit at Uncle Ernst's house was kept brief, because we were beginning to worry seriously whether we would get our visas to enter the Soviet Union, and decided to make a last-ditch effort in Berlin before the winter set in. The Soviet Consulate had no word but promised to send an air-mail letter to the tourist agency in London for information. We were also almost out of funds, and sent a cable to our parents asking them to cash in one of the insurance policies on our lives and cable the money to us in Berlin. They faithfully did so, posthaste. It was then November 11, Armistice Day, a day made even more painful by the election coming up on the morrow, which promised to be an offense to the very word *election*.

On election eve, Goering spoke, and we saw the enormous crowd go wild as he entered the Sport-Palast between row on row of his newly formed flying corps, followed by about 500 young Nazis bearing flags. His abrasive address had been preceded by the pathetic sight of the aged von Hindenburg, once a German leader of stature, repeating like a child the ideological clichés of the new regime. For many blocks around the Sport-Palast there were great concentrations of uniformed SA men and throughout the whole city that night huge trucks carried movie projectors and screens into the parks to show special election propaganda films and slides. The Hitler commercial repeated itself over and over: "For Peace, Work, Bread, Honor, and Justice."

As for the so-called election, there were no opposition candidates; all parties except the Nazis' had been banned. No one dared stay away from the polls or cast a dissenting vote.

The one bit of good news was that Roosevelt had recognized the Soviet Union, and this may or may not have been the reason why, when we appeared once again at the Soviet Consulate on November 13, our visas had been approved and all arrangements made for us to work in the Soviet Union.

CHAPTER 9

Tooling at Gorky

WE LEFT BERLIN with some relief on the evening of November 15, 1933, and stayed in Russia for almost two years, working eighteen months at the Gorky plant and for the balance of the time touring through the Ukraine and Black Sea area, Georgia, and the fabled cities, Samarkand and Tashkent. Then home via China and Japan.

But back to the beginning. Our train was called an express; it was strange for us, after having gone everywhere on bicycles, to whiz past the eastern provinces of Germany and through Polish villages we should have loved to explore. Still, having had our fill of sleeping outdoors or in hostels recently taken over by young Nazis, we enjoyed the luxury and peace of our compartment. We did not need to go to the expensive dining car because we had brought along bread, cheese, sausage, apples, hard chocolate, and a package of tea.

Reaching Moscow on the seventeenth, we were struck at once by the bitter cold. Unfortunately, our heavy clothing had been checked in our footlockers, along with our cycles, and we did not see our baggage again until we reached Gorky. We had only our essential tools, a change of underclothing, and the clothes we had on — short knickers, thin wool stockings and low-cut shoes, light wool jackets. Snow everywhere and subzero temperatures kept us from doing any sightseeing. An Intourist agent transferred us to the other railway station, where we waited most of the day for our train to Gorky, along with thousands of other passengers, who were sprawled on benches or the floor, lending their animal warmth to the unheated building.

The train to Gorky was a far cry from the international train: the compartments were spartan, and there were frequent stops as we lurched our way 250 miles northeast to ancient Nizhni Novgorod on the Volga, often called the gateway to Siberia. The morning we arrived the temperature was thirty-five below. The station was full to bursting and the stench was indescribable. The peasants, many looking as lifeless as the bundles beside them, covered almost every inch of the floor. They were clad in heavy quilted clothing, the women's heads wrapped in coarse scarves, the men in great felt hats with long earflaps, and all wore pressed felt boots, called *volinkiis*. We struggled through the crowd, carrying our suitcases and heavy rucksacks, reached the information office, and pronounced the only Russian word we had learned: *avtozavod*, "auto factory." Somehow we learned how to find the street car that ran out to the Gorky plant, six miles away.

Detroit at the changing of a factory shift was nothing compared to the logjam at this tramway; we were swept in and held immobile by the tight crowd. Many riders hung on the outside steps or sat on top of the car. After we got off and began hiking to the Administration Building, passersby pointed out to us what we had not yet noticed: our jackets had been neatly cut with a razor blade and the contents lifted out. Luckily, we kept our passports and hard currency in money belts. But we did lose important papers. It was a rude welcome to the workers' Fatherland. Later we discovered that there were many thousands of homeless, adolescent waifs roaming the countryside and cities, stealing for a living, in spite of the government's effort to get them into vocational schools and make citizens of them.

Factories were still under construction, and the smokestacks of a huge power plant dominated the far horizon. By the time Walter and I had filled out the routine forms authorizing us to live in what was called the American Village, about three quarters of a mile away, and had hiked there through the snow, I was as nearly frozen as I have ever been in my life. We found John Rushton's house, were warmly welcomed by him and his wife and daughter, and went through a painful thawing-out in front of their wood stove. We spent our first night in makeshift bunks in their kitchen.

The settlement was known as the American Village because there were so many technicians from Detroit and other U.S. cities. It had twelve or so two-story barracks-type apartment buildings and a number of small, jerrybuilt single houses, some communal rooms, and a special store where only foreigners were allowed to shop. We

were given a single room on the second floor of a barracks, a room
so small that when our footlockers and bikes were delivered, we had
to fasten hooks to the ceiling and hang them over our beds. There
was a single-burner electric stove in an alcove, central heating, a lav-
atory with a cold water tap in the hall. The walls were made of
sheets of plywood with six to eight inches of straw and manure
packed tightly between them — an age-old kind of insulation, efficient, and also a perfect breeding-place for roaches and vermin of
every variety.

About thirty technicians lived in the American Village. There was
a large contingent of Finns from the American Northwest. Luckily
for us, they had built a primitive sauna, and invited us to use it.
There were some Italians who had fled from Mussolini, some British, Poles, Germans. Later Austrians would arrive, after their unsuccessful 1934 uprising. The American technicians had come for
various reasons: a contractual arrangement with Ford, political idealism, or simple curiosity about a country in the initial stage of industrialization.

The Ford Motor Company had been a major factor in the development of the Gorky automotive works. Even before the 1917 revolution, even before the First World War, Ford had a large agency in
Russia for sale and distribution of the Model T. As early as 1919, a
Soviet trade mission opened an office in New York, and one of its
first contacts was Ford. The climate, however, was not yet conducive
to good trade relations; U.S. troops were still fighting in Russia and
the general apprehension about Bolshevism had led to the creation
of the Lusk Committee, which in the course of its activities broke
into the Soviet mission in New York, a miniature foreshadowing of
Watergate. Not even that committee uncovered the fact that on
March 14, 1919, the Ford Motor Company had signed a contract
with a Petrograd firm, Ivan Slacheef and Company, to sell them 400
vehicles. On March 31, Edsel Ford advised his foreign department
manager to "keep in as close touch with Russia, through various
channels in New York, as possible." He added, with an eye to a possible congressional inquiry, that the arrangement with the Petrograd
firm should be kept confidential.

As long as Russia appeared to be an expanding and profitable
market, Ford, like other big firms, did not worry about political
ideology. In fact, Ford's own paper, the Dearborn *Independent,* pub-

lished, in 1919, two articles by a Communist defending the Soviet regime, and only one, by a White Russian, denouncing it.

The most sought-after item was the small mobile Fordson tractor, and some twenty thousand were sold to the Soviet Union before the twenties. But the Soviets wanted more than just manufactured vehicles; they wanted Ford to train a cadre of Russian technicians so that they could build their own equivalent of the Model A. Hence the presence of fifty Russian trainees in the River Rouge plant when Walter was working there. In line with the Stakhanovite movement — the promotion of those workers who excelled in applying the new mass-production techniques — Ford was looked on as something of a hero in the Soviet Union, nearly as respected as Marx and Lenin.

Almost simultaneously with the start of the first Five Year Plan in October 1928, a delegation was sent to the United States to explore the possibilities of contracting for the construction and operation of an auto plant in Russia. The mission aborted when the chairman defected to Berlin and was never heard of again, but later in the year Valery I. Meschlauk appeared with a new technical group. He seems to have been an extremely purposeful man, and he made a deep impression on Charles E. Sorenson, the production manager at Ford. In 1929 the latter was sent to Russia to survey the situation before the agreement was negotiated.

Henry Ford was deeply committed to supplying practical assistance to the Soviet people, and not just for commercial ends. This was the period when he was actively promoting international peace. He accepted the reality that the less-industrialized countries would soon not be content merely to supply raw materials to the industrialized nations and then buy them back in finished products. He believed it was wise to help Russia industrialize. His architect friend and collaborator on the Gorky project, Albert Kahn, made this quite clear: "Our own attitude has been this — that we are not interested in their politics. We feel, as Mr. Ford has so well expressed it, that that which makes for the upbuilding of Russia is bound to prove a benefit to all nations, America included."

The Sorenson delegation was greeted with enthusiasm by the Russians and provided with a luxurious Pullman car on a private train. The Ford sales manager and the heads of the German and British Ford operations went along. They visited the Gorky site as well as

some of the older plants in Moscow and Leningrad, where, incidentally, in the great Petulov works, Sorenson was aghast to see that
they already had in production a smaller model of the Ford tractor — evidently without any formal agreement with Ford. Serious
negotiations went on inside the Kremlin with officials of Avtostroy
(the commissariat for auto manufacture). Occasionally Mikoyan
participated, or Stalin himself, who, they say, greeted Sorenson with
"Allo, Sharley."

An agreement was signed on May 31, 1929. Terms included
shipping seventy-two thousand knocked-down vehicles to Russia
over a period of three years; training of Soviet technicians in the
River Rouge plant; the promise to send experts to Russia to help
supervise the tooling of the new plant; and the sale to the Soviet
Union of all tools, dies, jigs, and special machinery related to the
Model A. It is interesting that the Ford Company tried to convince
the Soviets to tool for their new model, the V-8. The idea was
rejected — a wise decision, since the Model A was better suited to
the Soviet roads and had a much simpler engine. Furthermore, it
was less costly to buy the set of tools that Ford was ready to discard.

The Amtorg Trading Company persuaded Ford to intervene on
its behalf with the W. J. Austin Company of Cleveland, one of the
most experienced international engineering and construction firms,
to build not only an automotive plant but a brand new town, to
house some fifty thousand workers on the Gorky site. The Austin
Company was interested and a contract was signed in 1929, providing for the creation of a gigantic steam-generating plant, sewers,
roads, railway sidings, docks on the Oka River, plants and foundries
for the manufacture of automobiles, apartment houses, hospital,
schools, theaters, stores, laundries, social centers. The construction
got underway in 1930; some of the buildings were not yet up when
we arrived three years later.

The Soviet Union paid for all this by exporting its wheat and putting its people on a stringent diet. The Austin Company made a sizable profit. Its president, George A. Bryant, Jr., rather dis-
ingenuously justified his technical assistance to a country with an
unpopular ideology by saying, "No man or set of men responsible
for growing two bushels of wheat where one grew before, or mining
two tons of coal in place of one, can be said to be doing the world a
disservice, no matter to what radical political theory he or they may
subscribe."

By the end of 1930, the Radio Corporation of America, Du Pont, Bethlehem Steel, General Electric, Westinghouse, and other large corporations had concluded technical and trade agreements with the Soviet government.

The exchange of technicians began in 1931, when 150 Russians came to River Rouge, and Ford's top production man, Frank Bennett (no relation to Harry), set sail on the *Leviathan* with 40 Ford technicians to help with the tooling at Gorky. Henry Ford's parting words were, "When the first car comes off, would you send me a cable? It means very much to this company." When the first car, put together from knocked-down parts, did roll down the line, the Russian workers were so excited that Bennett was tossed in the air in a blanket like a hero. His major complaint was that the plant was so congested with Soviet officials and tourists come to see the miracle that the men couldn't get any work done. There was a long and hard road to travel before they could produce their own Model A, not a knocked-down American one, because so many of the subsidiary buildings needed for the production of the parts, were not yet finished. The manufacturing process had just begun when Walter and I got there. By that time almost all of the Ford technicians had gone home.

Much of the delay was caused by the inevitable snafu that occurs when a whole industrial process is transferred from one culture — and one language — to another. Some of the installation materials arrived in Russia before the buildings for which they were destined had been built. Some very expensive drill rods, for instance, stored in huge crates and awaiting installation in a still unfinished factory, were misplaced and not found before they had rusted in the weather. Then, apparently, Russian workers mistook them for the rods used in concrete reinforcement, and used them as such. This act of confusion was misinterpreted as sabotage. There was a long trial and some of the Austin engineers were under suspicion, though no action was taken against them. A number of Russians, however, were deported, presumably to Siberia.

The thirties were difficult years for the Soviet Union. The cost of industrialization forced it to export an unconscionable amount of its national resources. The agricultural collectivization program was not going well, and all food and clothing were under strict rationing. Walter and I soon became aware of the privations, and though foreign workers were given a more generous allowance than the

Russians, we did not feel we could take advantage of that arrangement, and surrendered our ration books to the general pool, thus
providing the children of the community with a little more butter
and meat than they otherwise would have had. We ate in the cooperative cafeteria instead of in the special restaurant for foreigners,
where a better grade of food was offered at no higher price. Again,
we did not want to abet that sort of caste discrimination. Usually
there was a large bowl of *schtchi,* or cabbage soup, a big piece of
moist black bread, and a cup of weak tea. Sometimes we could have
a dish of kasha, buckwheat groats, with a little vegetable oil on it.
One could get a glass of *kvass,* made of bread or fruit and slightly
fermented. We had no butter for many months; fresh meat was an
infrequent luxury, though occasionally there was some dried fish,
and fresh fruits were nonexistent. Things improved by 1935 and
during our last six months potatoes and vegetables were served
fairly often.

We enjoyed going to the cafeteria for the native workers and we
got used to the diet, even though each of us lost twenty pounds.
Walter once wrote a letter to the *Moscow News* about the cafeteria.
Most of his letters were protests against the obfuscation practiced
by Soviet bureaucracy, but this one was a note of appreciation:

> Imposing as the plant is, its human aspects are, to a Ford worker espe-
> cially, bound to be even more absorbing. In the *Red Corner,* at lunch in-
> tervals, a wonderful spirit is to be found among the workers. A fore-
> man produces a guitar, strums a few chords. A greasy mechanic and a
> red-kerchiefed Komsomolka [a young girl Communist], forgetting
> work, swing into gay dancing. Everybody keeps rhythms, shouts and
> laughs. I enjoy every minute here.

Soon after our arrival at Gorky, we participated in the well-known
Soviet *subotnik,* or volunteer labor, which was called upon whenever
an emergency project came up, such as the completion of a school or
hospital. Work of this sort was organized either by a trade union or
a youth group, and always came off with a great show of high spirits.
Music, dancing, sometimes extra food would be thrown in as incentive. Our first *subotnik* was a project to cut ice and store it for the
summer months. With other American Village workers, we walked
half a mile to the banks of the Oka River, where some of the local inhabitants had cut out the ice in big blocks. We snaked chains or
ropes around these and with the help of a team of horses pulled

them to a central area in Gorky, stacked them, and covered them with wood chips. The river bank, by the way, was also the site of a good deal of boat construction, much of it the hand-crafting of beams and timbers for the small barges that hauled supplies up and down both the Oka and the Volga. Small huts made there were floated downriver on log rafts.

John Rushton escorted us to our first day's work in the tool room. At long last we were able to hoist our tool boxes, which we had carried all over Europe, up to the bench and put on our white aprons, symbols of the skilled toolmaker. Our tool room was a small section of a vast building used mainly for the production of wheels and brake drums. Its location near the heat-treat department, where metals were tempered and hardened, was indeed a boon, for we were not used to working in subzero weather in a building that still had no heating. There was a high roof and a moving crane overhead, and one end of the shed had not been entirely enclosed. When big trainloads of steel had to be brought in, the tarpaulin curtains would be pulled aside, and the cold wind would really whistle through the craneway. We wore our sheepskin coats under our white aprons, but a man can't do precision work with gloves on! We would spend thirty minutes at our bench, go into the heat-treat department to thaw our fingers, then return to the bench. Work was not made any easier by the expansion and contraction of the metal as the temperature varied.

Though Ford had sent a reasonably complete set of tools and dies, some of the items were damaged in shipment or injured during their initial handling by an inexperienced crew, and had to be machined or ground or hand-worked, to within a thousandth of an inch, by technicians using precision micrometers and height gauges. Walter, who was in charge, and I, his assistant, served as leaders of a brigade of partly skilled workers. Many of the crew were young peasant lads, just off the farm, who had seen nothing more complicated than a wheelbarrow before they were enrolled in a technical training school operated by the factory. One worker came from an educated background and was eager to learn all our skills. We became very close friends with Vladimir Vladimirsky, and when we left, he took over the leadership of our brigade and finally became superintendent of the whole tool room.

We also had in our brigade two from the street waif population that made its living adventurously (by cutting jackets, for instance, in crowded street cars). These two boys had been rescued and sent to vocational school. One was so cynical — toughened, perhaps, by long years of homelessness — that he cared less than nothing about the quality of his work or his personal appearance. We nicknamed him "Nitchevo," after his favorite expression, which he always accompanied with a shrug of the shoulders that meant "What's the difference?" One day in the tool room we were wetting down a heavy casting with blue vitriol in order to copperize the surface and make it easy to inscribe with a sharp instrument. Vitriol is an acid that destroys any cloth. The factory was short on waste rags, and Nitchevo, who could not take the trouble to look for one, was using the sleeve of his jacket to wipe off the surplus acid. Walter rushed over, saying "Nyet, nyet!" and then hailed our interpreter to explain to the boy what would happen to his jacket. We got the usual shrug and "Nitchevo!" and the next day he came to work with pieces of burlap tied on with string to replace the sleeves of both jacket and shirt.

But most members of our brigade were fascinated by everything mechanical, and seemed to feel they were an important part of the nation's great effort to lift itself out of the mire of ignorance, need, and famine, which had been the peasants' lot in the feudal past. They were receptive to our teaching of techniques, and even studied technical literature in night school.

It still amazes me that the accident rate was not higher in Gorky as a whole. The majority of workers came from primitive surroundings; only a handful had had experience in Leningrad and Moscow factories. They came from peasant villages of the upper Volga, from the deserts and steppes of central Asia, from Uzbekistan and Tadzhikistan where almost all the people live in tents. They had to overcome an immediate and understandable fear of the strangeness and violence of modern machinery with its automatic propulsion. They wore entirely the wrong attire for factory work, especially for a tool room. We campaigned for practical work clothes, and I sent a letter on this subject to the *Moscow News:*

> On every occasion possible we have pointed out to Russian workers
> the . . . danger of being injured as a result of their loose baggy clothing
> being caught in the machines, but to no avail . . . We were on the verge
> of becoming discouraged and giving up the struggle when our lost
> hopes were revived by an editorial in your paper . . . issuing a chal-

lenge to all foreign workers to initiate a campaign through their shops for the mass purchase and production of practical work clothes.

Our committee met with the shop representative of ZOT [the safety committee], who referred us to another representative, who finally was convinced and agreed to purchase 120 meters of heavy cloth. When the aprons are finished they will be sold to the best *udarniks* [shock workers] and members of ZOT at the cost of production . . ."

Footwear was another problem. In winter the felt boots, *volinkiis*, were the best protection from the cold. We found that our leather boots cut off the circulation, and soon adopted the felt *volinkiis* ourselves. In the shop, however, there was not only oil on the floors but bits of metal cuttings, and the soft pressed felt became uncomfortable, full of imbedded metal chips, and wore out quickly. Early in our stay the factory passed a regulation requiring that workers wear proper shoes, but these were extremely hard to get, and cost more than a total month's income. At last a few pairs became available and workers were allowed to have the price deducted in small installments from their wages. I would say that the shoes caused, in many instances, a love-hate relationship. In the summer, I used to see the workers who walked a great distance to the factory approaching barefoot, carrying their precious mortgaged footwear, and when I asked them why they weren't wearing the shoes, they said it would be a crime to wear out good leather on the dirt roads. "We *must* wear the shoes in the factory, so we will save them for that."

Living indoors was a new sort of life for those who had been nomads on the steppes. There was a story about one tribal family that was assigned a second-floor apartment in one of the newest units and built a wood fire in the middle of the floor to cook the evening meal. And even in the severest cold, a number of workers went outdoors to relieve themselves, until the factory authorities exerted such pressure on them that they agreed to use the indoor toilets. Then, unfamiliar with plumbing facilities, they would stand on the seats, and bars had to be constructed across almost all of the toilets to encourage the users to sit down.

To raise living and cultural standards was one of the important aims of the Treugolnik, or tripartite administration of Soviet industry, composed of factory management, union leaders, and the Communist Party. Some of the incidents resulting from their efforts were equally pathetic and comic. Through the press or factory bulletin boards or speeches at departmental meetings, we were constantly reminded that Soviet society was dedicated to more than the increase of material wealth: "We are developing a new kind of human being who enjoys a cultural life and who has a proper social outlook." One department was pitted against another to think up ways to raise the "cultural level." An exhortation to speed up production in order to turn out a few more cars a day was easily understood, but precisely what did one do to implement the other aim?

Meetings were held in our tool room, and we challenged the neighboring brake-drum department in a so-called "Socialist competition." Weeks passed, we had many discussions, but nothing happened. Then one day we were brought up short by our neighbors' imagination. They had sent a delegation all the way to Moscow; it returned triumphantly with a truckload of artificial palm trees, which were scattered all through the department. They were so profuse around the punch presses, riveting machines, and other gear that the local shop artist made a cartoon of the brake-drum department's leader with palm fronds, ferns, and other greenery coming out of all parts of his body as he walked through the factory. This was displayed on the bulletin board and got a good laugh, but the truth of the matter was that we had been put to shame for our lack of cultural ideas, as our factory superintendent pointed out.

In desperation, Walter and I hit upon the idea of the spoons. We were still eating our cabbage soup and kasha with wooden ones, peasant spoons, which could not be properly sterilized and were a stigma of the past the Russians were anxious to forget. How about acquiring metal spoons? That would be a cultural leap forward. We sent out a committee to get some, but none could be found either in the Volga region or in Moscow. After more meetings, Walter suggested we take the scrap metal left over from the fender dies and organize our own volunteer labor group to make a simple die and stamp out soup spoons for the whole department. A big cheer, and we went to work in our spare time. We had no trouble building the die, but we lacked a tumbler to smooth the rough edges. Otherwise, the spoons looked fine. When we took them into the cafeteria and distributed them to the workers from our tool room, there was a big celebration, including a band, placards and banners, and speeches commemorating another milestone on the way to culture.

Unfortunately, the next day when we went into the cafeteria, looking forward to eating our lunch with the sanitary spoons, there wasn't one in sight. The workers had taken them all home with them. It was clear we couldn't supply the whole Volga countryside with soup spoons from that one small die. So a complicated procedure was devised: on entering the lunch room, the worker surrendered his or her factory pass with photograph and was supplied with a metal spoon; on leaving, the worker returned the spoon and was given back the pass. Such was the price of a cultural leap.

Thirty-four years later my son John was in Moscow for some special studies at the university in the field of U.S.–Soviet relations and was living in a student dormitory. He had heard the spoon story many times, and in his first letter home he wrote, "Dad, you remember those soup spoons you made in the Gorky auto plant? Well, we're still using them here at the university."

No amount of joking, however, can obscure the fact that great masses of people in the Soviet Union lifted themselves out of illiteracy and poverty with an extraordinary push of human energy. The spurs and the penalties were many, but somehow it truly became a personal as well as a social obligation to accomplish more than one normally could. A worker who went beyond the established production level was hailed as an *udarnik,* and on his workbench there was placed a little red flag. The worker who lagged behind the monthly quota was given a burlap flag. More pay, too, was given anyone who outdid himself, even though the society was not, supposedly, operated for profit. There was both individual and group piecework, so that one worked not only for his own but for the group's bonus, which added to the pressure.

Phenomenal progress was made in our tool room, for instance. When we got there, it took three weeks of struggle to produce one die, one complete tool that functioned properly. Eighteen months later, when we left, the tool room was turning out five to six complete dies each month.

We worked an eight-hour day and a six-day week. The tool-and-die department used 806 workers on three shifts, 172 of whom were women. There is no doubt that these women were encouraged to try their hand at every single job in the shop, whether it was operating a lathe or a milling machine, working in the heat-treat department or, for that matter, at the bench in the tool room. All in all the

Gorky plant employed some thirty-two thousand men and women. In many ways it was like an enormous trade school, with some Russian but mostly foreign workers as teachers.

All over the country workers were encouraged by a bureau called BRIZ to suggest labor-saving and cost-cutting devices. About two thousand out of the four thousand suggestions offered by Gorky auto workers in 1934 were put into effect, at a total saving of about six million rubles. In the wheel department, a worker invented a new layout for the presses, which saved some 7609 rubles. He was awarded a premium of 900 rubles, a handsome reward, considering that the average income was around 100 to 125 rubles a month. In the foundry department, a proposal for a machine to cast the pistons effected an economy of 203,000 rubles. Every worker felt it was possible for his own creative idea to be successful; this may have been one of the strongest and most valuable incentives used by the Soviet administration.

The *Moscow News* was constantly encouraging foreign workers to speak up about possible improvements. Walter made many suggestions that were accepted (he always refused the bonus), but there were many times when both he and I ran into a tangle of red tape that surrounded the operation of our department and of the factory in general. Some safety measures were turned down by the factory bureaucracy. This did not sit well with my brother and he finally took his case to the editor of the *Moscow News*. One safety device was especially important to him personally, because he had lost half of one of his toes in the Wheeling Corrugating tool room for lack of it.

In our department, for example, heavy dies and castings are moved by a heavy crane. In every efficient shop, safety holes are drilled . . . to allow for the use of lifting hooks. I could not find a single die in which these holes had been drilled.

What is the result? I watched a crane man and two hookup men trying to put a heavy casting on a machine; they struggled for an hour trying to get the casting to balance on the cable. Several times it slipped and fell to the floor. At last they hoped it would stay balanced and held their breath as they watched the crane man swing the casting over towards the machine.

As the casting swung over the edge of the machine, the jerk of the crane stopping threw it off its balance and it came crashing down on the machine, and as the machine man jumped aside to safety, the casting fell to the floor. It might have cost thousands of rubles if the casting had fallen on the vital parts of a delicate machine, or it might have cost a life.

Two rubles at the most would have been the cost of putting safety holes in this particular casting.

There were also problems that were the consequence of plain inefficiency. Blueprints often came too late in the month; part prints would be missing; programming was apt to lead to logjams at the end of the month. Walter emphasized at the beginning of this letter that "the shortcomings responsible for the greater percentage of the inefficiency in the Gorky Auto Plant are administrative in character."

The Bureau of Workers' Inventions had already heard about the crucial necessity of drilling holes in the castings, but it took that open letter to the press to get any action. The Gorky factory bureaucracy was eager to curry favor with the top brass in Moscow, and Walter firmly believed that the only way to beat the bureaucrats was to get Moscow's ear, because the men there had respect for technicians. Ford officials stationed in Gorky chose more discreet methods of complaining, sending long reports back to Dearborn, where they were quickly labeled top secret lest their contents damage commercial relations with the Soviet government. I might add that going over the heads of the local Gorky management created some unpleasant moments for Walter and me.

The daily production of bona fide Russian Model A's, made from scratch, began in 1933, pitifully small at first but gaining momentum until, at the beginning of 1934, the plant was turning out about 130 cars a day. It was really a very practical vehicle for the Soviet economy: sturdy, simply constructed, and high enough off the ground for the primitive Russian roads. It would have served the country's needs to continue that model as long as the tools and dies held out. But national pride and the ambitions of a few engineers at Gorky led them to modify the design and produce what they called their own "unique" model. It was merely a dressed-up version of the 1933 Model A.

The new car was heralded as the MI. Instead of the word *Ford* on the oval name plate on the radiator, this car had the initials *GAZ* (Gorky Avtomobil Zavod) plus a small hammer and sickle. The lines of the car were about the same as the original, except for a few angles stolen from the Dodge of that period. The MI was to be presented to the country at the May Day celebration, the traditional time for the awarding of honors to especially hard-working achievers.

Just before May Day, there was feverish activity at the Gorky plant as a mock-up of the "new" version was completed. A few skilled workers were involved, and a few engineers, including a young man named Kadarian, who had spent some time in the United States. An appropriate plaque, attributing the car to the skill and ingenuity of Gorky workers, was attached to the dashboard before the mock-up was crated and shipped to Moscow. The ingenious Kadarian had submitted to BRIZ many ideas he had found in American technical journals, claiming them as his own and thereby winning cash prizes. Now, apparently, he had made another plaque, which indicated that he, Kadarian, had designed the MI. Somewhere en route to Moscow the plaques were switched on the dashboard, and at May Day he was hailed as a great innovator and fighter for Socialist labor. Walter and I, as *udarniks,* were included in the Gorky delegation to May Day. We stood next to the diplomatic corps, only a stone's throw from Stalin, who was reviewing the parade from the podium on the Lenin mausoleum. This was our first trip away from our snowy village and our first real sight of Moscow.

To produce automobiles was only a first step for the Soviet government. Hitler had pledged himself and his military resources to the extermination of Communism, and the Soviets concentrated a large proportion of time and energy on preparedness. The public was alerted to the danger at every opportunity, and millions of young people were gathered into civilian defense activities; factories had marksmanship classes and parachute training groups. Soldiers of the Red Army were urged to build a working relationship with factory workers. And since an industrial complex dedicated solely to defense was not financially possible, the Gorky plant was earmarked from the beginning as a standby facility, tooled and geared to produce tanks, gun carriages, airplane parts, and the like. From the end of 1934 on, technicians and engineers from the Red Army would appear almost daily in the tool room to supervise the construction of dies and fixtures, which were then tested by a short run in the presses, oiled, and put on the shelf to be ready for emergency.

A few years later the Reuthers would be deeply involved in organizing the United Automobile Workers' Union, and embroiled in a tough dispute with the president of General Motors, C. E. Wilson.

The argument was part of a national debate on whether the American automobile industry could be tooled to produce airplanes. We knew for a fact, from our experience at Gorky, that the very machines that produce automobiles can be used to make parts for tanks or planes. However, Mr. Wilson and other auto industry leaders preferred to have our government underwrite the cost of entirely new factories, even though that would delay our reaching full defense capability for months, perhaps years. It turned out, of course, that by the end of the war the auto industry acknowledged that better than 80 percent of its machinery had been converted to defense production.

CHAPTER 10

Anomalies

I HAD GONE to the Soviet Union only partly skilled and had had some pretty tense moments in the tool room until I learned enough to take on a brigade of my own, on the evening shift. My most frightening experience was with an enormous casting, which was scheduled to be bored on the Swiss zip-boring machine. I had summoned the crane and moved the casting over the table of the boring mill, clamped it properly into position, and centered the cutting tool to the right point. Then, as I started the bore operating, I accidentally triggered the automatic feed. I was not aware of this until I found I couldn't stop the machine when the drill had reached the right depth. As I visualized the bore going right through the casting and into the expensive table of the boring mill, I felt pure terror. I knew how many bushels of wheat had been taken from hungry Russians to purchase these precision tools, and I was sure I would end up in Siberia. I let out a whoop that could be heard over the din of the tool room all the way to the other end of the craneway, and Walter came running and threw off the automatic feed just in time.

From then on I was considerably more cautious. I made myself familiar with every aspect of the tool room, and gradually was able to assume more and more responsibility.

The language problem eased up for me, too, mainly because I became impatient and frustrated at having to go through our interpreter, Dworney. He was a Czech who, as a matter of fact, did not know English. He did know German, however, so he could put our German words into Russian and switch into reverse when workers wanted to communicate with us. It was a tortuous process. Besides wanting to make myself understood more easily by the men at work, I wanted to be able to have conversations, without benefit of interpreter, with some of the very attractive girls working in the shop.

"How can I learn the language and learn it in a hurry?" I asked Dworney one day.

"Oh, that's easy," he replied. "You pick out a girl, go walking with her, and you will soon learn how to speak the language."

So with his encouragement and armed with my pocket dictionary, I summoned up my nerve to ask little Marussa in the tool crib if she would go walking with me. She indicated that she would be very pleased. Then it occurred to me that we should have an alternate plan in case it rained; we might go to the club house or theater. After consulting my dictionary, I asked — or thought I did — *"Yesli dozhd budyet?"* But instead of saying *dozhd,* I had said *doch,* which meant that I had asked her, "What shall we do in case there should be a daughter?"

I can assure you that the rumors about the immorality of Russian girls cannot be corroborated by me. This innocent creature blushed purple, turned on her heels, and would not speak to me. Desperate, I went in search of Dworney. *"Durak!* You fool!" he exclaimed and told me what I had said. "You must go back and apologize." Back I went, and by that time it must have occurred to her that I was just another stupid foreigner, so we went walking. There was neither *dozhd* nor *doch* and whatever else I learned has not complicated my life.

I made progress with the language, but not enough for me to serve as the perfect interpreter for our former professor, Dr. Walter Bergman, who happened to be in Moscow conducting a student tour during one of our trips there. He wanted to buy some Russian-made pipes to take home for presents and asked us to help him. In the store, I consulted my dictionary, and, in what I considered an authentic accent, asked the clerk to show us some of his pipes. He looked puzzled and asked me to repeat my request, which I did. Finally, looking pointedly at our clothes, he said to me in German, "Excuse me, citizen, but I cannot understand why you want to buy a smokestack." Needless to say, this story was too good to suppress, and we heard several embellished versions when we got back to Detroit.

When summer and our vacation time came, Walter and I took a trip on a river boat, following the Volga down to Kazan and the Caspian Sea, the Ukraine and the Black Sea area. We made a stopover to see the agrarian communes of descendants of the "Volga Germans," who had immigrated during the reign of Catherine the Great. We had heard about them from a woman in Gorky who came from their area. They still spoke German, we learned, not only at home but in their political meetings, too, in a dialect not very different from the Swabian. But they were extremely anxious to prove their loyalty to the Soviet Union and seemed to go overboard in their Communist Party activities. The effort was apparently wasted; the Soviet hierarchy even in 1934 was not comfortable with the presence of a large group of people of German ancestry in the heartland of the country. We heard later that the whole community was uprooted and forced to move to the interior of Siberia, and that many of them did not survive the migration.

Another group of German-speaking immigrants fared no better, though when they first came to the USSR in early 1934 they were given a welcome reserved for heroes. The Schutzbündlers, as they were called, were young Austrian Socialists who had made a courageous stand against the reactionary Heimwehr, or home guards. It was the Heimwehr that had paved the way for Hitler by smashing the trade union movement and destroying cooperatives. The presence of these young, brave exiles was considered a coup for the Soviet Union; they were fêted and displayed throughout the country, and workers, including 6100 in the Gorky complex, responded in a magnificent gesture of international solidarity by raising funds for direct relief and the support of surviving democratic factions in Austria. I suspect that the rush of events in Europe kept most of this money from reaching the right hands before the Anschluss.

A large contingent of Austrians was assigned to the Gorky auto plant; others stayed in Moscow or went elsewhere. Most of them were single; they soon found Soviet girl friends or wives and for a while, as long as they were being touted as heroes, their adjustment was smooth. It was obvious, however, that most of them had no special ideological commitments, except a strong belief in democracy.

In our community, their complaints were at first about superficial matters — no butter, limited diet, sugar rationing, — but when they began to express fundamental disagreement with the way the Soviet state was being operated, a commissar was assigned to do some political indoctrination. They bitterly resented the imposition of a political overseer, and the more outspoken ones soon disappeared. A few hard-core Communists among them took training for underground work in their own country and after Hitler's collapse played a role in establishing the short-lived Soviet control of a sector of Austria.

It is a sad fact that most of the Schutzbunders were never heard from again; they were either liquidated or sent to spend the rest of their lives in the cold reaches of Siberia. They were welcome only so long as their presence served as useful propaganda for the Soviet government in rallying the Russian people against Hitler.

The American Village became very popular right after the arrival of the attractive young Austrians; girls from villages all around found excuses to come to our social evenings. That is how Walter met Lucy, who came from Sormova across the river from the old city of Nizhni, a railroad and shipbuilding center. She was very beautiful, with a classic face and deep black hair, parted in the middle and plaited in long braids. She was both graceful and educated, though the first evening she was ill at ease and subdued, perhaps embarrassed at her own temerity in seeking out an evening's entertainment with perfect strangers. Walter tried to draw her out by means of his very limited Russian, then called me over to help him tell her he would be delighted if she would return the following week to attend our next party.

Walter saw Lucy frequently, and was finally persuaded to go over to Sormova to meet her parents. He took me along as much for moral support as for my interpreting (I was the better linguist) and though it was awkward, the occasion came off quite well. The father had been a railroad official, and the family's standard of living and its level of culture were above that of the average worker. The relationship grew into a full-fledged love affair and it was inevitable that Walter asked me, hesitantly, if I would mind getting myself a room in the compound. So I hung my bicycle and footlocker from the ceiling of a room across the street, above the cafeteria.

Many of the Austrians had invited Russian girls to move in with them and share a heated room and food considerably better than what was available outside the Village. The girls also had access to the special store for foreigners, where they could buy textiles, shoes, and other rationed items. Lucy, however, came from motives of genuine affection and soon turned our bleak cubicle into a small home, with curtains, needlework cushions, pictures, fresh flowers.

All this domesticity must have moved Walter to bring up the matter of a pledge he had made with me and Roy back in Detroit just before our trip abroad. We had promised that, no matter how involved we got in some romantic affair abroad, we would not get married, because we expected to lead lives of considerable hardship, possibly involving imprisonment, as soon as we threw ourselves into serious trade union organizing work. We were, of course, being overly dramatic in the way of the young, perhaps exaggerating the possibilities of a repressive American regime as an excuse to remain unencumbered.

At any rate, Walter reassured me that he had not changed his basic view, and that he had an understanding with Lucy that they would enjoy their companionship without permanent commitment or obligation. Young people today make such arrangements without the soul-searching one went through forty years ago.

Naturally I felt lonesome and deserted, cut off from the close interdependence that had grown up between Walter and me ever since I was eighteen. Something had to be done, and when Lucy told me with tears about an attractive young friend of hers who had come to stay with one of the Austrians and had had a falling out with him, I began to pay court to Victoria. She was good-looking and vivacious but very different from Lucy. In my naïveté, I did not at first understand how interested she was in the material advantages that went with life in our American Village. I invited her to share my room and all went fine as long as we were both working on the day shift.

As luck would have it, I had become by then efficient and secure enough in the tool room to head up a second brigade on the second shift, with Walter still managing the first. That left Victoria on her own each afternoon and part of the evening. Stories soon reached me about the callers she received when I was at work, but they didn't upset me as much as the reports that she was buying clothes in the foreign workers' store not for herself but for resale. The idea of black-marketing went violently against my grain. She admitted to it and I asked her to leave. It was a painful parting. Thus, after only a few weeks, I was alone again with my footlocker and my bicycle.

In our foreign community, even before the big purge got underway, we saw the first flashes of the political storm that was brewing. Near the end of August, a knock on the door at midnight prefaced the arrest by the secret police of an Italian worker who had been at Gorky long enough to marry and have several children. The next day the rumor was carefully wafted around that he had been in league with the Trotskyites and would be sent to Siberia. In the tool room we had known him as a gentle, sensitive person who rarely talked politics. There was no trial, no defense. It is hard to describe the foreboding felt by all of us in the Village, especially the Italian contingent.

The assassination of Kirov and its aftermath were even more alarming. Representing Leningrad in the Communist Party hierarchy, Kirov was the only leader with the qualities and stature to present a serious challenge to Stalin. He was a remarkable and unpretentious man who had established rapport with both intellectuals and workers. Leningraders, with a degree of elitist pride, felt themselves to be the heart and brains of the revolution, and Kirov was their great hope in Moscow — to them a backwater inhabited by country bumpkins.

After our experiences in Germany, Walter and I were not deceived when Stalin, Molotov, Beria, Khrushchev, and others hurried to Leningrad, with expressions of shock, sadness, and concern, to attribute the killing to a Trotskyist plot. Kirov was shot by a disgruntled party member named Nikolayev, and there seems to be no evidence linking him to Trotsky. But the assassination became the signal for the launching of an enormous purge by the Communist Party leadership of any possible challenge or opposition. When Khrushchev in later years began to expose the crimes of the thirties, he implied that Stalin himself had arranged for Kirov's murder.

Even in our factory, we felt the blast of the new wind when parts of Nikolayev's trial were broadcast over the public address system at every lunch break. Meetings were organized in every department to "review the evidence" and adopt resolutions calling for revenge against the traitors who were out to assassinate the leaders of the party. The lynching urge was encouraged in every factory in Russia. Anyone in the least suspect was placed on trial for conspiracy, and some workers were removed without any trial at all. Under these circumstances, political talk was taboo in the tool room, and it was only on those rare occasions when we were alone with friends on a walk through the woods or perhaps in a rowboat in the middle of the Oka that we could talk to any Russian worker about his opinion of the Stalin regime and the political oppression that was hanging like a sword over his head.

The majority of citizens in the Soviet Union had never known democracy; neither under Czarism nor Communism did they have the right of dissent, or true freedom of personal expression. Therefore, for most of them, Stalinism was at first no surprise. But as they became more literate and educated, and began to think and to analyze the political scene, they found it less easy to accept the Stalinist purge, which went on and on until it reached a crescendo of horror. There was, in fact, some question as to whether the workers were being told the whole truth by the official press. The great contribution of Nikita Khrushchev was his revelation of Stalin's intrigues and crimes. This is not to say that he replaced the Stalin years with an era of democracy. But from my own discussions, thirty years later, with workers I had known when I was at the Gorky plant, I can attest to a definite loosening of political constraint under Khrushchev. I even heard some humorous sallies at the expense of the party and the bureaucracy; in the thirties, this would have meant Siberia or worse.

Historians will probably debate for centuries whether so vast a country could have made the transition from feudalism to an industrial state without great sacrifice of individual freedom. But in the thirties, we were constantly disheartened at the price that was paid, while at the same time we were astonished at the progress manifest not only in factory production but in the rise of the standard of living.

By the time we left, young Soviet technicians, though not yet so skilled as the American toolmakers, had taken over the full responsibility of building replacement dies and designing new ones. Cars were rolling off the line in increasing numbers. Almost all the foreign workers were gone, and their special store had been abolished. Most of the essential consumer goods could be purchased in ordinary stores. What was perhaps even more gratifying was the sight of hundreds of thousands of peasants, from remote and primitive cultures, moving into the workers' flats, and enjoying, with their children, the kind of education, food, and health care they had never known before. One can measure a society by how it treats its children and its old people, and in some respects that still primitive Soviet economy seemed to do better than some of the advanced industrialized countries. I do not mean that medical care was equal to what we could have found in Detroit, assuming we had the cash to pay for it, but at least there were health centers, crèches, kindergartens associated with every factory and collective farm. Women were freed from the isolation of the home to learn skills and receive equal recognition at work, knowing that their children were being cared for and fed. The most apolitical tourist visiting the Soviet Union in that period could not help noticing that the children seemed remarkably well nourished and happy. And none of them worked in mills or went down into dark mines.

The catch, of course, was the intensely authoritarian regime; the catch was, and evidently still is, repression, forced labor, death or imprisonment or exile, without fair trial.

CHAPTER 11

Eastern Passage

THE SECOND LONG WINTER turned into 1935, and it was time to go home. We decided to travel a bit first, through the more exotic southern and eastern parts of Russia. We had accumulated a considerable supply of rubles, since our expenses had been minimal, and we were not allowed to change our pay into foreign currency. What better than to spend the rubles on a tour? And as special workers, *udarniks,* with a record of high production achievements, we were entitled to the papers of identification that would make travel a joy rather than a series of struggles to find places on the crowded trains.

Though there were scandals in the press now and then about the practice of favoritism, it was really built into the system. It began logically enough: the foreign experts who were helping the Soviet Union industrialize had to be allowed some special privileges and comforts so that others would not be reluctant to come. Also, the rewards held out to workers — travel passes and vacations at the resort facilities in the south — certainly heightened their enthusiasm to learn and to produce. Unfortunately, the special privilege habit became ingrained in the whole Soviet bureaucracy, especially among the party elite and the trade union officials. To this day officials feel free to claim space on any flight to any part of the country, bumping off even those who have advance reservations. As a member of a visiting delegation, I have cringed many times in airports when I've overheard the tearful complaints of those who have lost their reserved seats. I hope and expect the time will come when the Soviet people will insist that these class distinctions are not justified in a "classless society."

Our passports were more difficult to obtain than the authorization for food stamps, hotel accommodations, train tickets. Many efforts had been made to persuade us to stay at Gorky. The passports eventually came through, but Walter and I often speculated later about what uses they may have been put to when they were out of our hands.

Before checking out of the plant, Walter presented his leather-bound tool box, with all of his precision tools, worth at least $800, to the most promising skilled worker in the tool room, our friend Vladimir Vladimirsky. I gave my tools away, too, to a worker in my brigade. Our bicycles and white tool-room aprons were distributed to other shop workers. There is an ironic story connected with these gifts, which were accepted gratefully by our friends.

Nearly a quarter of a century later, when Khrushchev was an official guest of President Eisenhower, Walter and I together with a group of U.S. labor leaders, had dinner with the Soviet leader in San Francisco. The four-hour-long discussion sometimes turned rather acrimonious. We did not refrain from asking pointed questions, and Walter spoke his mind freely and forcefully. The next day there appeared in *Trud,* the Soviet trade union paper, a full-page spread slandering me and Walter for, among other things, "black marketeering with our clothing, our tools and our cycles." The article quoted our friends Rushton and Vladimirsky, who, it was said, thought us "evil and avaricious men." I am quite sure that neither John nor Vladimir was ever contacted by *Trud.* My trust in these men was reinforced when I spoke to their friends during a visit to Gorky some years later. Undoubtedly, the letter I had sent to the *Moscow News* in 1935, commenting on the inadequacy of the Russian workers' clothing, had never been forgotten by Khrushchev, and had fueled his anger. Certainly it was he who was responsible for the attack in *Trud.*

The rest of the article was even more unbelievable, maligning, to no purpose, the sincere and tender relationship between Walter and Lucy.

Walter's parting from Lucy made both of them miserable; they had been together for five happy months. There had been no marriage ceremony nor had they talked of one. A simple postcard to the factory authorities had made Lucy's residence in the American Village official. I think she might have gladly gone to America with Walter, but he stood by his resolve to stay single so that no girl would be harmed by the rough life he expected to throw himself into when he got home. Of course he felt great conflict within himself over Lucy and there was an emotional scene when we boarded the train from Gorky to Moscow.

Walter left forwarding addresses with Lucy and sent her cards informing her of our itinerary as we traveled through the Ukraine, visiting the Dnieper Dam, the vast collective farms, and the old Czarist villas on the Black Sea, which were now sanitariums or resorts for the workers. At Batumi, near the Turkish border, we had climbed the mountain to visit some tea plantations, and when we got back to our hostel, there was Lucy at the entrance, sitting on her suitcase, waiting for Walter. She had journeyed a thousand miles, all alone, to be with him once again. She wanted to stay with us until we left Russia, but since we had received permission to visit a part of Russia in Central Asia, where few Westerners had ever been, and since I knew that the longer she stayed with us, the more painful the final break would be, I tried to persuade Walter to say no to her plan.

Our immediate plans for the next few days were to hike up the Georgian military highway through the Caucasus Range to Ordzhonikidze, and Walter felt there was no reason why Lucy should not stay with us for that part of the tour. His decision, as we soon discovered, was a mistake. He carried Lucy's small grip in addition to his knapsack, but that was of little help. She was dressed in city clothes and thin-soled shoes — we could not find sturdy ones in the stores — and was, besides, a frail girl, unaccustomed to climbing. Walter helped her up the rough, stony terrain, but each delay played havoc with our daily schedule. The nights were very cold; often we borrowed the sheepskin coats used by the mountain herders to cover ourselves. When we at last got to Ordzhonikidze, Lucy realized she could not keep up such strenuous traveling and, after a tearful farewell, boarded a train for Gorky.

They corresponded for some time, through intermediaries like John Rushton, who helped put Walter's English into Russian. They had parted as many others lovers have, without recriminations. We learned soon after our return to the United States that Lucy had married another young American in the Village, an engineer in the Gorky factory, and in time had a daughter. She died on the same day as our brother Roy.

It is simply not possible that she said about Walter the lies attributed to her by *Trud*. Blaring headlines called Walter a bigamist who had deserted his Russian wife. Lucy was reported to have said:

> He vowed his love at first sight. He said that he had dedicated his life to the workers and needed a true girl friend. He spoke about the chains of capitalist labor which must be broken, about bloodthirsty exploiters — My God, what he didn't talk about! Anyone's head would have been turned, let alone an inexperienced girl. Soon after we got married he stopped talking about politics and I no longer heard beautiful speeches about the class struggle. He reiterated without end that one must be careful with money.

The tabloid style was certainly not Lucy's; the piece was obviously the work of a party journalist. What's more, Walter's Russian was certainly too limited for extensive conversation, and even if he had known more Russian words, he would not have been inclined to expound on the class struggle as he held a beautiful girl in his arms.

Official propagandists often overplay their hands. The reaction of most Americans who read about the *Trud* accusation was reflected in the comments of the Detroit *News:*

> The Russians, who have a talent for abuse that approaches genius, have surpassed themselves in their vilification of Walter P. Reuther. The UAW president has been assaulted with a variety of unkind nouns and adjectives in his own country, but it took Moscow to decide that he is a bigamist.

In the Soviet Union, perhaps more than in other countries, one's mind is forced into a constant balancing and juggling of the idealistic versus the cruel, the rational versus the stupid. In the Ukraine we were impressed by the great scale of the construction underway on the Dnieper River and by the resort areas in the Crimea. One can only hope that the government will build a sufficient number of such sanitariums so that many more factory workers, not just the privileged few, can enjoy them.

The Ukraine also revealed to us the devastating aftermath of enforced agricultural collectivization. There was a shortage of breeding cattle, which explained why there was practically no meat to eat in all the cities of Russia. It seems that the Ukrainian peasants, during the early days of Stalin, mistakenly believed that all farmers would enter the collective on an equal basis, whether they had no cattle or a thousand head, many acres of land or none. There occurred, therefore, a wild and indiscriminate slaughtering of cattle and an orgy of feasting, based on the assumption that all could "eat, drink and be merry, for tomorrow we join the collective!"

Samarkand restored some of our faith that the Soviet bureaucracy did not always act with heavy-handed ineptness and lack of sensibility. Here the approach was subtle, humane, and successful. It seemed to us that the government was proceeding with gingerly care to woo these people of varied cultures, different languages, and sharp religious contrasts. There was a new industrial group springing up, but artisans were encouraged to practice their wonderful ancient handicrafts. Moscow was subsidizing theater performances and literature in the native languages, and the people responded. Thus was Soviet political control further consolidated. Moscow also offered scholarships to bright young leaders to study at the university and take new ideas back to their people.

Crossing the Caspian Sea on the small steamer that took us to Samarkand, we met a husky young woman who had trained in Moscow and then returned to her region as teacher and social worker. She invited us to come and see her school in Samarkand and told us about her crusade to free the women of the area from having to cover their faces with the hideous horsehair veils they had been compelled to wear for centuries. We saw many veiled women on the streets in 1935, but they were mostly older women.

Her campaign had begun with a series of discreet meetings in private households; when she had built up a sufficiently large following, she held a public meeting one afternoon, in the course of which she urged her audience to break through — to take off the veils and throw them in the fire that had been built for the occasion. Hundreds of women had the courage to do so — though a number of them were murdered that evening in a counterattack allegedly mounted by the wealthy Muslim conservatives.

In Tashkent Walter and I were disappointed to find that we were not, after all, going to be allowed to go straight from there to Manchuria because we should have to travel through "sensitive areas" still in turmoil. We had to take the long ride back to Moscow and there board the Trans-Siberian Railroad for Harbin. This meant, once again, a trip of ten to eleven days. We took along bread, sausage, cheese, dark chocolate, and tea, counting on the hot water we knew would be available at the many local stops. Our compartment-mates were two handsome young British brothers named Bryson, who were on their way to China where their parents were missionaries, and a striking middle-aged Englishman named Hayley Bell, who had an uncanny resemblance to the movie actor C. Aubrey Smith, not only in physical appearance but in talk and manner.

We soon became friendly with the Brysons and learned a good deal about China from them. Over the years, we kept in touch. (Arthur, who became a missionary doctor in Africa, visited us in Detroit after the war.) Hayley Bell was a bit aloof, until he learned we were Americans fresh from almost two years in the Soviet Union, where we had worked on a factory bench, whereupon he evinced an active curiosity about Gorky. When we found out that he was a retired colonel and an aluminum manufacturer with offices in Shanghai, Walter decided he was an exploiter, and tried constantly to get his goat by pointing out what was being built all over Russia for the workers, by the workers, to be owned by workers. At last Hayley Bell exploded, and rising in all his British military majesty, said, "Good heavens, are there nothing but bloody workers in this country?"

"No, not really — no one but workers," Walter answered.

"Well," said Bell, "what do you suppose they would do with a chap like me?"

"Just who are you?" we asked him, and he replied, "I suppose, in addition to being an employer . . . you could call me an adventurer. Yes, an adventurer."

"Hell, they'd probably shoot you!" Walter said.

Bell burst out laughing, and from then on we got along very well. According to him, his main reason for hating the Bolsheviks was that they didn't know how to make decent tea, so we shared some of our precious package with him and showed him our method of steeping it in our little pail of hot water. It was very funny to watch him climb off the train at the frequent stops and make a dash to the local bazaar for a bit of shriveled fruit or a hard-boiled egg or some rice-filled pastries. I shall never forget the sight of his lanky six-foot frame trying to curl up on a too-narrow and too-short bunk, his feet stretching far out into the aisle, his snores almost drowning out the click-clack of the train wheels. It never occurred to us to question his story, or to wonder why a manufacturer and ex-colonel from the Boer War was traveling third class through Siberia.

At the border we thought we were entering Manchuria, but when we arrived at the godforsaken outpost of Negorailia, we discovered that the Japanese had just seized that area of Manchuria and established the state they called Manchukuo. Neither Britain nor the United States had recognized this new state, and it was therefore not included on our passports. A Japanese officer, the border official, whipped out a pen and said to the five of us, "You sign Manchukuo — you sign your name — I give you visa."

At this point Bell said indignantly, "Look here, my good man, I cannot issue myself a visa!" We all agreed with him, and refused to mutilate our passports in such a way. "Very well," said the Japanese officer, "no sign, no visa, no train."

We stood there in utter disbelief, watching the train pull away for Harbin, knowing there would not be another for days.

Haley Bell walked over to the officer. "I assume we are all now guests of your government of Manchukuo?" There was a smile and the demure answer: "Hotel across the street."

"Will your government pay the bill?

"No."

"Then we shall stay here," said Hayley Bell calmly, and began to unpack his clothing on the baggage examination rack, to use as bedding. We admired his nerve, and followed suit. All night long, the young Japanese on guard duty marched up and down, their long swords dangling and striking sparks on the cobblestones. The next morning brought another round of negotiations that got us nowhere, but on the third day I could see the colonel weakening as the train for Harbin appeared in the distance. With a flushed face and in absolute silence he took out his pen and signed his name boldly in his passport where the visa was to be attached, and, naturally, we did likewise. Still under his wing, we followed him across the street to the telegraph office and watched him send the following cable to the British Consulate at Harbin: "I, Lt. Col. Hayley Bell, have just recognized the state of Manchukuo. Now the six million British subjects may feel free to follow suit."

A charming man! We hated to part with the colonel in Harbin. As a final friendly gesture he invited us to take a rickshaw ride with him through this city, which he knew very well. Much as we should have liked to have such a guide, we were too horrified at the idea of being pulled around by another human being — the ultimate in exploitation, we said — to accept his kind offer.

"Silly asses, silly asses," he said, giving us a look of disdain. And hailing a rickshaw, he sat back in familiar comfort and was off. We thought sadly that we had probably seen the last of him.

Several hours later, after marveling at the latest models of Western cars and what seemed to us, after two years in spare and rationed Russia, an enormous display of low-priced goods at the five-and-ten-cent store, we were walking along when we heard our names called out. We turned and there in a rickshaw came Hayley Bell, all dressed up in a white linen suit and a white pith helmet. As he passed he tipped his hat and said, "Observe the British imperialist!" We had another good laugh with him and again said goodbye, promising to look him up in Shanghai.

It's a pity the colonel couldn't have observed his silly-ass friends on their way to Yenching University in Peking, which lay beyond the outskirts of the city. A professor at Ohio University had given us an introduction to Dr. Leighton Steward, then president of the university and later United States ambassador to China. We prepared to hike there, dressed suitably in short-sleeved shirts. We also wore pith helmets, which, since we saw coolies in them, did not seem too blatant a symbol of the imperialist class.

As we started out, we noticed several coolies with rickshaws following us. At each corner we turned, a few more joined the parade. They were chanting a sing-song sort of dirge, pleading with us to ride. We may have been the only hope of each of them to make enough for a good meal that night, but we had our principles and were not going to be party to using human beings as beasts of burden.

When the noise behind us became very loud — the rickshaw coolies were competing vocally — we were so embarrassed that we gave in, chose two of the rickshaws, and committed ourselves to traveling at what seemed a fantastic trot, considering the distance that had to be covered. Once outside the city and its observant crowds, we called a halt, got out, and told the coolies to take the seats — *we* were going to pull *them*. Of course they considered us completely insane. It took some time to persuade them. We were determined to convince them that we did not consider ourselves members of a superior class or that the labor they were performing was beneath us . . . and frankly, we also wanted to have the experience and to determine just how hard it was to pull another person in a rickshaw. Baffled and reluctant, they at last climbed in and we started pulling at a slow trot.

In a very few minutes, we were exhausted, and sheepishly resumed our seats in the rickshaws, letting the coolies pull us all the way to the university. For once in our lives we forgot how little money we had and splurged on the tips, though we had just left a country where tipping was looked on as degrading both for the recipient and the giver.

Later, in Shanghai, we became even more involved with rickshaw coolies. In that city they were harnessed in teams of five or six, and, straining at the ropes, pulled great loads of sheet steel through the streets. We talked with some who knew English and were told they had a union called the Rickshaw Benevolent Association. They invited us to visit their hall, an imposing building that housed facilities for Ping-Pong and other sports, reading rooms, and a small cooperative store, where their meager earnings went further than on the open market. They had a political committee that lobbied for reforms, and a cooperative health clinic.

We had found in Peking many things more disturbing than rickshaw-pulling. It was an alarming moment for northern China, according to Dr. Stewart; there were mounting threats from the Japanese, and the Kuomintang, which actually controlled only the major cities and the rail lines connecting them, was acutely unstable. Everywhere we traveled in the north we saw Chiang Kai-shek's soldiers guarding the trains against attack by the Eighth Route Army. Communists were executed daily, their severed heads remaining on show for days as a warning. What's more, the 1935 flood had left water standing so long over a vast area that the seeds had been destroyed, there were no crops, and thousands of refugees, searching for food, tried to reach the cities. Walter and I witnessed a scene that would have upset anyone — not just idealistic young Americans — with a modicum of sensibility.

It took place the night we boarded the boat from Nanking to Shanghai. A big crowd of starving peasants had gathered at the dock, trying to get on board. To deal with what was evidently a common occurrence, the ship owners had employed a private army of Sikhs, tall, swarthy men famous for their military valor, wearing magnificent turbans and tailored beards, and armed with outsized clubs. As the peasants fought to get on board, grabbing the railings, they were savagely clubbed, and sank in the muddy waters beneath us. No one made any effort to save them from drowning, and when we protested, we were told that they would soon have died of starvation anyway! I have never before or since felt as horrified — and as helpless.

We reached Hayley Bell on the phone in Shanghai and he asked us to the International Club to meet some fellow imperialists, as he called them. We were presented as a couple of "young American Bolsheviks." The club boasted the longest bar in the world. For a third time we said goodbye to our friend, but we still had not seen the last of him. We left the city at five in the morning on a boat headed for Japan, filled with people going home. The dock was crowded with friends and relatives who had come to say farewell in the customary way: they threw thick rolls of paper streamers on board. As the boat slowly pulled away, the passengers held tight to their ends of the streamers and the pretty paper stretched across the water, keeping contact between boat and land until it broke. We were feeling terribly alone and left out of this gala affair, when suddenly, as we were moving out, we saw a tall, lanky figure approaching the dock, towering above the crowd and waving his hat to us in a last and final salutation. He had not forgotten the day and hour of our going.

We wondered why we were always followed as we explored Japan on bicycles; every night as we checked into the remotest inn, three cups of tea would be automatically brought in: one for Walter, one for me, and one for the police officer who was soon to arrive. Some time after the Second World War, when I was in England as a member of the Anglo-American Council on Productivity, I learned what that was all about and who our good friend the colonel really was. We had exchanged letters with Hayley Bell until the war, when he returned to England, where he died. I was telling the story of our friendship with him at a meeting of British employers, trade unionists, and government leaders, including Prime Minister Attlee and my friend and colleague, Sir Vincent Tewson, General Secretary of the British Trade Union Congress. The latter turned to me and said, "Don't you know who that was?" I said that I didn't.

"Well, when he died during the war, Winston Churchill delivered a eulogy in the House of Commons to Leftenant Colonel Hayley Bell, and in the course of it disclosed that he had been the top British agent in all of Asia. Churchill also said that if the British government had given more attention to the reports of Colonel Bell and followed them more carefully, the course of the war in Asia might have proved less costly to the Allies."

Many things came clear to me then: why he had probed us so thoroughly on Gorky, and why the Japanese, after that incident at the border, had put a tail on us.

I went to pay my respects to the colonel's widow. Bombed out of their house, she was living in a tiny flat, jammed with memorabilia of the Far East. She invited me to have tea with her and her daughter. On a table was a very large colored photograph of her late husband, smiling that wonderful infectious grin, so full of vitality and humor. I told her of our experiences with the colonel, and she laughed and said, "Yes, that was my Hayley!" Their granddaughter is the talented movie star, Hayley Mills.

Japan was the last leg of our three-year journey around the world, and Walter and I were in a relaxed mood and able to enjoy ourselves for once as tourists, instead of self-appointed social scientists. We were delighted with everything, and the domestic architecture made such an instantaneous and permanent hit with us that when Walter built his own home he incorporated many ideas from Japanese houses. With the help of an Indian friend we had met on the boat from Shanghai, we rented cycles in Osaka. We rode through mountain country and villages; we slept in delightful inns, ate raw fish, took the traditional baths, and wore clogs and kimonos. In one village, children shouted at us and a small crowd gathered around: we must have looked like a pair of strange giants. Little children also giggled when we struggled with chopsticks. China had accustomed us to accept antiquity as the commonplace, but Nara, the capital city of Japan from A.D. 710 to 784, revived some of the excitement I had felt in Rome. One feels, in that beautiful city, in touch with the very origins — spirit and soul — of the Japanese aesthetic.

By the time we reached Tokyo we were flat broke; our last meals in Japan were rice, seaweed, and raw fish. We hoped to work our way home, and the American Embassy put us in touch with officials of various shipping lines. The situation was discouraging, but when several crew members of the S.S. *Hoover,* bound for Hawaii and Los Angeles, took sick, the captain interviewed us and signed us aboard. Walter worked below as a wiper in the engine room, and I polished brass and mopped decks.

At the dock in Los Angeles, we watched the passengers go ashore, finished up our chores, collected our pay, and in a few hours set our feet on native soil. It felt superb! Our one thought was to get back quickly to Wheeling and then Detroit — we had kept in close touch with Roy and knew of his work there; now we wanted to be part of it again. So we abandoned our usual thrift and, instead of hitchhiking, blew our wages on bus tickets to West Virginia.

As we started up the front walk of our home on Bethlehem Hill, Christine, who had spied us through the window, ran out into our arms. Tears were streaming down her cheeks. She was a teen-ager, no longer a little girl. Then our mother was there, embracing us, and our father too. That evening was a reunion in love as Ted, Ann, and their three children — one of whom we had never seen — joined us "up on the hill."

CHAPTER 12

Digging In

BACK IN DETROIT, we found the situation much as it had been —
hundreds of thousands still unemployed, trudging, with scant hope,
from factory gate to factory gate. But the extraordinary number of
strikes that had occurred since we left for Europe in 1933 was evidence of a surge of militancy among the auto workers, who not only
were resisting wage cuts but were trying to form unions with an industrial rather than a craft structure, allowing skilled and unskilled
to be united in one effort.

Supported by its various cannibalistic craft unions — Machinists,
Metal Polishers, Electrical Workers, Glass Workers — each fighting
for benefits for its own handful of workers, the AFL was still resisting the concept of industrial unionism as adamantly as any employer. In 1934, the Executive Council had yielded to demands
from some of the Federal Local Unions in the auto industry to convene a national conference, but had immediately dashed all hopes of
the delegates to elect their own officers. Instead, AFL leaders insisted that an eleven-man council, rigged to do their bidding, should
run the United Automobile Workers. In 1935, the same thing happened: some 250 auto industry delegates, from Michigan, Indiana,
Ohio, and other states, voted overwhelmingly to appoint their own
officers. But William Green stepped to the rostrum and announced,
"By virtue of the authority vested in me and upon orders of the Executive Council, I will now appoint the officers of this international
union." Whereupon he named Francis J. Dillon president, Homer
Martin vice-president, and Ed Hall secretary-treasurer of the United
Automobile Workers. The idea of an industrial union for the automobile workers was again rejected out of hand.

But the idea had not died. As we learned from Roy, many young auto workers had been meeting frequently at the Socialist Party headquarters in Detroit to discuss their hopes for a more democratic union, with officers chosen from the rank and file, and to work out ways of unifying the splinter unions within the automotive work force, which was being organized in somewhat random fashion in other cities. This discussion group included, besides Roy and Merlin Bishop, Robert Kanter, Allan Strachan, Norman Drachler, Al King, and Jean Seidel and May Wolf, active in the teachers' union.

Roy, Merlin, and Bob Kanter, unable to find jobs in Detroit, had gone to Madison for training sponsored by the Federal Emergency Relief Administration. All three served as instructors in Detroit under FERA, until Roy was transferred to Flint, Michigan, where he took charge of workers' education activities. Through this work, all three had helped train some of the alert new leaders coming up through the ranks, and had extended their contacts with the unions just beginning to gain strength in both Flint and Detroit. Then Roy was asked to join the staff at Brookwood Labor College in Katonah, New York, and was at work there soon after our return to Detroit in the early fall of 1935.

Walter and I actually got home just in time for the first big breakthrough — the birth of the CIO. As soon as we reached Detroit and made contact with our old friends and the newly formed Socialist Auto Council, which was aiming at an industrial trade union structure, we learned that there was genuine discontent in the AFL and that John L. Lewis was the leader of the disenchanted. We wanted him to address a rally in Detroit, so Walter went to the Atlantic City AFL fall convention to ask him to come. So it was that Walter witnessed the historic confrontation between Lewis and Bill Hutchison of the Carpenters' Union, who symbolized the arrogant attitude of the craft union leaders. Lewis responded to the profanity that Hutchinson directed against him with a good right to the latter's chin, and this bit of melodrama gave new hope to thousands of industrial workers. Within a matter of days, the Committee for Industrial Organization took form, a mewling infant destined to grow into a giant.

There were no factory jobs for Walter and me. We decided, therefore, to undertake a lecture tour through Michigan, Ohio, Illinois, and Wisconsin, organized by a professional bureau in New York, with help from the League for Industrial Democracy in ar-

ranging the student meetings. We wanted to get reacquainted with
the labor situation, which had been considerably transformed by the
impetus of the New Deal. We also wanted to meet personally the
people who would aid us in organizing the auto workers. Just before Christmas, we ended up at Brookwood Labor College, to lecture to the student body, to visit with Roy, and to renew our friendship with the director of the college, Tucker Smith. We had known
him through the peace movement and the LID, and I was very interested when he broached the possibility of my working with him on a
Quaker project to establish a labor division within the Emergency
Peace Campaign. This was an effort being made by many groups,
including churches, to arouse the country to the dangers of
war — an issue of enormous importance to me, and one with deep
family and ideological roots. Eventually I accepted Tucker's offer,
and worked out of the college in Katonah, traveling all over the
country, setting up seminars and speaking before trade union
groups. On my tours I met steelworkers, auto workers, glass workers, rubber workers, and sometimes members of the central labor hierarchy. My stay at Brookwood College itself was personally re-
warding — I met my future wife there.

Walter continued to lecture, but became increasingly involved with
automotive union activities. He, too, was asked to join the staff of
Brookwood, with the idea of heading up a branch of the college in
Detroit for the benefit of the new CIO. He was attracted to the idea,
but when he was in Akron, marching on the picket line in support of
one of the first and most dramatic of the sit-down strikes, at the
Goodyear Company, he changed his mind. This turned out to be a
decision that would prove most significant. Roy and I had written
him that we were against the idea, believing that he should remain in
Detroit, where the action was, working his way into union organizing
as a rank-and-file man, rather than as an educator, when the Depression began to let up. Roy himself was about to go back to Detroit.
Walter's letter to Tucker Smith acknowledges the pressure of brotherly advice, and includes other salient reasons for his refusal:

> Another matter which has influenced me greatly in making this decision
> is the fact that I have been able to join the United Auto Workers union
> and have been elected as a delegate to the central body. Then, too,
> there is the convention of the Auto International to be held before
> April 20, and there is much work to be done by the progressive group
> in order to mobilize all their forces for the convention.

It may seem strange that Walter, who had worked in the auto industry for seven years, had to make a special effort to establish his union membership. But when he returned to Detroit, his every effort to get a job in an auto plant had been frustrated: his name was on the backlist. It was the Ternstedt Local 86, UAW, that accepted him as a member and sent him as a delegate to the central body of the AFL, Wayne County, to attend his first meeting on February 19. This took place just before he went to Akron and made the decision to settle down to the hard job of building a base in the auto industry.

Decisions are never simple; another powerful factor may have tipped the scales. He had been seeing a good deal of the red-haired May Wolf, a very attractive and spirited young teacher in Detroit. They met at conferences, in the Socialist headquarters, and at several ethnic group meetings, where Walter went to campaign for trade unionism. Then there was the three-day state conference of the Socialist Party in Flint in January, which both attended. Less than two months later they were married, their courtship having been somewhat less than glamorous; most of their time together had been spent at union or Workmen's Circle branch meetings. May could hold her own in any political discussion. When it came to unionism and the defense of democracy, she was very much the evangelist, and was indefatigable in her efforts to build a strong teachers' union.

Her parents were Jewish immigrants from Russia — their name was Wolfman — and they were naturally quite baffled when May, with no lack of suitors from the professional class, chose instead an almost penniless young auto worker. They were sympathetic with his goals and his politics, however, and after he had visited in their home and had a chance to use some of his German and Russian words on them, they soon looked on him as a *landsman* and took him in as one of the family. Walter had known Frank Wolfman in the early thirties, when both were active in Socialist politics in Detroit. The fact that Walter was Lutheran and May was Jewish presented no problem; in both the Reuther and Wolfman families such artificial barriers meant nothing. On March 15, 1936, they were married in a civil ceremony, and, characteristically, spent their honeymoon attending a labor rally at Mount Clemens, Michigan.

The name Reuther was anathema to Ford personnel directors. Walter, using the name Walter Phillips, made several attempts to get jobs at Murray Body and at the Frederick Coleman Tool Company, but the long arm of Harry Bennett always reached in and plucked him out. But he carried many signed union cards in his pocket when he left each plant.

After a number of rejections, he accepted the fact that the influence of the reigning powers in the auto industry penetrated even the smallest plant, and realized that it would be impossible to fight the battle for industrial unionism in any one factory. He began to think in terms of pooling the separate, weak union forces into one amalgamated local, which would include all the West Side of Detroit, skilled and unskilled workers alike. The reason he was offered membership in the Ternstedt Local was that the few members of that local knew that he had already spent many years in the auto industry and was prepared to devote his life on a full-time basis to help auto workers build the sort of union they needed and wanted. Again they chose him as their delegate, this time to the historic South Bend Convention, to take place on April 27, 1936. He once gave a humorous account of the way in which he received this honor:

> I stood before this great mass meeting of organized workers — there were 5 there beside myself — and thanked them for the great honor . . . One of the brothers made a motion that since Reuther was unemployed and was devoting all of his time to the union without pay he should receive whatever money there was in the treasury to help finance his trip. Our financial secretary was a sister and she thought we were getting a bit reckless so she modified the motion to read that upon my return I would give back to the treasury any money that was left over. She opened her handbag and gave me five dollars. That was all the money we had.

As for the trip:

> I hitchhiked my way to South Bend and five of the brothers went along as observers. They too were unemployed. I checked in at the cheapest hotel I could find. It had running water and inside plumbing but that was about all. I rented a room with a double bed . . . We put the mattress on the floor — three of us slept on that and three on the box springs . . . We lived on hamburgers and not many of them.

The auto workers were in a belligerent mood when they gathered that April, determined to win their autonomy from the AFL hierarchy. Even Homer Martin, the UAW vice-president and no great militant, sensed the spirit of the men and at the last minute called on David Dubinsky to try to convince the AFL leadership to allow the auto workers to elect their own officers. Martin was understating when he said, "The situation in Detroit is the most pitiful I have ever seen. Dillon has completely betrayed the automobile workers."

The AFL bureaucracy was not the only obstruction. The La Follette Committee revealed later that General Motors was spending hundreds of thousands of dollars on espionage agents. It is a reasonable assumption that there were a large number of them at the South Bend Convention, their function being, of course, to keep any auto workers' trade union weak and ineffective.

When the Credentials Committee made its report at the beginning of the convention, some delegates from the East Side of Detroit protested the seating of Walter as a delegate. "Reuther has never been employed in the Ternstedt Plant since it was established." It was true, but he had worked many long years in the auto industry, and his fellow workers knew that he was an active unionist and that his forceful assistance was crucial to their cause. Everyone suspected, too, that the challenge was based not so much on the technical charge as on an effort by certain elements to hamstring the auto workers' union by denying it effective leadership. The convention voted by a huge margin to seat Walter.

Once seated, he moved with great speed to dramatize two issues. The first had to do with election of officers who would truly represent the rank and file. He laid emphasis on keeping the salaries of these officers very modest; it was more important, he said, to have a large number of organizers in the field than a few with bloated salaries. Second, he made an appeal to the press, pointing out the distortion in the Hearst headlines about the UAW convention, but making a strong distinction between the Hearst reporters who were writing accurate stories on the convention and the men who composed the headlines. He called on reporters of the Hearst chain to join the ranks of the CIO by affiliating with the Newspaper Guild. This move captured the imagination of the delegates and won the admiration of Heywood Broun, head of the Newspaper Guild, and of John L. Lewis, both of whom sent telegrams congratulating the convention on its stand.

By far the most significant event was the resignation of Francis Dillon as president of the UAW, and the election of Homer Martin, former Baptist preacher who had for a short period worked in an automobile plant, to succeed him. Wyndham Mortimer was then elected vice-president, and George Addes secretary-treasurer. Mortimer was a long-time loyal unionist from White Motor Works in Cleveland, and Addes, a strong and fiery personality, had just led the Auto Lite strike in Toledo. Walter was put on the Executive Board by a margin larger than that received by any other board member. This popular support, however, did not keep the same men who had challenged his being seated from objecting loudly to his election to the board.

Walter was especially pleased that at this convention, where UAW workers at last became their own masters, the final speaker was Norman Thomas. He gave a stirring description of the forces gathered together against labor in the country.

Walter returned to Detroit full of enthusiasm about an intensive organizing drive and the promise of industrial unionism now that the AFL had been challenged by the CIO. His election to the Executive Board provided no salary, but it gave him the status he needed to start building the strong amalgamated local union in the West Side that he had envisioned before the convention. It was actually chartered in September of that year as West Side Local 174.

Walter had written me at Brookwood in March about his marriage to May, whom both Roy and I had known for some time. Our family solidarity had been such that we were taken aback that Walter had abandoned our common vow not to get married for a while, and that he had done so without any family discussion. I was disconcerted, but pleased with his choice of May. His action also freed me to indulge in my emotional commitment. For I, too, had fallen in love — with a student at Brookwood named Sophia Goodlavich, a slight, rather prim girl with an eager mind. She was a hard worker and impressed one as never wasting a motion, quick-minded, not yet very worldly, curious, fearless in her search for new insight and new experience. She has joked in later years that I fell for her because she reminded me of my mother, who was also very neat, and organized her work in the same miraculously effective manner.

Though I had declared my love, I had not spoken of marriage, and suddenly, before I realized it, the school term was ending and the entire student body was soon to take to the road on a Chautauqua tour, performing union-oriented one-act plays across the country. We corresponded as best we could; I was also traveling on an assignment of my own. Then I learned that the students were playing in Aliquippa, Pennsylvania, for aluminum- and steelworkers, and that Roy was accompanying them and had invited the whole troupe of thirty or so to spend a weekend at our parents' house. I quickly altered my schedule, and so it turned out that I proposed to Sophie on Bethlehem Hill. She was hesitant at first, suggesting we wait until the end of the tour to see if we felt the same way then. We met again in Brookwood in July, and were married in Peekskill on the seventeenth, with Roy and Sophie's sister Jean attending.

Sophie's parents had come to America, when they were teenagers, from the section of Poland that has Vilna as its capital and that has changed hands and been fought over so often that the people never know whether to call themselves Russians, Poles, or Lithuanians. Because of the death of her father, Sophie had an arduous childhood, attending some seventeen different grade schools, helping an aunt in the home in Middleboro, Massachusetts, and working in shoe factories and later in chain stores all over Cape Cod. Constant labor and responsibility were her lot all through her teens. It was no wonder she exhibited the drive and determination to become the first woman organizer on the staff of the UAW during the period of crisis we entered as soon as we moved to Detroit late in 1936.

Her Catholic upbringing had its first painful shaking up under the influence of the Epworth League and a minister named Owen Knox in East Braintree, Massachusetts. Once her interest in economic and social as well as theological questions was stimulated, Sophie lost no time emancipating and broadening her mind. At twenty, she was enrolling in night classes and taking the train after work to Boston to participate in a Harvard Extension program. The Camden Shipyard strike erupted in the middle thirties and she joined with other Epworth Leaguers to solicit money and food for the strikers, speaking before church and community groups as well as the AFL hierarchy.

The Reverend Owen Knox was acquainted with Norman Thomas and must have mentioned to him on one of his New England lecture tours that in the Epworth League there was a remarkable young woman of considerable potential who had come up the hard way, working in New England shoe mills, and now helping feed shipyard strikers. Thomas recommended to Brookwood College that they admit her. At that time she was working in an A&P in South Brain-

tree, in charge of the bakery department. Before she left, her supervisor asked her where she was going.

"I'm going to Brookwood Labor College."

The man recoiled in horror. "Why, that's a Communist school!"

"Who are Communists?" asked Sophie.

"Well, if you have a wife and your friend has no wife, you share
your wife with him," replied the supervisor.

That didn't register with Sophie, and she went on questioning him
until he said: "Look, if you have a toothbrush and your neighbor
doesn't, you must share it with him."

So before she made her way to Katonah, New York, to enroll in
Brookwood, she saw to it that she had several extra toothbrushes, in
different colors, which she planned to keep in a tumbler on her
bureau to meet any emergency.

One couldn't plan or dream of a more propitious first few months
of marriage than ours in the summer setting of Brookwood. There
were no students around; there was a swimming pool not far from
our simple apartment; and we had the woods of Westchester County
to walk in. This idyll came to an end, however, when Tucker Smith
resigned as director of the Labor Division of the Emergency Peace
Campaign, and I became associated with Nelson Cruikshank, an ordained minister, who headed up the WPA workers' education project and was eager to move into active trade union work. The Peace
Campaign was shifted to New York where he lived.

My salary was extremely small. Sophie and I ended up in a tiny
apartment in a dilapidated and dirty brownstone block near Ninth
Avenue on Twenty-first Street, where we defeated cockroaches with
lye and kerosene, and Sophie made a charming home out of sparse
materials. My work was exciting; I was doing research on the major
United States corporations that stood to make a profit from war, and
I continued the campaign to educate workers concerning the proba-
bility of war. I was able to draw amply on my personal experiences
in Germany and other danger areas.

Working with a man of principle like Nelson Cruikshank, who was
not content merely to expound his ideas but tried to implement
them in daily life, was a most valuable experience. Nelson later became director of the Social Security Department of the AFL-CIO,
where he made a contribution to all Americans by promoting social
legislation. Now retired, he continues his labors of love as head of

the Senior Citizens of America, and is still fighting for social justice.

I was, of course, looking forward to the more vital job that lay ahead: the organizing of auto workers. When John L. Lewis came to New York in the fall to speak at a large rally in Madison Square Garden, Sophie and I were among the many thousands listening to him through the public address system rigged up outside. As he talked about the hopes of the unorganized industrial workers all over the country, my blood began to tingle, and I knew it was in that fight that I belonged. Two weeks later, when Sophie, Nelson, and I were in Philadelphia at a Quaker conference, I received a telegram from Walter and Roy: "If you are interested in the organizing of auto workers, come immediately back to Detroit."

I called Walter in Detroit for more information and he said the situation was ripe for a major push, what with the backing of the CIO and its resources. I was anxious to go, but I worried about Sophie. She said very calmly, "You go immediately and I'll go back to New York and pack our things and join you later." And Nelson, with his usual magnanimity, reassured me that he would escort Sophie to New York and, if necessary, would help her get to Detroit. I left that very evening, warmed by such loyalty and understanding.

As soon as I got to Detroit the next morning, I went at Walter's suggestion to the hiring gates of the Kelsey Hayes Wheel Company and was taken on as a punch press operator on the afternoon shift. Talking with Walter and other organizers late into the following night, I learned of the series of crucial meetings that had been held between workers at the Ternstedt and the Cadillac plants and, more important, with a group from Department 49 at the Kelsey Hayes Wheel Company.

Ever since the South Bend Convention, Walter had been holding small meetings in workers' homes or in the little back-room bars near the factory gates. He had, tragically, discovered that of the four or five present, one was sure to be a hired spy, and as soon as a worker signed up for the union in this private session, he would be fired. But in Department 49 of Kelsey Hayes, Walter had found a group that was insulated from treachery; these workers had developed a union loyalty and a courage that was unique in his experience so far. It had therefore been decided to concentrate as many dedicated union men as possible in the two Kelsey Hayes Wheel plants. Merlin Bishop had gone on the day shift in Department 49;

I was now on the second shift, with another friend and former student leader, George Edwards, who later became Detroit Police Commissioner, Justice of the Michigan Supreme Court, and is now a federal judge.

Nelson Cruikshank did drive Sophie out to Detroit, via Wheeling for a visit with my parents. They met me when I came off the shift. I remember that night well. I had walked a short block in the direction of the rooming house where I had found an inadequate temporary shelter for us, and there suddenly was Nelson's car, and Sophie in it.

Sophie was not one to sit idly at home in a dreary rooming house. The day after her arrival she went to the office of West Side Local 174 and offered her secretarial services. Because she knew Polish, she was of enormous help in dealing with the many Polish-born workers at Kelsey Hayes Wheel who spoke little or no English. Soon Sophie was hard at work on bilingual leaflets and bulletins, preparing for the imminent breakthrough.

Walter, after consultation with Dave Miller of the Cadillac plant, had set up shop at 3814 Thirty-fifth Street. The most important of the groups that made up Local 174 was the Automotive Industrial Workers' Alliance, organized mostly in Chrysler plants, under the leadership of Richard T. Frankensteen and R. J. Thomas. The price that had to be paid for getting this organization to join the local was providing a full-time paid position for Frankensteen.

Kelsey Hayes Wheel was chosen as the first target both because of its core of incorruptible union men and because, unlike the River Rouge plant, it was not too big to be unmanageable. But it was big enough, with two separate plants employing a total of about five thousand workers. It produced mostly for the Ford Company, which was dependent on it for wheels and brake drums. A victory there would give us a real push forward. The final decisive factor in the choice of Kelsey Hayes Wheel was that there had been few discharges among the union men who had been meeting with Walter, and it looked as if the two plants had not been deeply penetrated by stool pigeons. The fact that Bishop, Edwards, and I were allowed to work here, and under our own names, indicated that the company's security arrangements were not under the thumb of Ford's Harry Bennett. I am sure Bennett regretted this oversight later on.

Every day Merlin Bishop and I met with Walter to give our evaluation of strength in different departments of the plant. We estimated that Department 49 had the largest number of signed-up unionists, and it was decided that our efforts should be focused there. Fortunately I had on my shift in the brake-drum section a very husky Polish girl who was as staunch a defender of unionism and her own rights as could be found anywhere. She had for some time been speaking out against the vicious speed-up. Although she was strong, the constant increase in the tempo was more than she could handle: a few months before, she had fainted on the job. She was to prove an essential part of our strategy.

Wages were another vital issue. They were excessively low, even for those times, and of course the female workers were paid less. I hired in for 37½ cents an hour and many girls were doing exactly the same job, some more efficiently, for only 22½ cents. Many Kelsey Hayes Wheel workers had only $1.80 to show for eight hours of grueling labor — a weekly paycheck of $9.00. The national average weekly take-home pay for an auto worker, back in 1924, was $30.30. Ford increased it to $33.00 for a forty-four-hour week, but the Depression caused a nose dive to $19.80. The Kelsey Hayes Wheel average of $9.00 was, even by Depression standards, a gross exploitation.

On the first Sunday of December, about a dozen knowledgeable men from Kelsey Hayes Wheel met to discuss the situation in Department 49. It was revealed that tension was running especially high in the hub and brake-drum sector, where a foreman named Barnett was riding herd on the workers, creating such antagonism that there was open talk about organizing a committee to protest directly to the superintendent. It was clear that 49 was the key department at the moment. What was needed was some dramatic incident to spark the action and draw in the other departments as well.

Since the speed-up was the major source of resentment, we spoke to the Polish girl in my sector, and she agreed to faint again. This would be the signal for a strike in 49. Our contacts would not be alerted until the last minute, to prevent any leaks. Their part was to call for solidarity in support of Department 49. To take advantage of our membership in both shifts, we set the fainting incident for the hour when the shifts were about to change and both sets of workers would be present. D-Day would be on Tuesday, December 10, so that we could warn our men just before they went home on Monday that something would happen the next day. Only nine or ten people knew the precise details. Walter was to remain in the Local 174 office all day, and we would inform management that it was he who was to be contacted for any negotiations.

We organized picket squads, and since we were planning for a sit-in, a committee was formed to take care of feeding the strikers inside the plant and their families outside. May Reuther took a sick leave from her teaching job; Sophie was ready with a host of volunteers. Fortunately, Walter had persuaded Frank Winn, a former Brookwood student, to come from Texas to handle publicity on a volunteer basis. He had a quiet sense of humor and great dedication.

On the day of the strike, I reported to work earlier than usual to size up the situation before the deadline came. I saw Bishop and Edwards; they had already alerted the best unionists on the day shift. At precisely twenty minutes before that shift was to end, our faithful friend went into a dead faint, and I ran and pulled the main switch and shouted, "Strike! We've had enough of this speed-up!" The call for strike action spread through our whole department and into neighboring sectors, and we soon had an enormous gathering of both morning- and afternoon-shift workers crowding around us.

Within minutes, Kelsey Hayes Wheel's personnnel director, Paul Danzig, came pounding into the department. "What the hell is going on?" he yelled. Then he spied me up on a big crate, reviewing the facts for the workers: they had been the victims of an inhuman speed-up and every plea for slowing down had fallen on deaf ears; we needed a union to protect ourselves and to win an eight-hour day, forty-hour week, and a wage increase for all. Danzig came over and started pulling at my trouser leg. "What are you doing? What are you doing?" I told him I was explaining why we needed a union. "Get back to work," he said. "No," I answered, "we'll not get back to work. If you want us to get back to work, you will sit down with Walter Reuther and an elected committee."

Then Danzig said, "Who in the hell is Reuther?"

"He's the president of our union."

"Where do I reach him?"

I had Walter's number ready, and Danzig was soon on the phone to him.

"Is your name Reuther?"

"Yes."

"I want you to tell these men to get back to work."

"Where are you?"

"I'm inside the plant."

"But I'm outside the plant and can't tell anybody to get back to work as long as I'm out here. Send a car over to pick me up and take me into the plant and I'll talk to the guys."

Danzig agreed. I was still holding forth on the crate when Walter arrived. I stepped off the box and Walter stepped on and continued with the same speech. Danzig grabbed *his* trouser leg and said, "What the hell is this? You're supposed to tell them to go back to work."

"I can't tell them to do anything," Walter replied, "until I first get them organized."

Some 500 workers, from all sections of the McGraw Avenue plant (Kelsey Hayes Wheel's other plant was nearby on Military Avenue) were jammed into Department 49 for several hours. Finally the management agreed to hold a formal negotiation session at 9:00 A.M. the next morning, with representatives from all departments of both plants.

The talks were held, off and on, for two weeks. The men went back to work that Thursday, but the management canceled all second-shift operations for the balance of the day, fearful that the strike would sweep through other departments. Our organizers were on hand with sound trucks, leaflets, and membership applications, and many hundreds of workers signed up, impressed by the fact that we had caught the company off-guard and forced its representatives to sit down and negotiate.

What the company did, from then on, was stall for time. We heard that there was a council of war at the Ford Company, attended by George Kennedy, the president of Kelsey Hayes, Sorenson of Ford, and his strong-arm man, Harry Bennett, in addition to his sidekick, John Gillespie, and others. It was reported that Sorenson had advised Kennedy not to close the plant to one shift because the public would class it as a lock-out, and that Kennedy was not in a frame of mind to deal honestly with the men, believing he could satisfy them with some temporary raises. The most significant information we received was that Ford was at this point badly in need of brakes and other Kelsey Hayes Wheel parts, and that if the men struck again and work was shut down for a day or two, we might get tangible results.

A series of double-crosses began. Management constantly tried to break off negotiations, while their foremen were going through the plants, trying to buy off as many men as they could with offers of individual wage adjustments in return for their reneging on the union. They also tried to resurrect their own company union and use it as a weapon to vitiate support for the strike. They sent telegrams to all employees, inviting them to a company union meeting that first Sunday night after the strike. We countered by holding, that Sunday afternoon, the largest meeting of Kelsey workers we had ever convened, at Falcon Hall on Junction Avenue. After the meeting we marched, some 500 strong, to the company union's designated meeting place with our telegrams of invitation in hand, and proceeded to take over the company union, officially voting to disband it and join the UAW.

Monday morning brought the climax. Management had agreed that the results of the negotiations would be reported to workers in both plants, but when the union committee returned to the Military Avenue building to make its report, it was shut out of its own plant. Word of this came to us in the McGraw Avenue building in time for the conjunction of the two shifts. We called a general sit-down strike for the two plants. By refusing to negotiate with the union, management had brought upon itself a long and costly battle.

Approximately 500 workers were asked to remain inside the plants. Others were asked to report to the Falcon Hall strike headquarters and sign up for outside duties: picketing, setting up soup kitchens, soliciting food, and so on. It was suggested that I stay outside and help Walter with the organization, and I still remember the long list of small merchants in the neighborhood who responded to our appeals with both food and cash. By the second day of the sit-in, after hearing all the frightening rumors that were bound to circulate, including the report that police and vigilantes were coming to beat them up, the men inside became understandably worried. Merlin Bishop sent a message: "Walter, *please*, send some food in for us. We had only bread and coffee today so far and it is now 2:00 P.M. . . . Buy enough to feed the 200 in here; they have begun to get restless." This was in Department 49; there were hundreds more in the other plant. So we concentrated our efforts on giving the men inside not only food but some sense of security, which meant strong picket lines at all the gates.

A small strike bulletin was mimeographed by May and Sophie and other volunteers at the Thirty-fifth Street office, and Frank Winn briefed reporters on what was really happening, to counteract false statements put out by the corporation about what they had offered and we had rejected. Railway workers and teamsters agreed to respect our picket lines and not move anything in or out of the plants.

As the strike dragged on, the Kelsey Hayes Wheel management made a desperate attempt to move some of its tools and dies out, undoubtedly under pressure from the Ford Company, which was running short of brake drums, wheels, and hubs. The idea was to use the River Rouge plant, something Ford had done during the Akron rubber strike when tires became short. When the sit-in workers learned of this threat, they filled enormous dollies with all kinds of heavy auto parts and shoved them against the exits, making three-foot barriers. As soon as we heard that Ford trucks were coming to a certain gate, Walter, working with Frankensteen and others on the East Side, sent out an emergency appeal. Thousands of auto workers from all parts of Detroit converged on Kelsey Hayes Wheel in a mass demonstration, completely blocking access to the plant. I was manning the sound truck, speaking to a crowd that consisted in large part of Kelsey workers not yet signed into the UAW. On that day, one thousand new members joined us. No tools or dies left the plant.

In the East Side of Detroit another sit-down strike — by the Bohn Aluminum workers — began to make headlines in the press. General Motors, Ford, and Chrysler workers were watching these two strikes with intense interest, knowing their own future might be determined by what happened at Bohn. In a sense, the survival of the UAW depended on some sort of victory that December; auto industry management, of course, wanted to nip the Union in the bud right then and there, and keep its roots from spreading into the giant corporations.

On December 20, Sophie wrote a letter to Tucker Smith's wife, Myra, at Brookwood:

> The boys and girls have been sitting for six days and there are no signs of relenting till Easter. In fact some of the scissor bills are saying that if "they" don't hurry up and settle "we'll run the shop ourselves."

Merlin is one of the boys on the inside and he continues to remind the workers that "this is workers' education." . . . A few nights ago, the company imported a dozen professional strikebreakers; this was a Friday and there were a half dozen union meetings in town. We called all the unions and asked them to come in a body to enforce the picket line. When they did, there were a few thousand strong yelling, "Throw the scabs out, throw the scabs out!" It wasn't long before the scabs were thrown out.

The company made a last feeble attack. They called another company union meeting. This time it was done on the quiet. About 70 showed up (there are quite a number of foremen), our forces were mobilized, and the company union meeting ended in the police station. They got scared . . .

One of the teachers asked a pupil why her Dad was striking. The tot replied, "For more money and more toilets." Ford has been forced to lay off 20,000 of his workers because of lack of supplies. Several other plants are in the same position. We feel that this will be a hard battle and probably long drawn out. The folks in the plant are planning on using the conveyor belts for an Xmas gift displayer . . .

We knew that separation from their families at Christmas would dampen the morale of the sit-downers, so a special solicitation was made all over the city for food, trees, trimmings, presents for the men inside and their families outside. Boredom and loneliness were the worst enemies. Merlin Bishop had set up formal discussions: he and George Edwards had musical instruments brought in; and hillbilly bands and barbershop quartets suddenly formed. Then, just before Christmas, it began to look to both Kelsey Hayes Wheel and Ford that they could not get our men out of the plants until they took negotiations more seriously. The strike was really hurting Ford production. Harry Bennett evidently threatened Kennedy, Kelsey's president, that unless it was settled immediately, they would look elsewhere for supplies. This broke the deadlock. Kennedy knuckled under to Bennett, who told Gillespie to get in touch with Frankensteen, the city director of union organization. Frankensteen passed the information along to Walter, and things began to move.

It turned out to be one of the most glorious Christmas Days Detroit workers had known. The settlement came on the eve of the holiday. The terms called for a general wage hike for all and, what was of greater importance, a guaranteed minimum wage of seventy-five cents an hour. My wages were doubled, and for the girls who had been working next to me, they were tripled. We also won a shop steward system and a shop committee to be elected by the UAW members, and a seniority system by which the length of service of individual workers would govern the order of future layoffs and recalls. The final meetings took place in Ford offices, proving which one of the affected companies exercised the real power in that palaver.

The sit-down strikers marched out into the glare of flash bulbs and the cheers of thousands who had gathered to congratulate them on their fortitude and their victory. Everyone sensed that a new era had begun for auto workers. Within a short ten days, the West Side Local 174 increased its membership from seventy-eight to three thousand. Before the next Christmas would roll around, the count would have risen to thirty-five thousand. The significance of the signing of an agreement to allow unionization, right in the offices of the Ford Motor Company, was not lost on the workers; it was a turning point. After the Kelsey Hayes Wheel triumph, the phone at the West Side Local was ringing every hour of day and night: "Send us some soup and sandwiches; we're sitting down on strike."

Soon after Christmas, the industrial insurance agent who handled accidents at Kelsey Hayes Wheel came by to see Walter. What he had to say was an eye-opener for us all. It seems that he had previously negotiated the insurance contract with the personnel director at Kelsey, with whom he had obligingly split his commission. Now he proposed to let Walter, as leader of the union, have a third of the take. Walter was so irate that he threw the agent out of the office. This incident more than any other convinced him that some ethical codes had to be established to prevent the insidious and corrupting kickbacks, so long accepted by the business community, from creeping into the trade union movement. When Walter later became the UAW's president, he initiated, among UAW officers, staff, and local union leadership, lengthy and detailed discussions, which led to the creation by UAW convention action of a Public Review Board, designed to help the union and its leadership ensure democratic practices and procedures within the UAW.

"Where you find a weak trade union official who has been corrupted," Walter often repeated, "you will also find an employer who has been a party to corrupting him, and if you are going to send a weak trade union leader to prison for malpractices, then reserve the adjacent cells for the insurance agent and the personnel director."

When, at the end of 1936, Walter totaled up his income for the year, he knew he was fortunate to have something besides money to show for his efforts. He had earned $1760, which included lecture fees and occasional wages. He had received no salary for his union work, but he looked back on that year with a tremendous sense of accomplishment: at long last things had begun to move. The foundation had been laid for a democratic industrial union for auto workers.

Roy was caught in the turmoil of the General Motors sit-down strike in Flint at the very moment Walter was sitting at the conference table in Kelsey Hayes Wheel, just before negotiations were removed to the Ford offices. As Walter tells it, just when the meeting was about to begin one morning, someone put in front of Kennedy a newspaper black with headlines about Flint and a story about Roy Reuther, named as one of the chief organizers. It caught Kennedy's eye and he exploded: "Jesus Christ, is there another Reuther?"

At that point, from outside the gate, my voice, roaring away on the sound truck's microphone, penetrated the inner sanctum.

"Who the hell is out there?" asked the irritated Kennedy.

Paul Danzig answered, "Oh, that's another — Victor Reuther."

Kennedy blanched, and muttered, "My God, how many of those Reuther bastards are there?"

CHAPTER 13

Sit-Down in Flint

WHEN ROY had gone to Flint in October 1934 as an instructor in FERA's workers' education program, he built up contacts with auto workers in that one-industry, one-company town. In 1935, General Motors encouraged the Henderson Committee to undertake a witch hunt among FERA employees, and the whole project became suspect and Roy lost his job. Union membership dropped to a handful because of lack of AFL support and the thorough, intimidating spy system set up by General Motors.

Flint was a GM town down to the bone. Eighty percent of Flint families were dependent for their living on Buick, Fisher Body, Chevrolet, or AC Spark Plug. The rest of the working families were on relief. The people were gaunt and seedy-looking; years of unemployment had left hollows in their faces and fear in their eyes. Their housing was more miserable than that in any other highly developed industrial town in the country. In a sense, Flint was a segment of the deep South transported north, for General Motors had primarily employed white Southern workers, who were lured up during the twenties by the growing automobile industry. A large number of them went south again in 1929; the rest suffered the Depression out — on the welfare lines.

Flint's Mayor, Chief of Police, clergy, newspapers, and even its judges were under the thumb of General Motors, which had become the world's richest and most powerful corporation. But the New Deal had provided some hope, especially through the enactment of the section of the National Recovery Act that gave workers the right to unionize. The Automobile Labor Board under Leo Wolman, set up by Roosevelt to inquire into the management-labor situation in the auto industry, seemed another signal to workers that the federal government was on their side, saying to them: "Here are your rights. Stand up for them!" The upshot was that, in the spring of 1934, five thousand workers in Fisher Body Number One struck in protest against the discharge of twenty-five workers who had been in the process of forming an AFL union in that plant. Unfortunately, these Flint strikers had to taste the same bitter disillusionment so many rank-and-file industrial workers had suffered from the AFL. Once more there were unkept promises, the absence of any real assistance, and false leaders, who persuaded the workers to trust the words of corporation executives. William S. Knudsen and Alfred P. Sloan of General Motors made pious vows to the AFL leadership and to Roosevelt, none of which was kept: workers who had started the strike were not taken back; the union's bargaining position became weaker and weaker; and in the end the men found that their strike had accomplished almost nothing. Union membership dropped to a new low.

When Roy got there that fall, he began with great patience to meet with auto workers in small groups, often in their homes. He taught such basic subjects as parliamentary procedure, public speaking, labor economics, history of the labor movement. But, as Roy suspected and the La Follette Committee discovered later, at least 25 percent of those in attendance at these FERA classes were Pinkerton men paid by General Motors, and all too often Roy's students found discharge slips in their time-card racks. The company managed in this way to snuff out any hope of rebuilding a strong union.

After the CIO was born and the South Bend Convention gave the UAW a promise of new life, Wyndham Mortimer, the new vice-president, went to Flint to survey the situation and try to pool all the separate unions in the city into one amalgamated local, 156. He worked doggedly to recruit new members, but against him were arrayed stool pigeons, the Klan, and Black Legion members, some of whom, he suspected, were sitting right on the executive board of the union. He made house visits and distributed mimeographed letters, which might have appealed to a sophisticated work force. But in Flint the language missed the mark, and a delegation from Local 156 went to CIO leaders and asked that Mortimer be replaced by either Fred Pieper of Alabama or Robert Travis of Toledo. Travis was chosen, but it took him only a short time to realize that the task of bucking General Motors was too big for one man, and he asked to have Roy assigned as assistant director of organization. He had found many traces of the paths that Roy had trodden in Flint. So in October 1936, well before our Kelsey Hayes Wheel strike got underway, Roy returned to Flint to work with Travis. At that point, there were fewer than 200 UAW members in good standing in the whole city.

There was such suspicion of the Local 156 executive board that a general membership meeting could not be risked. Small groups gathered in private homes, and Travis and Roy began asking trusted unionists to undertake responsibility as volunteer shop stewards and organizers within key departments of Buick and of Fisher Body One and Two. Also, a union newspaper, the Flint *Auto Worker,* was started, headed up by Henry Kraus, former editor of an Auto Council paper in Cleveland.

Sporadic strikes began to break out in some isolated departments of the various GM plants, each followed by the discharge of the workers involved. One worker was discharged simply for wearing his union button. Roy asked for an appointment with Harry Coen, later to become GM vice-president.

"How come," asked Roy, "if you're a Mason, or K of C, or a member of the Elks, it's okay to wear a button, but if you wear a union button you get fired?"

"You're damn right," Coen replied. "Now what are you going to do about it?"

Roy did nothing that day, but made up for lost time later.

There had been more union militancy in the huge Fisher Body One over the past years than in the other Flint plants. In their "Body-in-White" department, a dedicated union man, Bud Simons, had become a volunteer steward and part-time organizer for the UAW. One Friday evening in November, several welders in his department, who had participated in a quickie strike the day before and won some concessions, were given notice. This became the signal for Simons to shut down the whole Body-in-White department, causing the laying off of some 700 workers. The company was beside itself with anxiety, and promised that if the men went back to work, the discharged welders would be re-employed the following Monday. But Simons told them this wouldn't be good enough, and that the welders must be located and brought right back, which took some effort on management's part, though it complied. When the welders came in, it was announced to the assembled department that the union had won their reinstatement. News of this success spread around Flint and gave hope to the new UAW Local 156. From then on, it was possible to hold citywide meetings in an effort to build morale and allay fear of reprisals.

The organizers were still plagued, however, by spies and stool pigeons, and Roy and Travis had asked the La Follette Committee to send in some investigators. Soon after the latter arrived, they turned up an agent, employed by GM, sitting on the local's executive board. So at the next big meeting in Pengelly Hall, on December 26, Roy rose from his seat dramatically and said they had come upon evidence that there was a stool pigeon in the union ranks. The crowd was at first stunned and dead quiet; then the shouts began: "Name him! Name him!"

Roy went on to describe the depths to which some human beings would sink for thirty pieces of silver, and the immorality of a corporation that would resort to such methods — but the crowd grew impatient and again shouted to Roy to name the traitor.

"Perhaps by now," said Roy, "this lonely creature would prefer to rise and confess his sins before I am compelled to identify him publicly. I will count to ten and if he has not by then risen to his feet, I will point him out." Silence — as Roy slowly counted to ten and no one stood up.

"His name is John Stott, and he is sitting in the center of the hall," Roy said, at which point Stott was on his feet, trembling. Four stalwart union members had previously been assigned to sit on either side of the stoolie, and they quickly surrounded him, to protect him from possible vengeance, and escorted him from the hall with the advice that he get out of town for his own good. This exposure was a shot in the arm for the audience and renewed its determination to achieve solidarity.

With a mere one thousand of the forty-seven thousand GM workers in Flint signed up so far, only the naïve would assume that there was a calculated strategy to strike General Motors at that time. As a matter of fact, there had been talk among CIO officials that, because Chrysler was more unionized and did not seem to be as fierce an antagonist as General Motors, it might be wise to take on Chrysler first. But despite the collective wisdom of the leadership, Fred Pieper, close friend and ally of Homer Martin, called a strike in GM's Fisher

Body plant in Atlanta. This precipitate action was taken without consultation with the officers of the international union, though Martin must have been in on it, since he sent telegrams alerting all GM locals across the country. Adolph Germer, CIO representative in Atlanta, had cautioned Martin against strike action, knowing that the national CIO would not have enough time to marshal manpower or money for a nationwide attack on the world's biggest corporation.

Soon after the Atlanta affair began, the Kansas City GM plant went on strike. Kansas City was Homer Martin's hometown, and his influence over the local there was perhaps greater than that of any other officer. At any event, with two strikes underway, Homer Martin wired President Knudsen of General Motors on December 20, requesting a conference. They met the next day, along with George F. Addes, secretary-treasurer of the UAW. Knudsen had said on December 18, when the Kelsey Hayes Wheel strike was threatening Ford's production schedule, that "General Motors believes collective bargaining is here to stay." But this new-found conviction had evidently not survived even a few days; at the December 21 meeting he refused to bargain collectively with the UAW on a national basis, suggesting instead that the Kansas City and Atlanta strikes should be negotiated separately. Unfortunately Homer Martin gave in immediately, much to the dismay and anger of the national CIO and the leaders of the UAW. They knew it was simply a ruse by which Knudsen could give the impression of bargaining with the UAW without actually doing so. When John L. Lewis heard about Martin's ineptness, he was furious; he realized it would amount to slow death for the UAW if the company could pick off one plant at a time.

But the die was cast and, prepared or not, the UAW had to summon all its resources to try to bring General Motors to terms. Hence the Fisher Body works in Cleveland was struck under the leadership of Paul Miley, and word was sent to Travis and Roy to get ready for strike action at Fisher Body One in Flint.

The GM management anticipated this possibility and made an attempt to move strategic dies out of the plant, so that the pressing and forming of auto parts might be shifted to factories not likely to be struck. This gambit by GM was what determined the Union's move. In both Fisher One and Two, a sit-down strike was called on December 30.

Whatever reservations John L. Lewis had about the general strategy, he rolled with the punch when strike action became inevitable
in GM plants, and served notice on the whole auto industry that
"employers who tyrannize over employees with the aid of labor
spies, company guards, and the threat of discharge need not be
surprised if their production lines are suddenly halted." He also ob-
viated the danger of Homer Martin's giving in to Knudsen's divide-
and-conquer technique by announcing that any effort to settle grievances through negotiations in local plants was a waste of time, for
the plant managers were "devoid of authority."

The sudden tempest took all of us in Detroit by surprise — even
Walter, who was on the UAW Executive Board. He had planned to
go to New York after the Kelsey strike was won, but the news from
Flint made it clear that the General Motors battle had taken priority.
Sophie had already gone, as the UAW's first woman organizer, to
Anderson, Indiana, where the Guide Lamp plant had been struck. I
was asked by Mortimer and Martin to hurry to Flint and join Bob
Travis and Roy as an auxiliary staff member, which I did on January
1, 1937, the day after the Fisher Body sit-down began.

It was obvious that the very nature of the sit-down strike would
provide a controversial element. Was it legal? The courts had not
officially ruled on the matter. The sit-down had been successful in
the Akron rubber strike and the recent skirmish at Kelsey Hayes
Wheel. The corporations were, of course, concerned about protecting their capital, invested in tools, equipment, and raw materials,
and could invoke the laws that safeguard property rights. Yet to the
workers it seemed natural to protest, by means of this essentially
peaceful technique, the years of exploitation they had suffered.
Their jobs were *their* investments, and they were protecting them.
They were no more concerned about the corporation's property
rights than was the corporation about the workers' legal rights to
unionize, as established by Congress in 1933. I should venture to
guess that those who doubted the morality of the sit-down in 1937
were fewer than the doubters among the population in 1775, when
American independence was won by challenging the tyrannical laws
and regulations of the British Crown.

The first court injunction against the sit-down was issued on January 2 by Circuit Judge Edward D. Black. He ordered the strikers
to evacuate the plants, and Sheriff Wolcott deputized 100 auxiliary

police — most of them "loyal employees" of GM. When the Sheriff appeared at the gates of Fisher One, where some 500 workers were sitting in, and read aloud the injunction terms, he was literally laughed out of the place, and retreated with boos and catcalls ringing in his ears. Meanwhile, Lee Pressman, general counsel for the national CIO, had been tipped off by an alert newspaperman that he might find it useful to look into Judge Black's GM stock holdings. To Pressman's amazement and glee he learned that the judge owned some 3365 shares, valued then at about $219,000. This fact hit like a delayed bomb in Flint, Detroit, and Washington. Black was asked to disqualify himself, and it was even suggested that he be impeached. GM's image suffered, and the UAW gained support in the community.

Once again Homer Martin showed lack of judgment. As soon as Judge Black had slapped on the injunction, Homer found it necessary to rush into public print to assure General Motors and the country at large that the strikers would respect the court order and evacuate the plants. He also implied a willingness to negotiate at the local plant level, in spite of all CIO and UAW objections. It was clear by then to the national leadership that Martin was out of touch with the reality of the situation; they arranged for him to undertake a speaking tour to increase union membership — and to be kept busy at a safe distance from the battlefield.

I have often been asked whether the idea of the sit-down strike was something brought in surreptitiously from Europe, by hired agents. I find that most unlikely. To my recollection, no one in Flint or Detroit or Akron was even vaguely aware that sit-in strikes had recently occurred in France. In Flint the concept gained support after the success of that first quickie stoppage in Fisher One, when the discharged welders were reinstated. During every short-term strike before that one, the workers had been promised concessions, only to find, when they returned to the plant a few days later, that everything was just as before, and as likely as not the ringleaders of such a strike would be discharged. Such betrayals had made the sit-down strike the only recourse.

Another reason for the workers to remain in the plant instead of marching in picket lines was that they might be free from intimidation by plant police, city police, vigilante groups, and other powers of authority that were always on the side of the corporation. Inside the plant, they gained a sense of security from the very walls and the familiar machines among which they had spent most of their lives. In 1936–37, only a small minority of workers dared to identify openly with the UAW. The sit-in technique, by allowing a small, highly organized group of laboring men to occupy key areas of a corporation's production process, gave workers control of a situation that affected them. Does this mean that sit-in strikes were immoral because they permitted a minority to force its will on a lethargic and fearful majority? No, I think the facts prove otherwise. Once the fear was calmed, the mass of workers in auto plants made incontrovertibly clear that they wanted a union to represent them — an industrial union to embrace all grades of employees. Furthermore, with all the money that was poured into it, the company's return-to-work movement was not able to persuade the majority outside the plant to act against the minority inside. There was obviously a conviction that the minority was acting in behalf of all.

Behind the scenes, the AFL, always opposed to the very idea of an industrial union, was trying to undermine the strikes. Frey, of the Metal Trades Union, got in touch with GM's labor relations director and elicited this statement from him in a letter:

> General Motors has no intentions of entering into any agreement with any other organization interfering with the legitimate jurisdiction.

"Legitimate jurisdiction," of course, referred to craft unions. Frey was not satisfied with this, and had two meetings with Knudsen himself. Other AFL leaders tried to get both President Roosevelt and Michigan's Governor Murphy to block recognition of the UAW. General Motors was delighted with the conflict between the AFL and the CIO, and tried to use it to avoid its obligation to negotiate.

Back in Detroit, Walter was holding meetings around the clock with some of the workers in General Motors plants, measuring the mood of the men as the news about Flint came in. There was strike fever on the West Side: on the ninth of January, 3800 workers struck at Cadillac, and Fleetwood Body Works followed suit with a sit-down on the twelfth. Both plants were evacuated on the fifteenth, and the strikes continued in the more conventional manner. There was action in Pontiac, Michigan, St. Louis, and Oakland, California, during that month. The countrywide battle had really begun.

The CIO turned on its full power, first sending Adolph Germer, a skilled organizer and orator, to Detroit; then Leo Krzycki from the Amalgamated Clothing Workers, Rose Pesotta from the Ladies' Garment Workers, Bill Carney from Akron, and, from the Mine Workers, those long-time militants, John Brophy and Powers Hapgood. All gave their time and energy at rallies and on picket lines wherever GM workers were on strike or on the verge of it. Their presence on the scene, symbol of active national CIO support, was a significant factor in our ultimate success.

The great contribution of Bob Travis cannot be underestimated. He inspired confidence and loyalty everywhere he went. Though not an effective public speaker — he left the oratory to Roy and me — his was a crucial role as we rapidly extended our trade union contacts, department by department, shift by shift, in every Chevrolet and Fisher plant, and made liaison with Buick and AC Spark Plug workers.

Roy and I handled most of the public presentation of our cause. We spoke at rallies and at the factory gates, attempting to stir the workers out of their apathy and to ease their doubts and fears. But it was not our oratory or Bob Travis's personal charm and dedication that set the workers marching. It was their long memory of grievances, near-starvation, layoffs, and arrogant and inhuman treatment by the corporation, together with the hope for the future that the union gave them. The natural bitterness and hatred that was the result of being exploited was the strongest motivation to fight back, once they became conscious of a nationwide army of CIO workers behind them.

Inside Fisher One and Fisher Two, the strikers showed their capacity for organization and self-control. A security committee was responsible for protecting the equipment and for blocking the doors against police, company men, or vigilantes. It also guarded against fire hazards; smoking was permitted only in specified sections. A health committee watched over the condition of the men and called a doctor when necessary, and another group provided entertainment.

The strikers' wives staunchly backed the cause, and indeed almost the entire population of Flint was ultimately caught up in the conflict. Small shopkeepers contributed supplies; they knew their survival depended on the steady income of factory workers and that they too would benefit from a wage increase across the board. It was no easy task to feed almost 700 strikers in Fisher One and several hundred in Fisher Two. The AFL Cooks' and Chefs' Union, unlike some of their national leaders, were in sympathy and assigned Chef Max Gazin to organize a soup kitchen, which took on the proportions of a facility to feed a regiment.

To get the food in was easy enough at Fisher One, where the strikers were on the ground floor. But at Fisher Two, the downstairs was patrolled regularly by company police, so most of the time the only way we could talk to those inside was to climb a tall ladder that was placed against the front windows. (Twice a day the guard opened the front door downstairs and allowed meals to be brought in.) We had some distinguished guests on that ladder — Jennie Lee from Britain, Ellen Wilkinson, and Mrs. Gifford Pinchot. The CIO organizers I have mentioned held chats and pep talks with the strikers, and newspaper reporters were sometimes allowed in to do human-interest stories.

Fisher One had a stronger group than Fisher Two because of its long history of unionizing efforts. Bud Simons was the chairman there; in Fisher Two it was William "Red" Mundale. When GM made its first overt effort to oust the strikers it chose Fisher Two, the easier prey. The attempt took place on the afternoon of January 11. The first indication of impending trouble was the arrival of a contingent of twenty-two plant protection guards, augmenting the force of only eight policemen usually on duty outside the plant. Then all heat in the building was shut off. Up to this time the company had refrained from using this tactic because of pleas from the state authorities and threats by the sit-downers to build wood fires, if necessary, to keep warm. But when GM decided to force a showdown, it did not consult state officials, and relied on the compliant Flint police force.

I was at strike headquarters with Roy and Bob Travis when word of this development came, and we rallied as many volunteers as we could and shifted most of our pickets from Fisher One to Fisher Two. We next heard that police, were gathering in some force not too far from Fisher Two. I had been using an improvised sound car, an old Chevrolet with speakers fastened to the roof, for my daily rounds at the two plants, giving news, playing music, talking to the pickets during their long vigil. My voice as well as the music penetrated to the strikers inside. That afternoon I took a circuitous route to avoid the police just beyond the railroad tracks on Chevrolet Avenue and reached Fisher Two's gate on that avenue by back alleys. Bill Carney was with me. We found a silent and grim picket line, slightly larger than before. There were now about 140 on the line, and the atmosphere was both ugly and solemn. As soon as we made contact with Red Mundale and the others and heard their story, we realized the men inside were in an even more bitter mood.

I quickly put on some music and went to consult with the picket captains and from them learned that the heat had been turned off, the ladder forcibly removed, and the front gate barred tight. No more food could be taken in. Then the men at the window shouted down to me, "Can the music, Reuther. Get us some food!" I did not wait long before deciding what to do. There was a truck nearby with food in large drums waiting to be delivered. I instructed Red Mundale, over the public address system, to select a small committee to go down to the door below and appeal to the guards to let the food through, as they had every other afternoon. If the guards refused, the strikers should open the door themselves and take in the food.

Mundale appointed Rosco Rich to go below, with a group of thirty, to ask Captain Peterson (he had a force of about twenty plant guards) if the gate could be opened to let the food in, and to make clear that if it was not they would force it open themselves. There was no response; the guards merely stood aside and, while the strikers snapped the lock and pushed open the gate, disappeared into the recesses of the first floor. As the strikers appeared at the outer gate to receive the food, a cheer went up from the pickets and for a moment the two groups mingled; then our supply truck moved up and the strikers took the food in and shut the gate and went back to the second floor. The picket line began to march again briskly, singing the familiar "Solidarity Forever." During the few minutes at the door, I gave Mundale instructions as fast as I could to go right back upstairs and make no effort to occupy the main floor.

As for Captain Peterson and his men, I suspect their hearts were not in their assignment to starve out the strikers, many of whom they had known personally for years. To cover their inaction, Peterson phoned the Flint police and reported that they were "being held captive by the sit-down strikers." In fact, they had chosen to remove themselves from the scene, wanting no part of a direct confrontation. They rather ignominiously closeted themselves in the ladies' rest room on the ground floor, and remained there throughout the long night of battle.

I had just returned to the sound car when I heard shouts: "The police! My God, the police!" Then I saw out of the corner of my eye the first burst of tear-gas shells from beyond the railroad tracks, in between Chevrolet Four and Five. From where I was parked, in the center of Chevrolet Avenue, I could see the police coming across the tracks and down the avenue. Over the bridge came a group of squad cars whose human occupants holding short, stubby muzzled guns, looked very strange in their gas masks. Then I saw more police on foot, shielding themselves behind the slowly advancing cars. As they got closer, they began lobbing tear-gas shells that had points hard and sharp enough to break through reinforced glass. They were aiming them at the second-floor windows of Fisher Two and into the midst of the pickets. And as they forced their way through, they hurled additional shells at the ground-floor windows, breaking several panes of glass, apparently unaware that all the strikers were upstairs.

We were not unprepared. The second-floor doors were barred with weighted steel dollies, and fire hoses were connected for any emergency. On the roof, at strategic points facing Chevrolet Avenue, the strikers had placed huge piles of pound-and-a-half hinges, and had stretched inner tube rubber between the big steel bars that were part of the roof's structure to use as giant slingshots. As soon as the police began using tear gas and breaking windows, I shouted to the men inside to defend themselves with everything they had. The response was immediate. Every tear-gas missile fired in their direction was followed by a barrage of heavy hinges that struck the cars and some of the officers.

The weather was on our side: it was only about sixteen degrees above and no day to be doused with cold water, so when the strikers brought the fires hoses into full play against the police below and the 150 pickets pushed with all their might, the police were driven back across the bridge to regroup and plan new tactics.

The pickets used this interlude to carry away those whose scalps had been cut open by police clubs or who had been directly hit by the tear-gas bombs. Unionists ready to assist the strikers crowded into the opposite end of Chevrolet Avenue. On the roof many more strikers from the second floor had come up to man the hoses and the slingshots. The remaining pickets began to gather up any objects that might be used as weapons — pop bottles, rocks, or hinges shot down during the first attack.

I continued to speak over the microphone, calling on the men and women both inside and out to stand firm and not permit GM to drive them into submission by the unwarranted use of police power. The onlookers had grown into a crowd of thousands. I reminded the strikers and all who could hear me that the UAW had tried to settle the matter over the conference table but had been turned away, that the promises of General Motors had never been kept, and that it was GM's choice to settle by means of force but that we were determined to defend our rights at any cost. I called upon those who stood looking on to come in and help the pickets. A great shout went up every time a group broke away from the sidelines and took up positions in front of the plant alongside the pickets.

Soon the police had regrouped and were marching in a solid phalanx toward us. They seemed intent on knocking out the sound truck. Thank God they hadn't yet brought in the long-range tear-gas missiles; most of their shots fell short but some bombs slithered along the pavement and came to rest immediately under the car. The fumes came seeping through the floorboards and mingled with the acid of the battery that ran the loudspeaker. Because of the possibility of a direct hit, I had to keep my head down close to that battery as I spoke into the microphone, so I soaked my handkerchief in some coffee I had in a thermos and held it to my nose, trying to breathe and keep talking. One observer later wrote: "From the sound car emanated one steady unswerving note. It dominated everything. Reuther's voice was like an inexhaustible furious flood pouring courage into the men."

The second police attack was directed more against those of us outside than at the sit-downers, but the heroic defenders on the roof did a spectacular job of pelting the attackers with hinges from their big slingshots, and kept pouring water down to freeze on the police uniforms, until the police were forced to retreat once again. As they went, they resorted to the vicious revenge I had dreaded: they began to use their firearms, and shot directly into the ranks of our pickets.

That night thirteen union men were seriously wounded.

I knew there would be another attack, and leaving the sound truck in the care of Bill Carney, helped the picket captains organize the building of barricades at both ends of Chevrolet Avenue. We used all available automobiles, including a sheriff's car disabled by a barrage of hinges and many belonging to the pickets themselves, who didn't hesitate to turn their vehicles over on their sides for the sake of a common defense. They had been risking their lives in this struggle — how much of a sacrifice was an old jalopy? I felt for one quick moment that we were all back in the days of the early settlers, defending a small enclave against the enemy.

Our greatest fear was that the police might race in squad cars down Chevrolet Avenue, firing, as they passed, at both pickets and the strikers on the roof. The barricades, therefore, gave us some sense of protection, though it cut off the possibility of more sympathizers breaking away from the crowd to join us. Actually the police had already cordoned off the crowds farther out on the avenue. I had returned to the sound truck and had been speaking only a few minutes when I suddenly noticed a window being slowly opened in the Chevrolet Two building across the avenue. Then I saw a double-barreled shotgun pointing directly at me. I shouted to the men on the roof that there was a gun aimed at us from across the way and immediately a bunch of hinges flew all the way across the avenue and smashed the window, and that was the last I saw of the gun. It was a short but terrifying moment.

The third attack came. This time they did bring long-range tear-gas missiles, and though the shells were fired from the other side of our barricades, they landed again and again in the midst of the pickets. At one point, with pickets choking and vomiting and staggering away, briefly, to get a whiff of fresh air, suddenly, as if it had been authorized from above, a gust of wind swept down, blowing the tear gas back into the faces of the police. I remember another incident: Genora Johnson (now Dollinger), whose husband, Kermit Johnson, was chairman of the strike committee and who was herself a picket, eating tear gas with the rest, came over and begged me to let her speak to the crowd of bystanders, especially to the women.

"Cowards, cowards, shooting unarmed and defenseless men," she cried into the microphone. Then she appealed to the women in the crowd to stand by their husbands and join in the defense.

I am convinced that the police lost not only that night's battle but the whole Flint war by providing us with the finest audience we had ever had. The drama the bystanders witnessed put our point across more cogently than any words could have done, and served to nudge thousands of Flint workers off dead center and into an open commitment to the UAW.

It was beyond midnight when the shelling stopped, and though we spent the rest of the night anticipating another barrage, the police had, we later learned, run out of ammunition. They had appealed to the Detroit police for more, but Detroit must have said, "No, we need ours down here." Thus ended the Battle of the Running Bulls. In the morning Chevrolet Avenue indeed looked like a battlefield of the industrial age — smashed and overturned vehicles, broken windowpanes, shattered bottles, stones, hinges, splintered picket signs, used tear-gas canisters, and everywhere the ice formed by the water that had served so effectively as a defensive weapon.

Rumors spread, of course. In an effort to explain the inglorious retreat by the police from unarmed workers, GM bruited about that we had been armed and had fired on them. The hospital record shows the indisputable facts: thirteen strikers with gunshot wounds, and one police officer — and he admitted that his wound came from a shot that ricocheted.

It was 6:00 A.M. when I left the sound truck and the scene of battle. By then only a few police were around, and some of the crowd beyond the lines could filter through. Roy and Bob Travis had been watching from the fringes, unable to get near. When they joined us, we all rejoiced that Fisher Two, which we had considered the weakest link in our chain, had proved heroically able to withstand the brutal onslaught. At a rally the following night Bob Travis dubbed me "General of the Battle of Bulls' Run." I said that if I ever became a general I hoped I would have troops as strong and faithful as the men and women who defended the sit-in at Fisher Two.

There must have been considerable bitterness among the General Motors executives, who had been frustrated in their move to use the courts against us, and now in their attempt to oust us with tear gas and bullets. They had not, however, exhausted their arsenal. For some time they had been secretly encouraging and arming a vigilante organization known as the Flint Alliance. This group was to be used to propagandize a back-to-work movement in the city. It was also the tool GM used when it wanted some CIO or UAW organizer brutally beaten up.

We discovered that we too had a strong extra resource: Governor Frank Murphy, a man of principle and sensibility, who had been elected the previous fall. I did not know him personally in 1937, though later in life we became very good friends. He was a true humanitarian: seldom have I met a man who anguished more over the prospect of violence perpetrated against a fellow human being. To be confronted with such a militant situation in Flint so soon after his inauguration created for him a personal dilemma. He was in Lansing, Michigan's capital, when the attack on the Fisher Two sitdowners began, and was kept informed by telephone by both John M. Barringer, Flint's City Manager, and by representatives of the UAW and the CIO. The conflicting reports convinced him that he urgently needed to have an independent view of the events.

Governor Murphy arrived in Flint around 1:00 A.M. on January 12, just when the battle on Chevrolet Avenue was letting up. He had ordered the National Guard in Flint alerted, and arranged for a meeting the next day with Flint officials, followed by one with union leaders. By then, Adolph Germer had hurried to Flint and was on hand to confer, together with Bob Travis and Roy, with the Governor.

We welcomed the intervention of Governor Murphy as a godsend. We had personal confidence in him — a confidence that was certainly not misplaced, as things turned out. And in spite of the tragic history of earlier instances of state intervention in strikes, we even welcomed the National Guard, as protection against the vigilantes we fully expected to have to contend with. The local police and Sheriff's men were also relieved, glad to be bailed out of a corporation campaign that had not brought them much glory or success.

It was Governor Murphy's delicate job to defuse a threatening situation in a neutral fashion, partisan neither to the corporation nor to the UAW. His first act was to mobilize two regiments of the National Guard: "Whatever else may happen, there is going to be law and order in Michigan. The public interest and public safety are paramount. The public authority in Michigan is stronger than either of the parties in the present controversy." He was obviously alarmed by the influx of angry unionists, who began to converge on Flint as soon as news of the violence at Fisher Two swept through

Michigan. Walter came with a group from the Detroit West Side local; Emil Mazey brought a contingent from the Briggs plant workers. GM used the arrival of these newcomers to influence the Governor, who mobilized more reserves. He did, however, reassure the sit-down strikers by appealing to General Motors not to deny them water, heat, or food, in the interest of public health and because "such moves only befuddle the already complicated situation."

The following day was relatively calm; both sides fought only with words. The union charged GM with direct responsibility for the violence, which had included the use of guns, and accused the police of collusion with the corporation. Knudsen sidestepped: "We were not involved in that riot. Our people were not in it." And he explained that the heat had been turned off because the plant office was closed and the plant was not in operation, a specious excuse, since the plant had not been operating from the time the strike began. Knudsen tried to put full blame on me for the battle, charging that there was no violence until the sound truck arrived and incited the pickets into storming the gates and taking the factory guards prisoner. But he agreed that, in deference to the Governor's plea, the strikers would not be denied heat, light, or food.

The Chief of Police declared he had not sent any men to the scene until he heard that the company guards had been taken prisoner. This was palpably untrue; we had seen them massed on Chevrolet Avenue just beyond the bridge. "They went out to see what was going on and to act if there was anything illegal," he said. Dr. Sidney Fine, the distinguished labor historian, has commented, in his book *Sit-Down*, on this fabrication:

> It is difficult . . . to view these remarks as anything more than self-serving. The evidence indicates that at least some police were in the area before the main gate was forced open from the inside, and the object of the police action seems to have been the ejection of the strikers rather than the rescue of the company guards. The Flint Police Department had added to its supply of tear gas only a few days earlier, and when its men made their appearance before Number Two plant on January 11, they were prepared to use gas equipment in a major action and not just ascertain the facts and proceed against the sit-downers only if they were doing something "illegal."

With the National Guard on the scene, the workers lost a good deal of their apprehension and union membership soared. The soldiers appeared in full battle regalia and set up field kitchens, and drab Flint took on the look of an occupied city, but the tension was reduced. I recall that there was considerable camaraderie between our strikers and pickets and the troops stationed near the gate. The commanding officer did ask Bob Travis and me to stop handing out copies of the Flint *Auto Worker* and addressing words of solidarity and friendship to the troops. He explained that his men could not take sides; their mission was to watch and wait. "Our troops include men of all walks of life and many of us are naturally sympathetic to one side or the other. However, as long as we are in uniform, our personal leanings must be made secondary."

On January 14, Governor Murphy brought together in his office in Lansing three men from each side: Knudsen, Smith, and Brown from GM; and Homer Martin, Mortimer, and John Brophy of the CIO. As chief executive, Murphy was sensitive to his responsibility to uphold due process, and since the strikers were "in unlawful possession" of GM property, he was most anxious to get the plant evacuated. But not at the cost of violence. He steadfastly refused to use the troops to force that evacuation. Instead, he worked untiringly to negotiate a compromise. His aim was to get a clear commitment from General Motors that it would negotiate with the UAW on a settlement involving not only the Flint plants but GM plants all over the country, and would cover a seniority system and a structure of representation for the union as well as wages. There was an immediate issue to be settled, too, and this seemed to be the stumbling block for both sides: General Motors was to deliver a signed promise that it would not move the strategic tools and dies from Fisher Two to "safer" plants once the men had evacuated. We in the UAW had a deep suspicion that the company planned to do just that the moment we left. GM refused to sign the promise.

After days of interminable consultations with both sides, early in the morning of January 15 the Governor, haggard and exhausted, announced an agreement, in the form of a letter signed by Knudsen, Smith, and Brown, addressed not to the UAW but to himself. It stated that the UAW had agreed that the strikers would leave the plant premises in Flint, Detroit, and Anderson, Indiana, "as soon as practicable," and that GM would meet with UAW representatives to bargain on the basis of our proposal of January 4. It was indicated in the letter that there would be no discrimination against any worker because of union affiliation and that GM would not remove any equipment from any of the struck plants while negotiations were taking place.

There was one other important clause: General Motors would not try to resume operations in the struck plants during the negotiations, which they would pursue steadily, unless those negotiations took more than fifteen days, in which case the corporation would be free to start up the plants again.

The Flint strikers were not enthusiastic about the terms of the settlement. They wanted a signed agreement that included more concessions before they evacuated the plant where they had endured the sit-down and where pickets had been brutalized. But Mortimer, Travis, Roy, Addes, and Hall reassured them it was a real turnabout on the part of the corporation — in fact, a victory for the union — and that GM could not afford to welch on the terms because the public would then turn against the corporation and more workers would join the union.

In Detroit, Walter met with the Cadillac and Fleetwood strikers and secured their acceptance of the agreement. They marched out of the plant and on that very same day, January 16, received telegrams from General Motors asking them to report for work on January 18, in direct contradiction to the terms of the letter.

In Anderson, Indiana, the Guide Lamp strikers also marched out on January 16, and even as they were leaving, some 150 policemen, augmented by company supervisors and guards, smashed and burned the picket headquarters, and threatened that no further interruption of work in the plant would be tolerated. Anderson had a very strong antiunion group, composed of Klan and Black Legion vigilantes, financed and encouraged by General Motors. I would soon experience personally their terrorist tactics.

The balance of power still lay with the Flint strike. GM had, for some weeks, been promoting an antiunion back-to-work movement of "loyal" employees through the Flint Alliance, headed by George Boysen, former Buick paymaster and former Mayor of the city. An elaborate PR campaign had been mounted to appeal to business and religious groups in the community to support the nonunion workers, who, it was charged, would suffer from more days of idleness. The reactionary group branded the UAW leaders Communists and outside agitators. Its following among the workers came mostly from the less unionized Buick and AC Spark Plug plants.

We had been aware of the threat of the Flint Alliance and had sent trusted UAW men to observe it from within. One of these, Kempton Williams, tipped us off to the plan to arm a large number of foremen and guards to march on Pengelly Hall, our strike headquarters, and drive all union organizers out of town. This was not as serious and alarming, however, as the telegram exchange between Knudsen and Boysen. The latter wired Knudsen, soon after the January 15 letter agreement with Governor Murphy, that the UAW spoke only for a minority of the workers and that the Flint Alliance wanted no settlement with that Union that would imperil the rights of the majority. Knudsen replied that "General Motors will never tolerate domination of its employees by a minority group." This exchange would not in itself have surprised us, but when Knudsen made the fatal blunder of agreeing by telegram to meet formally with members of the Flint Alliance to discuss collective bargaining, we realized that a double-cross was in the offing.

If it had not been for an alert newspaper reporter, Bill Lawrence of UP, who came across a copy of the press release including the exchange of telegrams and alerted Travis, the UAW would probably have kept its part of the agreement and evacuated Fisher Two, and General Motors would have proceeded to meet with a rump group that had not been a part of the January 15 settlement.

Travis immediately called Brophy, who spoke with John L. Lewis. Lewis was furious about this breach of promise, and instructed Brophy to call off the evacuation of the plants. The strikers, who were in the last stages of tidying up before moving out, courageously accepted the instructions. I am sure that no one was more incensed than Governor Murphy when he found that his peace formula had been jeopardized by the meddling of a group he had not even met, and he issued a statement asking "civic bodies and all other organizations to hold themselves in the background." Boysen got the message and quickly reassured the Governor that he would not press his request for a meeting with Knudsen.

But it was too late by now to resurrect the Murphy formula for conciliation. The lines had hardened once more; the atmosphere was tense and grim and remained so in spite of the personal intervention of President Roosevelt in private conversations with Lewis and Sloan. The settlement had been aborted by GM's patent lack of sincerity.

In the midst of this stand-off, GM made an effort to resume production in the Chevrolet units, which, like Buick, had closed down for lack of parts. They scheduled an opening for January 22, and Boysen of the Flint Alliance moved into action, announcing a big rally at which all Flint GM workers could express themselves on the subject of "forceful action" to re-establish their employment rights. This was obviously an open appeal to eject the strikers by force.

Governor Murphy was alerted to the possibility of more and bloody violence, and he called a meeting of the strike leaders along with Boysen, the Sheriff, and the Chief of Police, to discuss the rally. I remember Roy's description of walking with Travis to that meeting in the county courthouse. The streets were deserted, shades were drawn, and there was dead silence. The showdown in the movie *High Noon* reminded Roy, years later, of this scene.

The exchanges between Boysen and our union leaders were heated. Fortunately, the city officials made it clear to Boysen that they would not tolerate any behavior at the rally that would incite the audience to commit violence. At the actual rally, there were some angry remarks about the CIO, Lewis, and "outside agitators," but Boysen himself kept the commitment he had made to Murphy and cautioned the audience against any destructive actions. The rally, attended largely by about eight thousand Buick and AC Spark Plug workers, whose plants had not been called out on strike, reflected strong back-to-work sentiment. There is no question in my mind that had we been tricked into evacuating the struck plants most GM workers would have gone back to work under prestrike terms with few or no reforms, the UAW would have been broken, and Flint families would have continued to live in poverty and hopelessness.

Knudsen's letter to Governor Murphy promising a settlement became a thoroughly dead letter on January 28, when GM went back to the strategy of using the courts, and sought a new injunction, from a different judge, to evacuate the plants. Vigilante activity increased: organizers Ditzel, Federoff, and Mayo were attacked and badly beaten. Henry Kraus reports in his book, *The Many and the Few*, that City Manager Barringer, perhaps the most bitterly antiunion official in Flint, plotted the murders of Roy, Bob Travis, and Kraus himself. During my last days in the city, Roy and I slept with a volunteer bodyguard on a mattress on the floor beside us and another guard outside the door. Roy was dragged from the sound truck one day in front of Chevrolet Nine by a bunch of vigilantes, including GM foremen, who smashed the sound equipment and roughed up Roy and the men who were with him. This incident was a measure of the growing terror; it also confirmed our suspicion that the company was going to try to single me out as the major culprit when the court battle was joined. According to them, I was responsible for the Battle of the Running Bulls and they probably thought I was in the sound truck when they attacked it.

By trumping up charges, General Motors got the court to hand down a decision against Bob Travis, Roy, Henry Kraus, and me — a move to cripple the strike by imprisoning the leadership. UAW officers in Detroit recommended that we absent ourselves from Flint. As the others went into semiseclusion, I was asked to report to headquarters in Detroit. When I got there, I was quickly assigned to Anderson, where Sophie had been working since the end of December, to assume the responsibility of handling the approaching crisis in that city. I took the train for Indiana on January 25, thus spreading the Reuther brothers over a wider area, though only for a short time. Walter was soon to become more deeply involved, along with Roy, in breaking the Flint deadlock.

The UAW realized that unless the stalemate in Flint were resolved immediately the union would probably not survive. Inspired by desperation, Roy and Bob Travis devised one of the most daring and spectacular bits of strike strategy in the history of the labor movement.

Chevrolet was the biggest moneymaker within General Motors. Only one plant made Chevrolet engines for all the assembly plants around the country: Chevrolet Four. It had not been involved in the strike action, had small union affiliation, and by late January could have been quickly swung back into operation with the help of the Flint Alliance and its back-to-work propaganda. Unless the corporation's nerve could be pinched at this sensitive point, GM would win by waiting it out, and the strike would have been in vain. Roy, Travis, and a few trusted UAW staff members, therefore, plotted a plan of action used in many a military campaign: a feint, by which the enemy, distracted from the main thrust of troops by a minor deployment of forces, is taken off-guard.

Chevrolet Four was very well defended by the company because it was both important and vulnerable. Extra guards, whose motivation had been buttressed by long riot sticks and a pay increase, were installed in the plant. The building was somewhat removed from the main road, and it would have been foolhardy of the UAW to try to arrange a strike in that isolated, heavily armed fortress. It was decided to call an official strike at Chevrolet Nine instead, and let the plans leak out beforehand so that the guards, the riot sticks, and the tear-gas guns would be shifted from Four to Nine. If the ruse worked, then a strike could be brought off in the all-important Number Four.

The plan was cleared with CIO officials in Detroit, who were doubtful of its success but recognized that it just might be a great coup. Only four or five men in Flint besides Travis and Roy knew the real plot. The small, heroic group of union men in Chevrolet Nine, who were to become the sacrificial lambs, were not let in on the secret for fear of an inadvertent leak. They were merely asked, in a series of meetings, if they were willing to call a strike, and with considerable trepidation they agreed.

Walter's job was to bring several carloads of loyal unionists from Detroit's West Side to be on hand for the action, set for February 1. The day arrived. Precisely at three-thirty that afternoon, at the moment between shifts, the leading unionists in Chevrolet Nine threw the switches, downed their tools, and proclaimed a strike. Simultaneously, Roy and Travis brought a large group from a meeting in Pengelly Hall to demonstrate in front of the plant. They had earlier spread the word among the strikers in Fisher One that there would be action in Chevrolet Nine, sure that this decoy plan would reach the corporation through the omnipresent stool pigeons, which indeed proved to be the case. GM *had* been alerted, and when the open call came for a meeting in the union hall on the afternoon of February 1, the company quickly drew all its surplus security forces out of the engine-making plant, Chevrolet Four, and concentrated them inside Nine. When the strike was called, the union men in Nine were completely outnumbered. They defended themselves valiantly, hut they were badly mauled, and should be honored in the annals of the labor movement for their sacrifice.

Outside, meanwhile, one sound truck manned by Roy and Powers Hapgood led a big line of demonstrators noisily from Pengelly Hall to Chevrolet Nine, while another sound truck, operated by Merlin Bishop, quietly led a second group to the general vicinity of Number Four. When the demonstrators outside Nine heard the tear-gas

shells exploding inside and saw some windows being broken to let in
fresh air, they used their picket signs to break more windows and
reduce the fumes that were swirling around the uneven conflict.

Now that the General Motors defense was completely engaged in
Nine, a signal was given by Roy to Ed Kronk, a stalwart six-foot
press operator from Detroit, to pull an American flag out of his
shirt. This was the signal for the fifty Detroiters who had come with
him to proceed to the Chevrolet Four entrance, where they were
joined by Walter, coming from the opposite direction with an equal
number of men. They all entered the plant at once and gave the
sign to those union members who had been in on the secret plan to
throw the switches and declare a strike. Walter recalled later their
frenzied effort to block and secure the exit doors with heavy equipment, after letting out all those who wanted no part of a sit-down
strike.

The most vital sector of the General Motors empire was thus put
under siege. The strikers in Chevrolet Nine gave up around four
o'clock and came out, their heads bloody, but bowed only until they
heard what had happened in Number Four and realized that they
had played the bravest part in the whole affair. Then they became
jubilant and, in spite of their wounds and before they would go for
medical care, insisted on joining the Number Four picket line and
marching around a few times, singing. They bore no grudge, knowing that they could never have put up as convincing a fight as they
had if they had known the plan beforehand.

Once again the corporation officials responded by turning off the
heat, but when they were told the strikers would make wood fires to
keep warm, they turned it on again. This time, however, they were
determined to let no food in. The timing had been too close for the
organizers to lay in provisions, and there was no access from the
street. The idea of dropping food on the roof was frustrated when
the pilot was stopped by the city authorities with the threat of being
grounded.

Governor Murphy was again hard at work, meeting with National
Guard and police and city officials. By 6:30 P.M. the Chief of Police
and the Mayor were appealing to him to use the troops. He chose a
different course: he had the troop commanders seal off an area of
approximately eight acres, taking in Chevrolet Nine and Four, as
well as Fisher Body Two and Chevrolet Two, across from each other
on the avenue. Soldiers with fixed bayonets patrolled; the pickets

who had been marching and singing outside Chevy Four (Genora Johnson was again on the scene with her stalwart women's auxiliary) were dispersed or taken into custody if they resisted; and the sound car driven by Merlin Bishop was impounded. The troops were under strict orders to make no attempt to evict any of the sit-down strikers in the three plants.

Food was thus definitely cut off from all those inside. Governor Murphy's justification was that he had heard reports that individuals who were not Chevrolet workers were participating in the Chevy Four Strike and he did not propose to let food through to outsiders. Delicate discussions then got underway between the Governor and our leaders. The latter suggested that a National Guard delegation go in with them to check the badges of the sit-downers and ask those who were not legitimate to leave. The Guard refused to participate. Travis, Roy, and Henry Kraus went into the plant and found that Powers Hapgood and Walter were the only two who did not belong, the rest having already departed. Walter and Hapgood came out. Somewhat later the Guard made its own independent inspection and reported to the Governor that all the men inside were bona fide Chevrolet workers. The Governor then lifted the ban and allowed food to be taken in.

On that same historic day, Judge Gadola of Flint handed down what was perhaps one of the most sweeping injunctions ever issued during a labor battle. The public might have accepted it if it had not included a denial of basic rights. The judge declared that even peaceful picketing was now illegal in the State of Michigan, and then set a deadline of two days. If the strikers were not out by then, the union would be liable for a $15 million fine. When Sheriff Wolcott appeared at the struck plants to read the text of this injunction, there was no laughter, no cat calling — merely a grim silence. It was clear that the workers were as determined as ever to hold out against all legal and physical odds. They and all the UAW leaders in Flint feared that Governor Murphy would not be able to resist the pressure to use the troops to force evacuation, and that there would be a terrible and bloody confrontation. An urgent call went out to union members in other cities. They came in by hundreds and thousands from Toledo and from Detroit, from Pontiac and Saginaw and Bay City and Lansing, until, by the next morning, a gigantic crowd was milling around the gates of Fisher One.

The Fisher One sit-down strikers sent Governor Murphy an

urgent telegram, warning him of a "bloody massacre" that would be "on his head." The Fisher Two men, the heroes of the Battle of the Running Bulls, appealed even more effectively to the Governor's compassionate nature and deep moral sense. I suspect that their message was written in collaboration with someone on the CIO staff. It read:

> Governor, we have decided to stay in the plant. We have no illusions about the sacrifices which this decision will entail. We fully expect that if a violent effort is made to oust us, many of us will be killed, and we take this means of making it known to our wives, to our children, to the people of the State of Michigan and the country that if this result follows from the attempt to eject us, you are the one who must be held responsible for our deaths.

The injunction had set the deadline for 3:00 P.M. on February 3. It was a bitter afternoon, with temperatures near zero, but thousands of sympathizers and union workers participated in the huge demonstration in front of Fisher One. Everyone was waiting for the dénouement. The hour for the enforcement of the injunction came — and went. The National Guard did not appear.

The celebration that followed did not please the local police officials. It seemed as if almost all of Flint was supporting the strike. The City Manager was especially irritated and began that day, allegedly in collusion with the Flint Alliance, to deputize citizens, many of whom were probably vigilantes. If the Governor wouldn't act, they would take care of the evacuation themselves!

Again more meetings and consultations among the Governor, National Guard, and members of the UAW. The latter promised that if the vigilantes were demobilized they, in turn, would see to it that there were no more large demonstrations at the factory gates and that the large picket signs, which looked like weapons, would be banned. They also promised to give notice to the police if they planned any kind of rally or parade. By this time both sides were sincerely anxious to avoid any further violence, and that night a peace settlement between the union and the Flint authorities was reached and announced to the sit-downers and to the crowd of union pickets and sympathizers still congregated in Pengelly Hall.

What most Flint citizens didn't know was that, on that same February 3, negotiations between the UAW and General Motors resumed in Detroit, under the auspices of Governor Murphy and the able federal conciliator, James Dewey. That was why the Governor could spare himself the painful move of using the troops to evict the strikers. John L. Lewis had also come from Washington for the talks. Though Homer Martin was on hand for the beginning round, it was so obvious that he was not up to the rough-and-tumble of such negotiations that Lewis insisted he go on yet another speaking tour in the boondocks! The burden of the bargaining thus fell on Lewis and Wyndham Mortimer.

Frances Perkins, Secretary of Labor, had prevailed on President Roosevelt to make personal phone calls to Knudsen and Lewis to encourage compromise on the main issue that blocked any settlement: the union's demand for sole representation and bargaining rights in the plants that had been struck.

The AFL again began to interfere; Frey made direct phone calls to Knudsen. When Lewis heard of this, he used one of his famous dramatic ploys: he walked solemnly to the coat closet, got his hat and coat, and told the Governor that if the GM executives were going to play around with the AFL, he and his CIO officials would leave and let GM try to settle the strike that way.

The talks dragged on, and the Governor found it harder and harder to avoid his obligation to enforce the injunction and send the troops in to evacuate the plants. But he was backed in his determination to avoid violence by reassurances from President Roosevelt and by his own convictions. By February 9, when it looked as if he could hold off no longer, Lewis drafted a telegram right at the conference table and read it aloud to the Governor:

> I do not doubt your ability to call out your soldiers and shoot the members of our union out of those plants, but let me say that when you issue that order I shall leave this conference and I shall enter one of those plants with my own people . . . and the militia will have the pleasure of shooting me out of the plants with them.

According to reliable observers, the Governor went white, grabbed the draft from Lewis's hand, and fled the room. The order to send in the troops was never given, and on February 11 at 2:40 A.M. a completely exhausted but elated Governor announced that an agreement had been reached. The whole country heaved a sigh of relief.

Murphy was praised in the months and years that followed, but he was also cruelly condemned for his failure to enforce the injunction. There is no doubt in my mind that he chose the wiser course: he laid the foundation once and for all for a relationship between labor and management based on well-defined rules rather than on the sheer exertion of money power and military force. It is a temptation for statesmen who have soldiers at their beck and call to use them freely. To practice restraint and suffer the criticism of those who have no real desire for peace — this requires heroism and sacrifice. History has already commemorated Frank Murphy for his unique contribution to social justice in America. He was a man who had the guts to stand firm in support of his convictions.

The peace terms so long awaited hardly took up the space of one typewritten page, but in those few important words the world's largest corporation agreed to recognize the fledgling United Auto Workers as the collective bargaining agent for all employees who were members of that union. Bargaining, based on the union's January 4 demands, was to begin on February 16. It was promised that there would be no discrimination, interference, restraint, or coercion in any GM plant because of union membership or organizing activities. In return, the union promised to terminate the strikes as quickly as possible and get the facilities back into operation. The UAW also agreed that during collective bargaining negotiations it would not engage in strike action or interfere in any way with production. There would be, from then on, an established grievance procedure for the settlement of disputes, and all possibilities offered by the procedure would have to be exhausted before a strike was called.

As part of this package, GM agreed to withdraw the injunctions it had obtained from courts in Flint and Cleveland and to cancel any contempt proceedings or fines. The UAW did not get exclusive bargaining rights for all employees, union or nonunion, but the corporation agreed that, for a period of six months after resumption of work, it would not "bargain or enter agreements with any other union or representative employees of plants on strike." This, in effect, meant six months of exclusive bargaining rights for the UAW in seventeen plants. and this period was considered sufficient for the union to demonstrate, through general Labor Board elections or other appropriate ways, that it did in fact represent a majority of GM workers.

Roy wrote a description of the evacuation of the Flint plants:

When the boys came out, I never saw a night like that and perhaps may never see it again. I liken it to some description of a country experiencing independence. I was on the sound truck. We started at South Fisher [One], our sit-downers began walking out of the plant, some with beards — they had agreed not to shave until after it was over. We had a procession down to Chevrolet and Fisher Two. Women came greeting their husbands — some of the families being together for the first time since the strike began — kids hanging on to daddy with tears of joy and happiness. We converged on Chevrolet and Fisher Two down in the well between the two plants which had been the scene of the Battle of the Running Bulls, and when they came out there was dancing in the streets. It was a seething sea of humanity — a joy — fears were no longer in the minds of workers.

In 1966, thirty years later, Roy reminisced with a Detroit reporter about the Flint sit-down strikes. "People talk about the good old days. I would have preferred that we could have skipped that chapter. I felt it was very fortunate no one was killed . . . We got threats of bombings . . . threats that people were going to shoot us . . . I was very elated that the struggle was over and that we were moving along to a greater era of industrial democracy. I, of course, and in all humility, feel a great sense of pride in having been able to serve in the UAW at a critical point in what was the most crucial struggle in the glorious chapter of industrial unionism."

The early part of the Flint battle is especially remembered by me as the only time during the rise of the UAW that all three of us — Roy, Walter, and I — had the exhilarating experience of working side by side, united by family ties, but united even more firmly by intense commitment to a common cause. We were a small example of solidarity in the midst of confusion and possible betrayal.

Our solidarity and shared ideals were fortified by the extraordinary qualities of humanity summoned forth among the workers of Flint by the series of emergencies. They endured what seemed an unending nightmare; they suffered terror, broken heads, their families' hunger, and extreme risk, not just for another nickel an hour, but for the dignity and individuality denied them by an arrogant corporation. They won a richer life for millions of industrial workers in other towns and cities. They exhibited the most selfless quality men can possess: the ability to sacrifice immediate material security for desirable but as yet unrealized goals for humankind. They were the real heroes; it was our privilege to help them chart the narrow passage between defeat and victory.

CHAPTER 14

Anderson Rejoins the U.S.A.

ANDERSON, INDIANA, was a General Motors town, like Flint, but with far less union activity in its two important automotive supply plants, Guide Lamp and Delco Remy. The town officials and the police had no inhibitions about their antiunionism: when Bart Furey, veteran of the Toledo Auto-Lite strike, was sent to Anderson after the South Bend Convention, he was promptly run out of town and warned not to return. Later, Ed Hall, the secretary-treasurer of the UAW, set up the modest headquarters of Local 146 on Main Street, but GM protection men tore down his meeting announcements, posted near the factory entrances, and the town made it almost impossible for him to find a place to hold the meeting. A personal appeal to Governor Paul V. McNutt for a permit to use the state armory was at first refused, but McNutt capitulated after Hall threatened to go directly to President Roosevelt.

Late in 1936, when Hall could not get to Anderson very often because of the pressure of work in the International Union, Hugh Thompson, a CIO representative from New York, took over the organizing work, helped by a small staff. The going was rough: organizers were intimidated, and the workers in the plants were warned to steer clear of the union. At the same time, they were being pushed incessantly to speed up their work during the long nine-hour day.

The UAW had managed to recruit about 400 members out of a potential 11,500. When the moment came in late December for the CIO to call for strikes in all GM plants around the country, these few men in Anderson dared to step forward, certain they would receive the complete support of the majority once the fear of persecution and of layoffs had been overcome. They were fighting for a shorter work day, overtime pay, and, above all, a reduction of the speed-up. On December 31, they pulled the switches in the Guide Lamp plant. There was no resistance from the other workers, who marched out peacefully and left the union men in possession. No effort was made to strike the larger Delco Remy plant, but General Motors locked the employees out. Thus the entire economic life of Anderson was temporarily shut down, causing a crisis in the city. Soon after, GM was to reopen Delco Remy.

The reactionary elements quickly formed a Citizens' League for Employment Security — very similar to the Flint Alliance. Petitions were circulated in an effort to frighten the nonunion workers into breaking the strike, and the Mayor went to see the newly inaugurated Governor, M. Clifford Townsend, presumably to assure him that the town officials and police had the matter well in hand, but also, I suspect, to make sure the Governor did not intervene, leaving GM free to break the strike in its own fashion.

When Knudsen gave Governor Murphy of Michigan the letter of January 16, promising to negotiate with the UAW if the strikers would evacuate the plants, the Guide Lamp strikers in Anderson marched out and made their way to a victory meeting in the armory, only to hear, before the day was over, the bitter news of the General Motors double-cross. When I was sent to Anderson on January 25, 1937, all that the leaders in Detroit knew was that Guide Lamp had been evacuated and that a strong back-to-work movement was being organized by the company, in collusion with the Citizens' League. It was predicted that the union would have a hard time holding out.

Sophie had gone to Anderson at the end of December. She had been chosen by the International UAW because she had proved her competence in Detroit, and the union needed a woman to make contact with the large number of female workers in Guide Lamp and Delco Remy. She used a shortened form of her maiden name, Sophie Good, not wanting to ride on Reuther coattails, and also because she realized, wisely, that Homer Martin might have objected to her being given the assignment if he knew she was a Reuther. This all happened before I went to Flint. Communication between Reuther husbands and wives was so scanty in those days of crisis that when Sophie read in the papers about my participation in the Battle of the Running Bulls, she thought, "This is an error. It must be Roy, because he's in Flint and Victor's in Detroit."

I took the night train to Anderson on the twenty-fifth and on that very evening a mob of several thousand Anderson antiunionists assembled in the Granada Theater and spilled over into the surrounding area. Leaders of the Citizens' League were visible in the crowd, as were supervisors from Delco Remy and antiunion Guide Lamp workers. Plenty of liquor had been passed around by GM personnel directors, according to the La Follette Committee report. That committee also reported that a Guide Lamp personnel man addressed the crowd and urged it to drive the outside organizers out of town so that work could be resumed in the plants. The foes of the union were also supplied with clubs, eggs, and rocks as they moved en masse into the courthouse square. Here they recognized a union organizer named Charles Kramer and gave him a brutal beating, as the police stood by, watching. After he was beaten enough, the police took him to jail.

By then, word had reached Hugh Thompson and some twenty others gathered in the small union headquarters on the second floor above Main Street, and Hugh asked Sophie to go out and see what was going on, and find out if it was true that Kramer had been beaten. She switched coats with one of the other women in order not to be recognized and went out to mingle with the crowd, from which she quickly learned not only that Kramer had been injured but that a number of other union men had been locked up, too. The mob was by then on its way to our union headquarters. Apparently Earl Heaton, the local president of the union, and McNally, the financial secretary, had some foreknowledge, because they left the union office well before the crowd arrived to throw rocks through the windows, shout foul names, and splash eggs against the door below.

The crowd was obviously bent on driving the union men out of town, so Hugh Thompson, with glass breaking around his feet, called Governor Townsend in Indianapolis and described the situation, asking him to send in state troops to restore law and order. Townsend then made a routine call to Mayor Baldwin, who assured him that the police had the situation in hand, and the Governor called Hugh back, refusing to send any assistance. Hugh had hardly hung up when police vans arrived and Chief Carney and his men came up and arrested all the people in the office — most of them local workers on strike — and, labeling them outside agitators, whisked them off to jail through the angry and shouting mob, which at that point broke into the union office, smashed the furniture, rifled the filing cabinets, and threw everything into the street. Typewriters were wrenched off the desks and heaved out, too, along with the slashed picture of John L. Lewis. The mob's next diversion was a march to the Guide Lamp plant to set the small picket shack afire and drive off the few men on duty there.

When the hoodlums had accomplished all this, the manager of the Guide Lamp plant came out to congratulate them in behalf of General Motors and to thank them for having preformed their civic and patriotic duty. Chief Carney gave out a press release that the crowd was orderly and had responded to every police request. He had to admit there were no charges against the men who had been jailed. When they were released he ordered all those who were not Anderson residents to leave town and not return.

Sophie, who had just barely escaped, spent the next few days moving from one worker's house to another, always wearing a different coat to minimize the chances of being caught. She refused to leave when those concerned for her safety told her to go. She said, "The workers who are union members can't leave!"

Meanwhile, I had arrived unnoticed about five in the morning after the riot, and went to the Grand Hotel, a seedy place, its name notwithstanding. I knew Sophie had been living there. The lobby was deserted; I rang the bell and a maintenance man with mop in hand came out and asked me what I wanted. I said my wife Sophie Good, was registered there, and he looked at me blankly and did not respond. "Look," I said, "I know she's registered here, and I want to know what room she's in." He still stared, expressionless, until, becoming a little angry, I pressed him further. Finally he said, "Man, ain't you-all heard what's happened?" "What do you mean?" I asked, feeling a jab of fear. At that, he reached under the desk and brought out the morning paper, whose headlines were all about the riot. My eyes raced down the front page through the list of organizers who had been beaten and arrested, or just arrested and sent out of town. I was so angry I could not speak, but I thanked God her name was not listed. Then I fell back into a chair and read the whole article.

I wandered around town in a daze, taking in the gaping windows of union headquarters and the debris on the street, not knowing

where to begin to find union people, and terribly concerned about
Sophie. That night I put a call through to Walter in Detroit and
urged him to contact the national office to get some help. The following day, Hugh Thompson, whom I was to replace in Anderson,
reached Detroit and gave a firsthand account of the chaotic situation
to the UAW officials. On January 28, Ed Hall, accompanied by
the attorney Maurice Sugar, boarded a train for Anderson. We
must have had plenty of stool pigeons in Local 146, because the vigilantes were tipped off. It is reported that some 300 workers departed through a Delco Remy plant gate, without punching out, on a
special mission to the railway station to meet that train from Detroit.
But when the antiunionists raced through the railroad cars, they
found no Ed Hall and no Maurice Sugar. Fortunately some Anderson unionists had driven all the way to Union City at the Ohio-In-
diana border to get them off the train and drive them straight to Indianapolis to see the Governor.

That stalwart citizen again gave his standard reply: "I have been
assured by the Mayor and the Chief of Police of Anderson that
things are quiet and everything is in hand."

It took me several days to find Sophie; she was living in the basement of a worker's home, mimeographing leaflets, calling upon the
Anderson union workers to stand firm, reminding them that Flint
workers were still holding out. We tried to find a room to rent, but
most people turned us away, afraid of trouble. At last we persuaded
the couple running the little Stillwell Hotel to take us in. We repos-
sessed the union office and had it repaired, but we held our first
membership meeting fifteen miles away, in Alexandria.

Delco Remy and Guide Lamp announced they were going to resume full production. I called a meeting of our members and said
we were going to re-establish the picket line and that, though no one
should feel obliged to volunteer, I hoped some would find it in their
hearts to do so. All seventy-three who were there responded, "We'll
go with you!" We walked to the Guide Lamp plant, made a circle,
and started marching. Across the street, where the company union
had opened headquarters, a crowd of some 400 jeered at us. I expected some violent action, but that first effort to picket went off
routinely and served the purpose of sustaining morale. (We knew
we couldn't stop the resumption of work). I remember a tiny, gallant woman named Anna Marie Kailor, who pumped the accordion

with gusto, pouring out trade union and picket line songs to keep up our spirits. We were filmed by movie cameramen hired by Guide Lamp — a ploy to frighten the workers off — but our picket line was not diminished by one man or woman.

The second morning, I was slugged by a burly fellow, one of Chief Carney's new deputies. I knew he wanted to start a general ruckus, but I urged everyone not to respond and to keep marching; the important thing was the presence of the union on the scene and not any useless heroics.

Remembering my success in Flint, I got hold of a sound truck in order to reach with my voice the many workers standing on the fringe, confused and unaware of the issues involved. It was immediately confiscated by the police, but we found another and used it for a short time until General Motors got the city to pass an ordinance banning the use of any sound equipment on the streets. That really stripped me bare.

Each day the newspaper put out reports about the hundreds filtering back to work. We learned from various workers, however, that they were not making car parts, but blackjacks, or were grinding files into sharp daggers, or stamping out the large oval LOYAL EMPLOYEE buttons. With GM plants all across the country on strike, there was no reason to make parts: all the company could have done was stockpile them. By the second week of February, the betrayal by General Motors of its agreement with Governor Murphy and the UAW on the Flint strike brought new members into our union. Workers were also upset that the Anderson plants were encouraging the production of weapons, obviously to be used against fellow workers. During that time the Anderson membership swelled to over 600 strikers, plus sympathizers who joined us when we had a parade or demonstration. Our resources were still desperately slim — only two or three dollars at a time were granted to the family of a striker — since we received very little from Detroit.

The stool pigeons in Local 146 did not make our work any easier. Just as fast as we could sign up new members, the GM personnel department fired them. It was a bit too coincidental that Heaton and McNally had both cleared out of headquarters just before the crowd came. Sophie told me that she had steered clear of me those first few days because she did not want McNally to know of my whereabouts. She already suspected him. Until these problems were solved, I knew we could not increase our membership significantly. When the La Follette Committee and the Labor Department investigators came into Anderson, they soon confirmed our suspicions.

Then, on February 11, we had a telegram from Detroit announcing the final settlement that had been engineered with such determination by Governor Murphy. We felt a wonderful sense of relief; surely the period of terror was now over, and the union could grow in a climate of peace (though this was not yet the case in Anderson). I called staff and officers together to prepare a rally for that evening to proclaim the UAW-GM settlement to the workers.

Things went badly from the start. We couldn't find a building for the rally — the armory, school buildings, and churches were all denied us. In desperation I turned to a former member of the AFL who was now in the state legislature and was part-owner of the dilapidated, run-down old Crystal Theater, which had been closed for several years. The rally had been announced for 8:00 P.M. There was no heating, so we rounded up little kerosene stoves and put them in the aisles, and had an improvised hillbilly band to provide entertainment as the crowd came in. And in came our supporters, between 800 and 1000 strong; every seat was taken and many people stood. The workers had brought their wives and children and there was joy and relief on their faces; they felt they would soon be back at work, with paychecks coming in and the horror over.

I mounted the rostrum but had not uttered five words when there were shots outside the building. A crowd of vigilantes had massed at the entrance. Some shots had come through the windows; we could see plaster falling from where they had struck. Many of the women in the audience screamed; the children cried; and I had a gut fear that the stoves would be knocked over and we would have another Chicago fire, with a terrible toll of lives. I tried to calm the audience and told the ushers to put out the stoves immediately. After I had the hillbilly band start up again, I asked some trusted union men to try to ascertain the size and mood of the vigilante crowd by looking through the small windows above the balcony. They estimated that there were about three or four hundred, and reported that some had rifles and shotguns, some carried pitchforks and clubs, and all were obviously liquored up. They also said that Police Chief Carney was standing on the sidelines, watching.

The main fire station of the city was just across the street. One gust of cold water in that freezing weather would have dispersed the roughnecks, who were violating the law by shooting into the theater. But evidently it was we, instead, who were considered by the Police Chief to be the violators. The next act in the melodrama was the entrance of Chief Carney, who came to the rostrum to tell me that he had assurances the mob would disperse if I would submit to protective arrest. I did not believe that Carney could really control the rioters; he might have dispersed them but he could not alter their intentions. This was confirmed when I heard him tell one of the women in the audience, who asked for an escort home for herself and her children, that he could not ensure her safety. I was sure that the minute I stepped out of the hall, there would be a lynching party, and was determined that no one should leave until it was safe to do so. I asked Carney to get the Fire Chief if necessary, to use the hoses on the crowd outside, stressing that we were violating no law whatsoever, that we were going to insist on our right of peaceful assembly, and that it was his duty to protect that right.

After he left, I had a difficult time restraining several organizers, who begged to go out with some of our strongest men to scatter the crowd. I considered this dangerous: the mob might break in and cause harm to members of the audience. A few of the organizers lent us by the national CIO had a background of unionism in the southern Illinois mine country, and they were in the habit of going home to get their guns when a strike broke out and there was a possibility of terrorism; they could not understand our form of peaceful picket-line fighting. "By God, Reuther," one of them said, "now we are going to fight back!" and drew out his snub-nosed pocket revolver, which I had no idea he was carrying.

"Over my dead body you're going to fire back," I told them. "I'm not going to gamble with the lives of these thousand people here just because you want to fire back at that mob. You just sit tight. They can't stay there all night in this weather, and we'll sit it out until we can get the people home safely."

They cursed me out as yellow and everything else imaginable, but that was a minor problem compared to my anxiety about what would happen if someone triggered an open conflict. I was even more anxious — and angry — when I heard a report that the Governor had been called by one of our officers and had given the usual response: he was well aware that the local authorities had everything in control and could deal with the situation.

I think I put about ten years on my life that night, as the hours crawled by and the children became more hysterical and parents more concerned. People huddled together, trying to share human warmth and ward off the chill that was rapidly penetrating the leaky old Crystal Theater. We did our best to keep them occupied as pleasantly as possible under the circumstances. The hillbilly band performed tirelessly until about four in the morning, when the mob had thinned sufficiently to allow us to begin to escort the women and children out of the building under the protection of half a dozen of our strongest staff members and union workers. We took them out in small groups and everything was managed without incident. Then I called a council of war and we laid plans to take a small delegation to Indianapolis to see the Governor.

When we got to the capital, I told Governor Townsend about the two occasions when the police had permitted a mob, well provided with liquor, to terrorize unionists, and how a thousand people, including women and children, had been literally held prisoners in a cold building all night, with the police doing nothing about it. I appealed to him to declare martial law and send troops in to protect a large group of Anderson citizens from lawless vigilantes. He flatly refused.

I left that meeting feeling that somehow Anderson had been turned by General Motors and the city officials into an isolated medieval duchy, with some of its people denied basic rights. If Anderson was ever to rejoin the United States, it was obvious we would have to rescue it ourselves.

I called Detroit and reached Adolf Germer, a dedicated union man but well on in years and apt to be cautious, and told him we needed help if the union was going to survive in Anderson. I knew that request would not accomplish enough, so I called Walter, too, and asked him to organize groups to come in cars from Detroit and Toledo. Then I talked with Bob Travis and Roy in Flint, where they were celebrating the UAW victory in that city. When they told the Flint workers about Anderson, a wave of anger swept through the ranks. As a result of those phone calls, within a matter of a few hours there were cars loaded with staunch unionists converging on the Indiana border from Toledo, Detroit, Flint, and Pontiac, coming to aid their brothers and sisters. By the time they crossed the border, there were two hundred cars in the caravan.

State troopers were sent out to block the roads and prevent the cars from reaching Anderson. But by then our rescuers had got within twenty-five miles of the city, so they just parked their cars along the highway, and, putting white handkerchiefs around their arms for identification, filtered gradually through the fields into town. For some hours they made the rounds of the various bars and gathering places of the ringleaders of the Citizens' League, the Black Legion, and the Ku Klux Klan. Scuffles and shootings occurred. At that point the terrorizing of the UAW in Anderson was broken. Then martial law was declared.

Under martial law, no gathering of three or four people can be held without special permit. For the first three days, no such permits were granted. I occupied myself by bringing the Anderson crisis to national attention. I appealed to Roger Baldwin of the Civil Liberties Union, and asked Norman Thomas to come for a personal visit to test the right of freedom of speech in that beleaguered town. On February 15, Ira Latimer of the Midwest League for the Protection of Constitutional Rights wired Governor Townsend inquiring about the status of civil rights in Anderson, and informing him that the league intended to hold a meeting there. Townsend replied he was sure they could meet there "after submitting a request for a permit to Colonel Whitcomb." On that same day, we were authorized to hold small meetings.

But Mayor Baldwin was still not happy with the presence of a Reuther and other "outside agitators" in his town, and asked the Governor to have us expelled. We scheduled a rally for February 22 in our new union headquarters, which were commodious enough for a large meeting. I remember Homer Martin speaking to an overflowing crowd, with armed state troopers standing on guard inside the hall. It was clear from the large attendance that, once their fears of brutality were dispelled, the workers were ready and willing to join up. It was the turning point; after that, UAW membership in Anderson moved on and up.

Sophie and I returned years later to a completely different town. The new Mayor and Chief of Police spoke to us cordially at a reception in our honor, held by the city fathers in a new bank. The Sheriff's deputy who had slugged me on the picket line was now a

confirmed and respected UAW member. The union had comfortable headquarters and had led the citizens in the building of a magnificent center for older, retired citizens. The organization that had
been started by a dedicated few in the face of the fiercest opposition
was now accepted as a powerful force in the service not only of the
workers but of the whole community. It was so great a transformation that we wondered whether we had dreamed the whole desperate affair.

CHAPTER 15

Infighting

THE INK was barely dry on the settlement that ended the hard-fought General Motors strikes when Homer Martin began to wreak havoc within the UAW leadership, eventually splitting the union into two factions, one of which he led back into the AFL. Dissension, the prize that GM had failed to win by employing spies and provocateurs, was delivered to them gratis by Martin.

There were many reasons for the transformation of this rabble-rousing union evangelist into corporate stooge and provoker of internal warfare, but the basic one was his unstable and erratic personality. The leadership required of him was far beyond his capacity. Suddenly, head of an organization mushrooming from a handful into several hundred thousand members, he was faced with his own deep insecurity. During the drama of the sit-down strikes, he had been relegated to a minor role, twice sent on speaking tours to keep him from turning the negotiations into a fiasco. This demotion by CIO leaders in early 1937 rankled; he felt abused. He also resented the stellar role of John L. Lewis during the strikes and the subsequent negotiations. The loyalty of the thousands of new UAW members was naturally pledged to those leaders who had been most active in fighting for them in their plants. Martin became convinced that his personal control over the union was fast slipping.

He was therefore psychologically ripe for exploitation by one of the cleverest, most Machiavellian union-splitters ever to prey on the American labor movement: Jay Lovestone. Originally from Lithuania, Lovestone was one of the New York radicals who engineered the split in the Socialist Party that led to the founding of the American Communist Party. At the age of twenty-nine, he became the second secretary-general of that party.

Lovestone fell out of Stalin's good graces, however, and could not get reinstated even by actively supporting the 1934 purges. Having lost the support of American Communists, he about-faced and organized something called the Communist Party Opposition, which was a group opposed to Stalin but not to Communism as such. In every political or trade union crisis he suspected a Stalinist plot. His infiltration into the labor movement began in the mid-thirties, when he helped Charles Zimmerman, another party member, become head of Local 22 of the International Ladies' Garment Workers.

Lovestone had visions of leading the American proletariat, but in fact he was a leader without a following. He saw in Homer Martin's personal dilemma an opportunity to sidle into the UAW so that he might use it as a legitimate labor base. He coached Martin's every utterance and move, and gradually supplanted the UAW key department directors with his own people. Henry Kraus was arbitrarily fired and replaced, as editor of the *Auto Worker,* by William Munger (alias C. Neilson), an old and close friend of Lovestone. Alex Bail (alias George Milas) former editor of Lovestone's *Workers' Age* in New York, came to Detroit to assist Munger, and his wife, Eve Stone, was put in charge of women's affairs and was assigned specifically to Flint to undermine the leadership of Roy and Bob Travis. Other Lovestone invaders included Irving Brown, Larry Klein (alias John Wilson), and Francis Henson (alias F. Liggett). Henson was put in charge of the research and education departments. It was consistent with Lovestone's conspiratorial past that his political supporters within the UAW were encouraged to use aliases in their correspondence with him. Almost none of these new department heads had ever been auto workers.

On the advice of Lovestone, Martin indulged from time to time in a vicious McCarthy-style campaign, on radio and in the *Auto Worker,* denouncing a large proportion of the UAW leadership and claiming that those who had organized the General Motors strikes were guilty of sending the union into near-bankruptcy. All three Reuthers were accused, as were some others, of being Communists. A shady Lovestone friend named Maurice Silverman circulated a story in the Detroit and Flint locals that the entire CIO leadership was Communist, and made vicious verbal attacks on Brophy, Germer, Walter, Roy, and me.

Many important organizers were dropped by Martin under the

excuse of "economizing"; others were exiled to small outposts, where they would have no influence on new UAW members. Bob Travis had to turn to the National CIO for a staff position, but it was far from Flint, where he had done such outstanding work. On May 7, I was ordered to Jamestown, New York, to organize a minuscule group of auto workers, but I held off, with Martin's permission, until the court case against me in Flint was settled. I spent several months organizing the King Seeley plant in Ann Arbor and on June 4 reported my success there to Martin, who wrote back: "Your report on the Ann Arbor situation has been received. Since your case has been concluded in Flint, I desire you to report to my office Monday afternoon for assignment to another field." The upshot was that I was sent to a little agricultural community outside Detroit, where I had to live. At the end of September I was curtly notified that my services would no longer be needed. Sophie was also discharged from her job as staff representative as soon as Martin found out she was my wife.

Martin was not loath to exploit the natural conflicts arising between union members and management in the plants. The UAW had grown so fast — from 89,000 in February 1937 to 245,000 in April — that the orderly union processing of grievances in a shop was a new experience for thousands of members as well as for foremen and supervisors, who did not find it easy to give up their old practices. Nor was it easy for the workers, with their new-found power, to resist going into wildcat strikes. The number of these was greatly exaggerated by General Motors, who wanted to amend the contract with the UAW by the insertion of a clause authorizing the company to discharge anyone who was responsible for a stoppage in production before he had utilized the grievance procedure. Martin did not know how to cope with this situation; he procrastinated and vacillated, and then told General Motors, "We are prepared to cooperate and assist your position." When news of this statement, which is on record in the Wayne State University Archives, reached the rank and file, the men were furious, for they knew full well that most of the wildcat strikes had been deliberately provoked by foremen and superintendents, who resented the union and had increased the work loads and speed-ups in order to goad the workers into anger and recklessness.

Lovestone stepped in with the suggestion that Martin turn these wildcat strikes into a weapon against organizers like Travis, Roy, and me by holding us responsible, thus giving him an excuse to oust us. Others who lost their positions because of equally false accusations were Robert Kanter and Stanley Novak, Detroit West Side organizers, Emil Mazey of the Briggs Local, and Frank Winn, who had been handling Ford organization publicity.

The tragic split was made formal when Martin encouraged Richard Frankensteen, leader of the Chrysler Local, and Russell Merrill, member of the UAW Executive Board, to call a so-called Progressive Caucus several months before the 1937 convention. It soon became clear that the purpose of the group was to remove Vice-President Wyndham Mortimer and replace him with Frankensteen. Mortimer was accused of too close an association with the Communist Party. It was Lovestone, of course, who engineered the caucus for Martin.

The formation of the caucus naturally brought about a countermove by us: at a meeting in Toledo, the Unity Caucus was formed by Mortimer, Walter, Bob Travis, Ed Hall, George Addes, Emil Mazey, Roy, and me, among others. But at that point we had no desire to oust anyone, including Homer Martin. We who had fought through the GM strikes, and had seen the UAW unite and grow through victory, were appalled at the idea of sacrificing that progress by pointless infighting. Above all, we wanted to heal the rift, and we made it clear at the start that we were in favor of the re-election of existing officers, and would add, as a profession of unity and good faith, one more vice-president, Richard Frankensteen.

We decided to send a delegation to South Bend to meet the Martin forces in a preconvention gathering, and issue there our plea for unity. Walter was chosen as leader of the delegation. When he proposed a compromise slate of officers, he was booed by the Martin faction. He stressed, to no avail, the need for democracy in the union and for an end to the arbitrary dismissals of the last few months. He mentioned that the *Auto Worker* was now being used, under Munger, as an organ to promote a purge of certain staff members. He concluded: "Unity is possible not by squeezing people out but by using all constructive forces. We do not want to fight among ourselves. We want to fight toge her against General Motors and against Henry Ford."

Martin's response was to extend his purge in Flint and to discharge, without warning, Ralph Dale, who had been working closely with Roy and Travis.

The convention was held in Milwaukee and over one thousand delegates and hundreds of alternates and guests attended. It was a wildly enthusiastic crowd, meeting for the first time since the winter victories. I had been asked by our Unity Caucus to introduce at the beginning of the session a resolution to outlaw factional caucuses. My argument for unity was met by Frankensteen's rebuttal that such caucuses were essential because "certain powers outside this organization would continue to get together for their own secret sessions." I presume he meant by this the Communist Party. I doubt if he had in mind the secret meetings of Lovestone's Communists. At any rate, the important matter of healing the rift died in the early hours of the convention.

There was a terrible hassle over the seating of Roy as a delegate. He had been duly elected as such by the Flint Local but Martin did not want him to be elected to the International Executive Board, and used the Credentials Committee to effect his plan. There was pandemonium in the hall after George Edwards, a member of the minority on the Credentials Committee, told the audience that the committee majority, after three days of stalling, was "reporting simply to seat Morris Fields on the board in place of the man who was really elected." (Fields was a Lovestone man.) Martin strong-armed the committee's report through on a very ambiguous voice vote, claiming he had an electronic machine in the building that registered the ayes and nays. Delegate Ditzel stood up then and said: "Point of information. Are we going to register a vote according to a machine which will tell which side can yell the loudest?"

"That is the only way to decide an aye and nay vote," was Martin's answer.

On this elevated note of applied democracy, Martin adjourned the convention. Though a unity slate of officers had actually been elected, it was clear that there was something less than unity in the ranks when they left the hall.

Martin's behavior was not likely to enhance the influence or bargaining power of the UAW. Employers were quick to take advantage of the obvious rift by putting pressure on union workers through speed-ups and threats. To exacerbate the dismal situation, the country's economy was moving into recession, and each day brought new layoffs, which further weakened the union's strength. When management tried to push through a policy of wage cuts, there were bitter strikes in defense of the previously negotiated wage pattern. The auto workers became very angry when a front-page headline in the *Wall Street Journal* (January 1938) told them that Homer Martin had agreed to accept competitive wage cuts in Detroit. The article also commented that the West Side Local, one of UAW's "most powerful groups and a left-wing stronghold," did not agree with Martin's move, and that enthusiasm for the union among the rank and file was continuing to decline.

West Side Local 174 was a thorn in Martin's side. He tried to split it by separating union members in certain plants from the amalgamated local and granting them their own charters.

But when he acted alone in making a new agreement with General Motors about the wage pattern, and did not submit it to the membership for ratification, the Unity Caucus was stung into action against this complete travesty of democratic methods. We launched a serious campaign in union newspapers against Martin and the International for by-passing the rules.

Martin retaliated by suspending the publication of all union papers that he had not reviewed and censored.

By this time the whole UAW was divided into pro- or anti-Martin groups, and it became evident that the majority had shifted loyalty from the Progressive Caucus, dominated by Lovestone and Martin, to our Unity Caucus.

We represented essentially the same militant trade unionists who had been in the forefront of the great strikes and organizing drives that built up the UAW. We also represented the same political coalition as the National CIO. We had our traditional and somewhat conservative unionists, like John L. Lewis. But just as Lewis welcomed into the CIO former opponents of his who were Democratic Socialists, such as Brophy and Germer, the UAW had its Socialist component. The three Reuthers, George Edwards, Leonard Woodcock, Bob Kanter, Frank Winn, and many others were affiliated with the Socialist Party, but I know of not one instance when the Socialist group took a separate stand within the union and tried to impose their view on others. As a matter of fact, Roy, Paul Porter, and Andy Biemiller (later a U.S. Congressman), all of them active in the Socialist movement, introduced a bill in the U.S. Socialist Convention to the effect that Socialists would never act as a power bloc or caucus within the trade union movement.

As for the Communists, there were some who held influential

positions in the UAW by virtue of their achievements and the following they had earned during the struggle to build the union. Like the rest of us, they had agreed not to let their personal politics interfere with our work. Until the spring of 1938, the Unity Caucus had held to that commitment. But just at the moment when it had some chance of claiming the top leadership of the UAW, it was done in by its enemies.

Its demise occurred in April 1938, at the founding convention of the Michigan CIO Council, which had been conceived as a means of unifying all the CIO unions in the state. Both caucuses had their preconvention meetings and decided on their slates of officers. Both chose Adolph Germer, who had been CIO director in Michigan, as president. (The Martin people were not yet prepared to challenge him.) The real contest was for the post of secretary-treasurer.

The Progressive Caucus put forward Richard T. Leonard, president of the DeSoto Local 227 — a clever choice, since he was a sincere unionist with no political ax to grind. He was, however, completely loyal to Martin. The Unity Caucus drafted me to run against him, and though I was not enthusiastic about the prospect of what would be more or less a state lobbying job in Lansing, I accepted the draft because my election might serve to consolidate our Michigan leadership.

Richard Frankensteen was the floor leader of the Martin forces. He and Leonard were having breakfast on the second day of the convention. Frankensteen was called away to speak with someone and when he returned Leonard asked him who it was. Frankensteen said, "That was Gebert, and it's all set. You'll be the new secretary-treasurer."

Leonard was flabbergasted. He had heard of Gebert, who was not an auto worker, but a top official of the American Communist Party. Leonard knew he had been sent in to strengthen the party's influence in the UAW. What Leonard could not understand was why he himself was getting Communist support. The reason became clear later: Frankensteen realized that Martin was on his way out, and he wanted to build a personal coalition that would put him in a position to replace Martin. To do this, he had to split our Unity Caucus.

Walter realized something was afoot and on the third day of the convention, when Frankensteen asked for a ten-minute caucus to

work out a "deal which could unify the meeting," Walter followed
the group headed for the caucus room and found Frankensteen in a
huddle with some of the leading Communists: Gebert, William
Winestone, and two from the UAW, Nat Ganley and John Anderson.

Walter exploded. "What are you bastards doing? Don't you realize you are going to destroy the Unity Caucus, which is the only
thing that can save this union?"

"We know what we're doing," Winestone replied coldly.

"If you carry through this double-cross, then count me on the
other side, not only in this fight, but from here on out!"

Loren Lee Carey, a labor historian, has described, in his book
what happened after that:

> Amid shouts, confusion, and demands from Germer that the UAW
> fight be kept off the convention floor, the Unity group split and the
> Communist element threw its support to Leonard. The Communists
> probably preferred to back a relatively weak Martin man than to con-
> tinue working with the strong-willed and increasingly anti-Communist
> Reuther brothers. Their switch, in any case, carried Leonard to an easy
> 414 to 185 victory.

Martin's ultimate downfall resulted from his compulsion to make
compromises with the automobile corporations against the wishes of
the workers. It was hastened by his rabid outbursts against the CIO.
All efforts to persuade him to make peace instad of war were in
vain. At Lewis's invitation, Martin reluctantly agreed to meet with
the International Executive Board in Washington on June 12. But
nothing was accomplished; by that time Martin had decided to declare open warfare on his fellow officers within the UAW and to run
the risk of a clear break with the National CIO. He had barely returned from Washington when he announced the suspension of five
of our top officers, including the three vice-presidents, Mortimer,
Frankensteen, and Hall. On learning of this, five other officers,
among them Walter, walked out of the Executive Board meeting
and were themselves suspended by Martin. The secretary-treasurer,
George Addes, fearing a possible putsch by Martin forces, tried to
safeguard the union's funds, and was also given the ax. Eleven
officers were now either removed or suspended, and six more under
threat of supension. Democratic procedure had been entirely abandoned. Ward's *Automotive Report* of June 18, 1938, contained the

following observation: "It appears that the Martin bloc is losing support among the rank and file. Auto company officials would prefer the Martin group in power." Small wonder that General Motors and Ford preferred a man who seemed insanely bent on destroying a union.

It was inevitable that the AFL would start fishing in these troubled waters. Dillon, once UAW president and now general organizer for the AFL, said in a Toledo speech on June 21 that "the CIO is in its death throes . . . not just a split but the sign of disintegration of the entire CIO movement." He appealed to employers in Toledo to cooperate with the AFL and warmly invited all auto workers to return to the fold.

Martin then made a series of nationwide radio broadcasts, trying to justify his suspension of board members by labeling them Communists, aping the tones and even the phrases of Gerald L. K. Smith and Father Coughlin. If he had confined his charges to actual party members, he would have been more believable, but in his insecurity and desperation he flailed out in all directions, accusing many who had long opposed Communism within the UAW, like Walter, and even hitting at his erstwhile ally, Frankensteen, who was apolitical and concentrated only on his personal advancement.

The suspended officers carried their case to John L. Lewis, who, by the summer of 1938, was himself being viciously characterized by Homer Martin as a dictator and a threat to the autonomy of the CIO. Lewis must have been puzzled by Martin's malice. A letter dated August 3, now in the United Mine Workers–UAW files, shows that Germer tried to put the whole matter in proper perspective:

> The alliance between Lovestone and Martin began about March of last year which was also the time when I was edged out of the picture. During the early Chrysler negotiations I sat in and took the lead. I could sense the resentment on the part of Munger, research director and editor of the *Auto Worker,* who is really the fellow, I am sure, who brought Lovestone into the picture . . . From March of 1937 on, the CIO was shelved . . . It was about this time that Homer began to get cool on you and . . . began to talk of the importance of his job . . .

It was quite understandable that the National CIO would not want to intervene in our dispute unless it was pressured by an unmistakable majority of the UAW members. The Unity Caucus therefore set about getting in touch with local officials all over the country to tell them the truth they could not find in the Martin-dominated union newspapers. Eventually delegations were organized by Walter to journey to Washington and discuss with John L. Lewis the serious threat posed by Martin's unbalanced behavior. On August 20, the Unity Caucus scheduled a meeting between the suspended board members, officers and organizers who had been axed, and a large number of elected local officials from various areas. We adopted a resolution calling on John L. Lewis to intercede, and further resolved "that every local union that has the welfare of the UAW and CIO at heart adopt this same resolution at its next local meeting or special meeting and that copies be forwarded to Chairman Lewis."

This appeal brought an enormous response from the rank and file, and provided the ground swell of support that the CIO needed to justify stepping in to adjudicate and make peace. Martin's attack on Lewis and the CIO had been a major blunder: in those days the initials *CIO* meant more to the majority of workers, in terms of identification and loyalty, than did *UAW*.

Lewis finally agreed that a high-level CIO delegation should go to Detroit. Martin was very angry, but through the skillful intervention of Philip Murray of the National CIO and Sidney Hillman of the Amalgamated Clothing Workers, a peace meeting was arranged between the Martin group and the Unity Caucus leaders. The suspensions were lifted, and a twenty-point proposal agreed on. A semblance of harmony emerged, but it was short-lived. Martin took to the air again against the CIO, and, what was more serious, began to enter into private negotiations with Harry Bennett of Ford and his colleague, John Gillespie, over the heads of the UAW Executive Board, without reporting these meetings to any UAW officer responsible for the organizing drive at Ford. The time had come when there was no more tolerance of this erratic president, and the twenty board members, representing a sizable majority, placed him on trial and removed him from office.

CHAPTER 16

River Rouge

THE MARTIN PURGE made life difficult for many of us. Like my brothers, I had been blacklisted by industry and could get no job in an auto plant. I chose to return to home ground, Local 174, to work as a volunteer organizer. I was given transportation expenses but no salary. Sophie and I rented a ramshackle frame house on West Philadelphia Street and found friends to share space and rent: Bob Kanter, also a volunteer organizer, George Edwards, still on the payroll of the International UAW, and Dr. Frederick C. Lendrum, employed in the UAW Medical Research Division.

Both May and Sophie found the trade union way of life frustrating; their husbands traveled continuously, and all of us sweated out what seemed an interminable crisis in union affairs. The lack of a full family life was also painful for Walter and me. We were blessed with wives who shared our basic interests and political philosophy and were themselves active in the labor movement. But there remained an unending struggle on the part of all four of us to find time to lead a married existence. We wanted the best of both worlds — an impossible, youthful goal.

"The world is an empty place without you," Walter wrote to May from a distant city where he was attending an Executive Board meeting. Even when subject to enormous pressures, Walter wrote to May sometimes several times in one day when he was away from Detroit. Tenderness and humor shine through those early letters. From a National CIO Executive Board meeting in Washington: "Did you throw out the onions? If not, they will grow out of the kitchen into the parlor."

After the turmoil of Flint and Anderson, it looked as if there might be some way to maintain a family routine. But then the crisis

within the UAW began to go from a simmer to a boil. That called
for more trips away, more long hours among workers and organizers. In a show of irritation and independence, the two wives took
off together by bus for Gulfport, Mississippi, to have a vacation from
work and to indicate, perhaps, to Walter and me their need to establish the kind of home life and emotional relationship that would
be tolerable. May wrote from Gulfport with the natural ambiguity
of strong love:

> I have just taken a long walk on the beach along the Gulf by myself and
> all my mind could think of was Walter. And that I love you and miss
> you. And if I didn't know it was an awfully silly, silly thing to do, I'd
> come back in a minute to tell you that I love you and to forgive me for
> the way I've acted in the past two weeks . . . Gee, I want a long letter
> from you real quick . . .

It was after that trip that Walter convinced May to extend her leave
of absence from the school board so that she could continue acting
as his personal secretary at the West Side Local. At least he could
then have the joy of being with her many hours of the day when he
was in Detroit.

Off again to Milwaukee, he wrote:

> Last night on the train I felt guilty because I haven't given you more at-
> tention. I act like a perfect fool sometimes. I neglect you . . . I
> give the Movement all of my time only to find that by neglecting you I
> destroy a relationship without which I can never hope to accomplish
> anything.

And in a later letter, sent during one of the long meetings with John
L. Lewis and the UAW Executive Board, he assured May:

> I can't wait until you and I can get up into the north woods for several
> weeks — sunshine, swimming, hiking, reading, cooking, etc. Our main
> trouble is we have never had time together. I know the two weeks in
> the woods where we can be together every minute, just you and me, will
> be the happiest moments of my life.

Reunions were glorious, but the forces that pulled Walter in two
directions could not be easily reconciled. Both Walter and May were
strong personalities, with fixed, firm convictions, which made for a
number of ups and downs in their relationship.

From Washington, in November 1938, he wrote:

> My darling Mayichka, it seems we shall always be just a couple of bad
> kids. We both get mad and then I must leave and then I'm very sorry

and wish I had been nicer and sweeter to you because I love you. It seems we just keep going through this cycle . . . I wish I could say I will never leave you again for one minute . . . If I ever say I can live without you, please don't take me seriously for it isn't so . . . When I am away from the mechanical-like existence we live, I begin to see why we are on edge all the time. Please let's try to work out a schedule and stick to it. I know I have said this before but we must do something so that we won't keep going like two machines. Living in this hotel and alone every night is driving me mad. The other fellows have their poker and drinks every night, but that lets me out. I'd give a million dollars if you were here.

Sophie had her share of problems with me, but she did not waste her time trying to deal with grievances through correspondence. She had a more direct technique. I remember getting home one evening from a late meeting to find the house in complete shambles. Chalked on the dark brown living room rug were huge white letters: CONTRACT DEMANDS, followed by a list of same in numerical order. In the corner sat an empty pail with mop and broom, which, Sophie said, would never be used by her again until there were some concessions on my part. Sophie was a hard bargainer as well as a good organizer, and I loved her for it.

Walter and May bought their first home in the summer of 1941, a small white clapboard bungalow on Appoline Street in northwest Detroit, and to judge from the letters of that time, most of the planning for it was done by mail. I myself made the magnificent sum of $900 in 1939, and that was the year our first child, Carole, was born. With superhuman effort we scraped together enough for the downpayment on an FHA loan and bought a small colonial brick house on Mark Twain Avenue, one block south of the Kelvinator plant. The price was $6500.

Like many young fathers, I had had no idea of the ways in which a child changes one's lifestyle. The circumstances surrounding Carole's entry into the world were perhaps unavoidable, but they demonstrate how little I was prepared to accept my personal responsibilities. It was the eve of the March 1939 convention in Cleveland, following the dramatic upheaval in the UAW. Sophie had a difficult labor; after many anxious hours a healthy child was born, and as soon as I was sure Sophie was on the road to recovery I left for the convention. To this day I carry a feeling of guilt for leaving a new mother, who, without the kind help of friends, would have returned unaided to a cold, unheated house with a newborn child.

It would be some years before I would fully understand the quotation from Schiller that my father often used in praise of my mother: *"Ehret Die Frauen sie Flechten und Weben Himliche Rosen ins Irdishe Leben."* ("Honor the women who twine and weave roses of heaven in earthly lives.")

It was the battle to unionize Ford that made family life for the Reuther brothers not only frustrating but traumatic, during those years when threats of physical violence or outright assassination were heard almost daily. The bravery of our wives stood us in good stead. Sophie and I had two sons, Eric Val and John Stocker, who followed Carole. Walter and May had two daughters, Linda and Elizabeth, who was called Lisa (and a girl who died right after birth). All of our children suffered from our involvement in the labor movement. Unionism was still looked down upon by the social establishment and it was a constant source of embarrassment to them in school when they had to write on forms that their fathers were "union organizers."

For long periods after the Martin purge, Roy, who was still unmarried, was unemployed but continued to volunteer his efforts to local unions within his region. Later his children, too, felt the onus of their father's involvement in union affairs.

Our oldest brother, Ted, and his wife, Ann, were the only ones in the family who were able to rear their children — three sons and a daughter — under less hectic conditions. Our sister, Christine, married to a dedicated and socially motivated theology student, continued her career as supervisor of nursing in a large hospital even as her children — also three sons and a daughter — arrived.

On July 8, 1944, Roy married Fania Sasonkin. Like me, Roy found his future wife among the students at Brookwood Labor College. Fania's parents, Yitzhak and Doba, had settled in the little village of Rudensk in White Russia. They raised a family of four sons and three daughters, of whom Fania was the youngest. The family earned its modest income from the operation of a small general store. The Sasonkins were Jewish, and often suffered cruel persecution, instigated by Czarist soldiers. After the 1915 pogrom, the parents decided that if they were to be victimized by the army, then that army did not deserve the services of their sons. Soon three of the sons would leave for America by the circuitous route of Siberia. It was the father's wish that the entire family might be reunited in freedom in America, but he died in 1921 without realizing his dream. That year, the family quietly made preparations to cross the border, secretly, into Poland. Fania, though only eight at the time, still has vivid memories of the flight. However, the mother and children were arrested and were sent to Minsk. After their release, they successfully escaped to Vilna. They had first secured false Polish papers, which, with the help of an international Jewish relief agency, were converted into proper documents. These permitted the family to continue the journey, but only after sweating out two more years in Warsaw. Fania and the others arrived in the United States in 1923. At an early age, because of family influence as well as choice, Fania found herself involved in labor and Socialist activities. It was this interest that brought Fania to Brookwood and to Roy. In their life together, they shared a dedication to democratic political and trade union ideals. The birth of two sons, David and Alan, further enriched this close, warm family.

The Ford Company, the only significant holdout after General Motors, Chrysler, and some of the independents had been successfully unionized, proved the most difficult company to crack. That was because it engaged, perhaps to a larger extent than any other major corporation in the country, in open and shameless acts of terrorism, to prevent its workers from joining a trade union. Of the three Reuthers involved, Walter bore the brunt of the violence; he survived it with his particular combination of stamina and luck.

When he was employed at River Rouge in the early thirties, there were unsuccessful efforts made to unionize the workers. After the victories in the winter of 1937, the UAW felt ready to tackle the giant, which meant confronting the Ford Service Department and its master, Harry Bennett. With the rise of Bennett to the directorship of the Service Department, the several thousand members of that squad were soon transformed from fairly benign watchdogs over Ford employees into a bizarre collection of hired thugs and gangsters, noted for their ability to flex muscles rather than brains.

Bennett, who had been originally hired as bodyguard for Ford's children, became one of Ford's confidants, and then was awarded full decision-making power over labor relations and hiring and firing. He had early established a direct line of communication with the Michigan State Prison in Jackson, and prisoners were frequently paroled directly to his staff. They were, of course, indebted to him and eager to carry out any order, however outrageous or illegal. In the records of the National Labor Relations Board, one finds accounts of hundreds of brutal beatings of Ford workers who had shown signs of interest in unionization.

There were grisly stories coming out of Dallas, St. Louis, and Kansas City, as well as Detroit. A Mr. A. B. Louis, retained as temporary attorney by the Dallas UAW, was threatened by a thug in his hotel, and three days after he tried to get a grand jury warrant, he was, as George Edwards wrote to Walter in September 1937, "set upon by a dozen Ford Servicemen. He was knocked down, kicked and stabbed, and for several days he was in a serious condition." According to the same letter, "Two Socialist Party men who were showing the labor film of *Millions of Us* in a Dallas public park were set upon by a gang of twenty men who wrecked the sound equipment, slugged one of the men, and took the other out and tarred and feathered him and left him on the main street of the city without any clothes on. The same day, George Baer, Vice-President of the Cap, Hat and Millinery workers, was kidnapped in a downtown street and taken out in the country and beaten unconscious."

Meanwhile, Henry Ford pictured himself as a defender of the underdog, a promoter of a higher wage standard over the opposition of Wall Street financiers. He considered himself the person who kept the whole country's wages up. In a July 1937 editorial in his *Almanac,* he warned the workers:

> The next step in the game of the financiers will be wage standardization . . . The skilled worker will have lost the benefit of his skill . . . And should you sign away your rights, you will find out a little later on when all industries are under one control that Ford cannot raise wages in his plant as he has done so many times before. . . . If he did, it would cause trouble in the other plants controlled by the financiers' wage dictators. There's something to think about.

What they also had to think about was that the slightest wage increase at Ford was converted into an enormously increased output, through the pressure of foremen, supervisors, and the Service Department to speed up the line. What it was like was captured in Joe Glazer's ballad, "You Gotta Fight That Line."

> They put me to work on the assembly line;
> My clock-card number was 90–90–9.
> Those Fords rolled by on that factory floor,
> And every fourteen seconds I slapped on a door.

> *Chorus:* You gotta fight that line
> You gotta fight that line
> You gotta fight that line . . . all the time.

Those Fords rolled by all day and all night,
My job was the front door on the right.
Foreman told me the day I was hired,
"You miss one door, Mr. Jones . . . you're fired."
(Well I'll see my union representative about that.)
I slapped those doors on always on the run
Every fourteen seconds, never missed a one.
And I staggered home from work each night,
Still slappin' 'em on — front door right.

Henry Ford was not interested in conditions on the assembly line or in the criminal acts of Bennett's minions. He was preoccupied with the medal awarded him by Adolf Hitler. Like Charles Lindbergh, he became a tool in the hands of clever European fascists.

River Rouge was called Sweat Shop or Butcher House. When its workers heard about the added job security and improved working conditions that followed unionization in GM and Chrysler, they began to get interested in the UAW, and would drop by our West Side headquarters, somewhat surreptitiously, to whisper about their right to organize. Since our office was under constant Ford surveillance, Walter devised a decentralized organizing scheme, opening small branch offices in neighborhoods remote from the Ford plants. We issued general informational bulletins and leaflets in Polish, Serbo-Croatian, Hungarian, Italian, inserted short ads and news items on Polish radio programs, directed especially to Ford workers, and bought space on well-situated billboards for open appeals for members.

The UAW relied heavily on loyal union members in Chrysler and GM to let us know of relatives, friends, neighbors who worked at Ford and were ready, though frightened, to join up. We found at least a hundred prominent citizens — clergymen, jurists, professors, leaders in ethnic communities — to help with the distribution of union literature. On several occasions Walter and I made a dramatic bid to win the attention of Ford workers by renting a plane that had broadcasting equipment in its belly and circling River Rouge, shouting organizing slogans into the microphone. The maneuver, alas, made press copy rather than converts. At the height we had to fly, almost no one on the ground could hear us. A more effective stratagem was used by wives and friends of unionists; they would take the tourist trip through the River Rouge plant and, once in the midst of the workers, would put on UAW caps or pull out our small signs reading GET WISE. ORGANIZE.

Unlike Flint in the twenties, Detroit now had a large percentage of black workers. They presented a real problem. They had been urged to come north specifically to work at Ford, and many of Detroit's black preachers had been carefully wooed in order to turn them into recruiting agents and to make sure they disseminated the views of the Ford Company from their pulpits. The black workers inevitably felt a sense of obligation to the company. Moreover, unions were not very popular with blacks; in the South unions had excluded all but the lily white from their memberships. We had a few staunch supporters, however, who played a central role in its final unionization: Paul Kirk, Tommy Williams, Lebroun Simons, Nelson Crawford, Percy Key, Waldo Thomas, Doyle Duckman, and others.

Walter's own years in River Rouge, and the intimate friends he had made among the skilled tool workers, gave him credibility. He also depended on a "Jimmy Higgins," whose real name was William McKie, and who had been discharged after years of service in the Ford plant because of his militant unionism. His knowledge of the various plants and contacts with rank-and-file workers made him an indispensable member of our team.

However, at the time, it was clear that if the Ford workers were going to find the courage to overcome their terror of Bennett and his Service Department, the organizing campaign would have to be carried right to the factory gates. We laid plans for a massive leaflet distribution at all of the main gates to River Rouge. Since we had to apply well in advance for a license to hand out material in the city of Dearborn, and Dearborn officialdom was completely in the pocket of Ford, one can assume that interested officials were notified of our application. The leaflet consisted mainly of quotes from the Wagner Act on the right to organize, with an appeal to auto workers to join the UAW.

We briefed our hundreds of volunteers on how to conduct themselves during the distribution, giving them diagrams to indicate what was public and what was Ford property. The focal point was Gate 4, through which most workers entered River Rouge. Here an elevated bridge crossed Miller Road to permit those arriving in street cars to cross the highway into the plant. Ford had constructed this walkway but had leased it to the Detroit Railway Commission for public use; it was not, in effect, private property, and it was crossed by all sorts of people with no Ford association. This footbridge became a battleground.

The time was the change of shift on the afternoon of May 26, 1937. Walter has written a graphic description of the occasion:

> I got out of the car on the public highway, Miller Road, near Gate 4. Dick Frankensteen and I walked together over to the stairs. I got up the stairs and walked over near the center of the bridge. I was there a couple of minutes and then all of a sudden about 35 or 40 men surrounded us and started to beat us up. I didn't fight back. I merely tried to guard my face. The men . . . picked me up about eight different times and threw me down on my back on the concrete and while I was on the ground, they kicked me in the face, head and other parts of my body. After they kicked me a while, one fellow would yell, "All right, let him go now." Then they would raise me up, hold my arms behind me and begin to hit me some more. They picked my feet up and my shoulders and slammed me down on the concrete and while I was on the ground, they kicked me again in the face, head and other parts of my body . . . Finally they got me next to Dick who was lying on the bridge and with both of us together they kicked me again and then picked me up and threw me down the first flight of stairs. I lay there and they picked me up and began to kick me down the total flight of steps . . .
>
> There were about 150 men standing around . . . I should say about 20 were doing the actual beating . . . I never raised a hand . . . They started to hit me again at the bottom of the stairs and slugging me, driving me before them, but never letting me get away . . . The more we tried to leave, the worse it was for us . . . They drove me to the outside of the fence, almost a block of slugging and beating and hurling me before them . . . If I ran it would make it all the worse. Finally they drove me to the other end. I was on the outside of the Ford fence by the streetcar tracks, Frankensteen on the inside of the fence . . . While I was being driven down I had glimpses of women being kicked and other men being kicked and when I got to the end of the fence, I found Dick.
>
> In the meantime some newspaper photographers came along and they picked us up and we managed to get away from the thugs by getting into the car . . . It is the only way we could have escaped. Bob Kanter was also with us. And all the time I had the permit to distribute the leaflets in my pocket, but no one would look at that. I might add, the police standing around did nothing to prevent the slugging.

Bob Kanter recalls how his glasses were ripped off his face and smashed against the wall by the hoods as they began pummeling him and slamming him against the concrete before kicking him down the long flight of stairs. When he tried to climb up again to be with Walter and Dick, Walter's body hit his and they both went down together.

William Merriweather, a UAW member, was trying to help some of the women who were being attacked and was pounced on by the Ford men shouting, "Get that union son of a bitch." His back was broken, and he suffered other internal injuries. Mrs. Katherine Gelles, who saw the attack on Merriweather and later testified before the NLRB, said, "Oh my God, he looked as if he were dead. Blood was coming out of his nose and mouth. He was unconscious. I said, 'For God's sake, let's get out of here.' "

The Reverend Raymond Sanford, chairman of the Committee for Church and Industry of the Chicago Church Federation, was an observer of the whole affair, and told the press, and also testified before the NLRB, that he saw Walter "crouched down with arms shielding his face. His face was bleached . . . Blood was trickling all over his face . . . Eventually he was thrown down three flights of stairs with men attacking him from all sides." He saw Frankensteen "kicked in the groin and kidneys and knocked down . . . lifted to his feet and then knocked down and beaten again." He saw women hit and pushed around, girls "called all manner of vile names usually attributed to women of the streets. A well-dressed man kicked one of the girls in the abdomen and she fell at my feet. I shot an imploring glance at a mounted policeman, and he, in a pleading and for God's sakes tone, asked the well-dressed man not to hurt the women. He seemed to speak as one not having authority."

Victor Beresford, a Detroit reporter, and Herbert Bauer from UP were cruising around near the footbridge at eleven that morning and saw "about 25 carloads of men parked under the overpass." When Bauer tried to take pictures, they stopped him and, surrounding the car, escorted it and the two reporters to the main gate. They did not want their pictures in the paper, they told Bauer. The two reporters returned later and saw and photographed the whole scene. As they said to an NLRB lawyer, "Everywhere you looked, someone was getting kicked around." At the same hearing, Mrs.

Gelles testified that she appealed to a policeman standing nearby to call an ambulance for a leaflet distributor named Stella, who had been badly beaten up and was leaning against the fence in great pain. "Oh, let her go back the way she got out here. We didn't invite her," the officer said.

There were many other reporters and photographers who were on the overpass before Walter arrived, and some extraordinary pictures, printed in papers all over the world, showed clearly and in sequence just how the union leaflet distributors were attacked and by whom. One could easily identify Sam Taylor, for instance, a Ford foreman who was also president of the rightist Knights of Dearborn; Wilford Comment, a Ford Serviceman, with handcuffs dangling from his rear pocket; and Ted Greis, another Serviceman who was a wrestling referee. As this trio mounted the stairs and approached Walter, Dick Frankensteen, and other UAW leaders, a phalanx of men numbering well over seventy-five sprang into action, claiming the bridge was private property, and the well-documented and photographed acts of mayhem began.

Even before the brutality had stopped, Harry Bennett issued a press release, claiming complete innocence of any involvement. He fabricated the story that Ford workers had been so insulted by names shouted at them by the union people that they had exploded in rage. Evidence that he was lying was clearly established by Arnold Freeman of the Detroit *Times,* who had preceded Walter to Gate 4 and questioned one of the individuals hanging about, a man he had recently questioned in police headquarters in connection with a holdup. The man freely admitted, "We were hired, as far as I know, temporary, to take care of these union men that are to distribute these pamphlets," adding that the Ford Servicemen had organized the setup and assigned four hired thugs to every single UAW person arriving to distribute leaflets.

The techniques of the hoodlums were certainly those of professionals: they would pull the victim's coat over his head, for instance, as they did with Frankensteen, making him completely defenseless. Walter and Frankensteen had obviously been subjected to more than punches. Walter had been kicked in the temples so many times he could hardly open his eyes. *Time* magazine ran a detailed story, concluding, "It looked very much as if that brutal beating might hurt Henry Ford as much as it hurt Richard Frankensteen."

Thereupon the Ford Motor Company withdrew all advertising from *Time, Life,* and *Fortune* for a total period of seventy weeks.

A remarkable book entitled *We Never Called Him Henry,* written by Harry Bennett (with the aid of Paul Marcus) after the death of the elder Henry Ford, reveals some of the things that went on. Bennett, who seems to have written the book so that he could blame Ford for all the brutal and illegal acts committed, denies that he had anything to do with bringing in John Gillespie, former Detroit Police Commissioner, to work in Ford labor relations.

> Gillespie . . . began working directly under Mr. Ford and usually at cross purposes with me. For example, Gillespie began trying to break up union meetings by such stunts as putting tear gas in the radiators of cars at meeting halls and when John succeeded in something like this, Mr. Ford would rib me about it, "Well, I see John broke up another meeting," he'd say . . . But I had no part in this sort of thing which was childish to me.

How was it possible that one of the world's largest industrial firms could have had such a barbaric labor relations policy? Certainly the elder Ford must be held responsible for giving Bennett carte blanche and never questioning his methods. How did he condone the fact of Bennett's deal with underworld characters? Bennett, who, as of this writing, is eighty-three years old and living in seclusion in Las Vegas, granted an unusual interview to David L. Lewis of the Detroit *Free Press* in 1974. Lewis quotes Bennett as saying that Ford had no confidence in law enforcement agencies and told him to hire anyone he wanted. So Bennett made a point of keeping in touch with leading downriver gangsters, including Chester LaMare — the Al Capone of Detroit — and Joe Adonis of Murder, Incorporated. LaMare told Bennett, "I am the king. You deal with me and nobody gets killed." He was involved in illegal drugs, bordellos, and hijacking of trucks and freight cars, and owned many nightclubs. He also had a fruit company, and Bennett gave him the concession to supply all the caterers who provided the Ford Company lunches. Joe Adonis was given a Ford contract to deliver cars from the Edgewater assembly plant to dealers all over the East Coast.

Bennett knew how to exploit to the full Ford's confidence in him, and ended up as a virtual general in charge of three thousand full-time Servicemen — perhaps the largest private army in the world at that time. He had complete charge of hiring and firing a work force of one hundred thousand at River Rouge. He did well with his personal finances too; old Henry was always slipping him bundles of cash for bizarre projects, and titles to valuable pieces of land. The result was very luxurious homes, yachts, hunting lodges. Bennett admitted to having title to "about a million dollars worth of farms."

The Battle of the Overpass and the physical trauma of the beatings did not stop our West Side Local from pressing on with the Ford campaign. When Walter recovered, he was more determined than ever to bring the Ford plants within the laws of the United States and to free the workers from what amounted to serfdom. But the Reuthers had more than Bennett and his army to contend with. Homer Martin, as described in the preceding chapter, was using every possible means to undermine us in the UAW. He was furious about the nationwide publicity that both Frankensteen and Walter received after the massacre at the River Rouge gate.

Since he was still friendly at that point with Frankensteen, he tried to play him off against Walter by naming him organizing director of the Ford campaign, and insisting that Walter turn over all records, names, and addresses of River Rouge union members. Rumors were circulated by Martin men that forced Walter to issue a press statement from the Executive Board meeting held in Milwaukee in the fall of 1937.

> Contrary to the streamer headline in the afternoon Detroit *Daily,* I have not quit the Ford organizing drive. Quite the opposite. I came to Detroit Tuesday evening to lead the distribution of union literature at the Ford Dearborn plant Wednesday. I came because I had been in charge of the first union literature distribution on May 26, and because I am not in the habit of asking any union member to do anything I would not be willing to do myself. However, I was compelled by vote of the General Executive Board, under threat of suspension, to return to Milwaukee early Wednesday before I could lead the distribution in the afternoon. I was not called back by President Martin, and there is no rift with him . . .

That second distribution at the Ford gates went ahead. George Edwards, William McKie, and Bob Kanter reported to Walter that it was a "magnificent success, in perfect order, and high union spirits. Ford employees taking papers in great numbers. West Side Local had 600 at hall."

In spite of Martin's efforts to pull Walter off the Ford drive, it was clear that his West Side Local continued to be the main source of contacts and volunteers. And it was on his initiative, supported by George Edwards, that the International Union set in motion a special paperback printing of two hundred thousand copies of Upton Sinclair's *The Flivver King*. This mass printing made an enormous contribution to the ultimate success of the drive to unionize Ford, and brought joy to its author, in all respects a remarkable man.

Widespread national indignation at the brutality of its antiunion activities certainly made the Ford Motor Company re-evaluate its methods of dealing with us. From then on, the physical violence was less overt, directed only against certain individuals, among them Walter. His views and intentions were well known. It was he, for instance, who vigorously supported the continuing distribution of literature at the River Rouge gates. Frankensteen wanted, instead, to arrange for an hour of radio time, using the Detroit Symphony Orchestra for public relations — an expensive and, Walter felt, ineffectual stunt. After years of experience, Walter knew that unless the union continued to inspire confidence, by courageously carrying the campaign right into the midst of the auto workers, the Battle of the Overpass would have been in vain. He was a stubborn fighter, and it was no secret that he was a marked man. This was, unfortunately, proved true in the spring of 1938.

April 9 was Sophie's birthday, and we were celebrating it at Walter and May's apartment instead of our own, because Walter had come down with a cold that day. Roy was there, and Ben Fisher, a steelworker organizer, his wife, Hannah, Lewis Steigerwald, our old friend Tucker Smith from Brookwood, Frank Marquardt, active unionist at the Briggs plant, and Al King, a rank-and-file member of the UAW. No one was aware that for some weeks the apartment had been under constant surveillance by two of Bennett's hirelings, who had rented an apartment close by. Walter phoned a Chinese restaurant to send up dinner. About an hour after he had called, there was a knock on the door and Sophie and I, who were closest, opened it. Instead of the delivery boy, there stood two toughs with drawn revolvers. They pushed their way into the room, shouting, "Okay, back against the wall!" At first it was as unreal as a clip from an old silent movie. The shorter gunman wore a dark hat with the brim turned down to conceal his eyes; he was obviously the trigger man. The other gangster spotted Walter immediately, put his gun in its holster, and drew out of his rear pocket an enormous blackjack with a leather strap, which he twined around his wrist.

"Okay, Red, you're coming with us," he said.

Only gradually did we realize this was no joke. George Edwards muttered, "You're not getting him out of here. You may shoot some of us, but you won't get out yourselves."

The attackers were obviously surprised by the presence of so large a group; they would have known, by watching the house, that Walter seldom had meetings in his own home. The shorter gunman kept his .38 pointed at us and toyed with the trigger. Walter, who happened to be standing somewhat apart, slowly maneuvered himself into a corner, where he could best fend off the blows. The bigger of the two hoods broke a glass floor lamp over Walter's head, trying to get him off balance so that he would come within striking distance. That failed to put Walter out of commission, so the thug threw a glass-topped coffee table at him. Walter was then on the floor in the corner, using both feet and arms to keep off the swinging blows of the blackjack, and at some point he managed to grasp the end of the weapon and wrench it loose from its leather thong. He tossed it over the man's head in our direction, yelling, "Catch, George!" Comparing notes later, many of us confessed to a sensation of hot lead going through our guts when that happened, and no one made the slightest motion to catch the blackjack before it fell to the floor with a thud.

"Kill the son of a bitch," the larger bruiser shouted to his companion.

Four or five of us moved a few inches toward the man with the gun; it was the slightest of movements, but it gave meaning to George's earlier threat that they could kill some of us but wouldn't themselves get out alive.

During the commotion, little Al King, who had been standing near the kitchen door, slouched down, backed into the breakfast nook, jumped out an open window into the concrete alleyway two flights below, and started to shout for help. This brave action woke up the neighborhood and broke the deadlock. Sophie, at about the same time, decided to distract the killer; she reached her hand into the kitchen and as Al jumped out the window a pickle bottle came sailing in the direction of the trigger man. We all felt there would surely be shooting now, but after Al's "Help! Help!" had gathered a group in the street, the two professional hoods decided they had better retreat before they got caught, and abruptly fled the apartment.

May and Roy rushed to Walter to see how seriously he was injured. There were some cuts on his face from the broken glass but he had avoided any direct blow from the blackjack. We all collapsed into giddy hysterical laughter. There was an eerie unreality about that attempt to take Walter on what would have been his last ride. I can't even remember if the Chinese food ever came. I know we bolted the door and propped furniture against it, and immediately called the police. They took an hour to arrive and we let them in only after they had passed identification cards under the door. As they came in, whom should we see in the doorway but three men dressed in civilian clothes wearing dark hats with wide brims pulled down over their eyes! We told them what had happened, and I shall never forget Sophie's wonderfully blunt response when they asked for a description of the two thugs. In light of what would later unfold, it seemed clairvoyant. She looked the officers straight in their faces, and said, "They looked very much like you."

That birthday party made a change in our way of life that was to last for years — until Detroit's criminal element, backed by corporation money, was removed from power, and the workers could win a measure of security and protection. Walter and I got permits to carry revolvers and bought .38s. Neither of us had ever fired a revolver in our lives, though we had hunted a little with rifles in the West Virginia hills. We went for target practice to a firing range operated by the Sheriff of Macomb County; we had no confidence in the Detroit police. The idea of carrying a gun in order to fire at another human being was alien and uncomfortable, and I don't think that Walter wore his every day; I certainly did not carry mine. But the guns gave us some security at home. For quite a while after the birthday party, Sophie carried the revolver under her apron when she took the garbage out to the alley.

The police were not overly anxious to find our attackers, but in the underworld there are always individuals who will squeal for a fee. Within two days, Walter received an anonymous call, met the informer in a bar — filled with husky union men in case the call was a trap — and bought the names of the gunmen: Eddie Percelli, alias Eddie Tall, and Willard "Bud" Holt. Percelli was a former rumrunner who had been held as a suspect in the Harry Millman slaying. Bud Holt had once been a Ford Serviceman, and had recently been employed by John Gillespie. Each one of us who had been at the birthday party, brought in separately to view a police line-up, recognized both men at once.

The trial in September of 1938 was a farce. Over eighty prospective jurors were rejected for one reason or another, and the jury, it was reported, was composed of people chosen at random off the street. From the final verdict, one might surmise that many members of this jury were waiting on certain street corners to be picked "at random." Sherman, the defense lawyer, who had championed many other underworld characters, told the jurors: "We contend that Reuther arranged with Holt to come to his apartment at 13233 La Salle Boulevard and stage a sham battle before witnesses to embarrass Homer Martin, president of the UAW, with whom Reuther was at war." An attorney for the Ford Company, working with Sherman, repeatedly spoke of the "radical background" of all the guests at the birthday party, and implied that Walter and I were sinister revolutionists undermining the American way of life. After all, we had lived and worked in Russia for a year. The state prosecutor mentioned nothing about possible motives for an attack on Walter, though everyone knew he was on Ford's blacklist and that until two weeks before the event Holt had been employed as bodyguard for Ford's Gillespie. I strongly suspect that Judge George B. Murphy was as shocked as we were when the jury acquitted Holt and Percelli.

We knew we had many enemies: in the Ford Company; among other employers still urging Ford to hold out; among the racketeers who were paid by Bennett and saw a threat to their graft in the rise of the union. And, of course, we had foes within the UAW itself: Lovestone Communists who wanted power, and hard-core Communists who put their party above the interests of the union and whom we had openly opposed. But we had never anticipated the extent to which Homer Martin would make common cause with Harry Bennett. The very existence of the union was threatened by the possibility of Bennett and his Service Department controlling an enormous bloc of membership brought in not by worker vote, but by a deal between Bennett and Martin.

This collusion, unknown to those responsible for the Ford drive and to the Executive Board, began in the fall of 1938, during the last desperate months of Martin's presidency. Bennett has written:

> The UAW was by this time raging with factional disputes. This intra-union warfare was at least in part stimulated by a man named John Gillespie . . . While I was carrying on negotiations with Homer Martin, Gillespie injected himself into that situation by carrying on negotiations with Homer without my knowledge . . . Soon the factional wars within the UAW reached a climax in which Homer's desire to get along with us was used against him. He was expelled from the union . . ."

According to a letter from Adolph Germer to John L. Lewis, the secret agreement between Martin and Bennett stipulated that Ford would reinstate all workers discharged for union activity on condition that they were approved by Homer or his representative. "So far as I know," Germer wrote, "nothing is said about paying for the time lost in accordance with the order of the Labor Board with respect to at least 29 of the victims." The second condition was that Homer Martin, not the UAW, would be recognized as "sole bargaining agent for the employees." Third, Bennett's army of toughs would be available to Homer to enforce the agreement.

When the Executive Board summoned Martin to an emergency session and asked for an explanation of this incredible deal, he said he was making a "legitimate agreement." When the board called his bluff and asked him to produce the agreement, he panicked, and once again tried his earlier tactic: the suspension of Executive Board members. This time fifteen out of twenty-four were axed, and three who had not been suspended promptly joined the fifteen in denouncing Martin's action as arbitrary and unconstitutional. The time had at last come when there was no more tolerance of this erratic president, and twenty board members placed him on trial and removed him from office. The Executive Board took charges of conspiracy between him and the Ford Company to the NLRB, claiming unfair labor practice.

Martin then revived his plan to take the auto workers into the AFL. Bennett was in on this, too. In his book he explains that after Martin was expelled from the UAW-CIO

> I got Bill Green and his attorney in my office. I told them I'd sign an AFL contract covering the whole plant, providing they'd take Homer over. Green agreed to this and Homer went to work trying to organize an auto workers union within the AFL. Homer worked on this about a

year. His efforts were not particularly successful and finally Green called me up and backed out . . . When this happened, Homer was pretty hard up. Mr. Ford came to see me about Homer's plight and said, "Harry, I guess this is our fault. Let's help Homer." So we gave Homer a couple of accounts. One with a chemical company. We also gave him a completely furnished home in Detroit.

Both Bill Green and Bennett thought that Homer Martin had the auto workers in his vest pocket, ready to be delivered to the AFL. But the auto workers had other ideas. At the rump convention called by Martin after he had been deposed, he gathered in delegates representing only 17,500 workers, compared to the 371,213 who were represented at the legitimate UAW-CIO convention in Cleveland in March 1939. The Ford workers in particular distrusted any leader who connived with Harry Bennett. They had watched the strength of the CIO grow in major sections of their industry, and knew that crucial gains had been made in the standard of living, grievance procedures, and in ending the intimidation of the open-shop days.

The time was ripe for the National CIO to mount a large campaign of assistance to the struggling UAW forces, and a National Ford Organizing Committee opened headquarters in Detroit in July of 1940, with Michael Widman as assistant director of organization. Walter and his West Side Local wholeheartedly supported this committee and stepped up efforts among Polish and Italian workers in River Rouge. It was not until March 1941, however, that the death blow was given to Bennett and his antiunion army. By direction of the Supreme Court and the NLRB, after long months of research and hearings, the Ford Motor Company was instructed to post notices at the River Rouge plant stating that the company had ceased its opposition to the UAW. At least twenty-two UAW workers who had been fired in 1937 were to be reinstated with back pay. In California, Kansas City, St. Louis, Dallas, Somerville in Massachusetts, and Buffalo, the decisions all went against Ford.

This breakthrough boosted the morale of the Ford Organizing Committee, and new membership applications swamped the locals. But it soon became obvious that Ford and Harry Bennett were stalling. Bennett even reneged on the agreement that had been made with Michigan Governor Van Wagoner, federal conciliators, and the UAW. He abruptly ended a meeting with the UAW Grievance

Committee on April Fool's Day, and fired all participating members. This turned out to be his undoing. Calls for a strike spread rapidly through the plant. Widman was reluctant to approve, but he could not stem the tide. All efforts of Federal Conciliator Dewey to arrange a meeting between Ford and UAW officials were frustrated by Bennett. When Walter and Jim Dewey drove up to the River Rouge gate — the same gate where Walter had been unmercifully beaten — their car was stopped by Servicemen: "They will not meet with you. Get off our property." Small wonder, then, that the UAW Executive Board, knowing that the anger of Ford workers inside the plant had risen to fever pitch (though only 30 percent of them were signed up with the union), realized that it would be useless and wrong to try to stop them from striking. At noon on April 2, a majority of workers in River Rouge downed their tools and staged a magnificently effective strike, showing in the course of it their courage and their self-discipline.

After ten days, the Ford Motor Company finally threw in the sponge and agreed to recognize the UAW-CIO as bargaining agent for their workers, pending, of course, official elections under the auspices of the NLRB. It was also agreed that Ford wages would be raised to the levels of Detroit competitors. Until the NLRB elections could take place, there was to be an appeal board made up of R. J. Thomas, new president of the UAW, Alan Haywood from the National CIO, Governor Van Wagoner, Dewey, and Harry Bennett and six other Ford officials. Finally, all federal injunction suits against the UAW were to be dropped. It was indeed a victory.

According to Bennett, in an interview with a reporter:

> Mr. Ford was mad over the UAW-CIO strike in 1941. He told me, "I've never done anything against labor." He was so mad he wanted to shut the plant down. He asked me, "What is this check-off system the UAW wants?" I explained to him that we'd take union dues out of the employees' paychecks and that we'd be the UAW's banker. He liked that idea. "What's wrong with that?" he said. "We'll go along with it."

Ford and Bennett thought the check-off might be a way of exercising some control over the union because neither was capable of understanding that a democratic trade union insists on being independent and on managing its own affairs.

Over 25,000 Ford workers packed the fair grounds auditorium on April 10, 1941, to give their approval to the terms of the settlement.

The NLRB set the elections for May 21, and on that day the UAW won 51,866 votes as against 20,364 for Martin's rump organization, in spite of all Bennett's propaganda. Only 1958 voted for no union at all in River Rouge. In the Lincoln plant, it was a five-to-one victory over the splinter group. Even the pattern makers at River Rouge, long a separately organized craft group, and sought after by the AFL, gave the UAW-CIO 161 votes as against 90 for the AFL. It was a total repudiation of Martin and what he stood for. It also meant the end of the atrocious labor policies of Harry Bennett. His reaction was typical: "It's a great victory for the Communist Party, Governor Van Wagoner, and the NLRB."

The agreement negotiated with the Ford Company and ratified at an enormous rally of all Ford workers was hailed as one of the best in the entire history of the labor movement. Most people were amazed to find that Ford had agreed to the union shop, the check-off of union dues, and the affixing of a union label to all Ford cars. What's more, Ford Servicemen, plant police, and intelligence men were to wear uniforms with insignia designating their positions.

Perhaps the full scope of that victory for human values was best expressed by an old Polish auto worker who remembered Walter from the days when he worked with him in the tool room:

> I thank you, brother Reuther, for what you and UAW has done for me. Once in the Ford plant they called me "dumb Polack," but now with UAW they call me "brother."

CHAPTER 17

A Letter from Gorky

IT WAS DURING the period of sit-down strikes, sound truck oratory, and the consolidation of the UAW that the once innocent letter from Russia was first used against me. Later on, during Red-baiting epidemics, it would be used, with tedious repetition, against Walter, who, as president of the UAW, was more vulnerable to slander.

The facts are quite simple. One evening in the winter of 1934, as Walter and I sat in our small room in the American Village catching up with our correspondence, I wrote a letter to Melvin (brother of Merlin) and Gladys Bishop, in which I tried to share some of our excitement about participating in the growth of a huge modern automotive plant right in the middle of a primitive society and landscape. With youthful enthusiasm, I described our first Soviet experiences in terms of unqualified admiration. Such positive views were not unusual at a time when the U.S. was extending technical and financial aid to the USSR. In retrospect, I am amused that the antilabor-baiters and the rightists, who could have had a field day by using my actual words as "smears" against active unionists, bothered to resort to doctored versions of my letter. It was these forgeries that they circulated in their campaign against us. The original ending of my letter read: "Let us know definitely what is happening to the YPSL [Young People's Socialist League], also if the Social Problems Club at City College is still functioning and what it is doing. Carry on the fight. Vic and Wal."

By 1958 there were at least five different versions of that ending to be perused by the McClellan Committee (the Senate Select Committee on Improper Activities in the Labor and Management Field) during an investigation that Walter and I had asked for in order to clear the matter up once and for all. The first of these versions was on a mimeographed sheet passed out at the factory gates of the GM plants in Flint after my participation in the Battle of the Running Bulls. It ended with: "Carry on the fight for a Soviet America. Vic and Wal."

The minute I read that closing sentence I knew that it was a phony. I denounced it as such, and so did Walter. But beginning with its use by General Motors, which wanted to get rid of the Reuther troublemakers, the forgery was used by right-wing organizations and individuals for twenty years. It was almost certain that every time the UAW entered significant contract negotiations or called a major strike, an employer, or a manufacturers' association or its spokesman in Congress (such as Clair Hoffman of Michigan) would, as if on cue, distribute some variation of "Yours for a Soviet America."

Walter and I were not ashamed of the views we held when we were in the Soviet Union. Moreover, we were proud that on our return home we, together with hundreds of other dedicated unionists, had helped build one of the cleanest and most democratic unions in the world, free of both Marxism and gangsterism. Our record made it very clear that we had led the fight to prevent Communists or any other political group from dominating the UAW. Yet no matter how many times we stated publicly, often under oath, that we did not subscribe to the Communist philosophy, none of our denials made a dent in the ultraright wing, which was determined to squeeze every drop of political advantage out of that altered letter. Even trade unions, competing against the UAW in a National Labor Relations Board election, stooped to the same calumny; the Machinists' Union in California and the Southwest was one such union.

Upton Close and Gerald Winrod frequently reprinted the doctored text. Gerald L. K. Smith gave it its widest distribution, with the help of *Human Events,* Dan Smoot, the *American Mercury,* and *National Republic.* On at least twenty-seven occasions, spokesmen for the reactionary right quoted the "Reuther letter," not only to vilify Walter and me but, what was more serious, to try to weaken the UAW's position.

Clair Hoffman put two different versions in the Congressional Record. The first, in 1955, read: "And let no one tell you that we are not on the road to Socialism in the Soviet Union." This obviously did not serve his purpose, so in 1958 he substituted: "And let no one tell you we are not on the road to Socialism in the United States."

I wouldn't go so far as to advise young Americans traveling abroad not to write home and express their honest views, but I would caution them to use a typewriter wherever possible and make carbon copies. Quite naturally, the letter became a touchy matter for Walter, though his sense of humor never failed him, and we would all have a good laugh when Roy would say, in our intimate family circle, "I'm sure glad I never learned to write letters!"

Although I had publicly acknowledged that it was I who wrote from Gorky to the Bishops, there was never any doubt that whatever views I expressed were shared by Walter, or I would not have signed "Vic and Wal." I was never personally upset about the ridiculous distortion of my words for political smearing, but, then, I was not president of the UAW and did not bear the major responsibility for safeguarding it from attack. It was, however, very shocking to me to read, in early 1941, an interview that Walter had given to reporter Blair Moody (later to become a U.S. senator). The conversation had turned inevitably to the famous epistle, and Walter was reported to have said, "Victor wrote that letter in the flush of enthusiasm at seeing all those uneducated Russian peasants, who had never had anything, working in a fine factory." He then added, according to Moody, that he did not agree with the letter in the first place and still didn't. I was furious with Walter. This led to a confrontation in which Roy participated. Walter, insisting that Moody had misquoted him, apologized profusely. All in all, much good came out of the incident: it cleared the air and reinforced the bond between us, and helped Roy and me delineate our status as individuals in relation to Walter, who was both our brother and our superior in the UAW.

The ranting of the fanatics against the UAW and the Reuther brothers reached its peak in 1958, when the McClellan Committee was inquiring into unethical labor practices. The Teamsters' Union in particular made many headlines. Republican senators, such as Goldwater, Curtis, and Mundt, were determined to bring the UAW into the limelight, ostensibly to investigate the violence that had marked the Kohler strike in Wisconsin and the Perfect Circle strike in Indiana. Actually, they wanted to curb the union's political influence. The UAW was pressing for equitable tax laws, broad legislation on civil rights, improved Social Security and labor laws. If the conservative senators could label us Communists, they might be able to transfer the tag to some Democratic candidates. Many industrialists did their part by contributing to a slush fund for full-page ads in the *Wall Street Journal,* headlining once again — for lack of any other ammunition — the same old "Carry on the fight for a Soviet America."

It was at this point that the UAW requested to have its spokesmen appear before the McClellan Committee. For years, Walter had endured slander against himself and the union he headed, and he wanted to describe, on a nationwide telecast, the democratic nature of the UAW. We were granted a hearing, and UAW men testified freely, hiding nothing and eschewing the Fifth Amendment. The union proved invulnerable to any attack by the senators. But when Clair Hoffman asked to appear and do some questioning, it was a sure sign that the letter from Gorky was about to pop up once more, like a jack-in-the-box, to be exploited before the TV cameras.

We decided we had to exorcise that demon then or never. Our friend Hubert Humphrey agreed to write to the McClellan Committee to suggest some research into the letter smear: "Apparently, despite their long and distinguished anti-Communist records, the letter continues to be circulated in a number of different versions by hate groups and fanatics . . . . I would like to be in a position to answer inquiries and to help clear up the matter." Robert Kennedy, counsel to the committee, also used his influence to start an investigation of the forgeries, and put Carmine S. Bellino, formerly with the FBI, on the case.

It seems to have been Joseph Kamp (who spent six months in jail for contempt of Congress) who was more persistent than anyone in keeping the nonsense going. In 1937 he used the letter in his booklet entitled *Join the CIO — and Help Build a Soviet America.* This booklet was peddled again before the 1956 election. In the intervening nineteen years, he had frequently used the letter in one version or another, and in 1958 he accused Walter of having captured the Democratic Party in order to sovietize America. Then there was the *Saturday Evening Post* version, taken from the Congressional Record. There it was used as part of a general attack on the educational efforts of organized labor. A Committee of Constructive Conservatives used it in a pamphlet called *The Man Who Will Win in the*

1956 Elections, that is, Walter Reuther. Incidentally, the man who did take over the government in 1956, Dwight D. Eisenhower, stated publicly, in a campaign speech:

> Today in Europe, Irving Brown for the AFL and Victor Reuther for the CIO are working night and day with the European labor in the still free countries. They are explaining the difference between competition and class warfare, the difference that has made American trade unionism effective within the framework of industrial progress and the individual freedom of the workers.

The McClellan Committee tracked down the earliest published version of my letter. It had appeared in July 1934, when Walter and I were still in Russia, in a newspaper called the *Challenge,* the official organ of the Young People's Socialist League. It ended as I have quoted it at the beginning of this chapter: "Carry on the fight." The committee's researchers logically decided that the best way to determine the sources of the twenty-year slander was to subpoena the individual who had received the original handwritten letter.

Melvin Bishop had made a vicious attack on us at the 1946 UAW convention where Walter was elected president. He had been fired by Walter from his UAW-CIO job as soon as Walter found out, right after he became president, that Bishop had been using his union position to put pressure on the officials of the Briggs plant to grant the waste contract to the son-in-law of a notorious gangster. The McClellan Committee found out that "Bishop allegedly stated he would get even with Reuther if it took him all his life. He was a prime suspect in the shootings of Walter and Victor Reuther."

When asked by the McClellan Committee if he had the original letter, Bishop first said yes, it was locked in his vault, and he would not bring it out. The committee insisted, so he backtracked, saying he had not seen it since the thirties, when he had shown it to a number of friends, among them May Wolf, who, he said, had typed a copy of it in his garage and forwarded it to the *Challenge* in Chicago. May testified that she had not then learned to type and had neither seen the letter nor been in Bishop's garage. Bishop then mentioned a former teacher at Fordson High School, who, contradicting Bishop's recollection, gave a legal deposition that she had never received the letter, though she remembered having the Reuthers as students.

Closed in excutive session with the committee, Bishop then falsely swore that the phrase "for a Soviet America" was in the original. The editor of the *Challenge,* however, who had printed the letter without those four words, said under oath that he had received it as a handwritten document from Melvin Bishop and had printed it exactly as it was, deleting only some references to mutual friends. He swore that if the last four words had been there, he would have printed them. "Not only would it have been contrary to editorial practice but it would have been contrary to the spirit of the times to eliminate any reference or statement of a political nature, however extreme or exaggerated." He had earlier wired Robert Kennedy to the same effect: "If there was any such phrase . . . it would have been reproduced, and if not reproduced, it was never in the original."

Senators Mundt, Curtis, and Goldwater soon realized that their key witness was less than convincing. When Walter appeared before them to give testimony and answer questions, they never mentioned the letter, though they had been passing a copy of it among themselves all during the morning session.

The upshot was complete clearance by the committee. McClellan, a man noted for his conservatism, wrote to Humphrey:

> As a matter of precaution and to preclude anyone's charging the committee with not having looked into it, I placed Mr. Bishop under oath and took his testimony in executive session. He admitted he has not seen this letter for over twenty years, and his story concerning the disposition of it is completely contradicted by reliable information the committee has obtained.
>
> I think it is significant that, with the established unreliability of Mr. Bishop and the fact that the existence and text of the letter were so questionable, no member of the committee saw fit to ask Mr. Reuther any questions about it.

The expression of political differences is the very lifeblood of democracy, but I think we should revise our ground rules on character assassination, and confine our quarrels to disputing the merits of our respective positions. On the whole, Walter and I had little to complain about compared to the back-stabbing suffered by today's public figures, as revealed through testimony about Watergate. Even the official documents of a martyred President of the United States were recently in serious danger of being forged and distorted for political ends.

CHAPTER 18

War on Two Fronts

"500 Planes a Day"

By 1940, Western Europe had fallen to Hitler's blitzkrieg. The Luftwaffe was pounding Britain. Within the UAW there was uneasy peace under the compromise presidency of R. J. Thomas, a genial, tobacco-chewing rank-and-file Chrysler worker, unexpectedly thrust into leadership. Weak leadership, to be sure, but far sounder than that of George Addes who, though probably not himself a member of the Communist Party, was quite willing to have the party do all his political thinking — at a time when Communists all around the world, including the U.S., were at their most demagogic. In spite of the realization of what a Nazi victory would mean to Europe and the world, the die-hard American Communists began to oppose our entry into the Second World War as soon as Stalin signed the infamous pact with Hitler, betraying not only Poland but the spirit of the Russian revolution. Thousands did tear up their cards in disgust, but the hard-core Communists within the UAW, like Mortimer, John Anderson, Nat Ganley, Fred Williams, and others, hewed to the new Moscow line, denouncing Roosevelt as a warmonger, and serving notice on Britain that "the Yanks are not coming!"

To the Reuthers, despite our skepticism about the two major American parties, Roosevelt made a difference; we wanted to see him re-elected. He spoke to the issues, and he had moved the nation off dead center toward essential, long-needed reforms. His first term had made him the idol of American industrial workers. (Even that lifetime Socialist, Valentine Reuther, voted for FDR in 1940.) It was over this political issue that we had our first real skirmish inside the union since the dismissal of Homer Martin.

It happened at the 1940 UAW convention in St. Louis. The Executive Board put forth a resolution calling for the re-election of FDR against Wendell Willkie, whose record and political platform aroused no enthusiasm among working people. The Communists called the resolution, which I had a hand in drafting, a "Reuther plot," and when it hit the floor, Mortimer shouted that it was "a direct kick in the face to the greatest labor leader this country or any other nation has produced." He was referring, of course, to John L. Lewis, who had turned against Roosevelt because he had not been chosen as his running mate. The Communists in the CIO knew very well how to push Lewis into an increasingly isolationist stance; they tried constantly to use him as a smoke screen to hide their own allegiance to Stalin and the party line.

Nat Ganley charged that the resolution would shove the United States even closer to war. Walter was soon on his feet, holding aloft the 1939 convention proceedings:

> Brother chairman, I wish I had time to read through this book of proceedings of the last convention and review the beautiful resolutions that Brother Nat Ganley introduced praising Roosevelt, because those were the days of collective security and the People's Front. That is no more: there has been a deal between Stalin and Hitler and therefore the People's Front and collective security have been put in the ash can once and for all.

The auditorium resounded with cheers of approval for Walter, catcalls and whistles for those who tried to delay the vote further. Support for FDR passed by a vote of 550 to 30.

This became, at last, the turning point in the balance of power within the UAW. Only a handful opposed another resolution condemning "the brutal dictatorship and wars of aggression of the totalitarian governments of Germany, Italy, Russia, and Japan." I was part author of that resolution also, and was labeled Red baiter for calling the Soviet regime a dictatorship. Lewis Stark, a veteran labor reporter for the *New York Times* who had previously swallowed the Lovestone-Martin line about the Reuthers being captives of the Communist faction in the UAW, sent a dispatch to his paper that the convention "marked the first clear-cut defeat of the left-wing and Communist-supported group in the union on a question which linked Russia to the dictatorships."

Our firm stand against the Hitler-Stalin pact brought added

strength to the Reuther forces within the UAW, but only a cynic, unaware of our fundamental ideology, would conclude that we were being opportunistic. Walter and I had seen Hitler's terror firsthand and had retained close personal contact, through Paul Hagen and his anti-Nazi *Neu Beginnen* group, with friends inside Germany, and, through Haakon Lie of Norway, with many who had fled into exile. The Soviet occupation of Poland, the obliteration of democracy there, the arrest and execution of Polish union and political leaders Ehrlich and Alter — both of whom we had known in Paris in 1933 — all these personal concerns were involved in our decision, along with the sober realization that only the survival of Britain lay between us and the Nazis. We could not possibly stand by and watch Britain fall. Substantial material aid had to be moved there immediately, and this meant backing FDR and the lend-lease program. We therefore crisscrossed the country, campaigning for Roosevelt, and were violently attacked by Communists and Trotskyites in speeches and publications as "imperialist warmonger lackeys." But the vilification merely gained us supporters.

John L. Lewis was a serious problem. Millions of American workers had come to worship him for his aid in their fight against the gigantic corporations and were incredulous when they heard of his endorsement of Wendell Willkie. I remember the night his announcement came over the air. Walter and I were at a special joint council meeting of our West Side Local, and we saw many veterans of the sit-down strikes, tears streaming down their faces, leave the hall in anger and bewilderment. From the wall of the auditorium, a more than life-size portrait of John L. looked down at the stunned assembly.

We realized that Lewis's speech had to be answered lest large numbers of workers be too demoralized to go to the polls at all. The Executive Board called a conference of 700 UAW leaders from all over the nation, and invited FDR himself to come. He demurred, but he did invite R. J. Thomas, Walter, and Frankensteen to meet with him at Hunter College in New York, where he was to give a speech. He expressed his strong appreciation of their continued support, and his belief that such support would be significant during the months ahead.

Walter enjoyed describing the circumstances of this meeting. On their arrival, the three labor leaders, to their chagrin, were ushered by the Secret Service into a janitor's storage cubby. Soon, however, FDR was wheeled in and, while the assembled crowd waited, he asked to hear — and was delighted by — the details of how the UAW had adroitly managed to support Lewis on union matters and Roosevelt for political leadership. Still eager to hear more, the President ordered dinner for his labor friends and the discussion continued in the janitor's cubby.

After this meeting, Walter took to the air in a thirteen-city hookup to answer Lewis specifically: "The personal spite and hatred of one man will not switch labor's votes from Roosevelt . . . The issue is wholly and simply: Roosevelt or reaction. American labor will take Roosevelt."

John L. Lewis was never quite the same after FDR's 1944 victory. His ego had sustained a beating, and his stature as a great and wise leader of American workers was considerably diminished. Actually his stand was not really out of character, because Lewis had been a practicing Republican throughout much of his adult life. It was more out of character for him to have supported Roosevelt so enthusiastically in the second campaign. The great personal appeal that John L. had for industrial workers did not stem from any example of democratic methods he offered. It was, rather, his stubborn courage in standing up against powerful special interests and in helping the unions organize.

Within days after the election, the CIO held its national convention in Atlantic City. Lewis had threatened that if his advice to support Willkie were disregarded by the membership, he would step down from the CIO presidency. He kept that pledge and returned very much a loser to his fortress, the United Mine Workers. After that, he retreated more and more into isolationism. In his place, a soft-spoken, gentle, Scottish coal miner, Philip Murray, was elected head of the CIO and he made it his primary goal to restore internal unity in spite of the rifts developing over foreign policy.

The hard-core Communists, who still had a good deal of influence in the UAW-CIO, especially on the Executive Board, remained as isolationist as Lewis, simply because the Stalin-Hitler pact was still in effect. When Hitler attacked Russia, they made a complete about-face. But that was not until June 21, 1941; in the meantime, they set about obstructing both UAW unity and the war effort by promoting a series of wildcat strikes that had no justification in terms of eco-

nomic demands or workers' rights. In Allis Chalmers, where tur-
bines were being made for vitally needed lend-lease destroyers, they
pulled off a seventy-six-day strike. The strike at the North American Aviation plant on the West Coast was even more blatantly ob-
structionist: the workers had had assurances from both the National
UAW and the National Mediation Service that their wage demands
would be met. Yet Wyndham Mortimer, Lewis H. Michener, Jr.
(regional UAW director), and Elmer Freitag (president of the Los
Angeles local union) took matters into their own hands and called a
strike, bringing to a halt $300 million worth of contracts, about one–
fifth of the total defense aircraft output. FDR had to send out
twenty-five hundred troops to seize the plant.

The flip-flop of the party at the end of June, when Hitler broke
his pact with Stalin and marched into Russia, had its ludicrous side.
The Detroit Plymouth Local 51, then under Communist influence,
had adopted, earlier that month, a resolution denouncing the war
effort. But before the Wayne County Council had time to meet and
act upon this resolution, the events of late June came along, and the
Plymouth Local hurriedly adopted another resolution, denouncing
the Nazis and reversing by a 180-degree angle its previous position
with regard to the U.S. defense effort. The two resolutions came up
before the Wayne County Council at the same time, and I remember
that those of us who had been supporting Roosevelt all along advocated that both resolutions be adopted, in an attempt to reveal the
asininity of the Communists within the union. For with them, it was
always: "Yours not to reason why. Just follow the Moscow line!" It
was a good lesson for the auto workers — one they did not forget.

Walter, meanwhile, had been asked by the Executive Board to
take over the directorship of the UAW General Motors Department,
the largest single unit within the union, representing auto workers in
almost every section of the U.S and in Canada. A new contract was
up for negotiation in the spring of 1941, and Walter, focusing the
workers' attention on the expansion of GM production and profits,
mobilized 165,000 GM employees for strike action against car production if it became necessary. All of us were aware that the corporation held defense contracts in the amount of $600 million. We
expected that enormous pressure would be brought to bear to prevent the union's exercise of its right to strike. It took three separate
strike deadlines before the corporation agreed to a 10-percent-an-

hour increase. And though the workers were forced to give up their demand for a union shop, they won an overall package that contained one of the largest increases in the history of the auto industry. Walter's victory was all the more remarkable in that he achieved it without a single strike, a great relief to him, since he did not relish the prospect of tangling with FDR on the defense production issue.

Months before Hitler's armies marched eastward into Poland, Walter and I had had a conversation with Ben Blackwood, a trusted aide in the General Motors Department and himself a skilled toolmaker, about Roosevelt's call for aid to Britain and the kind of help America was best equipped to give. Because of the unremitting Luftwaffe offensive, it was obvious that England needed planes, not only guns and tanks, for her defense. As toolmakers we knew it would be many years before American industries turning out civilian goods could be tooled to produce weapons in any quantity. But, as Walter said, we should not romanticize about the nature of the airplane, though the aircraft industry had for so long made a fetish of the highly specialized expertise involved. A plane was made of steel and aluminum, like other vehicles, and its component parts could be manufactured by essentially the same kind of machines and machine tools that stamp or turn out the parts of an automobile. We had seen the conversion of peacetime tools — and helped make it — in the Gorky plant, when Russia was arming itself against the inevitable German invasion.

Of course, the automobile manufacturers, asked to take on enormous defense contracts, assumed that they would gradually close down their automobile plants, keeping them on a standby basis, while the government proceeded to build and put at their disposal spanking new factories, equipped with millions of dollars' worth of machine tools, most of which would be duplications of the tools sitting idle, or about to sit idle, in the automobile plants as we moved into an all-out war effort.

A careful survey taken by Ben Blackwood and me in GM plants all over the country corroborated Walter's hypothesis and became the basis of his proposal for a "500 planes a day" program, to be undertaken by the automotive industry. He had informal meetings with R. J. Thomas and Philip Murray about his plan. They were both enthusiastic, and Murray submitted it to President Roosevelt on December 20, 1940, under the title "A Program for Utilization of the

Automobile Industry for Mass Production of Defense Planes," by
Walter P. Reuther. It is still so listed in the Hyde Park archives.
When he presented it, Murray said:

> Believing again that labor is entitled to play an important part in our
> nation's well-being, some three months ago I asked Mr. Walter Reuther,
> in association with a group of expert mechanics and tool and die makers
> who are members of the Automobile Workers' Union to make an ex-
> haustive study of the ability of the automobile industry to produce air-
> planes. I had in mind the use of existing facilities plus the preparation
> of new dies and tools to produce airplanes with a minimum of delay.
> Mr. Reuther and his associates have now submitted to me such a pro-
> gram, which I have enclosed. I believe this will meet the requirements
> of our government in manufacturing airplanes in sufficient quantities.

Roosevelt responded with interest, and sent a memo to Knudsen,
codirector with Sidney Hillman of the Office of Production Management: "I do not know whether you have seen all of this. It is well
worth our while, I think, to give a good deal of attention to his program." Jerome Frank, then president of the Securities and Exchange Commission, sent a note to the President suggesting that a
personal interview be arranged for Walter to explain his proposal,
and that the OPM might appoint a public committee to hold open
hearings on the question. FDR sent this along to Knudsen, with a
personal note, "Speak to me about." (All these notes are in the
Hyde Park Archives.)

William Knudsen, though deeply devoted to FDR and to the defense effort, must nevertheless have felt put out that Walter
Reuther, the "red-headed upstart" who had so often clashed with
him across the General Motors bargaining table, should presume to
tell the nation what the automobile industry could do about mass
tooling for aircraft production. Yet an editorial in Knudsen's hometown newspaper, the Detroit *News,* stated, on January 6, 1941, that
"no industrial leader has paralleled Reuther's initiative and ingenuity in presenting such a plan for consideration."

There was a meeting of top officials of the OPM, the Air Force
and the Navy, Knudsen, Hillman, R. J. Thomas, and Walter. A
courtesy call was paid on the President after the discussion, and as
the men walked in, Roosevelt warmly greeted Walter with, "Oh,
here's my young engineer." Burly R. J. Thomas, his ever-present
wad of tobacco tucked in one cheek, was annoyed by the publicity

Walter was getting. He promptly blurted out, "Hell, he's not an engineer; he's only a toolmaker."

Walter had made a public appeal on the radio the week before. It was a long speech, and an emotional one. Some of it is well worth remembering:

In London they are huddled in the subways praying for aid from America. In America we are huddled over blueprints praying that Hitler will be obliging enough to postpone an all-out attack on England for another two years until new plants begin to turn out engines and aircraft.

Packard has just finished pouring the concrete for its new engine factory and Ford may soon be ready to begin digging ditches in which to sink the foundations for his. Not until the fall of nineteen forty-two, almost two years hence, will these bright, shiny new factories actually begin to turn out the engines. This is snail's pace production in the age of lightning war . . .

We believe that without disturbing present aircraft plant production schedules we can supplement them by turning out five hundred planes a day of a single standard fighting model by the use of idle automotive capacity. We believe that this can be done after six months of preparation as compared to the eighteen months or two years required to get new plane and engine factories into production . . .

Fortunately, despite the headlines which tell us of unfillable orders and labor shortages, we have a huge reservoir of unused machinery, unused plants, unused skill, and unused labor to fall back upon . . . The tool and die workers . . . are also partially idle . . .

The plane, from certain points of view, is only an automobile with wings. Our greatest need is for plane engines . . . The plane engine is the more delicate and compact combustion engine but it is still a combustion engine, containing the same parts . . .

There stand idle in the Cleveland Fisher Body plant toggle presses huge enough to hold and operate a draw or flange die weighing seventy to eighty tons. Such a machine can stamp out airplane parts as well as automobile parts . . . It would take years to install in new aircraft plants the same type of presses which now stand idle fifty percent of the time . . .

Equipment at the Chevrolet Drop Flange plant in Detroit operates at sixty percent of capacity even at this time, which is a peak period for the automobile industry. The machines and hammers in this plant could produce all the drop forgings required for five hundred airplanes a day and still supply the Chevrolet Company with sufficient forgings for one million cars during the coming year. Labor asks: Why not use this equipment instead of duplicating it? . . .

Labor's plan springs from the pooled experience and knowledge of skilled workers in all the automotive plants, the same skilled workers who are called upon year by year in the industry to produce new machine marvels. Each manufacturer has the benefit of his skilled workers. We of the United Automobile Workers, CIO, have the benefit of the skilled manpower in all the automotive plants, not just in one of them.

Labor asks only in return that its hard-won rights be preserved . . . only that it be allowed to contribute its own creative experience and knowledge and that it be given a voice in the education of its program . . .

No question of policy needs to be settled. The President has laid down the policy. We must have more planes . . .

Quantity production was achieved in the Reich and is being achieved in England by the methods labor now proposes to apply to the automotive industry.

The difference and our opportunity is that we have in the automotive industry the greatest mass-production machine the world has ever seen. Treated as one great production unit, it can in half a year's time turn out planes in unheard-of numbers and swamp the Luftwaffe. This is labor's answer to Hitler aggression, American labor's reply to the cries of its enslaved brothers under the Nazi yoke in Europe.

England's battles, it used to be said, were won on the playing fields of Eton. America's can be won on the assembly lines of Detroit.

The swollen wartime bureaucracy, with its myriads of dollar-a-year men jammed into Washington, consigned many proposals to limbo, Walter's among them. It was not, of course, attractive to the automobile manufacturers, but it was both imaginative and timely, and was finally given serious consideration by the War Department. It stirred up debate in the press and even inspired Charles E. Wilson, Knudsen's successor as president of General Motors, to challenge Walter to a face-to-face verbal duel in Detroit. The debate was inconclusive and served only to give the proposal more publicity. Alsop and Kintner, in their New York *Herald Tribune* column, did not mince words on some of the personal aspects of the matter:

Certain officials of the Defense Commission are really downright silly. These men, one or two of whom are unhappily to be found in Knudsen's immediate entourage, have carried all the domestic conflicts of the past over into their defense work. Again because the plan came from Reuther, they took it as a personal insult. They had hardly had time to read it through before they were busily disseminating stories that it was ridiculously impractical and dead wrong . . . Fortunately, Undersecretary of War, Robert Patterson, and his new special assistant in charge of aircraft production, Robert Lovett, were giving very serious attention to the Reuther proposal.

No one was more outspoken against Walter's plan than the chairman of General Motors, Alfred P. Sloan, who declared categorically on November 20, 1940, that automobile plants were not adaptable to the manufacture of any other products. "Only about ten or fifteen percent of the machinery and equipment in an automobile factory can be utilized for the production of special defense material." He was, in effect, saying: Leave our plants alone on a standby basis, and build new plants for aircraft and tanks and gun carriages; tool them completely for that sort of specialized work though it may take two years to get them into real production.

The tragedy of this two-year delay was compounded by the insanity of saddling American taxpayers with the enormous cost of building new plants, which the corporations would later argue were "special purpose defense plants unsuited for civilian production" and ask that they be turned over to them, for a token fee, to be converted to their own purposes. The auto industry seemed ready to sacrifice the very life of the nation to its profit interests.

Many American workers paid dearly for this intransigence, which, of course, enriched the owners of industry. Corporate profits and the incomes of auto, steel, and other executives went up considerably during 1941. Eugene Grace of Bethlehem Steel, for instance, enjoyed a salary increase that year, boosting his remuneration from $478,000 in 1940 to $537,000 in 1941. Even the small Willys Overland Corporation provided for its president a 71 percent salary increase. Tom Girdler of Republic Steel had his salary raised by 56 percent, bringing it up to $275,000. When these men advocated business as usual, they knew what they were defending — and it wasn't the nation's survival.

Our UAW survey had indicated that at least 50 percent of auto-producing machinery was suitable for defense production. The refusal of General Motors to put at the disposal of the defense effort even its idle machine tools meant that in the urgent first six months of 1941, a crucial period, GM, out of a total production of $1,350,000,000 worth of goods, delivered only $131,000,000 worth of defense products.

Most American industrialists were trying at that point to make money from civilian *and* military sales. Their continued production of civilian cars and other consumer goods brought them huge profits, to which they intended to add the lucrative cost-plus defense contracts. With all their patriotic protestations and "victory councils," they had, in fact, to be shoved, against their will, into a maximum defense effort.

The final assessment of the merits of the Reuther plan came much later. It could be found in the reports of the auto executives themselves when, at the war's end, they boasted, as did K. T. Keller, Chrysler's head, that 89 percent of their machine tools had been converted to war production and could now be easily reconverted into making civilian cars. *Fortune* magazine gave Walter his due: "Reuther was on the right track compared with many industrialists who sat back and hugged profits . . . The red-headed leader exhibited atomic spirit of action. He never let up." Fully a year before the official declaration of war, the UAW created a special task force, the Defense Employment Division, on which I served as chief administrative officer. The purpose was to facilitate the conversion to defense production, involving modifications in our collective agreements to make possible the orderly transfer of workers with the full protection of their accumulated seniority rights. It was also expected to encourage workers to upgrade themselves by performing such new skills as the defense effort required. In addition, the division was determined to remove any racial or sex discrimination in hiring that might inhibit the rapid expansion of the labor force. Another of its functions was to act as a clearinghouse through which the UAW was represented before the many defense agencies. We dealt with the Selective Service Agency, for instance, with regard to the deferment from military service of those whose skills were urgently needed in defense work, and the obtaining of employment rights for certain aliens whose abilities made them invaluable in fulfilling sensitive defense contracts.

Labor was of course well represented in the OPM through the wisdom of Roosevelt, who had made Hillman, one of the top CIO leaders, codirector with Knudsen. Hillman was totally committed to the defense effort. I remember many occasions when Walter and I would journey to Washington to meet with him late at night. Exhausted by the enormous burdens he carried every day, he would still sit and talk with us in the quiet of his bedroom about what could be done to speed the tempo of production. Yet he was hardly a match for Knudsen and the natural allies the latter had in the armed services; it was a rare general or admiral who was not thinking beyond the war to the prospect of a cushy job in one of the large corporations after he retired. The result was that Knudsen's judgments too often prevailed. For trade union spokesmen like Walter and me it was strange to have to travel to the capital to urge our government to curtail the production of civilian cars, knowing full well that this would lead to large-scale unemployment of our own union members.

Hillman was, however, able to convince Knudsen to join with him in creating an Advisory Board within the OPM, made up of representatives of the major auto, steel, electrical firms, and spokesmen for the workers from the AFL and CIO. Walter was a full member of that board and I was his deputy. Among those on industry's side was Conrad Cooper of the Wheeling Steel Corporation in West Virginia, who happened to be the immediate supervisor of our brother Ted. There were many open clashes between Cooper and us, and Ted told us that whenever Cooper returned to Wheeling from Washington and was particularly uncivil to him, he knew Cooper had been having a rough time at the OPM. Actually, Conrad Cooper was one of the more constructive representatives from industry, and played a useful role in helping us develop the Six-Point OPM Labor Transfer Agreement to facilitate the orderly movement of workers into defense work. This agreement later became basic policy, and was applied to industry in general.

Finally, in December 1941, there was a decree to cut back by 51.5 percent the passenger car production of the "big three" auto producers, and the quotas of the smaller firms like Studebaker, Hudson, and Nash by 15.3 percent. A month before, I had challenged automobile executives to concentrate on fewer models in order to eliminate waste of materials and machinery. When the cutback was made an official order, serious pockets of unemployment appeared, as we had anticipated, lasting for six to eight months, and this at a time when the nation was calling for the labor of every person in a combined defense effort.

Within hours after the Japanese air attack on Pearl Harbor and before declaration of war by Germany against the U.S., I reported to the press:

The President's appeal for increase of production seven days a week in defense industries has received the unanimous support of the UAW-CIO . . . This will not only speed defense production, but will also provide immediate defense employment for additional thousands of workers displaced by auto curtailment and whose skilled labor would otherwise be unused.

Needless to say, the automobile industry went on dragging its feet and it was urged that the cut-off date for passenger cars should be extended to the middle of February.

The CIO and the UAW began to carry their case to the public by writing an open letter to the OPM:

> Half of the nation's auto plants are today closed down. Virtually all of them will be down by the end of January. Blacked out not by Hitler and Japan. Approximately 25,000 automobile workers, men trained in precision, mass-production methods, and highly skilled tool and die makers are now idle. Fully 400,000 will be idle by the end of January. The nation has lost two million man days every week in war production . . . Only a few plants are turning out the vital materials of war . . .
>
> The program drafted by Walter P. Reuther and other members of the CIO-UAW was referred to you for study and recommendation. You did nothing about it. Similar plans for increasing production of steel, aluminum, copper and other materials vital to the war program were proposed. You did nothing about them. Labor is ready and determined to do its part . . . willing to accept the bitter necessities of a righteous war. Labor had the right to expect industry to do its part.

The formal declaration of war had led to the reorganization of the OPM into the War Production Board under Donald M. Nelson. As one of his first acts, Nelson announced that by January 31, 1942, all production of passenger cars had to end. About 350,000 workers were thereby put on the unemployment list in Michigan alone. General Motors' estimates had set the time needed to convert from passenger car to war production at from ten months to one year. The adoption of the essential elements of Walter's plan for 500 planes a day would have reduced that time to a matter of a few months.

There was a widespread fear among American workers that war profiteers would use the emergency as an excuse to undermine labor's hard-won collective bargaining system. Fortunately, FDR had an uncanny sensitivity to the changing moods of his people, and had early recognized that a program of equality of sacrifice was essential, and that there must be a limitation set on corporate profits and a greater involvement of labor in the councils of war. There were those who brought this message strongly to him, including Robert Patterson in the War Department, who became one of Walter's close friends and gave encouragement to both him and me during those frustrating early years of the war. Others were Harold Ickes and his bright, able deputy, Abe Fortas, later to become a Supreme Court Justice, and Felix Frankfurter, already a Justice, as well as Gardner "Pat" Jackson, an early supporter of the New Deal and a valiant journalist, who almost single-handedly (despite the jury's verdict) proved the innocence of Sacco and Vanzetti, depleting his family fortune in their behalf. Pat became an intimate friend and shared our feeling that labor should play a more important part in shaping wartime policies. Eleanor Roosevelt took to Walter's ideas and prodded FDR, who incorporated the concept of victory through "equality of sacrifice" in a fireside chat delivered early in 1942, and advocated a Labor Production Division of the War Production Board. He also proposed a $25,000 limit on personal income. Moved by the same concern, Philip Murray advanced his own excellent program for the forming of industry councils in the basic mass-production industries, which would have given both labor and consumers a voice in policy-making and could have overcome the resentment and alienation felt by those who were doing most of the sacrificing.

There is every reason to believe that President Roosevelt was serious about giving the trade union movement an important role in advancing the war effort. In April of 1942, he summoned CIO and AFL officials to a meeting to discuss the proposed Labor Production Division. At that meeting, as reported in the Detroit *Free Press* of April 30, 1942, he told them he thought Walter was the "logical man for the War Production Board Labor Production post." What happened to FDR's suggestion was revealed by Drew Pearson in his "Merry-Go-Round" column:

> For months the AFL and CIO have been loudly demanding more labor participation in the war machinery. The Labor Production Division is of the utmost importance to labor. But when it came to proposing a chief of this key labor agency, the laborites did not offer the name of a labor man. Because of personal jealousies and petty personal politics, they passed over such outstanding production experts as Robert Watt, AFL head of the International Labor Office, Clinton Golden, brainy head of the CIO Steel Workers, or Walter Reuther, dynamic young

director of the General Motors Department of the UAW. Instead, the
politics-playing labor moguls got together on Lund, a lawyer with very
limited industrial experience and no knowledge at all of the War Production program. Around the White House it is no secret that the
President is getting awfully fed up with this kind of labor "statesmanship."

Sad and true as this was, there were other kinds of "moguls" making
sure that labor was kept in its subordinate place.

Meanwhile in Great Britain, where the bombs were falling on London and other cities, Churchill appealed for the support of all seg-
ments of the population and invited many key trade union and
Labor Party figures to occupy important policy posts in virtually
every single significant wartime agency, involving not only production but price control, rationing, transportation, fuels, and, of
course, the home defense and security. There can be no doubt that
Britain's chances of survival were enormously enhanced by the roles
offered to labor and the rigid adherence to the rule of equality of
sacrifice. British labor performed so gallantly and effectively during
the war that at the war's end the British people felt their future
would be more secure in the hands of a Labor government. I suspect that employers and other conservative forces in the U.S. denied
labor any extensive leadership roles in wartime production precisely
because they were certain that labor would expect to continue such
leadership roles in postwar America. And why not?

On the Home Front

We were representatives of labor; our support of the war effort
did not mean that we condoned a moratorium on economic justice
and workers' rights. On the contrary, we believed that freedom and
equity must be nurtured all the more carefully at home while we
were fighting to restore them on foreign soil.

There were four areas that labor had to defend vigorously so that
it might not lose ground: 1) maintenance of the forty-hour week,
eight-hour day, and overtime pay; 2) abolition of piecework; 3) the
end of racial discrimination; 4) the assurance of decent housing for
workers.

The first was one of labor's most treasured gains. The payment of overtime had never been a deterrent to increased output, and certainly the hour-wage factor was not what was keeping industry from going all-out for war production. In January 1943, Walter submitted to the War Manpower Commission a four-point program requiring all war plants to provide full employment of forty hours a week for sixty days, after which the work week should be lengthened to forty-eight hours, with payment for the overtime. Two other points were the immediate release to defense plants, with complete seniority protection, of all employees who could not find full employment in their home factories; and the guarantee by the government of forty hours of work for those employees who, through no fault of their own, were forced to work fewer hours. The fourth was an industrywide master plan for ensuring equal pay for equal work in all defense plants.

The proposal was particularly urgent because many manufacturers were holding on to their employees who worked only part-time by threatening that those who left would lose their accumulated seniority rights. Meantime, younger workers with less seniority were snapping up the full-time defense jobs, sometimes receiving considerable overtime pay. This was an injustice as well as a waste of skilled, experienced workers.

We advocated a swing shift allowing for continuous operation of the machines — hardly an innovation in the auto industry. Ever since unionization, there had been three shifts, with overtime pay for Saturdays, Sundays, and holidays, for work in excess of eight hours a day and forty hours a week. Now suddenly a small band of Communists within the UAW and other unions was preparing to call on American workers to sacrifice their collective bargaining gains and go back to working overtime for no extra pay.

The failure of that proposition did not stop these men from launching, in the fall of 1943, a campaign for the restoration of piecework, or incentive wages, in the auto industry, with all that meant in terms of the vicious speed-up system we had worked so hard to abolish. There was no more vital issue in the fight for unionism, or one that raised deeper concern among auto workers. Yet on September 5, 1943, Earl Browder, in a double-page editorial in the *Daily Worker,* advocated a return to the "system of incentive wage rates under the control of collective bargaining machinery,

backed up by a strong trade union movement." In support of his
idea, he pointed out that Philip Murray, president of the CIO and of
the Steel Workers' union, had taken the initiative by pushing
through incentive wages in the steel plants. The truth was that
piecework in that industry had never really been eliminated to the
extent that it had in the auto plants. After presuming to tempt wage
earners by reminding them that the War Labor Board had approved
all pay increases that had come before it on the basis of incentive
pay, he zoomed in on his target:

> The United Auto Workers' Union, however, has been restrained from
> adopting the incentive wage policy by opposition led and organized by
> Walter Reuther and his brother Victor. In this opposition Walter
> Reuther has been vigorously supported by the *New Leader,* organ of
> Dubinsky's Social Democratic Federation, although Dubinsky's own
> union, the Ladies' Garment Workers, has always worked under the in-
> centive wage scheme.

In obvious reference to our support of the legitimate demands of
the coal miners led by John L. Lewis, Browder attacked us as op-
posers of the war effort,

> about which Walter Reuther keeps silent but of which his brother
> openly speaks . . . Reuther is not an ordinary fool. He is young, ener-
> getic, aggressive, capable, clever and ambitious . . . Unlike his brother
> Victor, who has been openly against the war throughout, Walter has
> shown an ability to support the war with great energy when that also
> serves the purpose of his ambition.

Those were strange charges coming from a man who not too long
before, when we were pushing for FDR's defense program, had
called the President a warmonger. The unions that were Communist-controlled echoed his sentiments in their local newspapers.

Both Richard Frankensteen and George Addes spearheaded a
fight to reintroduce incentive systems into the auto industry, and in
spite of the opposition of R. J. Thomas, Walter, and Richard Leonard, the motion was approved. The issue continued to divide the
leadership of the UAW, but the rank-and-file workers remained
firm in their opposition to the punishing piecework system. Walter
refused to be intimidated:

> We care not how the corporation may dress up the piecework in sheep's
> clothing nor how many others it may confuse by this tactic. The GM

workers will have nothing to do with piecework, and if the GM Corporation is genuinely interested in increasing war production, let it set up bona fide labor-management committees in its plants . . . Piecework will not increase production. It will cause dislocation of schedules. It will lead to layoffs and unemployment. It will pit worker against worker in a speed-up contest which will lead to chaos, rate cutting and destruction of labor morale.

The fact that Walter held his ground, not only against General Motors but against a majority of the UAW Executive Board, considerably enhanced his standing among the rank and file. Their own sentiments ran so high that the incentive pay resolution was defeated by a two-thirds majority vote at the 1943 UAW convention. There was also a drive there to run Richard T. Leonard against the Communists' spokesman, George Addes. Leonard failed by only 71 votes. That year Walter defeated Frankensteen by 345 votes in the race for the first of the two vice-presidencies.

Fortunately, in spite of the political infighting that erupted from time to time, the entire UAW leadership shared the same firm policy with regard to nondiscrimination in employment, and equal rights for all to advance into jobs demanding higher skills. As defense plants expanded production, new opportunities opened up for both non-whites and women. It took effort and persistence to see to it that the enormous pool of available and qualified labor would for the first time be properly utilized. The UAW leadership pressed hard for an end to all discrimination at the hiring gate. Since the work force in Detroit and many other Michigan cities included a high percentage of southern whites, the racial barriers were not easy to break down. We had some difficulty in getting our own workers to understand that abolishing the color bar was a matter of justice. I remember that twenty-four hundred Packard workers went on strike when three black girls were hired, after consultation with the UAW, the War Production Board, and the War Manpower Commission. Our International officers stood firm, and the strike was ended with those three girls still on the job and many other blacks on the employment muster.

One might have expected that at Ford, where more blacks had always been employed than in any other Detroit plant, there would have been less resistance, and the company would have increased its non-white work force of its own volition. Instead, Ford resisted

upping its black quota, and, though its total employment rolls had
increased by around thirty-two thousand, fewer than one hundred
additional blacks had been taken on. The first brush with Ford
came in January 1942 over the hiring practices at the new Willow
Run bomber plant on the outskirts of Detroit. The UAW concluded
a wage agreement, and in the course of the talks asked the company
to see to it that at least 7 percent of the women employed in the new
plant were black. No females had as yet been hired. Ford pointed
out that all women at the bomber plant had to meet certain specifications of height, weight, manual dexterity, and education; and union
representatives responded that of course black employees should
meet the same requirements as whites. The company then agreed
to hire some, but refused to designate a percentage; shortly after, its
representatives told the union it was inadvisable to hire any black
women. After further talks, it tried to get the union to let it put the
black women in a separate department, away from all whites, and to
agree that it hire fewer than previously agreed upon. These proposals were rejected. On April 14, Ford said it feared that the white
women already employed would refuse to work with blacks. The
union held two meetings with the white women employees and
found that they had no objection to working with blacks. Ford management still did not budge, saying it already had more employees
than it needed at the bomber plant. The following week it took on
about 360 additional men and 130 more women, all white.

We knew there was strong sentiment building in the Detroit community in opposition to this example of Ford's stubbornness. We
decided to air the matter in public and encouraged a group of distinguished citizens to intercede with Harry Bennett, still the head of
the personnel department. The meeting was attended by professors, doctors, ministers, and was recorded verbatim by Miss Zaioa
Woodford. Her minutes, dated June 1, 1942, are in the Wayne
State University Archives.

Harry Bennett conceded that there were no black but about
1100 white women in the bomber plant. No reason, he said, why this
committee or any other should come to the Ford Company and tell
them what to do . . . Mr. Ford had been very generous to the colored
people. He couldn't see any reason why the Ford Motor Company
should be made a guinea pig of. Furthermore, this wasn't a white
problem but a colored problem, for they were perfectly capable of tak-

ing care of themselves and when white people took to injecting themselves into the Negro problem, they were simply causing race hatred.

Bennett went on that he did not need any executive order and didn't see why this administration . . . should continue to cause Henry Ford trouble. The unions were a bunch of cutthroats and liars, and now they had the payroll locked up and he couldn't get into it. He was going to cancel all their agreements and not believe anything they said. There were a few Communists causing all this difficulty and they would not hire any colored men sent by those Communists. . . . And what's more, they were going to transfer all those women from the bomber plant to the Ford plant as the men left there, for the women were not working out; they were causing such scandal there. There was one instance, Bennett said, where a grandfather working next to a 20-year old girl did not go home all night. Seemed he attempted to drive her home and did not get home himself. That was one thing the Ford Motor Company was not going to stand for. Mr. Ford was old-fashioned. He, Mr. Bennett, had four daughters and he wouldn't let them work out there. Anyway, there were a lot of men unemployed and they should be taken on instead. The women should "go home and stay home."

So it went, every step of the way. There was an enormous pool of qualified women workers, both black and white, already living in the metropolitan area, who could fill the defense jobs. There would be no need to aggravate the housing shortage by drawing in more families from the farms and the South. Fortunately there were those in the armed services who stood by us. In the War Manpower Commission, Robert Weaver, chief of the Negro War Manpower Service, was firm on this issue, along with Walter White and national leaders of the NAACP. In Detroit we were helped frequently by Gloster Current, local NAACP representative, and Walter Hardin, one of the early black members of the UAW.

The fourth sore point was housing. It is incredible how insensitive our society is to the industrial workers' basic need for decent housing and transportation. The situation was worst, of course, in the black ghettos of Detroit. When the huge Willow Run bomber plant was built in rural Ypsilanti, outside Detroit, little or no thought had been given to housing the work force, which eventually grew to fifty thousand persons.

Our concern about this problem was shared by two magnificent men, John Edelman, long associated with the textile workers and at that time employed by the War Production Board, and the distinguished architect Oskar Stonorov. Walter and I were proud of our

friendship with them. Through our many meetings and letters, the
four of us devised the plan for the development of a "bomber city"
for ten thousand Willow Run defense workers. Walter and Richard
T. Leonard, director of the UAW Ford division that included Willow
Run, presented the proposal to the Housing Authority in Washington in December of 1941. As one of his last acts as associate director
of the OPM, Sidney Hillman disclosed the fact that he had talked
with President Roosevelt about the idea and that FDR had told him
such a Defense City would be "a city of homes well planned and
designed, and owned by defense workers, as a symbol of the
America we are defending and the America we are rebuilding for
the future."

A large housing project was finally built, though more flimsy in
construction than we had hoped for.

John Edelman continued through the years to. work for good,
nondiscriminatory housing. Oskar Stonorov was a close friend for
twenty-eight years. We worked together on many plans to improve
the quality of life of workers both in this country and abroad. The
last act of cooperation between Walter and Oskar was the development and fulfillment of one of Walter's dreams — a Family Education Center in the beautiful woods of northern Michigan. It was on
a flight to the site of that construction that both Stonorov and Walter
were killed in a plane crash.

There was one management-labor committee on which I served
that made a contribution to the desegregation of Detroit housing:
the Detroit Victory Council, a tripartite body composed of men from
industry, labor, and the general public. It was organized by George
Romney, then my counterpart on the industry side. (He was executive head of the Automotive Council for War Production.) Our purpose was to mobilize support for essential wartime measures. One
of the trouble areas was housing. With the help of Carlton Sharp, a
regional director for the Public Housing Agency, Romney and I
were able to initiate some successful desegregation policies.

Romney moved on to become Governor of the state, head of the
American Motors Corporation, and secretary of the Department of Housing and Urban Development. While I did not always
agree with him, our clashes were usually confined to collective
bargaining issues. In the broader area of public policy, we enjoyed
mutual respect and cooperation. Romney, a devout Mormon, often

pontificated, not always with data to back his pronouncements, on social issues; and he was on even less firm ground when dealing with basic economic questions. When he was head of American Motors, he once launched a campaign against "monopoly trade unionism" with the same kind of fervor his company used in condemning the "huge gas-guzzling monsters" produced by the big three auto companies. I remember hearing him complain, during a Senate hearing, about the immorality of unions in demanding of the small firms like American Motors the same wage scale they asked of the larger companies. When the noon break came, I took Romney's arm and led him out to the corridor!

"George," I said, "I would not have raised this question if you had not used the term 'immorality.' Tell me, when you order a ton of steel, to produce your cars, from U.S. Steel, does U.S. Steel say, 'Now Mr. Romney, you represent a small automobile firm. You obviously can't afford to pay the same price for a ton of steel as General Motors pays, so we will give you the ton of steel at a discount? No, because what happens is just the opposite. General Motors, because of its bigness, places a larger order with the steel companies and gets steel at a more favorable price than you can with your small order. Since you apparently don't consider this practice within the free market economy 'immoral,' why then do you ask an American worker to sell his labor in the marketplace under circumstances less favorable to him than those that govern the sale of a cold ton of steel?"

When I finished, George looked at me with an expression of confusion and bewilderment.

"You know, I never thought of it that way before," he said.

Early in the war, Roy left Detroit for Washington to help set up the War Production Board's Labor Production Division, which had been suggested by FDR in April 1942. It was created essentially to enlist the support of the unions in handling relations with employers with a minimum of difficulty. Even more important, it was to get labor involved in a variety of related government activities, such as price control, rationing, car pool arrangements, sale of war bonds, and so forth. When the U.S. formally declared war, all three of us, of course, felt we should enlist. Though we knew we were performing necessary work on the production front, it was impossible for us, when we heard of the deaths, in battle, of many friends, not to feel conscience-stricken. Also, our political enemies both inside and out-side the union made none too subtle jibes at the Reuther brothers for allegedly avoiding service in the armed forces.

Roy, who was still single, finally made the War Production Board, against its will, waive its request for his deferment and let him be in-ducted into the Army. He was sent to the Southwest for boot train-ing. His health had never been good — he had been plagued for years with a circulatory problem — and the heavy strain of boot camp landed him repeatedly in the Army hospital. He was finally given a medical discharge and returned to the War Production Board.

Walter's deferment was insisted upon by Philip Murray and R. J. Thomas, who intervened with Selective Service, so that he could con-tinue as director of the General Motors Department of the UAW as well as a member of the War Production Board and the War Manpower Commission's National Advisory Committee. I was de-ferred by normal procedures at the beginning of the war because I was the father of three children. Later, the War Department in-sisted on my continued deferment, maintaining that harmonious in-dustrial relations were essential to the speedy production of defense materials. When the Army stepped up its inductions, I was called up, passed my physical, and prepared to report for duty. Sophie resigned herself to a long separation. Important meetings had al-ready been scheduled for me in Washington during the two weeks before I was to report. I did not want to miss them, yet I wanted to be with Sophie, so we left our three children with my parents in Wheeling and went to Washington, certain it would be our last time together for many months. But, while we were there, Selective Ser-vice suddenly revised its policies and exempted all fathers my age and over. Once we were back in Detroit, Sophie remembered she had planned to give me a send-off party like Roy's, with Polish kilbasa and all the trimmings. In spite of the changed circum-stances, the kilbasa was enjoyed by all.

My work as director of the UAW's War Policy Division and as a member of the Detroit Victory Council was supplemented by my function as a radio broadcaster to workers in Germany, France, and other countries. Early in 1942, Roy and I had established a close working relationship with Sigmund Jeremias, formerly active in the German trade union movement and now in exile in the U.S. He worked at the Office of War Information preparing propaganda, and through him the OWI approached Roy and me about the possibility of recruiting American workers fluent in the languages of the occupied European countries. I myself made many shortwave broadcasts in German beamed at strategic hours to the workers in Poland, Germany, and Austria.

In those broadcasts I urged industrial workers in Europe to believe that the postwar years would bring them the opportunity to rebuild their democratic trade union movement: "The time is growing close at hand when you will have the opportunity to . . . act in defense of your own rights."

I also took part in some special broadcasts directed at French workers, calling upon them to resist Nazi efforts to entice or draft them for work inside Germany. I was encouraged to go on when I heard through the BBC and the OWI that the recorded messages were getting through. "A German worker who happens to be living in France at this moment and has means of getting letters out to the BBC was most enthusiastic in his comments on the program," said a BBC official, and then added, most gratifyingly, "By far the best program on American labor that has come to us so far has been the speech by Walter Reuther's brother Victor . . . I'm asked to say that further material of this Reuther kind would be most welcome." In that speech, I had told the workers who were members of the resistance: "We send a message of thanks. To such workers who may be listening to me today, we also send a message of hope . . . Today you are hunted men, facing daily the dangers of terrible reprisals from the Nazi warlords and their quislings. Tomorrow with the support of American labor and American democracy, you will be the builders and masters of a new land, freed forever from the spies, the bayonets, and the machine guns of terrorism."

It was difficult to make my broadcasts during the period when American and British planes were carrying out the saturation bombing of German cities — cities that Walter and I had come to know so well. These were more than pins on the map; they represented many people whom we had come to call friends, and many to whom we were related. How could one explain to them adequately why the bombs were raining death upon them?

In my mind, the real issue was much broader than the defeat of Hitler, and had been paramount long before the outbreak of World

War II. The present war was just another phase of the long historical struggle of people to free themselves from authoritarian rule and win a measure of individual freedom. Therefore, even while the war against the Axis demanded our immediate attention, we could not afford to forget the subjugated colonial countries that would soon be fighting for national sovereignty and social and economic justice. In the summer of 1943, I joined with Florence Cassidy and Ralph Ulveling in sponsoring a Detroit Inter-American Center to make direct contact with those in our area of Latin-American background as well as with the organizations in Latin America itself. That summer I also renewed relations with friends on the Jewish Labor Committee and met its New York field director, Charles Sherman. It was the beginning of a long friendship. I also worked closely with the Federation of Jewish Labor (Histadrut), some of whose members would become Israel's political leaders.

Just as the trade unions wanted a voice in the special agencies created to push industrial production, they felt they deserved some position in the State Department. After the war, they did, in fact, serve there. Matthew Woll and Robert Watts from the AFL, and James B. Carey and Michael Ross from the CIO worked hard and effectively to implement the Marshall Plan. The State Department also established a labor attaché program. The War Department asked for our cooperation in recruiting particularly knowledgeable unionists for key roles in the military governments that were to be set up in Germany and Austria and other occupied countries. Recruitment and training for the Army of Occupation were undertaken even before the war ended. In connection with this work, the names of Clarence Bolds, George Silver, Newman Jeffrey, William Kemsley, and Henry Rutz come to mind. Clarence, for instance became military governor of Bavaria, and the other four, together with Joseph Keenan, who had served on the War Production Board, played important roles not only in Berlin but throughout Germany in the re-establishment of a democratic trade union movement. I remember cautioning Clarence that his task would not be easy, because no people can feel friendly toward military forces occupying their homeland. How often I was to hear Austrian and German workers, soon after the war, lamenting that although they had been liberated from the Nazis, they still had to "liberate themselves from their liberators."

I was most concerned as to whether the American soldier could really understand what was needed to plant the seeds and nourish the tender roots of democracy and self-government. I had had too much experience with the military mentality, which inevitably makes an emotional and intellectual adjustment to authoritarianism. I tried to impress on OWI officials the importance of briefing sessions for those who were to be in the Army of Occupation. Obviously, Germany's future security depended on the understanding and dedication of truly democratic elements within her society. Many of us were disturbed that so little education in democratic ideas and processes was being carried out among the German soldiers in U.S. prisoner-of-war camps. Gerhart Seger, a refugee from Hitler and editor of the oldest German-language newspaper in the United States, the *Neue Volkszeitung,* spoke to our local chapter of the German-American Congress for Democracy, expressing his dismay that any German prisoner who showed an interest in America or in democracy was punished by the Nazi organization in the camps. "Several have been murdered by their colleagues . . . Men have been beaten for reading my newspaper."

Unfortunately the U.S. military was ill prepared to take on any such responsibility.

CHAPTER 19

Perils of Peace

As THE FIGHTING neared an end, our thoughts turned frequently toward what was going to happen in our own country after the war. Roy, who possessed long political antennae, was especially sensitive to whatever might have negative effects on labor. His long months in the Army hospital and his War Production assignments on the West Coast had given him the time and the range to get a realistic perspective on what lay ahead. In his letters to Walter and me, he worried that the CIO had not begun to push a full-employment program for the postwar period. Millions of returning veterans would find no jobs unless concrete steps were taken to stimulate the economy. He warned about the prospect of continuing wage controls without any check on rising prices. An economy turned completely free again would tend to be inflationary, and labor would be in a bind. Thought should be given to mammoth public works programs, not WPA leaf-raking, but the gearing of defense plants back to domestic production — of prefab housing, for instance, and construction of schools, hospitals, new highways, parks, and engineering projects like the TVA. He saw an urgent need for a thirty-hour week with the take-home pay of a forty-hour week:

> Wages must somehow be geared to the technological developments in industry. This could be done with periodic adjustments on a national basis the same as could be done with any cost-of-living adjustments. In this way, you could maintain the high purchasing power that is the key to prosperity and full employment.

Roy cautioned us about relying on Roosevelt. We needed an organized public demand on Congress for the proper legislation. Otherwise, Roosevelt would merely say, "Sorry, Congress won't go along," and labor would be out in the cold again.

Walter began working on a program to meet peacetime contingencies, and on March 16, 1944, he made a speech, incorporating many of Roy's ideas, before the New York Times Hall Forum, which was broadcast by WMCA.

> The last war taught us that democracy cannot be saved if we fight only with the implements of war. We won the last war to save democracy only to reap a bumper crop of dictators. We won the war on the battlefield but lost it on the economic and political field . . .
> Halfway measures did not meet the problems of war, they will not meet the problems of peace. We must be prepared to fully mobilize our human and material resources to fight a total war against poverty and human insecurity with the same determination with which we are now fighting the Axis.

He then offered specific programs. He proposed a Peace Production Board, to be composed of government, management, labor, farmers, and consumers, to direct the conversion of industry back to civilian production in such a way as to ensure full and continuous employment. He talked of area tooling pools and "control of materials on the basis of social priority." He suggested continuing government control over monopolistic industries, which, with their cartel agreements, had imperiled our nation's defense program. The government-owned war plants should be leased to private industry, but with guarantees from those industries that would protect both labor and the consumer. Special provisions would be necessary to rehabilitate and guard small businesses during the conversion. A "central research clearinghouse would make certain that patents and technical knowledge are not hoarded by the monopolies but used for the general welfare of the public."

Ideally, housing would become the number one postwar industry. Government-owned aircraft plants could be converted to the manufacture of prefabricated, mass-produced, low-cost homes. Prophetically, Walter declared:

> We must have the courage and imagination to rebuild backward sections of our economy which have not kept abreast of technological progress. Our railroad system must be unified and modernized. The development of light metals and diesel power has made most of our rolling stock obsolete and uneconomical. We should not continue to pay for hauling dead weight simply to protect dead investments.

Restoration of devastated parts of Europe and the assimilation into our economy of our own returning soldiers were also high on the priority list. Finally, Walter said, elaborating on Roy's suggestion, the Peace Production Board should establish the thirty-hour week, which, "with the full realization of our productive potential," could be the equivalent of our prewar forty-hour week. Postwar security for the individual workers must be based upon a "guaranteed annual living wage."

The war ended; soon one began to sense that the auto workers were in an ugly mood. The long strain was beginning to show. They had an instinctive feeling that their employers had feathered their nests exceedingly well during the crisis, while they themselves had suffered under wage ceilings and constantly rising prices. They often took their resentment out on their union leaders, criticizing them for not pressing the bosses hard enough. Walter's militancy in defense of workers' rights during the war had earned him popularity and respect. But he was aware that the real test lay ahead, and General Motors would be the area of conflict.

During that period a gifted and dedicated economist and expert in consumer affairs, Donald Montgomery, resigned from his Washington post when the Department of Agriculture refused to undertake a program of grade-labeling to protect the consumer. Sophie saw the notice of his resignation in the papers, and a few days later we happened to be sitting at the same table with him at a dinner honoring Senator George Norris. I asked Montgomery what his plans were; he said they were still fluid, and I immediately called Walter, urging him to try to secure the services of this talented man. It worked out remarkably well, and Montgomery proved to be a most ingenious innovator in the area of national, social, and economic policy, as well as legislative strategy.

In line with Roy's admonition that the union should not be tricked into a position where it would appear that the wage increase it won was in direct conflict with the interests of consumers, Montgomery and Walter developed a voluminous economic brief, which they filed with the federal price control agencies on June 30, 1945. It was based on the premise that "wages *can* be increased without increasing prices. Increased production must be supported by increased consumption, and increased consumption would be possible only through increased wages."

To traditionalists in the labor movement, like John L. Lewis and even Philip Murray, this was a most unorthodox approach to a demand for a wage increase. In the past, labor leaders usually demanded raises without giving a thought to whether the employer would promptly pass on all (and sometimes more than all) of the cost of such increases to the consumer by marking up the price of his product. It was actually the first time in the history of collective bargaining that a conscious effort was made to win the consumer as an ally in the wage struggle, and to put the onus for any inflationary spiral right on the backs of employers, where it belonged.

The next step was to challenge the employers to prove that they could not afford the wage increase we were demanding unless they raised their prices. The UAW knew its case was sound, and would be substantiated by the facts if we should ever be able to get a true financial picture from the auto company executives. Throughout the war, the "Little Steel" formula had frozen wages to no more than a 15 percent increase, leaving the auto workers, among others, victimized by the inflation, which had risen to near 45 percent. There was pressure from the rank and file, and a showdown was in the offing, when President Truman, at the end of the war in the Pacific, authorized wage increases *providing they did not add to the rise in prices.* That act of Truman's gave the UAW and Walter precisely the opportunity they needed to challenge General Motors to tell the truth about its profits. A formal demand was made for a 30 percent wage increase, with the contractual proviso that retail prices on passenger cars, trucks, and other products would not shoot up.

There were some who thought Walter was overstating his case when he declared that not only could the auto manufacturers afford to pay the 30 percent increase without raising car prices, but that they could pay it and even reduce car prices, without losing their handsome profit. His claim was backed up by William S. Davis, director of the Office of Economic Stabilization, who was convinced that the industry could afford a 50 percent raise without having to boost prices.

Walter was playing for high stakes. He knew that his only hope was to mobilize broad community and consumer support for the UAW's position. He had to defend himself against the old-timers who, as he said, pretended "to promote the interests of the workers by conspiring with management, as in the coal industry, to exact higher prices for consumers." He infuriated John L. Lewis and other conservative leaders in both the AFL and the CIO who did not want their chances for striking private deals with industry made more difficult. Walter irrevocably threw in his lot with the consuming public, which included all the auto workers who were terrified of greater inflation and further erosion of their hard-won gains. "We shall realize and hold on to our gains only by making progress with the community and not at the expense of the community." This principle was to remain one of Walter's tenets throughout his career and become a guideline for all of the collective bargaining demands by the UAW.

General Motors procrastinated for six weeks before responding to the demand, and then Wilson rejected the whole thing outright. "We shall resist the monopolistic power of your union to force this 30 percent increase in basic wages." He added, "Automobiles would shortly cost 30 percent more to produce." The economics involved did not support his claim. Walter carried his case to the public through the *New York Times,* radio appeals, and a debate with George Romney on the "Town Meeting of the Air."

When the negotiations got under way on October 19, Walter suggested to General Motors that, because of the general public's stake in the issue, some newsmen should be allowed in, but the request was refused. Harry Coen, assistant personnel director, called the idea "more of Reuther's grandstanding." Walter countered by bringing in a public stenographer, who kept accurate minutes. The verbatim transcript proved most helpful later when, once things came to an impasse, the UAW put its case before the public.

It was a classic confrontation between entrenched power and a new breed. The young unionists represented pragmatism, social vision, and an understanding of economics the older labor leaders lacked. On one side sat Charles Wilson, fifty-five-year-old president of one of the world's richest corporations, whose annual salary was close to half a million dollars. Opposite him sat Walter, aged thirty-eight, with a $7000 income, surrounded by a shop committee of workers directly out of General Motors plants across the country. Next to Wilson was his personnel man, Harry Coen, who was always careful to stress the spelling of his name. Obviously not Jewish, he enjoyed anti-Semitic jokes. When he later became GM vice-president, he said, "I'm vice-president in charge of Jews and niggers." Since the "expletives deleted" process had not been invented in 1945, the verbatim transcript of the negotiations is replete with Coen's dirty language as he clashed with Walter.

Walter hammered away at the issue of consumers' interests, and Coen, his face getting redder and redder with anger, finally blurted out: "Why don't you get down to your size and talk about the money you'd like to have for your people, and let labor statesmanship go to hell for a while? It's none of your damn business what the OPA does about the prices!"

"But unless we get a more realistic distribution of America's wealth, we don't get enough to keep this machinery going," Walter persisted.

"There it is again," Coen complained. "You can't talk about this thing without exposing your Socialistic desires."

"If fighting for equitable distribution of the wealth is Socialistic, I stand guilty of being a Socialist."

"I think you are convicted," Coen retorted.

"I plead guilty," said Walter, and that was the end of that exchange.

Meanwhile President Truman, though he did not plug the welling spring of price increases, established a new wage policy, adjusting salaries to the cost of living. This bolstered Walter's contention that a substantial wage increase was essential; it would support with purchasing power an expanding economy that could provide job opportunities for all. He was under no illusion, however, that the President would pull any chestnuts out of the fire for the UAW. Labor had to depend on the solidarity of its membership and the backing of the general public. He also knew, from experience, that General Motors would not yield until it was threatened by strike action. Therefore, with the approval of the Executive Board, he took a strike vote and the results of that vote strengthened the UAW hand at the bargaining table. It turned out that 70,853 GM workers were in favor of strike action as compared with 12,438 who opposed it.

It was not until November 7 that General Motors made its offer: a mere 10 percent raise. In view of the disparity between the existing wage scale and the rise in the cost of living, the proposal was an insult. It was rejected out of hand as a cheap bribe to rank-and-file workers to give up their fight for economic justice. The corporation was not surprised by the rejection of offer, but it was certainly taken aback when Walter countered with a proposal to arbitrate the wage demand on two conditions: 1) that General Motors open its books and records to members of a board of arbitration, who would make a realistic estimate of the extent of the company's ability to raise

wages, and 2) that General Motors agree not to increase the price of
its cars on the basis of any wage increase. Walter's point was that,
since the wage issue could not be settled by a show of strength of the
two sides, an objective board of arbitration would judge the equity of
the workers' demands in relation to corporation's assets and profits.

General Motors was asked to reply within twenty-four hours, and
when no word came, 175,000 workers in ninety-five plants across the
U.S. went on strike. Two days later, the anticipated response came,
from GM's vice-president, H. W. Anderson, who declared it was "not
an offer of arbitration but a demand for abdication." General Motors, he said, was not prepared to give over management decisions to
any board of arbitration. This decision to refuse even to consider
opening its books to an impartial board was another blow to GM's already poor image. Walter moved with all speed to capitalize on the
favorable public sentiment building up for the UAW in this first
postwar strike. He summoned a meeting of a broadly representative
citizens' committee to hear a reading of the transcripts of the negotiations of the last months, and asked that the committee issue an independent report on the controversy.

The Citizens' Committee was made up of men associated with the
YMCA, the NAACP, banking, religion, education, and other profes-
sions. It fell to me to read aloud most of the transcript. Members
of the committee were then allowed to examine, at their leisure, any
sections they wished.

Walter suggested to the committee — his suggestion became
known immediately to the corporation — that the wage demand
could be reduced all the way down to a 1 percent increase if the
company would open its books and prove it could afford no more
than that unless it raised car prices. The committee members were
invited to ask the GM management what it thought of that offer;
they were flabbergasted when they learned that the corporation
would not even consider such a proposal. Many of them said to me
in private that they could not understand how the company could let
itself be manuevered into such an untenable position. It was an eye
opener for many of the community leaders, who had never been involved in collective bargaining or industrial relations and who had
often wondered why trade unions did not give more thought and
consideration to consumer interests, especially on the subject of
prices. In their final report they praised the UAW for lifting "the

whole matter of collective bargaining to a new level by insisting that the advancement of labor's interests should not be made at the expense of the public."

There was no such praise from the labor leadership. The collective bargaining stance assumed by Walter looked like one that would cause difficulties for Philip Murray in steel, and certainly for Lewis in the coal industry, both of whom wanted to get a settlement without bothering about the price of steel or coal. Among the UAW leaders also there were those who resented the national publicity that the strike and his innovative approach had brought to Walter; they were afraid it would strengthen his position both within the UAW and the CIO. Even though the UAW Executive Board had approved every basic decision he had made, rumors were circulated that the strike was untimely and ineffective.

President Truman was finally convinced by certain individuals opposed to the strike that it was "a major obstacle holding up our reconversion program," and appointed a three-man fact-finding board to investigate the strike. From talks with Chester Bowles, the new head of the Office of Economic Stabilization, Walter had gathered that Truman and his staff were sympathetic to the idea of considering wages in relation to the ability of the corporation to pay, and that they welcomed the UAW's efforts to hold down inflation. He also knew that General Motors would refuse to promise not to raise prices of its cars. The pivotal question at that point was whether General Motors would participate in any meetings with a government board of inquiry.

The reply was not long in coming. When the fact-finding panel — consisting of Walter P. Stacy, Milton Eisenhower, and Lloyd Garrison — convened in Washington to meet with spokesmen from the corporation and the union, the General Motors officials refused to take their seats until they had an answer to one important question: would the hearing be conducted in terms of *their ability to pay*? By coincidence, a telegram was delivered to the chairman at exactly that moment, before he had time to answer them, and he interrupted the proceedings to read it aloud. It was from President Truman, setting forth his views and those of his administration favoring a study of the relationship between wages and prices. Whereupon the General Motors delegation stamped out of the hearing room, leaving the UAW a clear field in which to express its views before the panel and the press without interference or rebuttal. GM's arrogant determination to conceal its actual production costs and the true level of its profits was so strong that it would not yield even to a presidential commission. The fact-finding panel in the end recommended a wage settlement of a 19½-cents-an-hour increase, without a boost in the price of General Motors cars. This was less than the wage increase Walter was seeking, but the recommendation that there should be no price increase was interpreted by the UAW and, I think, by the rest of the country as a vindication of the course we were pursuing.

The panel's recommendation was immediately rejected by General Motors.

So the strike went on and on, and the hardships suffered by the strikers' families reached emergency proportions. We had no strike fund in those days, and could pay out only modest amounts to care for the sick, to try to prevent evictions by advancing small payments toward a month's rent, and to buy some food for the neediest. Walter set an example that he and his fellow officers were to follow during every major strike: he turned his salary back to the UAW for strike assistance. A national Committee to Aid the Families of GM Strikers was set up with the help of Leo Goodman, and drew into its ranks such outstanding citizens as Eleanor Roosevelt, Senator Wayne Morse, and Republicans Henry Luce and Harold Stassen. There was a rally in Madison Square Garden, which gave me the opportunity to explain the issues, describe the negotiating efforts, and solicit the aid of many not directly involved in labor's struggle. Dozens of UAW staff members and hundreds of volunteers held solicitation meetings across the country, and did some effective educating on the relation of profits to wages to prices. Buttons were printed with the slogan, "We fight for a better tomorrow. I gave to win higher wages — no price increases."

While Walter was holding out at General Motors for a settlement in line with the recommendation of President Truman and his fact-finding panel, he was being undercut by enemies within the labor leadership. The strike at General Motors had been followed by strikes in steel, electrical equipment, and packing-house plants, involving in all about 1,750,000 workers. But it was actually the leadership of the small United Electrical Workers (the UE, not to be confused with the IUE, whose president was James B. Carey) that struck the first low, unanticipated blow. That union, representing a minor segment of the CIO, had long been under Communist domination. It had only 30,000 members among GM workers as against the better than 150,000 organized into the UAW. United Electrical Workers officials met secretly with General Motors executives while the strike was in progress and signed an inferior agreement, settling for an 18½-cents-an-hour raise, without, of course, any reference to price levels. This was one cent less than what had been recommended by the government panel, but even worse, it was a double-cross by a sister trade union that had often ridden on the coattails of the UAW and benefited from its strength during previous struggles with General Motors. It was not only an attack against Walter; it was a sellout of the 150,000 GM auto workers.

When General Motors finally came around to offering Walter the same 18½ cents an hour agreed to by the United Electrical Workers, Walter exploded: "I won't be made a damned fool of forever. The President's offer of nineteen-and-a-half cents was a compromise of our demand and I'll be Goddamned if I'll compromise a compromise! We're not going to take less than this and this is all horseshit about going back to work!"

An even more devastating wallop came from Philip Murray, who settled a U.S. Steel strike of four weeks' duration on the basis of 18½ cents an hour. Within a matter of weeks, the federal government gave its approval to a five-dollar-a-ton increase in the price of steel! This pulled the rug out from under the union and spelled disaster for his carefully planned strategy to protect the consumer from further inflation. It was a victory for the old-fashioned concept of unionism: "Give us our share and the devil take the hindmost!"

All Walter's efforts to get the White House or the Secretary of Labor to back up the 19½-cents-an-hour decision failed; his work to hold the line on prices went down the drain with the Electrical, Steel, and then Rubber Workers' wage settlements. There was nothing to do but agree to the 18½-cent increase and settle the strike, which had by then run for 113 days. General Motors made a few concessions, which were a mild palliative: provision for a check-off of union dues, which laid the basis for a larger and stronger membership; and modest improvements in the seniority system. Disappointing as the terms were, the most disheartening aspect was the failure to hold the line against inflation. Salt was rubbed into the

wound when the auto industry, by August 1946, had been granted
at least three separate price increases, and Congress turned its back
on the whole system of price ceilings that had existed during the
war.

Some of Walter's colleagues in the labor movement took pleasure
in seeing him confounded. R. J. Thomas charged later that the
strike was "called six weeks too early and ended a month too late."
Others announced that Reuther's "statesmanship" should be replaced by "bread-and-butter unionism." They misjudged, however,
the impact that long strike had on the rank-and-file GM workers,
who were proud of their struggle and who understood there was
little to gain in being paid off by the "wooden nickels of inflation."
They also understood that, though the UAW had not won this particular battle against rising prices, the union membership and the
public at large now had a better grasp of basic economic facts. Indeed, the strike and the national publicity it gave to the subject of
wages and prices was to lead in time to the introduction of an escalator clause in our contracts, automatically protecting the workers
against cost-of-living increases and guaranteeing an annual wage
raise to reflect the growth of national productivity.

The controversy had its effect on General Motors. Collective
bargaining in the years ahead was never to sink to the previous low
level. In the future the corporation was to show much more respect
for the strength, the economic logic, and the morality of the issues
the UAW laid before it.

It was during this strike that Walter resolved that something drastic had to be done to provide more stable and forward-looking leadership for the United Automobile Workers; to remove for all time
the danger that certain elements within the union could betray a
great mass of workers who were willing to suffer a long strike in
order to achieve reasonable economic aims; to eliminate from the
union leadership all those who placed partisan politics above the
well-being of the membership. By the same token, he was soon to
feel obligated to make a bid for the presidency of the UAW and to
try to build a spirit of unity and democracy.

Our parents, Valentine and Anna Stocker Reuther, pose for their engagement photographs, 1903.

The Reuther family, c. 1920: Gathered around my father are (from left to right) Roy, my mother, Ted, Walter, and myself.

Our grandparents, Christina and Jacob Reuther, at their home in Effingham, Illinois, 1923.

Walter and Roy strike a muscular attitude behind their athletic trophies, 1925.

Walter put on his Grandmother Stocker's clothes when we visited our Uncle Ernst in Ruit, Germany, 1933.

I took this snapshot of Hitler returning from a Berlin rally
in February 1933.

Walter (right) and I, dressed for the Russian winter, leave for work in the Gorky auto plant, 1934.

Palm trees and a huge portrait of Stalin were supposed to "elevate culture" along the Gorky assembly line.

Crowds gather around the Fisher Body plant in Flint, Michigan, after its take-over by sit-down strikers. It was here, in January 1937, that the strikers repelled a police attack in what came to be known as "The Battle of Bulls Run." *Archives of Labor History and Urban Affairs, Wayne State University*

At a rally in 1937, Roy exposes GM "stool pigeons."

Walter, my wife, Sophie, and myself at the UAW Milwaukee Convention, 1937.

FORD MOTOR COMPANY

May 26, 1937: Ford Motor Company
thugs at the River Rouge works approach
UAW organizers (left to right) Bob
Kanter, Walter, Dick Frankensteen, and
Jack Kennedy. *Detroit News*

The "Battle of the Overpass" begins, as
Frankensteen (right), his coat pulled
over his head, is pummeled. *The
Archives of Labor History and Urban
Affairs, Wayne State University.*

As I look on (far left), Walter speaks to GM tool and die workers on strike strategy, 1937. *Archives of Labor History and Urban Affairs, Wayne State University*

Walter and his wife, May, in a rare playful moment.

To be with Walter more, May worked as his secretary. *Associated Press Photo*

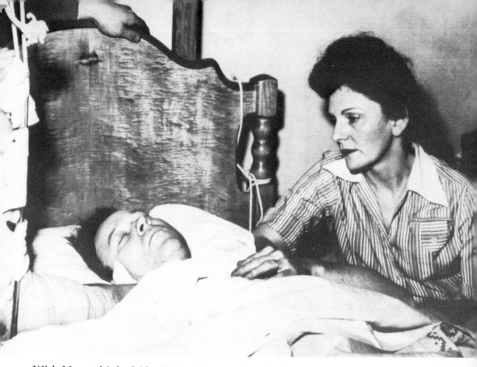

With May at his bedside, Walter lies near death after the attempt on his life in 1948. *UPI*

My turn came next. Here I am with Roy and Walter in May 1949, my first public appearance after being gunned down by a would-be assassin. *Photo by Clayton W. Fountain*

Walter, a lifelong abstainer, pledged to have a smoke and take a drink if he was elected President of the CIO. He was — and he kept his promise. *Life*

George Meany and Walter shake hands and hold aloft a gavel, marking the merger of the AFL and CIO in 1955. But their cordial relations proved short-lived. *Ransdell Inc., Washington*

At the summer home of Swedish Prime Minister Tage Erlander, Walter (back to camera) rows while (left to right) Hubert Humphrey, Willy Brandt, and Erlander enjoy the ride. But a Brazilian newspaper seems to have gotten the wrong idea. "Leaders of Junta Gather," it captioned this picture.

Sophie and I are received by coal miners at Asansol in India, 1965. *USIS photo*

"You are still the best cook," Walter tells our mother in the Reuther family kitchen, as our father looks on. The year is 1950. *Life*

The Reuther family, 1954: Gathered around our parents at their 50th Anniversary celebration in Bethlehem, West Virginia, are Ted, our sister, Christine, Roy, myself, and Walter. *Jim Yardley, UAW*

My mother and Eleanor Roosevelt at the 1956 UAW convention in Atlantic City.

At the same convention, Walter introduces an "old soap-boxer" — Valentine Reuther. *Chelsea Studio, Atlantic City, N.J.*

Leonard Woodcock, the new president of
the UAW, presents me with the union's
"Social Justice Award" on my retirement
in 1972. *UAW Photo*

"He was the only friend I had":
Alexander Cardozo, retired auto worker,
breaks down in front of Walter's coffin.

CHAPTER 20

"Teamwork in the Leadership, Solidarity in the Ranks"

FOR A NUMBER OF YEARS Walter had been under pressure from the rank and file to seek the presidency of the UAW. The union's strength was being sapped by the fever of political dissension, and it was often so weakened by internal fights that it could not win from employers the wages and rights that were the workers' due. Walter had resisted that pressure because he knew that Murray and other CIO officials preferred to maintain a delicate balance between the Addes–Communist Party caucus and the Reuther caucus by supporting the presidency of the well-meaning but ineffectual R. J. Thomas. Now Thomas was giving increasing support to the Addes–Communist group. Its betrayal of the workers, during the war, on the piecework issue and overtime, and the treachery it perpetrated on the General Motors strikers immediately after the war, left Walter no choice but to run for the presidency in March 1946. It was a gamble: his announcement would certainly hasten the marriage of convenience between R. J. Thomas and the Communists in the union, and if R. J. should be re-elected, the balance of power might be shifted permanently to the far left.

Intensive campaigning got underway months before the convention. The Reuther strength lay primarily in the General Motors unions, where Walter's leadership had earned him loyalty and respect; we could count, too, on the Association of Catholic Trade Unionists, which had a strong following in the Chrysler plants. Finally, and most important, there were the thousands of unionists who were fed up with the efforts of the Communists to call the tune in their unions, and who wanted leaders who were loyal to the basic trade union commitments and did not change their positions to meet every new national or international political fashion.

Walter won . . . by only 124 votes! That evening, we were exultant, but on the third day of the convention we suffered a severe comedown as we watched the Thomas–Addes caucus win almost every important post on the Executive Board. R. J. Thomas became first vice-president, R. T. Leonard second vice-president, and George Addes continued as secretary-treasurer. Our man, Emil Mazey, still stationed in the South Pacific and unaware that he had been nominated, was elected a member of the board. Frankensteen, who a short time before had lost his bid to be Mayor of Detroit and had been condemned for vacationing in Florida while his Chrysler workers were picketing in the snowy streets, made a less than graceful exit from the UAW leadership.

Back in Detroit, it seemed as if the presidency itself might be an illusion. The first hurdle was getting physical occupancy of the president's office at UAW headquarters. Walter's previous office was identical to Thomas's but was on the floor above. The ex-president balked at making the switch and for a few days I thought we might have to resort to calling in the Briggs and West Side Local flying squads. When R. J. finally relinquished his chair, packed up, and moved to the third floor, it was with an air of defiance that as much as said, "Redhead, you may get my chair and the office, but we'll see to it, by God, you won't get the power of the presidency!"

The opposition miscalculated if it thought Walter could be stalemated. His first step as president was to tighten control over all expenditures by enforcing the constitutional rule that the president of the union must cosign all checks. When the Executive Board refused to honor that rule, Walter notified the banks not to honor any check that did not bear his signature. It did not take him long to realize that the financial condition of the UAW was far worse than Addes had reported at the convention. What better way to stymie an "upstart" new president than to offer him a bare treasury! Walter flew to New York and consulted Sidney Hillman, who was genuinely pleased by Walter's election. A $250,000 loan to the UAW from the Amalgamated Clothing Workers was soon arranged. What's more — and this could never be measured in dollars and cents — Hillman gave Walter invaluable advice on strengthening his position within the UAW.

How tragic it was that when his leadership was so urgently needed a sudden heart attack snatched Sidney away. Both he and Walter were an unusual blend of pragmatism and social idealism, almost ascetic in personal habits and needs, both fiercely dedicated to the movement that had produced them and that they were able to influence so that it conformed to patterns of democracy. Each of them considered a position of power in a trade union a public trust, to be used for the advancement of the country's general welfare.

The "mechanical majority" on the Executive Board tried various means to box Walter in and restrict his authority. They called meetings without notifying him; they refused to ratify Walter's appointments, though under the constitution it was his responsibility to appoint department heads and directors of the major units within different corporations, subject to the approval of the Executive Board. The result was a temporary standstill, since the board would not accept Walter's choices but could not proceed on their own. It was clear that Walter had to play for time, and work out some sort of quid pro quo with the board, if we were to remain alive as a force in the union. Thomas, for instance, was in a bargaining mood, seeking some major assignment that would allow him a large personal staff and help him rebuild his eroding influence. He wanted the directorship of the Competitive Shop Department, a loosely knit catchall organization whose function was to search out and organize plants that offered unfair competition to those already organized.

Walter at the same time was pushing to have me named director of the Education Department, then in the hands of a person slavishly loyal to the Addes faction. Walter considered the Education Department of strategic importance because it had direct access to the rank and file through seminars, summer schools, and publications. It could be a powerful instrument in developing the workers' understanding of his goals and objectives. He also wanted to appoint Frank Winn, the genial, experienced public relations expert, to head the Press and Publicity Department. He finally got Thomas to agree to these two appointments in exchange for the directorship of the Competitive Shop Department.

Walter's own staff began to grow with the hiring of Jack Conway, a young Chicago auto worker who also ran the Chicago University "Round Table" radio program, and would in later years become deputy administrator of HUD in the Kennedy administration. Nat

Weinberg, an old friend of Roy's from Brookwood days, came on to
help with general research, wage and bargaining matters. Nat
found the factionalism in the UAW astounding, even after his experience with squabbles in the ILGWU. His immediate boss in the
Research Department was James Wishart, who gave him no assignments and even denied him use of the department's secretarial staff.
"If I had something I wanted typed for Walter," Nat recalls, "I
would walk around the building and find some girl who had a few
minutes free and who was on Walter's side."

The Education Department proved to be a useful vehicle, indeed,
for helping us break out from under the hard-core group that dominated the Executive Board. I began my task by searching, in every
local, for articulate and creative auto workers willing to work tirelessly to attract other activists into the education program. At headquarters, I was lucky to acquire for staff such talented, down-to-
earth educators as Joseph Kowalski, Brendan Sexton, Ed Lee, and
Lewis Carliner. Lew, who had been wooed away from the Department of Agriculture in Washington, was a talented writer, layout
man, film producer, and jack-of-all-trades. Between us, we converted the monthly UAW magazine, *Ammunition,* from a dull house
organ into a lively, illustrated manual with essential do's and don't's
for training shop stewards, local committeemen, and local union
officers to become informed and active leaders. In our publication,
corporation financial reports were made intelligible to shop workers;
grievance procedures and parliamentary rules lost their awesome
qualities and became tools for daily combat. In addition to the
monthly magazine, film strips and illustrated lectures were produced
by the thousands for circulation within the plants.

Weekend and afterwork seminars were organized in hundreds of
communities across the country. Within the first year of Walter's
presidency, the Education Department had enrolled more than
thirty-five thousand local leaders in formal education classes — in institutes or summer schools established near automotive plants or in
some spot convenient for a whole region. The most important central area for summer school training was the FDR Labor Education
Center in Port Huron, Michigan, purchased by the Michigan CIO
Council, but used extensively by the UAW. It serviced more than
the Michigan region; it was used for special seminars to educate
leaders recruited from all regions of the United States.

During that same first year, Addes hatched a plot that, had it been successful, would have destroyed once and for all any chance for Walter to exercise his power as president. It involved the Farm Equipment Workers' Union, a small independent group within the CIO known to be under Communist domination. The UAW by that time was more than a union of auto workers; it included aircraft workers and a large group of Farm Implement Workers. Addes began a series of secret discussions with the Farm Implement Workers, inviting them to merge with the UAW and offering them very attractive terms: they would remain an intact body, a "union within a union," while the UAW would pick up the financial tab for their operations. The Addes forces would stand to gain a solid bloc of some 500 convention votes belonging to workers fanatically loyal to their cause and able to swing any national election in their favor.

The discussions had gone on for some months without Walter's knowledge. In late June, on the very last day of an Executive Board session, as Walter prepared to adjourn the meeting and take a plane east for a speaking engagement, Addes sprung his bombshell — the merger proposal. Walter and his supporters on the board realized the magnitude of the danger, but, confronted with the majority on the board, could do nothing to prevent the adoption of the motion. Every effort to hold it over for more study and consideration was brushed aside. Fortunately, John W. Livingston, regional director from the St. Louis–Kansas City area and a Reuther man, moved that the final decision be subject to a referendum to be voted on by the entire membership of the UAW, local by local, during the next month. The Addes group, fearing that opposition to the referendum might be regarded with suspicion by the rank and file, and smugly sure that its proposal would be affirmed, allowed the Livingston amendment to go through.

Now that the matter was up to the entire union, Walter moved with speed to line up his lieutenants and carry the debate into every local. In fact, the Addes group had unwittingly presented Walter with a strong weapon. Our summer school classes were suddenly turned into forums for heated arguments and discussions. The Farm Implement Workers' merger was labeled a Trojan horse, which indeed it was, and the membership was informed that the proposal was an effort to bring into the union a sizable bloc of pro-Communists so that orderly democratic processes would be hampered. The debates gave Walter a chance to tell the story of the continuing attempts of the majority on the Executive Board to deprive him of his presidential powers. The many thousands of new recruits we had enrolled in our seminars, and countless numbers of loyal staff members and local officers, understood what was involved and responded with determination to "beat the pants off them in this referendum." On July 11, 1946, at a rally in Detroit, Walter debated with Addes on the merger proposal. It was clear from the response of the twenty-five hundred in attendance that night that the referendum would bring about a resounding defeat for both the merger and Addes. Some days later, the vote across the country quashed the proposal by a two-to-one ratio, and gave Walter assurance of rank-and-file support at a moment when he desperately needed it.

Our National Education Conference, called for January of 1947, was another milestone. It was colorfully described by Francis A. Kornegay, a leader in the Detroit black community, in his Detroit *Tribune* column:

> The conference was well attended by workers coming from all sections of the nation. Many representatives of other organizations took part to observe what goes on there. Well, to be sure, plenty went on. Hats off to Victor Reuther, Director UAW-CIO — old thrills and frills were regimented to the zoo and shortcuts were substituted. All of which put the facts that the rank and file of labor should know right at their door. To go further, education was injected into the circulatory system of the labor movement. These veins, arteries and capillaries will carry these messages back to all parts of the great body of the UAW-CIO network . . . This must be said to industrial management. Organized labor has come of age . . . Management, counselors, psychologists, industrial psychologists, employment personnel, labor relations persons should start now a new movement. A new movement towards a convergence series in respect to labor officials.

Eleanor Roosevelt, who had become very fond of Walter and had invited him and his family for visits to Hyde Park, came to address our conference. The Roosevelts, especially Eleanor, were still favorites among the auto workers. She had continued her courageous probing of problems that were of immediate importance to wage earners; she never stopped fighting for civil rights, and our black workers, whose ranks had increased over the years, held her in great honor and respect.

Mrs. Roosevelt saw in Walter more than a bright young trade

union leader. She recognized the social visionary who always related his trade union commitments to other broad social responsibilities, which all Americans should share. He had been her strong ally in support of basic social legislation. Her attendance at our conference and her praise of Walter had a profound effect on the twelve hundred delegates and increased his influence within the union.

Walter White, the NAACP leader, was also a guest speaker. He spoke enthusiastically about Walter, and realizing that we were troubled by warring factions, he reminded the delegates that such quarrels could mean destruction of the union. Walter White's words had a sobering effect on many of the black delegates, which I could sense even before he left the rostrum. As I wrote him later, he had "helped turn the tide against the attempts of the Communists to capture the meeting."

Walter's concern with unity drew him closer to Philip Murray. Walter conferred with him as frequently as possible, and when Phil came to an Executive Board meeting at Walter's invitation, he commented that the factional strife within the UAW had "sunk to a level of complete moral degeneracy."

The duplicity of some members of his own staff was an affront to this devout Catholic. At the 1947 National CIO Convention, Murray was outspoken on the subject of factionalism and insisted that the convention ratify a resolution to "resent and reject" efforts by the Communist Party to interfere in CIO affairs.

When it saw that Murray had become an open ally of Walter's, the Thomas-Addes caucus turned to acts of desperation. They circulated a brochure, entitled *The Boss's Boy,* in which Walter was portrayed as an agent in the pay of certain manufacturers. Mortimer, who no longer held any official union position, went so far as to label Walter a "bastard and stool pigeon," referring to Walter's open denunciation of Communist activities within the union. Walter, however, was equally frank in speaking out against right-wing extremists, charging that "the reactionaries of the country have launched a Red hunt, whose ultimate victims are intended not to be Communists, but all effective labor leaders and labor unions." He agreed with James B. Carey, secretary-treasurer of the National CIO and president of the IUE, when he said that the purpose of an organization of labor is "to serve workers. It is not to serve governments or bureaus or political parties or any groups."

When the opposing majority on the UAW Executive Board circulated a forged document, supposedly written by the anti-Semitic and antilabor Gerald L. K. Smith, applauding Walter for the excellent job he was doing in curbing the influence of the Thomas-Addes faction, Walter countered immediately by filing a libel suit against both the publisher and the alleged author of the pamphlet. Hot on the heels of this affair came a widely circulated rumor that Walter was eyeing the United States presidency and feeling out the possibility of Robert A. Taft as a running mate. The Thomas-Addes forces were able to convince Drew Pearson that this ridiculous fantasy was the truth.

The intent of these attacks was to keep us so constantly on the defensive that we would have no time to pursue the basic work of the union, and, in fact, they did greatly weaken the UAW during direct wage negotiations with the corporations. The first year of Walter's presidency saw no significant advances in collective bargaining. The majority of the workers, however, were neither on the defensive nor immobilized. The national caucus, organized in support of Walter and the program he stood for, included thousands in the field, our few supporters on the Executive Board, and the small staff personnel we had available to serve as liaison between Detroit headquarters and the locals.

At headquarters, Frank Winn, Nat Weinberg, Jack Conway, Brendan Sexton, Roy, and I, together with Don Montgomery in Washington, took on the task of keeping detailed documentation of every incident of sabotage or destruction that prevented the union and its president from functioning effectively. Incidents of this sort ranged all the way from sloppy bookkeeping by the Addes office and padding of expense accounts to help bankroll partisan political campaigns in strategic locals, to wildcat strikes deliberately provoked in order to embarrass the Reuther presidency and dissipate its resources. The scheme to bring in the Farm Equipment Workers' Union was carefully documented in all its details, and this affair became a matter of public record, which Walter laid before the union in accordance with his constitutional obligation to submit a report to the membership.

Because the Executive Board held secret meetings without Walter, he felt justified in making the report to the membership without discussing it with the Executive Board. He did so in a special issue of the *United Auto Worker,* printed and mailed before the Thomas-Addes people had had an opportunity to look at it. Naturally, all hell broke loose, but the only recourse they had was to prepare their own special issue, which they would slant so as to exonerate themselves. But the effect of their special was to focus still more attention on the basic charges and to substantiate the evidence that Walter had put before the membership. The "Report of the President" had raised a stir in every shop and union hall, and at that propitious moment we made intensive efforts to strengthen our caucus, especially in those great concentrations of unionism like River Rouge Ford Local 600, which had for some time been a Thomas-Addes stronghold but was now fair game for conversion. Here Emil Mazey, Ken Bannon, and Jack Conway did magnificent work, with the help of the personal contacts that Frank Winn had built up over the years.

The proof of the pudding would come at the 1947 UAW convention, scheduled for November. From late September through October all locals were involved in the election of delegates to this crucial gathering. There was a ground swell of indignation against the sabotage performed by the Thomas-Addes group, and a campaign was underway to re-elect Walter and to vote for a slate of Executive Board members who would support his programs. Even in such opposition quarters as the Tool and Die Local 155, we were successful in winning a majority of the delegates. A few days before the convention, a national caucus of Reuther supporters met in Detroit and selected Emil Mazey to run for secretary-treasurer against George Addes, and two new men for vice-presidents: Richard Gosser from Toledo and John Livingston from St. Louis. Similar caucuses were held in each significant geographical region in close consultation with Walter and his staff to ensure that the strongest candidates would be selected to challenge the Thomas-Addes men at every level of UAW leadership.

Walter went to Washington to see Murray, who was doubtful that Walter could pull off the challenge to Addes, but indicated there would be no interference from CIO leaders at the convention. As thousands gathered in Atlantic City there was none of the feverish tension of the previous year; there was, rather, a jubilant spirit, since every delegate was sure of the outcome. We also were confident enough to ask our father and mother to be with us in Atlantic City to share the moment when at last there would be solidarity in the ranks.

From the moment that Walter rapped the gavel for the convention's start, he seemed firmly and confidently in control of the great gathering. Philip Murray's warm endorsement removed any idea that there might be a strong opposition to Walter's re-election. Two self-starting candidates did run, but between them chalked up only 399 votes against Walter's 5593. At the urging of the Addes caucus, 1219 delegates abstained from voting. But even if their votes had been cast against Walter, he would have won by nearly four to one. The real test came in the election for secretary-treasurer, and certainly in that contest no voter abstained. Emil Mazey was a popular, militant rank-and-file worker who had organized the Briggs plant, become president of its union, had run up a splendid war record in the South Pacific, and had been elected the year before to the Executive Board. He swamped George Addes with a remarkable vote that ran only 760 short of Walter's plurality. With John Livingston and Richard Gosser easily winning the vice-presidencies, and fourteen of the eighteen regional director posts going to Reuther men, the victory was impressive.

During the festivities that night, Walter made his traditional convention concession to his colleagues: he sipped at a glass of whiskey and coughed through a few puffs on a cigar. The next day brought his real moment of joy: he introduced to the convention Valentine and Anna Reuther, who were standing with him on the rostrum. "A good pal of mine," he began. "An old fighter in the ranks of labor, a trade unionist from way back when the going was rough, who indoctrinated his boys when they were pretty young and told them the most important thing in the world to fight for was the other guy, the brotherhood of man, the golden rule."

There was a standing ovation from the floor, then Walter asked Dad to say a few words. Without any notes and with great poise, he said to the crowd, "I am extremely happy that the seed I tried to sow in the minds of our children is bearing fruit, and that they are engaged in the trade union movement that has always been dear to my heart." The delegates, perhaps for the first time, understood what made all the Reuther children tick. There were motions made from the floor to declare Valentine Reuther a lifelong honorary member of the UAW.

Before Walter introduced Mother, he couldn't resist telling the story, already recounted here, about the shirt she had made for him out of the black umbrella he had tried to use as a parachute. It was a very happy, very moving occasion for the four brothers and for our sister, Chris, and their respective wives and husband. We were all together for the first time in many years, and what's more, there was a feeling that perhaps now, after the long period of struggle and combat, we could lead more normal lives.

The delegates insisted on upping the salaries of the UAW leaders. The union was known for paying its officials the lowest salaries paid by any union — a tradition Walter was proud to retain. When they voted him a $2000-a-year increase, he refused to accept more than $1000, bringing his income up to $10,000. The regional organizers were at long last able to enjoy a weekly wage of $100.

The convention ended on a serious note as Walter stated his belief, and his pride, in the fact that the UAW was "in the vanguard of that great crusade to build a better world." Then, sensitive to the danger that some columnists might take the ousting of the Communist-oriented leaders as a signal of a swing to the right and conservatism, Walter declared that the UAW leadership was still committed to militant unionism and economic and social reform. With the election of a supportive team of officers and Executive Board, Walter had at last achieved his goal of "Teamwork in the Leadership and Solidarity in the Ranks."

There was no purge, although Walter was in a position to have refused reappointment to the staff those who had opposed him. Many staff supporters of the Addes faction were retained and, as Walter had predicted, made valuable contributions to the future vitality and success of the union. R. J. Thomas, for instance, was personally assisted by Walter in securing a post with the National CIO, as was Richard Leonard, who was to become one of Walter's important assistants in the Industrial Union Department of the merged AFL-CIO. George Addes himself chose to leave the labor movement.

The Reuther sweep within the UAW, and the growing sentiment among Murray's own steelworkers that it was time to face up to the Communist issue, finally brought National CIO action. With Walter's approval, Murray and the CIO Executive Council brought some eleven unions to trial for violating National CIO policy and espousing Communist Party doctrine. Their charters were lifted, and in most instances new charters granted, as their members, appealing over the heads of their old officers, were brought back into the CIO fold under proper auspices.

In dealing with the Communist problem, Walter always insisted that "Exposure, not repression, must be our goal. We must get the Communists out of the political back alleys and walk them up Main Street in the full light of informed opinion." It took five years to break their power in the Ford Local 600, mainly because Walter would not use the autocratic methods John L. Lewis had used in dealing with Communist infiltration of his mine workers. The democratic process required time-consuming efforts to educate the rank and file, but that is what Walter preferred.

The cleavage between the Western powers and Stalinist Russia over postwar policies was an additional factor in further isolating the Communists in the United States from the rank-and-file workers. Both the AFL and the CIO fully supported the Marshall Plan; the Communists tried to obstruct it. I remember that, after my journey in 1948 as CIO representative to talk with trade union leaders in Germany, Italy, France, Austria, and England, I told Walter how impossible it was to go on working with the World Federation of Trade Unions, by then Communist-dominated. A year later, Walter joined with others in the launching of a new world labor organization at a congress in London — the International Confederation of Free Trade Unions. For this he was blasted by *Trud* as a "traitor and strike breaker"; it was also implied that he was a pet of the U.S. Chamber of Commerce!

At the same time, the Republican Party continued to hammer away at him as the "most dangerous man in America and a Communist." The Reuther brothers had stepped squarely into the middle. In that unenviable position, they became targets for shots from both sides. Soon, some enemy would make use of real bullets.

CHAPTER 21

An Unholy Alliance

The Background

The months immediately after Walter's re-election and the spectacular victory of the Reuther slate were hectic ones for all of us. We had been given a mandate. We would not pass the responsibility to others; we were determined to deliver what the membership hoped for — and expected. So with his key staff members, Walter began to coordinate the basic demands to be laid before the corporations. The union had been shortchanged for many years and it was clear that the auto workers were in line for a whopping wage adjustment, along with some genuine protection from the runaway inflation. It was at this time that the concept of an escalator clause, described in Chapter 19, was born.

The strategy devised in the staff sessions was to reduce by many millions of dollars the auto corporations' swollen profits. We knew they would resist with every weapon they had. They had certainly not yet made up their minds to live in peace with the UAW. For them, Walter's victory was bad news. Now that he had the union behind him, he would, they knew, be a tougher, more confident antagonist than ever before.

But there were other enemies waiting to attack. We had met them during the days of unionization of the River Rouge plant: underworld characters who ran the numbers racket and had the lucrative commissary concessions in the Ford plants. Any interruption of work in those plants meant a reduction in their payoffs. They did not welcome Walter's consolidation of power and feared the effects of a stronger union.

Nor could we underestimate our political enemies, both from the

left and from the right. Our espousal of the Americans for Democratic Action (the ADA) after Roosevelt's death, and our eventual
endorsement of Harry Truman against Henry Wallace further alienated the Communists in the UAW. There were the rabid peddlers
of hate on the extreme right, who never wearied of accusing the
Reuthers of fronting for Moscow and being secretly bent on destroying the free enterprise system. And there were the racists, frightened by our promotion of equal opportunities for blacks.

So it was not surprising that we frequently received threatening
telephone calls and letters. As I write this chapter, violence has
become almost commonplace in America. Presidents, presidential
aspirants, distinguished men in the field of human rights have been
brutally murdered, and all too often the assailants remain unknown
or unapprehended. What is little understood by those born after
World War II is that for many decades before presidents and civil
rights leaders became fair game, these men and women who fought
for the right of American workers to join unions of their choice were
subjected to brutal beatings and assassination. In my father's day it
was the Pinkerton Agency that provided the criminals who preyed,
for the most part, on the steelworkers. In our day it was the underworld of thugs, in cooperation with vigilante groups, who helped
General Motors in Flint and Anderson intimidate the growing
UAW. But in no city in the country was there such an unholy alliance among hired gunmen, high-level executives, government officials, and police agents as openly existed in Detroit.

The memory of Harry Bennett's nearly successful efforts in the
late thirties to contain and control the UAW with his army of ex-con-
victs was not easily forgotten. And in 1945, just before Emil Mazey
returned from the war to become regional director on the Detroit
East Side, replacing Melvin Bishop, a number of important union
leaders in the great Briggs plant, who supported Mazey and the
Reuthers, were assaulted by what were obviously professionals. On
May 31, 1946, Ken Morris, recording secretary of the Briggs Local
212 and a close associate of Mazey and the Reuthers (now an International Executive Board member), was waylaid and beaten so badly
that he almost died. It was indeed strange that when the police
started to investigate the case, the lead pipe and the man's hat recovered by police officers at the scene of the slugging, and stored in the
Police Department's property room, mysteriously disappeared.

When Emil took up his new duties and occupied the office that had been Melvin Bishop's, he found in the desk drawer a personal telephone book. Thumbing through it, he accidentally came upon the private, unlisted number of one Santo Perrone. Perrone was a well-known underworld character suspected of having close ties with the Mafia. He usually went under the name of "the Shark" or "the Enforcer." His base of operations was the Detroit Michigan Stove Works on East Jefferson Avenue near the Detroit River, opposite Windsor, Ontario. A history of Santo Perrone and his brother Gaspar, compiled later by the Kefauver Crime Committee, contains much that is relevant to the events that nearly put Walter and me into early graves. (The transcript of the committee's report is in the Wayne State University archives.)

The Perrones were employed for some years as strikebreakers for the Detroit Michigan Stove Works' Jefferson plant. They took a crew of strikebreakers into the plant on April 7, 1934; a riot started; and a police detail escorted the strikebreakers out and arrested the union pickets. On the fourteenth of that month, with the strike still going on, a picket named Victor D. Joughe was attacked on his way home by unknown assailants and taken to the hospital with a lacerated right arm. Shortly after, the police arrested Santo Perrone and a man named Bart Fasio for carrying concealed weapons. The arrest was made at Mack and McDougall streets, where Perrone had established a loading station for strikebreakers. They were released on their own recognizance and no further police action was taken.

Around June of that year, Santo Perrone was granted a scrap contract by the Detroit Michigan Stove Works, which meant that he could buy its scrap at low prices and sell it for considerable profit. At the same time, Gaspar was granted a contract in the foundry of the same company to produce his own castings. The Crime Committee later estimated that both contracts eventually netted the Perrones about $65,000 a year.

Early in 1937, two of the Perrones' other activities, bootlegging and still operations, caught up with them, and they went to Leavenworth on February 19. Within days, the employees at the Detroit Michigan Stove Works organized themselves into the UAW-CIO and, after a strike of only three hours' duration, obtained a blanket wage increase and an agreement negotiated and signed on February 26. By June, a charter, Local 305, was issued to them.

With the Perrones in jail, there were two years of peace at the

Stove Works. Their contracts for scrap and foundry work, however, remained in force, supposedly administered by their wives, who reaped the profits. Then in 1939, Gaspar (on May 17) and Santo (on June 1) were paroled to John A. Fry, president of the Stove Works, on condition that they remain employed by Fry during their parole. Two month later, the UAW union at the Stove Works had completely disintegrated! There is no clear picture of what happened except for unauthenticated stories of bribery of union officers, intimidation of committeemen, window smashings, and so on. The UAW charter was carried by the last active members for safekeeping to the nearby union office of the CIO Rubber Workers, where it was later recovered by the UAW.

In 1942, Santo, Gaspar, and a third brother, Matteo, were arrested by Detroit police in conjunction with the FBI for possessing a veritable arsenal of unregistered guns, ammunition, and dynamite fuses and caps in their lockers at the Stove Works. Again the employees began to re-establish a union, with UAW help, and petitioned the NLRB to hold elections. But the latter decided in July 1943 that the petitions were premature and they would have to wait until December. Unfortunately the Perrones, charged with violating the federal Firearms Act, got off scot-free. By December 1, their intimidation of union organizers began again with the beating up of Joseph LeBlanc, who came out of his house to go to work, noticed that some of his tires were flat, and, while trying to repair them, was attacked with lead pipes. His head, shoulders, and arms were hurt so severely he had to be taken to the hospital. There was no police action.

When the UAW won elections at both of the Detroit Michigan Stove Works plants (the second, called Metal Fabricating Company, is located at 6450 McNichols Avenue, East Detroit), and was certified as bargaining agent in April 1944, the Perrones turned on the heat in earnest, circulating petitions among the employees against the UAW contract and using divers methods of intimidation to get signatures. On June 2 union committeeman John McCarthy, asleep in his house, was awakened by a series of crashes and found that three windows on the ground floor had been smashed in with a long steel pipe. Three nights later a heavy chisel was thrown at the rear of the house, hitting a screen and cracking the window. In July, Sam Mazzolla, chief shop steward, was attacked from the rear by "Frenchie" Girard, one of the Perrone gang, and beaten so severely with a steel bar that he was in the hospital for some weeks. (Girard had been convicted in 1928 of smuggling in aliens from Canada.) On leaving the hospital, Mazzolla entered a civil suit against Girard for damages, but the day before the trial his car was stopped and searched by police and a gun was discovered. Mazzolla insisted it had been planted. The police held him in custody until his case was dismissed by the court for his failure to appear. He was then released.

John McCarthy, whose windows had been smashed, was threatened in October by two hoodlums with lead pipes who said they would smash his head in unless he promised to resign from his union job and get out of the UAW. He promised and they let him go. He then conferred with Mazzolla; both men were so terror-stricken by now that they agreed to resign together at the next union meeting. Three weeks later, the union had completely melted away at the two Stove Works' plants.

When Emil Mazey reviewed the contract conditions in the various East Side plants and discovered that the Stove Works' membership had vanished and the contract was not being complied with, he assigned Jess Ferrazza to undertake reorganization efforts. While passing out leaflets, Ferrazza was threatened by a person calling himself Gus and advised to stay away from the Detroit Michigan Stove Works. Gus later offered Ferrazza a $1000 bribe, but backed away from the payoff when he apparently became aware of the UAW lookouts lying in wait for him. This same Gus was often seen in the early fifties frequenting Perrone's Gas Station, which was situated, by a not too strange coincidence, directly across the street from the main gate of the Detroit Michigan Stove Works.

Leaflet distributors were viciously threatened in July 1946 by a bunch of thugs directed by Tom Moceri and his brother Joe, who had both been in jail several times for armed robbery and income tax violations, and who figured prominently in the Detroit numbers racket. Before they could do serious damage, Ferrazza shouted, "Here come the cops," and the hoods ran to their cars and disappeared. It was obvious that one Tino Orlando had engineered the whole attack from his position in front of the gas station.

Reorganization of the union at the Stove Works was then discontinued, pending a grand jury investigation to take place in late summer, during which Judge George Murphy uncovered some interesting facts about the Perrones and their gang. Born in Alcamo, Sicily, in 1895, Santo emigrated to the U.S. in 1912 and had his first tangle with the police eight years later. His brothers also emigrated and both Santo and Gaspar were employed by the Detroit Michigan Stove Works as core makers. However, as soon as they had proved themselves ardent and efficient strikebreakers, John Fry entered into an unwritten agreement with them whereby Gaspar would run the Stove Works and use it as a front for his numerous other projects and Santo would be given the scrap metal contract. Santo himself told Judge Murphy that he cleared a profit of roughly $4000 a month from the scrap contract.

The friendly arm of John A. Fry continued to protect his henchmen, and when Detroit made him Deputy Commissioner of the Detroit Police Department (while he was supposedly heading up the Detroit Michigan Stove Works) he once again paroled his protégés out of Leavenworth to work under his supervision.

It also came out during the grand jury investigation that Fry was a close friend of Dean Robinson, son-in-law of the founder of the Briggs Company. Robinson had served as labor relations director until he became president of the company in 1945. Although the latter vigorously denied he had even talked with Fry about using the Perrone gang for union-busting, it was revealed that the Briggs firm had a contract for scrap metal hauling with Carl Renda who, it was revealed, was Santo Perrone's son-in-law. The contract with Renda was signed on April 7, 1945, just seven weeks before the first brutal beating of a UAW officer of the Briggs Local.

Renda's testimony made it clear that, like his father-in-law, he had had no previous experience in scrap hauling; he did none of the actual work but subcontracted it to professionals. Nonetheless, he earned $53,000 in 1946, and $101,000 in 1947, from the Briggs contract. Judge Murphy wondered why a reputable firm like Briggs would grant such a lucrative contract to someone who had no experience. The Briggs comptroller, George N. Lilygren, who was responsible for the financing of salvage operations, testified that he had complained about the arrangement to W. J. Cleary, director of purchasing. When the judge asked Lilygren, "Is it not a fact that Mr. Cleary told you he had orders from Robinson and there was nothing he could do about it?"

"That was my understanding, yes."

"And you had an opinion as to what the cause of that was, did you not?"

"I had an opinion. There was some relief from labor trouble. We had a considerable amount of wildcat strikes there during that period of time."

The records of the grand jury inquiry showed that in 1946, after the Renda scrap iron contract went into effect, there were only 600,000 hours of labor lost, compared with 1,600,000 in 1945. The grand jury sought to find Mr. Cleary for interrogation. They learned that he had died under mysterious circumstances. They did get the testimony of Max W. Temchin, a professional scrap dealer, who said, "The whole tie-up seems to work."

"What indication have you that it works?"

"Well, Briggs has less strikes. See, it's evident that Briggs haven't had any trouble at all in the last year or so. That wasn't settled in a day."

The grand jury investigation led to no convictions against the criminals responsible for the Briggs beatings; no action whatsoever with regard to collusion between automobile executives and the Detroit underworld. Nor did anything come of the arrest of Melvin Bishop and Santo Perrone, who were hunting together in northern Michigan, where Santo owned a hunting lodge — hunting illegally by "shining"; that is, using a bright spotlight to transfix the animals. The two men said they did not know each other, but the arresting officer remarked, "They were not strangers. I know that." Melvin Bishop, who had Perrone's unlisted number in his phone book, refused to discuss his acquaintance with Santo, and also refused to take a lie detector test when later questioned by the Detroit police.

It is significant to remember that it was Walter who initiated the grand jury investigation into the Briggs beatings and, consequently, into the scrap contracts between the Perrone gang and the leading Detroit auto manufacturers; the petition was signed only a few weeks after he was first elected president of the UAW.

Though little came of the investigation, a former federal investigator, Ralph Winstead, who was helping the UAW try to uncover the source of the violent attacks against its officers and members, was able to give some significant information to Michigan State Police Senior Inspector Slack:

In 1943 and 1944, a series of meetings had been held by large employers, Messrs. Fry, Bennett [of Ford], Dean Robinson and others for the purpose of discussing ways and means to eliminate unions at the termination of World War II. These meetings were attended by Perrone and Tony Dana. Information indicates that Sam Perrone was likewise to get a scrap contract — from Ford and Chrysler. A similar meeting was held May 12, 1950, at the Book Cadillac Hotel attended by Messrs. Bennett, Fry, Dean Robinson, Hutchinson and other persons.

In January 1950, acting on a tip, Chief James Butterfield of the U.S. Immigration and Naturalization Service, raided the Michigan Stove Works, searching for aliens smuggled into the country. Twenty Sicilians were arrested — the biggest haul he had ever made. Subsequent federal inquiry revealed the Stove Works was more than a center for the smuggling of aliens; it was a convenient by-station for the rumrunning that originally sent the Perrones to prison.

Some years later, after both the Detroit police and the FBI had failed to find the would-be assassins of Walter and me, the Kefauver Committee came to Detroit for hearings. Among other things, they uncovered the fact that Carl Renda, Santo's son-in-law and holder of the Briggs scrap iron contract, had been issued a hidden weapon permit in 1946 by the Detroit Police Department. According to testimony, Perrone introduced his son-in-law to a high Immigration Department official, who endorsed the application to carry a concealed gun.

Some auto industry die-hards were determined to keep Detroit an "open-shop town," but it seems they had their own closed shop, uniting into an unholy alliance the criminal underworld, themselves, the Detroit police, and federal agents too.

The Terror

Walter, Roy, and I learned to live with the threatening letters and phone calls. We traveled around the city as usual; even late at night, Walter often returned home alone to the bungalow on Appoline Street in northwest Detroit, the first real home he and May had. He had enjoyed fixing it up himself; it was his sanctuary, and with the exception of an occasional meeting with a few of us in the basement "buttermilk bar," it was kept completely free of union business. The house sat on a corner lot, and Walter usually parked his car on the side street and entered through the kitchen door.

On April 20, 1948, five months after his re-election, Walter was detained at a meeting in the Cadillac Hotel in downtown Detroit and phoned May to say he could not make it for supper and would like something kept hot for him. It was about nine-thirty when he reached Appoline Street, unhappy that he was too late to see his two small daughters, who must have gone to bed. By some chance, he deviated from his usual custom: he parked the car in front of the house and went in by the front door.

After greeting May, he took off his coat and shoes, opened his shirt collar, went into the kitchen, and ate most of his meal. Then he went to the refrigerator to get the dessert. As he turned to May to make some casual remark, there was an enormous explosion and the noise of shattering glass, and Walter fell bleeding to the kitchen floor. A twelve-gauge shotgun, the kind usually used for hunting big game, had been fired through the kitchen window by someone who had been waiting in the bushes near the kitchen door. If Walter had not turned to speak to May at the very second the trigger was pulled, the full load of both barrels would have hit him in the chest and undoubtedly killed him immediately. Also, if he had entered the house in his usual way — the killer was obviously familiar with his habits — he would indeed have been a sitting duck.

As it was, four of the big slugs smashed his right arm just above the elbow, all but severing it, and a fifth entered his back above the waist and ricocheted around the ribs from right to left, exiting from the front of his body. The shots that missed him ripped out huge chunks of plaster and wood from the cupboards, wall, and hot air ventilator.

May recalls that she screamed and Walter cried out, "My God, I'm shot." She rushed to the phone to summon police and an ambulance. Richard Ruen, a neighbor, awakened by the roar of the shotgun, jumped out of bed, dashed across to the bungalow, and seeing Walter sprawled on the floor, bleeding profusely, ran down the street to get another neighbor, Dr. Angelo V. Lenzi. The doctor gave Walter morphine for the pain and worked to staunch the bleeding. "Those bastards had to shoot me in the back," Walter said between gasps. "They couldn't come out in the open and fight!"

He told me later that his mind at that moment flashed back to the accident he had had in his youth at the Wheeling Corrugating Company, when a heavy die severed his toe and he had begged the doctors to sew it back on. This time he was afraid that the morphine would make him lose consciousness, and his arm would be removed.

He begged Dr. Lenzi not to let anyone cut off his arm and was reassured when the doctor fashioned an emergency splint. "The arm was hanging at such a crazy angle," Dr. Lenzi told me later, "I decided he would have a better chance to save it if I got a splint on before he was taken to the hospital."

The ambulance took Walter to the New Grace Hospital, where he went through two and a half hours of surgery and received three pints of blood and a pint of plasma. His body was put in a cast from the waist up and his arm into an unusually complicated traction device. Electric shocks were given the arm to keep up the circulation.

May, of course, had gone with Walter in the ambulance; neighbors came in to be with the children, who had miraculously not been awakened. The house was already buzzing with police and detectives. I was fortunately at home that evening and rushed to the hospital as soon as I heard the news, joined Roy, and got there just as Walter was being prepared for surgery. Though he had been given some sedation, he was fully conscious. I walked to his side, tears in my eyes, took his good hand in mine, and leaned over and whispered in his ear, "This is Vic. You've been hurt bad, but we've been through many things together and you'll pull through this one. Don't give up. Hang with it." He pressed my hand feebly and I knew he had heard me. May soon joined me and told him we would be at his side throughout the night.

As they wheeled him off to surgery, I went to the waiting room, which was crowded with people talking about what the police had found. I was anxious to get word to Wheeling, for I knew that Mother and Dad and Ted would want to be with Walter. I had to locate Christine at the Pittsburgh hospital where she worked. I did not know then the extent of Walter's injury — just that his arm was almost gone and he was still bleeding profusely at the waist.

I reached Ted and asked him to break the news to Mother and Dad and let me know if they were coming. When I finally got Christine on the phone, even though she was a nurse and used to human suffering, she wept openly, repeating over and over, "Oh no! Oh no!" Ted, Ann, and my parents drove to Pittsburgh to pick up Christine and continued through Ohio to Detroit. Each time they stopped for gas or a cup of coffee, they saw new editions of newspapers with big headlines on the assassination attempt. "What has he done to deserve this?" my mother kept repeating.

May, Roy, and I took turns at Walter's bedside and by dawn the whole family had come. I would rather have been beaten into insensibility than go through the pain of escorting our dear mother into Walter's room that morning. He was a pathetic sight — pale, his eyes closed, and his right arm in the grotesque traction. Mother sat with him for a while, saying little, just holding his hand and urging him not to talk. On the day following, when we knew he was out of danger, she did say what was on her mind: "Why don't you give up your union work? Go into some other field? You could even go back to your trade and earn good money." Walter was still dazed with drugs, but he opened his eyes slightly and, looking at her quizzically, murmured, "I'd probably make more money." "Then do it," Mother urged. Walter was silent for a while and then in a low and clear voice, he said, "No, I must do what I'm doing; it's bigger than I am, and we can't run away from it." And our Mütterschen, who had survived many storms and crises and had enormous inner strength, knew in her heart there was no turning aside for any of us.

Meantime, the police had gathered bits and pieces of information from Walter's neighbors, who, when they had heard the shot, had gone to their windows and seen a new Ford sedan, either red or maroon, parked around the corner on Chippewa Avenue, its lights off, motor running, and a man at the wheel. They had seen the assassin run to the car and jump in, and watched the car race off. Deep footprints had been found under the kitchen window. Crowds of the curious gathered around the house, so that the two little girls, Linda and Lisa, who had been told that Walter had fallen against the window and cut himself, soon realized this was no ordinary accident. There were police on guard, but Jack Conway, Emil Mazey, and other officers of the union, who had little confidence in the Detroit police, had organized their own guard duty, not only of the house but of Walter's hospital room. (From then on, for the rest of Walter's life, whether he was home or in distant parts of the world, a silent figure was always somewhere near him: his UAW security officer. It was hard for him to answer Linda's recurring questions: "Daddy, why can't they leave us alone? Why can't I be like other kids?")

The savage attempt to assassinate a prominent American in his home shocked the nation; expressions of outrage came from the President, Supreme Court Justices, senators, congressmen, the City Council of Detroit, religious leaders, corporation officials, and from

political leaders and trade union compatriots all over the world.
There was a clamor for speedy police action. In a burst of activity
the day after the shooting, the Detroit Police Commissioner ordered
a search of "every garage in the city," and told his staff to bring in
for questioning anybody who had any personal animosity toward
Walter, especially "Communists or anyone in industry or a union."

Walter stayed in the hospital for many weeks. And as if the pains
from the wounds were not enough, he was to suffer intermittent attacks of hepatitis and even malaria, with which he was infected by
the blood transfusions. What disturbed the surgeons most was their
inability to get any response in the radial nerve, which controlled the
movements of Walter's right hand. Dr. Barnes Woodhall, a consulting neurosurgeon, told Walter he did not believe he would ever
move his arm again and should decide in what position he wanted to
have his hand and arm permanently fixed. Walter rejected the idea.
He had already vowed that he would use his arm and hand again.
The doctor's comment was that he admired his spirit but his medical
judgment was bad. In the end, Walter proved the impossible.

He had further surgery later in the summer at the Duke University Center, followed by therapy in a Detroit clinic. One day he let
out a war whoop and the clinic attendant came running.

"I knew I could do it!" Walter cried in glee and excitement.
"Look, I can move this finger!"

Then, because he had incredible will power, he got his hand working. For months one saw him always with a sponge rubber ball,
which he would squeeze to make the rubber force the fingers open
again; the radial nerve had not yet regenerated sufficiently to allow
him to make a fist. When his arm was at last out of the sling, he
painfully forced himself to hold a hammer in his right hand and do
repair work — even build furniture in his basement workshop. He
knew that use of the arm was the only means of restoring the nerve.
Many people who knew Walter in later life marveled that the arm
that was nearly severed could become a functioning part of his energetic body.

The house on Appoline Street was no longer an island of privacy.
Tourists came to satisfy their ghoulish curiosity, and there was grave
concern in the UAW about the family's staying there any longer. So
later in the summer Walter and May purchased a two-story house,
closer to the center of town and situated in the middle of a block,

with houses close on both sides. The rear yard was carefully fenced in, floodlights installed, and bulletproof glass placed in all the exposed windows. Even police dogs were insisted on by the UAW officers. A special bulletproof Packard was put at Walter's disposal, but he used it seldom and reluctantly. Soon after his recovery, he developed a practical philosophy about the continued threat to his life. After our nation had lived through the assassinations of President Kennedy, Martin Luther King, and Robert Kennedy, Walter turned to me and said: "And we were concerned about protecting ourselves . . . when even the President of the United States can't be made safe and secure in this land!"

The police got nowhere on the case, though rewards totaling $117,800 were offered by the City Council, churches, and many labor organizations — the bulk by the UAW.

A number of congressmen and cabinet members urged the FBI to enter the case. UAW lawyers Irving Levy and Joseph L. Rauh, Jr., were instructed to approach Attorney General Tom Clark to seek his help in involving the FBI. Clark was most sympathetic and said he would talk with J. Edgar Hoover and let them know the next day. Joe Rauh remembers Clark's exact words: "Fellows, Edgar says no. He says he's not going to send the FBI in every time some nigger woman gets raped."

Though Walter's assassin was still at large, I was naïve enough to begin to feel safe, as if the violence that had marked the labor movement in Detroit were now a thing of the past. Walter was recovering fast, and his life was under as much protection as he could endure. With the excitement dying down, and my own Education Department projects moving ahead smoothly, I felt free to branch out into the international work that had always appealed to me and that was to occupy much of my time for almost thirty years.

I had received a cable from General Lucius Clay, head of the U.S. Military Government in Berlin, asking me to fly to Europe and speak to West Berlin trade unionists, who were under pressure from the Russians in East Berlin to join them in a completely Communist-dominated trade union organization. So I flew to Frankfurt and took an overnight military train into the section of Berlin that was still under four-power military rule. The municipal government had not as yet gained the full support of all the citizens of Berlin. But there was one organization that not only the working class but all Berliners felt truly represented them: the UGO, or Independent Trade Union Federation, a provisional body created to meet the exigencies of the postwar period. Because the USSR had precipitated a crisis that immobilized the new, still untested, local government, the UGO was the only authentic voice of the population. It was probably the only thing that stood in the way of the Russians in East Berlin, who were determined to absorb all of the city and were promoting a Unified Trade Union. The West Berlin workers wanted no part of it, and they looked to U.S. officials for assistance and the encouragement to stand firm. An election to determine the issue had been scheduled, and General Clay had appealed to a number of American trade unionists, especially those who could speak German, to come over and lend advice and moral support.

I welcomed the opportunity to help out in that delicate and vital situation. Those were exciting days, hurrying about the battered city in a small, beat-up car with Ernst Scharnowski, leader of the trade unions in Berlin, meeting workers who were literally trying to pull industries out of the rubble and were resisting the dismantlement programs of both the U.S. and the Soviet Union. In that connection, I had an opportunity to impress upon General Clay views that Walter, years before, had expressed in a letter to President Truman. He had attacked the idea of tearing down Germany's industries, showing how that would play right into the Russians' hands. I pointed out to General Clay that the USSR was continuing to dismantle factories that the workers in Berlin had just put back into working order at great sacrifice and was shipping the equipment eastward just as fast as it could be taken apart. (I learned later that many trainloads of precious rebuilt machinery had been unloaded on docks and left to rust in the weather.)

Our delegation was urged by the Berlin workers to intercede with the American military to let them repossess and rebuild their own property, most of which had been badly damaged by the Nazis. They also needed mimeograph machines, typewriters, and other office equipment, without which they were at a great disadvantage in their attempts to avoid the takeover by the Communist trade unions, which were being supplied with such equipment from Eastern Europe. I must say that, while Clay was not immediately responsive, his final record on that score was excellent.

I renewed my acquaintance with George Silver, a former U.S. trade unionist and member of the Jewish Labor Committee in Philadephia, who had come to Berlin as a GI and wound up in military government, fortunately in the section that dealt with labor. He and my old UAW friend, William Kemsley, did prodigious service in providing practical assistance to the genuinely democratic forces emerging in the UGO. Together we were able to convince General Clay to make available the former palatial home of von Ribbentrop, which had been stripped almost bare by the Russians when they left West Berlin, for a UGO Youth and Education Center.

A tempestuous campaign to rally the workers of Berlin was successful; the votes were overwhelmingly in favor of the Independent Trade Union Federation's independence; this victory ensured its survival. General Clay told me many years later that it was doubtful the U.S. military could have stayed on in West Berlin without that show of public moral support.

That same summer I was invited to England to participate in the founding conference of what became the Anglo-American Council on Productivity. This was a joint U.S.–British undertaking initiated by Paul G. Hoffman, economic cooperation Administrator under the Marshall Plan, and an old friend from the days when he had been head of Studebaker, and Sir Stafford Cripps, Chancellor of the Exchequer of Great Britain. Both employer and union representatives came together from both sides of the Atlantic: General Electric's president, Philip Reed, and Ernest Breech from Ford represented U.S. management. Some of my fellow trade unionists were Harvey Brown, president of the Machinists' Association, Lee W. Minton of the Glass Workers, Joseph Scanlon from the Steel Workers. On the British side, there were such prominent labor leaders as Sir Vincent Tewson, Sir Thomas Williamson, Sir William Lawther, and Sir Lincoln Evans.

The purpose of the council was to encourage a more rapid and uniform application within Britain of methods to increase productivity and speed up postwar recovery. Cochairmen were selected from management and labor to underscore the partnership. Philip Reed and I were chosen on the U.S. side. I was very enthusiastic about my new involvement in international labor and when I returned to America, I took every opportunity to speak in public about the importance of promoting free trade unions in Europe and to warn that our aid must *not* go to restore the great prewar cartels, but to finance democratic institutions.

Home again, I found things quiet around our house on Mark

Twain Avenue. The attack on Walter had not brought many
changes to our household: I traveled without security men stepping
on my heels; we had no floodlights or police dogs. We had made
one concession to security: we had bought a small cocker spaniel, a
good watchdog and a companion for our children. I admit now that
there were times in the early part of 1949 when, coming home late
from a meeting, parking the car at the entrance of the garage, and
getting out to slide the door up, I would notice a parked car nearby
suddenly start its engine and roar away. But I dismissed it easily;
probably a couple spooning in the dark.

In mid-May, we began to get calls from the local police station to
the effect that the neighbors were complaining about our dog's bark-
ing. We were not aware that our dog had been a nuisance, though
sometimes late at night Blackie did kick up a fuss. I would usually
go down to see what was causing it and at those moments, too, I
would see a parked car start up and speed away. I had the feeling
that if the dog barked, he had a good reason.

Once, when the police called, I asked for the names of the neighbors who had complained but this request was turned down. A few
days later an officer came to the door to talk about the dog and I
asked him for the names, saying I wanted to talk personally to the
neighbors and try to iron things out. The policeman said he could
not give the names and added, "This is the last time I'm notifying
you. You'll have to do something about the dog."

We had a family conference that evening, and though the children
were very upset about the decision, we gave Blackie to friends who
lived in a Detroit suburb.

The very day after the dog was gone, May 24, 1949, just thirteen
months after Walter was shot, I spent the whole evening at home
with Sophie. After the children were in bed, we had a visit from our
friends the Lowries. Dr. William Lowrie had for a long time been
the family physician as well as a friend. They stayed until about
eleven-thirty. Sophie had a batch of clothing that needed mending
and I wanted to read an article in the *New York Times*. Sophie told
me that the reading lamp at the foot of the stairs near the sofa
where she was sitting needed a new bulb. I replaced the burned-out
bulb and sat down to read. All of a sudden there was a terrible
blast, and buckshot from a double-barreled shotgun tore through
the front window, ripping the right side of my face, tearing out my

right eye, plowing into the jaw, and scattering bits of tooth and bone throughout my head. Some of the lead shot ripped open my chest and smashed the collarbone. I was wearing glasses, and bits of glass and frame were driven into my skull. A partial denture was pushed deep into the back of my throat.

Sophie screamed, thinking the light bulb had exploded. I staggered to my feet and felt as if I had been electrocuted — an enormous voltage of electric current seemed to be going through my entire nervous system. I felt no pain then, only numbness. I could not breathe and knew I was choking; as I fell to the floor I managed to reach into my bleeding mouth and pull out the twisted denture and throw it across the room. As so often happens with those at the threshold of death who live to tell the tale, I saw my life as a whole, and I knew it was too soon to die. I prayed, "Dear God, no, not yet, there is still so much to do. And so much to live for with Sophie and the children." I was swept by an intense feeling of remorse for all the times of crisis at home when I had not been there to help Sophie and she had to bear the heavy load alone. I prayed for another chance to lighten her burden.

At the sound of the gun blast, Mrs. Tessie Kominars, who lived directly across the street, rushed from her house in time to see an old-model car race east on the side street, Elmira, directly away from our house. At that moment Sophie emerged from our front door screaming for help. As she turned to come in again and saw all the broken glass scattered on the carpet along with leaves from our window plants, she realized I had been shot and dialed the operator for police and an ambulance.

How ironic that I had put in a bulb of stronger wattage than the one I replaced, making myself a brilliant target for the assassin on the very first evening we were without a watchdog!

Ten-year-old Carole was awakened by the blast and came running down. When she saw me lying in a pool of blood and the stairs cluttered with broken plaster from a hole in the stairway as big as a football (the shot in the choke barrel had missed my head by a few inches), she became hysterical. To this day Sophie and I are grateful to our neighbors, the Austin Heys, who took her in for the night, and to Mrs. Kominars, who came in to stay with Eric and John, who fortunately had not been around.

The ambulance took me to the Redford Receiving Hospital, but as soon as Dr. Lowrie had been reached, he made arrangements to transfer me to the Henry Ford Hospital, where he was on the staff. I was conscious all the way, and as I went into shock and had terrible chills, I was aware that Sophie, riding with me in the ambulance, was also in a state of shock — I distinctly recall her moaning. I knew the pain and terror she was feeling.

Walter, returning from a meeting with Jack Conway, heard the news on the car radio. They rushed to the hospital and made their way to my room through the crowd of newsmen and police jamming the corridors. Sophie had asked neighbors to call George Edwards, our close friend; he was the first to reach the hospital, along with Roy, who lived in nearby Birmingham, Michigan, and was called by Sophie from the hospital. This time Roy had the sad task of calling Ted and asking him to wake our parents once again with tragic news. The blow of this second murderous attack was too much for Dad; he was not up to making the trip and remained in Wheeling.

I couldn't see Walter when he came in because my left eye was too bloodshot and my face heavily bandaged. My right arm was paralyzed by the shots that had smashed my collarbone. Walter took my left hand and pressed it gently, as I had done his thirteen months before, and spoke words of encouragement. I remember Roy also grasping my good hand and saying, "Keep fighting. You've got to pull through."

I shall be forever grateful to Dr. Lowrie, who pulled together a group of skilled surgeons to give me the emergency care I needed. Among them was Dr. Conrad Lam and the eye surgeon Dr. James Olson. Sophie was asked that night to sign papers, required by law, to authorize removal of my right eye. But to impose such a responsibility on her then was little short of barbaric. No one needed such authorization. There was no eye. It had been shot out. I vividly recall Dr. Olson working over me that night — they could not give me much more than local anesthesia for fear I wouldn't regain consciousness. I apparently mumbled something about the disfiguration and handicap of having only one eye. Dr. Olson was not only a great surgeon but a kind man. As he operated, he said to me in a soft quiet voice, "You know, there are many people who are not handicapped though they have vision in only one eye. How would you feel if you knew that many a surgeon with only one eye performs delicate operations?"

That was indeed a consolation. Just before a later operation on my tongue, however, I remember saying to the oral surgeon, "They can take out my eye and take off an arm or a leg, but please fix up my tongue. I've got a living to make."

It was 5:45 A.M. before Sophie was taken home. "Vic is bad," she said, "but I think he's out of danger." The house was full of detectives and police, some making themselves coffee in the kitchen. The living room was a shambles. It was fortunate that Sophie's half brother, Edward Bezuska, was able to take time off from his job as mechanic with the Detroit bus company to help her during those first difficult days.

This time the assailant had dropped his shotgun on the ground and the police found it in the bushes in front of the house. They were also able to make very good plaster of Paris imprints of the footprints left by the murderer in the soft dirt — not that this authentic evidence seemed to do them much good in their investigation. The gun was similar, perhaps identical, to the one used against Walter.

Cordons of police were thrown around our house and Walter's and, for the first time, around Roy's. He and Fania and their two small boys lived in a renovated garage-guest house. That night when the reporters asked him if he felt he might be the next victim, he answered: "Naturally, I've thought of it. The State Police have offered to post guard and I've accepted it. I'm not going to resign or go into hiding or anything like that. We're fighting for good clean unionism. Our record stands by and for itself. After Walter was shot, Victor and I talked this over and agreed to continue the good fight. Whoever has done this represents forces that are against clean unionism. Whether they are employers, fascists, or Communists makes no difference. This can't be fought be resigning!"

Fania, sober-faced and holding tight to Roy's hand, silently nodded her head in agreement.

During the painful weeks of convalescence, as I went through successive operations for the rebuilding of my face, I received personal messages, from all over the country and from abroad, that gave me strength and comfort: a note from Paul Hoffman and one from Averell Harriman, who was then administering the Marshall Plan in Paris; messages from Governors and members of Congress. Dr. Kurt Schumacher, leader of the German Social Democratic Party and survivor of twelve years in a concentration camp, a man I had long admired, wrote, "The enemies of the workers' movement will not succeed in stopping progress of democratic powers in spite of their terrorism." British and European trade union leaders sent me condolences and good wishes. Dear friends in Detroit, knowing I didn't want them wasting money on flowers, thought up an ingenious way of putting their good wishes to work: Hans Scherber and Bill Kemsley of the American Association for a Democratic Germany started a Victor Reuther Get Well Quick Fund, with all contributions to go for supplies for the struggling trade union forces in West Germany.

When I was finally released after the first series of operations and allowed to recuperate at home, my neighbors dropped in from time to time to see me. I had read in the Detroit *Times* that some of them had given the police many valuable clues:

> Police are still hopeful that the neighbors' description of two men seen prowling in the neighborhood of the Reuther home at 11304 Mark Twain for several nights before the attack could be pieced together. Three neighbors of Reuther saw the men sitting in a parked car and driving past the Reuther home occasionally as if to map the crime that was to come. One of the neighbors, whose name was withheld, said he was walking his dog between 9:30 and 10:00 Monday slightly more than 24 hours before the shooting and saw the men in their parked car two blocks from the Reuther home. He first saw the car, a '39 or '40 Mercury five passenger coupe, standing in Freeland between Orangelawn and Elmira, and when the two occupants noticed him, they pulled away, drove past the Reuther home, circled, and returned to their original parking place.

I was therefore surprised to learn from one of my neighbors five weeks later that, although he had been able to give a very detailed description of the men in the car, no police officer returned to talk with him, nor had they shown him any photographs of suspects. I called this to the attention of the chief of the detective squad investigating the case, Detective Sergeant Albert DeLamielleure. He was irritated, but the next day arrived at our neighbor's home and dumped off four or five shoe boxes full of photographs of individuals who had previously been arrested. This did not seem to me a professional way to try to zero in on criminals.

What was really disturbing and sad for us was that, only a few days after the delivery of the boxes of photos, the same neighbor received several anonymous phone calls, threatening him and his family with death if they gave any more information to the police. He suffered a heart attack as a result of the calls and the family finally sought refuge in a secluded area in Florida. Why didn't the calls come earlier? Why did they come right after my complaint to DeLamielleure?

As I talked with other neighbors, I remembered the police telling us we had to get rid of our dog, and I asked the neighbors whether they had ever made or heard of any complaints about our spaniel. (Many times, in those days, Sophie would exclaim, "Oh, if only we had had the dog! He would have warned us.") I was not surprised when every one of the neighbors answered no, because I reasoned that if anyone *had* complained, he or she would now be remorseful and would not want to admit it. I phoned the local precinct station, and asked if it had a record of the people who had phoned about our dog. The officer on duty called back to say there was absolutely no record of any complaint about our dog.

The question remains and probably always will: were the calls about our dog really from the police? Was the officer who came to the door the day before I was shot an impersonator? Or did someone on the police staff remove from the files any record of the calls — just as the lead pipe and the hat belonging to Ken Morris's assailant disappeared from the police property room?

I had, in fact, an astonishing conversation with DeLamielleure even before I saw my neighbors. Shortly after I came home from the hospital, still weak, and scarcely able to talk because of the facial surgery, DeLamielleure insisted on seeing me alone, so Sophie left the room. He pulled his chair close to me and, looking me straight in the eye, said in a hushed voice, "Mr. Reuther, have you had any recent difficulties with your wife?"

If I had had the strength, I would have picked up a chair and hit him over the head for his sordid insinuation that Sophie hired someone to murder me. After that incident I found it difficult to consider him credible, and later events proved that he had a much greater stake in not making a proper investigation of the crime than any of us dreamed.

Of all that was written or spoken in the national media, in Congress, and around the world about this second assassination attempt, it was a New York *Post* editorial that most closely hit the mark:

The methods of the would-be assassin who shot Walter Reuther more than a year ago and the assailant of his brother Victor are so similar as to suggest that both these cowardly attacks were the work of the same criminal, but even if the assault on Victor Reuther were the work of an imitator, it was undoubtedly encouraged by the failure of the authorities to bring to trial the man who tried to murder his more famous brother. The fact that this earlier assault remains shrouded in mystery is a serious reflection on the competence of the Detroit police force to deal with the turbulent elements of that great industrial city.

Michigan's Senator Ferguson had spoken from the Senate floor on May 25 to urge the Justice Department to help solve the two crimes, saying it was no time to quibble over jurisdiction. "I called on the Justice Department a year ago to help investigate the attempted assassination of Walter Reuther. Those who assaulted Walter Reuther were never caught and now the calamity has happened again. His brother is seriously wounded and there is grave doubt as to whether he will live."

The next day, in an unprecedented move, the Senate adopted a resolution requesting President Truman to direct the FBI to investigate the shootings. An appeal also went to Truman and to Attorney General Tom Clark from Michigan's Governor G. Mennen Williams for FBI intervention. The UAW posted an additional $100,000, bringing to $217,800. the reward money offered for information.

By May 27, however, the Detroit *News* appeared to have solved both crimes all by itself:

> Walter Reuther was way over on the vicious side when he said after the shooting of his brother Victor that "diehard elements among employers, or Communist or Fascist agents could be responsible . . . ." He knows very well that dragging the employers into such a line-up of possible assassins is mere hokum. He knows very well that it is a million to one that both he and his brother were shot by men moved by CIO union political quarrels which by all we hear have reached a stage of bitterness far beyond that existing between employer and employee.

Thus spoke a mouthpiece of the unholy alliance, reflecting an attitude all too prevalent among the authorities in Detroit, including some within the Police Department who wanted the public to accept the view that it didn't matter too much "if one union gangster bumped another union gangster off."

Meanwhile, on the insistence of the UAW officers, our small house was converted into a fortress surrounded by a six-foot wire fence with its posts imbedded in concrete. Bulletproof metal window shades were installed on all windows exposed to the street; there was an electric light system with alarms, an automatic lift for the garage door, and an intercom on the front door so that visitors could be identified. There were bodyguards always underfoot. This was not a pleasant sort of life and Roy and I both bridled at having guards around us, though we recognized the necessity. Walter and I bore physical scars all our lives but there were deeper, if invisible, scars left by those events on the Reuther women and on all our children. For a long time it was impossible not to imagine who might be lurking in every dark shadow and not to be terrified of every strange noise in the night.

Terror struck twice again that year. There was an ambush attempt, which failed, on the life of Ken Bannon, our UAW Ford national director. It was no coincidence that this came immediately after a Ford pension plan had been fought through and finally ratified. The second atrocity was an attempt to blow up the headquarters of the UAW-CIO two nights before Christmas Eve. Disaster was averted by a tip relayed to the police by its recipient, Detroit *Times* reporter Jack Pickering.

> The bomb contained enough explosives, the police said, to blow the four-story brick building sky-high and to cause heavy damage and possible loss of life in the seven-story General Motors research building 25 feet away . . . The bomb, planted in an outdoor stairwell leading to a side basement entrance, contained two fuses and detonators showing the dynamiters' deliberate attempt to touch off a devastating blast. The dynamite was contained in a cardboard box brightly wrapped in white candycane striped Christmas paper. To add a bizarre touch, a blue ribbon was tied around the box. The bomb was apparently meant for Walter Reuther, President of the UAW, because the anonymous caller, who informed Pickering of the plot, said: *"It was planted when the big guy was in the building."*

CHAPTER 22

Justice Aborted

"Till then sit still, my soul: foul deeds will rise,
Though all the earth o'erwhelm them, to men's eyes."

Hamlet (Act I, Scene 2)

WAS THERE EVER a sincere investigation of the two shootings and the attempted bombing? The answer has to be *no* with regard to the Detroit police and the FBI. Only the Kefauver Crime Committee and the investigators hired by the UAW uncovered any significant clues. These were either bungled or not followed up by law enforcement officials.

None of us in the UAW wanted to take on the role of detective; we were not competent as such, and it would have been both time-consuming and emotionally harrowing. On the other hand, it was urgent that the UAW try to maintain some kind of working relationship with the lawmen working on the three crimes. This was possible with the Michigan State Police — Jack Conway and others in the UAW had good liaison with them — but the Detroit police were another matter altogether. The UAW, therefore, turned to two highly qualified investigators: Heber Blankenhorn, who, as a representative of the NLRB in 1936, had laid the groundwork for what became the La Follette Committee inquiry into corporate spying on labor, and Ralph Winstead, the skilled federal investigator who had helped uncover the connection between Bennett and Perrone. When Blankenhorn was with NLRB, he almost single-handedly broke the case in Texas involving the violence provoked by Harry Bennett and his Ford Service Department. In 1942, the Army commissioned him for a post on the General Staff.

The task of these two men was to pull together as much information as they could about the forces antagonistic to the Reuthers and/or the UAW who might have hired the would-be assassins and dynamiters. They were also to provide a proper method of keeping in touch with the various law enforcement agencies without meddling with the basic responsibilities of the police. With the Detroit police, it must be said, they drew a blank. Every time they approached the detectives who were theoretically working on the Reuther shootings, they were advised to hunt out various Communist suspects in distant countries. There was one thing the Detroit police definitely did not want investigated: the link between the underworld and prominent automotive executives. They did not want it known how many scrap iron contracts were signed, and who was paid how much to do what to whom.

The FBI, which entered the scene shortly after the dynamite threat, was evidently not very interested in that, either. A memorandum from Blankenhorn to the UAW, dictated in January 1950, provides an amusing, if slightly sinister, account of the way in which the FBI investigation was conducted. Parts of it are worth quoting:

> After two conferences in which the union's investigators, as ordered, put everything at FBI disposal, we have encountered the typical FBI secrecy. Everything goes in; nothing is ever communicated . . . so I talked with FBI Deputy Director E. G. Conley from Washington, apparently in charge of the case here . . .
> The FBI entry into the Reuther cases had visible effects on local police authorities. They seemed to sit further down on their fannies than they had, if that was possible . . .
> E. G. Conley is a lean, graying, compact man with a confident manner, a poker face, and a complete master of the FBI habit of talking platitudes to evade giving any information. His personal manner was very friendly . . .

Blankenhorn then gave us a sample of his conversation with Conley. He said: "The police records are supposed to include data on a car equipped to hide a gun — a confession and a gun found. None of these papers are available to the Prosecutor's office . . . A second general question has been heard: Is the FBI in as investigator or as undertaker?"

Conley replied: "If you mean strings on my investigation, you are wrong. The orders are to go into everything — both shootings, dynamiting, etc. I am not saying the FBI is always successful; this is the most difficult case I have had in thirty years in the FBI. We may have to go way back — it may take five years to solve it. But I am not classifying it as insoluble, not yet."

(As it happened, the case was closed only two years later.)

Blankenhorn then asked Conley if his agents ever had difficulty getting labor people to talk.

"We never do," Conley answered, "except the left wing, you know who. The right wing always comes to us and talks."

When Blankenhorn told Conley how he himself had been investigated by the FBI when he was directing the NLRB probe into Ford's labor spying and other antilabor practices, and asked him if he didn't find that rather strange, Conley answered, "The FBI investigation might have been under the Hatch Act."

"How could any investigation of Ford's violation of labor law be considered a private political activity? asked Blankenhorn.

"Might be," replied Conley.

Blankenhorn confessed in his memorandum that that reply left him winded. He asked Conley if, as an American, he didn't feel ashamed that in this country well-known labor leaders could be shot and a union office almost dynamited yet no solution found.

"There is no protection against somebody who wants to shoot you," said Conley. "I know. I've been shot at more than once — you just take it. There is no question they meant to kill; both records make that plain."

Blankenhorn then checked through the ten suggestions he had given the FBI with regard to leads in a previous case. Conley offered no indication of what the FBI had done with them, nor did he ask for any more information. Blankenhorn asked if there was anything about theories on the cases he wanted to discuss.

"I know all the theories," answered Conley. "It's a bit early to discuss that."

After a few more futile exchanges, Blankenhorn said: "The union's position has been clear for a long time. It wanted the FBI on the cases; it realizes the difficulties of cases so long unsolved. The union also realizes that the local police authorities have shown less rather than more effort since the FBI came in. If the union finds no evidence of any effective police work, local or federal, anywhere, it is not likely to be silent. You would agree that the union had a right to be nervous if it thought that the criminal underworld responsible for all this came to believe that no law enforcement agencies were really after them?"

Conley's response ended the interview. "Of course, of course. But the FBI can't promise to deliver overnight. It may take years."

My own interview with Attorney General J. Howard McGrath in the summer of 1950, a year after I had been shot, was equally appalling. I was then back in full swing, and had ahead of me many missions overseas. But I was most uneasy about leaving the country, since I did not feel my family was safe. I no longer feared for my own life, but knew that the limited security provided for the family could not possibly give it any real protection. I would have had some peace of mind if I had thought the FBI was actively searching for the killers. Even the press had begun to imply there was little force in the investigation. So I asked our Washington attorney, Joe Rauh, if he could arrange for us both to have a talk with the Attorney General.

McGrath, when we finally were given an interview, said he made it a practice never to interfere with the FBI's work, and then added, "By concentrating on the Commie cases, the FBI might break this case through some Commie angle." According to him, that was the best bet.

Rauh, in a confidential report, said that this statement conflicted with Deputy Attorney General Peyton Ford's opinion, expressed earlier, that the assassins obviously were not Commies since the Department of Justice "would know if it had been them."

Mr. McGrath's most significant remark was: "The FBI is working on the bomb case and *not the earlier crimes.*" (Italics mine.) It was clear then that there would be little help coming from that direction.

The Attorney General, who, to understate the matter, had been cool during the first part of the interview, became openly hostile when I brought up the Kefauver Crime Committee, which had already uncovered some amazing links between the underworld and the great corporate units. I asked if he thought the committee might be of help in breaking the Detroit cases. Both the FBI and the Justice Department were very negative about the idea of the Crime Committee's nosing around in Detroit; McGrath actually told us that such a development would definitely dampen the FBI's enthusiasm for pursuing any of the crimes. But if I wanted to talk to the Kefauver Committee, he assured me, I was free to do so.

Pressure was meanwhile mounting from some Michigan officials and private citizens to get the Crime Committee to come to Detroit. Gerald K. "Pat" O'Brien, the Wayne County Prosecuting Attorney, who had always held himself somewhat independent of local and state police, made his own appeal on February 26, 1951, to the Kefauver Committee "to delve into the Reuther shootings and the Briggs beatings," and offered his full cooperation. More pressure came from the UAW and two prominent clergymen, Father Raymond Clancy, director of Social Action for the Catholic Archdiocese of Detroit, and the Reverend G. Merrill Lenox, executive secretary of the Detroit Council of Churches.

Blankenhorn had established personal relations with Senator Kefauver and his staff, and responded to specific questions they had raised, some of which involved FBI action on the case. Blankenhorn wrote Kefauver in August of 1950:

> FBI had two squads on it last spring; they have fewer now and Hoover's Deputy Director in Charge never appears . . . FBI does not take us, mere non-governmental experts, into confidence. They have to preserve their secrecy and they are right, up to the point where they have to ask us, or local authorities, for facts they don't know. I know that point, having been in the Government and working with FBI and I know that is where they fall down — on labor cases, which after all are Greek to the FBI . . . They are now following bum steers that we cleared up for them months ago . . . Time and again they have said, "If we need anything further on that we'll call you up." Net result: they have never asked us, even after we gave them what we thought were main clues — documentation which we have now put into the hands of your Senate Committee. Most particularly was the listing and analysis of famed gambler-racketeer characters, nearly 100 of them, from whom, we feel, the Reuther gunmen came, together with our lead to the main instigating suspect . . .
>
> Your Committee has clear jurisdiction over the corruptive gangster operations in the auto underworld, one segment of which seems to lead into the Reuther shootings, on which the FBI has been assigned for eight months without turning up anything for a grand jury."

When Kefauver received the documentation from Blankenhorn and Winstead, he gave them a clear commitment that the committee would come to Detroit and conduct hearings. The hearings were delayed by events described by Blankenhorn: "Some fool shoots two prospective Kefauver witnesses in Chicago, and New York throws out its Police Commissioner for graft. Result: my Detroit Reuther shootings drop in the Senate Committee's priorities. So now they say, 'Sure, we will get to you, but not now.' "

By February of 1951, the Kefauver Committee had amassed enough information in American cities to issue a report called "How Gangs Sap U.S. of Billions," in which they refer to "a secret government within government, which rules the underworld with a 20 billion dollars a year budget."

Just a month after the report was made public, Santo Perrone and the Detroit Michigan Stove Works were back in the news. This time federal immigration agents had found sixty Sicilian aliens making their way into Detroit via the Stove Works. And in August, Police Commissioner George F. Boos lowered the boom on the Canton Bar, across the street from the Stove Works on East Jefferson Avenue. It was the hangout of many of Perrone's men and had figured in the plotting of the antiunion activities that had kept the UAW out of the Stove Works for many years. It was also frequented by many of those suspected by the UAW of involvement in the shootings. At this point it was publicly announced that Detective Sergeant DeLamielleure was under investigation as the possible hidden owner of the Canton Bar, which was listed as being owned by his brother-in-law, Gaston Williams, and in which DeLamielleure's wife worked. After investigation, the Police Department found that the very same DeLamielleure was guilty of having a substantial and illegal interest in the Canton Bar. He was demoted to the rank of detective, suspended for fifteen days, and took a loss of $355 a year. Stern justice!

When it became clear that Kefauver would not come to Detroit for some time, Heber Blankenhorn felt he could no longer justify the expense to the UAW of two full-time investigators, and suggested that he resign and Ralph Winstead stay on and act as liaison until the Senate Crime Committee should need his services on the case.

"This has been a thankless task," he wrote in his final memorandum, "tougher than I guessed last year, because of the new recalcitrance of three so-called law enforcement agencies. But I owe thanks to a hundred UAW officers and members, top to bottom, who cooperated every way they could . . . and if any fool of an ex-police commissioner or other attempts to reiterate that lack of UAW cooperation blocked solution of these crimes, I will testify . . . that it was the UAW that organized the investigation and thrust its facts at 'law enforcement agencies' — who stifled them."

By the autumn of 1951, the UAW was successful in organizing the Detroit Michigan Stove Works and had negotiated a two-year contract. One reason for the success was that Santo Perrone had been confronted with some serious problems related to the Kefauver Committee hearings, which had at long last commenced in Detroit. He had been compelled to give up his lucrative scrap iron contract with Fry. And he and four others, including his son-in-law Agostino Orlando, were found guilty of bribing Detroit Michigan Stove Works workers to resist efforts at unionization, were fined $1000 each, and placed on probation.

With the shootings still unsolved in 1953 and the statute of limitations about to expire on the case of the attack on Walter in 1948 (The Michigan statute of limitations was later extended to ten years), our private UAW investigators, in cooperation with Jack Conway and Emil Mazey, stepped up their search for a man named Donald Joseph Ritchie, a Canadian ex-convict and the nephew of Clarence Jacobs, a member of Perrone's gang. Both of these men had been tied in to various Perrone operations. Jacobs and Ritchie fitted perfectly the descriptions by my neighbors of two men they had seen several times dawdling in parked cars near my house. Conway dispatched Sam Henderson to make contact with Ritchie in Canada. He found him on November 18, in a Canadian jail.

"I know what you want, but see me when I get out," said Ritchie.

He also told Henderson that if he were to accept money under the UAW's reward scheme, he would surely be murdered, and suggested an alternative arrangement, whereby $25,000 would be turned over to his common-law wife, who went by either of two names, Betty White or Elizabeth Ritchie.

A Windsor, Ontario, lawyer was hired to serve as go-between, and after conversations with Pat O'Brien, the Windsor lawyer was presented with a UAW check for $25,000, with instructions that $5000 of it was to be an initial payment to Betty White in Canadian hundred-dollar bills, once Ritchie had come to Detroit and told his story under oath.

Ritchie came across the river with Henderson at the end of December 1953 and met with Prosecutor O'Brien. Six days later, the latter announced that he had solved the Reuther shootings, and issued warrants for the arrest of Santo Perrone, Carl Renda, Peter Lombardo, and Clarence Jacobs. This same Jacobs, Ritchie's uncle, had been convicted in Detroit in 1928 for smuggling in aliens and was deported back to Canada; he returned to Detroit illegally in

1940, was again arrested for illegal entry but freed, pending trial, on $5000 bond posted by — guess who? — Santo Perrone.

O'Brien made public the following statement by Ritchie:

> I was in the car the night Walter Reuther was shot. For about four or five years I had been working for Sam [Santo] Perrone. I made about $400 to $500 a week. In the occupation I was in — well — it just wasn't what people would call work. Clarence Jacobs approached me for this particular job. He told me I would get five grand. I was approached about five days before it happened and asked if I wanted to go. The conversation took place in Perrone's gas station. Perrone asked me several days before the shooting if I was going on the job. I said I was. I didn't ask a lot of questions. These people don't talk things over very much. All I knew was that Perrone had once said, "We'll have to get that guy out of the way."

Ritchie was asked if he meant Reuther.

> Yeh. The night of the shooting I was picked up at the gas station. The car was a red Mercury. I don't know who it belonged to. I sat in the back seat. Jacobs drove and Peter Lombardo was in the front seat with Jacobs. I was there in case there was any trouble. If anything happened, I was to drive the car away. Jacobs did the shooting. He was the only one who got out of the car. I don't know how long he was gone . . . I heard the report of a gun. Then Jacobs got back in the car and said, "Well, I knocked the bastard down."
>
> We took off in a hurry. After the job, they dropped me back at the Helen Bar, about 200 feet from the gas station. I don't know what they did with the car. I heard later it was demolished and junked. Haven't any idea what happened to the gun. I had some drinks at the bar and then went and saw Carl Renda. Why? I always went in to see Renda. He said, "I have something for you." He got a bundle of cash and handed it to me. I went downstairs and met a girl. I stayed with her until four in the morning. Then I took a taxi to Windsor. I didn't count the money until I got to Canada. It was exactly five grand.

After signing the statement, Ritchie was kept under close police surveillance in the Statler Hotel in downtown Detroit, since he was to be a material witness. It was a three-room suite and he was guarded by Detectives Wayne Glisman and William K. Krupka. On January 8, 1954, Ritchie, telling the detectives he wanted to take a shower, went into the bathroom and turned on the water. About an hour later, the detectives seem to have become mildly curious and went to investigate. When they got the door open, they found Ritchie gone.

Not long after that, a Detroit *Free Press* reporter received a phone call from someone in Windsor, Ontario, who identified himself as Ritchie and said that everything he had told the police about the Reuther shooting was a lie, and he would fight extradition to the United States. At the urging of the police, the *Free Press* did not publish a report of Ritchie's escape; it merely stated that a witness had disappeared. But on his own, the reporter who had got the call, Ken McCormick, pursued the matter and confirmed that a person answering the description of Ritchie had recently been in Chatham, Ontario, had deposited $3500 in a bank there, and on January 8 purchased a 1952 Dodge for $1000 cash. He was accompanied by a woman.

When a red-faced Prosecutor O'Brien learned what had happened to his key witness, he blurted out: "I felt — and I still feel — we have the solution . . . We have a lot of evidence along the same lines, but he is the case."

Detectives Glisman and Krupka were found to have neglected their duty and each had to forfeit thirty days' pay.

In December 1957, the frozen body of Ralph Winstead, who for eight long years had been investigating the Reuther shootings for the UAW and was the greatest source of information that might have led to the application of real justice, was recovered from Lake St. Clair. He was dressed in fisherman garb; his death was pronounced accidental. This happened four months before the statute of limitations on Walter's shooting ran out.

The FBI made no effort to have Ritchie extradited.

I learned this and many other discouraging facts twenty-five years after the shootings. Attorney General Elliot Richardson had decreed that "investigatory records of historical interest" might be examined by certain qualified persons, and I asked my attorney, Joe Rauh, to gain access for me to those records of the Justice Department and its agency, the FBI, that related to the attacks on Walter and me. Copies of documents and letters pertaining to the entire matter will be found in the Appendix.

After eight months, the director of the FBI, Clarence M. Kelley sent to me through the mail, with a covering letter, some 120 pages of heavily censored "summary reports."

These reports, with many names and other facts deleted, raised more questions than they answered, and as a follow-up, we drafted a series of specific questions directed to Kelley. He made his reply on October 15, 1974.

First of all we learned that although the Michigan statute of limitations had been extended to run ten years, which gave the law until 1958 to find the criminals, the case was closed in May 1952. No reason was given.

We asked Director Kelley why J. Edgar Hoover had written Congressman Rabaut that there was no federal jurisdiction involved in the Reuther shootings when it was a fact that on May 26, 1949, right after I was shot, Assistant Attorney General Alexander Campbell, with the approval of his boss, Tom Clark, had sent Hoover a memorandum listing reasons why the FBI should go in:

> The prominence of these men in the labor movement has resulted in these attempted murders being given a nationwide and even worldwide publicity. Moreover, press dispatches have indicated for some time past that the Reuthers actively fought the Communist element in the labor movement . . . and consequently incurred their enmity. The latter fact gives significance to these attempted assassinations which impel the Department of Justice to take every possible step at once to ascertain the identity of the guilty party or parties and to vigorously prosecute any violation of federal law.

Reference is also made in the memo to a possible violation of the Fugitive Felon Act, "since it is quite likely that the guilty party or parties would flee the jurisdiction to avoid prosecution." A possible violation of the federal Firearms Act was also mentioned as a reason for the FBI to take action.

Director Kelley's reply was:

> A thorough check of the files of this Bureau disclosed no record of receipt of the memorandum from Assistant Attorney Alexander Campbell dated May 26, 1949. Our files do contain a memorandum to the Attorney General dated May 26, 1949, stating it was the Bureau's position that there was no FBI jurisdiction in the shootings, but we were offering cooperative services of the Laboratory and Identification Division to local authorities. In view of this, we did not reverse ourselves and did not inform the public we were assuming jurisdiction. The investigation initiated pursuant to the request of the Department on December 21, 1949, was thorough, extensive and completely objective.

It is obvious that Hoover had chosen to ignore the May 26, 1949, memo from Campbell, destroying his own copy (but unable to destroy the one still in the Attorney General's files) and substituting his own disclaimer of jurisdiction. This way Hoover covered both flanks: should a break in the case occur, he could claim he had secretly pursued the investigation and be credited with victory; at the same time, he was protected from any responsibility for failure by claiming he had never entered the case.

Director Kelley's letter informed me that not only was there no effort made to extradite Ritchie from Canada, even after he had confessed, under oath, to being an accomplice (lying about it later probably out of fear of the Perrone gang), but that there was also no investigation made of DeLamielleure or others in the Detroit police force who may have been involved in a massive cover-up or in the assassination attempts themselves.

Nor was Harry Bennett ever interviewed, though his close ties with the Detroit underworld were well known, and his own employees had been involved in the earlier attempt on Walter's life witnessed by many of us in his apartment.

Our last question was brushed off summarily. We asked: "In view of the evidence that underworld figures, Perrone and others, may have been involved in the Reuther shootings, and in view of the use to which these underworld figures had been put by employers such as Michigan Stove and Briggs Body, did the Bureau ever seek to identify the employers or underworld figures who might have financed such physical attacks on the Reuther brothers to win 'labor peace?' "

Mr. Kelley's response was: "All logical investigation was conducted in this matter and results furnished to the Department of Justice, which advised in May 1952 that in view of the extensive, unproductive investigation, it was suggested no further action be taken unless additional information was received indicating a violation of Federal statutes." All of which seems to suggest that corporate officials were immune from landing on any FBI list of suspects.

To end on a sweeter note, and to defend human nature and citizens of Detroit, I quote from a letter written to the President of the United States by a private nurse who was asked by the nursing registry, when I was first admitted to the Henry Ford Hospital, if she would be willing to take care of me. Apparently the registry had told her, "We think you should know that the injured man is Reuther, the union man."

Astonished by the implications of the statement, the nurse, a rock-ribbed Republican, retorted: "What difference does it make who he is? He needs nursing, doesn't he?"

A few weeks after she had finished tending to my needs in the hospital, and without my knowledge, she dashed off this letter:

Dear Mr. President:

Here in this America of ours we are proud of the privileges we possess. One of our most democratic privileges is the assurance that we, the "little people," can reach our President to rectify an injustice. A grave injustice is being permitted today. Victor Reuther has been the victim of attempted murder. Walter was the object of a similar attempt very recently, and the perpetrator is still at large. As a Detroit resident I am not proud of our police showing . . . A newspaper story stated that the unions were withholding information. I am not a union member, nor can I see eye to eye with them over many of their policies, but you who know Walter Reuther and I who know Victor Reuther extremely well are sure of their integrity, high aspirations and deep sincerity. The Senate passed a resolution recommending that the FBI enter this investigation but it is being stalemated while Attorney General Clark decides a question of jurisdiction. This is the time to break down barriers. These men are not local but national, more, they are international figures.

Won't you demand and force your demand that the FBI enter this case at once? It is unthinkable that here in America men cannot sit quietly in their homes without being murdered . . . You will have the lasting gratitude of millions if you come out with a public stand on this matter and a strong private insistence that this matter be expedited. I somehow feel you won't fail us, Mr. President, and the Reuthers will live and give many more years of unselfish service to this country.

Very truly yours,
(Mrs.) Dorothy Townsend

New Dimensions for the UAW

Innovations in Collective Bargaining

Under Walter's guidance, collective bargaining became more than the instrument with which workers could win economic equality and decent working conditions; it became a tool for the UAW to use in organizing the workers' power and strength so that they might reach out beyond the work place and gain for themselves and their families a larger measure of security and dignity. He knew that innovative patterns for collective bargaining negotiations, in an industry as large and influential as auto, could be copied by workers across the land and bring new benefits even to unorganized employees.

Above all, Walter urged that unions recognize their social responsibility to the community at large as well as to their members. He viewed the labor movement as a way to bring about social change by nonviolent means. This implementation of Valentine Reuther's belief, that there was a relationship between the bread box and the ballot box, became central to the UAW's philosophy.

Moreover, the democratic heritage of the UAW ensured that all major collective bargaining and legislative goals became the demands of the membership as a whole, not simply of the leaders. The members understood this, and supported the proposals that were formulated in open convention. They fought hard to bring them to reality in the form of contractual obligations.

The development of collective bargaining demands, the collective bargaining process itself, and the tactics and strategy employed to achieve the union's objectives required complete cooperation between the union's leaders and a militant, enlightened membership. Walter invariably consulted with his fellow officers and the Executive

Board before critical decisions were made. It was team effort in fact, not just in words.

Walter, perhaps more than any other union president in the country, insisted that job opportunity and advancement should be open to all, without racial or sex discrimination and without regard to a worker's national origin or religious convictions. It was therefore necessary to use trade union economic leverage to achieve any reforms.

Of course, we in the UAW were fortunate that across the bargaining table from us sat employers who were among the most economically privileged in the whole country, representing, indeed, the most powerful segment of the world. (Considering this fact, it is noteworthy that, before the advent of the UAW, auto workers were paid on the whole less than workers in other strategic and basic industries, such as coal and steel.) As we pressed for higher wages and other benefits and fringe provisions, we did not run the risk of bankrupting the industry. Far from it. Walter often lamented that the union had never pressed for quite enough. In his very last address before a UAW convention, as he prepared once again to undertake negotiations, he referred to the efforts of the auto magnates to make the public believe that the woes of the industry were due to the "cost squeeze" the UAW was exerting:

> We have talked in the past about this being a kind of golden goose and no matter how much fat we take off that goose at the bargaining table, it has the capability of coming back and the next time it is even fatter. There are periodic times when the fat accumulation is not as great, but in the long sweep of history, it is fantastic. The profits of the big three from nineteen forty-seven through nineteen sixty-nine . . . were thirty-five billion dollars or equal to fourteen times the invested worth of those three corporations . . . In twenty years they got back in return fourteen times more than their total investment.

Those twenty-two years, one must remember, were years of unionization, years when during every bargaining session there was hysterical propaganda in the press that any more concessions to labor would bankrupt the auto industry and destroy the very basis of free enterprise.

Even as far back as the GM strike in 1945–46, Walter raised issues reaching far beyond wage adjustment. As he said later, "The strike was about two questions. It was about the right of a worker to share — not as a matter of collective bargaining muscle, but as a matter of *right* — to share in the fruits of advancing technology. The second issue was: why should workers be victimized by inflationary forces, over which they had no control, and which eroded their true wage position?"

Though the UAW did not win that strike, its arguments evidently left a deep impression on the leading auto industry executive, GM president Charles E. Wilson. "You did not persuade us on those two basic principles during the negotiations," he once told Walter, "but when it was all over, I began to realize you were right and that the two principles you had advanced were sound." Louis G. Seaton, the GM chief labor negotiator during that period, claims that Wilson had begun toying with the idea of tying wages, prices, and productivity together as early as 1942, when he was in the hospital recuperating from an illness. However long it took for these ideas to germinate in Wilson's mind, one can say with certainty that the war years, with their rigid controls on wages, were not propitious for such changes.

By the 1948 negotiations, Walter had sufficiently consolidated his leadership within the union (it was enhanced by the aura of martyrdom following the assassination attempt) so that the UAW had become something like an irresistible force, ready to take on the most immovable object. It was too bad that Walter, still convalescing, could not be present when Wilson made his innovative offer, which came in two interrelated parts. First was the establishment of an "annual improvement factor" representing the amount that management and union jointly agreed should be added to each worker's annual income as his share of the increase in national productivity. At the outset, this amounted to a 2 percent wage increase, or an adjustment of three cents an hour. Second, the corporation proposed a "cost of living escalator formula," by which wages would be adjusted according to the fluctuation of price levels as reflected in the federal government's index of living costs. The adjustment would be made at each quarter point of the year. Walter, though incapacitated, was kept abreast of the negotiations by Mazey, Conway, Weinberg, and Johnstone, who was appointed UAW-GM Department director after the 1947 convention.

Some twenty years later, Walter estimated that the annual productivity factor plus the escalator clause had brought the average GM worker an additional $18,000 in hard cash.

It was easy for General Motors to make these concessions in 1948 because the year ahead promised to be an extremely good one for car sales. They also wanted to avoid a confrontation with the union every year, and hoped that by making these concessions they could get a five-year contract with the UAW. The union rejected that idea, but did agree to a two-year agreement instead of the usual one-year contract.

In wage negotiations over the years, Walter called not only for equity for workers, but *equity for consumers* as well. It was his argument that the profit position of the corporations could and should permit a substantial reduction in the prices of their cars. Only a few weeks before his death he declared: "General Motors could have cut the price of every car two hundred dollars at the wholesale level and even two-fifty at the retail level and still would have made a greater profit than the average manufacturing company after that price reduction."

Nothing nettled the auto executives more than Walter's refusal to ignore the consumer.

On the eve of the 1970 negotiations, Walter told the UAW convention:

> Mr. Nixon has told us we ought to exercise restraint when we go to the bargaining table . . . Well, we want to dampen the fires of inflation, but the place to start is not with the workers who are victimized by inflation but with the people who are the culprits — these hungry, greedy corporations who have been milking the American and Canadian consumers . . . It's a crazy, cockeyed kind of economic philosophy where the drum beaters who say to us, "Slow down, take less than your share," are the people who are responsible. Who gets laid off? I don't know of one top GM or Ford or Chrysler executive, or any executive in the Agricultural Implement Industry who has been laid off or who is working short weeks . . . Here is a story in the Detroit *Free Press* and the headline says "Auto Executives Paychecks Cut Back." Let me read the fine print: Mr. Roche [then GM president] — I feel so sad about him — took a cut in nineteen sixty-nine. His bonus was cut $4,991. How sad, because after that cut, he made a paltry combination of salary and bonus of $789,943 . . . Lynn Townsend, chairman of the Chrysler Corporation, lost his bonus, but here again he does not seem to qualify for the poverty program. In the last seven years, he has averaged in salary and bonuses $428,952 . . . When we sit across the table from the management people in the middle of July . . . I intend to look them right in the eye as we need to look Mr. Nixon in the eye and say to those corporation executives: "Whenever UAW members . . . get ten percent

of the income you get, we will demonstrate one hundred percent more restraint than you are demonstrating in the fight against inflation.

One of Walter's deepest interests was the plight of the senior workers, those who had given their lives to industry and were facing retirement or were already retired. A society can be measured by the way it treats its children and its older citizens. In both cases, the United States has a pitiful record. Under FDR the Social Security Act was passed, yet all he really accomplished was to establish a principle — a vital principle to be sure. Thirty-two dollars a month was a pathetic sum: inflation soon eroded every dollar, and American workers, lacking political clout, were unable to win any upward adjustment in Congress.

The UAW, therefore, carefully prepared its case and went to the bargaining table with the demand that employers set aside a portion of their profits to help employees retire when they were "too old to work and too young to die." The industry screamed "Socialism!" but Walter responded it was no more Socialistic than was providing executives with a yearly income to maintain them in their old age — since evidently they had not been able to set aside any of their annual half-million-dollar salaries and bonuses for that purpose. Why was it Socialism only when it pertained to the hourly rated workers?

"If you make $258 an hour," Walter told a rally of seven thousand Ford workers who were sixty years old and over, "they give you a pension, but if you make $1.65 an hour, they say you don't need it, you're not entitled to it, and furthermore it's socialistic."

Walter may have coined it, but I have a feeling that the phrase "too old to work and too young to die" was a catchy line by Paul Sifton, a colleague of Don Montgomery's on the Washington staff of the UAW. However it was born, Walter made that slogan part of the vocabulary of millions of industrial workers as he hammered away at the idea during the negotiations. In fact, it became immortalized by the labor balladeer, Joe Glazer, guitar-strumming troubadour and former education director of the United Rubber Workers:

> They put horses to pasture, they feed them on hay,
> Even machines get retired some day.
> The bosses get pensions when their days are through,
> Fat pensions for them, brother, nothing for you.
> Who will take care of you? How'll you get by
> When you're too old to work and too young to die?

Glazer told me he was first inspired to compose the ballad when he heard Walter telling a story about the mine mules that used to pull the coal cars in West Virginia: "During slack times, the mules were put out to pasture. They were fed and kept healthy so that they would be ready to work when the mines started up again. But did they put the coal miner out to pasture? Did they feed him and keep him healthy? They did not! And you know why? Because it cost fifty bucks to get another mule, but they could always get another coal miner for nothing."

In dealing with the auto companies, Walter, unlike Lewis, who had been apt to force the coal industry into a united front, always held to a one-at-a-time strategy, playing off one section against the other, knowing that the shareholders in General Motors were eager to reap any competitive advantage over Ford or Chrysler and vice versa. "Fords are never built on a Chevrolet assembly line," Walter used to say. Other practical considerations favored this strategy. If it came to a strike, the whole membership would not be involved; other UAW auto workers would be urged to continue to work and pay their dues, which would make the financing of the strike easier. Then, too, a strike throughout the whole auto industry might quickly bring the federal government into the picture. Walter was sufficiently realistic to know it was preferable to take on General Motors, Ford, Chrysler, or American Motors than the U.S. Government, for, as he said, "GM doesn't have the U.S. Army at its beck and call."

Once a set of collective bargaining demands had been developed and passed by convention action, and the rank and file had given its approval of the goals and the reasons for setting them, the respective negotiating committees would present them simultaneously to each of the major corporations. As the contract deadline approached, the Executive Board would consider the tactical questions: which industry was most vulnerable at that time, and where to begin the showdown? Over the years, a pattern took shape. The union leadership reasoned that with the Ford Motor Company, a single-family corporation, it was relatively easy to accomplish breakthroughs of broad new principles in the area of collective bargaining. If, as sometimes was the case, it was cash that one needed to finance the implementation of that new principle, the place to go was General Motors. This, however, was not a hard-and-fast strategy, since there were times when Chrysler or American Motors was chosen as the target company.

The battle for retirement funding that took place in 1949 was not supported only by the older workers; younger workers were concerned with the thought of growing old without any income for retirement. They were fiercely independent and did not want to become burdens on their children. Since Social Security provided only thirty-two dollars a month, considerably less than half what they were earning per week, the prospect of retirement income appealed to the young worker; his future would be taken care of, and his father would not be a burden to him when *he* retired.

The demand laid before the industry called for guaranteeing every worker who reached the age of sixty-five, with thirty or more years of credited service in the firm, a pension benefit of $100 a month, including the Social Security payment. The industry was thus being asked to pay into a special fund enough money to assure this monthly income of up to $100. What was most significant — and this is a tribute not to Walter alone but to the very skilled staff working with him — the UAW insisted that the program be "actuarially sound," which meant that sufficient money had to be set aside each year so that it would be there for every worker going into retirement. This was much more satisfactory than the program established by the United Mine Workers, in which funding was dependent on the amount of coal mined, and often the level of payments had to be reduced because of a lack of sound funding. The UAW insisted also that the general plan was to be noncontributory, with the full cost borne by the company, and that it was to be jointly administered.

Under threat of strike action, the Ford Motor Company, in October 1949, signed with the UAW the historic first pension agreement in the industry, establishing the $100 monthly benefit for thirty years of service, based on three stipulations; there was to be actuarial funding, noncontributory payment, and joint administration.

Armed with this victory, the UAW turned its guns on the Chrysler Corporation, which quickly agreed to the $100 a month (Social Security making up a third of that, of course) but would not agree to actuarial funding and joint administration. Although the Steel Workers that same year accepted a nonfunded program, the UAW felt the principle was sufficiently vital to call a strike, which lasted 104 days, and force through the funding principle, with the plan jointly administered. If there were Chrysler workers who did not know, when the strike began, what the words "actuarially sound" meant, those words, as Doug Fraser recalled, had become, by the end of the strike, a part of their everyday speech. Chrysler gave in. Later on, the UAW was to take the lead in urging Congress to enact legislation to make funding mandatory in all private pension programs, so that a worker would be protected even if he was employed by a smaller firm confronted with financial liquidation.

In 1961, on the occasion of the twenty-fifth anniversary of Walter's leadership in the labor movement, Frank B. Tuttle, rank-and-file UAW philosopher and gadfly, who also had the distinction of being the first Chrysler pensioner under UAW contract, wrote to Walter:

> On my 65th birthday in January 1950 I had three important messages before me from Social Security, telling me that I had an assured life income of exactly $38.69 a month; from Chrysler Corporation, declaring it would never grant the "preposterous" pension demands of our union; and one from you saying that those demands would be won, either at the bargaining table or at the picket line.
>
> Chrysler managed to reverse the sequence — we went to the picket line first and the bargaining table afterwards, but today I am looking at pension checks of $157.46 a month. And even a little Social Security of $38.69 was due to action of our union . . . Without the protection of our union it is highly improbable that I would have lived to be 65 at all and without the union who would want to? Before our union, the best a worker could hope for was to die on the payroll — before he became old enough to be replaced by a younger worker. In 1830 Daniel Webster said in Congress, "Union and liberty now and forever, one and inseparable." Probably few auto workers would know who said that — or when. But millions of workers in our own and a host of other unions feel in our hearts that union and Reuther are one and inseparable. Today at 76 I have not only an economic competence, but an inheritance to leave to three generations of descendents — and my common stock in Reuther is a large part of it.

People from one end of the country to the other were the beneficiaries of the UAW victory. And most of those people had never paid a dollar into a labor union treasury. Because we had touched on the employer's sensitive nerve — the "pocketbook nerve," as Walter called it — Social Security payments were increased in 1950. Big employers like the auto manufacturers suddenly realized that if the federal government gave more to retired workers, they themselves would be able to give less to make up the stipulated $100 a month. Though labor unions had not been strong enough in Washington to get the basic Social Security payment raised, the employers were, and once converted to the idea that their financial interests would be served, they became allies — for the first and perhaps only time — in advocating an increase. Congress passed legislation raising the Social Security benefit, and every retired citizen who received his Social Security check had the labor movement to thank for the first breakthrough, the first increase in twenty years.

I am certain the industry was not surprised, when 1950 rolled around and the contract with GM opened up, to hear the UAW asking General Motors to negotiate a pension plan calling for $125 instead of $100. Thus, with the principles nailed down, the UAW moved to improve the benefits. This was done. In those negotiations the UAW also wrested from GM a modified union shop, which required new employees to join the UAW. This provision did much to stabilize the relations between GM and the union and to provide the UAW with the needed financial security to face the future.

The next great innovation was the guaranteed annual wage. The auto industry had always been notorious for its seasonal work. Once the factories were tooled for a new model, there was an enormous effort by the industry to rush out the new cars as rapidly as possible in order to stock posthaste all the showrooms. Often this meant hiring thousands of extra workers for the peak period only. Once the frenzied production was over, working hours would be cut and finally the surplus workers were dropped from the payroll, to fend for themselves or become public charges. This boom-and-bust procedure had come under criticism from many, especially FDR, who inveighed against it but could not push through any legislation to compel stabilization of production. Fifteen years had to go by before the auto workers would be in a position to do something about it themselves.

1955 was the target year for the UAW's campaign for a guaranteed annual wage. Preparation for this major undertaking had taken years of careful work on the part of a skilled professional staff. It was anticipated that the struggle for such an innovation would make the pension program battle look like a tempest in a teacup. Nat Weinberg, our economics brain-truster, was the head of a special task force preparing the data to substantiate the UAW's claim for annual wage security. The group studied the experiences of other countries that had striven for employment stability; it examined, state by state, the great variety of legislative provisions; it charted the country's employment and layoff patterns over a long span of years.

During the course of the task force's study, the UAW gave notice to the large corporations with which it would be negotiating that it was aiming toward this goal, well aware that the latter had the resources to employ the foremost economists and actuarial experts in the country to prepare their defense. The UAW knew it had to have the best documented case possible. Walter was sure that the union's claim for a guaranteed wage was morally justified. But he was determined to have at hand logic and economic justification. In a sense the big three auto companies played into the UAW's hands on this issue by failing to schedule production more sensibly and with due consideration of the welfare of the workers, who lived all the time with uncertainty and insecurity. Anticipating that the major defense of the industry would be that the UAW was seeking pay for workers who were not working, Weinberg underscored in each of his presentations that "the main purpose was not to get pay for idleness but to compel the industry, by imposing penalties for instability, to schedule steady employment for its workers, week by week throughout the year."

When the idea took clear shape, it was laid before the membership in meeting after meeting and was approved with enormous enthusiasm. The Education Department concentrated on organizing special seminars and institutes in every region that might be affected by the guaranteed annual wage demand. Articles appeared in both popular and professional journals, and the UAW leaders made a point of accepting every radio and TV opportunity to present or debate the issue. With the able assistance of Weinberg and Leonard Lesser, a member of the UAW's Social Security Department staff, Walter wrote a thoughtful article for the *Annals of the American Academy of Political and Social Science,* in which he described the stake that the public had in the guaranteed annual wage. "It is more than a matter of economic justice to the wage earner; it is a matter of economic necessity to our nation, for freedom and unemployment cannot live together in democracy's house."

The UAW did not claim to have invented the concept of linking privately funded unemployment benefit schemes with the federal or state unemployment compensation program. To the best of my knowledge, that idea originated in the fertile mind of Murray Latimer during World War II, when he was making a special study for the Office of War Mobilization. In this connection, however, the UAW nearly ran into what some of our own people considered an almost insurmountable problem, because there was a widespread belief that in order to develop a guaranteed yearly wage scheme integrated with the federal and state unemployment benefit system, it would be necessary to amend many of the various state laws. In negotiating the private pension supplement, we had dealt with only one piece of federal legislation — the Social Security Act. Trying to integrate our new guaranteed wage scheme with all of the widely differing state-administered programs raised the horrid possibility that many rural states, whose legislatures had an antilabor bias, might deduct from the worker's unemployment benefits any amount he would receive through a privately funded program. For a while, Leonard Lesser stood almost alone in his strong conviction that the privately funded benefits would not jeopardize state benefits. After he had won Weinberg to his view, Walter and the Executive Board determined to run the risk of providing money hard-won at the bargaining table to relieve the states of paying part of the unemployment compensation.

To strengthen our hand in case of possible confrontation with state governments, the UAW assembled a Public Advisory Committee, which included some of the nation's most outstanding economists, Harvard's Alvin Hansen and Seymour Harris among them. The creation of this committee must have convinced the corporations that the UAW was in dead earnest about establishing a precedent in this major area.

In a pioneering situation of this sort, the most important collective bargaining lesson for us all to learn was that we must retain a high degree of flexibility and not become so committed to a particular solution as to lose maneuverability. The main problem to be solved was simply that many auto workers never knew from one day to the next how much work they would be given, a fact that created for them intolerable insecurity. The union was not wedded to any one way of solving it, though it had developed some specific ideas. Since it had informed the corporations of its program, the auto executives would not suddenly be confronted with new proposals without being given a chance to research them in order to determine costs, feasibility, and other factors.

With equal foresight, the UAW had seen to it that the expiration dates of both the Ford and GM contracts were within a few days of each other. This gave the union the option of choosing one or the other company as the first target. The UAW also began to build a strike fund, and when the showdown approached, the workers had the protection of a $125 million strike reserve. Though the Ford Motor Company seemed to have a mind open enough to consider the subject, there was every indication that General Motors had shut the gate completely on this new demand and was prepared to endure a long strike and wage a tough battle to prevent the UAW from undermining what it considered its fundamental corporate prerogatives. GM made a proposal that contained no consideration of the basic concept of a guaranteed annual wage; the union immediately rejected it.

Ford was therefore chosen for the initial showdown. The company had earlier indicated it was preparing some positive response to the guaranteed wage issue. It was all the more dismaying, therefore, when John S. Bugas, an ex-FBI investigator and director of Ford's labor relations, began to read Ford's proposal and lo, it was the General Motors answer, word for word, with only the name of the company changed. Walter was furious. He immediately responded, "John, please don't insult our integrity and your integrity when you know and I know this is the GM proposal which we rejected two weeks ago — and you haven't changed a word of it. You have a perfect right to change your mind. We do not question your right to stooge for the General Motors Corporation, but I'd like to suggest that it's very bad policy and will get you nowhere. You guys have rocks in your head."

Then he said to Bugas, "By God, this is the first time I've seen a Chevy coming down a Ford final assembly line."

The General Motors proposal was essentially a stock option plan in lieu of the creation of a special fund out of which supplemental unemployment benefits would be paid. Walter warned Bugas, "You have just bought yourself a strike." And as he packed his briefcase, he reminded Bugas that the Willys Overland's decline had begun when the company proved unwilling to face up to collective bargaining responsibilities, and that Chrysler, because it suffered a 104-day strike, lost its chance of becoming number two in the auto industry. As the UAW negotiators were leaving, however, Bugas made a comment that let the cat out of the bag. He said it was ridiculous for the UAW to call a strike when the workers themselves really didn't want the guaranteed wage program and preferred, he said, to have the same money in another form. We knew the facts were otherwise. Walter therefore took advantage of a suggestion that Henry Ford II had made to him when Walter invited him to address the UAW's Ford Council during the early stages of serious negotiations. Ford had declined to speak but suggested that his workers should have an opportunity to indicate their views on management's offer. Walter remembered this and decided to outfox John Bugas and play Henry Ford against his own labor relations director. So he said to John: "Will you agree to have a referendum vote by Ford workers on our proposal? If they prefer yours, we'll sign a contract containing your proposal. Since you say they want yours by nine-to-one, you're not taking any chances."

"Poor John," Walter said later. "I thought he'd die."

It certainly must have been a glum crowd that gathered in Ford headquarters to consider whether Henry Ford's suggestion of a referendum would now be accepted by Bugas. Of course the Ford negotiators realized that their goose was cooked. The company withdrew its copy of the GM counterproposal and settled down to negotiate the UAW demands. Unfortunately they had already put full-page ads in the papers extolling the proposal they were now withdrawing. After that blunder, they were willing to accept the UAW's suggestion of a news blackout, and began genuine bargaining.

Having successfully split the Ford–General Motors united front, Walter, Ken Bannon, the technical staff, and the negotiating committee finally brought Ford, under threat of strike action, to the position where it offered a Supplemental Unemployment Benefit Plan, to be known as SUB. Thus was established the principle of guaranteeing an income over a specified period. We knew that once the principle was accepted, subsequent negotiations could enlarge the benefits.

Ford agreed to place five cents an hour per employee into a special fund, which would be used to supplement the weekly unemployment benefits to an amount of twenty-five dollars a week for a maximum of twenty-six weeks. ˙ This, together with the state's unemployment compensation, would provide the laid-off worker with approximately 65 percent of his normal take-home pay for the first four weeks of any layoff and 60 percent for the next twenty-two weeks.

After five days of round-the-clock bargaining General Motors finally accepted the SUB formula also. Harry Anderson, then GM vice-president, was quoted as saying: "I would like to congratulate Mr. Reuther for having gone to Ford first, because we never would have agreed to this otherwise."

We knew that once the principles of the program were solidly established, subsequent negotiations would widen the range of benefits. As with pensions and health care, it became a matter of "building brick by brick," as Walter used to put it, fleshing out the bare bones of a basic fringe benefit. Thus, in time, the Supplemental Unemployment Benefits (SUB) plan came to cover payments for short work weeks (50 percent of gross pay for the difference in hours between the standard forty hours and a lesser number of hours scheduled), severance pay, payment of health care premiums, and improvements in the duration of benefits.

Between the beginning of January 1974 and May 5, 1975, the GM-UAW SUB plan alone paid out more than $400 million to some eighty-eight thousand workers on layoff. This money came from GM earnings, not from general tax revenues. How much deeper the current Nixon-Ford depression would have gone, and how much slower the rate of economic recovery, had these purchasing-power dollars not been paid to those unemployed. To the workers who receive these benefits under their union agreement, no justification is needed.

Many of Walter's innovations, including this last one, were ridiculed by some leaders in the trade union movement. However, when the first recession hit after the SUB funds were initiated, more than $13 million were paid out in supplemental benefits to over 877,000 UAW members. And by 1967, the program was sufficiently improved to guarantee an eligible employee in any of the big three auto companies 95 percent of his normal take-home pay for up to fifty-two weeks (less $7.50 for work-related expenditures). The guaranteed annual wage became a reality. The total impact of this program on the whole community, not only auto workers and their families, has received less acknowledgment than it deserves. The cost to the employer was such that he had an incentive to organize and schedule the flow of work in such a way as to lower the peaks and raise the valleys and, in general, to stabilize employment.

Few questions absorbed Walter more in the later years of his life than the impact of automation on industrial workers. He was not one to regard the new technology as a bogy or some mysterious disease that could not be cured. He embraced the benefits of technology and was frightened only by the apparent blindness of many in responsible positions to the "social fallout" involved, the toll it took on human lives.

He said at a 1954 nationwide economic and collective bargaining conference convened by the UAW in Detroit:

> The first Industrial Revolution had a tragic impact upon the lives of many people. Ruthlessly workers were displaced by the first power-driven machines. They were turned into the streets to wander about homeless and hungry. In desperation the workers struck back at the callous indifference and social irresponsibility of the owners of the primitive early machines. In France, Germany, and mostly in England, the Luddites, inspired by mythical King Lud, burned factories, wrecked machinery, rioted, and inspired a guerrilla war that lasted for almost twenty years . . . Out of these early struggles came our modern labor movement. Now we enter the second phase of the Industrial Revolution and the impact of automation — for good or for evil — is magnified a thousandfold . . . Automation must be met sanely and constructively so that the miracle of mass production — and the even greater economic abundance made possible by automation — can find expression in the lives of people through improved economic security and a fuller share of happiness and human dignity.

Such concerns gave new impetus to the drive for earlier retirement, and for counseling of those about to retire to encourage better use of leisure time. The UAW also stepped up its efforts to offer retraining and upgrading of less skilled workers, who might be replaced through the introduction of automated equipment, so that they could fill the industry's needs for a higher degree of competence. Throughout the debates on the effects of the new technology, Walter's theme was that society must find ways to expand purchasing power to meet the expanding ability for mass production;

otherwise the new technology would cause disastrous dislocations in the form of widespread unemployment.

Another unfortunate consequence of automated assembly-line production is the growing depersonalization of work and the destruction of the sense of creativity a worker used to have in performing something more than an endlessly repetitive, monotonous operation. The great challenge is to enjoy the benefits of greater efficiency without losing dignity and the satisfaction one should find in work. Modern industries are only now beginning to experiment with ways of "humanizing the work place." Walter followed with avid interest the pioneering work done in this connection by the Scandinavian unions in conjunction with their employer associations. They were seeking to find new ways of organizing the allocation of work at the shop level to diminish the effect of monotony. And from the seeds that Walter planted in the UAW there are the healthy shoots of interested and continued exploration within the union today. In 1973 negotiations, the union and the corporations appointed a joint national committee to undertake experiments and demonstration projects designed to improve work life.

The refusal of the auto companies to make small, efficient passenger cars that would reduce expense to the consumer is an example of ruthless greed and blindness to their own interests. In 1948 General Motors, in its publication, *Folks,* justified its stand by writing, "Folks in the U.S. are inclined to like class and dash. Because of that, the popular American cars are big, fast, high-powered, advanced in styling, and a-sparkle with chrome." There was an element of brainwashing here. Also American car-buying habits did not bear out the propaganda. That very year the one fifth of families in the higher income bracket purchased 47½ percent of the splashy big new cars. What were the majority of Americans buying? Those in the lowest two fifths of the earning bracket purchased only 11.5 percent of the new cars. Low- and middle-income families, if they wanted transportaton, had to content themselves with used cars, which needed more fuel and were costly to maintain.

In January 1949, the UAW, in an article entitled "A Small Car Named Desire," proposed the manufacture of a small car in the U.S. This did not accord with the profit plans of the auto corporations (large cars are more profitable than small ones) and it took the great success of European small cars in this country to persuade them that the American people were not completely satisfied with their long and highly gadgeted products. Even so, the industry did not introduce the small car until 1969 and 1970; for twenty years it left a vacuum for European competition to fill.

In Germany and Austria, because of similar irresponsibility on the part of the private sector, the workers demanded a voice in the management of industry. In Germany this sharing of responsibility is called *Mitbestimmung,* or "codetermination." Because the great Ruhr barons during the Hitler period had been bankers for the Nazis, and as a part, too, of the general postwar democratization program, the workers refused outright to entrust important economic decisions to corporate executives who had proved themselves unsympathetic with democracy.

For twenty years the UAW asked the auto industry to tool for the production of smaller cars, with less expensive maintenance and lower mileage costs, to meet the budgets of working men. The answer was essentially that given years earlier by GM vice-president Coen where he heard the broad views expressed by Walter. "Reuther, get down off your soapbox. Stop trying to save the world . . . Tell us how much you want in wages for your guys and let's settle the contract." After the Second World War, when Volkswagens, Fiats, Renaults, and several entries from Japan began to flood the U.S. market, and their sales climbed, and they began to threaten the very jobs of American auto workers, even then the industry did not try to produce in any quantity what the consumers clearly wanted. They restricted their small car manufacture to as few as possible in order to maintain the profits they had for so long garnered from the sale of big cars. Twenty years elapsed between the publication of "A Small Car Named Desire" and the production of the Vega by GM, the Ford Pinto, and AMC's Gremlin — years during which the public was gouged and the atmosphere polluted by gas-eating mastodons.

Yet nothing has really changed since the UAW declared, in 1949, "Monopolies are organized economic power without social responsibility . . . Monopolies are organized to increase profits, not to meet human needs." When I think of the recent oil crisis, and the fact that the major oil producers put their own profits before the needs and the safety of the nation, I am not surprised that some Americans are thinking as did the German, Austrian (and later the Scandinavian) workers, in terms of democratizing the whole process of decision-making at the corporate level, so that the voice of the workers and the voice of the consumer will also be heard in corporate councils.

Internal Union Democracy

Everything the UAW accomplished under Walter's leadership through collective bargaining would have been far less meaningful without the crowning factor: democratic management of the union. The democratic process was always a Reuther obsession. Walter was well aware that those at the top of a large organization can all too easily lose touch with the needs and sentiments of the rank and file, and fall victim to bureaucratic practices that deny others their fundamental rights. (Our experience with Homer Martin had left a scar; we were exceedingly anxious to avoid a repetition of that kind of "rule.")

The writing of legal collective bargaining agreements was an important first step toward the goal of justice for the workers. But no written agreement can possibly anticipate all the disputes that arise during the life of such a contract. Special democratic machinery was needed to take care of the thousands of unsettled grievances that accumulated, many of which involved interpretation of contract terms. As far back as 1940, the UAW moved, with General Motors, to appoint an impartial umpire, whose salary would be paid jointly by union and corporation. According to Walter, "The principles of [contract] interpretation established by umpire decisions have been a sort of common law of labor relations at General Motors. Thousands of grievances are settled every year because the parties realize that the umpire has already ruled upon the question in dispute."

From the moment the contract provision establishing the impartial umpire was written, General Motors insisted on a "strict constructionist" interpretation of his power, resisting virtually any move to grant him the latitude the UAW thought proper for his role. Yet experience can teach corporations to bend. A case in the Fleetwood plant had both its humorous and its painful side. During an argument between the obstreperous UAW committeeman Glen Brayton, a body trimmer, and his foreman, things became more than usually heated. It was right after the holidays and the foreman was sporting a loud multicolored tie his wife had given him for Christmas. When Brayton took the foreman by the tie and drew him closer, the foreman responded with language that made Brayton madder. As a trimmer, he was handy with the shears, which he happened to be holding in his other hand, and he reached up and snipped off the foreman's tie.

Brayton was immediately suspended from his job for several weeks as a disciplinary layoff, and when he returned, there was a notice in his rack telling him to report to the office. There he was told that the corporation had reconsidered his penalty; he was fired. In those days I was stationed on the West Side of Detroit as representative for the International UAW, and it was my duty to handle appeal cases that went before the umpire. It was obvious that Brayton was guilty of insubordination and improper behavior. However, I argued the case against the summary discharge before the impartial umpire on the grounds that there could not be double jeopardy for a single offense. Brayton had served one penalty and should not be subject to further punishment. It took months for this dispute to go through all the lower stages of collective bargaining and finally reach the umpire. Meanwhile Brayton was without work or income.

The umpire handed down a decision in favor of the union's view that it was a case of double jeopardy. It was clear that he did not question Brayton's guilt and felt that, though outright discharge was too severe, a few weeks' layoff had not been sufficient punishment. But since the corporation would not grant him the leeway to alter the degree of the penalty, he had no choice but to rule in favor of the union's position. When GM had to write a back paycheck to our overmilitant shop committeeman, it learned a painful lesson. Soon after that, it conceded much more authority to the umpire.

As the UAW grew larger and, of necessity, more centralized — and once the union shop and check-off provisions were in effect — it was inevitable that the members would gather infrequently and in too few numbers. A structure was needed to help both the officers and the rank and file police themselves in accordance with the ideals and purposes for which the UAW had originally been formed. In 1957, after consulting with the officers and the Executive Board and with the leaders of locals across the country, Walter made the unprecedented proposal that a Public Review Board be established to strengthen the democratic structure of the union. This called for an amendment to the UAW constitution, which was approved in convention:

> For the purpose of ensuring a continuation of high moral and ethical standards in the administrative and operative practices of the International Union and its subordinate bodies, and to further strengthen the democratic processes and appeal procedures within the union as they affect the rights and privileges of individual members of subordinate bodies, there shall be established a Public Review Board consisting of impartial persons of good repute not working under the jurisdiction of the UAW or employed by the International Union or any of its subordinate bodies. The Public Review Board shall consist of seven members including the Chairman.

The UAW Executive Board was to recommend seven outstanding citizens whose names would be submitted, at the annual convention, to some three thousand delegates for their approval or rejection. The Review Board was to be in no sense beholden to the UAW. The convention created the Review Board, and over the years clergymen of different faiths, distinguished jurists both black and white, educators, and other professionals served on it. What made it important was that this body had "the authority and duty to make final and binding decisons on all cases appealed to it." After ten years, Walter said that, in spite of the initial apprehension within the union about giving such power to outsiders, all fear was dissipated as "the Public Review Board proved its capacity to render objective judgments, and the evidence mounted that in serving individual members it was serving the UAW as a whole by making a democratic union even more democratic." Not that we had reached some ideal democracy, but we now had a reliable feedback mechanism to uncover and remedy the bureaucratic injustices that crop up in any large organization.

Hundreds of grievances have been aired and the board has made significant policy decisons that have had a profound effect on the union. Some of them have overruled decisions made by the International Executive Board. Some of the PRB's recommendations proposed changes in the UAW constitution, which were acted on favorably at an annual convention. After ten years of operation, the board's chairman stated: "We have discovered no instance of corrupt

practices, and in a number of our decisions we have pointed out pro-
cedural deficiencies which have subsequently been corrected . . . It
is at the same time a source of disappointment that others have not
followed where the UAW has led, for surely the labor movement
would be instantly strengthened were but these procedures for voluntary self-discipline adopted by other major labor unions."

After another five years, the new UAW president, Leonard Woodcock, commented: "We are a better union because of the Public
Review Board . . . Our commitment to equity and integrity is not
only real, it is known throughout the world. It is not extravagant to
say that the Public Review Board is a key part of the UAW reputation."

In the 1950s several Congressional committees uncovered the
shocking degree to which some unions had been penetrated by racketeering and self-seeking elements. Dave Beck and James Hoffa of
the Teamsters' Union went to prison. Unfortunately most government inquiries have focused too little attention on those who offer
bribes and too much on those who accept them. The searchers must
look in both directions if corruption in our society is to be checked.
In 1952, when Walter succeeded Philip Murray as National CIO
president, he was dismayed to find that some CIO-affiliated unions
had been penetrated by racketeers — not a great number, but
enough to send alarm through the ranks. At a New York City press
conference Walter emphasized that union welfare funds are a sacred
trust: "It is shocking beyond words to find any single instance of
these funds' being used as a special financial reserve with which to
enrich the officers of the union or the administrators of the welfare
fund . . . I have said time and again that I will fight corruption
wherever I find it, within or without the labor movement."

Under his urging, the CIO executive Board created a standing
committee on ethical practices. The distinguished president of the
Amalgamated Clothing Workers, Jacob Potofsky, was chairman of
the Ethical Practices Committee, and Arthur J. Goldberg (later Secretary of Labor, Supreme Court Justice, and UN Ambassador) was
its director. This committee took prompt action to clean up corruption wherever it was unearthed, and also made it clear that legislation was needed if the administration of welfare funds was to be
handled in the proper "goldfish bowl" manner in order to cut down
the possibility of malfeasance.

The concept of an Ethical Practices Committee was carried over into the merged AFL-CIO on the insistence of the CIO. Al Hayes, then president of the Machinists Union, a man respected for his integrity and forthrightness, was appointed its chairman. Under his guidance, the committee functioned effectively, but not for long. Walter soon saw that the AFL-CIO Executive Council had no wish to support vigorously the activities of the Ethical Practices Committee. This became one of the factors contributing to the final break between the UAW and the AFL-CIO.

The story has it that soon after the appointment of Hayes, John L. Lewis met him on the street and noted wryly: "So you're now chairman of the AFL-CIO Ethical Practices Committee. Have you found any yet?"

The upheaval in the auto industry that gave birth to the UAW was, in essence, a demand on the part of the workers to be recognized as valuable citizens in an industrial democracy. No one who was part of that struggle could underestimate the determination of those workers to safeguard their right to put the final stamp of yes or no on every contract. Sometimes bad agreements, with unfortunate provisions, are negotiated by elected officers or members of a bargaining committee and blitzed through the membership because they have been sweetened up with sufficient wage gains to discourage the membership from reading the fine print. Not so with the auto workers. I don't know what it is about the mentality of auto, aerospace, and agricultural implement workers, but I sometimes had the feeling they were all lawyers on the side. They were masters at reading the fine print. Often there were sharp differences between the unskilled and highly skilled workers that were not easily resolved at the bargaining table, since no one could agree on how the total package of wage gains should be divided between the two groups. In the UAW it finally became necessary to specify in the constitution that the two types of workers were to hold separate votes on the terms of a given contract, and that no contract would be operative until voted through by both. (The application of this principle continues to create difficulties.)

One can therefore imagine Walter's horror when, in February 1970, he read the Washington Post headline: MEANY WOULD END UNION VOTES FOR RATIFICATION OF CONTRACTS. He was proposing that all contracts worked out by "labor leaders and management

should be final and not subject to the approval of union members."
George Meany, president of the AFL-CIO, was obviously irritated
because some agreements had been rejected by the rank and file and
a number of wildcat strikes had resulted. When Walter addressed
his last UAW convention shortly afterward, he had this to say on the
subject:

> We have our differences with the AFL-CIO. They are not differences
> of personality. They are differences that relate to the basic purposes
> and the role and responsibilities of a modern labor movement. I don't
> waste my time sniping at George Meany, because I don't think it's im-
> portant whether he likes me or I like him. But I do believe I am
> obligated to respond to a proposal which George Meany made at the
> last meeting of the AFL-CIO Executive Council in Miami Beach,
> Florida.

Pulling the clipping out of his pocket, he read the whole news item
and then declared with fervor:

> I want to make the record clear that as long as I have a voice in the
> labor movement, the rank and file are going to ratify the contracts and
> the conditions under which they work. If anybody in Congress tries to
> pick up Mr. Meany's proposal, we are going to march on Washington
> and do the most effective legislative job we have ever done.

If the majority of workers found it hard to identify with Walter as
someone who would frequent the bars with them or spend the night
in a poker session, still they identified closely with him as the leader
and the person who fought most tenaciously to protect their vital interests. And Walter certainly understood their habits better than
those union leaders who enjoyed plush hotels in Miami or Puerto
Rico — at the union's expense. That sort of thing ran completely
counter to his convictions and his lifestyle. (His frugality became so
famous that it was often said that he would ease his conscience, when
forced by his position to go to Miami or San Juan, by squeezing his
own orange juice in his hotel room.) Walter never forgot who really
paid those big bills: the rank and file.

Another fanatical protector of union funds who was determined
the UAW could never be accused of payroll or expense account
padding was our secretary-treasurer, fondly referred to as "Cash-
box" Mazey. When the Teamsters' Union scandal broke out, some
members of the McClellan Committee made snide reference to possible chicanery within the UAW. Walter demanded a day in court

and produced our records, and I remember that after Carmine Bellino, the committee's accountant, had checked those records, he commented that he had never seen a set of books kept more meticulously for any corporation than those of Emil Mazey for the UAW. He also called attention to an item that was both amusing and symbolic. Walter had once, when submitting an expense account, forgotten to delete a cleaning bill for $1.75. Cashbox Mazey's office spied it immediately and deducted it. Not even the UAW president was granted any special privileges — which was just as Walter wanted it.

Early in Walter's presidency he decided that the temptation to supplement his income with fees for lectures or for articles in major publications must be resisted, and he therefore set up a special scholarship fund to be the depository of all such honorariums. The fund was administered by individuals on his staff designated by himself, and grants were made to worthy students. He also made it clear that no official funds of the union, no income from the dues paid by the workers, could be used to finance internal political activities, and that any caucus or group that was bound to spring up within such a large and diverse organization had to finance its special causes or campaigns by soliciting contributions from workers or staff. Such funds for internal politicking were often referred to as "flower funds." The McClellan Committee repeatedly sought to prove that the administration of these funds was a sinister phenomenon. But the result of the committee's inquiry made clear that this was a legitimate function within a democratic trade union.

To understand well the degree of internal democracy within the UAW, one would have to attend a UAW convention and contrast it with a convention held by some other trade union. Walter leaned over backward to give the minority the fullest chance to have its say. Even if it represented only 3 to 5 percent of the delegates, it would be guaranteed 50 percent of the debating time. An astute, if not always friendly columnist, Murray Kempton, observed this democracy in action at the UAW convention of July 1949:

> Always at the end when you watch the auto workers you come down to the leader who seems so unlike them and yet is so much of them and you keep coming back to the taut, tired man on the platform even though there is no exterior symbol in this whole convention to remind you that he exists. There is not even a portrait of Walter Reuther on

the backdrop — just pictures of kids and a doctor and two old people. Those are pictures of a program and not of a leader, and it is strange that his command of you and of his union is the fruit of not one small trick of the ham actor. He leans so far the other way that during this convention he hasn't dropped a hint to remind the delegates that he was shot hardly a year ago and still goes every day to the hospital — he had very carefully and conspicuously not done what so many of us thought he would do — turn the UAW into an iron personal machine.

Wednesday morning on a minor administrative issue he did a thing which proved more than ever before what he thinks of the rank and file. Reuther had recommended to the convention that it split the UAW's Wisconsin region in two and add a new director. When the issue came up on the floor, Reuther called for a show of hands. From the press tables, the vote looked even enough; he ruled that his recommendation had passed. That turned the convention into an uproar. Reuther could have stood by his ruling . . . He could have ordered the sergeant at arms to clear the aisles and gone on to further business, but he didn't. He stood on the platform for twenty minutes and joshed the delegates into calming down. After a while he got them to vote again with tellers from both sides. Reuther won the final vote by a close margin but throughout the byplay you couldn't escape the sense that he was perfectly ready to chance defeat of an issue he felt keenly rather than cut off the rank and file protest.

You get the sense too that no one is more worried than Reuther by the fact that his own complete victory has left him with no ideological opposition in the UAW except from the communists. This worry explains for one thing the remarkable role played here by the six delegates present belonging to the offshoot of American Trotskyism which calls itself the Independent Socialist League . . . They're smart kids, good union men and steadily throughout this convention they've risen from the left to criticize Reuther for his abandonment of the labor party ideas and his suggestion that the communists be expelled from the CIO. Each time Reuther beams upon them with a quite obvious wish that they weren't so few in number. That's why they have to come back to him. The big news of this convention is that Reuther is still a democrat. He doesn't think anyone not even himself should win every argument in the UAW.

CHAPTER 24

Postwar European Labor

AT THE END of the Second World War, when the peoples of Europe began to pull themselves out of the rubble, Walter, Roy, and I volunteered to help in any way we could, through our work with the UAW, and we became deeply involved in the Marshall Plan.

As I have described in Chapter 18, while the war was still going on, U.S. trade unions had suggested to the government many excellent programs (several of which were rejected) for stimulating maximum production. Considerable financial aid was also mobilized. Through AFL organizations, through a special wartime relief committee established by the National CIO, millions of dollars went to refugees forced to flee their native lands, and to help finance hospitals in the Soviet Union, the Philippines, Britain, and many other countries. These programs brought American trade union leaders into some degree of personal contact with their sister organizations in other countries.

As early as 1944 there gathered in London several hundred trade union delegates from the various allied countries to discuss ways of continuing cooperation after the war. The meeting was, in itself, an expression of the hope that the closer relationships brought about by the war might reduce the barriers of race, color, and politics around the globe. "We must not only win the war but we must also win the peace," was becoming a watchword for many of the Allied nations.

Delegates from the European countries, where there was a long history of trade union involvement in politics — many from union ranks had served in their countries' legislatures; some had become prime ministers — were naturally anxious to put into concrete terms their postwar goals. As a result of plans made at the 1944 London conference, a further meeting was scheduled for October 1945 in

Paris, with the purpose of founding the World Federation of Trade Unions. The CIO, which had participated informally in the London conference, sent official delegates to the 1945 founding congress of the WFTU.

For the first time in history, a world congress brought together union delegates from the Western world and from the Soviet Union and other Eastern European countries. Only the CIO, however, represented the United States, as the AFL insisted that the Soviet unions were not bona fide trade unions but agents of the Soviet government and the Communist Party. The CIO had no illusions that the Soviet trade unions were autonomous, but peace had just been won by an alliance of Britain, France, the U.S., and the Soviet Union, and there was a feeling of good will and eagerness to get on with constructive work in a cooperative spirit. The sentiment among British and Swedish union leaders, not to speak of those whose countries had recently been liberated, was a sense of gratitude to the people in the Soviet Union, who had borne the brunt of the force of Hitler's armies. In the view of most of the CIO leaders, to have slammed the door shut on the Soviet unions at that time might have increased rather than reduced their isolation and further strengthened the dictatorship under which they and the rest of the Russian people lived. It was a period of experimentation in mutual aid, and the onus should not be placed on the Western trade unions because cooperation turned out to be impossible.

Which it did, and not long afterward the Soviet Union mounted attacks on the European Recovery Program through political channels and also through its trade unions, in conjunction with Communist-controlled labor unions in France and Italy. They were clearly out to undercut Western Europe's chances for industrial recovery. Specific examples were the flooding of the mines in northern France and the efforts to prevent the unloading of crucial supplies on the docks of southern France. There were, as well, the numerous political strikes promoted in Italy to frustrate the establishment of a stable government. Even in the face of strong resolutions adopted by the WFTU to support rehabilitation programs, the Soviet bloc managed to use the WFTU as an instrument to sabotage the efforts of both Europe and the U.S., and finally, in spite of the perseverance of James B. Carey, secretary-treasurer of the National CIO, working with many European trade union colleagues, the WFTU refused to support the Marshall Plan. By May 1949, the CIO had withdrawn from the organization. Carey's statement is straightforward: "When the Communists . . . sought to pervert this organization to serve their ends they irrevocably split it in two. The WFTU became ineffective. There is nothing left to split."

Soon all the major trade unions of Europe, except those in France and Italy that followed the Moscow party line, also withdrew. This paved the way for the founding in London in late 1949 of a truly democratic world organization, the International Confederation of Free Trade Unions. The leadership of the AFL joined with that of the CIO as charter members. Walter was one of the National CIO delegates at the London founding congress, and was elected chairman of the committee that drafted the ICFTU manifesto calling for "bread, peace, and freedom." Jacob Potofsky, in his capacity as chairman of the CIO's Committee of Foreign Affairs, had a very active role in shaping, and providing maximum support to, the newly formed ICFTU.

One of the major problems threatening to restrict the scope of the membership of this new organization was the age-old division among religious faiths. In France, Italy, Belgium, and the Netherlands, each political party, with its own religious orientation, had historically tried to build a trade union base, so there were Protestant trade unions, Catholic trade unions, and now, under the new order, Communist federations as well. Walter was pressed into the role of mediator as we tried to draft a constitution for the ICFTU that would leave the door open for all those trade unions that were essentially democratic but had, perhaps, been divided from the mainstream of the trade union movement of their countries by religion. At least he was successful in writing such a constitution. But to this day the wounds caused by those divisions, although not so deep as they were, have not been healed.

The attitude of the AFL posed another problem. It was participating largely to try to turn the ICFTU into an anti-Communist coalition and to advance the Cold War interests of the West against the Soviet block. Walter had warned, even before the ICFTU was formed, about such a negative approach. "The chief weakness of American foreign policy is the predilection of our State Department for dealing with anybody who will promise to hate Communism. It is fatal to resist Communism by courting reaction." This was especially true in the field of international labor. To make common cause with anyone who was opposed to Communism would open the door to alliances with the most reactionary politicians, employers, military juntas, and dictatorships, all for the sake of defeating Communism.

The true strength of the ICFTU was the fact that this organization was committed to European recovery within a democratic framework that permitted free and democratic trade unions to function.

Prior to the London congress, the AFL had maintained an office in Paris, with Irving Brown as its roving ambassador; the CIO had a more modest office there, under the direction of Elmer Cope, whose major duty was to maintain liaison with the WFTU. Later, after withdrawing from the WFTU and helping to found the ICFTU, CIO leaders decided they themselves should keep in touch with European trade unions, and discussed sending a delegation to survey the general situation. Because I had spent some time in occupied Germany and Austria at the invitation of General Clay, and had been in England in connection with the Anglo-American Council, Philip Murray asked me to head a three-man delegation to undertake a mission to the trade union centers of Europe between January 7 and February 19, 1951.

Although I'd only a short time before recovered from my long series of operations, I was delighted to accept the job. There followed an exhausting six weeks. We spoke personally with over five hundred key trade unionists in France, Italy, Switzerland, Austria, Germany, Scandinavia, and of course Britain. We also met with the political leaders who had contacts with the trade union movement.

In this connection, I must point out that there is a misconception in the United States about the relation between unionism and politics in European countries. Our foreign policy makers, both in the State Department and in Congress, usually think of European trade union leaders as individuals concerned only with wages, hours, and working conditions. In the Scandinavian countries, the Social Democratic or Labor parties, in coalition with the unions, formed various governments. Immediately after the war, Britain voted in a Labor government; in Germany today, as it was during the leadership of Willy Brandt, the party that best speaks for the trade unions — the Social Democratic Party — is the one in power. Four members of Chancellor Schmidt's cabinet carry union cards as active members of the German Trade Union Federation. In France and Italy, were it not for division in their ranks, the labor parties might easily form the government.

If the United States wants to establish influential relationships with European nations, its emissaries and statesmen must understand the roles of trade union leaders and their political allies and spokesmen and gain their support.

Our delegation submitted a long report to the officers of the National CIO, describing, country by country, the difficulties trade unions were experiencing, their strengths and weaknesses, and the ways in which they were participating, or failing to participate, in economic recovery programs. We outlined what CIO unions might specifically do to help their sister unions in terms of material aid, exchange of delegations, and the kind of counseling that might smooth their way in dealing with U.S. agencies in Europe. Finally, we made recommendations for enlarging the staff of CIO's European office and broadening the scope of its activities.

Not long after that mission, Murray asked me to be director of the CIO's Paris office. Nothing could have been more welcome, in spite of my exhaustion. I quote here some descriptive excerpts from Murray Kempton's column in the New York *Post* in November 1951, six months after I took Sophie and the children to live in Paris.

There is a story that goes back 20 years to the time when Walter and Victor Reuther were bicycling around Europe. In England Walter Reuther fell off his bicycle and hurt his arm and every morning for a few weeks afterwards Victor would help him aboard, give him a push and send him off on England's rolling roads, intense and purposeful and forgetful of pain. Victor Reuther was a younger brother and it has been enough for him many years just to give Walter a push . . . Victor Reuther was shot in the spring of 1949. He made a tragic and ruined appearance at the auto union convention that summer and then he went painfully back to work as the union's Education Director. He is not put together like Walter and the routine of life under the shadow of a bodyguard was visibly heavy on him. Last winter Victor Reuther was assigned to represent CIO in Europe . . . CIO has lagged far behind the AFL in international affairs; he would be breaking new ground where the Communists are far more powerful than their democratic labor opponents. He came to New York to sail to Paris, frail, tired, and his voice low-keyed. He seemed no figure then on whom to bet very much, but Victor Reuther went to Paris and he is back now for the first time in six months. Since then he has traveled 50,000 miles. He was in

Helsinki, Finland, where the bravest free trade unionists on earth fight for their lives under daily Soviet threats of reprisal. He was in Germany helping its unions fight through a law which gives them a voice in the management of the industries they work in, while an emissary of the NAM went about telling businessmen that they could not expect a cent of American capital if the law passed. He was in Austria pushing American authorities to deal with the Socialist unions who have beaten the Communists to a standstill.

Most of all, he was in France, the key to European labor where coal costs $49 a ton, where wages are a third of the American standard and where the Communists still run the unions. He sits in an old sweatshop in a Paris slum and talks to men who still belong to Communist unions and are looking for the kind of strong labor movement that can lead them out, and wherever he goes the Communists chalk on his car "War Propagandist." Victor Reuther came back to the CIO platform yesterday. His shoulders were straight, his head was up and the wounds on his soul were gone. He will go back to Europe with a big new allotment from CIO as organizer not out for dues but to help restore the soul of European labor . . . The audience got very quiet as Victor Reuther reminded them that this is a fight still undecided and that we dare not rest on our battalions alone, and at the end the applause welled up because though he seems a softer man, he is as indestructible as any other Reuther.

The idea of going to Paris was exhilarating. And it gave me the chance to take Sophie and the children away from the depressing climate in Detroit, where we were always conscious of the bodyguards, and where all of us feared still more attacks. The idea of establishing a somewhat more normal family life was most attractive, though uprooting the children from their school and playmates, and Sophie from her circle of friends, and packing off to a strange country with a strange language and culture was not an entirely easy undertaking. At a party before we left Detroit, my friends and colleagues presented me with a shortwave radio set. When I explained how it worked to the children, their only response was, "Does this mean we can still hear 'The Lone Ranger' in Paris?"

There was talk among worried UAW officers about our going to Paris without security arrangements. No one in Detroit had been (or ever would be) apprehended for the criminal attacks; there had been a lot in the press about the possibility that the assassination attempts were Communist-inspired, and Paris was a well-known center of organized and disciplined leftists. But Sophie and I were set on sailing for Paris with no bodyguards. I solved the problem by assuring the UAW officers that we would take our trained boxer, Taffy, with us and that if the Paris police permitted, I would take my .38 Police Positive revolver, to have in my home at least. Friends at the U.S. Embassy in Paris cooperated, and I was instructed to carry the weapon in a briefcase and declare it at customs in Le Havre. There was the usual confusion at landing — each of us carried some hand luggage; Sophie had two children in tow; I had my left hand occupied with holding the leash on a very excited boxer who had been cooped up for many days, and my right arm, in the possession of another child, clutched the briefcase containing a few papers, a 35 millimeter camera, and the .38 caliber revolver. No wonder that I caused an incident through a slight error in my declaration form, on which I described the pistol as "38 millimeter"! As the French customs officer ran down the list of declared items, his eyebrows suddenly began to flutter and he sputtered out, *"Mais ce n'est pas possible. C'est un petit canon!"* He was right. I apologized profusely; nevertheless a senior customs official had to be called. Fortunately he had been informed in advance by the Paris police, and we went ashore with no difficulty, secured our car, and enjoyed our first day in France with a leisurely drive to Paris, which was to be our home for several years.

As might be expected, the children made the adjustment to a foreign land and language with greater ease than their parents, though the first few months were difficult. We lived in a little village called Enghien-les-Bains on the outskirts of the city, known for its great casino as well as its thermal baths. We thought the best thing for the children would be to put them in the French school in the village because in the long run it would be less painful than having them tutored in French after classes at an American school. There were, of course, days when they would come home weeping, asking why they couldn't go back to Detroit. But before long they were all babbling away in French, thanks to intensive training in school and their friendship with the neighborhood children. Sophie and I, trying to communicate in our halting French, soon became a source of embarrassment to them. On many occasions we pressed them into service as interpreters, especially when Sophie went to the nearby open markets to buy food. Eric went along with her but tried his best to stay a safe distance as she negotiated a purchase. One day

Sophie, who especially loved the French goat cheese, could not remember the word for it, and as the saleswoman obligingly ran down
the very long list of cheeses, the line of impatient customers behind
Sophie got longer and longer and still Eric did not come to her aid.
In sheer desperation she put her fingers on each side of her head
like horns and blurted out "Baa! Baa!" There came a chorus from
the line behind her, *"Ah, chèvre, Madame."* Eric by then had fled the
scene.

Once again, freed from the chains of fear, family life became a
joy. We were not exactly living in the lap of luxury, for we had
none of the fringe benefits normally provided to those on official assignments overseas, but our stay was a delightful experience. We
loved the city and the wonderful countryside surrounding it, especially the Compiègne Forests to the north. We had short holidays in
Switzerland or on the beach in Holland and an unforgettable
Christmas in Algiers.

Though the shooting had robbed me of all sense of taste and
smell, I enjoyed the French cuisine and also drank with pleasure the
superb wine. It came as a shock to us that French children start
drinking wine at an early age. I have seen suckling infants given a
pacifier made of cloth soaked in wine. Sophie, a good American
mother, insisted that growing children needed the proper amount of
milk every day — but where to find pasteurized milk in the country
of Louis Pasteur? We finally located a dairy establishment but there
was no guarantee that the bottles were sterilized. It became the
daily chore of our younger son, John, to carry on his way home
from school a little metal wine rack holding four liters of bottled
milk, but he had to bear the taunts and jokes of his schoolmates, who
thought it a ridiculous amount of milk to consume every day. "Hey,
what do you do? Bathe in it?" Day after day John came home in
tears, asking if arrangements couldn't be made for someone to deliver it. But such things were not easily arranged there, and Sophie
insisted that it was one of John's responsibilities. Finally, one night
when the subject had once again been raised, John looked at us, and
with his characteristic pragmatism, asked, "Why can't they put the
milk in wine bottles?"

Before I went to Europe, I had stressed to Phil Murray that our
CIO committee should confine its efforts to assisting all sorts of
democratic trade union organizations, at all times respecting

their rights to set their own policies. I recommended that we avoid any impression of rich Americans going to Europe to throw money around and dictate policies and practices. This image was all too common. Of course, even if we had wanted to play the rich uncle, the budget provided by the National CIO would have made it impossible. So my first move was to shift the Paris office from the Boulevard Haussmann to a more proletarian address, 15 rue du Temple, a 400-year-old tenement building around the corner from the famous market, Les Halles. The inevitable comparisons were drawn between our quarters and those of the AFL on the ritzy rue de la Paix.

For staff, I had as assistant Charles Levinson, a French-speaking Canadian who had considerable trade union experience in both Canada and Europe, Lewis Carliner, who came with me from the UAW in Detroit to handle our publications, and several bilingual secretaries, who made it possible for us to carry on correspondence in four languages. Later we added to our German staff Helmuth Jockel, who edited and published our CIO bulletin in German.

In France, the trade union movement, which had once been the backbone of Léon Blum's Popular Front, was becoming splintered. The majority of the organized workers remained in the historic General Confederation of Labor (the CGT), now becoming Communist-dominated. The complete take-over of this union by the Communists was helped along by the AFL's Irving Brown, who encouraged, with American funding, the withdrawal of non-Communists from the CGT. The split was engineered by Léon Jouhaux, the popular secretary-general of the CGT, who had suffered long Nazi imprisonment in Germany and was persuaded to take the democratic minority out of the mainstream of the French trade union movement and establish a new union called Force Ouvrière. The fact that the split was poorly organized and premature was demonstrated by the small number of non-Communists who followed Jouhaux. He remained a somewhat lonely figure during the last days of his life, though he was honored with a Nobel Peace Prize. He confided to me one day that the split was a mistake and that had he and his group remained within the CGT and encouraged other democratic workers into stronger positions, they might have been able to challenge the Communists and recapture control.

What cannot be questioned is that even that small split could not have been organized without encouragement from certain Americans and the cost of it heavily underwritten by U.S. Government funds.

Irving Brown alienated Jouhaux by an insulting reference to the French workers, during an AFL convention. Jouhaux responded with a press release:

> We are happy that in our debonair republic there is enough freedom for Mr. Irving Brown, welcomed as an American citizen without the need for a visa on the soil of France, to attack with powerful means a movement of ideas and action that is honored by the support of many distinguished Frenchmen. We are determined to fight against the setting up in Paris of an Un-French Activities Committee on the model of the Un-American Activities Committee in Washington. The former could, incidentally and usefully, investigate the action of Mr. Brown, who in a speech made at the last congress of the AFL and widely distributed in France, declares that the French masses are "indifferent, cynical, and inert."

Charles Levinson reported to me that Jouhaux was even more disturbed by Brown's activities in France than by his speech to the AFL; he considered asking the French authorities to have him expelled from France.

The AFL, through Brown, kept at arm's length the smaller, Catholic union called the Christian Federation of Trade Unions (the CFTC), because there were times when it cooperated with the CGT in support of specific economic goals. This was considered treason by the AFL.

In keeping with CIO ideology and policy, I set as my first goal good personal relations with the representatives of all democratic French trade unions, with the officials in their national headquarters, and, even more important, with the leaders of their industrial branches, such as metal workers, chemical workers, transport workers, and others. The next goal was to help them prepare a new cadre of young trade union leaders, because the war had taken its toll of the old. Fortunately the Swedish trade unions had come into possession of a lovely old château, La Brevière, in the Compiègne Forests, which they had renovated and offered for trade union leadership training purposes. I was pleased to be able to play a part in organizing some of the first postwar educational seminars. They were attended by delegates from both the Force Ouvrière and the CFTC — representing the metal, mining, and transportation industries. Where the CIO saw the need, and direct requests were made of us, we extended some limited financial help to these unions organizing training sessions.

The workers who attended the La Brevière seminars were compensated for their lost wages and their travel expenses to this base in north-central France. Soon after their arrival, I learned something new about collective bargaining and experienced a minor cultural shock. By the second day, the students had elected their own committee to deal with staff and administrators of the training program. Their first demand was that they should receive compensation for refreshments, which seemed reasonable and was rooted in French tradition. The second demand was for a special allowance to compensate them for loss of marital joys — a claim they based on numerous French court decisions. I was aghast, but after consultation with more knowledgeable Francophiles, I conceded there were legal precedents. Yet how could one put a dollar or franc value on such a loss? We compromised on a round sum; it was not necessary to check prevailing rates on the Champs Elysées.

The personal relationships we helped establish during that period were a factor in eventually bringing unions affiliated with both the Protestant and Catholic federations into worldwide organizations, such as the great International Metal Workers' Federation, representing nearly thirteen million workers in fifty countries.

How fortunate it was that Harry Truman, who was admittedly little experienced in foreign affairs when the mantle of the presidency suddenly fell on his shoulders, had at his side a general whose outlook and whose compassion for the vanquished were more civilian than military. George C. Marshall, who became Secretary of State and fathered the Marshall Plan, had the vision and courage to push vigorously for the economic recovery of war-devastated Europe, especially Germany.

The desire to strip Germany of its basic industrial strength was, alas, shared by many unthinking Americans. Dismantling Germany's basic technological power — and thereby, of course, making sure it could not rearm itself — was the objective of the policies advocated by Secretary of the Treasury Henry Morgenthau, Jr., and enthusiastically endorsed by our wartime ally, the Soviet Union. I have already described what the Russians were doing along these lines when I was in Germany in 1948; they were shipping to their own country great amounts of German industrial equipment that the workers in Germany had tried to reassemble and put to use. Quite understandably, the USSR feared the resurgence of an economically powerful Germany, and seemed to believe that it could be reduced to an agricultural country, serving as a buffer on the western flank of the Soviet Union and its newly acquired satellites.

The truth is that the industrial know-how and productive ability of Germany have always been crucial factors in Europe's economic balance. Preventing the re-establishment of a German industrial society would have led to chaos and social upheaval, and would have precluded the creation of a democratic society in Germany. Nothing would have better prepared the way for future Hitlers than the prolongation of bitterness and starvation. It was not merely compassion; it was a realistic appraisal of the condition of Europe that led Marshall to propose his plan. Nor was his plan limited to Western Europe: it was made explicitly clear to the Soviet Union that the U.S. was prepared to give it the same kind of massive economic help.

The Soviet Union, however, did not want to play ball; it preferred to harrow the ball field and despoil the opponents.

The Marshall Plan did not win Congressional approval with ease. There was no certainty that an America still jubilant over the defeat of Germany would be willing to finance the start of Europe's recovery. Winning acceptance of the program took much arm-twisting of senators and congressmen and behind-doors lobbying. I recall with satisfaction the many times Walter and I testified before congressional committees in support of the plan.

President Truman was being urged to take a hard line against it. R. J. Thomas, I remember, then president of the UAW, made a trip to Germany in 1945 and, along with some National CIO leaders, advised Truman that Germany should be punished economically. Truman's response at that time was: "The amount of German steel production, now under discussion, will be determined in the light of the severe terms there laid down . . . We propose to cause to be removed much industrial equipment from Germany by way of reparations and industrial disarmament."

During my first postwar trip to Europe, I had fortunately met with many German political leaders, such as Dr. Kurt Schumacher, and with heads of the newly established German Trade Union Federation (DGB), such as Hans Boeckler, leader of the coal miners. It was indeed a blessing that within the U.S. Military Government there were some who learned quickly from practical experience, especially in Berlin, where they had their fingers on the pulse of German politics. General Clay and others soon understood the pitfalls of the whole dismantlement program. I began to pull together documentation for a letter that Walter was to send Truman on May 10, 1949, spelling out in detail why German industry had to be rehabilitated:

Dear Mr. President:

I am writing you in hopes that through use of the great prestige and authority of your office and of the United States Government you will be able to avert the senseless destruction of industrial capacity in Germany.

I am writing specifically with regard to six steel and three chemical plants found by the ECA to be necessary for European recovery. I hope, however, that the proposal which I shall outline in relation to these plants can be extended to cover all the non-munitions plants now scheduled to be destroyed under the reparations program.

The six steel and three chemical plants referred to were recommended for retention in Germany by Mr. Paul Hoffman . . . Despite that recommendation, the Three Power agreement recently concluded in Washington earmarked those plants for reparations. In the normal course this would mean dismantlement. The nature of these plants, however, makes dismantlement equivalent to destruction . . . The destruction of these plants would, in my opinion, be in direct conflict with the domestic and foreign objectives of your administration.

You have called for expansion of steel capacity in the United States to relieve a shortage that is world-wide in scope. Dismantlement of German steel mills would intensify that shortage . . . and deprive American workers in the automobile and other steel-consuming industries of opportunities for full and regular employment.

You have sought and obtained from Congress billions of dollars to speed European recovery. Part of those funds are being spent to supply Europe with steel and fertilizer. Destruction of German plants able to supply these needs thrusts an unnecessary additional burden on the American taxpayer and diminishes the effectiveness of the funds which we are spending in Europe's behalf.

A major goal of your foreign policy is to prevent the spread of Communist totalitarianism and to preserve and strengthen democracy throughout the world. Establishment of a vital democracy in Western Germany is crucial to that goal. Needless dismantlement of German plants will deprive German workers of employment and will drive them, out of desperation, into the arms of the Communists. . . .

We must recognize, of course, that fears still exist with respect to restoring German industrial power because of its military potential. But the security which Germany's neighbors desire can be assured by controls which will promote the purposes of the European Recovery Program rather than by destruction of Germany's productive capacity . . .

I suggest, in brief, that the plants in question be left intact at their present locations, operated under the Law 75 trusteeship of the Western occupying nations; and that nations entitled to reparations be assigned the output of these plants up to the value which they would have received through dismantling . . .

The full text of the memo is in the Wayne State University archives.

The selection by Truman of Paul Hoffman to direct the Marshall Plan was very good news. An able administrator, a compassionate man, a moderate Republican, Hoffman was able most effectively to win friends in Congress. Moreover, as the Soviets increased their pillage of industrial equipment and their sabotage of European recovery, Truman became angrier, and lost his enthusiasm for the Morgenthau dismantlement program. He began to embrace enthusiastically the plan of his Secretary of State, and within six months John J. McCloy, high commissioner for Germany, announced in Berlin to the world press that the United States had called a halt to the dismantlement of German industry.

This was one of the most dramatic of all postwar decisions. The German workers would achieve full employment, and Germany would be able to develop a prosperous economy in cooperation with other West European industrial countries. Later, Dr. Fritz Baade, economic consultant to the West German government, was to recall gratefully "the help of the American trade unions, with the UAW at the head."

When I went to West Germany in 1951 with a CIO delegation, I wrote a letter to Michael Ross, CIO director of International Affairs in Washington, summing up the situation as of that date:

We met with the top officials and General Council of the metal workers in Frankfort, as well as the General Council of the railroad workers. We were very much impressed especially with Jahn, the head of the railroad workers, and the work he is doing with those from the Eastern Zone . . . The timing of our arrival was perfect. The *Mitbestimmung* issue was just coming to a head and we were there to see the whole issue buttoned up rather tightly before we left . . .

Berlin has its usual problems: unemployment is proving especially irritating at the moment because it is hitting new sections of the labor force, particularly the retail field . . . I was much impressed with the progress made on housing. Of course it still remains one of their most serious headaches . . .

The political situation in Berlin is as you know complicated by the differences between [Ernst] Reuter and Schumacher. We spent the good part of the morning with Reuter and his right-hand man Hertz and also a full evening with Franz Neumann and his close trade union associates . . . It gave us important background information essential to understanding a number of issues that are very hot and explosive. One of these involves the right of the Berlin trade union, the DGB, to organize the police, a right which DGB has enjoyed for a long time in the Western Zone . . . Ex-Nazis and extremely conservative members of the *Beamten* Group have wormed their way into the Berlin Police Force and give the democratic forces in Berlin real cause for concern. We hammered away at this issue with McCloy and with General Taylor in Berlin. We feel reasonably sure that the DGB will get the right to organize the Berlin police within a short time.

We went to a conference of metal workers, with two thousand delegates participating, at Bochum; we met with the general executive of the Miners' Union and spent a day going through the steel and mining areas. From there I wrote: "When I go through places like the Ruhr and see how it is, I wonder why the Communists aren't actually stronger, for God only knows there isn't much there that seems worth defending. There is a very urgent need for more emphasis on housing."

Divided Berlin was the place where the Soviet Union's harassment took its most dramatic form. It was essentially the workers of West Berlin who strengthened the fiber of democracy in all of West Germany by rebuffing Soviet efforts to draw them into a Communist-dominated trade union. What is little understood and appreciated outside Germany is the extent of significant opposition to Hitler among the Germans themselves. While it is true that the Jews suffered most through his brutality and barbarism, there were many thousands of trade unionists and outstanding political leaders who went to concentration camps rather than submit to Nazism. One of these was Mayor Konrad Adenauer (later to become Chancellor) and another was the gallant Ernst Reuter, who was the Mayor of West Berlin during the dark days of the airlift. The workers had their heroes, too, such as Hans Böckler of the Mine Workers, who became the first president of the DGB at the end of the war, and Otto Brenner, leader of the Metal Workers' Union. None of these was ever to forget or forgive; one and all they were determined not to permit the Nazis to come back into power either in uniform or in the suits of bankers and corporate employers. I recall Böckler's telling me that soon after the war's end, when there was an effort to get coal production underway again, the U.S. Military Government chose a well-known previous employer to head up the program — a man who had been a Hitler collaborator. Böckler and his miners were infuriated. Their protests were considered an affront by the American general involved. It came to the point where Böckler had to tell the general there would be no coal mining done under the direction of the ex-Nazi. The general warned that strikes were not permitted and that if Böckler called one he would be arrested and possibly imprisoned. The latter, in a low quiet voice, stretched out crossed wrists, inviting the general to arrest him. "Herr General," he said, "you may arrest me, but I doubt if there is anything in your jails which I have not already seen in Hitler's prison."

There was no strike. The manager was changed.

The same determination on the part of the workers, aided by their political friends, made them push for *Mitbestimmung*. Not even in Scandinavia or Britain, not to mention the United States, had the workers got to the point where they would advance such a proposal. It was the holocaust that had given them such courage, and made it absolutely necessary to keep the new Germany from falling back into the hands of the very men, such as Krupp and Thyssen, whose support had made Hitler's coup possible in the first place. Legislation for *Mitbestimmung* first became operative in the coal and steel sectors of West Germany. As the military occupation phased out and political power was fully transferred to the West Germans, the question of worker participation in management became an issue sharply dividing the political parties.

Konrad Adenauer's personal commitment to genuine democracy cannot be questioned. He was, nevertheless, the spokesman for the most conservative elements in West Germany, and his support came primarily from the employer class. His party, the Christian Democrats, fought tooth and nail against the extension of codetermination to the rest of industry. It is to the credit of every segment of the American trade union movement that it brought pressure to bear to help West German workers win their point. The National Association of Manufacturers, on the other hand, openly opposed any such legislation in the U.S. After twenty-five years, the association continues to lobby against it. In a release dated April 1, 1951, I said:

> Nothing is better calculated to persuade the working people of Europe that Communist charges of American imperialism are well founded than the current campaign of the National Association of Manufacturers of the United States against the German labor movement's drive for codetermination. The people of Europe should know that the NAM does not speak for the American people either in this matter or in others. NAM certainly does not speak for the 16 million organized workers of CIO and AFL who are united in their desire that the free labor movement of Europe pursue its own path toward economic democracy . . .
>
> We do not believe that we have the right to demand that the rest of the world conform to the American pattern of economic organization in exchange for economic assistance . . . After the bitter experience of the Nazi years, we feel that the German workers are entitled to demand and to secure sufficient democratic controls over the direction of their national economic life to protect themselves against the power drive of a selfish minority of German big businessmen whose allegiance to democracy is, to put it mildly, suspect.

Adenauer, for all his conservatism, did a great service to the West Germans by leading them through their initial period of economic growth and re-establishing relations with other nations. Like Winston Churchill, he was a great man for a very special time. But as the West Germans became more prosperous, they grew impatient with the continuation of the Cold War and looked with greater hope toward a slight opening in the wall between East and West Berlin. They also thought seriously about enlarging the social benefits of workers, small farmers, and consumers. Just as the British electorate turned to the Labor Party to meet peacetime goals, so the West Germans turned away from Adenauer to an attractive young man who became Mayor of Berlin after the tragic death of Reuter — Willy Brandt. Walter and I knew Brandt; we talked with him whenever we were in Berlin and encouraged labor delegations to go there and see for themselves the tragedy of the wall and meet the dynamic new Mayor. We also helped promote appearances for Brandt in Washington and elsewhere in the United States.

Later on, Brandt met John F. Kennedy and the two men hit it off immediately. Brandt was impressed with Kennedy's refreshing approach to both domestic and world problems, and admired his polit-

ical pragmatism. He sent several members of his staff to observe
Kennedy's fight for the presidency. (He asked me to help arrange
for them to travel with the Kennedy party, which I did.) Roy
Reuther was heading up the campaign on the labor front, and
Brandt's team was so impressed by the role that U.S. trade unions
had played in helping to bring about victory that they invited Roy to
come to Germany and advise them in Brandt's forthcoming campaign for the chancellorship.

The city of Berlin, divided as it was, was a constant symbol of West
German determination to resist any Soviet encroachment on its freedom. Many times during the days of the airlift I sat on bags of coal
and rode in cold planes into the besieged city to talk with Mayor
Reuter, with Scharnowski, and with the workers. I spoke to many
hundreds of thousands of Berliners at one of their first May Day
rallies since the end of the war, and listened to their city leaders and
to spokesmen from the rest of the free world pledge their continuing struggle for freedom. The event left such an impression on me
that I urged Walter to accept an invitation to speak at the 1949 rally.
He wanted to speak in German as I had, and I worked with him on
the text of his speech. He did not feel at home in the language, as I
did, but I convinced him that he should say at least the opening
paragraph in German. Before the great sea of uplifted faces, he
promised the Berliners, "We shall stand with you in Berlin no matter
how strong and cold the Soviet winds blow from the East." He
ended on a positive note: "The only war in which the American people wish to engage is the war against poverty, hunger, ignorance,
and disease. The promise of a world at peace, dedicating its combined resources to the fulfillment of human needs everywhere, will
kindle the same hopes and warm response in the hearts of the Russian people as among the people of the free world."

What we all feared most was that the USSR would take some hasty
action, not realizing the will and determination of the West to resist
any aggression against West Berlin or West Germany. Brandt therefore stressed the importance of seizing every opportunity for dia-
logue with the Russians. Yet he also knew there was no chance of
the Social Democratic Party's coming to power unless it could shed
its outworn Marxist ideology and create an image comparable to that
of the British Labor Party: a coalition of wage earners, middle-income people, and farmers. He achieved this by internal party re-

form and by rewriting his party's basic declaration of principles, aligning its goals with the needs of modern, postwar Germany.

It was difficult to overcome the doubt felt by many that the Social Democratic Party was fiscally responsible and had the capability to govern. Adenauer had stature and personal popularity. The electorate became so evenly divided between the two parties that small splinter groups held an almost unhealthy power to shift the balance. Adenauer, knowing the importance of U.S. support, tried to make the voters believe that he alone had the confidence of Washington and he alone could guarantee continued American aid. In this he was helped by George Meany, who encouraged him in his opposition to the views of the German Trade Union Federation and Brandt's *Ostpolitik.*

Adenauer tried to use Walter, too, to promote his campaign of weaning the German workers away from their traditional loyalty to the Social Democratic Party. Walter and I were in Italy attending the World Conference of Automobile Workers when Walter was invited by Adenauer to come to Germany and accept the highest civilian award in appreciation for his help in preventing the dismantlement of German industry. Naturally Walter felt honored, yet we could not shake off the suspicion that the timing of this award in the midst of a political campaign was designed to create the impression that Walter and the UAW were as pro-Adenauer as George Meany. Walter accepted, but at my suggestion called Brandt and arranged an advance meeting with him in Berlin, with press coverage and photographs, in order to print clearly on the public mind our support of Brandt and the Social Democrats. We also contacted Willy Richter, president of the Trade Union Federation, who had not even been informed by Chancellor Adenauer that Walter was arriving to receive an award.

Brandt, sensing the slimness of his margin, conceived the brilliant idea of a grand coalition in the nation's interest, which would include both major parties, with Adenauer to remain Chancellor at first, and Brandt himself as Foreign Minister. This strategy achieved immediate results; it won over the electorate and freed the West German government to undertake the politically risky "opening to the East" that Brandt desired — to be more fully realized when he became Chancellor himself.

Brandt's most spectacular successes as Chancellor were his bold and dramatic moves to normalize relations with the Soviet Union and her satellites bordering Germany — Poland, Hungary, and Czechoslovakia — all to go through violent upheavals and suffering in their efforts to loosen the tight Soviet control. No one better understands the reasons for the awarding of the Nobel Peace Prize to Brandt than the Poles, Czechs, Hungarians, and East Germans, who owe him a personal debt for the larger measure of autonomy they enjoy today.

Even the United States, after long years of waging the Cold War, has at last accepted the political realities and is establishing diplomatic and trade relations with mainland China and Russia. Undoubtedly the advance work done by Brandt eased the way for new Western overtures to Moscow and Peking. In no other European country did I observe anything equal to the stoicism of the Austrian people. This small nation, though occupied by foreign soldiers and divided into zones for years after the war, maintained its sense of political identity, and in the face of stupendous odds was able to retain a degree of satirical humor that was perhaps more troublesome to its conquerors than open opposition. With realistic awareness of their limitations, the Austrians skillfully took advantage of every chance to improve the level of their economic status without prostituting their national independence. I remember being escorted by Austrian friends, during the early days of military occupation, through the French, American, and Russian zones. At the end of the tour, one of them wryly remarked, "Perhaps some day we can introduce you to the Austrian zone."

Historically Austrian trade unions have played an important role in government affairs, and it was natural that, as we made postwar union contacts, we were at the same time meeting the future political leaders of the country, including Bruno Pittermann and the man who is the present Chancellor, Bruno Kreisky. Walter and I enjoyed the friendship and cooperation of the president of the Austrian Trade Union Federation, Johan Boehm; of Karl Maisel, head of the Metal Workers and later to be Minister of Labor; and of Anton Proksch. We had such warm memories of Austria before the Hitler coup, it was a joy to know that the commitment to a democratic government with an active social policy was still alive. Full credit must go to the trade unions, which had the courage to include within their unified movement the Christian and Catholic opposition groups, just as the Social Democrats prepared to move into coalition and cooperate, under difficult circumstances, with their political opposition.

I was happy that Roy, who was not to be as active in international affairs as Walter and I, was able to bring Fania to Germany, Italy, and Austria to study the political and trade union situation and share some of our experiences. I was in Vienna the night that Austria won its full independence under the State Peace Treaty, signed by all the great powers, which meant that at long last the Russians would evacuate their Austrian zone. What jubilation swept across that small country! Karl Maisel and I joined the celebrants on the next evening in the little city of Rust just across the lake from the Hungarian border.

I know there were skeptics in our State Department (and, of course, in the AFL) who thought that the Austrians paid too heavy a price for their independence by agreeing to follow a policy of "neutrality and non-alignment." What naïve nonsense. How else could Austria survive, belted in on the east by Communist satellites, and on the west by a divided, still uncertain Germany? Within a year — 1956 — Soviet tanks were rumbling through the streets of Budapest, brutally crushing a Hungarian revolt. *Neutral* Austria was the first to provide succor to the heroic Hungarians, who fought with their bare fists. I myself saw the first caravan of relief supplies organized and sent by the Austrian trade unions and the Social Democrats under the leadership of Fritz Klenner. This display of Austrian courage prompted the officers of the UAW to dispatch immediately a contribution of $25,000 to assist the Hungarians escaping to Austria.

At this point I came home to speak across the country in an effort to raise additional funds for the ICFTU to donate to the refugees who were fleeing across the Austrian border. The Austrians were themselves running the risk of having their country invaded by the Russians as they opened their borders to 200,000 refugees. Trade union headquarters, churches, public buildings were converted into asylums until more facilities could be organized. Later this same remarkable courage and compassion would be tested by the plight of the Czechoslovakians.

Accompanied by a UAW staff member, Guy T. Nunn, Walter was able to visit Yugoslavia and take May along, which was a great joy for both of them. Nunn had been a Rhodes Scholar, had served with the OSS during the war, and parachuted behind the German lines into Yugoslavia on a mission to make contact with Tito's partisan forces. He had served with them until they were overrun and taken by the Germans; he later escaped with them from a Berlin prison. His reunion with the men who had saved his life was a happy experience. Nunn was a most fortunate companion for Walter: he arranged an interview with Tito and contact with trade unionists, specifically the Metal Workers' Union under the leadership of Milan Rukavina.

I had already made a trip to the country and had laid some of the groundwork for Walter's visit. Tito has had the courage to insist on his independence from Moscow, while at the same time remaining completely unaffiliated with any of the Western powers. Although Yugoslavia is not a democracy, and its people do not enjoy full freedom, the good will of its leader was important to all of us who hoped for an end to the Cold War. We had no illusions about any significant short-term gains. It would always be a long hard road to peace.

The trade unions in Italy were plagued by much the same kind of divisiveness — though to a more serious degree — as existed in France. There was a Christian minority, who, together with a smattering of right-wing Socialists and republicans, split away from the main segment of the Italian trade union movement, the CGIL, which was dominated by Communists. This splinter group was encouraged by the U.S. Government and AFL anti-Communists.

Later there came into being in Italy a small but potentially significant Democratic Socialist trade union called the UIL. We of the CIO did not believe it was our prerogative to favor a particular organization; what we stressed was the advantage of belonging to a union that was essentially democratic and nonauthoritarian. Both the Catholic Trade Union Federation (the CISL) and the Democratic Socialist UIL met those conditions, and we encouraged each to expand its influence, to cease attacking each other, and to collaborate wherever possible on the improvement of the workers' economic and political status.

As in France, the split from the major trade union body had been premature; it left the Communists firmly in control of the larger federation and in possession of all its physical assets, including buildings, printing presses, and financial assets. With its major source of opposition removed, the CGIL was thus permitted to follow slavishly the Stalinist line.

Nowhere in Europe was the political situation as volatile as in Italy, where no single political party was ever in power long enough to create a stable government. The matter was exacerbated by a host of political strikes called by the CGIL, clearly for the purpose of sabotaging the political process. Furthermore, allied with the Communist Party was the old-line Socialist, Pietro Nenni. Walter and I had come to know him in 1933 in Paris, where he lived in exile. We considered his marriage of convenience with the Communists to be unnatural and destructive. Fortunately for the existing Italian government, which was essentially Christian Democrat in character, the liberals and moderates were in the ascendancy under the leadership of Fanfani, who later became Prime Minister.

The State Department under Eisenhower's presidency had treated Nenni as part of a permanent coalition of Communists and left-wing Socialists. Walter and I knew from personal conversations with him that he was unhappy with the arrangement, a precarious one at best, and that he sincerely wished to play a constructive role in reshaping the social and economic conditions of postwar Italy. He needed some sort of face-saving device to break with the extreme left and join with the Christian Democrats. This association would have assured Italy a greater degree of political stability and would have isolated the hard-core opposition in such a way as to immunize Italy against incessant political disruption.

Walter and I had many frank talks with Averell Harriman, who in my opinion had the best grasp of the political realities in Italy of any American diplomat. He headed the Marshall Plan assistance program for all of Europe and later became trouble-shooter for President John F. Kennedy. At that time Arthur Schlesinger, Jr., also made numerous trips to Italy to speak with political leaders; he frequently talked to Walter and me about the matter. We all came to the conclusion that Nenni should be encouraged to sever his ties with the Communists and enter into the larger democratic coalition. This move would also have profound effects on the trade unions, since he had a large following in the CGIL. Finally the uprisings and brutal Soviet suppressions in Hungary provided Nenni with the appropriate issue for divorcing himself from the Italian Communists.

The question was: would the Christian Democratic Party, which was the heart of the governing coalition, welcome Nenni, thus expanding the scope of the coalition? There were those in the State Department, the Pentagon, and in the merged AFL-CIO headquarters who bitterly opposed any acceptance of Pietro Nenni. Walter and I talked with Schlesinger and with Arthur Goldberg, then Secretary of Labor, and a breakfast meeting was arranged with Attorney General Robert Kennedy at his home in McLean, Virginia. Walter and I reviewed the situation in Italy, as we understood it, and cautioned Kennedy and Schlesinger that new directives would have to be given to the CIA and its operators in Italy. Kennedy suggested this question should be raised directly with the National Security Council and asked us to attend a meeting and present our view. We gathered in the old State Department building under the chairmanship of General Maxwell Taylor and reviewed the material we had covered at the previous meeting with Kennedy and our earlier ones with Harriman, suggesting a basic change in U.S. policy. At no time did we propose any special program to be undertaken in the trade union field in Italy, nor did we offer our services to carry out any program there. We merely recommended that the U.S. cease to put all its eggs in the same basket, and sponsor, instead, a broad coalition that would include Nenni. The members of the NSC listened attentively, asked many questions. No decision was made in our presence.

I was therefore shocked when I read, the next day, a column written by Victor Riesel in which he stated that Walter and I had met with the NSC and requested a million-dollar fund for an undercover plot to penetrate and win over union leaders within the Communist CGIL in Italy. There is little doubt in my mind that this distorted information was fed to Riesel by the CIA to block any change.

Events, however, moved inexorably in the direction we anticipated. Fortunately there were men in Italy, such as Ugo La Malfa and Aldo Moro, who favored just such an "opening to the left." One of the most knowledgeable U.S. correspondents in Italy, Leo Wollenberg, summarized the events of that time:

> In 1956 the sharp rifts which already divided the majority of the Socialists from their old allies, the Communists, became evident, especially as a result of Khrushchev's disclosure of Stalin's crimes and the Soviet intervention in Hungary. At the same time the meeting between Nenni and Saragat . . . gave for the first time concrete shape to the prospects

of reunification of PSI and PSDI (the splintered remains of the Socialist movement). However, for the American Foreign Service nothing was changing, nothing ever could change in Italy. To those who hinted at the new prospects in the Socialist camps the snap answer was "we cannot trust Nenni."

The Kennedy administration seemed to promise a change in the traditional American policy toward Italy. The rise to power of a center-left government supported by the Socialists began to appear probable — with most of the Socialists splitting away from the Communists. Harriman had an important part in convincing the American foreign policy makers of the wisdom of this move, and he was aided by progressive elements of American labor, including some of the Italo-American leaders of the Garment Workers' Union.

Wollenberg wrote of President Kennedy's visit to Rome in 1963: "Kennedy did not hesitate to underscore in public form his position and his propensities. The most conspicuous manifestation was his long talk with Nenni during the reception at the Quirinale Palace . . . It ended, as Nenni told me a few days later, with Kennedy extending a warm invitation to visit the United States."

No single factor had such a profound impact on postwar life in Italy as the building of this new coalition. For the first time, the political system was fortified by internal stability, to be reflected in the significant economic and social advances made in the years immediately following the change.

Going to Sweden was like moving onto a smooth lake, away from the storms of the war-torn countries. Over many years, some of our most fruitful international labor relationships had been with Scandinavian union and political leaders. Shortly after the war, Walter and I met the head of the Swedish Metal Workers, Arne Geijer, a man about Walter's age, who quickly established rapport with all of us in the UAW and in the Reuther family. The Swedish leaders have for a long time shown a mature regard for the living standards of their people, and have skillfully balanced the political influences of industry and the trade union movement. Geijer was pleasantly surprised to find in the U.S. more mutuality of interest, in terms of socioeconomic goals, than he had expected. Our involvement with him deepened as we all cooperated in the work of the International Metal Workers' Federation and the International Confederation of Free Trade Unions. He was elected president of the latter in July 1957.

Through Arne we came to know Prime Minister Tage Erlander and his successor, Olof Palme. During an evening's discussion in Stockholm with Erlander and Arne, we developed the idea for a series of international, high-level, off-the-record seminars, which turned out to have great significance during future political developments in Germany, Britain, and the U.S. These seminars, held in the early sixties, came to be known as the Harpsung meetings. (Harpsung was the summer residence of the Swedish Prime Minister, situated on the outskirts of Stockholm.)

Harold Wilson and Brandt, then Mayor of Berlin, were at the first conference, as well as Ludwig Rosenberg, president of the German Trade Union Federation, and George Woodcock, general secretary of the British Trade Union Congress. From Scandinavia came Geijer and Erlander of the host country, and the Prime Ministers of both Norway and Denmark. Hubert Humphrey was there (Arne had met him on one of his American trips) as were Walter and I. The group was kept small enough to permit informality and frank discussion. The agenda covered international economics (the Common Market was still in the offing), east-west relations, arms limitations, and other topics.

At one of the Harpsung meetings Wilson, who was soon to announce his candidacy for Prime Minister, listened with great attention and took detailed notes as Walter spoke about the developing new technology and how it should not be feared but, rather, harnessed in the service of man. A few weeks later Wilson sent Walter a letter enclosing the text of his opening campaign speech and, with remarkable humility for a politician, admitting that he had plagiarized some of Walter's Harpsung remarks. In Wilson's book, *A Personal Record: The Labour Government 1964–70*, he makes a handsome tribute:

> I had been greatly impressed over the years by my contacts with Walter Reuther, leader of the American Automobile Workers. It was his sophisticated approach to the challenge of automation, which we had discussed in Sweden in July 1963, which partly inspired my Scarborough speech of that year. He had been my guest at No. 10, and at my request had given me a brief on modern union organization. His approach was to force the pace in industrial efficiency . . . This was the basis of my appeal to the AEU and through them to the union movement: insist on high wages, but force the pace on productivity so that every organized firm could meet them.

As Prime Minister, Wilson added a new cabinet post, Minister of Technology, to which he appointed our friend Frank Cousins, general secretary of the Transport and General Workers' Union.

I do not know how much our Harpsung meetings helped Brandt in his campaign for the chancellorship, but I do know that everyone left those seminars enriched and strengthened by the close association among individuals who shared ideals for their respective countries.

One effect was felt in America soon after President Kennedy's election. Erlander came over for discussions, and one evening at the home of the Swedish Ambassador, he met with Arthur Goldberg, Walter, and me. We talked a good deal about one of Walter's favorite subjects: the need to implement the Full Employment Act, adopted under Truman but so far almost inoperative. Walter and I knew that Sweden had much to offer on the problem of the utilization of manpower, which they had solved by developing a unique relationship among industry, labor, and government. We thought this solution should be described to American political leaders; and as a result of that evening's talk a delegation, consisting of spokesmen for workers, employers, and the government, was invited by a Senate committee to come to the U.S. That was the first time, to my knowledge, that Congress had ever extended such an invitation. A rereading of the proceedings shows how far we still have to go in this country before we can say we are dealing on any responsible, effective, civilized basis with the problem of unemployment.

As a member of the Anglo-American Council I had many opportunities to visit Britain and to encourage the maximum application of modern production techniques. The actual dollar aid to England in those days was not large. In retrospect, I believe that what helped the British most in their efforts to recover from wartime dislocation was the challenge to examine their own society, where the most advanced technology existed side by side with the most antiquated — the latter being protected by cartel arrangements within employer associations. It was obvious that the British had far more to learn from themselves than from others.

Whatever seed money was made available produced far greater results than a comparable amount given to countries that had not come so far industrially. This was true also with regard to Germany, Austria, and the Netherlands, where workers' skills and political in-

volvement were already well developed. Under postwar governments sensitive to the social needs and rights of workers and consumers, recovery was more rapid than under the unstable and less
enlightened regimes in Italy and France.

It was a pleasure to re-establish personal friendships in England.
I especially enjoyed seeing Aneurin Bevan again and his wife, Jennie
Lee, who were living in a small flat in Cliveden Place. Nye Bevan
was head of the housing effort in Britain, as well as a member of the
cabinet, and he had made certain in his egalitarian way that he
would not be among the first to receive panes of glass for his
bombed-out windows. They were still covered with tarpaper on my
first postwar visit in 1948. Food was scarce. There was much more
sharing of the hardships of the war among the different classes in
Britain than in any other country I visited. Nye and Jennie, though
both members of Parliament, subsisted on the same rations as all
other citizens. I remember flying to London from Paris one day,
bearing eggs, butter, a bit of good French cheese, and a small bottle
of cognac in order to give them an unfamiliar feast that evening.

Talking with the Bevans, I realized why the people of Britain at
the end of the war turned their backs on their wartime savior, Winston Churchill, though they were grateful for what he had done, and
why, for the peace, they chose Clement Attlee and the Labor Party.
Attlee may have lacked personal magnetism, but he was completely
dedicated to a social evolution that included national housing and
national health programs. He and his Labor Party believed that
Britain's people, having made the terrible sacrifices demanded by
the war, deserved a higher level of economic justice than they had
had before. It was this belief that the electorate chose to accept in
place of a return to the status quo, offered by Churchill.

We in the UAW followed with intense interest the struggle in Britain to establish a national health program against the organized and
bitter opposition of the proponents of private medical care. We had
always felt that, with our science and technology, no American,
when injured or ill, should be stopped at the hospital door and
asked whether he or she could afford to come in. Again and again I
returned from England armed with bundles of Labor Party pamphlets on housing, health care, urban planning — all the problems I
knew would soon be confronting us at home. Every time the Labor
Party's programs were harshly attacked in the U.S. press, Walter

came strongly and openly to their defense. In September 1949, he forwarded copies of one of his arguments to some British friends, including Ernest Bevin, then Foreign Minister. Walter had met Bevin when he was head of the British Transport Workers. From his United Nations office in New York, Bevin responded:

Dear Walter:

My cordial thanks and those of HMG for the spirited defense you have put up for the Labour Government here in America. We are fully alive to the propaganda which has been carried on here . . .

We were under no illusion when we took office as to how difficult the task would be. We had been mobilized one day in three in the last thirty years. That means ten years of war, and to pull a country around after such a waste of slaughter and destruction has been no easy task. However, the Labour Government decided to ride whatever storms might blow up and to take decisions whether they were popular or unpopular on the basis of what was right for the people in the long run . . .

With regard to what is called the Welfare State, we are determined to look after the health of the people. I am sure it will pay handsome dividends, and while it is very costly at the beginning, it would have been fatal to have neglected it. Incidentally, one of the heaviest costs of this field is the hospital and what has amazed us is the amount of equipment that was needed to bring them up to date in accordance with the latest medical discoveries . . . The whole scheme is worthwhile and it removes a great anxiety particularly where there are large families. I am very glad, therefore, that you are following the problem closely and I think the article which you enclose is particularly encouraging.

Yours sincerely,
Ernest Bevin.

The success of the British National Health Service was to have a deep effect on Walter. Some years later a national committee of distinguished health experts drafted, under Walter's chairmanship, the basic elements of what has become the Kennedy-Gorman-Griffiths Health Bill.

All in all, the visits we made to European countries directly after the war, and those we made afterward to developing countries in Africa, South America, and the Near East, were undertaken with the idea of emphasizing our common interests and minimizing the conflicts. Any hope of peace must rest upon the understanding by people in all lands of how much they have to gain from international cooperation.

Since the founding of the United Nations, there have been far greater possibilities than the nations have taken advantage of. In 1949, Walter drafted a resolution, which the UAW adopted: "We hold that the United Nations offers the best immediate hope and mechanism for establishment of groundwork agreements and rules of conduct which must ultimately be forged into world government." He enjoyed his long, fruitful relationship with the American Association for the United Nations and its then executive head, Clark Eichelberger. He and Clark were among the few who first pointed out the enormous economic potential of the seabed, stressing that it must not be exploited by competing private interests or become the subject of national rivalries.

United Nations affairs were frequently discussed by Walter with Eleanor Roosevelt and, later, with Adlai Stevenson and Arthur Goldberg when, in turn, each served as our UN Ambassador. President Kennedy wanted to name Walter to the U.S. delegation to the UN, but George Meany always threatened to make political waves. Walter remembered that, in one of his last conversations with Kennedy, the President said to him: "I need you at the UN. Your practical collective bargaining experience needs to be brought to bear on building a coalition with other nations concerned with the struggle for freedom." Meany said no, and the President yielded.

In 1964, Walter sponsored a UAW resolution stating that "in the age of thermonuclear weapons and missile delivery" disarmament is absolutely essential. And one of Walter's last public services before his untimely death was to encourage the United Nations to focus the world's attention on the dangers threatening the human environment. In 1969, he and I went together to talk about ecological problems with UN Secretary General U Thant and our old friend Dr. Ralph Bunche. We discussed the UAW's efforts four years earlier to bring the United States and Canadian authorities and its members together in a Great Lakes Clear Water Conference in order to stimulate action on pollution by both countries. We knew that the UN was moving toward a worldwide conference on ecology, and Walter wanted to make certain that not only governments but the people themselves, through their lay organizations, could contribute to improving man's environment. He had recently become involved in the construction of the great UAW Family Education Center in northern Michigan. It was near completion at the time, and he proposed to U Thant and Dr. Bunche that it be the site for a joint conference, to be undertaken by the United Nations and the UAW, to explore on a tripartite basis — government, industry, and labor — the impact of urbanization on the human environment.

Walter did not live to participate in that conference. But the UAW asked me to continue to promote it with UN officials, and in the summer of 1970 delegates, some of them outstanding ecological experts, came from seventeen nations. Out of their working papers emerged excellent background and briefing documents for the delegates who were to meet the following year in Stockholm at the UN's first world conference on environment.

CHAPTER 25

Merger

THE SUDDEN DEATH in 1952 of Philip Murray and, a few months later, of William Green, president of the AFL, set in motion the merger of the two great American trade union federations. Twenty years had elapsed since John L. Lewis angrily led his industrial union out of the AFL, denouncing its leadership as aged, feeble, inept, and indifferent to the needs of the millions of unorganized workers in our country. The formation of the CIO had dramatically changed American society: union membership had more than tripled, and huge giants in the auto, steel, rubber, electrical, and agricultural implement industries had accepted the discipline of trade union democracy. The CIO alone accounted for five million new members, and its competition had stimulated the stodgy AFL to increase its membership from three to nine million. The combined influence of the two organizations began to affect federal social legislation; Presidents and cabinet members sought out CIO and AFL leaders for counsel and advice.

Walter succeeded Murray as president of the National CIO. During a long summary of its twenty years, he said:

> CIO has fought for decent schools and adequate health programs and housing for the people; CIO has fought for civil rights and civil liberties and human dignity; CIO has been a voice at the collective bargaining table where unions and mighty corporations participate in the bargaining process essential to the evolution of our free economic system and the growth of democracy.
>
> CIO has been the man or woman on the picket line, the witness at the legislative hearing, the voice on the Board of the Community Chest, the organizer outside the factory gate, the doorbell ringer urging Americans to know the issues and vote . . . We have fought not only for bread and butter! . . .

Look back over these eventful years. Who were the realists? Who were the practical people? Who initiated programs, who supported policies for our government that have long proven their essential strength and validity? Who, in the years since 1935, have had the faith in the dynamic potentiality of our economic system? . . . In the perspective of history, the facts sort out from the myths and the facts show this: the faith, the confidence, the spirit were there to an unparalleled degree in the ranks of the CIO.

While the CIO was creating a new image for labor, the AFL, even though its membership had been augmented, remained essentially the same. The CIO was the result of a crusade, and hundreds of its young dedicated organizers were out in the field, working together to storm the fortresses of certain monolithic industries. In contrast, the AFL, still dominated by men over sixty, still bureaucratic, had practically no national organizing staff to reach the unorganized workers, depending often on employers to organize the workers — especially employers who feared they might be attacked by the more aggressive CIO. Furthermore, the old established craft unions never hesitated to depict the CIO as dominated by Communists, in order to exploit the conservatism of a large group of American workers, not to mention employers.

The withdrawal of the industrial unions from the AFL left the traditional building trades and crafts unions in firmer control of the AFL than before. Their full-time officials were properly referred to as "business agents"; they were more concerned about the extra nickel in the pay envelope than in advancing social benefits. A deep-rooted discrimination against women and blacks persisted.

The CIO, to be sure, had to contend with the efforts of small but well-organized groups intent on capturing the leadership. These constituted an internal threat because in every crisis they turned to outside cliques for their directives instead of respecting the mandates of the membership. (Their stand on overtime and the forty-hour week in wartime, and their open sabotage of lend-lease through strikes are examples of their disruptive tactics.) The scourge of the AFL, on the other hand, was racketeering and corruption, which had never been dealt with energetically. Thus the commitment of the CIO unions to ethical standards was a matter of great moment during the merger discussions.

Another divisive factor was the wide distribution of responsibility in the CIO. Many specialized committees had been set up, each assigned a particular goal and all of them expected to implement agreed-upon policy. Virtually all the power of the AFL lay with the Executive Council, and even members of that council, acting as heads of select committees, were seldom allowed initiative.

I have already indicated the sharp differences that existed between the CIO and AFL in the field of international affairs, a natural result of ideological differences at home.

Perhaps the most graphic symbol of the gulf between the two organizations was the quarters they chose for the winter meetings of their respective Executive Councils. AFL officials periodically journeyed to Florida to stay for several weeks, spending a few hours each morning in formal session, then going to the races or golf course or whatever for the rest of the day. The CIO Executive Board, under Philip Murray and then under Walter, usually met in a hotel conference room in some northern industrial city — Pittsburgh, Chicago, New York, or Washington — never too far removed from industrial workers who wanted to come before it to discuss urgent problems.

In my judgment, the merger of the AFL and CIO in 1955 was premature — more or less a shotgun wedding. Its failure to achieve the hopes expressed on all sides, and the eventual rupture when Walter took the UAW out, can be traced directly to the fact that a solid foundation for a workable merger had not been laid.

Why did it happen? It is true that the leaders of every union in the country had dreamed that the labor movement might some day be reunited. For some, especially the leaders of the Amalgamated Clothing Workers, there was a commitment to the slogan, "In unity there is strength." What was not realized was that there is something worse than disunity and separation — stagnation, stultified bureaucracy, inaction, and reactionary behavior. Evidently some leaders of the National CIO did not recognize the dangers of affiliation with the AFL.

As so often happens, personal ambitions can profoundly affect important events. Philip Murray, at the time of his death, was president both of the National CIO and of the United Steel Workers. Walter replaced him as CIO head, but David McDonald, who had begun as Murray's private secretary and had successfully schemed to become his successor in the Steel Workers' Union, felt that he should have succeeded him also as head of the CIO. McDonald, never himself a steelworker, had none of Murray's commitment to the workers in the shops; he was an egocentric and ambitious man who enjoyed luxury and preferred to spend his evenings in nightclubs rather than meet with steelworkers. He had been flattered by the attentions of Hollywood stars and of steel tycoons.

When he realized he was not going to be nominated for the CIO presidency, he threw his weight behind Alan Haywood, who challenged Walter and lost. The good relations built up over the years between Walter and the Steel Workers under Murray deteriorated into envy, hostility, and increasing isolation on McDonald's part from the new leadership of the CIO. He even let it be known that he was considering withdrawing the Steel Workers from the CIO and affiliating with the AFL. Had he carried out this threat, it would have further undermined the merger bargaining position of the CIO.

There must have been others who were tired of the rigors and hardships of trade union life and were tempted by the prospect of being a member of a merged AFL-CIO Executive Council and of basking in the Florida sun every half-year. What Walter feared most was that other CIO affiliates, encouraged by McDonald's behavior, might return to the AFL fold, like errant children going home. It was no secret that some of the older AFL spokesmen demanded repentance as the price for accepting, once again, a union that had strayed.

As the difficult merger negotiations went on, Walter's energies were directed toward keeping the ranks of the CIO unbroken, and on extracting commitments from the AFL that the fight for civil rights, equal opportunity, ethical practices, and social legislation, would not cease. Recognizing at the outset that the CIO members were outnumbered by the AFL's and that the CIO ranks had been somewhat eroded by internal dissension, Walter recommended to his fellow CIO officers that they request no paid positions in the merged organization, and concentrate their efforts on structure, program, and policy. Walter himself had little interest in any post except the presidency of the UAW. While it is true that he fought hard to be president of the CIO, he always considered the UAW his home and power base, and he never thought of giving up his UAW position in exchange for any other.

In the terms of the merger agreement, and later in the language of the constitution, were anchored the major principles and organizational demands of the CIO. A new Industrial Union Department (the IUD) was created; it accepted all the unions previously affiliated with the CIO and any AFL unions that had industrial membership and chose to join. Walter was elected to head this department, and James B. Carey served as secretary-treasurer. Jack Conway, after a stint as deputy director of the Federal Housing Authority, became Walter's chief administrative assistant at the IUD. Conway's previous duties at Walter's right hand in UAW were assumed by Irving Bluestone, a sensitive, able, and experienced administrator, who came from the UAW's ranks and was almost as close as a brother to Walter.

UAW vice-president John W. Livingston was named director of a new Department of Organization. Provisions were made for an Ethical Practices Committee and for committing the merged AFL-CIO to advance the cause of civil rights and antidiscrimination. Everything looked fine on paper. As Walter knew only too well, however, words are one thing, deeds are another. He cautioned his CIO colleagues:

> The constitution makes provision, for instance, for methods of organizing the still unorganized workers of America, but our constitution cannot do that organizing job. My own union — the UAW — has indicated its willingness to contribute generously from its treasury to provide the necessary finances for an organizing campaign worthy in size and scope of our new trade union movement . . . We will press forward, in cooperation with like-minded colleagues from the AFL, to carry the torch of an organizational crusade . . . to the millions of Americans who today have no union.

He then repeated that corruption could not be tolerated, or Communist infiltration, "or any other totalitarian influences which do not share our common faith in the democratic process."

The merger agreement was signed in February 1955. George Meany and Walter issued a joint statement pledging the new organization to the service of the American public. As thousands of CIO delegates gathered for their last National Convention in New York City in December 1955, there was a strong undercurrent of nostalgia and, though everyone tried to put a good face on the situation, there was a feeling that an era had come to an end. A moving narration, by Melvyn Douglas, of the CIO's struggles and achievements of twenty years, and the singing, led by Joe Glazer, of the old familiar songs of the picket line brought tears to the eyes of many of labor's veterans.

Meanwhile in Washington, D.C., a large, modern building on six-teenth Street, just across from the White House, bearing on its cor-nerstone the initials *AFL-CIO*, was already under construction. And the most frustrating experience of Walter's life was about to begin.

The first disappointment was the failure of the AFL-CIO to launch an extensive organizing campaign to enroll millions of work-ers still without benefit of trade unions. Many were in the pe-trochemical industries and in the textile industry, which had moved south to escape unionization; a vast number were white collar workers — civil servants, schoolteachers, nurses — and there was the most exploited group of all: agricultural laborers. John Brophy's hopes for a "new era," which would unionize twenty-five million workers and give them increased wages, shorter hours, adequate pensions, and welfare provisions, could have been realized. The moment was ripe; perhaps never better in the United States. News of the amalgamation had raised the expectations of workers all over the country. The merged labor movement had potential financial resources never before available. The political climate was favor-able; the Wagner Act was firmly rooted; U.S. unions had already es-tablished a firm collective bargaining base in pivotal industries; and there was far greater understanding and support for labor in Congress than there had been a decade earlier.

The golden moment was lost. It is true that an organizing depart-ment was set up, but it was inadequately staffed and given little ma-terial support. Walter's offer, in behalf of the auto workers and the National CIO, of $4 million for an organizing campaign if the larger and much richer AFL would match the money, was turned down by Meany and his staff, dashing the hopes of hundreds of organizers waiting to do active work in the field. Some of the AFL-CIO leaders adopted a cynical attitude and said that it was risky to upset the ex-isting leadership of trade unions by inviting in large numbers of perhaps unsympathetic workers. Why not maintain the status quo and play it safe? John Livingston was treated with such disdain that he was not permitted to sit in on the meetings of the council to learn about the policies under which his department would be operating.

The gulf between the leadership and the rank and file widened. Although the first of the Eisenhower recessions had begun and unemployment was growing, the old AFL types went on renting hotel suites at Miami Beach. Such extravagance was distasteful to Walter, who resented taking meals in a Miami hotel dining room even when essential committee work was done over lunch or dinner. He finally raised the point openly in 1957 at a winter council meeting, suggesting that there might be a more appropriate, less expensive place to meet. He was surprised when the council accepted his idea and Meany promised to arrange something else for the following winter. Where? At the Caribe Hilton in San Juan, Puerto Rico!

This first meeting in San Juan, as a matter of fact, brought into the open another schism in this merger of incompatible partners. Meany was absent the first day. Walter held a meeting of his Economic Policy Committee and took to the Executive Council its recommendations for a march on Washington, organized by the AFL-CIO to dramatize the unemployment crisis and to demand from the President and Congress effective countermeasures. When news of this proposed march leaked to the press, Eisenhower and his publicity aides did not ignore the ludicrousness of such a plan emerging from the "sunny beaches" of Puerto Rico. Walter's angry response was, "Mr. President, I have spent no time on the sunny beaches of Puerto Rico, nor have I been with you and your many big business friends on the golf course, the duck blinds, and the quail hunts." The publicity by both sides was wasted, because Meany immediately quashed the initiative taken by the Economic Policy Committee and demanded that it withdraw its proposal. Walter threatened to resign as chairman of the committee; Meany persisted; eventually a compromise was reached when he approved a less dramatic Unemployment Rally.

Though the merger actually failed to strengthen the labor movement in America, the AFL-CIO from the outside looked like a giant threat to the right-wingers. The peddlers of hate and anti-Semitism, the Chambers of Commerce, the Manufacturers' Associations, the Milk Trusts, and other lobbies were frightened into making greater efforts and bigger financial contributions to restrict the social and economic progress of the trade union workers. Though the merger failed to increase significantly the membership of the AFL-CIO, it filled the coffers of its opponents.

In 1961, Walter, as chairman of the Standing Committee on Organization, submitted a detailed proposal to the Executive Council for an intensive membership drive, a step-by-step plan for soliciting the cooperation of each affiliate of the AFL-CIO. Walter's proposal was approved "in principle" by the council, but no steps were ever taken to implement or adequately to finance the program. Meany made his first dodge at a meeting of the presidents of approximately twenty unions in the distributing and retail industry, which had a direct interest in the program since their industry was still mostly unorganized. All the union presidents except one were prepared to work out a sensible solution to jurisdictional problems, but the single dissenting voice was accepted by Meany as a veto of the entire program. The tactic of permitting a veto by one union to block the cooperative efforts of nineteen others was a convenient way for the AFL-CIO president to confirm a do-nothing stance in organizing activities. Some years later he was to admit openly that he felt no particular need to increase the size of the membership; it was large enough already. At that point only 2 to 3 percent of AFL-CIO money, above administrative costs, went into organizing work within the U.S., while, Meany boasted before the House Foreign Affairs Committee on April 30, 1963, 23 percent went into overseas activities.

There were a few brave affiliates that recognized the opportunities for increasing their membership and pressed ahead. One was the American Federation of Teachers, a former AFL affiliate, which appealed directly to the Executive Council for support. These appeals initially went unheeded, but the IUD, made up, for the most part, of former CIO unions, collected funds to provide some assistance. In fact, the records show that, beginning in 1961, under Walter's presidency, the IUD extended well above $1 million to the organizing campaign of the AFT. Later, the AFL-CIO did respond to the federation's appeals.

Another point of difference between the old-line and the progressive leaders of the AFL-CIO was the matter of the farm workers, led by Cesar Chavez. Excerpts from a long administrative report to Walter in 1967 show clearly the fundamental contrast between the Reuther and the Meany philosophies.

"No segment of the American working population has been more neglected than the farm and migratory workers and the working poor. They represent the most deprived and disadvantaged of the work force . . . A breakthrough in Delano, California, may well symbolize the beginning of a new forward surge in bringing the benefits of union organization and collective bargaining to these forgotten workers.

"Following the merger of the AFL-CIO, repeated attempts were made to persuade the president . . . that a major effort should be made to help organize farm and migratory workers and to improve their conditions . . . When the campaign to organize farm workers in California did not yield early and encouraging results, the AFL-CIO, upon the insistence of its president, curtailed the organizing activities. Instead of responding to the difficulties and adversities experienced in this effort by offering greater commitment and more adequate resources, the president of the AFL-CIO proposed the termination of all efforts to organize farm workers, using the narrow argument that the amount of dues dollars collected did not measure up to the expenditures of funds to organize them . . .

"In September of 1965, strikes began among grape workers in California led by AWOC [Agricultural Workers' Organizing Committee]. Within a few days, the National Farm Workers' Association, an independent organization led by Cesar Chavez with a larger membership than AWOC, led his workers off. In its most elemental form, the strike was a long overdue bid for freedom and dignity by America's poorest and most disadvantaged workers.

"Week after week passed with no sign of a settlement of the strike in sight. Members of the clergy, students, civil rights groups, and representatives of individual unions such as the UAW and the Packinghouse Workers provided major on-the-scene 'outside' support to the strikers. By December, however, the struggling effort was faltering.

"At the time of the AFL-CIO convention in San Francisco in December 1965, the Delano grape strike was at a critical stage. A resolution to support the strikers, introduced by Walter P. Reuther, was adopted by the convention but the leadership of the AFL-CIO made no special effort to provide practical and needed help. Walter asked Meany to join him in a visit to Delano, but Meany refused . . . A delegation from the UAW and the Industrial Union Department, headed by Walter, went to Delano immediately following the AFL-CIO convention, met with strike leaders, and addressed the grape strikers at an enthusiastic rally there. He held a meeting with the Mayor and the City Manager of Delano and met with a group of grape growers in the effort to obtain union recognition for this budding union. The UAW and the Industrial Union Department committed direct economic support, made contact with lawmakers in Washington, and urged that a Senate investigation be held in Delano. Senators Robert Kennedy of New York, Harrison Williams of New Jersey, and George Murphy of California held investigative hearings in Delano.

"The moral and financial support pledged by the UAW, the Packinghouse Workers, and the Industrial Union Department was a turning point in the Delano strike. New hope was infused into the strike; the strike gained momentum and national prominence and the struggle of the farm workers in Delano, symbolized by their cry of 'Huelga,' gained recognition among the people of the nation . . .

"During these months of ferment, the AFL-CIO . . . continued to provide at best only minimal support to the strikers, although when the Schenley Products finally recognized the NFWA as bargaining agent, the then director of Organization of the AFL-CIO, William Kircher, was helpful in negotiating a contract settlement. He was also helpful in the campaign at the DiGiorgio vineyards. Throughout the bitter months of hard and determined strike effort, however, the critical and major moral and financial support from within the labor movement still came from UAW, IUD, and unions such as the Packinghouse Workers . . .

"At the Executive Council meeting of the AFL-CIO, held in Chicago in August 1966, the independent National Farm Workers' Association agreed to affiliate with the AFL-CIO . . . An AFL-CIO charter was issued under the title United Farm Workers' Organizing Committee. The president of the UAW urged the creation of a top-level committee composed of AFL-CIO Executive Council members to raise adequate financial support and to aid and assist the farm workers in their strike and in their organizational campaigns. This proposal was at first resisted by the president of the AFL-CIO but he ultimately, though reluctantly, agreed to set up such a committee of Executive Council members. But he very carefully denied UAW representation on the committee even though he knew that the UAW leadership perhaps more than the leadership of any other union had been deeply engaged in the strike struggle of the grape workers and had been actively involved in assisting them in their organizational campaigns."

Meany's exclusion of Walter might be considered a symptom of the incompatibility of the two men. No other Executive Council member at that time except Walter had ever visited the farm workers in the field.

Actually, the very first prominent union man to visit the agricultural workers and discuss matters with them was Roy. It was he who encouraged Chavez to bring his cause to the attention of national labor. When the farm workers won their first small victories in Delano and were able to build a simple structure for headquarters, they dedicated it to the memory of Roy, who had died of a heart attack on January 10, 1968.

The AFL-CIO executives not only failed to provide Chavez with the initial assistance required; they also tried to keep him from appealing to individual affiliates for contributions. In 1967, Chavez was invited to Detroit by the UAW to do some fund-raising. Meany's on-the-spot man, Kircher, heard about it and warned Chavez against going to Detroit or, indeed, having any contact with the UAW. But Chavez came anyway, and had a most successful visit, collecting, with the help of the UAW, money, food, and clothing for the migratory workers. He also arranged for Walter to go with him to Mexico to lay the groundwork for an agreement between the Mexican trade union movement and the U.S. migratory workers for dealing with the problem of the Mexican strikebreakers, brought in illegally by the growers. Again Kircher cautioned Chavez — unsuccessfully — not to go to Mexico with Walter. Useful contacts were made with the Mexican trade union and an arrangement was worked out.

When Chavez launched his consumer boycott of grapes and tried to extend it to European cities, where large quantities of California grapes were being marketed, I was surprised to learn that the AFL-CIO, in spite of its extensive contacts in Europe, had opened no doors there for Chavez. I therefore set up meetings with key unionists, in particular the transport workers in Scandinavia, Germany, England, and Holland, which made possible the first efforts toward an extension of the boycott to Europe.

The most serious threat to Chavez was to come from the Teamsters' Union. When Walter was alive, the Teamsters' Union respected the agreements they had made not to enter into a jurisdictional fight over the workers in the vineyards and the lettuce fields. After Walter's death and the deterioration of the UAW-Teamster relationship within the Alliance for Labor Action, the Teamsters undertook a vicious strikebreaking campaign to destroy the Chavez union. It was only at this point, with the gauntlet thrown down by the Teamsters, that the AFL-CIO responded with any worthwhile amount of financial aid and manpower to the struggling farm workers' union.

Walter was by no means the sole object of Meany's high-handedness. There was perhaps no more lonely figure within the old AFL than the distinguished and courageous leader of black American labor, A. Philip Randolph. The sole black member on the AFL Executive Council, he was insulted before an AFL-CIO convention when Meany bellowed, "Who in hell appointed you the spokesman for the black workers?"

The historic hesitancy of the AFL leaders to acknowledge the necessity for equal rights and opportunities for minorities was little changed by the merger. In Atlanta, Montgomery, Selma, and finally in Memphis, wherever Martin Luther King, Jr., marched, Walter and Roy and CIO colleagues marched at his side. The UAW, in particular, felt that moral and financial support were not enough; personal presence was needed to give visible evidence to the nation as well as to blacks that the cause of civil rights was a concern of all who cared about preserving American democracy. It was a great sadness to Walter that he could get so few of the other AFL-CIO leaders involved.

In the summer of 1963, the civil rights fight reached a climax with the August 28 March on Washington. Meany was in Europe at the time the plans for the march were being made. Immediately after his return, Walter phoned him and suggested that the AFL-CIO should become actively involved. He told Meany that leaders of all the civil rights groups, of church groups, and of 122 other organizations had met in New York and agreed to cooperate in the legislative fight and participate in the march. Meany replied that nothing could be done until the Executive Council met on August 12. Walter said this would be too late, and finally persuaded him to convene the committee on July 18. But on July 15, Meany sent Walter a wire: "Unable to reach you by telephone to advise there will not be a meeting of the Executive Committee July 18th, which we had discussed." Some weeks later, Walter, refusing to be thwarted, met with President Kennedy and certain civil rights leaders at the White House. At this point Meany agreed to set up a special task force on civil rights, a committee to consist of himself, William Schnitzler, Phil Randolph, Neil Haggerty, and Walter.

The committee met on August 2, and Walter raised the question again of supporting the March on Washington, stressing the need for participation by a broadly representative group of white Americans from labor and church groups. Meany refused to endorse the march and said that a number of members of the Executive Council also opposed it; he doubted it would be approved at the next meeting, which was to convene on August 12. And he saw to it that that was exactly what happened. However, a good number of AFL-CIO–affiliated unions worked hard and effectively for that dramatic, orderly, and very impressive event; namely, the Radio and Electrical Workers (the IUE), the Ladies' Garment Workers, the Distributive Workers of America, Amalgamated Clothing Workers, the State, County and Municipal Workers, the Packing House Workers, and of course the United Automobile Workers. Walter was one of the featured speakers.

It was the strike of an AFL-CIO–affiliated union, the State, County and Municipal Workers, organized by the garbage collectors in Tennessee, that brought Dr. King to Memphis and to his tragic death. Walter was the only member of the AFL-CIO Executive Council to march at King's side in that Memphis demonstration, and the only member to attend his funeral, though the president of the State, County and Municipal Workers, Jerry Wurf, later elevated to the Executive Council, was in the forefront of the Memphis fight and stood on many occasions at the side of Martin Luther King, Jr.

There was no doubt that Meany could always count on an overwhelming majority of the Executive Council to sustain him on any issue he felt strongly about, no matter what the facts or the logic of the case. How did he manage this? The average age of the members of the Executive Council, always the subject of jibes and humorous comments, was certainly one of the main factors. There has long been a tradition that AFL presidents never retire; they die in office. Gompers died at the age of seventy-four after thirty-eight years in office; William Green died on the job at seventy-nine years.

(John L. Lewis did not retire until he was eighty, after forty years as president of the Mine Workers.) Meany, at this writing over eighty years old, encouraged members of his Executive Council to remain, even when they wished to retire. When Meany tried to urge Leland Stanford Buckmaster of the Rubber Workers to stay on the council he told him: "You don't need to be tied to the labor movement. You can stay on the council as long as you wish," and indicated that other people were making a lifetime career of it so there was no reason why Buckmaster shouldn't follow suit. Some on the council had already retired from active work in their own unions, and no longer represented the workers. But they enjoyed the life led by members of the council, and it is easy to understand why they remained slavishly loyal to their domineering leader.

One might truthfully say that Meany treated some presidents of affiliated unions and members of his own council as vassals. James Carey was often the butt of Meany's vulgarity and anger. At an Executive Council meeting he snorted to Carey: "Move the hell down to the other end of the table. You give me hives."

Another matter of contention was Meany's desultory manner of lobbying for labor legislation and of participating in the work of advisory commissions that several Presidents set up to deal with labor relations and wage-price adjustments. On August 11, 1961, as Walter recalled, there was a meeting of the subcommittee of the President's Advisory Committee on Labor-Management Policy; George Meany, George Harrison, and Walter were the labor representatives. The meeting was set for 9:00 A.M. Harrison had already notified George Taylor, chairman of the President's Labor-Management Policy Committee and nationally known arbitrator, that he would be unable to attend. Those present included representatives from the White House and some influential men from industry, such as Henry Ford II and William Goff Caples of Inland Steel. Meany did not show up. There was to be an afternoon session on economic growth and development, a subject of critical importance to American workers. Walter had lunch with Meany at twelve-thirty to discuss the Eleanor Roosevelt Cancer Foundation, and urged him then to attend that afternoon, but Meany never appeared, leaving Walter again as the sole representative of labor.

A year later, the same President's Advisory Committee met to complete the paper on collective bargaining and the emergency disputes prodecure under Taft-Hartley. A full contingent of top management officials attended, as did Secretary of Labor Arthur Goldberg, Secretary of Commerce Luther Hodges, and William Simkin, director of Mediation Conciliation. Meany made only a perfunctory appearance on the first day and did not come at all the second day. This left Walter alone to do labor's homework during most of the entire two-day session.

Meany's attitude toward Executive Council meetings was equally irresponsible. When it was pointed out to him several weeks before the August 25, 1961, meeting that four of the members were inextricably involved with pressing collective bargaining negotiations, a strike, a crucial maritime situation, and a Steel Workers' National Convention, and that perhaps he should postpone the meeting, Meany's reply was, "I don't give a damn if no one shows so long as Dubinsky is there with his deck of cards." After Walter told me about this, he added, "Unfortunately, he wasn't joking."

In 1963, President Kennedy set up a ten-man committee to study all U.S. foreign aid programs, under the chairmanship of Lucius Clay. The single member from labor was George Meany. On March 3, 1963, the Detroit *Free Press* reported that the committee had held many intensive sessions to review the whole aid program, then under heavy attack by the conservatives. According to their report, "George Meany did not attend or participate in a single session."

Meanwhile — and this was the area of my particular concern — relations between the AFL-CIO and the International Trade Union movement were going from bad to worse, especially in regard to the World Headquarters of the International Confederation of Free Trade Unions. In spite of convention resolutions and Executive Council policy statements pledging support and funds, it turned out that international affairs continued to be conducted privately by Meany, Lovestone, Brown, and their minions. In the public press, Meany called the ICFTU headquarters staff a collection of "fairies," and made ugly personal remarks about its general secretary, Jacobin Oldenbroek, an experienced international union leader from the Transport Workers who had, ironically, been hand-picked by the AFL-CIO. He was humiliated and forced to resign. Though Meany at first gave full support to his successor, Omer Becu, he too became the object of public and private insults because he would not transform the ICFTU into an appendage of the AFL-CIO.

Financial obligations to the world organization, which had been voted by the Executive Council, were used for bargaining purposes. On one occasion, Meany, at an ICFTU Executive Board meeting, pulled out a check for several hundred thousand dollars, representing the per capita installment of the AFL-CIO's contribution, and then returned it to his pocket when the ICFTU balked at rubber-stamping AFL-CIO wishes. The ICFTU refused to give in to this blackmail. Soon Meany was insisting that some $800,000 already paid into the worldwide assistance fund be returned to the AFL-CIO, which was done. For all practical purposes, this was the end of active participation by the AFL-CIO in an organization it had helped create. Unable to dominate it, the council set out to scuttle it. From AFL-CIO headquarters, and on official stationery bearing the names of many individuals, such as Reuther, Potofsky, and Carey — as well as Meany — Jay Lovestone sent out scurrilous letters to a former AFL employee on the staff of the ICFTU in Brussels. In this correspondence, he tried to blacken the characters of certain leaders of the ICFTU and also vilified Walter, Carey, Potofsky, and other officials of the AFL-CIO, an organization of which he was a paid employee. He could not have done this without the encouragement of the old guard of the AFL-CIO.

Although the AFL-CIO withdrew from the ICFTU, it retained control of the western hemisphere branch, the Organización Regional Interamericana de Trabajadores (called ORIT) and also set up its own instruments in South America (the American Institute for Free Labor Development), in Africa (the American-African Center), and in the Far East (the Asian Institute for Free Labor Development).

The fur really began to fly when UAW officers learned from a Detroit newspaper that the AFL-CIO was raising havoc with the International Labor Organization in Geneva. The ILO was created on the initiative of American labor and had always been a source of pride both to the AFL and the younger CIO. After the birth of the United Nations in 1945, the ILO was reorganized as an agency of that body, and included the Soviet Union and other Communist nations. The ILO is a unique organization because its membership equally represents official government delegates, employer delegates, and delegates from workers' organizations. The American labor movement, responding to this broadening of the membership, continued its support and urged U.S. employers to stay in the ILO as an effective means of meeting the Communist challenge. In 1955, when the employer group threatened to walk out because of the admission of Soviet delegates, Meany himself had forcefully stated: "We are not going to walk away from the ILO. We are not going to fall into a Soviet trap and aid them in destroying this organization."

In 1966 the AFL-CIO delegates, in a complete reversal, walked out of a Geneva meeting because, in a democratic secret ballot election, a Polish delegate was elected chairman instead of the candidate supported by the AFL-CIO and other Western trade unions. The UAW was shocked, declaring, "Having made the decision to participate in the ILO, the American labor movement as well as other parties were morally obligated to accept the democratic process in the ILO even when it was not to their liking."

The AFL-CIO not only left the meeting but declared it would boycott the ILO, which was utterly unreasonable since the chairmanship in question was largely a ceremonial post that expired at the end of the ten-day conference. U.S. Government and business delegates did not leave, nor did any delegate from labor, business, or government of any other nation involved in the conference.

The day of truth was slowly approaching. The UAW learned that the boycott of the ILO had been under consideration at AFL-CIO headquarters for about a week prior to the walkout, so there had been ample time for consultation between Meany and members of the Executive Council before the drastic step was taken. Walter was instructed by the entire UAW Executive Board to fire off a protest to Meany to register the UAW's

> strong objections and sharp disagreement . . . A decision of such grave importance cannot properly be made except on the basis of a vote taken at the highest policy level of the AFL-CIO after thorough review and discussion . . . The action of the delegates in walking out of the ILO Conference was unwise, undemocratic, contrary to established AFL-CIO policy, and unauthorized . . . It is a gross disservice to democracy . . . This is precisely the kind of action for which American labor has in the past justifiably condemned Communists. If delegates from the U.S. Government were to take similar action when a Communist is elected to any post in the UN, the UN would soon be destroyed and with it mankind's best hope for world peace and survival.

At an Executive Council meeting after the fact, the Meany loyalists supported the walkout and boycott by a vote of eighteen to six.

The UAW thereupon declared that the vote in no way bound it to agree with the decision and that it intended to exercise its right to express its views "on all policy matters both foreign and domestic that relate to the welfare of UAW members and the well-being of our nation."

There were some who tried to describe the deep ideological differences between the UAW and the old guard as a mere clash of personalities between Walter and Meany. That was an oversimplification, though one must in honesty face the fact that they held diametrically opposed views about the mission and purpose of the trade union movement and about the necessity of maintaining democratic procedures in running the AFL-CIO.

Disagreement on the Vietnam War was the final blow to the wedge splitting the UAW and the merged AFL-CIO. In educational seminars, in local union halls across the nation, the UAW democratically debated resolutions protesting the continuation of that war. In 1966, at the first conference, held in Chicago, of the Labor Assembly for Peace, which we helped to found, hundreds of union delegates were addressed by Martin Luther King, Jr., Norman Thomas, and others; and Emil Mazey and I also spoke. At the end of the conference a resolution was adopted, calling for an end to the war. Some of the participants in that conference were elected, by their unions, to be delegates to the upcoming AFL-CIO convention in Miami. When a group of observers at that convention indicated its negative feelings about the Vietnam War, Meany thundered from his rostrum, "Throw the kooks out!" Mazey insisted on speaking, and Meany charged that the resolution we had adopted in Chicago "had been written in Hanoi." This hysterical remark was reminiscent of the most sinister tactics of Joe McCarthy.

Meany has recently said publicly that had he known earlier what he knows now he would have been opposed to the Vietnam War. If he had not consistently suppressed democratic debate and discussion, he would indeed have known it. Perhaps a united CIO-AFL effort might have resulted in a quicker end to the war — and the preservation of many lives.

The withdrawal of the UAW from the merged organization was not, as it may have seemed, a consequence of the antipathy between Walter and George Meany. At grass roots of the UAW there was growing anxiety and dissatisfaction. When, in early 1967, the International UAW Executive Board met in special session to review its relationship with the AFL-CIO, the board unanimously concluded:

> It is sad, but nevertheless true that the AFL-CIO is becoming increasingly the comfortable, complacent custodian of the status quo . . . In the eleven years of merger the officers of the UAW . . . have seen the great promise of the merger go unfulfilled . . . Repeated efforts have been made to get the AFL-CIO . . . to accept new ideas and new concepts, to meet new problems and new challenges. Even when such efforts were successful . . . the actions taken have not always been carried out. Basic provisions of the constitution have been violated. On occasion even a completely unanimous mandate of the AFL-CIO convention itself has been thwarted when [it] did not meet with the personal pleasure of the President of the AFL-CIO.

Thereupon all UAW officers on the Executive Council, the General Board, and on standing committees sent in their resignations. Walter was directed by the UAW Executive Board to resign from the Board of Directors of the American Institute for Free Labor Development and from the African-American Center. Actually, Walter had already resigned from AIFLD two years earlier, since he took sharp exception to the policies being carried out in Latin America.

Shortly after the resignations, the UAW Executive Board set forth an outline of a concrete program to be considered by the entire American labor movement. It included proposals for internal reform; a Public Review Board for the AFL-CIO; strengthening of collective bargaining machinery; a United Defense Fund for workers in vital public jobs who were denied the right to strike. The manifesto also stressed labor's responsibility within the community for the rebuilding of inner cities — better schools, more security for older citizens — and for the protection of natural resources and the reduction of pollution. The labor movement was challenged to step up its cooperation with the international trade movement, to resist totalitarianism, and reduce Cold War tensions by bringing together people of different languages and economic systems.

At the May 1968 convention in Atlantic City, the UAW delegates, after reviewing the deteriorating relations with the AFL-CIO, voted to place future per capita payments in an escrow account, pending remedial action by the AFL-CIO. Such action was not forthcoming and by July 1, 1968, on the unanimous instruction of its officers and Executive Board, the UAW gave the AFL-CIO formal notice of disaffiliation.

It should be made clear that though the UAW felt it could no longer silently and slavishly acquiesce to the policies and practices of the AFL-CIO, it made no effort to encourage other unions to disaffiliate. Even Walter's bitterest opponents would have admitted that his influence was such that, had he chosen, he could have persuaded some of them to withdraw along with the UAW.

Over seven years have passed since the UAW's disaffiliation and I sense little sentiment within the ranks for a return to the monolithic AFL-CIO. There have been few changes in the latter's policies. In the field of foreign affairs it continues to stand considerably to the right of the U.S. Chamber of Commerce. It remains outside the International Confederation of Free Trade Unions. Its membership has expanded very little, though over ninety-one million working Americans remain unorganized. Trade unions now represent only 19 to 20 percent of the work force not engaged in farming, a decrease from 35.5 percent in 1945. Were it not for the substantial growth of such unions as the teachers' union, and the State, County and Municipal Workers' Federation, the actual membership of the AFL-CIO would have dropped since 1970. Jerry Wurf has taken up the cudgels of reform. He has pointed out the far greater percentage of unionized labor in country after country of Western Europe. He has called attention to the "jurisdictional messiness" of the American labor movement, declaring that the poaching is one reason for the failure to organize workers. The time, money, and manpower spent on raiding another union's membership or in fighting the "conglomerate unions," which recognize no jurisdictional boundaries, should be devoted, he says, to seeking out and signing up nonunion workers. It will be interesting to see if any of Wurf's proposals will be implemented or even seriously considered.

It is easy, with the benefit of hindsight, to fault Walter for his delay in withdrawing earlier. He knew a break was inevitable; in my opinion he waited too long. It was clear after the first few years that internal democracy within the merged organization was a farce. He might at any time have allowed the conflict of ideologies to come to a head. The truth is that he did not want to be responsible for causing a split, so each time he pressed only so far and no further. But after eleven years of frustration he finally had to admit that the troops he had so often marched up the hill could not endlessly be marched down again.

His regret for the loss of precious years that should have been

spent in the positive work of trade unionism led Walter, I think, to
the hasty decision to join with the Teamsters' Union in creating, on
July 28, 1968, the Alliance for Labor Action. About a year later, the
International Chemical Workers also joined the ALA. Without encouraging any member unions of the AFL-CIO to split off, Walter
was trying to form another focus for trade union action, which
would have the resources for the launching of organizing campaigns, and could undertake projects in the ghettos and in farming
areas. In 1967, he had written:

> A new concept of union organization has been developing in areas such
> as Delano and Watts, California. Properly nurtured and motivated, it
> can spread across the face of the nation, changing the social character
> of the inner city structure and uplifting the lives of millions of slum
> dwellers. This new organizing effort is called "the community union."
> It is designed to provide the poor with their own self-sufficient eco-
> nomic organization . . . community and cuts across many areas of so-
> cial and economic need . . . health care, schools, public transportation,
> sanitation, building maintenance, etc. These and many other facets of
> community life become integrated in the work and effort of "commu-
> nity unionism."

The ALA represented around four million trade unionists. It
provided manpower and money to Chavez's struggling United Farm
Workers and directed the preliminary agreements that, for a while
at least, prevented the destructive jurisdictional warfare between
that union and the Teamsters. As long as Walter lived, and the
ALA lived, the terms of that mutual understanding were respected.

The ALA also helped the State, County and Municipal Workers'
Union, the American Federation of Teachers, District 65 of the
Wholesale and Retail Workers, and the Packinghouse Workers.
Chicanos in East Los Angeles were organized with the help of ALA
into a self-help organization called TELECU. Similar projects got underway in the Newark ghettos, in Chicago, in the St. Louis Tandy
area, in Daytona Beach, Florida, and other areas.

At a time when the AFL-CIO was ballyhooing its support for
Nixon's program to enlarge our antiballistic missile arsenal and to
expand the Vietnam War, the ALA lobbied with great vigor against
both.

But the ALA had far too short a life to leave any lasting imprint.
As soon as it dissolved, after Walter's death, the Teamsters re-

established their close alliance with Nixon, broke their commitments to the farm workers, and joined with the fruit growers and Nixon's White House gang to launch one of the most despicable strike-breaking campaigns in American history.

The need for ethical codes and public review boards in every union to help labor police its governance was never more obvious than during the turmoil that wracked the United Mine Workers and culminated in the murders of Jock Yablonski, his wife, and daughter, and the trial of Tony Boyle. The crimes of the latter's administration were a scandal of such magnitude that they threatened the entire trade union movement. I was pleased to lend my voice, through recordings used in West Virginia mining towns, to help the election of Arnold Miller as president of the Mine Workers. There must be a smile on Val Reuther's face as he looks down on the changes that have restored that great union to its position of honor in the annals of labor.

Another great union, the United Steel Workers, had a serious ethical upset when it failed to guarantee proper procedures for the election of important district directors. In a re-election ordered by the Department of Labor, insurgent Ed Sadlowski won by two-to-one over the administration's candidate. Many, including our friend and counselor Joe Rauh, see him as "a coming Walter Reuther." Challenged elections are painful experiences for any union, but I am certain that the clean-up of their own houses by the Mine Workers and the Steel Workers will give hope and courage to rank-and-file reform movements throughout the country.

Labor for Peace
Around the World

BEFORE THE MERGER, when Walter became president of the CIO, he asked me to return to the United States from my Paris assignment to serve as one of his administrative assistants at the National CIO in Washington. In August 1953, therefore, after the World Congress of the ICFTU, we came home. The move, of course, was not so traumatic for Sophie and the children as the one we had made over two years before, though the children did mind not going back to Detroit.

John had learned to read and write French; in fact, he read French better than he did English. During our years in Paris, the nearest thing to an American experience for the children was an occasional visit, at the invitation of a friend on the U.S. Embassy staff, for a hamburger and a milkshake or a bit of shopping for American items at a nearby Army PX. I had not fully realized the effect of these visits until, strolling up New York's Fifth Avenue, looking at the shop windows, we heard John remark, "Gee, there are a lot of PX's in *this* country!"

As we drove to Washington we passed through an area of Baltimore that had been razed in preparation for low-cost housing projects. Eric exclaimed, "I didn't know the war was fought here too!" It was obviously high time that we brought our brood home.

We stayed in Washington with Dorothy and Arthur Goldberg (he was then general counsel of the National CIO) until we found a huge, rambling old house in Northwest Washington that was to become our permanent home. It had been unoccupied for some time, and we set to with hammers, saws, and paintbrushes to make it habitable. To this day it is a sanctuary, a place for relaxation and renewal for the members of our scattered tribe.

In those first months we had a real family life. I was home in the evenings; and we visited relatives and friends to catch up on all that had happened since we had gone. But it turned out that I was soon on the go again, because, in addition to being Walter's assistant, I directed the CIO's Department of International Affairs during the years before the merger with the AFL. This meant continuing my personal contacts in Europe as well as breaking new ground in many of the developing countries on other continents. As usual, I was so absorbed and excited by my work that I was blind to the hardship that my frequent absences — many beyond the reach of even a late-night reassuring phone call — inflicted on Sophie and the children. A year later, when filling out income tax forms, I turned to Sophie in amazement: "My God, do you realize I was away from home over two hundred days this past year?" With a patient wry smile she responded, "We don't need any tax forms to remind us of that."

Walter's schedule was equally hectic, though his trips were usually within the U.S. and Canada. Yet there were many times when we met in Israel, Europe, the Arab countries, Africa, India, or Japan. When the CIO and AFL were formally merged, I chose to return to the UAW staff to work for a liberal and progressive policy on international affairs. My sharp conflict with the Meany-Lovestone negative attitude toward international cooperation precluded any consideration of me as International Affairs director of the merged federation. Furthermore, Michael Ross of the CIO International Affairs staff was acceptable to Meany and his AFL colleagues; and I had personal misgivings about the chances of the merger's fulfilling its purposes and also knew I would have a freer hand working from a UAW base. Events have certainly corroborated this judgment. It is a source of satisfaction that the UAW still holds to its commitment in the field of foreign affairs, a commitment that accords with its traditions and democratic ideals.

Nowhere is this more obvious than in our continuing relations with Israel. Here is a country that was pioneered by Socialists. Its trade union federation, Histadrut, was a vigorous organization in the U.S. and in Palestine long before Israel existed as a sovereign state. In many respects, Histadrut was almost a state by itself; it was the broadest single organization in Palestine, concerned with every aspect of the economy. It comprised numerous separate trade unions; an agency to help newly arrived immigrants; and many cooperative farms, which it owned and managed. It also embraced a huge construction corporation, through which it built and managed small industries and large housing developments; a school system that employed the most comprehensive education apparatus in Palestine; and finally, through its trade unions, it operated what was in essence a social security program, complete with medical insurance, accident compensation, unemployment insurance, and related needs. Histadrut, the embodiment of the political philosophy of the founders, gave a strong labor character to the new state. In 1950, soon after the founding of Israel I was invited to join a group of religious leaders who were journeying there. I had not quite recovered from the surgery, but I seized the opportunity eagerly. Friends in Detroit and New York sent word ahead, and I was able to meet Histadrut leaders at their headquarters in Tel Aviv.

Physical evidence of Israel's war for independence was still apparent everywhere, and those difficult days were vividly described by members of kibbutzim, by young soldiers still in uniform, and by leaders of the great building cooperative, who had taken their places in the front lines. We traversed little Israel from Dan in the north to Beersheba at the southern desert's edge. Everything was hustle, bustle, and continuous activity, especially in the great tent cities, where thousands of new arrivals were housed temporarily and trained for productive work. I was deeply impressed as I watched Histadrut representatives conversing and writing in five different languages, dealing with émigrés from the Middle East, Europe, indeed from the whole world.

The kibbutzim near the border were honeycombed with the trenches and battlements from which the settlers had defended themselves against Arab attacks. The children were happy and carefree in spite of the constant danger; near where they played were underground bunkers in which they could sleep in case of an emergency.

Never have I met a people who looked ahead with such hope and confidence — a confidence symbolized by the brand-new forests and orchards and vineyards planted on mountainsides that had, for so many years, been parched and barren. At a later time I was to look over from Arab land at the lush greenery of Israel, so startling in contrast to the drabness of the rest of the Middle East.

It was clear that the infant state was founded on a truly democratic base; freedom of speech and press were firmly guaranteed, the existence of minority parties was protected, and some significant measures were taken to assure the rights of the Arab minority. Histadrut, for instance, welcomed Arab workers into its trade unions.

Walter, Roy, and I established personal relationships with David Ben-Gurion, Golda Meir, and Abba Eban. We had made friends with Ben-Gurion even before Israel was founded, when he was on an American lecture tour in the U.S. Walter visited him several times in his kibbutz in the southern desert, where he lived after his retirement. To counteract the threat that has hung for many years over the very existence of Israel, the UAW had done what it could during every crisis by lobbying and by talking with American Presidents and leaders abroad to mobilize public support for Israel's just cause. How sad it is that the vast sums of money spent for military defense cannot be plowed into programs for social well-being. I am sure the Israelis would prefer this not only for themselves but for their Arab neighbors, who are burdened by frightful poverty and by inadequate education and housing.

In Jerusalem, before its unification, I had spent some time with workers in the old quarter of the city, and became acquainted with a very able and bright young trade union leader who had organized the Arab taxi drivers. I admired his dedication, his sincerity, his general outlook. Returning several years later, after the west bank of the Jordan had been occupied, to Histadrut headquarters in Jerusalem, I was delighted to find that this same young Arab had been placed in complete charge of the training center for Arab workers.

In 1954, before the AFL-CIO merger, both Walter and George Meany were named honorary cochairmen of the American Trade Union Council for Histadrut. As a living memorial to its former president, Philip Murray, Walter encouraged the National CIO to establish a Philip Murray Community Center to be administered by Histadrut in Elat, Israel's southernmost city. Later both the UAW and the Industrial Union Department of the AFL-CIO, of which Walter was president, provided grants to found the Afro-Asian Institute of Histadrut in Tel Aviv, which trained young African and Asian trade union activists. In 1958, Walter was presented with Histadrut's Humanitarian Award at a huge dinner in New York, where funds for scholarships and for needy children were raised.

The Reuthers' friendship with the Israeli people is expressed in the form of several institutions. One of them is the Walter Reuther Youth Center, a splendid building, with a library, in Holon, a working-class suburb of Tel Aviv. And in 1968 the Weizmann Institute of Science in Rehovoth established a Walter P. Reuther chair in the peaceful uses of atomic energy.

India is another country that has always aroused in members of the Reuther family a passionate concern. This enormous subcontinent, on gaining its independence after more than two centuries of British rule, faced the herculean task of dealing with unimaginable poverty, hunger, and superstition. Walter and I were both drawn, in our early days in Detroit, to young Indian students who were involved in the struggle for freedom. Wartime goals expressed by Roosevelt and Churchill raised high hopes among the people of India, China, and the Philippines that they might shake off colonialism and avoid subjugation by Japan. The UAW passed resolutions and set up a campaign of letter-writing in our local unions to urge Roosevelt and Churchill to make specific pledges. During the war I had discussions with Pearl Buck, just returned from a mission to Asia arranged by our Secretary of State, about the importance of establishing contact with our trade union counterparts over there and with their political leaders.

On August 9, 1944, the second anniversary of the arrest of India's popular leaders by the British, I was among the Americans signing an appeal to Lord Halifax for their release. The appeal was organized by an old personal friend, President J. J. Singh of the India League of America, and included, along with Pearl Buck, Stuart Chase, Louis Fischer, Dr. John Haynes Holmes, Max Lerner, Dr. Reinhold Niebuhr, Oswald Garrison Villard, Matthew Woll, vice-president of the AFL, and two staunch Republicans, Representatives Clare Booth Luce and Karl E. Mundt.

We followed with concern and admiration the successful struggle of Gandhi and Nehru. When the UN was established, Nehru's sister, Madam Pandit, was one of the first Indian delegates to journey to New York. Walter came to know her well through Eleanor Roosevelt.

The new Indian state had very many internal problems to solve; it could not afford to become involved with any of the major political power blocs. Nehru's decision to maintain his country's neutrality is even more understandable when one realizes how close India lies to both Soviet and Chinese borders. He believed that India's most important contribution to world peace lay in providing leadership for the growing group of developing nations that were interested more in implements of agriculture and industrial production than those of war. Hard-liners in the Pentagon, however, and in Dulles's State Department, and, of course, George Meany decided that those who were not with us must be against us. Meany, in a characteristic overstatement, condemned Nehru as an "aide and ally of Communism in fact and effect if not in diplomatic verbiage." It meant nothing to him, nor, evidently, to Dulles, that India, the most populous country in the world outside of China, was also the only major nation in all of Asia that had established a parliamentary democracy. To dismiss this vast area, with its millions of souls longing for a better future, as pro-Communist was not only insulting but stupid, and was certainly a great disservice to our country; we needed a strong Asian ally in our diplomatic confrontations with Russia and China.

Our good friend Chester Bowles, who had been U.S. Ambassador to India, was disturbed by the negative impact of Meany's statement on the Indians; he felt that the most effective antidote would be a response delivered in India by an eloquent and liberal American trade unionist. John Sherman Cooper, then the U.S. Ambassador, agreed. Soon invitations came to Walter from the Prime Minister and from the Indian National Congress asking him to make an official visit. The *New York Times,* in an editorial, expressed great relief that Walter was going on a "mission to India," as did the Washington *Post.* The *Times* said: "Mr. Reuther can do a great deal to assuage their injured feelings and to correct misunderstandings they may have about American opinion, especially that of organized labor."

Careful and thorough preparations were made for Walter's visit. I was able to convince an experienced journalist, Sig Harrison, to go with him; we were also lucky to have stationed at the U.S. Embassy in Delhi a former CIO official, David Burgess, the first labor attaché in the State Department to receive the Distinguished Service Award.

From the moment he arrived, Walter was swept up in a triumphal tour through waves of chanting humanity. They placed a white Nehru hat on his head and took this American to their hearts. In the textile mills of Gandhi's home, along the docks of Bombay, the steelmills at Jamshedpur, they hailed Walter as a person to whom they could relate. He had several long private conversations with Nehru. No words were wasted on explaining away hostile American comments in the press. They talked mostly about the world's search for peace, and, in particular, the problems of India, lying like a crushing burden on the shoulders of the gentle Prime Minister. What reassured Nehru most was Walter's strong conviction that each of the great industrialized countries was obligated to set aside a percentage of its gross national product to help emerging nations. Nehru was aware of the specific proposals Walter had submitted before the U.S. Congress for the creation of a United Nations Development Fund.

On April 5, 1956, Walter made a moving address before the Indian Council on World Affairs in New Delhi:

> India and America have much in common . . . Both of our nations were conceived and dedicated to the proposition that all men are created equal. [They] contributed to the world and to the ages two . . . great moral giants, Gandhi and Lincoln. In an age of nuclear giants, we need more than ever a rededication to the human and moral values of both . . . for neither peace nor freedom can be made secure in a world of nuclear giants and moral pigmies . . . Lincoln said, "America cannot endure half slave and half free." In the world in which we live, peace and freedom cannot endure with the world half well fed and half starving.

Referring to the trade union forces of our time, Walter said the struggle should be geared "not to be a negative program of anti-Communism, but rather to a positive program for social justice." He described some of his experiences as a worker in the Soviet Union, and his observation of the harsh reality that the Soviet workers won more bread but not more freedom. He quoted Gandhi: "As I look to Russia, the life there does not appeal to me . . . It is beneath human dignity to become a mere cog in a machine. I want every individual to become a full-blooded, fully developed member of society."

Admitting America's weakness in its treatment of its black citizens, he drew a parallel between the passive resistance campaigns of Gandhi and Martin Luther King, Jr., and voiced the hope American Negroes would eventually "take their place as free and equal citizens." In concluding he said: "If we shape our policy in the image of our common faith instead of our common fears, I am confident that men of good will everywhere can march forward together and together they can build a better tomorrow fashioned in the image of peace, in the image of freedom, in the image of justice and in the image of human brotherhood."

There was a broad grin of satisfaction on the face of Ambassador Cooper and an embrace from Prime Minister Nehru. And from the lowliest "untouchables," whose hands Walter had taken in his own, to the highest officials of India there was a feeling that Walter had expressed ideas they could share. His was an America they could understand.

When John F. Kennedy was elected President, he seemed to put new hope into the hearts of many insecure and impoverished peoples. While the Arabs and Africans never had a chance to demonstrate, as did the Latin Americans and Europeans, the enthusiasm his name evoked everywhere he went, they were attracted from afar by the magnetism of his personality. With his election the time seemed right for something I had long tried to persuade Walter to consider: a delegation from the UAW to the French- and English-speaking parts of Africa, and to the Arab countries in the Middle East. Because the Israelis were our special friends, it did not follow that the Arabs were our enemies. We were convinced then, as I still am, that the Israelis would like nothing better than to live in peace with their neighbors. We wanted to help bridge the gap.

With great care, Walter selected a delegation of UAW local union officers, staff members, and Executive Board members, some of whom were fluent in French and Arabic. After weeks of briefing, including sessions at the UN in New York, our delegation departed. One third was to concentrate on Arab lands — Morocco, Algeria, Tunisia, Egypt, Lebanon, and Jordan; the rest planned to visit Nigeria, Uganda, Kenya, Ghana, Tanganyika, Guinea, Senegal, the Congo, and Northern Rhodesia. At the end of the mission, all would meet for a seminar at the Afro-Asian Institute of Histadrut in Israel.

In many lands we were the first U.S. trade unionists ever to appear and talk with workers and political leaders. Egypt had been previously considered off limits by some because of its quarrel with Israel. Guinea had been taboo because, after winning independence from France, it had come for a short time under Soviet and Chinese influence, and its new president, Sékou Touré, whom I had met many times in Brussels at ICFTU headquarters, had rebuffed every offer of American economic aid.

The ICFTU extended its appeal to the growing trade unions in the Third World, and many of the men whom we had first come to know at the union level became the leaders of their countries. In Guinea, there was Sékou Touré, former secretary-general of the postal workers' union; Nkrumah of Ghana, the "father of his country," began his life as a worker and unionist (once during a stay in the U.S. he belonged to the CIO); in Kenya, Tom Mboya, an active ICFTU leader and a widely respected spokesman for black union workers in English-speaking East Africa, became Minister of Justice when his country achieved independence, and undoubtedly would have succeeded President Kenyatta had he not been assassinated. In Tunisia, after the French finally pulled out, Ahmad Ben Salah, active member of the Executive Board of the ICFTU for many years and a dear friend of Walter's and mine, served as Minister of Education, Agriculture, and Economic Development. It was not surprising that a population on the threshold of freedom from colonial rule should turn to such men for leadership. Their unions cut across tribal lines and through the language barriers that often exist in a single colony; and the prominent unionists had been in the forefront of the struggle for economic justice as well as social and political independence.

Ahmed Ben Bella had just come into power in Algeria. Trade union relations with him had become strained, and our visit there was of considerable importance; I believe it encouraged the democratic unions struggling to avoid complete domination and control by the new government. With Tunisia we had enjoyed friendly relations over a long period, and in 1963 our friend Ahmad Ben Salah, former head of the Tunisian Trade Union Movement, had been named Minister of Economic Development, and was second only to President Bourguiba in popularity.

In Libya, we helped establish the Tripoli health clinic by shipping large quantities of medical supplies. As a result of on-the-spot conversations, the UAW initiated, in conjunction with UNESCO, the first training courses for automotive mechanics in Lebanon; it was part of a program for the Palestinian refugees. In Northern Rhodesia, we had already made available to Kenneth Kaunda (after his first visit to the U.S. under the auspices of the American Committee on Africa) several jeeps with loudspeakers to help him rally his people to fight for independence.

South Africa, a technically advanced section of Africa, was not on our itinerary. We had sought unsuccessfully on several occasions to send Ken Bannon, UAW director of our Ford Department, to meet automobile workers and their union leaders in that country, but each time the visa was refused. A visa was also refused for a UAW member of an international delegation sent to South Africa by the International Metal Workers' Federation. The UAW's history of civil rights activities and its denunciation of racism and apartheid certainly did not endear us to South Africa.

In Guinea, we saw firsthand the terrible condition of the transport system. When the French left, they had taken all their technicians and mechanics, and there were no nationals trained to take their places. The union leaders and President Touré, no longer a thrall of the Communists, asked the UAW to help train personnel. They preferred it on a union-to-union basis. Bearing in mind our union's limitations in undertaking such an extensive project in so distant a country, I suggested to Sargent Shriver that perhaps the Peace Corps could cosponsor the training project. He agreed to the idea and the Guineans found it acceptable, with the result that the UAW recruited trained mechanics to go to Guinea together with some bright and adaptable young university graduates. The mixed group, after boning up on French, set out on the same modest basis as any other Peace Corps volunteers. Fortunately we were able to secure as director of this project an able administrator and diplomat, Henry Norman, who steered the group through many a crisis, including a break in diplomatic relations between Guinea and the U.S. provoked by the arrest of Guinea officials, ordered by Nkrumah, when they landed at Accra in Ghana.

Despite all snafus, our UAW–Peace Corps volunteers did a heroic job of getting public transport and dock equipment at the harbor back into working condition. When they left, they were given a royal send-off, with three ministers of Touré's government in attendance to express appreciation. The whole experience proved how effective blue-collar volunteers with the needed practical skills can be in the developing countries. Everywhere we went, we tried to set up some ongoing practical program to demonstrate our desire for a continuing friendly relationship. In Guinea, we accomplished something that the U.S. Government had tried alone but found impossible.

The idea of the Peace Corps had been germinating several years before that day in 1960 when Kennedy, not long after he had won the nomination for the presidency, asked Walter to drop in at his home in Hyannisport for some discussions. The talks were wide-ranging, covering the mechanics of getting out the vote as well as probing the sorts of issues that might excite new interest among younger voters. Robert Kennedy had seen at the Democratic convention the result of the very effective work done by Roy, and had noted even before then his innovative techniques of promoting registration and marshaling the workers for an election. It was decided that Roy would be asked to head up a nationwide registration drive, and the two Kennedys cleared the appointment with Meany.

During the Hyannisport talks Walter urged Kennedy to lay before America new ways of "waging peace" as a substitute for the building of bigger and bigger bombs. He suggested as an example that the youth of the country be challenged to volunteer, in lieu of military service, for two to three years of strenuous work overseas in the cause of peace. Walter had actually proposed this idea at least seven years before at a UAW-CIO Full Employment Conference in Washington, saying, "The more young Americans are sent to the places in the world where people are hungry, and sent with slide rules and textbooks and medical kits . . . the fewer of our sons we will have to send with guns to fight Communism on the battlefields of the world."

I had also proposed such a plan in February 1958 before a Point Four Conference on International Economic and Social Development, saying that we should set in motion the training of at least a hundred thousand of our most promising young graduates to assure the success of our aid programs. They would constitute "a human reserve from which the underdeveloped countries could draw in their efforts to fight poverty, hunger, ignorance, and disease."

Kennedy was taken with the idea of the Peace Corps as Walter presented it, and made copious notes. Later Walter sent him statements both of us had made on the subject, and as the campaign heated up, the idea of a volunteer army for peace became part of his own speeches. After he was elected, he implemented the program. The Peace Corps, at first recruiting only college graduates with few mechanical skills, later recognized the importance of enlisting blue-collar workers with the technical knowledge that was needed by the developing lands, as was proved by the experience in Guinea. I am sure that the benefits of the program, for the U.S. and for the countries where the volunteers served, though not amenable to statistical measurement, will be shown to be great in the light of history.

Contact with workers in the Soviet bloc was more difficult to achieve. There were two significant encounters in the late fifties between Russian political leaders and some of our labor officials. Early in 1959, Deputy Premier Anastas Mikoyan came to the U.S. for an official two-week visit. Twenty-four hours after his arrival, he expressed a desire to meet with a delegation representing American labor. I encouraged Walter, Jim Carey, and others to take him up on it. Walter in turn urged Meany to take part, but that intrepid Cold Warrior brusquely rejected any contact with a Communist and belittled as naïve those who "feel they can meet the Soviet challenge at the conference table" (the implication being that military confrontation was inevitable).

Mikoyan's schedule was already crowded with meetings with bankers, businessmen, politicians. So Carey, whose Electrical Workers' national headquarters were right across from the Soviet Embassy, telephoned Ambassador Menshikov and invited him to bring Mikoyan over to lunch the next day. It was so arranged; the Russian group included Mikoyan, his son Sergei, and an interpreter named Troyanovsky. On the labor side, in addition to Carey, were Walter; William Doherty, president of the Association of Letter Carriers; Joseph Beirne, president of the Communication Workers' Union; Karl Feller, President of the Brewery Workers' Union; George L. Weaver, Carey's assistant; and others.

The Americans were direct and to the point. Both Carey and Walter referred to the brutal suppression of the Hungarian uprising, and the Soviet responsibility for the continuing crisis in Berlin. Mikoyan employed his formidable talent for sidestepping in his attempts to defend Soviet policy, but Walter was in no mood to let him off the hook.

When questioned by the press about the luncheon, Walter said: "I am told there is ever present a danger that totalitarian leaders, unaccustomed to soliciting or heeding the views of others, may underestimate the mood and determination of free people to resist encroachment on their rights. For this reason I thought it wise to tell Deputy Mikoyan to his face . . . that on the question of safeguarding the rights of free Berlin and securing a Germany united in freedom and democracy, the American people are united."

Such frank talk was welcomed in West Berlin. John Sherman Cooper, at the time a senator from Kentucky, remarked that Walter had done "a major service for peace by his blunt exchange with the Kremlin's number two man." Because of the historical significance of this first exchange between American labor and a Soviet leader, it was reported in some detail by the distinguished labor journalist, John Herling, in the *New Leader*.

President Eisenhower invited Nikita Khrushchev for a visit later that same year. Again Meany made it clear in the press that he wouldn't be caught dead in the same room with the head of a government that did not permit free trade unions. He was not alone; refugee groups from Eastern Europe were understandably bitter about the Khrushchev visit, as were some fundamentalist religious groups. Dr. Carl McIntire said it was "morally wrong for this nation to receive a bloody-handed tyrant who intends to bury us." At the AFL-CIO Executive Council meeting, Joe Bierne asked, "How are we going to understand this guy if we don't communicate with him?" and Doherty echoed him. Yet both men voted with Meany, as usual. Only Walter, Carey, and O. A. Knight of the Oil and Chemical Workers objected.

When the time came for the famous dinner, however, there were seven union presidents who dared to break bread with the Russian delegates; they spoke for the Electrical Workers (Carey); the United Paper Workers and Paper Makers (Paul L. Phillips); the National Maritime Union (Joseph Curran); the United Brewery Workers (Feller); the Oil and Chemical Workers (Knight); the Textile Workers (Emil Rieve); the United Auto Workers (Walter).

Khrushchev, a more colorful and bombastic character than Mikoyan, received far greater press coverage. As he fraternized with businessmen and politicians, he kept complaining loudly, "Where are the *workers?*" He wanted to meet their spokesmen. We watched him on television; his antics were obviously amusing, especially since his American-educated interpreter had a genius for converting his crude peasant expressions into familiar American idioms. I knew enough Russian to understand what he was really saying, and I was anxious that the American people get an unvarnished view of this man who represented such a powerful force in the world. We also wanted Khrushchev to find out what was in the minds of Americans.

After he had implied several times that the American workers were afraid to exchange ideas with him, our State Department called my office and asked whether something could be arranged in spite of the determined aloofness of the AFL-CIO. I called Walter and the above-mentioned union presidents, and the result was a dinner in the Mark Hopkins Hotel in San Francisco on September 20, 1959. The rest of our contingent consisted of George Weaver; Les Finnegan, Carey's press representative, who was there to take notes; and me, as director of the UAW's international affairs.

The Russian group, in addition to Khrushchev and his interpreter, Sukhodrev, included Ambassador Menshikov; Mikhail A. Sholokhov, the famous Soviet novelist; Pavel A. Satyukov, editor of *Izvestia;* Khrushchev's son-in-law, Aleksei I. Adzhubei; and the chairman of the Ukrainian Economic Council, Nikolai A. Tikhonov.

I had been asked to handle the arrangements. We researched carefully a wide range of domestic and international questions and even had suggestions for discussion and factual material typed on cards for each of our labor participants — including actual quotations of statements made by Russian leaders in their press, with sources and dates.

I was still concerned about the problem of interpretation, but Walter insisted we could not possibly insist on an interpreter of our choice. At the last minute I suggested that I greet Khrushchev, as he entered, in Russian, to indicate to the interpreter that our side understood Russian and would brook no tampering with the translation. To this Walter agreed.

We had been asked to arrive an hour in advance so that the entire floor could be sealed off and a security check made by both U.S. and Soviet intelligence men. The draperies, every inch of the floor, and even the table under the flower arrangement — everything was examined not only for dangerous objects but also, apparently, for any recording equipment. Khrushchev later wrote in his inaccurate memoirs that I had had the whole dinner taped and photographs taken. This was simply not true. The only record we had was made in shorthand by Les Finnegan, a union newspaperman and an experienced reporter, who sat at a small table nearby after it was found there was not enough room at the banquet table because Khrushchev had brought unannounced guests. There were no cameras in the room.

At eight o'clock sharp the door to the Golden Empire Room opened and Nikita Khrushchev led his party in. I was near the door, and when he extended his pudgy arm, I shook his hand and said in a loud voice, "здравствуй." He looked at me in amazement.

"You speak Russian?"

I answered him in his own language. "Mr. Chairman, have you forgotten that I spent several years in your country?"

"When?"

"In nineteen thirty-three and nineteen thirty-four."

"Where?"

"In the Gorky Automobile Plant, named in honor of Molotov."

Then, still speaking Russian and looking directly into his eyes, I asked, "Tell me, Mr. Chairman, is the Gorky plant still named in honor of Molotov?"

Molotov had recently been exiled to Siberia. Khrushchev turned white with rage, stammered, then blurted out a loud "Nyet! Today we call it only the Gorky Auto Works," and turned to greet the other members of our party.

Thus began three and a half hours of completely candid discussion between spokesmen for free and democratic trade unions and the head of the world's most powerful autocracy. The knowledge that everything was being taken down in shorthand by Les seemed to inhibit no one.

Jim Carey probably would turn over in his grave if he knew that in his memoirs Khrushchev wrote, "I was the host, so I arranged for us to serve snacks and drinks — just refreshments, no hard liquor." The Industrial Union Department of the CIO-AFL picked up the tab for a most sumptuous dinner accompanied by generous supplies of whiskey and cognac, which were enjoyed by all the guests, with one exception — Walter. As a matter of fact, Walter was annoyed that some in our party did not have the Russians' capacity to hold liquor.

In spite of the seriousness of the discussion and obvious clash of ideologies, there were many friendly toasts proposed from each side. Peering across the table Khrushchev noticed that Walter was merely touching his glass to his lips.

"Gospodin Valter," said Khrushchev, using the term that meant Walter was not a *comrade,* "what is this? You are giving only lip service to the toast?"

Walter ignored the first two jibes and went on with the discussion. But after the third — irritated as much by some of his colleagues as by the Soviet leader — he put his glass down and responded in a solemn voice; "Mr. Chairman, I think you should know that when the revolution comes to America, there will be at least one sober trade unionist." That ended the "Gospodin Valter" comments.

It was not an easy evening for Nikita Khrushchev. He was not used to individuals so far below him in rank speaking as directly and bluntly to him as we did. We used the same straightforward manner in which we spoke across the negotiating table with American employers. Later he took out his irritation on Walter in his book: "Here was a man who had betrayed the class struggle. At the head of a big trade union, he organized strikes — but always within certain permissible limits so as not to endanger or weaken the capitalist regime." He accused Walter of making as much money as Henry Ford. "In other words, the capitalists have bought him off; they paid him enough to make him represent their interests rather than those of the workers." (In 1959, Walter's salary was $22,000. Henry Ford received, in salary, bonus, and dividends, a total of $445,000.)

As the discussion became more heated (fueled, in part, by alcohol) Khrushchev, mimicking can-can dancers and turning his derrière skyward, mocked the "degenerate and pornographic" exploitation of sex by bourgeois society. And as the questions about Hungary and East Germany and the suppression of protest in Soviet society became more insistent, he rose to his feet three separate times, threatening to call a halt to the dinner party. It was an idle threat; how could he ever explain back home that he had got along with U.S. bankers and corporate officials but had fallen out with the spokesmen of American workers?

I was, however, impressed by the fact that he did not dominate the entire conversation, and that he let members of his entourage correct him if he got some detail or statistic wrong. There was no slavish deference as to one all-wise and all-powerful. His own program of de-Stalinization was beginning to have some effect and I admired him for his courage within the context of his own society.

Walter and I had riled him; he soon had his revenge when *Trud*
ran the headline GET ACQUAINTED WITH MR. REUTHER, LACKEY OF THE
MONOPOLISTS, along with the story I have mentioned in an earlier
chapter of Walter's alleged marriage to, and desertion of, Lucy, his
friend in Gorky. Two years later he was more truthful, when he
said to President Kennedy in Vienna, after some mention of Walter,
"We hanged the likes of Reuther in Russia in nineteen-seventeen."

But the party ended on a jovial note, with Khrushchev inviting the
trade union leaders to come to the Soviet Union and see things firsthand; and there were toasts to the hope that Russia and the United
States would improve their relationship and thereby contribute to
world peace.

Leaving out only some anecdotes and incidental by-play, the *New
York Times* ran a completely accurate account of the Soviet-American
exchange, supplied to them by the indefatigable Les Finnegan, who
worked most of the night with secretaries and me to get it into the
papers the next day.

Khrushchev had a much better time with Harry Bridges, president of the International Longshoremen's and Warehousemen's
Union centered in California, and long considered a fellow traveler
if not an actual Communist Party member. He invited Khrushchev
to visit their headquarters on the waterfront. In his memoirs,
Khrushchev praised Bridges, who was "unlike Reuther and his
kind," and lamented that not too many people showed up. "Perhaps
we were already a bit spoiled since we were accustomed to big
crowds. But the longshoremen made up for it by receiving me
warmly and sincerely. A few gave speeches expressing friendship
toward the Soviet Union." He referred to the longshoremen as "the
true representatives of the American working class."

Later, when Walter and I traveled to the various lands whose
problems we had discussed during that well-publicized dinner, we
received many thanks for our firm support of their national interests
and rights — especially from the people of West Berlin, and from
the Israelis, whose very existence was jeopardized by the continuous
flow of Soviet armaments to the Arab states.

I am certain that the arguments at that dinner did not damage
Soviet-American relations but, rather, helped clear the atmosphere.
Soon a delegation from the UAW (despite the U-2 incident, which
precipitated an explosion from Khrushchev and forced a cancella-

tion of Eisenhower's visit to Russia) was invited to travel to the Lake Baikal region in Siberia to visit the enormous hydroelectric plants at Bratsk. That gave me a chance to make a sentimental journey back to the Gorky factory. The UAW group was housed in a villa that had been built especially for the Eisenhower visit, on the shores of a beautiful lake and overlooking the newly built Bratsk. I hope that many American Presidents and diplomats will be received in those cool and invigorating surroundings, where the very air may stimulate a reasonable approach to our ideological differences.

In retrospect I have a friendly regard for Khrushchev. His vulgar displays of temper notwithstanding, he will be remembered for exposing the crimes of Stalin and for loosening, to a degree, the grip of a bureaucracy that for so long had held tight reins on Soviet society. The Russian people are warm and compassionate; they have suffered much; they have contributed much to our civilization. We must not identify the people as a whole too closely with the regime under which they now live. In time they may be freed from internal oppression. It cannot be denied that the lot of the working people and peasants has been improved and that the level of education and general understanding is higher than under czarist rule. As their thirst for contact with the rest of the world becomes greater, there will, I am sure, be greater pressure on the government for relaxation of police security, for freedom of speech, press, travel, and communication. Hope for these is something we must cherish and nurture by seeking opportunities for further contact, for exchange at all levels.

CHAPTER 27

International Solidarity and Subversion

The UAW Responds to the Multinational Corporations

Lincoln spoke prophetically to the wage earners of the world when he said, "The strongest bond of human sympathy outside the family relations should be one uniting working people of all nations and tongues and kindreds."

In the early days of trade unionism, discussion about the need for international labor solidarity generated more hot air than action. Ironically, it was the capitalistic private industries that in the end unified world labor. Not until large conglomerates began to see the whole world as their marketplace, and leapfrogged across borders and oceans to advance their commercial operations, were workers forced to counter multinational exploitation with international measures of their own. Where Marx, Engels, and Lenin failed to unify the "workers of the world," General Motors, General Electric, Ford, and others succeeded to a surprising extent.

International Business Machines Corporation is not just the name of a company; it's a symbol of a process at work in almost every country in the world. General Motors manufactures products in more than twenty-three nations; Ford workers draw wages in Canada, Brazil, Bermuda, Australia, South Africa, Southern Rhodesia, New Zealand, the Congo, the United Arab Republic, England, France, Italy, Portugal, Belgium, Switzerland, Germany, Norway, Sweden, Denmark, Finland, the Netherlands, and Japan.

The forward thrust of the twentieth-century technological revolution has spread the tools of production so widely that these gigantic corporations are now able to switch orders, jobs, and finished products on international control boards. Frederick Donner of GM put it succinctly on September 27, 1961, at a meeting of world accountants at the Waldorf-Astoria, calling the phenomenon "a new kind of capitalism." President Thornbrough of the Massey-Ferguson Corporation told the New York Society of Security Analysts on February 20, 1964, that his agricultural implement firm, with twenty-seven plants spread through ten countries, could "take a transmission from Detroit, an engine from Italy, other components from England and build a tractor to prescribed specifications in France — or the other way around . . . We live and think internationally."

The trade union movement had to develop a parallel multinational structure or find itself impotent to cope with the firms that called the shots on a world corporate basis, just as earlier American unionists had to follow our big firms to our South, where they had moved to exploit cheap labor. The result then was a pattern of national collective bargaining agreements pertaining to both North and South. But it was no easy task to respond to the new strategy whereby an employer, without any discussion with the union or unions involved, could gradually phase out home operations and dismiss thousands of workers, only to move its plants to other lands and bring back the finished products to sell in the United States. It was this bitter experience, not the exhortations of ideologues talking about world brotherhood, that opened the eyes of U.S. workers to the absolute necessity of establishing closer international ties. Industry by industry, employees were forced to join some sort of common structure at a world level in order to protect themselves.

It was after the Second World War that the multinationals began to swell. U.S. industry had the obvious edge over European corporations because the war had not damaged our shores, and we were in a better position to respond to the pent-up demand for consumer goods, and for the machinery to help rebuild the ravaged industries of Europe. U.S. capital was eager to move in and take the lion's share of trading areas long dominated by Germany and Japan.

As I have said, there was a World Federation of Trade Unions in existence before the Second World War, but its membership was on the whole restricted to the older trade unions, and was concentrated in Europe. Metal workers, transport and mine workers, and others had their international trade secretariats. We in the automobile trade unions were mainly concerned with the International Metal

Workers' Federation (the IMF) then based in Berne, Switzerland. Founded in 1893, it was the largest, most strategically situated of the trade secretariats because it included workers engaged in steel manufacture, auto and agricultural implement production, ship building, machine tool construction, and all phases of the production of electrical appliances and generators. Many metal workers had separate unions in the U.S. and Canada, but in Europe it was customary for them to group into a single, centralized federation.

The rise of Nazism had crippled most of the trade secretariats. One million members of the IMF came from the German Metal Workers' Union and were out of the running for many years after the putsch. It was not until 1947 that the American Machinists' Union, an AFL union, became affiliated with the IMF and attended its first World Congress. We in the CIO were too involved in our own survival in the thirties and early forties to devote much energy to international trade union concerns.

When the war ended, the Machinists' Union invited a committee to come to Washington for its meeting, and alerted American steel, shipyard, and electrical workers, and of course the UAW. Konrad Ilg, general secretary of the IMF and former head of the Swiss Watch and Metal Workers, had kept lonely vigil during those years when contact with even the British and Scandinavians was difficult. Thanks to the efforts of British unionists in the metal industries, especially Lincoln Evans and Jack Tanner, Ilg was supported in his drive to re-establish communications after the war and give aid to those democratic metal workers in Germany who had survived.

Ilg brought to Washington with him the stalwart Arne Geijer, president of the Swedish Metal Workers, a union numerically strong and very influential politically and socially, which had emerged from the war years in far better financial position than most. From Belgium came Arthur Gailly, general secretary of the Metal Workers, a devoted Socialist who saw each confrontation with employers as a skirmish in the class war. Evans and Tanner came from England, and Walter Freitag from the German Metal Workers' Union.

Konrad Ilg was a stubborn mixture of humanism and union pragmatism. He had made up his mind, before coming to America, to procure the affiliation of the great new CIO unions in the metal field. He felt quite rightly that it would be ridiculous to call the IMF a world organization if it did not embrace the millions of newly organized metal workers in the United States; also, without their financial contributions, it would be impossible to penetrate the Third World, the newly industrialized areas of Latin America, Africa, and Asia. But he knew, too, that merely continuing the prewar fraternal relations among metal workers was not enough. American workers were too deeply occupied on the home front to use funds for traveling great distances to listen to lectures. The IMF's goals had to be transformed into practical measures in order to attract the U.S. workers.

Without discussing many details in advance with his colleagues, Ilg had decided to broaden the structure of the IMF by creating special trade or industry departments for iron, steel, auto manufacturing, shipbuilding, and possibly for general metal manufacturing — or engineering, as it is called in Europe. Ilg thought that in this way he could provide American unions with the inducement to participate actively and to help shape policy.

At the Washington meeting, Ilg approached Walter privately and asked if he would accept the presidency of a World Automotive Department within the IMF, a position predicated, of course, on the affiliation of the UAW, which was certainly in the cards. It should be pointed out clearly that we did not affiliate because of any protective posture on imported cars. At that time — 1949 — the U.S. auto industry so dominated the world market that it stood almost alone; there were few low-priced imports from low-wage countries. The UAW, by convention vote in July 1949, joined the IMF because it saw "an opportunity to work with representatives of the free labor movement throughout the world who have membership in metal-working industries, in developing a program to protect the working conditions, the wage standards and general interests of the workers in these basic industries."

Ilg's idea for special industrial departments did not meet with general enthusiasm among the European leaders of the IMF, who were worried that it might lead to a fracturing of the metal workers whom the IMF had taken so many years to unify. I suspect they were also doubtful whether the leaders of the U.S. metal-working unions shared their social and political goals. Might not the U.S. unions return to a practice of isolationism, or perhaps reflect the "free enterprise obsessions" of American capitalism?

Walter's speech, when he first met with the IMF at their Zurich conference, did much to dispel the apprehension. He began by explaining in detail the tremendous struggles American steel, auto,

shipyard, and electrical workers had waged in their recent efforts to
unionize and to wring from the great corporations valuable collective bargaining gains. Then, echoing the recent UAW convention
resolution on international affairs, he called for full support of the
Marshall Plan. He attacked the power bloc tactics of the Soviet
Union and its satellites. He called for aid to four hundred thousand
European refugees and a democratic approach to the control of industries in the Ruhr; he voiced his opposition to the Franco regime
and warned that "without substantial U.S. tariff reduction, the Marshall Plan will prove illusory as a device for permanent recovery."
Perhaps the most significant item of his talk was the emphasis on the
need for international fair labor standards with codes to control the
policies of trading nations. This concept lay dormant for some time,
but was to become one of the IMF's major demands in later years.

The European metal workers, justifiably concerned about the
need for full employment, were impressed by Walter's statement
that the vast unused productive capacities of the Western world
must be harnessed if we were to enter an era of abundance. In
concluding, he said, "Neither Communism nor Wall Street is the
solution to our problems." That warning against both the perver-
sion of Socialism and effects of unrestrained capitalism was characteristic of the Reuther position. It was the first time many of the Europeans had heard such ideas expressed by a U.S. union leader, and
they received him enthusiastically. Ilg, without waiting for further
discussion, took advantage of Walter's reception to obtain approval
for the creation of his industrial departments, and publicly invited
Walter to head the Automotive Department.

Ilg was indeed prophetic about the role the industrial departments
would play in cementing closer relations among the metal and iron
workers of many nationalities. Soon after their creation, metal
unions like those in Germany began to convene national conferences
for their auto workers. If American, Scandinavian, or English workers found it difficult to understand that the IMF headquarters in
Switzerland were really their headquarters, one thing at least was
clear to them: they had a common interest, to be defended at the
bargaining table, with the workers employed by Ford, General Motors, General Electric, and similar multinationals. These corporations, which were spreading rapidly over the globe, helped, unwittingly, to unite international labor.

Walter's first act as president of the Automotive Department of the IMF was to set up a massive research project that would accumulate for the first time all the details of every collective bargaining agreement signed with automobile companies in every country of the world. Never again would a group of auto workers on any continent enter into negotiations with a multinational employer without prior knowledge about exactly what concessions that firm had already granted to unionized workers in other lands. This was especially important to the isolated unions in the industrially emerging areas, which were handicapped, in dealing with such Goliaths as General Motors, by limited resources and small memberships.

A Steel Department was soon established under the joint leadership of the presidents of U.S. and British steelworkers' unions; the Germans assumed chairmanship of the Machine Construction Department; the Scandinavians directed the World Shipbuilding Department. Later, as the Japanese became unionized and affiliated with the IMF, they undertook the direction of the World Electrical Department.

Along with research, these units started training cadres of activists for each industry sector. Soon at international conferences there was a demand for the coordination of collective bargaining provisions in order that a united workers' front could be presented during negotiations. The provisions would cover uniformity of hours, overtime pay, vacation allowances. Finally, there was a call for uniform termination dates for contracts, so that the combined power of the unions could be called upon during negotiations with any single industry sector.

A further refinement was needed in the structure of the automotive section if we were to see concrete results, so world councils were created: one for Ford workers, one for General Motors, and a third to lock together Chrysler, by far the smallest of the giants, with its allied small firms in Europe and elsewhere, such as Simca, Fiat, and the British Rootes. Not long after there was a world council for Volkswagen and Mercedes workers, and still another for the Japanese Nissan and Toyota.

As director of the UAW's International Affairs Department, and a member of the IMF's Executive Committee, I became responsible for organizing and often participating in the educational seminars, which provided technical assistance to IMF-affiliated automotive unions around the world. Soon skilled negotiators, researchers, and technicians were journeying to Brazil and Mexico to deliberate with their counterparts in outlying Volkswagen plants. UAW staff members held training sessions to assist Ford or General Motors unionists in Latin America and Europe. Pat Patterson, a regional director, was asked by the GM Holden auto workers in Australia to come down under and help them present their wage brief. Walter and I led one of the first U.S. labor delegations to go to Japan after the war; we encouraged the auto workers to resolve their internal differences and support the aims of the International Metal Workers. A basis was laid then for the founding in Japan of a Wage Research Center.

Although the corporations had gone global years before, they were in no haste to deal with labor on a world basis, and frequently displayed an arrogant disregard of the traditions of their host countries. They liked to say that each branch could behave autonomously, though this was far from the truth. When Ford decided to open a branch in Antwerp, it put in charge an American manager, who remained stubbornly oblivious of trade union traditions and employer obligations in Belgium. Workers in the metal industry there had always received a Christmas bonus, which had become no small portion of their salary; it was approximately equal to three months' income for the average wage earner. While the Ford Company paid slightly more than the prevailing hourly wage, it absolutely refused to pay the year-end bonus. Word reached us at the UAW in Detroit, via the IMF in Berne, that a strike over this issue was pending, and that the Antwerp workers wanted to know whether it really was against Ford policy in Detroit to pay a bonus. They also asked how they could negotiate with their employers in Detroit, since the Ford manager in Antwerp had told them he was powerless to change the policy.

We knew full well that the UAW had no contractual right to intervene directly. But we wanted to clarify the issue in order to assist our fellow unionists, so Walter suggested that Ken Bannon and I request an off-the-record conference at Ford, to include representatives from its world operation headquarters. The meeting took place, and we were told that the plant manager in Antwerp had full authority in this matter. We sent the news to Belgium, only to be cabled once again: "The bonus seems to be prohibited by general Ford Co. policy." This sent us back to the Detroit people. We told them:

We realize we have no contractual right to bargain with you in behalf of the Belgian workers, but we want you to know that if you continue this policy of speaking out of both sides of your mouth at the same time, you are inviting serious trouble, and if it comes to a strike in Belgium over this issue, we will blanket every Ford establishment and every retail car dealership with leaflets informing the workers and the public of the duplicity and arrogance of the Ford Motor Co., and furthermore we will extend all possible financial strike assistance to our Belgian brothers and sisters.

Ford got the message. The Antwerp workers received their traditional bonus!

The multinational corporations, almost without exception, have refused to meet with any federation of international labor representing unionized workers in their far-flung foreign plants, and continue to exercise their vast economic power in a manner that can be described only as blackmail — of governments as well as trade unions. (It is good to report, however, that the IMF has recently enjoyed a breakthrough with the International Harvester Company.)

An example of the typical strategy of the multinationals is the 1971 affair in Dagenham, home of England's Ford works. A strike over wages was underway; Henry Ford II flew to London and insisted on an immediate conference with Prime Minister Heath, during which he warned that unless the British government compelled the Ford strikers to accept their present wage offer, he, Henry Ford, had no recourse but to shift the British Ford operations to the Ford works in Cologne.

Fortunately the IMF was scheduled to meet in London the following week. The IMF's president at that time was Otto Brenner, also president of the two-million-strong German Metal Workers' Union. He was joined in London by Leonard Woodcock, who succeeded Walter as head of the UAW and of the IMF's Automotive Department. When they learned what had taken place between Henry Ford and Heath, the IMF officials met with the Prime Minister and told him that any effort by the Ford Company to shift strike-bound plant work to Germany would meet with no success because the German metal workers would not perform the work. So Henry Ford's blackmail package proved to be a bag of wind, and the company had to settle with its workers in Dagenham. Such a dispute would not have ended so happily if the machinery had not been set up to balance labor solidarity against the power of a giant multinational corporation.

Closer to home, General Motors, Ford, and Chrysler had monopoly control over Canadian car production, and identical vehicles were marketed at a higher price in Canada, although Canadian workers were paid fifty to sixty cents an hour less than their U.S. counterparts. Even after the U.S. and Canadian governments agreed to lift all duty or tariff charges on vehicles or parts shipped across the border, the big three took no steps to eliminate the discriminatory difference in wages and in the price to the Canadian consumer.

At a UAW convention it was resolved that the Canadian auto workers, who had their autonomous division within the UAW, would be supported in their demand for a wage policy similar to that in the U.S. It was a long fight, but the UAW was finally able to get Chrysler to sign in 1964, followed by Ford and GM in 1967, thus eliminating the long-standing U.S.–Canadian wage differential.

This advance in U.S.–Canadian collective agreements bolstered the European unions in their efforts to equalize conditions within member countries of the Common Market. Since, for the purposes of employment, Common Market countries consider all Europe as a common labor market — and it is a rare major industrial European country that does not reach deep into Greece, Turkey, southern Italy, Spain, and Yugoslavia to augment its work force — then why not a common labor policy for the men and women of different nationalities who journey to Common Market countries to be employed?

Not only the workers, but many countries are threatened with the dwarfing of their national resources by the incredibly rich multinationals. Even in Germany, Scandinavia, the Netherlands, and Britain there is anxiety about maintaining financial stability as the conglomerates move heedlessly ahead, making private economic decisions that can jettison the best conceived national stabilization program. The control of this situation is a matter being debated in the legislatures of many countries; even the Social and Economic Council of the UN itself has created a special task force to prepare recommendations.

Meanwhile, the international trade secretariats must continue to bear the burden of financing research, underwriting the traveling costs of delegations, paying for the training of local cadres, and covering the expenses of skilled experts who assist with negotiations or strike situations. All this is a heavy drain on the resources of international labor, even of the IMF, the most affluent of the eighteen separate trade secretariats. We in the UAW, therefore, felt there was an urgent need for a Solidarity Fund, which would guarantee assistance to affiliated organizations, especially those in the developing countries. We devised a fairly painless method of establishing it. By resolution and vote at the 1962 convention, the UAW took the historic step of allocating all the interest earned on the investment of our own strike-assistance funds to a special UAW Free World Labor Defense Fund. Our strike fund then had a capital accumulation of $25 million, which gave us, even at an interest rate of 4 percent, $1 million a year for the Solidarity Fund. As our strike fund grew, exceeding $100 million, the income permitted us to meet not only the needs of labor abroad, but the needs within our own country of such groups as the struggling farm workers, civil rights organizations, and others. As President Kennedy said, at the 1962 UAW convention: "You have not confined yourselves to getting the best possible deal at the bargaining table, but instead, year after year, you have worked to strengthen the entire United States and the free world, and your action taken at this convention, of spending, over a period of two years, over one million four hundred thousand dollars per year to build strong free trade unions around the world, is an example of the public service that this union has rendered, and I commend you."

Confident of our own resources, we called on the IMF to create an International Solidarity Fund. I remember going to Norway to propose at an IMF meeting that the federation set a target of $1 million a year. With the Germans, Scandinavians, and the UAW each pledging to meet one quarter of this goal, and the IMF the remaining quarter, it was possible to raise $800,000 the first year. As the IMF grew from a membership of a few million to twelve million (It now represents some seventy centers in fifty countries), the need for the fund grew, but it also became possible for each affiliated union to contribute not just on a voluntary basis but as a portion of its fees. It is now an established amount of the normal income of the IMF.

Out of our UAW Free World Labor Defense Fund, we were able to assist, with $50,000, the heroic Spanish coal miners striking against the Franco regime. The Greek trade union movement (Greek Confederation of Labor) was given a loan of $25,000, which

we would have written off as assistance to a sister union had not the
junta seized power and the generals headed unions that no longer
spoke for the workers. We insisted that the government pay back
the loan, which it did, over a number of years. We sent cash grants
to both the Hungarian and Czechoslovakian refugees after the
bloody uprisings; we helped with the training of African unionists;
we aided in establishing the Wage Research Center in Tokyo.

When we became more realistic about conditions in the less developed countries, we realized that the normal incentives that lead to
unionization — the promise of higher wages and fringe benefits —
did not exist in a number of lands that were to remain agrarian for
many years. Their national economies simply would not involve the
kind of wages one would normally expect from industrial firms, except in the case of the privileged few singled out as an industrial elite
as compared to the majority of the population. Many governments
imposed such rigid controls on the unions that any wage increases
were impossible.

But there were many needs we could fill. A small cooperative
pharmacy, for instance, that could make essential drugs available at
reasonable cost turned out to be a service perhaps more valuable
than a direct raise in wages. We also found that the educational activity of a union was often completely stymied by the lack of a typewriter or mineograph machine; at the same time we found at home
and in some European countries machinery and office equipment
that was being discarded. These discoveries gave rise to the UAW-
STEP; that is, Social, Technical, and Educational Programs. Since
elected UAW officers held precisely equivalent posts in STEP, and I
was the director of the International Affairs Department, it became
my baby. It was, in effect, a nonprofit organization born of our
belief that freedom withers where there is poverty, disease, hunger,
and ignorance.

STEP became the central agency for collecting and repairing material to be sent to far-away lands. UAW local unions across the U.S.
sent in to our huge Detroit warehouse used hospital equipment — x-
ray machines, surgeons' tools, operating tables, everything down to
simple items like bedpans and lamps. Some of our Detroit workers
gave their hours to help repair, recondition, paint. Since for years
major drug companies had made contributions to church and other
relief groups, which they wrote off as tax deductions, we saw no
reason why they could not do the same for STEP. A number of

drug firms responded to our appeal, and our volunteers crated the pharmaceuticals and sent them off with the repaired equipment. During the first year, our output exceeded $1 million in cash value. We refurbished a hospital in southern Chile that had been gutted by fire; furnished operating rooms and patients' rooms in a cooperative hospital belonging to sugar workers at Shrirampur, India; sent large shipments of equipment and drugs to the metal workers of São Paulo and to the unions of South Vietnam. From old school buses we made mobile health clinics and shipped them to union Vicomptu in the Philippines, to unions in Kenya, to farm workers in Texas, and to remote areas of Mississippi, where doctors and clinics were non-existent.

Transportation and trucking equipment was made available to union metal workers in Turkey, Tunisia, Mexico, France, West Berlin, and to some of the lands in Africa still seeking their independence. For one African country, sizable shipments of medical supplies were of vital help in their final overthrow of Portuguese colonialism.

If it is true, as it is so often said, that the United Auto Workers is the best known and most respected of any single trade union in the world, then the bouquet should be given to the membership, to the rank and file, for their understanding and their acceptance of their responsibilities in an interdependent world. Their devotion to the cause of freedom wherever it is threatened, and the conviction that unionism must keep up with technological and economic change, encouraged the UAW leaders to raise their sights and develop tactics to cope with the multinational corporate octopus.

The Seduction of AFL-CIO by the Central Intelligence Agency

> *All, all of a piece throughout,*
> *Thy chase had a beast in view;*
> *Thy wars brought nothing about;*
> *Thy lovers were all untrue.*
> *T'is well an old age is out,*
> *And time to begin a new.*
>
> — JOHN DRYDEN,
> *The Secular Masque*

The other, less rosy side of the international labor story reflects a sad image of some of our countrymen during the decades between World War II and the seventies. The revelations of the Nixon scandal even now continue to cast light on some of the more melodramatic domestic and foreign adventures. Among these are the extended CIA operations, some of which, under the guise of international trade union work, brought corruption and shame, weakness and betrayal to the cause of international labor solidarity.

Soon after I accepted the European directorship in behalf of National CIO (before the merger with AFL) I became aware of a suspicion, pervading European labor and political circles, that some of those acting in the name of U.S. labor were spending money far beyond what normal trade unions would have had available at that time. The activities of the AFL's Irving Brown were especially mistrusted; it was thought that he was receiving incredibly large funds from some U.S. Government source in an effort to get European trade unions in his pocket and to dictate the foreign policy of both European and African countries. In plainer words, the hysterical fear of Communism that produced McCarthyism in America was being spread, by means of CIA money, first by the AFL and later by the merged AFL-CIO under Meany's autocratic rule.

I have already described how Brown caused the splintering of the French trade union movement and financed the establishment of the Force Ouvrière. Soon after, when the Communists instigated strikes in Marseilles in an effort to block the unloading of Marshall Plan supplies, Brown recruited the notorious Ferri Pisani and his entourage of Corsican thugs, gave them the title of Mediterranean Committee of Transport Workers, and bankrolled their strikebreaking operations. The Comité Mediterranée was never a formal division of any bona fide trade union; it was a front financed by the CIA to achieve specific objectives. The tragedy was that Ferri Pisani and his gang, after successfully breaking the strike, refused to go out of business, and for decades plagued the unions in southern France. Brown and the CIA had to pay them off for years. Though Pisani was dead, the remnants of this American-funded organization were involved in pilfering and drug dealing in the harbors of South Vietnam.

The CIA funding was heaviest in Italy, France, North Africa, and Greece — areas where democratic trade unionism has remained weakest. But nothing that I suspected in the mid-fifties, nor the worst apprehensions of European and African union leaders at that time, could match what was uncovered by an alert U.S. press in 1967. On February 26 of that year the Washington *Post* printed in its editorial section an exposé of the intricate ramifications of the CIA's use of private foundations and dummy corporations as fronts to finance their operations. Another front, unfortunately, consisted of many AFL-CIO affiliated groups, including some international trade secretariats. The truth is that many millions of taxpayers' dollars were used by the CIA, with no public accounting whatsoever, to influence the political posture of nongovernmental organizations throughout the world — and in the United States.

The obscure and muddy channels through which the CIA poured public monies were accidentally discovered in 1964 by Congressman Wright Patman while he was conducting a routine examination of certain foundations to see if they were abusing their tax-exempt status. He suddenly realized that he was being "trifled with" by the CIA and the Internal Revenue Service, both of which were very uncooperative in responding to his questions about the J. M. Kaplan Fund of New York City. Although he refused to elaborate on the matter, Patman did state publicly that the Kaplan Fund had been used as a "secret conduit."

His investigation revealed that the Kaplan Fund was the recipient of at least $1 million in grants from the Gotham Foundation, the Michigan Fund, the Andrew Hamilton Fund, the Borden Trust Fund, the Price Fund, the Edsel Fund, the Beacon Fund, and the Kentfield Fund. The *New York Times* listed these in 1964, but several years had to pass before the press zeroed in and asked the hard questions. Then reporters came up with the fact that these were phony foundations, used for funneling money to numerous other fronts. The Kaplan Fund, for example, made direct grants to CIA-chosen projects, like the Institute of International Labor Research, a school for political action in Costa Rica, later moved to the Dominican Republic. This school turned out to be a boomerang — many of its graduates were active in the Dominican revolution of 1965, which the U.S. Government quashed by sending in the Marines.

In Europe, the founding and financing of the International Federation of Petroleum and Chemical Workers (the IFPCW) was a covert CIA maneuver, carried out through the services of the Oil,

Chemical and Atomic Workers (the OCAW), a legitimate U.S. trade union then headed by Jack Knight and affiliated with the AFL-CIO. It was he who was the driving force behind the IFPCW. Except for the OCAW, most of the petroleum unions were in the Middle East and were weak, poorly organized, and almost without funds. The few Venezuelan unions were relatively better off, but it was obvious from the start that the OCAW would be carrying the major part of the financial load of the international federation.

As an affiliate of the IFPCW, with fifty thousand members and with the monthly contribution set at two U.S. cents per member, the OCAW was obliged to send in only $12,000 a year. However, Knight contributed $44,000 in 1960 and the same in 1961; in 1962 the sum rose to $66,000, more than four times the amount agreed upon by the membership. In addition, he made contributions, over and above affiliation fees, totaling $137,880. This sort of money did not exist in the OCAW's treasury. It came from direct grants, arranged by Knight, from the Midland Foundation and the Hamilton Fund, both of which turned out to be CIA conduits.

What did the CIA get for the taxpayers' money? It got information it wanted from Venezuela, Argentina, Brazil, India, Indonesia, Italy, Japan, Lebanon, Malaya, the Netherlands, Nigeria, Turkey, Iran, Saudi Arabia — wherever petroleum refining was done.

Fortunately, Jack Knight's retirement and the refusal of the American petroleum workers of OCAW to accept at their convention the CIA-favored W. J. Forrester to succeed him, turned the tide. Although four or five IFPCW staff members flew in haste from the Middle East, South Asia, and Latin America to that Miami convention in order to twist arms and protect with massive propaganda and plenty of expense money the spy apparatus that had been set up, the workers' choice, Al Grosperin, won the election. One of his first acts was to sever all ties with the foundations and funds that had been used to turn his staff members into government agents; he returned the union to the control of its membership and turned its attention to the collective bargaining purposes for which it had been founded. He also saw to it that all fees to the International Federation of Petroleum and Chemical Workers were henceforth paid out of legitimate OCAW funds.

Another victim was the Newspaper Guild, an AFL-CIO affiliate, which accepted CIA money from the Warden, Granary, and Hamilton funds, and from the Chesapeake Foundation and the Broad-High Foundation to the tune of $944,000, to be used to promote closer contacts with journalists in other countries and help train newspapermen in the emerging nations. When the news of this broke, the Guild officers said they had no knowledge that the money came from the CIA, explaining that "initial assistance was sought and received from the AFL-CIO and the Solidarity Fund of the ICFTU." Only $10,000, however, of the roughly $1 million it received came from a legitimate international labor source. It was a traumatic realization for the Guild, and to the best of my knowledge it terminated all such grants after the disclosure.

One could go on and on. Perhaps the saddest examples were the cases where the AFL-CIO compromised old and reputable international trade union organizations, which represented the legitimate aspirations of low-income workers. One of these was the International Union of Food Workers (the IUF), with headquarters in Geneva. It was led by the admirable Jules Poulsen, who had won for his small federation a unique stature. It was not, however, affluent enough to send a large staff into outlying regions. During a trip to Washington, Poulsen discovered that, under the auspices of Andrew C. McLellan, the AFL-CIO Latin-American representative chosen by Meany, a good-sized staff had been financed to work in Latin America in behalf of the IUF without consultation with Poulsen or his Executive Committee. This spurious group had been provided with false credentials and, of course, plenty of CIA money.

Poulsen was quick to act when he returned to Europe. With his Executive Committee he reorganized his western hemisphere programs, closing down regional offices in San José, Costa Rica, and Santiago, Chile, and substituting a provisional committee to direct the Latin-American work and report directly to Geneva.

One of the most brazen examples of the CIA's use of an AFL-CIO union to do its dirty work was the overthrow of Cheddi Jagan, who had been elected Prime Minister of British Guiana in 1961. The U.S. Government preferred the more pro-American Forbes Burnham.

That an all-white, rather middle-class union could be used as a weapon to topple a foreign government seems almost too fantastic to believe, but with money and skilled agents, the CIA can sometimes achieve the impossible. They had already started, in 1959, the fund-

ing of the American Federation of State, County and Municipal Employees through its president, Arnold Zander, to set up, ostensibly,
an educational program for state and municipal workers in Latin
America. The Gotham Fund in New York was handy for the first
funding, which it increased each year until 1964. This money,
routed through Zander, persuaded pro-Burnham public employees,
as well as some workers on the British Guiana docks, to organize
strikes. Zander's agents also stirred up latent racial bitterness between the black supporters of Burnham and the East Indian followers of Cheddi Jagan. Strikes were sustained long enough to
disrupt the economy and eventually oust Jagan. All of this was supposed to be a legitimate activity of the PSI, the Public Service International, which had a long, distinguished history, was an amalgam of
125 unions in 62 nations, and represented European civil service
groups. The *New York Times* reported: "At one point one of the
agents even served as a member of a bargaining committee from a
Guiana dock workers' union that was negotiating with Dr. Jagan. It
is doubtful that the PSI officials at the world level were fully informed of all that was being done . . . but it is also certain that they
were less than vigilant about inquiring about what was being done in
their name."

By the beginning of the sixties, Meany's lieutenants in the arena of
international intrigue had woven a worldwide net financed by huge
sums. Sometimes they used dummy international or regional trade
union structures. At other times they penetrated bona fide international trade secretariats. The monies they manipulated made them
vulnerable to the control of the donor. In 1962 the AFL-CIO officially created the American Institute for Free Labor Development
(the AIFLD), which was to open wide the doors to U.S. Government
funds on an even larger scale. Initially it was to have been a joint
undertaking of trade unions and American universities, with the
purpose of extending training to union members in the western
hemisphere. It was on this basis that Walter supported the founding of the AIFLD. But Meany had something else in mind, and suddenly laid before his Executive Council the blueprint for a tripartite
structure, to have representatives and funds from AFL-CIO unions,
from the U.S. Government, and from corporations with Latin-
American interests.

In the long history of the American trade union movement, no legitimate official would ever have considered giving U.S. corporations a joint role in training union members for union leadership posts. Not only would the idea have been treated with contempt, but any person promoting it would have been booted from his official position. In this case, the notion that Latin-American workers — so often exploited by Standard Oil, Anaconda, Grace Lines, and other corporations — would have allowed the multinationals to subsidize the training of their union leaders boggles the imagination.

Though Meany assumed the presidency of the AIFLD and Joseph Beirne became secretary-treasurer, the chairman of the Board of Directors turned out to be none other than J. P. Grace, president of W. R. Grace and Company, which held all the capital stock of Grace Lines, Incorporated; 50 percent of the Gulf and South American Steamship Company; 50 percent of Pan American–Grace Airways; 80 percent of Griswold and Company, Incorporated; and 53 percent of Cosden Petroleum Corporation. It owned and operated petroleum-refining, paper, chemical, and food-processing industries as well as banking and insurance operations throughout Latin America.

Ironically, just when Mr. Grace assumed the chairmanship of the board of the AIFLD and began contributing to its treasury, the UAW was beginning to organize the employees of Airmold Products in Tonawanda, New York, also owned by the Grace Company. The manager there, a Mr. Schurman, began mailing out to all his employees, on Grace Company stationery, a series of vicious attacks against the UAW and the entire concept of unionism. The leaflets even attacked Meany and the AIFLD: "Do you want to pay dues to help finance foreign unions in foreign countries? Ask the paid organizer about this foreign aid plan . . . Mr. Meany recently told the House Foreign Affairs Committee that his AFL-CIO . . . has been subsidizing foreign unions since the days of Nazi Germany."

Walter objected strenuously to the inclusion of corporation executives and to the acceptance of their money and of government grants to finance the AIFLD. He didn't have a prayer of a chance in the Executive Council meeting. With some members of that council already raking in government money for their pet programs, it was easy for Meany to get a majority to approve his plans.

Training programs were undertaken in each of the major Central and South American countries. The most promising trainees from several unions came north for indoctrination at a center in Front

Royal, Virginia. These were then offered paid positions, lasting from six to eight months, as representatives of the new institute in their own unions. Obviously they were charged with AIFLD directives well soaked with both U.S. corporate and CIA juices. It was, in effect, an exercise in trade union colonialism, paradoxical as those words may seem.

The AIFLD began with a modest budget of $681,237, of which $100,000 theoretically came from the AFL-CIO treasury and $10,050 from affiliated unions, $133,500 from a list of twenty-one corporations that reads like Dun and Bradstreet, and the balance from the State Department, through its American International Development Agency (AID). This program grew like a weed and by 1965 the total budget was $5,095,661, of which AID provided about four and three quarters million. It was estimated in later years that AIFLD ran a budget in excess of $8 million a year. The AFL-CIO and corporate contributions remained at approximately the 1965 level, though there seems to be some question as to whether there were any donations from the AFL-CIO treasury at all, since they are not listed as such on the official union financial budget, which is required by law. (See Appendix for a breakdown of the AIFLD budget.)

One might assume there would be larger "labor" programs in countries with important industries and trade union movements, such as Venezuela. But that nation received practically nothing until 1966, when its receipts suddenly jumped to $201,000. All in all, Venezuela received considerably less than the little agrarian Dominican Republic, which had big injections of money just before and after the overthrow of the Juan Bosch regime. Enormous Brazil, with its concentration of industry and its powerful trade unions, received nothing in 1962 and a mere $54,500 in 1963. However, with President Goulart knocked out of the way in 1964 (with the help of the CIA), Brazil suddenly deserved a budget of $518,352. Bolivia's budget, after the military had taken over in 1966, went from zero to nearly $245,000.

It must be remembered that these AIFLD funds were only the tip of the CIA iceberg. Many additional millions were negotiated on a project-by-project basis and paid by AID or out of special U.S. ambassadorial funds.

Taking Brazil as an example of what the AIFLD was really doing in the name of labor solidarity, we find that, though João Goulart had enjoyed widespread support among the workers and throughout the Brazilian trade union movement, when he was overthrown in 1964 the Executive Council of the AFL-CIO passed a resolution that included the following pious statement: "The recent events in Brazil which culminated in the successful military revolution of April 1st demonstrated the great determination of a freedom-loving people to end the grave threat to their constitution and democratic processes." It is now an accepted fact that the CIA was behind the coup against Goulart. The AIFLD's part was revealed in a more candid manner than Mr. Meany may have cared for by William Doherty, Jr., director of the AIFLD's Social Projects Division, when he returned from Brazil to Washington and talked on the AFL-CIO–sponsored radio program, "Labor News Conference." Henry Conn of Press Associates asked Doherty about the Brazilian trade unionists trained by the AIFLD. "What happened to these individuals who learned the techniques and the programs of Free Trade Unionism in recent developments?"

Doherty's answer must have appalled some people:

> Well, very frankly, within the limits placed upon them by the administration of João Goulart, when they returned to their respective countries they were very active in organizing workers and helping unions introduce systems of labor-management relations. As a matter of fact, some of them were so active that they became intimately involved in some of the clandestine operations of the revolution before it took place on April first. What happened in Brazil on April first did not just happen — it was planned — and planned *months in advance. Many of the trade union leaders — some of whom were actually trained in our institute — were involved in the revolution and in the overthrow of the Goulart regime.* (Italics mine.)

Worse was to come. Soon AIFLD representatives were urging Brazilian workers to accept a freeze on their wages suggested by the new and brutal military regime — and this at a time of rapid inflation. Our UAW friends and associates in the IMF were pressing hard for the cost-of-living adjustment to which they were entitled under existing contracts. But in Brazil, as the *New York Times* reported: "Steel executives advised the labor ministry this week that they would not fulfill a contract signed with 50,000 workers in Minas Gerais and São Paulo during the Goulart regime. This provided for quarterly adjustments that would now require the industries to pay a minimum wage of 70,000 cruzeiros [$55] a month." Doherty commented on this in his radio interview. Among other sage remarks on inflation, he said, "You can't have the poor suffer more than the rich or the poor less than the rich, and if these proper checks and balances are built into the system, the Brazilian labor movement will cooperate in any type of wage freezes that may have to be employed to bring about stability."

I transmitted the text of the whole interview to Walter in one of my letters warning him about what the AFL-CIO was getting mixed up in, and told him that "to speak of the hope of price controls in an economy so irresponsible, where employers and big landowners traditionally seek to evade their income and property tax payments is the height of naïveté . . . Not even the most servile company union in the U.S. would dare to advocate this kind of sellout. I am horrified that all of this is being done in the name of establishing a 'strong, free, virile trade union movement in Latin America.' . . . With this kind of friends, who needs enemies?"

The housing mess was another source of bitterness. The AIFLD's sponsors had tied up $67 million in AID-guaranteed funds for housing. At the end of 1965, only 3394 individual units had been completed. In São Paulo, two leaders of the Shoe Workers' Union accused Doherty in November 1966 of promising to build housing though he had no intention of doing so, in order to cause the downfall of the trade union leaders who had trusted him. This would open the door for new leaders, to be hand-picked by the AIFLD. Such false promises were made in Guanabara, Recife, Joinvile, Porto Alegre, and some other cities; they were undoubtedly intended to precipitate the ouster of certain labeled Communists by the AIFLD.

The AFL-CIO not only embraced the military regime in Brazil; it even boasted of bringing it to power. Military men were soon substituted for presidents and general secretaries of unions; the right to strike was gone; the jails were full of dissidents who refused to be silent under this totalitarianism. The truth is that the AFL-CIO was having its usual love affair with generals who took a strong stand against Communism. That's why they tried to bolster the Batista government in Cuba. Jay Lovestone sent an emissary to Castro to offer support if he would promise to retain Mujal, the pro-Batista general secretary of the Cuban Trade Union Confederation (the

CTC), but Castro refused and Mujal had to flee the country. The AFL-CIO arranged for a cushy job for him, and later he was often seen in its Washington headquarters.

In the Dominican Republic, the AIFLD wanted a military dictatorship rather than the return of the democratic Juan Bosch, to whom most of the working people in the country felt great loyalty. Bosch was in no way an ally of the Communists; the only alliance he made when he was President and when he attempted to be re-elected was with the Christian or Democratic Catholic Party, a party similar to the one that was in power for many years in Chile, led by Frei. Because Bosch had trade union support, the AIFLD's Andy McLellan set out to develop his own method for splitting the workers. He created, with the financial help of the U.S. Ambassador, an organization named Conatral, provided it with $50,000, and said it was "AIFLD's answer to the Communist attempt to cash in on the current political turmoil in the Dominican Republic and take over the labor movement." The program called for organizing campaigns in all regions and for "a specially trained mobile unit of educator-organizers for emergency situations. These will be used to confront and battle the 'Goon Squads' of the extreme left." McLellan had used the same tactics some years before when he employed stevedores to roam the streets of the Dominican Republic "to clear away the leftists."

When our Marines were sent in to overthrow Bosch, there was an outcry of protest from all branches of labor throughout the world, including the two Americas — except for one group: the AFL-CIO. And, of course, Conatral.

All of this open collaboration with antilabor military regimes became too much even for some of the AIFLD's own staff members. Brazil's program director, Xavier M. Vela, for instance, protested to Doherty that the AFL-CIO should "disassociate itself from any program which is part of a larger plan calculated to deprive workers of basic union rights by offering transparent palliatives instead."

This foreign policy of the AFL-CIO was worked out in a hush-hush atmosphere in the Washington headquarters, usually in conjunction with the State Department and other agencies. Rarely was there any discussion beforehand with Executive Council members; there was not even a pretense of democratic process. In 1966, aware of the corrosive effects of the CIA in Latin America, I wrote to Lovestone, by then the director of the International Affairs Department, that the policies of the AFL-CIO should reflect the views of its members and not those of the State Department, the U.S. AID Agency, the U.S. Information Service, or the CIA. I made clear my strong feelings that only designated representatives of AFL-CIO affiliates should be present at the Washington meetings. Although the UAW was the largest of the AFL-CIO affiliates, my letter was not answered.

When I heard rumors, which proved to be true, that the covert setup was beginning to encircle the globe, with an Africa-American Labor Center to be directed by Irving Brown and wholly financed by U.S. AID, I filled Walter in on the subject with a long letter that ended: "When you read the enclosed memorandum of developments in Brazil, you will understand why, as a trade unionist, I feel a sense of revulsion."

To facilitate the expansion of conduits into all countries, a new Labor Advisory Committee on Foreign Affairs was set up by the State Department. Minutes of this committee's meeting (at AFL-CIO headquarters) show in attendance Meany, Doherty, Boyle of the United Mine Workers, Lovestone, Ernest S. Lee, Meany's son-in-law and now successor to Lovestone, and McLellan. From the State Department came Joseph Palmer, Assistant Secretary of Foreign Affairs, Philip C. Habib from the East Indian Bureau, and people from the Department of Labor. Frequently Rutherford M. Poats, deputy administrator of AID, would be there, too, with ten or twelve of his agency men.

Four years after the African operation was started, the Asian-American Free Labor Institute was established in Vietnam. The funding became more and more complicated. Many millions channeled into the AALC in Africa and the AAFLI in Asia would then be diverted into separate contractual arrangements covering "social projects" programs or so-called labor seminars. But the AFL-CIO was not satisfied with all these special institutes or fronts, so Ernest Lee negotiated a remarkable contract with AID's Poats, authorizing the State Department to "utilize the American Institute for Free Labor Development [Latin America], the African-American Labor Center, and the Asian-American Free Labor Institute as instruments to provide financial support to American labor organizations involved in and capable of developing and strengthening free labor unions throughout the world."

(The full text of Lee's letter is in the Appendix.)

Lee signed an agreement with AID for three separate grants to the above-mentioned organizations, totaling $1,300,000. These three would in turn assist seven specific trade union groups who had in the past been receiving large funds from the CIA via the grants from the dummy corporations. Same operation — new cover.

Thus the AFL-CIO became, quite literally, a disbursement agent for the State Department. My personal knowledge of this arrangement before it all came out in the press weighed heavily on my conscience. I felt that Walter, I, and the UAW should no longer remain silent. Walter agreed that it was a serious concern, but felt that a full exposé would mean a definite split between the UAW and the AFL-CIO. He thought it wrong to precipitate such a break over foreign relations rather than over the domestic issues, which were of more immediate importance to rank-and-file workers. He also said that, while he knew as I did that the CIA was using the trade union movement in disgraceful ways, I would never be able to produce enough documentation to stand up against the barrage of fabricated documents the agency could produce so easily.

In 1966, however, I did speak my mind in an interview with Harry Bernstein of the Los Angeles *Times,* during the UAW convention in California. I told him frankly that the AFL-CIO International Affairs Department was involved with the CIA and the tragedy was that it was "a vest pocket operation run by Jay Lovestone," who enjoyed the confidence of Meany. I said the membership was not really involved and there was little chance of an early shift in policy. "Mr. Lovestone," I ended, "seems to have brought into the labor movement the working habits and undercover techniques that he learned when he was in the highest echelons of the Communist Party. I guess it's awfully hard to break those habits."

The Bernstein interview created a flap in labor circles. Meany and Beirne pronounced my remarks "a damned lie." Walter was annoyed that I had spoken so openly, and said so before the UAW International Executive Board, though he added that he knew I had spoken the truth. The AFL-CIO Executive Council adopted a resolution criticizing me for making irresponsible charges.

Less than a year later the whole CIA thing began to come apart at the seams as the press discovered the secret funding of student groups, cooperatives, and certain AFL-CIO unions. The agency was seriously wounded; it fought back by answering all questions with "no comment" — just as it did during the furor over the Bay of Pigs. Memoirs of former agents, evidence of prospective witnesses, articles, and books were censored — *with one exception.* A high official, Thomas H. Braden, Dulles's right-hand man from 1951 to 1954 and chief of the International Division of the CIA, wrote a long article, which was published in the May 20, 1967 *Saturday Evening Post,* in order, he said, to defend the agency against "wild and scurrilous charges."

In the article Braden set forth in some detail what had already been ferreted out by the press: the CIA's part in the Congress for Cultural Freedom in Europe; its subsidizing of the British magazine *Encounter;* its penetration of the World Assembly of Youth; the founding of the International Committee of Women; its funding of students and professors in their "battle with Communist fronts"; and its paying for overseas trips by the Boston Symphony Orchestra. He also indicated that the foreign activities of Jay Lovestone and Irving Brown had been oiled by some $2 million a year, under his supervision. He then took off against the Reuthers, me in particular: "Victor Reuther ought to be ashamed of himself. At his request I went to Detroit one morning and gave Walter $50,000 in fifty-dollar bills. Victor spent the money, mostly in West Germany, to bolster labor unions there. He tried to keep me from finding out how he spent it, but I had my own undercover techniques . . . In my opinion and that of my peers in the CIA he spent it with less than perfect wisdom, for the German unions he chose to help weren't seriously short of money and were already anti-Communists."

When pressed by reporters about this attack on the Reuthers, Braden admitted it was just his personal opinion and not meant to be a "serious charge." He was just twitting me, he said, in return for my remarks in the Bernstein article. Later, he was to call Walter and me "responsible and patriotic citizens in a time of great crisis for the United States and the free world," and say he believed I had behaved in a most responsible fashion. He also admitted that the Detroit money transfer was the only direct payment to the Reuthers that he knew anything about.

There were, naturally, reactions in the press about the "righteousness and bold hypocrisy" of the Reuthers. John Herling, the distinguished labor journalist, in his "Newsletter," wrote about my "short-sighted behavior . . . When he lowered the boom on Messrs.

Lovestone, Brown, etc., why did he not bring to light his own involvement fifteen years ago? . . . Was Victor so wrapped up in the
cocoon of certainty of his own moral position as to feel secure
against all misunderstanding and the possibility of disclosure? To
the eye of the beholder, he was vulnerable."

I can sympathize with that harsh and critical comment. There was
much that was not then known about the $50,000 incident. There is
no question that it would have been far wiser had Walter revealed
this unfortunate involvement with the agency long before all the
sinister CIA details became public knowledge. Neither of us, however, felt tainted by the real facts, and told the whole story immediately after Braden's article came out. Walter's statement went:

> Following the end of World War II, the American labor movement
> made a great effort to assist in the rebuilding of the free labor move-
> ment in Europe which had been destroyed as the first victim of Hitler's
> tyranny and brutality. The labor movement of Europe was weak and
> without resources and therefore especially vulnerable to Communist
> subversion. In this emergency situation fifteen years ago the UAW did
> agree reluctantly on one occasion to the request to transmit government
> funds to supplement the inadequate funds being made available by the
> U.S. labor movement. These monies were merely added to the trade
> union funds to intensify the education and organizational programs
> then underway in Europe. The content of the programs was no way af-
> fected or altered.

Braden had failed to mention in his article that the CIA had made
a careful plan to enmesh the UAW in its network. I never solicited
financial help from him or anyone in the CIA. I was still in Paris
when the transfer of the fifty-dollar bills took place. The $50,000
was obviously an attempt to silence us, at least, if we would not play
ball. The money was not used, incidentally, in Germany; the funds
sent to me by Walter were specifically allocated to assist democratic
trade unions in France and Italy. I challenge Mr. Braden to name
any CIA-funded projects I was involved with in West Germany.

When I first met Braden in the early fifties, I had hardly
even heard of the CIA, and was under the impression that he was
an employee either of the State Department or of the European
Recovery Program. In carrying out the request to transmit financial
assistance to certain unions in Italy and France, I was, I must admit,
acting with what was probably unjustified innocence about the

source of the money. I learned better sometime later when I was asked, by a Mr. Thayer, whom I had met casually and believed to be a political officer at the U.S. Embassy in Paris to meet Braden. In Thayer's office, Braden said he had been following my activities in Europe with great interest, made the first reference to the $50,000 transferred to Walter in Detroit, and told me that for some years the CIA had been providing direct financial assistance to the AFL through Irving Brown. He would like to make a similar arrangement with me. I would not have to leave my CIO international post, he said, as I could be much more helpful if I worked under the cover of that job, but I would have to keep the whole arrangement a secret from my employers and colleagues.

I was shocked and angry, and rejected the idea on the spot, saying I could not possibly take on secret work unknown to my employers, who had given me their confidence as a trade unionist and were entitled to the assurance that I was responsible only to them and their policies. I left the office immediately, filled with new — and unpleasant — knowledge. I had known that Communist and fascist unions operated with government funds, both overtly and covertly; now I knew that our own government resorted to the same methods, but entirely covertly. Indeed I had been naïve! I was so disturbed that I felt it essential to report the affair to Philip Murray.

Braden, as he himself stated, made no more offers to the Reuthers. It is sad that I could not persuade Walter to pull out of the AFL-CIO sooner and let the whole truth be revealed. It was not until he fully understood the corrupting role of the AIFLD in Brazil, and heard Meany hail the overthrow of the Goulart regime, that Walter understood what he had, in all conscience, to do.

Meany, Beirne, Lovestone, and Brown persisted in their categorical denial of having received CIA funds, and when the exposé of false foundations and trusts hit the news, they moved quickly to get under a new umbrella — U.S. AID Agency — in order to proceed with the same sort of subversion of foreign governments and unions under the guise of labor work in Latin America, Africa, and Asia.

It is to the eternal credit of the UAW that its extensive overseas aid to democratic trade unions has been financed exclusively by the interest earned from investment of its strike funds. All expenditures were, and still are, approved by duly elected officers and members of the Executive Board, and are regularly reported in the audits of the UAW. The revelation of the CIA's dirty tracks through various trade unions in no way changes the fact that throughout the world hundreds of thousands — yes, millions — of union workers in legitimate federations are making their small, often heroic, contributions to the well-being and security of other working men and women far from their own lands. No exposure of dirty work, or of weak, negative, or plain stupid human nature can detract from the significance of those efforts and that faith in democracy.

CHAPTER 28

Under Five Presidents

JUST AS I had specialized in international labor as a representative of the UAW and National CIO, so Roy became the UAW expert in the field of U.S. political action; his span covered the terms of five Presidents. More than any other unionist, Roy developed imaginative programs for pushing labor legislation, ensuring the civil rights of minorities, and campaigning for candidates; these programs won for the UAW its reputation as the strongest political arm of the trade union movement.

The UAW was never just a "nickel in the pay envelope" union. Its forces having been tempered in the struggle with the world's most powerful corporations, it was not likely to permit these same economic giants to continue their monopolistic control over political life. The thirties had been a decade of organizing; the forties were spent largely on internal consolidation, in addition to the tasks related to spurring war production. By 1947, the UAW was able to give some attention to mobilizing its latent political strength. Michigan was a natural challenge; our membership concentration was great in this auto state, and the opponents primitive in their political outlook. During eighty of the previous ninety-four years, a Republican had been Governor, and the party had exercised iron control over a state legislature oriented toward the interests of big business and the rural constituency. And in 1947, of one hundred members in the state House, only five were Democrats; on the Senate side, only four out of a total of thirty-two. The Democratic Party was moribund, suffering from too little grassroots support and too much reliance on federal patronage.

At the war's end, Roy pointed out to the UAW leadership the importance of encouraging the CIO, in every city, county, and congressional district, to join with other forward-looking political organizations in each community in revitalizing the political process so that the instruments of government would become more responsive to people's needs. Walter, Roy, and the Michigan Executive Board members met with August Scholle, president of the Michigan CIO. Neil Staebler, later to become head of the Michigan Democratic Party, and other liberals, like G. Mennen Williams, who would be Governor for twelve consecutive years, contributed greatly to this new beginning. Recalling the defeat of the "labor ticket" in Detroit some years before, Roy hammered away at the need to explain that labor, in establishing a relationship with the Democratic Party, was not out to "capture it"; he argued that if anyone were even to imply this, labor would end up capturing only itself and, in the process, would antagonize the very element in the community that should be the natural allies of labor and the Democrats. Hence, he steered the discussions toward the building of a broad coalition of labor, church, ethnic minorities, and blacks. Roy cautioned that, just because union leadership had gained in stature by winning at the collective bargaining table, it could not take for granted worker support for its favored political candidates. It had to earn a following by demonstrating leadership, and by carrying out intensive political education to win the same support for social and political goals. Under his stimulus, each local union in the state was encouraged to set up a Political Action Committee (PAC) to focus attention on priority issues and mobilize the membership and the electorate. In a sense, Michigan became the arena, the testing ground, for the UAW's quest for "social democracy." In addition to a grassroots structure, we were blessed with dedicated candidates and pertinent issues. "Soapy" Williams was a tireless campaigner who, it is alleged, "campaigned 365 days every year" — at least! He took seriously our admonitions to make politics the "people's business"; no town was too small or remote, no gathering unimportant if qualified voters were in attendance. He took them all in his stride, pumping hands, kissing babies, calling square dances, and always sporting the familiar campaign symbol, his green polka dot bow tie.

So began the story of an impressive coalition of enlightened political forces, motivated not by patronage, but by the need to redress the imbalance in the state capital and to get on with the job of working for the people. This coalition, which Roy labored so long and effectively to bring into existence, permanently altered, for the better, the political character of the State of Michigan and, by example, that of many other states. Today, millions enjoy the benefits of better health insurance, education, training for unemployed workers, and the vigorous application of the laws protecting human rights. The iron control of Michigan politics by monied interests was broken.

Similarly, throughout the entire country, every local was called upon to develop its own PAC, and each of these in turn was coordinated into larger committees for every congressional district and for every state of the union. Delegates from these committees monitored congressional proceedings on labor and social questions. Day by day and week by week in each local PAC, the entire gamut of workers' concerns — health, housing, wage security — became proper matters for debate and discussion. When national conferences were held, usually addressed by members of the federal House and the Senate, delegations organized by congressional districts would visit Washington for personal talks with their representatives. Unlike the Democratic and Republican party structures, which between campaigns undertake minimal activity, the local PAC's stayed in action the year round.

Roy worked patiently to strengthen the coalition of black unionists. In collaboration with the Leadership Conference on Civil Rights, he worked with Clarence Mitchell of the NAACP, Herman Edelsberg of the Anti-Defamation League, and Joe Rauh, Washington counsel for the UAW. They fought unceasingly to abolish the filibuster, which gave a bigoted minority in the Senate a tool with which to block the majority's will.

At the historic signing of the Civil Rights Act of 1964, there gathered at the White House many who, over the years, had actively supported its enactment. As President Johnson began the complicated process of using fistfuls of pens to affix his signature and as the guests closed in, each hoping to claim one of the pens, Roy noticed Robert Kennedy, head bowed, standing toward the rear. Surely no one had contributed more to this moment than he. Roy walked over and, taking Robert by the arm gently but firmly, escorted the Attorney General to the President's side. He said, "Mr. President, I know you have reserved a pen for your Attorney General." The President did not give Kennedy only one; he gave him several, and asked that they be given to Jackie, John Doar, and Kennedy's stalwart deputy, Nicholas Katzenbach. Nor did the President overlook Roy, who had earned numerous presidential pens, but none that he treasured more than this civil right memento.

Roy was often described as more gentle and sensitive than Walter or me; certainly he was more vulnerable. Every crisis, either in his work or in the family, he took as a personal burden. He was involved in the same bitter controversies as his brothers, striving by different means toward the same goals, but he never incurred the animosity and antagonism of others, as Walter and I often did. Some people referred to Roy as "the only Reuther who seems to get on with George Meany." There was more than humor in that remark; it underscored one of his fundamental traits. He was a far better listener than Walter or I; he was sought out by many in the labor movement and in politics as a sounding board, and was often used as an intermediary to influence Walter's decisions. But Roy was also a true innovator: he was the inspiration behind the building of bridges between the union movement and its natural allies among the civil rights movement, church organizations, ethnic groups, older citizens, youth groups, farm workers. His practical skills and achievements in this regard led both John F. Kennedy and Lyndon Johnson to put him in charge of national registration drives to get out the vote among workers from coast to coast. Nothing perturbed Roy more than the prospects of a continued decline in voter participation in the essential housekeeping chores of our country's political system.

There were reasons, obvious to many, why millions of Americans were being denied their right to vote, especially in the South, and there were also identifiable obstacles being put in the way of millions of others, blocking or discouraging their political participation. Roy complained, "In some states, it's easier to get a hunting or fishing license or a pistol permit than to register and vote." For years, inside the labor movement, Roy was the spearhead of local and national campaigns to increase voter registration and participation. He knew, however, that the task was enormous, and that the roadblocks were both legal and psychological; only a concerted national effort, involving all sections of the American society, could turn it around. He was among those who urged President Kennedy to take the initiative in this effort. On March 30, 1963, Kennedy issued an

Executive Order creating the President's Commission on Registration and Voting Participation, under the chairmanship of Richard
M. Scammon and with Roy one of its members. The commission
made public its findings after eight months of intensive study of the
election laws and practices in the fifty states and the experience of
other democracies. The report confirmed that one third of our
adults do not participate in presidential elections, and that over 50
percent stay home when there are congressional elections. The picture is even more dismal when contrasted with voter turnouts in
other contemporary democracies:

  Italy: 92 percent in each of the last four national elections.
  West Germany: 78.5 percent to 87.8 percent during last fifteen years.
  Canada: 80 percent in last 3 general elections.
  Scandinavia: In Finland, Sweden, Norway, and Denmark, turnout is sig-
    nificantly and persistently higher than in the U.S.

The commission charged that "many election laws and administrative practices are unworkable, unfair, and outmoded; they obstruct
the path to the ballot box, disenfranchising millions who want to
vote," and issued specific recommendations. Most states still have a
long way to go in implementing these recommendations. Nonetheless, Roy found considerable satisfaction in having played a part in
focusing national attention on the need for election reform and in
revitalizing the entire political process.

He imposed on himself a heavy work load and spent weeks at a
time, especially during campaigns, away from his family and the
home that he and Fania had built on the outskirts of Detroit. I
remember the great pleasure he took in working with his sons,
David and Alan, grading and landscaping the grounds, and planting
about fifty small pine trees (part of a larger order Walter had bought
for his beloved Paint Creek home in Michigan), and how much he
enjoyed the all too rare evenings at home with Fania, listening to
classical music.

It was characteristic that one of the last journeys Roy made for the
UAW was to Rio Grande City, where he marched with Mexican-
American farm workers striking for union recognition and a $1.25-
an-hour wage. Roy walked the streets of that Texas border town as
he had walked other streets before — with and for the poverty-
stricken. At the height of the civil rights struggle, he walked with

Walter and Martin Luther King, Jr., on the streets of Selma and Jackson.

It is unusual for three brothers to develop and maintain the affectionate yet professional relationship that Roy, Walter, and I enjoyed. Virtually every major decision about our work, and most of those dealing with family, were tested out first by discussion among the three of us. Our characters, though so different, meshed into an efficient working unit. Walter was high-strung, aggressive, puritanical sometimes to the point of intolerance, and had such a strong body and so high a morale that nothing could block him. He suffered violent attacks, both physical and verbal, from his enemies, shook them off, and maintained his incredible energy to the end, when an act of fate felled him. Roy had empathy for all human beings; tactful, wrung by suffering, and weakened by a circulatory ailment, he softened what some called the "self-righteousness" of Walter and me. As Roy said of himself, he was not a man of words. I was the rhetorical one; Walter often turned to me for expression of the ideas we held in common and for help with articles, letters, hundreds of communications sent to Congress, the press, and prominent leaders all over the world when he became the leader of millions of laboring men and a confidant of American Presidents.

One should never underestimate, however, the importance of Roy's work at the grassroots. The PAC's were essential in maintaining contact with congressmen, who, once they are elected, are apt to do as they choose, regardless of platform commitments. FDR brought into existence a unique coalition of political forces; over many years it was the key to repeated Democratic success at the polls. The New Deal projected a concern for the problems of low-income citizens and for racial and ethnic minorities; it attracted a group, including intellectuals, that sustained Roosevelt's policies through the Democratic regimes that followed his. But this amorphous group did not constitute an integral part of the Democratic Party. It became a coalition on the eves of elections and ceased to function between elections. Moreover, the Southern Democrats were likely to stop at the water's edge when it came to voting on broad social issues, and helped Republicans defeat efforts for improving the minimum wage and Social Security. The unions quickly discovered that they had to organize themselves on a year-round basis to prevent the undermining of labor's Magna Carta, the

Wagner Labor Relations Act. They could not rely, as did most of their European trade union cousins, on any one political party's loyalty. Paul Sifton, a UAW legislative representative in Washington, once wisely observed, "A politician is only able to stand erect as he is subject to countervailing pressures from both sides." It was Roy's political action committees that worked to counter the influence of the well-heeled lobbies of the Manufacturers' Association, the Medical Association, the Milk Trust.

Those lobbies were able to get laws passed that restricted the political role of trade unions by denying them the right to use any income from dues in support of candidates for federal office. (Corporations later came under the same sort of restriction.) This meant that voluntary contributions had to be solicited from union members. Most unions limited these to one dollar per person, and it was a rare union that collected from even 50 percent of its membership. In spite of this there persists in the public mind a myth that the financial support of politicians by "big labor" is to be equated with that of big business. For even though corporations cannot legally dip into corporate earnings for political contributions, the financial potential of the wealthy certainly exceeds that of the daily wage earners. It takes ten thousand workers to make up for one $10,000 contribution of a high-salaried executive. That is why Walter, twenty years before the scandal that broke around Nixon's Committee to Re-Elect the President, advocated to a Senate committee that a law be passed restricting political contributions to five dollars per person. The burden of his testimony was that public financing of political campaigns would give substance to the cherished American dream of one person, one vote. (All of his testimony is on record in the transcript of the October 9, 1956, hearings of the Senate Subcommittee on Privileges and Elections.)

During Walter's twenty-four years as president of the UAW, he appeared nearly one hundred times before congressional committees in connection with almost every social or economic issue that came before the lawmakers. His testimony was noted for its innovation and factual accuracy, supported by careful research. He often suggested ambitious conferences in Washington at a strategic moment, when the House or the Senate was considering important labor legislation. One of these was a dinner meeting at the Mayflower Hotel with several thousand persons as guests of the AFL-CIO Industrial Union Department. Cabinet officers, thirty-five senators, and one hundred sixty-seven representatives (fifty-five of them Republicans) were there, and before such an audience Walter naturally could not restrain himself from giving the usual forty-five–minute speech. This provoked one of his closest aides to joke: "Walter had a joint session of Congress there. I knew he couldn't resist a State of the Union message."

Harry Truman remained a close personal friend long after his presidency. Walter often went to Independence for a warm reunion with the former President. The UAW chipped in generously for the Truman Library and the restoration of the birthplace home in Lamar, presenting original Truman family furniture and other period pieces in a ceremony in 1959, at which time the property was transferred to the State of Missouri.

Down-to-earth politician that he was, Truman recognized the importance of the "common" people when it came to election day. He launched his campaign on Labor Day from a rostrum in Detroit's Cadillac Square (now Kennedy Square), and on the eve of the election, which flabbergasted the pollsters as much as it did Thomas Dewey, Truman addressed one of our national PAC conferences. As he ticked off the "do-nothing Republican Congress," our UAW delegates gleefully began chanting, "Give 'em hell, Harry," which started that phrase moving all across the country. Truman's plain talk endeared him to the workers; he was a no-nonsense President. With his own painful memories of the Great Depression, he was determined that anyone able and willing to work should find employment. As he said, "We have rejected the discredited theory that the fortunes of the nation should be in the hands of a privileged few. We have abandoned the 'trickle down' concept of national prosperity . . . The American people have decided that poverty is just as wasteful and just as unnecessary as preventable disease . . . The government must work with industry, labor, and farmers in keeping our economy running at full speed."

He did not spare his friends from outspoken criticism any more than he did his opponents. Once, in 1962, Walter invited him to come out of retirement to Flint to attend an anniversary celebration of the great sit-down strikes. Truman wrote back:

Dear Walter,

I appreciate very much your letter of the 11th and I want to say to you very frankly that I don't like sit-down strikes. I am sorry to say that it will not be possible for me to be with you on February 4th anyway,

but between you and me and the gatepost I don't think you would want
me there because I would tell them exactly what I think about sit-down
strikes . . . I am for labor and the right to strike, but when you destroy
a business, especially a little man, it just isn't right and you know it as
well as I do."

Both the Republican and Democratic parties schedule open hearings
on platform issues prior to every presidential election. At one of
these, Richard Nixon, then a senator, asked Walter if there was any
aspect of the Truman foreign policy with which the CIO disagreed.
Walter said there were some. Then he added, "The essential difference between the CIO and the Republicans is that we criticize the
Truman administration for its deficiencies, and the Republican
Party criticizes it for its virtues — that is a fundamental distinction."

Eisenhower had integrity, but no zest for the political process; he
was inept at mobilizing even his own party's support for the issues to
which he committed the country. He was bored by the day-to-day
White House duties, though he enjoyed the prestige of the office.
The U.S. was just coming out of years of artificial economic stimula-
tion caused by the war and postwar needs in Europe and Korea, but
he did little to encourage the transition back to peacetime high levels
of employment. When Herling asked him during a press conference if he knew why the Republican leadership had refused to back
legislation, which he, the President, favored, for the relief of depressed areas in about fifteen states, Eisenhower gave a shocking answer: "No, you are telling me something now that I didn't know. As
a matter of fact it is one piece of legislation I was disappointed was
not passed, and I don't know the reason lying behind it."

Walter wrote President Eisenhower a long letter about the large-
scale unemployment and the "inability of the American people to
buy back a fair share of the vast and steadily increasing amount of
goods and services the American economy can produce." He wrote
that the Employment Act of 1946 needed to be implemented, now
more than ever. *Fortune* magazine was predicting the unemployment of, perhaps, five million.

Eisenhower's response was friendly but only vaguely promising.
In his 1953 inaugural address he had mentioned a few forward-
looking proposals, such as an increase in Social Security benefits, but
on the whole he was an advocate of laissez faire. He did not refer to
the minimum wage, then only seventy-five cents an hour, to control

of inflation, to civil rights, to public housing, or public works programs to bolster the declining economy. Nor did he speak of the Point Four Program, the cornerstone of our foreign policy. Walter kept at him, urging him to assume bold leadership in these areas.

As the UAW won extensive gains at the bargaining table and as its political influence expanded, Walter became more and more the whipping boy of the extreme right. I have described in Chapter 17 how the triumvirate of Goldwater, Curtis, and Mundt tried to bring both the Reuthers and the UAW down, aided by Joseph Kamp's libelous pamphlets, by alleging that Walter was a fascist who wanted to become the ruler of America.

> He is a smart, smug, arrogant labor boss. He is a bold, shrewd, foulmouthed agitator. He is a vile purveyor of vicious slander. He is a ruthless, reckless, lawless, labor goon. He is a persistent prevaricator. He is a cunning conspirator. He is a rabid anti-anti-Communist. He is a slick, sordid, conniving politician. He is a doubletalking rabblerousing opportunist who glibly repeats the fallacious fulminations of his red-tinged ghost writers . . . Walter Reuther is an evil genius.

This charming essay was published in September 1958, and included an appeal for anti-Reuther funds. It found response among many businessmen and corporation heads. Several full-page ads appeared in the *Wall Street Journal*. According to the Washington *Post*, Senator Goldwater had offered Joe Kamp assistance and encouragement to keep the stuff coming.

The protracted strike by the UAW against a despotic and backward employer in Wisconsin, the Kohler Company, which lasted twelve years and cost the UAW $13 million, became a cause célèbre among the Republicans. The *Wall Street Journal* reported that a GOP official in Washington had frankly conceded that "the labor issue is just about the only national issue worth anything to us. We have to hit it for all it's worth."

To a greater extent than American labor ever realized, some of the fast proliferating hate groups had collaborators in the AFL-CIO, joining together with the reactionary right-wing organizations that had their origins in the McCarthy period. One of these was Serafino Romualdi, Inter-American Representative for the AFL-CIO, who was responsible for liaison with Latin-American trade unions. He lectured to many right-wing assemblies; his fellow speakers often were Birchers. Groups included Fred Schwarz's Christian Anti-

Communism Crusade, Robert Morris's Defenders of American Liberty, the Cuban Freedom Committee. The latter has been cited as a major recipient of CIA funds and had five radio stations, one of them directed by Donald Bruce, whose "Manion Forum" was one of the most disgusting antilabor programs on any U.S. network.

The American Security Council was perhaps the most ambitious of all professional propaganda groups, with an annual budget of more than a quarter million. It operated initially in the blacklisting era, about 1956, "to help companies screen personnel for Communist affiliations or sympathies." Many innocent people were ruined. Lovestone served on the board of this council.

The list is almost endless. Group Research, which monitored these coalitions of hate, estimated that the combined budgets of some thirty organizations rose from $5 million in 1958 to $12.2 million in 1962, and $14.4 million in 1963. The annual budget of the ADA, often under attack from the right, was a mere $150,000 in those years. The only thing that equaled the upward spiral of verbal attack on liberalism was the sale of handguns. Schlesinger, in his *A Thousand Days*, reports that in the two years after November 1961 there were, according to the Secret Service, "thirty-four threats against the President's life from the state of Texas alone."

The nomination of John F. Kennedy for the presidency had the real, if not already declared, support of the UAW, with Roy and our Chicago Regional Director, Robert Johnston, working tirelessly in his behalf. But among the labor delegates to the Democratic convention, all hell broke loose over the naming of the candidate for Vice-President. No one had ever thought of Lyndon Johnson for the job. Walter was conferring with Leonard Woodcock, Jack Conway, Joe Rauh, Roy, and Milly Jeffrey when he received word of Kennedy's choice. There were angry cries of "double-cross!" Though Lyndon Johnson was a New Deal Democrat from FDR days, he had recently locked horns with Walter and others who had joined with civil rights leaders to try to eliminate the filibuster. Johnson had also been less than supportive of urgently needed health-care legislation. It was little consolation that Robert Kennedy had apparently not been consulted and was equally shocked.

There was a rumor that Johnson had been offered the post in the expectation he would turn it down, but Robert soon told Walter that his brother stood firmly behind the nomination and that Johnson would accept it. The long years of realistic collective bargaining taught the UAW leaders not to wallow in their disappointment but to set to work immediately to preserve unity among our labor allies. G. Mennen Williams, leader of the Michigan delegation and just recently re-elected Governor, with labor's massive backing, was considering calling for a roll-call vote on the vice-presidental nomination, and George Meany was emitting ugly sounds through his cigar smoke.

Woodcock was dispatched to talk with Williams and the Michigan delegation. After hours of wrangling in closed caucus, the delegates were brought in line behind the nomination, thus avoiding a floor fight. But it took all of Arthur Goldberg's skills and two and a half hours of hard arguing by Walter and Dubinsky to bring George Meany and his Executive Council around.

Before Kennedy left the city, he said to Walter, "I need to sit down and talk with you. I'm going to need your help. I'll give you a ring." And this led to the meeting in Hyannisport during which the idea of the Peace Corps was born and Roy was urged by Robert Kennedy to direct a nationwide registration campaign. Roy spent the next months in constant travel, often accompanying Robert and sometimes the candidate himself. At the Hyannisport meeting Walter expounded on many of his ideas on the deteriorating economic situation, health care, civil rights, unemployment. He traveled extensively during the campaign, often speaking at Kennedy rallies. We were all deeply committed, and excited by the possibilities.

The Republican nominee, Richard Nixon, following the Joseph Kamp strategy, labeled Walter "a labor leader turned radical politician," warning that if Kennedy were elected Reuther would "have a lot to do with calling the tune in the White House." It was never Walter's desire to call the tune, nor did he dance to any tune, except in the most literal sense when he and May were invited to gala affairs at the White House under both Republican and Democratic Presidents.

The margin of victory over Nixon was so razor-thin that any person or small group that helped had the satisfaction of knowing that its efforts had made a real difference. Despite our qualms, Johnson's name on the ticket and his personal efforts during the campaign certainly brought the ticket some needed strength.

John F. Kennedy's election increased the growth of hate crusades and he became the object of systematic vilification, reminiscent of the attacks on Franklin D. Roosevelt. In the world of the right wing, Kennedy had against him his youthful charisma, his wealth, intelligence, New England and Harvard background, his religion, his wife, brothers, advisers, his support of the blacks, his refusal to drop the bomb. He sounded a rational note on the subject of hate-mongers in a speech in the fall of 1961:

> In critical periods there have always been those on the fringes of our society who have sought to escape their own responsibility by finding a simple solution, an appealing slogan or a convenient scapegoat . . . They look suspiciously at their neighbors and their leader. They call for a "man on horseback" because they do not trust the people. They find treason in our churches, in our highest court . . . They equate the Democratic Party with the welfare state, the welfare state with Socialism, Socialism with Communism . . . Let our patriotism be reflected in the creation of confidence in one another, rather than in crusades of suspicion — above all, let us remember, however serious the outlook, however harsh the task, the one great irreversible trend in the history of the world is on the side of liberty.

Some time before President Kennedy's assassination, he talked with Robert and others about how to cope with the many threats he had received, especially from Texas. Robert turned to Walter — Walter knew a lot about the subject firsthand — and to Joe Rauh and me to put some concrete suggestions on paper. The final draft was approved by Walter on December 19, 1961; it was a twenty-four-page memorandum on the radical right in America, ending with, "It is very late in the day to be dealing with these problems, but it will never get earlier."

Soon some of our recommendations were implemented and right-wing groups cried out that they were being "persecuted." Parts of the memorandum leaked to the press and added fuel to the campaign to "get Reuther, the man to beat." Many of our suggestions were distorted and twisted by right wingers, yet we did not feel free to release the true text of a document that had been requested in confidence by the President, and we stuck to that policy over the years. Now that both the President and his Attorney General are dead, the memorandum is a matter of public record, and can be found in the Appendix of this book.

I feel that if more of our urgent recommendations had been acted on, the American tragedy that began with the two Kennedy assassinations, the murder of Dr. King, and continued with the Nixon election might have been avoided.

For newly elected John F. Kennedy, the Bay of Pigs' fiasco left scars. Though the unwise venture had been planned during the last days of the Eisenhower regime and was too far underway, the young President was told, to be canceled, he took full responsibility for the tragedy.

The fate of the twelve hundred men rotting in Castro's prisons weighed heavily on him. Many were badly wounded; others were being physically abused; and their continued presence behind bars was a source of almost daily propaganda for the cocky Castro. In May 1961, in a speech exhorting the workers and peasants of Cuba to increase industrial and farm output, he challenged the U.S. to exchange the more than 1200 prisoners for 500 bulldozers or tractors, and without waiting for any response, recruited ten of the captives from Brigade 2506 to go to Miami to dramatize his offer. That was the beginning of the Tractors for Freedom affair, which in its own way became a fiasco too.

President Kennedy could not put the United States officially in a position of yielding to a barter offer so reminiscent of Hitler's demand for trucks in exchange for concentration camp prisoners. Nor could he ignore Castro's proposal and thus give him a political weapon with which to embarrass the United States. He therefore sought to achieve through a private committee what could not be done officially. He first telephoned Mrs. Roosevelt, then Walter, and later Dr. Milton Eisenhower, brother of the former President and head of the Johns Hopkins University. He asked them to join together to form a special committee to respond to Castro's proposal and raise the necessary funds for 500 agricultural tractors. The three agreed to serve.

Time was of the essence. The delegation of prisoners had arrived in Miami on May 20. A few days later Kennedy, in announcing the formation of the committee, said:

> The Tractors for Freedom movement is a wholly private humanitarian movement aiming at saving the lives of several hundred men . . .
> When Fidel Castro first made his offer to "exchange" the lives and liberty of twelve hundred prisoners for five hundred agricultural tractors,

the American people responded with characteristic compassion. A number of private committees were organized to raise the necessary funds . . . My concern was to help make certain that a single, representative group of citizens headed this effort in the United States. I am grateful to Mrs. Roosevelt, Walter Reuther, and Dr. Milton Eisenhower for their leadership. The United States Government has not been and cannot be a party to these negotiations. But when private citizens seek to help prevent suffering in other lands through voluntary contributions . . . neither law nor equity calls upon us to impose obstacles in their path . . . I hope that all citizens will contribute what they can.

The President obviously felt such a long explanation necessary because some Republicans were already beginning to place obstacles in the committee's way. One was Richard Nixon, who pontificated about "lives being bartered." The President's response to this display of partisan politics was to broaden the committee by the addition of another Republican, Joseph M. Dodge, Detroit banker and former director of the Bureau of the Budget. He agreed to serve as treasurer.

The Tractors for Freedom Committee wired Castro that it would raise the funds to provide the tractors and would meet the delegation of ten prisoners at any mutually convenient place. The Immigration Department quickly cleared them and escorted them to Washington, where I had arranged to meet them at the Statler Hotel on May 22. Since the committee did not want to spend any of the contributors' money for administrative purposes, the Washington office of the UAW was made available, along with my services as an executive director.

The ten men told us in confidence that if they failed to receive a positive response within seventy-two hours, they were to return to Cuba, but if assurances were given, they could stay four days more. If they returned empty-handed, they would be sentenced to twenty-five to thirty years of hard labor. They said that Castro wanted D-8 Super Caterpillar tractors, and therein lay the first frustration of our committee. Super D-8 tractors are not designed to pull plows and harrows; they are used for the building of expressways and the clearing of land for gigantic airstrips and/or missile sites. It looked very much as if Castro was deceiving his own people when he told them he would help them increase agricultural crops by means of the exchange. Our committee had no intention of providing Castro with equipment to build missile sites nor would the State Department have authorized an export license for it. The prisoner delegation told us that Castro resented the use of the word *exchange* and insisted that the process be called *indemnification.* This produced another, even more serious problem later on.

In the course of talking with agricultural experts recommended by Secretary of Agriculture Orville Freeman, and culled from various universities, we discovered that in the whole United States there were no more than fifty or sixty D-8's in use. By putting 500 of them on the island of Cuba, we might well be helping Castro return some favors to the Soviet Union or China. There was hardly a bridge in Cuba that could carry the weight of the D-8, nor would the roads stand the strain. We therefore cabled Castro that we would send him an assortment of smaller tractors with attachments suitable for improving Cuban agricultural production.

We also asked for official confirmation from Castro that he would carry out the release of the 1214 prisoners, as proposed in his speech of May 17, and would send us a list of the names of said prisoners. We made clear that we could not proceed with any shipment until we heard from his government, and that we did not think it unreasonable to insist that the official confirmation come no later than June 7.

From then on it was cables back and forth, with Castro backing and filling, changing the game, indulging in polemics. We sent a team of agricultural experts to Cuba to see what the farmers there really needed. The team was accompanied by an interpreter who had been recommended by the State Department, a Dr. Pineda, assistant professor of Spanish at American University in Washington. He was a U.S. citizen of Chilean origin, and a former American GI. John Hooker, young Nashville lawyer who was a close friend of the Deputy U.S. Attorney General, and I escorted the team to the airport. After we saw them off, Hooker and I were having a drink in the VIP lounge at the National Airport when a phone call came from Hooker's friend, the Deputy Attorney General, telling us that his office had just been told that the interpreter we had sent to Cuba, and who had been cleared completely by the intelligence division of the State Department, was in reality a Castro agent. At that point I exploded, and tried to find out on whose authority Pineda had been chosen. Later that day I talked to Pat Greathouse, UAW vice-president and chairman of the delegation of agricultural experts, and he agreed with me when I said I thought someone was trying to blow the President's efforts sky-high and that he should go on as planned but keep a close watch on the movements of Dr. Pineda.

Nothing in the course of their Havana stay aroused any suspicion on the part of the experts as to the loyalty of the interpreter, who remained close to the group and acted in a most responsible way. This confirmed the suspicion that the CIA was trying to throw a monkey wrench into Kennedy's plan — perhaps still taking revenge on him for not turning the Air Force loose in support of its ill-conceived invasion.

When the experts talked with the prisoners, they complained that Castro had told them the equipment offered by the Tractors for Freedom Committee was not worth the $28 million he considered compensation for damages; he wanted the 500 giant D-8 bulldozers or their total dollar value.

Our team learned from Cuban technicians, who were overseeing agrarian reform, a very significant fact: Cuba had already ordered smaller tractors from other countries. They said they wanted the heavy equipment for road-building. They admitted that some 41 percent of the plots of land under cultivation in Cuba were so small that oxen were usually used. When our experts met with Castro, the ambiguities increased, but the upshot was that he insisted on calling the whole exchange "indemnity" for the material damage caused during the invasion of April 17, and indicated that money, to the tune of $28 million in cash, would do as well if not better than tractors.

We had made clear to Castro from the beginning that as private citizens we were not authorized to enter into any discussion of indemnification claims and we at no time agreed to a specific price tag. Now Castro's shift was making any further negotiations almost impossible, though it is just conceivable that we could have drawn up a list of agricultural equipment, excluding the mammoth D-8's, that would have brought the dollar value of the package close to Castro's $28 million figure, and the prisoners would have been freed that year.

Meanwhile at home the final kibosh was put on the committee. While Nixon made public remarks about "this submission to blackmail," Republicans put enormous pressure on Dodge and Dr. Eisenhower to withdraw from the committee. Some even said they would cut off their contributions to Johns Hopkins if Dr. Eisenhower would not change his ways. It was Castro's constant harping on indemnification that gave the Republicans their weapon. Neither Dodge nor Dr. Eisenhower "could stand the heat" — in Truman's words — and so "got out of the kitchen." They threatened to resign from a committee they had joined with considerable enthusiasm.

The Tractors for Freedom Committee decided, to avoid embarrassing President Kennedy, that it should disband. It did so with sorrow and with regret "that Dr. Castro had switched his offer from 500 tractors to 28 million dollars . . . knowing full well that a proposal for cash indemnification or prisoner for prisoner exchange is legally and practically beyond the scope and authority of our voluntary citizens committee."

The sad result was that in March 1962 the captives were put on trial in Havana and there was every indication that a large number would be executed. Some had already died in prison of injuries or illness. Finally Robert Kennedy, with the assistance of Richard Goodwin, who had worked closely with our committee, persuaded James D. Donovan to intercede with Castro and exchange the surviving prisoners for $62 million worth of food and medical supplies.

Thus the partisan Republicans who brought down the Tractors for Freedom effort, which might very possibly have succeeded in 1961, upped the final cost to the people of the United States from $28 million to $62 million.

Every single contribution to our committee made by an identified donor was returned; those not identified were turned over to the U.S. Treasury. All the administrative expenses — mailings, the trips to and from Cuba by the experts — were not paid by John F. Kennedy, the State Department, or the CIA. The bill was footed by the Industrial Union Department of the AFL-CIO, of which Walter was president. All of us who worked on the committee received personal letters of thanks from President Kennedy.

The all too short Kennedy era was exciting more by reason of its youthful aura and the hopes it held out rather than for any great policy changes or actual socioeconomic progress. Access to the White House and its staff had never been so easy; there was a willingness to listen even to bold suggestions on foreign policy. Able

men were enlisted for important positions, and the nation again had
the feeling it was moving forward.   In the area of civil rights, the denial and procrastination of one hundred years were being rectified
by firm leadership in the White House; the paths were being cleared
to prepare both the country and Congress for long-delayed legislation.

I was in Tunis, about to join a large UAW delegation for a series
of discussions in African and Arab countries, when the terrible news
came.   The U.S. Embassy phoned my host, the labor attaché, whom
I had known since Detroit days.   The message was that there were
unconfirmed radio reports that Kennedy had been shot in Dallas.
No word yet from Washington.   Dead silence; shock; disbelief.
"Those bastards." I burst out.   "They've finally killed him."   There
flashed before my mind bitter memories of the hatred and prejudice
that had been nourished and broadcast across America for so many
years.   I realized then that I had always been afraid of exactly this
moment.

We went to the Embassy and waited through the night, a sad and
solemn group waiting for the confirmation of what we feared, that
all hope was gone.   The next day we decided we could not possibly
continue our trip and canceled all reservations for the delegation except for those who were homeward-bound.   Rarely have I seen such
a public display of grief over the death of a foreign leader as in the
streets of Tunis.   All sorts of men and women, especially the young,
had identified with that energetic, imaginative American, who had
held out hope to them as he had to us.   Long, long lines formed at
the American Embassy; the Tunisians wanted to express their sympathy.   I rushed back to Washington to meet Walter.

I met Walter in the Washington hotel suite of Willy Brandt.   Soon
Harold Wilson joined us, Olof Palme, and Hubert Humphrey — all
of us glued to the television set, watching Lyndon Johnson trying to
comfort and unify a nation in shock.   Because of my own outrage at
the assassination, I am sure I gave strong credence to the suspicions
of our overseas friends that the murder had been plotted carefully
in advance.   The shooting of Lee Harvey Oswald added to everyone's doubts that the assassination was carried out by one psychotic
individual.

Walter's immediate reaction was to draft a statement for me to
transmit to trade union and political friends around the world, reas-

suring them of Johnson's basic integrity and our belief that he would continue the Kennedy programs. On Saturday, after returning from the White House to view the body of the slain President, Walter began to compose a telegram to President Johnson, offering his prayers and expressing his confidence in Johnson's "courage, competence, and compassion." Just then Humphrey rang up to tell Walter that the President would call him around four-thirty that afternoon. Johnson's first words were, "My friend, I need your friendship and support now more than ever before." He wanted to sit down and talk with him, but in the meantime would Walter rush off to him a brief memorandum setting down those issues he felt were most crucial at the moment.

Walter's memorandum stressed the need for strengthening national unity and rejecting extremism and hate campaigns. He called for a pledge to continue to seek peace; to improve the quality of our society and utilize our potential. Civil rights and equal job opportunity, better education, a decent job for every American able and willing to work — all these were long overdue.

There is a familiar ring to these recommendations; Walter had been making them all his adult life to one U.S. President or another. His relationship with Lyndon Johnson had grown over the years. In 1958 they had an exchange of letters when the Kohler strike was on, and Walter insisted on clearing the reputation of both the UAW and the Reuthers before a Senate investigating committee. Walter wrote to Johnson, among others things, that in that hearing Goldwater, Mundt, and Curtis were obviously digging for political pay dirt and not facts about the strike, and that he had advised them they would get more votes if they showed some concern for the plight of the unemployed, the problems of farmers, school and hospital needs. "As was to be expected, they did not appreciate my advice." Johnson wrote back: "I was strengthened by your warm and generous letter . . . It is my experience that those who dig for political pay dirt usually find themselves digging their own political graves."

Walter's hopes were buoyed by Johnson's inaugural address and especially by his taking on the war against poverty as a national goal. He was also reassured to see a Southerner so genuinely concerned with civil rights. Walter pledged the enlistment of "the officers and the one and a half million members of the UAW . . . for the duration of the war against poverty." There were many phone calls and meetings between Walter and the President in the ensuing months. After Walter and Roy marched with Martin Luther King and demonstrated in Selma, Walter was so upset by the events there that he sent what was perhaps his strongest message to Johnson:

> Americans of all religious faiths, all political persuasions, and from every section of our nation are deeply shocked and outraged at the tragic events in Selma, Alabama. And they look to the Federal Government as the only possible source to protect and guarantee the exercise of constitutional rights, which is being denied and destroyed by the Dallas County law enforcement agents and the Alabama state troops under the direction of Governor George Wallace . . . Mr. President, I join in urging you to take immediate and appropriate steps, including the use of Federal Marshalls and troops if necessary, so that the full exercise of . . . free assembly and free speech may be fully protected. Sunday's spectacle of tear gas, night sticks, whips, and electric cattle prods used against defenseless citizens demonstrating to secure their constitutional right to register and vote as American citizens was an outrage against all decency. This shameful brutality by law enforcement agents makes a mockery of America's concept of justice and provides effective ammunition to Communist propagandists and our enemies around the world who would weaken and destroy us.

In the area of social reform no U.S. President since Roosevelt (and perhaps to an even greater extent than he) was as able and willing as Lyndon Johnson to push through basic legislation for improvement of the rights of minorities and for headlong attack on that most insidious enemy: poverty.

Yet Johnson's great successes with Congress were to be overshadowed by his blindness to international realities. He was influenced by slogans; too ready to accept the judgment of generals and admirals. He lacked Truman's determination to keep the military under firm civilian control.

The Vietnam War was doubly painful for Walter: first, the senseless killing in a lost cause; second, the evidence of the fatal flaw in his relationship with President Johnson, whom he could not help admiring for achievements on the domestic front. Olof Palme summed it up many years later when he recalled a meeting at the home of Gunnar Jarring after the burial of Kennedy:

> The drums were silent. So was the lonely trumpet at Arlington. We had walked far . . . There was Walter Reuther and there was Hubert Humphrey. We discussed the future. Walter was stubbornly vindicat-

ing his conviction that Johnson had to carry on the Kennedy policies. He told us, "He got his education during Roosevelt's New Deal. He will, better than Kennedy himself, get Kennedy's policies through Congress . . . He needs labor and we need him and Humphrey will be the next Vice-President. Goldwater has no chance in the election. But in foreign policy Lyndon Johnson is an unknown quantity, almost surely ignorant especially regarding Southeast Asia and Africa."

Palme concluded: "Many have forgotten the first success of Johnson in home politics. Nobody has forgotten his failure in the field of foreign policy." (The records of our conversations are in the Victor G. Reuther papers in the Wayne State University archives.)

Later, when Humphrey was Vice-President, I tried my hand at convincing him to take some initiative on the question of Vietnam, but to no avail. His personal loyalty to Johnson would not permit him to exercise his own judgment. In the latter days of that administration I had a talk with him about his political future. It was obvious he wanted the Democratic nomination for President, and I told him very frankly that because he had not made a clean break with Johnson's foreign policy he might get the nomination but would not win the election — nor did I think he deserved to.

I left his office discouraged and sad. The Reuthers, all of us, had had a long and close friendship with Humphrey over the years. I knew, too, that he was committed to the cause of peace, though he could not see his way clear to express his own feelings and opinions. The sadness was increased by my knowledge that without Walter's solid and energetic intervention Humphrey probably would not have been chosen by Johnson to be his Vice-President.

The Democratic convention of 1964, which nominated Johnson for his second term, had been torn asunder by the seating of delegates from Mississippi. Johnson's old-line traditionalists had chosen the lily white group that was being challenged by the black Mississippi Freedom Democratic Party. Johnson's floor manager tried to smooth things over by offering the Freedom Party seats in the gallery and proposing for the convention a new set of rules, to apply in the future, that would ensure a better racial mixture in Southern delegations. Our UAW lawyer, Joe Rauh, who was also acting as counsel for the Freedom Democrats, proposed the compromise of seating both groups with equal privileges, but many Southern delegates threatened to walk out if the blacks were handed delegate credentials under any circumstances. This was a spectacle Johnson wanted to avoid. He appealed to Walter to go down to the convention and take a personal hand in the negotiations. Walter was hesitant because he was engrossed in crucial bargaining with General Motors and was preoccupied with our father's grave illness.

He gave in to Johnson, however, and arrived in Atlantic City around midnight on August 25. After being briefed by some of Johnson's advisers, including Humphrey, Walter began shuttling back and forth between the two groups of delegates.

Walter had known Joe Rauh personally as well as professionally over a long period, and nothing could have put such a strain on their relationship as this delegation fight. There was no illusion that Walter was there as a free agent; he was avowedly there in behalf of the President, trying to avoid an open break. He finally worked out a new version of the original Johnson compromise, which called for seating two of the Freedom Democrats, Aaron Henry and Ed King, with full voting rights, and included a stronger guarantee of fair treatment for blacks at future conventions. I can understand Joe Rauh's feeling irate at Walter's doing Johnson's legwork.

At any rate, the all-white delegation walked out rather than sign the loyalty pledge, and the Freedom Party rejected the compromise. Walter gained little from his all-night efforts except to increase his influence with Johnson, and when he went to the White House the next day and learned to his dismay that the President was considering choosing a running mate from a group we considered unacceptable, Walter bore down heavily, at this eleventh hour, for the choice of Hubert Humphrey as Vice-President. This healed the rift with Joe Rauh. And, for once, George Meany agreed with Walter.

There was more than a touch of irony in Johnson's asking Roy to do for him what he had done so effectively for John Kennedy; namely, to get out the vote of the entire country for his presidential campaign. Not so long before, he was after Roy's scalp and, perhaps unwittingly, became involved in a macabre maneuver to have Walter do the hatchet job. Frank W. McCulloch, then administrative assistant to Senator Paul H. Douglas, recalled the hectic lobbying efforts by a coalition of liberal, labor, church, and civil rights groups to effect a change in Senate Rule 22 (that is, to end filibustering), and the crude arm-twisting that the then Senate Majority Leader, Lyndon Johnson, and his assistant, Robert G. "Bobby" Baker, were employing to maintain the status quo, so dear to the Southern bloc.

On Thursday evening, January 8, 1959, McCulloch was speaking with Baker in the first-floor hallway of the Capitol. Roy came by and McCulloch introduced him to Baker. Roy, welcoming a chance to express his feelings to an emissary of Johnson's, said to Baker, "Our people are deeply disturbed by the pressures being placed on senators to oppose a real rule change and support the proposal of the Majority Leader. Our people go out and ask for votes for these candidates, tell people the candidates are going to support the Democratic platform, or have given their backing to this civil rights and antifilibustering campaign, and to help them win. Then they find the party leadership here working for just the opposite, and they're mad."

Baker sought refuge in some gobbledygook about "diversity within the party being one of its sources of strength," but Roy reminded him that "diversity requires that the views of all senators be reflected, and elected officials resent being pressured to conform to the views of the Majority Leader." Baker countered that there could be only one leader, that Johnson had been elected unanimously, and that he had every right to exercise the functions of a leader for what he believed was right. "Not so," replied Roy, "when the Majority Leader's views are opposed to the views of the Democratic Party and the platform commitments."

Roy and all who worked for civil rights felt betrayed. While the exchange between Roy and Baker was "not the honeysuckle treatment to which we are accustomed from some of our Southern friends," recalled McCulloch, "there was nothing dishonorable in Roy's stating frankly his concerns; it is probably fortunate that someone had the courage to express a critical view about this directly to the Majority Leader's representative rather than to have the wounds from these types of operations fester . . ."

Fester they did, and everyone knew about them. Soon Baker was promoting an open campaign to discredit Roy. What better way than to undercut him with his influential brother? Personal telephone calls started coming in to Walter from Johnson, Speaker of the House Sam Rayburn, and even from David Dubinsky, protesting Roy's alleged "dressing down" of the assistant to the Majority Leader. On Roy's return to Detroit, Walter said, "I hear you've been a busy little boy." Both were amused that anyone believed he could pit one Reuther against another, and on an issue to which both were so unalterably committed.

(The letter and memo from Frank McCulloch, and the memo from Fania Reuther are in the Wayne State University archives.)

The Johnson-Humphrey campaign was launched at a big Labor Day rally in Detroit, where Walter introduced the President to his hometown audience. In spite of his own opposition to the Vietnam War, Walter insisted that any change in foreign policy must be made by the appropriate means. He blasted the president of the Longshoremen's Union for refusing to handle wheat bound for the Soviet Union, accusing him of "trying to become the Secretary of State." Foreign policy, insisted Walter, cannot be made by marchers on the picket line any more than by right-wing groups. In the summer of 1967, when negotiations were underway between the UAW and the AVCO Corporation, which was heavily involved in defense work for the Vietnam War, both Labor Secretary Willard W. Wirtz and President Johnson pressured Walter not to let AVCO's work be interrupted.

Our father, in the meantime, had reached what looked like the last stage of his last illness; he had suffered a heart attack, and Walter was, of course, in Wheeling. President Johnson sent him a subtle but insistent telegram: ". . . My prayers are with you both and you can call on me for assistance. I know how much your father will be comforted by your presence. His pride in you is confirmed again by recent courageous and effective efforts on your country's behalf. Secretary Wirtz shares my great hope that you will be able to see it through despite this family tragedy. You have all my sympathy and encouragement as does your dear mother who I know will find you a tower of strength at this time."

Walter felt forced to yield to this plea and left the bedside of our father, who had been in the intensive care unit but who recovered sufficiently to leave the hospital. He lived for several more months.

Yet as President Johnson continued the incredible escalation of our military activity in Vetnam, the UAW could not be silent; the Reuthers could not be silent. At the outset of the hostilities, the rank-and-file auto workers were sympathetic with the official government position, and Walter moved with caution in his break with Johnson on the Vietnam War lest his personal views separate him too far from the membership. He countenanced the vigorous antiwar views of Emil Mazey, Paul Schrade, regional director on the West Coast, and me. Sometimes he tried to rein us in if he thought we were too far ahead, but there was no doubt as to what his convictions were: the U.S. never should have become involved in the first place. Also, the U.S. had violated the Geneva accord, under which we were to do everything we could to promote free elections in Vietnam after the French evacuation. President Roosevelt had earlier made a commitment to Ho Chi Minh to the same effect in return for his assistance against the Japanese, when they were sweeping down through Southeast Asia. President Eisenhower himself admitted that had elections been held under proper international control the North Vietnamese would have won overwhelmingly. Instead, there were no real elections; there were only deals, excused because they were made in the name of anti-Communism.

Finally, in spite of reluctance to break with the President, the UAW and other important trade unions took a firm stand against the continuation of the war. (I myself had the opportunity to go to Vietnam and talk with the unionized workers in Saigon; I saw the miserable condition of the people and understood their longing for peace.) As nuclear weapon testing increased, both Walter and I became involved with SANE, founded in the U.S. with the issuance of an "appeal to the men in Geneva," signed by Albert Schweitzer, Trygve Lie, Bertrand Russell, and Eleanor Roosevelt. By the time the Moscow Agreement (the nuclear test-ban treaty) was signed in 1963, the UAW had become one of the strongest groups working for its ratification, and received the Eleanor Roosevelt Peace Award in 1971.

On the seventeeth of November, 1967, our father died. It is of some consolation to remember that three years before that, my mother and father had had their whole family around them for their sixtieth anniversary. Over thirty descendants, including great-grandchildren, gathered with them in a little Italian restaurant, Figarretti's, in a suburb of Wheeling. It was the last time the entire family would be intact.

Valentine had survived persecution and discrimination during World War I because of his national origin, his political beliefs, and his trade union vocation. He and my mother overcame the lean years of unemployment; he suffered the tragic loss of one eye; they grew a family that made them proud and happy. At their jubilee I had a small tape recorder. Many speeches were made, praising our parents and affirming, as Walter put it, "what we lacked in our childhood in material things were more than compensated for in terms of spiritual things . . . because you can grow up the son or grandson of a multimillionaire and you can be the poorest human being in the world . . . We went through troubled times together, but we never lost our faith in the things that we believed in . . ." Ted and Ann were thanked by us all for carrying "the major load and responsibility of the family . . . with great credit and integrity" while the other three brothers were out locking horns with Ford and General Motors and traveling all over the world.

Roy said to the younger members of the family, "I want to let you in on a family secret. We did have horns. Walter had horns, Victor had horns, and Ted did; but I want to tell you how we got the horns. Grandma Reuther — Mütterschen, as we call her — had a broad wedding ring. And when we did things that we were not to do, she wouldn't spank us; she'd just sort of 'kaplunk' — tap us. And later on a doctor . . . wondered what all those bumps were on my head."

Chris, who came last, said, "What can a kid sister say following four gassers? There's one thing that bothers me — I didn't get in on this . . . 'clunking' but I still got the lumps. That makes me feel good because I know I'm really related even though I was at the tail end. And it really is a great occasion!"

I said I had been lucky to know members of our family on the other side of the water because it was part of our heritage, and I told about taking Dad and Mother to Edigheim in the Rhine Valley. It was exactly sixty years since my father had last set foot on European soil when he and my mother came to visit Sophie and me in Paris. "Two wars had taken place in this little village since he left as a boy of eleven. I remember Dad looking around trying to orient himself and the only thing he could possibly recognize was what remained of an old church steeple. And from there he could begin to figure out where once his family home stood . . . As we were wandering around . . . an old man approached from the opposite direction. His hair and beard were white; he was hump-shouldered . . . Dad looked at him and called him by a nickname. The man stood in utter amazement.

" 'Why do you call me by that name?'

"Dad replied, 'When I was a little boy there was a man in this village who looked just like you and that's what we called him.'

"The old man answered, 'That was my father.' "

" 'That's a pretty good memory,' I said to Vater."

After my remarks about Europe, Walter joked: "We'd like to point out that the reason Victor is getting a bit broad in the midsection is that he's carrying a responsibility on both sides. If you make proper allowances you can understand this." I said I enjoyed every extra inch.

The young were asked to speak and several of them recalled the wonderful vacations spent with their grandparents on Bethlehem Hill.

From Theo and Robert: "We'd walk over to Seel's with Grandma and get eggs over the years when she didn't have her chickens and then we'd walk down the path toward the little outhouse and there were red raspberries and strawberries and gooseberries and there were currants and there was a cooler cellar underneath the wash-house and you'd go down there and there'd be something good to drink down there . . . I remember Grossvater taking me down to the workshop and we made a map out of plywood with a band saw."

"When he took me down to the workshop it wasn't for such light affairs!" put in Roy.

We ended with a German song. Within three years Vater was gone. After the June 1967 heart attack, Mütterschen's efforts were valiant, but she could not manage the essential care; so he was transferred to the Peterson Home near Elmgrove and was visited every day by her, or Ted, or Ann, or by Roy, Walter, or me whenever we could get there by rearranging our schedules. He had periods of lucidity. But on one occasion, after taking each of our hands and smiling in recognition, he whispered to the nurse, "These are guests of mine. They have traveled far. Would you please serve them a beer?"

Solicitous of others to the end, he died on November 17, 1967, with Mütterschen holding his hand in her two palms and the five of us in a semicircle around his bed, singing softly the old German folk songs he had loved and taught us so well. His eyes opened for a second and a fleeting smile passed across his face. He was saying thank you and farewell.

He was spared the sufferings of the Reuther family and the nation that began in 1968. Only two months after his death, we were dealt the unbelievable blow of a second break in our close family circle. Roy had not been well at Dad's funeral. By January, he was working strenuously to crank up the machinery for the 1968 Democratic presidential campaign, as he had in 1960 and 1964, and he was burdened by the possible division in the party as several presidential hopefuls — Humphrey, Robert Kennedy, Eugene McCarthy, and others — announced their intentions. A very heavy work schedule probably contributed to the heart attack, the first signs of which came early on the morning of January 10. Fania wanted to call an ambulance but Roy insisted that they drive to the hospital. Fania herself had not been well for some time, but she took the wheel. On the way, he suffered a massive attack — and was gone.

Walter, who had been telephoned by Fania, dropped everything and rushed to join her; May was left to call me with the terrible news. I was so shaken that it was some time before I could believe what had happened. Finally I summoned the composure to telephone the rest of the family. How could it be broken to our mother, still not used to the void left by our father's death?

Once again we gathered, full of the sorrow that never runs dry in the human heart. A multitude of Roy's friends were with us — from every walk of life. We heard the same question from many lips: "Why this sweet man and why at this early age?" There was one among the mourners who came and sat with us in the small private room reserved for family, and his presence gave solace to each of us. He knew only too well what we were feeling. The boyish look had gone from Robert Kennedy's face; there were deep lines of grief there. With his sympathy, he gave us, too, an unspoken exhortation to carry on.

Many projects would be undertaken in Roy's memory but none that would touch us as tenderly as the gesture of Cesar Chavez and the United Farm Workers in Delano, California. Roy had been the first trade union leader of any power and influence to recognize the justice of their struggle; it was he who had tried to arouse an indifferent trade union movement and nation to their cause. When Chavez and his union completed a small building for their national headquarters, they dedicated it to Roy. Walter and Roy's younger son, Alan, flew to California for the cornerstone ceremony and the placing of a commemorative plaque by Chavez: "In memory of our brother, Roy L. Reuther, who understood our struggle."

Walter and Roy and I had had such a close relationship that Roy's death left a sense of emptiness that has never gone away. Walter sought comfort in realizing the dream he and Roy had shared — the Family Education Center for UAW workers in a wooded area on the shores of Black Lake near Onaway in northern Michigan. Together they had tramped through the snow when the property was first purchased, talking about where the buildings might best be placed on the site. Walter was to live long enough to see that vision made real.

1968 rapidly because a year of tragedy for the nation and for us: the assassination of two friends who might have changed the course of public events — Robert Kennedy and Martin Luther King, Jr. — and the ushering in of the Nixon era. Johnson's obsession with the Vietnam War, and the failure of Humphrey to dissociate himself from the military escalation, were largely responsible for the Democratic Party's losing the confidence of the American people, and brought to an end many of the constructive domestic programs that the Johnson administration had initiated.

There had never been any secret about how the UAW or the Reuthers felt about Nixon, who had used lies and underhanded means to defeat reputable political leaders, such as Jerry Voorhis and Helen Gahagan Douglas. Nothing in his career changed our opinion about his opportunism and questionable motivations. The Great Society was dismantled as quickly as possible.

There was some futile correspondence between Walter and President Nixon on the causes of inflation. Walter asserted that the UAW had never pressed demands contributing to rising costs.

> I think it is pertinent to note that wage increases did not trigger the current round of inflation. In the manufacturing industry, for example, wholesale prices began their rise in 1964 at a time when unit labor costs were actually declining. The ratio of profits to sales was already rising, pointing up the fact that *labor costs provided no justification for the price boosts.* Unit labor costs did not begin to increase until about a year and a half after acceleration of the rise in consumer prices compelled workers to seek larger wage increases to protect their family living standards. Secretary of Labor Shultz publicly acknowledged recently [this was in October 1969] that the present inflation is not the result of exorbitant wage increases . . . Our concern has been increased by reports . . . that the leaders of big business in America consider an increase in unemployment to be "desirable." (Italics mine.)

Strangely enough, it was in October of that fatal year that Walter and I had a brush with death as we flew to Washington in one of the

Executive Jet Aviation, Incorporated, planes that Walter sometimes used. (The UAW had an annual contract with that charter airline.) A slight rain was falling as we circled for an 11:35 P.M. landing at Dulles Airport in Washington. At 500 or 600 feet the copilot called, "Runway in sight," and the pilot went visual. The sky at this point was clear and the plane was allowed by the tower to continue its descent toward the runway. At that very instant, both pilots realized the aircraft was too low.

As the pilot leveled, there was a jolt, the plane shuddered, and when the wheels touched there was a loud dragging and scraping sound, and then enormous sparks as the metal hit the concrete. The plane whipped from side to side, nearly capsizing, but the pilots held it to the runway until it had slowed sufficiently to allow them to maneuver it onto the soft surface of an open field. The engines and all electric power were cut off and we were told to leave the plane at once. Suspecting a fuel leak and fearing a fire, the crew even cut radio contact with the tower. For a period of minutes that seemed an hour, they went all over the craft. We could see that we had struck a steel girder as we landed: some four feet of it were rammed into the tail section and another six feet projected from the tail section to the ground. It was later determined that this steel object was "the inner marker antenna which is approximately 12 feet above the ground and 82 feet below the proper glide angle for an ILS approach." The altimeter setting was reported to have been 29.96.

When the crew decided it was safe to resume radio contact with the tower, which had no idea where we were, a rescue car came out to retrieve us. Driving into Washington, Walter calmly remarked, "I guess this wasn't intended to be our time."

CHAPTER 29

Servus

THERE WAS virtually nothing constructive Walter could do under President Richard M. Nixon. In mid-April of 1970, when the UAW met in its annual convention, for the last time under the gavel of Walter Reuther, the delegates heard him say: "Three recessions in eight years, and now Mr. Nixon is making the same mistakes again . . . Mr. Nixon says the way to stop inflation is to soften the economy, slow it down . . . So Mr. Nixon has given us both more unemployment and more inflation in one economic package."

During 1969, Walter gave more and more of his energies to the building of the beautiful center where workers could study, play, bring their families, train to be leaders in the trade union movement — "leaders who combine technical competence with social vision, idealism, and commitment."

He had been impressed and influenced by Scandinavian and Japanese architecture as well as by the treatment of landscape in our national parks, especially Yosemite. Under his loving care, the UAW Family Education Center became more than a facility or a group of buildings; it became a community within a park. One of its great charms is the way it nestles around a series of trout ponds, connected by a winding trout stream. It reminded Walter and May of the serenity of their own Paint Creek land near Rochester, Michigan, where Walter had built his retreat home, mostly with his own hands. Every tree was cherished; he even shifted roof lines to save a most precious one. At the Black Lake site, Walter tramped for hours, identifying trees that must not be disturbed, marking them with yellow plastic bands. Woe to any construction man who backed his truck or tractor into one of them!

He had as architect his close friend Oskar Stonorov, internationally renowned as a planner as well as an architect, and a sculptor to boot. The center was built to provide year-round housing for nearly 500 students or guests and a permanent teaching and management staff; it has a large dining hall and lecture complex, a gymnasium that can serve as a concert or lecture hall seating 1200; and an indoor swimming pool. The intellectual nerve center is the library; there are a dozen separate classrooms nearby for small study groups.

The outdoor scene was so beautiful that wherever possible he and Stonorov planned to invite it indoors through the use of large areas of glass. Long months in advance of the actual construction, Walter's office in Detroit was covered everywhere with blueprints, samples of timber, cross sections of cement construction, coverings for walls, light fixture samples, and other materials. No detail was too small for his attention. And nothing was as exciting to him as sprawling over an enormous table and projecting his visions on paper. Oskar would have been the first to admit that he had a coarchitect.

As clearing began for sewage lines and electric lines to be laid underground, the tree removal equipment was put to good use for replanting, and all areas were quickly restored. There was to be no pollution of the clear waters of Black Lake: a sewage disposal plant, which became the envy of many townships in that part of the Midwest, was erected on the site.

The architectural brilliance of the Center has been praised in many countries. Large student lounges look down on the treetops. Laminated, handsome Douglas fir beams support the roof in the great dining hall, some as long as seventy-two feet, cut to size in our Northwest with equipment once used to turn the masts of sailing ships, then shipped from Portland, Oregon, on flat cars. The warm-colored stone (about 15,000 tons of it) covering most of the buildings comes from Wisconsin, because it was both more beautiful and less expensive than the local stone.

All the structures are connected by covered walkways; even when the snow is three feet deep one can walk comfortably from one's room to any part of the compound.

In the camaraderie that developed among all those involved in this materialization of a social ideal, Walter was presented by the workers with a red construction hat bearing the initials CABGF, for

"Chief Architect, Builder, and General Flunky." He wore it with pride, except when he was conducting some of the first UAW member-students through the site, at which time he wore with relish a green velours Tyrolean hat he had bought in Salzburg. He was being tour leader, telling stories about buying the hat and about my appearance, on one occasion, in lederhosen. Walter's sense of humor was rarely submerged, nor was he a prude, in spite of his famous teetotalism. Irving Bluestone recalls that one day at an Executive Board meeting, Walter was holding forth solemnly, and at length, about our monthly UAW newspaper, *Solidarity,* and ended with, "You know, after all, a house organ is a kind of sexless piece." There was a moment of silence before the burst of laughter.

Onaway was an area of farmers, small town people, and resort owners. It depended heavily on the tourist trade, and the people were obviously becoming apprehensive about "those union guys from Detroit" moving into their own backyard. Many of the fears had to do with the problems the people expected because a large number of blacks might come to the center. Walter, no innocent in the field of prejudice, sensed all this and moved to deal with it head-on even before construction work began. Convinced that ignorance nurtures bigotry, he sent out invitations to well over a hundred of the leading citizens of Onaway, and others from all walks of life, to come to the old lodge that was on the place when the UAW bought it. There he told them the UAW's plans and showed them the architect's model of the site, with all its buildings and transplanted trees. He did not wait for a question period but plunged right into some of the ugly subjects he knew were in their minds and dealt openly with them. This session did much to clear the air. The UAW's interest in preserving the environment and avoiding any pollution or devastation appealed to the local people, as did the interest of the UAW in helping to promote, through the state, the development of a park in and around the Great Bear Dunes.

May did her part in community relations by her sincere interest in the scattered American Indian communities. She supported educational projects for the children on the reservation, and worked hard on the drive for a new hospital, which was built, and to this day receives financial support from voluntary donations made every two weeks, when a new group of UAW worker-students comes to the center.

As Walter presided over the 1970 UAW convention of nearly four thousand delegates, a confidence and optimism exuded from him that could have come only from the knowledge that his ranks were solidly behind him. Although the economic situation was deteriorating, he looked forward to an improvement of pension benefits and a sturdier relationship between skilled and unskilled workers. He also predicted an expanded role for the UAW in world affairs, especially in the battle against the multinational corporations. He had already talked with Dr. Ralphe Bunche and others about a conference to be sponsored jointly by the United Nations and the UAW. But he was not optimistic about the Vietnam War and its serious disruption of our country.

A few days after the convention, our troops were sent into Cambodia, a tragedy that spawned tragedy on the campuses of Kent State and Jackson State. I was on the phone to Walter constantly from Washington at that time, having prepared a statement I suggested he send to Nixon. Walter wanted to send a message that would be tougher and sharper than the one I had drafted. He called to give me the corrections he was making in the telegram, and to authorize me to release it simultaneously in Washington and Detroit. It was our last conversation.

At the end of it, he asked me how I was coming on the outline of a book we planned to write together. Then he said that he and May and Oskar Stonorov were planning to go away for a few days to the Black Lake center to check on the construction. It was Mother's Day, and Walter and May were looking forward to the trip with great pleasure. There was not a single achievement in Walter's whole life that gave him more joy than the Black Lake center. (Only days before, the UAW convention delegates had voted, as a show of appreciation, to call it the Walter P. Reuther Family Education Center, but he had insisted that until his retirement at sixty-five his name should not be used.)

At 9:28 on the evening of May 9, 1970, Walter and May, Oskar Stonorov, and May's young nephew William Wolfman, who was serving as Walter's security officer, were killed, along with the two pilots, when their plane crashed at the Emmet County Airport in Pellston, Michigan. I cannot possibly express in words what this meant to me, to all the families involved.

The six-passenger twin engine Lear Jet M43EJ was operated by the aforementioned Executive Jet Aviation, which the UAW often chartered to carry top personnel when their schedules required them to be in places and at hours not covered by commercial airlines. It was a well-established, reputable line operating extensively both in the U.S. and Europe. The pilots were experienced, and Walter had flown with them on many occasions — in fact, the plane was identical with the one Walter and I had taken to Washington the night we had our brush with disaster.

Like others, I have been haunted continually by the question, "Was the crash accidental?" There had been so many attempts on Walter's life. But from the intensive investigation made by the Federal Aviation Authority, the facts seem to say clearly that it was caused by human error, not neglect.

The FAA had a team of thirty-three men investigating the crash of the jet into fifty-foot elm trees approximately two and a half miles southwest of the approach end of Runway 5 of the Emmet County Airport. The jet engines were immediately choked and stopped by the branches. The momentum of the plane took it 269 feet farther, cutting a swath through the trees; then it exploded into a ball of fire, a pyre from which no one could escape.

Weather conditions were reported by Pellston as "scattered clouds at 400 feet, measured ceiling 800 feet overcast, visibility 7 miles, thunderstorms and light rain showers, temperature 45 degrees Fahrenheit, wind 100° at ten knots." A significant fact about the airport emerged later in an official report: "Runways 23 and 32 are equipped with runway and identifier lights [called REIL's]. The FSS specialist stated that . . . one of the REIL's at the approach of Runway 23 was not operating. A notice to airmen was not issued to that effect. Subsequent to the accident REIL and a visual approach path indicator (VAPI) were installed on Runway 5."

The investigating team included experts from the Transportation and Safety Board; the FAA, which certifies airplanes; General Electric the Lear Jet firm; and the Coast Guard and Air Force. Because of the prominence of the passengers and inevitable suspicion of sabotage, the Safety Board took the unusual step of having the chief pathologist of the University of Michigan conduct the autopsies. His conclusions were that it was highly unlikely that any explosives were involved. The Lear company maintained that it was impossible for anyone but trusted officials of their firm to have known who was to use the plane, which was assigned initially to a ferry job from Columbus to Akron. The plane refueled at Akron and took Glen

Campbell, the folk singer, to the Detroit City Airport, landing at 7:00 P.M., and after debarking its passenger was ferried immediately to Metro Airport. It was on the ground only twenty minutes, taxiing in and out before it loaded Walter and his party a 8:44 P.M. The crew was seasoned — Captain Evans with 7760 flight hours, most of them in jets, and his copilot, Karaffa, with a total of 6533, half of them in jets. Neither had flown during the twenty-four hours prior to that evening.

The crucial part of the evidence has to do with the captain's altimeter. The report states that "while all systems were irreparably damaged, information was nevertheless obtained from a few units. The captain's altimeter showed a reading of 1400 feet msl with an altimeter setting 29.75 inches . . . During the disassembly of the altimeter it was observed that a brass screw had fallen out and was lying loose in the case . . . Considering that the screw may have loosened because of heat, a similar calibration arm mechanism was placed in an oven and heated for two hours at 1100 degrees Fahrenheit. This screw was found to be tight when examined."

Further examination of the altimeter revealed that an incorrect pivot was installed in one end of a rocking shaft. At the opposite end of the shaft, an end stone was missing. A ring jewel within the mechanism was installed off-center. A second rocking shaft rear support pivot was incorrect.

The Transportation and Safety Board decided that, "while the evidence is not conclusive, the captain's altimeter was probably reading inaccurately . . . The pilot would not have flown at an altitude of 166 feet above the runway heading [which is why he struck the trees] so far from the threshold, since this would require a turn at a dangerously low altitude, particularly at night. *However, an altimeter which read too high could have caused the pilot to have believed he was sufficiently high so as to safely traverse the area.*" (Italics mine.)

The accident set shock waves around the world. As for myself, I was so stunned, it was almost impossible to make all the necessary calls to my family, the Wolfmans, and to the Oskar's widow, Betty. What a magnificent person she is, with such strength and courage — I found her consoling me! After I had called Ted and Chris, all of us wondering how to break the news to our mother, already in her late eighties and in fragile condition, I called Fania, who proved to be another tower of strength.

The clan gathered; Eric came from East Los Angeles, where he was working with Mexican-Americans, bringing with him Walter and May's daughter Linda from San Francisco. Sophie and I finally reached our son John at the University of Moscow, where he was finishing two years of study in U.S.–Soviet relations.

Walter and May's other daughter, Lisa, had been one of my first concerns when we heard the news of the crash, even though we were still not completely sure that Walter and May had been on that plane. Lisa was alone at home in Detroit. Sophie and I were still in Washington. I finally located Irving Bluestone, Walter's closest assistant and confidant in Detroit. We begged him to make arrangements to have someone go immediately to Lisa and talk to her before the reporters went swarming in. The press badgered us in Washington, where, to add to the difficulty, we were putting up students who had arrived from all over for a huge demonstration against the Vietnam War, the invasion of Cambodia, and the Kent State and Jackson State killings.

Somehow we got through the next days. There was a separate funeral service for young Bill Wolfman. Then all of us except Mütterschen, who remained in the hotel in Detroit to greet the friends who were dropping by, went to the main auditorium at Solidarity House, UAW headquarters, where the entire staff and all the top officers had gathered for a "family session" as a last tribute to Walter and May. After several of the UAW national staff members had made a few remarks, I was introduced by Emil Mazey. It was not easy to speak in a room filled with so many associates of long years and so many memories. I told them how touched we were that they had asked to meet with us and said:

> In a very real sense you have always been an extension of the family to Walter and to May and to all of us and we have drawn strength from you. Walter could not have conceivably achieved even a small beginning of the great goals he set for himself and the UAW if it had not been for a very skillful, talented, devoted, and loyal team of officers, who stood solidly together, who did not let divisions enter their ranks; and the staff that has grown enormously in recent years, but still reflects the same dedication and loyalty to those things for which this union has always stood . . . Our thoughts are with Earl Wolfman, for in one tragic incident he lost both a sister and a son and he is much more alone than we are, who have all of you close at hand to support us. . . .

I described Walter's last act as a UAW official: the sharp and bitter telegram denouncing Nixon for the waste of lives and resources in

Indochina that were needed at home to fight poverty, renew our cities, build hospitals and schools to make life more meaningful for our people. I reminded them that on the morrow, when we would have the memorial service, Walter and I had been scheduled to be in New York to announce to the press, with the UN, that there would be a UAW-UN June conference on the impact of urbanization on the human environment. I knew of no other occasion, I said, when the United Nations had agreed that a trade union should serve as cohost for an official United Nations conference.

But our union was not the run-of-the-mill union. It was concerned about the brotherhood of man and all phases of the life and well-being of men, women, families. That was the meaning of the new Family Education Center, toward which, ironically, Walter and May were winging when they lost their lives. "That center," I said, "will help transmit the kind of philosophy that our union has acquired over thirty years, as it is transmitted to new generations of leadership."

Emotionally wrought, I spoke of a great many other things, including a tribute to Ted.

> Maybe some of our UAW friends thought there were only three Reuther brothers. We were the ones around where speeches were to be made; we had our photographs taken; we had the great joys that go with the achievements of the UAW. But there is one Reuther brother who preceded us all, the oldest, who carried a heavy burden during all those years. Walter, Roy, and I always felt a deep sense of guilt because our responsibilities kept us so far removed from Wheeling, where we could have taken more of a personal hand in helping our father and mother . . . I want to acknowledge to my brother Ted and his loving wife, Ann, our deep and everlasting appreciation.

I spoke also of Irving and Zelda Bluestone, "who had helped us, every time tragedy struck, to handle problems that in times of crisis husbands, wives, and children shouldn't have to deal with." How pleased we were, I said, that Irving would be speaking in behalf of the UAW at the memorial service.

I concluded; with Walter's own words: *"To men of good will, we extend our hand. Together we shall build that better tomorrow in the image of peace, in the image of freedom, in the image of social justice, and in the image of human brotherhood."*

There was a light drizzle on the morning of May 13 when the

doors to the Veterans' Memorial Building beside the Detroit River were opened to the throngs who for days filed silently past the two simple oak caskets, Walter's draped in the emblem of the UAW. Between the two lay a bouquet of white daisies from their daughters; and four flags stood as silent sentinels: of the United States, of Canada, of the United Nations, and a flag bearing the familiar peace symbol, at the request of Linda and Lisa. Prime Ministers, heads of state, workers from factories and fields telegraphed their deep sorrow. Many would travel long distances to express that same sorrow in person — from Australia, South America, Europe. Rich and poor, black and white, old and young filed along the royal blue carpet.

Among the first were the Rhydolms: Clarence was a seventy-one-year-old retired Cadillac worker who had joined the union in 1936 during a strike. "We felt he was just like a father to us," said Mrs. Rhydolm, with tears in her eyes. They had attended together, they said, just about every meeting held in Detroit when Walter was speaking.

Sam Smith, a stocky forty-four-year-old black worker, came at 7:30 P.M. on his way to his third-shift job as janitor in the Dodge plant, carrying his lunch pail. "He bargained for the broom pushers like me, too," he said. "He wanted the laboring man to live good and to make money like others with prettier jobs."

For fourteen hours each day came officers of international and local unions, secretaries, retired workers, and staff members. We in the family took turns as members of an honor guard. Schoolchildren, books in hand, mingled with the others.

"My grandfather worked at Hudson Motors," said Catherine Dent, a high school sophomore, "and Mr. Reuther did a lot of great things that helped my granddad. It made his life much better and I guess it made mine better too."

Walter Cotes of Local 600 touched the casket and wiped the tears from his eyes. "I feel so bad. Nobody can take his place. He had honest guts. He stood up for people."

Sadie Schweitzer, aged sixty-three, who helped tend the soup kitchens during the thirties, came because she wanted to be part of the honor guard. "It was the least I could do." As a member of Chrysler Local 7, she had helped Ford workers organize after her own working hours.

Alexander Cardozo, a retired black Chrysler worker, fell to his knees before Walter's casket and wept, repeating over and over, "He was the only friend I had in the world."

It would be inappropriate to list here all the tributes paid to May and Walter in the press, by trade union and political leaders, by heads of state, by automobile corporation executives, by citizens from all strata of American life. There were mountains of handwritten messages, including poems.

Thirty-four hundred people crowded into the Ford Auditorium for a simple, emotional ceremony of farewell. They had come by invitation, but thousands more jammed the sidewalks to hear the voices of the eulogists over loudspeakers. Our mother, frail and shaken, leaned heavily on Ted's arm as she came into the auditorium. The enormity of Walter's death, after the loss of Val and Roy, was too much for her to absorb, and she never recovered from it. (For months, she did not accept the reality. Once, while staying with Sophie and me in Washington, Mütterschen greeted me when I returned from a trip, and then said, "I guess Walter was too busy to get away.")

Space allows me to quote only excerpts from the farewells spoken at the Memorial Service:

"Whenever the going was tough, Walter Reuther was with us . . . He knew. He was a believer. He was a man." — Whitney Young, Director, National Urban League.

"He did not live to see the kind of world he visualized but in his years upon this earth he touched the lives of millions of people and made them better." — Dave Miller, Chairman, National UAW Retired Workers' Advisory Council.

"She was an endless searcher and learner . . . She quietly but firmly and enthusiastically supported aspects which focused on involving members of the community in planning and implementing programs . . . And she gave strong encouragement to our increased efforts to recruit minority students to our campus." — Dr. William Rioux, President, Merrill Palmer Institute, Detroit.

"He was not a selfish man; that's why we have so much to inherit." — Senator Philip A. Hart.

"For blacks, he was pre-eminently the most widely known and respected white labor leader in the nation . . . He was there in person when the

storm clouds were thick . . . We are all better off — black and white —
as beneficiaries of his creative life." — Mrs. Martin Luther King, Jr.

"I knew May and Walter Reuther as early and unwavering colleagues in
the establishment of the Meadowbrook Music Festival and the Meadowbrook Theater so their people, too, could share in the riches and beauty
and dignity of the arts." — Dr. Durward B. Varner, Chancellor, University of Nebraska.

"I came to know him not in bargaining sessions . . . but in the struggle
for peace in Vietnam . . . The strong, clear voice of Walter Reuther
provided another voice and another vision, a vision of peace and justice
. . . I saw the substance of those dreams of Walter Reuther in the
UAW Family Education Center at Black Lake . . . We walked together
by the lake and he talked about paths where families could walk among
the trees." — Sam Brown, National Youth Leader.

"The words of Chaim Nachman Bialik, the poet of the Hebrew renais-
sance, flashed before me: 'There was a man, and behold, he is no
more.' " — Rabbi Jacob J. Weinstein.

"The international labor movement is also mourning a great leader . . .
It is on their behalf . . . that I have come here to pay tribute to Walter
Reuther and what he stood for. Walter Reuther clearly realized that in
modern society the trade unions must take a stand . . . on the great
problems of social policy of our times and throw all their powers into a
democratic transformation of society." — Ivar Noren, General Secretary, IMF.

"In this indescribably painful hour, I am deeply honored to have been
selected in behalf of the UAW, its officers and its members, to speak
this last farewell . . . Where shall we find such men who can lead us, as
did Walter with boundless energy, to a new and brighter day? Who can
dream for humanity and realize their dreams? . . . We shall find them
among the countless men and women of good will and deep commitment . . . in all corners of the earth, whose voices will respond exul-
tantly to the challenges of a new day . . . Walter had faith that these
voices will prevail. He never wavered, never faltered in this faith, nor
can we waver or falter if we are to be true to his memory." — Irving
Bluestone, Administrative Assistant to Walter P. Reuther.

At the conclusion, Henry Ghant, president of UAW Local 212,
sang a workers' song (Walter's favorite) written during the Depression in honor of an executed trade union organizer. The words
came through in his rich, mournful voice:

> I dreamed I saw Joe Hill last night
>   Alive as you and me.
> Says I, "But Joe, you're ten years dead."
>   "I never died," says he.
>   "I never died," says he . . .
>
> And standing there as big as life
>   And smiling with his eyes,
> Joe says, "What they forgot to kill
>   Went on to organize,
>   Went on to organize."

As the song was ending, my mind went back to happier days when Walter and I were in Vienna. The Viennese had taken into their language an ancient word, *Servus,* that is used both as greeting and farewell to good friends. Walter and I had used it over the years whenever we met or parted. So, with my eyes clouding up, as I joined the rest of our family to file out for the last time past the caskets, I whispered quietly: *"Servus,* Walter; *Servus,* May."

Sophie and I went to Philadelphia the day after the ceremony in Detroit to take our leave of another dear friend, Oskar Stonorov. We joined his wife, Betty, their three daughters, and their son, with his wife, in the small and lovely Quaker meetinghouse so familiar to us from the early days of our marriage, when we had gathered there with friends in the peace movement.

Then one more ceremony: this time in Washington, conducted by Dean Francis B. Sayre, at the National Cathedral, where tributes were given by the Honorable Earl Warren, Sam Brown, Jack Conway, the Honorable Tage Erlander of Sweden, Anna Roosevelt Halsted, James Jordan, Clarence Mitchell, the Honorable Willard W. Wirtz, and our son John Reuther. Once again "Joe Hill" was sung, this time by Joe Glazer.

Some months later the officers and Executive Board of the UAW and invited staff members, along with the Reuther family, dedicated a small plot of land directly across from the main student lounge at the Family Education Center as a Reuther Natural Sanctuary. It was a charming small knoll, beloved by Walter and May and Roy. We nourished it with their ashes and three memorial trees. There are no markings to indicate it is a burial place, for in all of our minds there was and is the feeling that the center must not be associated with sadness and the past, but with joy, and hope for the future.

The International Executive Board officially named the center the Walter and May Reuther UAW Family Education Center.

Trade unions from Europe, Latin America, the Middle East, Africa, and Australia sent to the center beautiful trees, indigenous to their countries; they have been planted in a memorial arboretum.

Stunned as the UAW was by the sudden loss, there was no thought that Walter's death would signal a division in the ranks or a diminution of the union's commitment to the economic issues at the bargaining table or to the efforts at social reform it had always sponsored. Walter had surrounded himself not with sycophants but with strong and independent-minded people, already leaders in their own right. Planning to retire at sixty-five, Walter had thought of Douglas Fraser, one of the UAW vice-presidents, as his successor, since Leonard Woodcock was nearer his own age and would have had only one short term to serve. Now things were different, and there was a natural competition between the two men. Emil Mazey withdrew from the running. He played a highly constructive mediating role in helping the Executive Board eventually come to a choice, though the vote was so close that for days it was a tossup between Woodcock and Fraser. By a vote of thirteen to twelve, the Executive Board elected Woodcock. Doug Fraser, in a magnanimous gesture, urged the board to cast a unanimous vote for Woodcock. This prompted me to send Fraser the following quotation from Disraeli: "Next to knowing when to seize an opportunity, the most important thing in life is to know when to forgo an advantage."

Immediately after Leonard's elevation to president of the UAW, he departed for Georgia to join in the Poor People's March, organized by the Southern Christian Leadership Conference, which had been created by Martin Luther King, Jr. "I will be there in Walter's stead," said Leonard before he left. "I will also be there to signify that our alliance with the progressive institutions in this country has not only not changed but that because of the tragic loss we are doubly dedicated to that type of activity . . . We have a united union. Our slogan, 'Teamwork in the leadership and solidarity in the ranks,' is not just words on paper."

The Executive Board confirmed Irving Bluestone, who had worked so closely with Walter during the last ten years, as director of the General Motors Department. At the very next convention, Bluestone was elevated to the vice-presidency by an overwhelming vote, further evidence that Walter's concepts would be carried forward.

One of the UAW and Walter's great innovations, Supplemental Unemployment Benefits (SUB), has lately been in the news because of our disastrous depression-plus-inflation. William Safire, in the *New York Times,* April 10, 1975, praised it as "Detroit's Better Idea."

> This was an indirect approach to Mr. Reuther's dream of a "guaranteed annual wage" in an industry notorious for boom-and-bust production . . .
>
> SUB's shock absorber, like state unemployment insurance, is not welfare; it is essentially insurance paid for by the worker, as about ten cents an hour of fringe benefit is set aside in a fund for lay-off emergencies. It was designed for the auto industry's fluctuation, not an extended recession, which is why funds are now running out . . .
>
> Of course Detroit's SUB funds are depleted. But having proved their worth in transforming what surely would have been hard times into what amounted to a paid vacation for unemployed auto workers with seniority, SUB funds will be replenished at a faster rate than before when the economy picks up.
>
> And other workers — particularly those in the vulnerable building trades — will wake up to the need for putting something aside for a rainy season . . .
>
> The example of SUB is trying to teach us something . . . Perhaps we have been listening too raptly to the theories of Lord Keynes and underestimating the practical genius of Walter Reuther.

In the spring of 1972 I decided to retire from the UAW and write the book that Walter and I had planned to do together. To note my departure from active duty, the ADA arranged a party in Washington, attended by hundreds of friends. They secured as sponsors some eighty prominent prople to permit the use of their names on the invitation — members of Congress, diplomats, leaders of labor, civil rights, religion, education. A copy of this Salute to Victor Reuther letterhead fell into the hands of some of Nixon's gang, and a confidential memo was directed to John Dean and Pat Buchanan, instructing them to add the eighty names of sponsors to the White House enemies list. Had not this surfaced during the Ervin Committee's Watergate inquiry, I would never have known that Sophie and I had played a role in honoring so many of our friends by causing their names to be placed on such a distinguished list. I could not resist the temptation to reproduce the White House memo and send copies, on the Christmas following Watergate, to all eighty on the list, congratulating them on the honor of "making it" on the enemies list of Richard Nixon. One of them, Melina Mercouri, with whom I had been working to try to deny U.S. support for the Greek military regime, answered that she felt she really hadn't done enough against Nixon to earn the distinction.

The tragedy of that regime is of course not a joking affair, especially the campaign of 1972, which gave Nixon his "popular mandate" against one of the most honorable and sensitive candidates for President that the Democratic Party ever nominated, Senator George McGovern. One would have thought that labor at least would have known better. Roy's presence was sorely missed in that presidential campaign.

As we go to press, Watergate-style revelations are implicating the two highest U.S. intelligence-gathering agencies, the CIA and the FBI, in surreptitious and illegal activities against many thousands of American citizens. Senator Walter Mondale, a member of the Senate Select Committee on Intelligence, has made public the names of some whose personal mail was illegally intercepted. Among those he listed were "Nobel Prize-winner Linus Pauling, author John Steinbeck, and labor leader Victor Reuther." Thousands of students and black organizations were penetrated by hired FBI informers, not just to obtain information, but to provoke actions designed to bring discredit on those organizations. Most frightening of all is the extent to which both agencies were a government unto themselves, with no person of authority exercising any degree of appropriate supervision over their activities. Under the guise of national security, U.S. agencies, charged with upholding the law, were themselves undermining individual liberties and eroding the foundations of constitutional government. The American people are still not fully aware of how close our nation came to being converted into a police state. The truism, "eternal vigilance is the price of liberty," was never more valid than at this moment, when America prepares to celebrate its bicentennial.

George Meany maneuvered the AFL-CIO, then at its numerical peak and presumed peak of political influence, into a position of *nonendorsement*, which was actually a big plus for Nixon. John Herling, in an election eve column, said, "Never before has the labor movement been pervaded with so much dismay, so much uncertainty as to its prospects in the period ahead." Half the members of the AFL-CIO Executive Council, representing the larger, more dominant unions, were actively campaigning for McGovern. But four presidents of building trade unions and two maritime unions openly endorsed Nixon. Meany puffed on his cigar and, with a hypocritically nostalgic sigh, said, "If only Norman Thomas were alive!" He fooled no one; he had not voted for Norman Thomas any of the six times he could have.

Perhaps Meany's unspoken but effective support for Nixon in that campaign achieved something that Walter's pleading over the years had failed to do. In the AFL-CIO, and in some of the outside unions, such as the UAW, there are signs that the members intend to exercise their own political judgment. A new coalition seems to be forming, embracing the Machinist's Union, the UAW, the State, County and Municipal Workers, the Radio and Electrical Workers, the Communication Workers, and others. What's more, the Democratic Party is moving toward genuine internal reforms.

In October of the year I retired, 1972, our dear mother died at the age of ninety. The will to live and to be independent had remained amazingly strong, though near the end she was in a nursing home, since Chris, with whom she had been living, could no longer adequately manage her care. Three surviving children, fifteen grandchildren, thirteen great-grandchildren mourned her passing in a simple Lutheran ceremony in Elmgrove, West Virginia. She was laid to rest beside her husband, Valentine.

Earlier, in the spring, at my last UAW convention, after the showing of a very moving, newly produced film entitled *Walter*, I was presented by Leonard Woodcock with the UAW's Distinguished Social Justice Award, and gave my last speech before the friends and colleagues I had worked with almost all my life. Arne Geijer, president of the Swedish Labor Federation, and Ichiro Shioji, president of Japan's Federation of Auto Workers, had journeyed from afar to honor me.

I told the thousands of UAW members sitting before me in the hall that it had been a privilege to serve as their spokesman in the international field. I referred especially to the multinational conglomerates, which could be so destructive to workers unless they were countered with worldwide trade union solidarity. I then spoke with some optimism about future leaders of labor:

> There is a new generation coming into industry that begins on the platform which we have built as a foundation, but they have set their eyes

on a new goal beyond all that we have sought in the past. It strikes at a very crucial question . . . the right of workers to participate in some of the corporate decision-making that bears so heavily on our own lives and the lives of our children. We are far from knowing the answer to that problem, but lest we become frustrated and believe this is a peculiar problem unique to the United States . . . Arne Geijer and Ichiro Shioji will tell you they struggle with it in Sweden and Japan, and in Germany and Italy and France, in Brazil and Argentina — wherever there are auto workers, wherever the new generation is moving into the plant. The Swedes call it a search to humanize industry. The Germans call it codetermination or joint management. By whatever name it is called we will have to search for an answer . . .

What a flood of unsolved problems passed before my mind's eye — unemployment and runaway inflation, the decay of urban centers, the rise of crime and racial tensions, the waste of lives and resources while nations squander their wealth on arsenals of destruction. Must our aimless drift as a people continue? The progress of our union developed from clear guidelines held firm by years of struggle in pursuit of social justice. This heritage is a compass that can hold us on a steady course now and in the days ahead.

Where is the leadership to meet this challenge? My thoughts returned quickly to the sea of delegates I was addressing. In that audience were many young leaders I had come to know and respect. They have "stars in their eyes" and they have courage and persistence. They are the response to our urgent need. As they serve their union, so will they better serve their nation and mankind. More than a torch has been passed to this new generation of leaders: what they have is a clearer vision of a better world, more productive tools with which to fashion it, and the will and determination to settle for nothing less.

APPENDICES

A. Documents and Letters Pertaining to the Assassination Attempts

Senate Resolution 120 in the Senate of the United States, May 26th (Legislative Day, May 23rd), 1949

"Whereas requests have been made by the Detroit Common Council, the Mayor of Detroit and the Governor of Michigan for the immediate assistance of the Federal Bureau of Investigation in the apprehension of the assailants who attempted the assassination of Victor G. Reuther and earlier of his brother Walter P. Reuther. Now therefore be it resolved that it is the sense of Senate of the United States that all law enforcement facilities of the Department of Justice be made available immediately to investigate and cooperate with the local authorities in apprehending the criminals who attempted the assassination of Victor G. Reuther and earlier of his brother Walter P. Reuther. Signed by Leslie L. Biffle, Secretary of the Senate."

This was transmitted to the Department of Justice. The Justice Department's file number in the attack on the life of Victor Reuther is 146—7—5433.

* * *

May 26, 1949
A memorandum from Alexander M. Campbell, Assistant Attorney General, Criminal Division to the Director of the Federal Bureau of Investigation

The attention of the Criminal Division has been called to the attempted assassination of Victor Reuther in Detroit, Michigan. Reuther is said to be educational director of the CIO Auto Workers' Union. His brother Walter, president of the same organization, last year was the victim of a similar crime.

The prominence of these men in the labor movement has resulted in these attempted murders being given nationwide and even worldwide publicity. Moreover, press dispatches have indicated for some time past that the Reuthers have actively fought the communist element in the labor movement with which they are identified and consequently have incurred their enmity. This latter fact gives significance to these attempted assassinations, which impel the Department of Justice to take every possible step at once to ascertain the identity of the guilty party or parties and to vigorously prosecute any violation of federal law. This is therefore to request that you immediately cause the Bureau to make a thorough investigation into the facts of this reprehensible crime.

Basis for federal entry into the investigation lies primarily in the fact that these acts of violence are quite logically suspected to have arisen out of communist subversive activity in this country.

Your attention is also directed to the fact that the attempted slaying is of the "gang" type and the perpetrator or perpetrators may have violated the Fugitive Felon Act since it is quite likely that the guilty party or parties would flee the jurisdiction to avoid prosecution.

We are informed that a stolen automobile may have been used in the perpetration of the act or flight of those responsible for the crime for that reason the National Motor Vehicle Theft Act may have been violated. Your investigation should, of course, be directed to ascertaining whether or not the car was stolen, whether it was moved in interstate commerce and to follow out all leads which may develop with reference to the automobile.

It is also our information that a sawed-off shotgun may have been used in the attempted assassination. For that reason both the Federal Firearms Act (15 USC 901, et seq.) and the National Firearms Act (26 USC 326, et seq.) may also have been violated. While investigations of alleged violations of these acts have been handled by the Treasury Department, any information which develops in your investigation indicating a possible violation of either of these acts should be furnished to the Commissioner of Internal Revenue as well as to the division. It is requested that copies of your reports be currently furnished to the Criminal Division. Approved by Peyton Ford, Assistant to the Attorney General and Tom C. Clark, Attorney General.

* * *

July 11, 1949

Congressman George P. O'Brien transmitted to Attorney General Tom C. Clark a telegram from a group of Michigan citizens asking for FBI intervention. The telegram represented "a cross section of Detroit community represented by 39 organizations speaking for 850,000 affiliates in a special meeting held July 5th." The message continues that they are "firmly convinced that the safety and security of our homes and our persons and of our community requires an immediate and full measure of participation on the part of the FBI in the investigation of the attempted murders of the Reuther brothers." Within the Justice Department the Assistant Attorney General Alexander M. Campbell in transmitting the attached lengthy telegram indicated that "maybe we should give a cautious acknowledgement."

However, when it reached the desk of Mr. Whearty, he informed Mr. Campbell, "Alex, I'd just file these and forget them. However, you're the boss."

Among the signatures to that lengthy telegram were: George Schermer, State President of the Michigan Committee on Civil Rights, I. Pokempner of the Labor Zionist Organization, Edward Swan of the NAACP, Mrs. Pearl Harris, the Detroit Association of Women's Clubs, The Reverend William B. Sperry, Chairman of Social Relations Department of the Episcopal Diocese of Michigan, Myra Silverman, President of the East Side Merchants Association, Rabbi Leon Fram, Temple Israel, Mrs. Helen Moore, President of the Federation of Teachers, Arthur Elder, Vice President of the American Federation of Teachers, Dr. E. Shurley Johnson of the Central Methodist Church, Mrs. Geraldine Bledsoe of the American Council of Human Relations of the Alpha Kappa Alpha Sorority, Borris Joffe, Executive Director of the Jewish Community, Andrew Brown, Vice President Detroit Chapter Americans for Democratic Action, Mrs. Mary Kornhauser, Mr. and Mrs. Abe Zwerdling, Mrs. Mildred Jeffrey.

* * *

Honorable Louis C. Rabaut   July 19, 1949
House of Representatives
Washington, D. C.

My dear Congressman:
   Mr. Tolson has informed me of your letter to him dated July 5, 1949 concerning the shooting of the Reuther brothers.
   Copies of the telegram which you enclosed have been brought to my attention previously by other prominent individuals. In each instance it was necessary to advise them that this Bureau cannot investigate this matter in the absence of any indication that a Federal law within the Bureau's investigative jurisdiction has been violated. Senators Vandenberg and Ferguson who expressed an interest in an investigation by this Bureau were similarly advised.
   Although the Attorney General has advised me that there is no basis for Federal jurisdiction we will, of course, be most happy to make the facilities of our Laboratory available to the local authorities in Detroit and any information which the Bureau may receive relative to the shootings will be promptly furnished to them.
   I am returning the telegram addressed to you from Mr. George Schermer, State President, Michigan Committee on Civil Rights, and others.
   With expressions of my highest esteem and best regards,
                                                      Sincerely yours,
                                                      J. EDGAR HOOVER

* * *

CONFIDENTIAL   August 8, 1950

Dear Senator Kefauver:
   At our conference yesterday you asked me three puzzlers: 1 — what would I suggest as to how your Crimes Committee could work with FBI on the Reuther shootings; 2 — had I in behalf of UAW-CIO turned over to FBI every clue we had; 3 — how many agents did FBI have working on it and where were they getting.
   Taking them in reverse order: FBI had two squads on it last spring; they have fewer now and Hoover's Deputy Director in Charge never appears; he never had a grasp of what he was supposed to be after; FBI does not take us, mere non-governmental experts, into confidence; they have to preserve their secrecy and they are right, up to the point where they have to ask us, or local authorities for facts that they don't know; I know that point having been in the Gov't and working with FBI and I know that is where they fall down — on labor cases, which after all are Greek to FBI. That is the point where apparently they are now falling down on the Reuther shootings.

They are now following bum steers, that we cleared up for them months ago. And to this day they have never had enough common sense investigative gumption to sit down with the responsible UAW-CIO representatives — Cranefield, Associate General Counsel, and me, and Ralph Winstead, investigator, to say "We have got so far with this, and we're stumped on that, and what can you get on it?"

Point 2: we have *offered* to FBI in Detroit everything the UAW has; but time and again they have said "If we need anything further on that we'll call you up." Net result: they have never asked us, even after we gave them what we thought were main clues, for the documentation which we have now put into the hands of your Senate Committee. We gave them the leads, and I even suggested to them why the FBI might hesitate to go into the leads, and the net result was silence. Most particularly, was the listing and analysis of named gambler-racketeer characters, nearly 100 of them, from whom (we feel) the Reuther gunmen came — together with our lead to the main instigating suspect — and the FBI either out of ignorance or fear has never asked us for the documentation now turned over to you.

Your point 1: *suggestions* are what I hesitate about, to a Senator who as Chairman of the Crime Committee has conferred with the Atty. Gen., with the Asst Atty. Gen., with the Director FBI, and others. Yet I will presume to suggest —

First, a clear declaration by your Committee, in conferences, that these shootings have got to be solved. As Americans we can take no pride in having prominent leaders like Walter Reuther heard with respect by Europeans on government levels and then have them, Britishers, French, etc. saying "Now he goes home to where he may be shot again, in that gangster land where they never even find out who did it."

Second, your Committee has clear jurisdiction over the corruptive gangster operations in the auto underworld, one segment of which seems to lead into the Reuther shootings, on which FBI has been assigned for eight months without turning up anything for a grand jury. You have Senate subpoena power, and a list of leads, which should turn up facts aplenty both for your general purpose and the particular objective. And you don't care in the joint effort whether FBI gets the "credit" for solving the shootings or your Committee.

Third, a team of your investigators working in Michigan without publicity at first could be bringing in named persons for examination and steadily asking FBI in Michigan, "Have you got this? Can you find that one? Between us we want the long distance phone calls for two years from this point in California, and the records of plane trips, and where such-and-such met up in Detroit."

In other words your team in Michigan going to work practically with FBI there and an end to high level jurisdictional disputations in Washington.

And I don't think it would be many weeks before pay dirt would be flying.

In pressing these suggestions, for which you asked, I recognize clearly that many other factors may enter the decision which of course rests only with you.

Respectfully
Heber Blankenhorn

* * *

April 4, 1951
Memorandum from Francis X. Walker, Chief of the General Crime Section, Criminal Division, to the Assistant Attorney General James McInerney:

There is reference to the basis for an inquiry into the attack on the lives of the Reuther brothers. "An investigation of the shooting had previously been requested. On the basis of a possible violation of Section 241, Title 18, USC (Conspiracy Against the Rights of Citizens) this section, of course, refers only to rights secured by the constitution and the laws of the United States. And Section 372, Title 18, United States Code (Conspiracy to Impede or Injure Officer) in view of the fact that Victor Reuther had been employed on a consultant basis by the Economic Cooperation Administration and that the shooting may have been in connection with this employment. The investigation into the bombing of the UAW-CIO National Headquarters was made to discover if there had been any violation of the Federal statutes."

* * *

Mr. Clarence M. Kelley   September 3, 1974
Director
Federal Bureau of Investigation
Pennsylvania Avenue at 9th Street, N. W.
Washington, D. C. 20535

Dear Mr. Kelley:

Mr. Victor Reuther is in receipt of your letter of August 27, 1974, transmitting two FBI summary reports of the attempted assassination of Mr. Reuther and his brother Walter. Mr. Reuther's check for $65.60 is enclosed as requested by you.

Both Mr. Victor Reuther and I have reviewed the two summary reports and believe they raise more questions than they answer. There certainly must be much additional information in the files of the Bureau that would be of assistance to Mr. Reuther in preparing his detailed autobiography of the three Reuther brothers.

We request answers to the following questions in the belief that the FBI files must contain the additional information necessary to answer them and in the further belief that your answers will materially assist Mr. Reuther in detailing the story of the shootings:

1. You forwarded summary reports dated May 9, 1951 and January 18, 1952. It seems incredible that there were not both earlier and later reports — earlier reports because of public pressure for Bureau action on the Reuther shootings and later reports because the summary reports you forwarded end with the word "PENDING." We would, of course, under the rules promulgated by the Attorney General, be entitled to all additional reports whether denominated "summary" or something else.

2. In connection with the two summary reports forwarded to Mr. Reuther and in connection with any additional reports we may receive under paragraph 1 of this letter, we refer to our understanding with the representatives of the Department of Justice that the only deletions were to

be the names of *existing* FBI informants. Quite obviously the two summary reports made available to Mr. Reuther contain delegations far beyond any such concept and even delete the names of dead people. We are, therefore, requesting that the additional reports furnished be in accordance with our understanding and, in addition, that the Bureau transmit to Mr. Reuther the names deleted from the two summary reports already furnished him with the exception, of course, of the names of persons presently informants for the Bureau.

3. In connection with the previous questions, we would like to know when the FBI closed out its investigation of the attempted assassinations. Mr. Victor Reuther was permitted to examine a small "Reuther" file in the Department of Justice which indicates that the investigation of the bombing of the UAW-CIO International headquarters on December 20, 1949 was closed out in February, 1952. What Mr. Reuther wants to know is whether the investigation of the attempted assassinations of Walter and Victor Reuther was closed out at the same time (February 1952) and if so, why, especially since the statute of limitations under many statutes had not yet run.

4. On May 26, 1949 the United States Senate, by unanimous resolution, asked that "all law enforcement facilities of the Department of Justice be made available immediately to investigate and cooperate with the local authorities in apprehending the criminals who attempted the assassination of Victor G. Reuther and earlier of his brother Walter P. Reuther." On that same day, Assistant Attorney General Alexander M. Campbell, with the approval of Attorney General Tom Clark, forwarded to the Director of the FBI a detailed communication setting forth the Justice Department's views that there were a number of grounds on which intervention by the Bureau could be legally justified. Questions:

(a) In view of the fact that Mr. Campbell's memorandum, approved by the Attorney General, fully demonstrates the jurisdiction of the Bureau, why did Mr. Hoover, two months later, that is on July 19, 1949, write Congressman Louis Rabaut that the Attorney General had advised Mr. Hoover "that there is no basis for federal jurisdiction . . ." In other words, is there a memorandum cancelling the Campbell memorandum of May 26, 1949?

(b) Did the Bureau reverse itself at any time after the Rabaut letter and assume jurisdiction?

(c) Was the public ever informed that the Bureau was assuming jurisdiction in the Reuther case?

(d) Finally, and most importantly, is it fair for Mr. Victor Reuther to conclude that the failure of the Bureau to crack the Reuther case was the result of the fact that the investigation was half-hearted since the Bureau never decided whether it would or would not accept the Attorney General's directive that it did have jurisdiction?

5. Soon after Mr. Walter Reuther was shot in 1948, UAW legal representatives, Mr. Irving Levy and Mr. Joseph L. Rauh, Jr., met with Attorney General Tom Clark to urge FBI intervention into the search for the would-be assassins. The Attorney General indicated he would immediately transmit the request to the Bureau. What was the response of the Bureau to this request?

6. On June 28, 1950 a similar conference was held with Attorney General McGrath and participating in that conference were Mr. Victor Reuther, Mr.

Rauh, and Mr. William Farnum, of the UAW. What was the content of the report submitted by the Attorney General to the Director of the FBI as a follow up of this meeting and what was the response of the Bureau?

7. The Kefauver Senate Crime Committee investigated the attacks on the Reuther brothers and their published hearings are more comprehensive than the Bureau summaries we received. The correspondence between the Bureau and the Kefauver Committee would be most useful to Mr. Reuther and we request copies of same.

8. The two summary reports made available to Mr. Reuther repeatedly refer to the incredible theory that UAW leaders themselves planted the bomb in the UAW headquarters on December 20, 1949. Why was so much emphasis placed on this theory in those summaries? Did the FBI then or does it now have any evidence whatever to support that theory?

9. One alleged suspect in the case was a certain Donald J. Ritchie, of Canada, who came to Detroit, gave a sworn statement to the Prosecuting Attorney of Wayne County, Gerald K. O'Brien, to the effect that he was in the get-away car of those who shot Walter Reuther. While in Detroit Police custody, Ritchie was permitted to escape and return to Canada, and enjoy $5,000.00 in reward monies. Was any request made for the extradition of Ritchie from Canada? Was the Bureau successful in interrogating Ritchie after his escape? If so, may Mr. Reuther have the report of the interrogation?

10. The two summary reports made available to Mr. Reuther omit any reference to the possible complicity of members of the Detroit Police Force. For example, Detective DeLamielleure, assigned to break the case, was heavily involved with Perrone and others, prime suspects in the attempted assassinations. Did the Bureau make any investigation of DeLamielleure or others in the Detroit Police Force who may have been involved in a massive cover-up or even in the assassinations themselves?

11. The Kefauver reports indicate that meetings took place between Perrone, Michigan Stove owner Fry, Briggs Body officials and Harry Bennett of the Ford Motor Company. Did the Bureau ever interrogate Mr. Bennett as to any of his discussions with Perrone? In view of the long and violent history of Bennett's years at Ford and in view of the fact that an earlier attempt on the life of Walter Reuther involved individuals who were on the payroll of Bennett and the Ford Motor Company, was Mr. Bennett ever questioned as to whether he or individuals under his direction might have been involved in any violent attack on either Reuther? If so, may we have the report of such interrogation?

12. In view of the evidence that underworld figures Perrone and others may have been involved in the Reuther shootings and in view of the use to which these underworld figures had been put by big employers such as Michigan Stove and Briggs Body, did the Bureau ever seek to identify the employers or top underworld figures who might have financed such physical attacks upon the Reuther brothers in the effort to win "labor peace"?

Mr. Reuther is presently completing his book. It would be most helpful if we could receive a response to this letter in a reasonable time.

Sincerely,
Joseph L. Rauh, Jr.

* * *

Joseph L. Rauh, Jr., Esq.   October 15, 1974
Rauh and Silard
1001 Connecticut Avenue, N. W.
Washington, D. C. 20036

Dear Mr. Rauh:
  Reference is made to your letter dated September 3, 1974, and my letter
dated September 20, 1974, concerning the request of Mr. Victor Reuther
for information in the files of the FBI under the Freedom of Information
Act.
  With respect to the questions you posed in your letter of September 3,
1974, I wish to advise you of the following facts:
  Question 1: You were advised in my letter dated September 20th, the
FBI has begun processing the additional reports contained in this file.
  Question 2: The deletions we make in the reports which are furnished
to the public are based on Departmental Order 528-73 which provides for
the deletion of names and other identifying data of informants. In our
discussions with the Office of Legal Counsel, Department of Justice, during the past year, they have indicated this protection extends to inactive
informants and even to informants who have died in order to insulate
their families from harassment and reprisals.
  Question 3: The investigation of the attempted bombing of UAW
Headquarters in Detroit, which included inquiries into the attempted assassinations of the Reuther brothers, was closed in May 1952.
  Question 4: A thorough check of the files of this Bureau disclosed no
record of receipt of the memorandum from Assistant Attorney General
Alexander Campbell dated May 26, 1949. Our files do contain a memorandum to the Attorney General dated May 26, 1949, stating it was the
Bureau's position that there was no FBI jurisdiction in the shootings, but
we were offering cooperative services of the Laboratory and Identification
Division to local authorities. In view of this, we did not reverse ourselves
and did not inform the public we were assuming jurisdiction. The investigation initiated pursuant to the request of the Department on December
21, 1949, was thorough, extensive and completely objective.
  Question 5: We could locate no record of any request by Attorney General Tom Clark urging FBI intervention into this case.
  Question 6: Similarly, we could locate no record submitted by the Attorney General to the Director of the FBI as a follow up to a June 28, 1959,
meeting.
  Question 7: A search of our files reflects several references to the Kefauver Senate Crime Committee, but we could not locate any correspondence between this Bureau and that Committee.
  Question 8: The 2 summary reports previously furnished to you contain results of partial investigation conducted, including comments of persons interviewed and do not contain "theories," conclusions or opinions of
the FBI.
  Question 9: The FBI did not request that Donald J. Ritchie be extradited from Canada and he was not interrogated by the FBI.
  Question 10: No investigation was conducted by the FBI concerning
Detective DeLamielleure or other members of the Detroit Police Department in connection with this matter.

Question 11: A search of our files fails to indicate Harry Bennett was ever interviewed by the FBI in conjunction with this investigation.

Question 12: All logical investigation was conducted in this matter and results furnished to the Department of Justice which advised in May, 1952, that in view of the extensive, unproductive investigation, it was suggested no further action be taken unless additional information was received indicating a violation of Federal statutes.

Sincerely yours,
Clarence M. Kelley
Director

B. Agreement Between the AFL-CIO and the State Department

Mr. Rutherford M. Poats
Deputy Administrator
Agency for International Development
U. S. Department of State
Washington, D. C. 20523

May 15, 1968

Dear Mr. Poats:

This will confirm our recent discussions in which the Agency for International Development may utilize the American Institute for Free Labor Development, the African-American Labor Center, and the Asian-American Free Labor Institute as instruments to provide financial support to American labor organizations involved in, and capable of, developing and strengthening free trade unions throughout the world.

In order to provide a basis for this assistance program, we believe that funds in an amount of $1,300,000 should be made available to the AIFLD and AALC by amending, or modifying, their existing relevant task orders with the Agency for International Development, and to the AAFLI by initiating a new task order under their recently completed basic agreement with the Agency.

These regional AFL-CIO organizations will allocate funds through legal instruments approved by A.I.D. to those trade union organizations approved by the AFL-CIO and named hereunder to obtain their specialized assistance in the international field. Such agreements will govern the detailed expenditure of funds in accordance with the following schedule:

Union	Estimated Total	AIFLD	AAFLI	AALC
Retail Clerks International Association	$ 300,000	$195,000	$ 65,000	$ 40,000
International Federation of Petroleum and Chemical Workers	300,000	120,000	90,000	90,000
Communication Workers of America	300,000	200,000	50,000	50,000
Brotherhood of Railway, Airline and Steamship Clerks, Freight Handlers, Express and Station Employees	100,000	50,000	25,000	25,000
Clothing and Textile Workers Unions	75,000	60,000	5,000	10,000

Entertainment Workers Unions	75,000	60,000	10,000	5,000
Food, Drink and Plantation Workers Unions	50,000	30,000	10,000	10,000
Sub Total	$1,200,000	$715,000	$255,000	$230,000
Administrative and Supervisory Travel	100,000			
TOTAL	$1,300,000			

In a general review of the requirements of AFL-CIO affiliated unions and labor organizations, relatively minor administrative expenses, chargeable to regional activity, are incurred by their representatives resident in European headquarters. Such expenses are directly attributable to regional activity and are, therefore, shown under the regional budgeting in this schedule above. We favor the writing of the individual union agreements with our regional organizations permitting this type of administrative aid which is grounded in regional performance.

One other matter obvious in the schedule of expenses above is the line item on Food, Drink and Plantation Workers Unions. At this time, we favor that the allocation of $50,000 broken down regionally, be administered through the regional organizations (AALC, AIFLD, and AAFLI) so that maximum efficiency can be achieved with this relatively small support. The regional organizations will create a better basis of performance for the entrance of U. S. unions internationally in these jurisdictions and the regional organizations will call upon appropriate American trade union organizations for specialized support in this work during the coming year.

Additionally, you will find attached a suggested agreement form for use between the regional organizations and specific unions, papers in support of each union's program, with the exception of Clothing and Textile Workers Unions and the Entertainment Workers Unions. These two documents are now being responsibly prepared by AFL-CIO Vice Presidents Kenin and Pollock and should be available to you by week's end and for insertion with the others attached.

The last area of concern to us and requiring explanation is the line item above, titled "Administration and Supervisory Travel" in the amount of $100,000. This item will be utilized for the coordination of the entire program allocation directly to the regions. However, at this time, we cannot be sure of the requirements of each region and can only estimate this need in an overall way. To break this item down by region would be merely guess work. We would seek your good advice as to how to allocate the funds without precisely earmarking them to each region.

I am confident that this program will provide the AFL-CIO, through its regional organizations, with additional means to enable affiliated American unions to cooperate with those free trade unions abroad and unionists who believe in democratic principles and strive to build strong institutions in their countries.

Sincerely yours,
Ernest S. Lee
Assistant Director
Department of International Affairs

C. Budget for the American Institute for Free Labor Development

Estimated Budget Comparisons/All Years

	1962	1963	1964	1965	1966
Washington Head-quarters	146,237	895,660	2,204,780	1,621,735	1,381,755
Washington Training Center	485,000	678,100	515,765	659,700	945,705
Argentina	—	59,500	24,000	118,260	186,440
Bolivia	—	—	75,000	191,992	244,936
Brazil—Urban	—	54,500	150,000	394,952	484,690
Brazil—Rural	—	—	—	123,400	—
British Guiana	—	—	—	—	99,410
Caribbean	—	—	—	37,350	31,400
Cen. Amer. ROCAP:	—	60,000	142,000	271,025	341,500
Costa Rica	—	—	—	10,000	62,000
El Salvador	—	—	—	15,000	30,250
Guatemala	—	—	—	12,500	30,000
Honduras	—	—	—	—	51,365
Nicaragua	—	—	—	50,000	60,000
Panama	—	—	—	15,850	30,000
Chile	—	—	55,000	248,825	330,857
Colombia	—	120,000	132,000	244,395	346,402
Dominican Republic	—	—	67,500	181,870	243,003
Ecuador	—	30,000	—	173,500	199,980
Jamaica	—	—	141,000	—	—
Mexico	—	—	—	125,000	160,800
Peru	—	60,000	156,137	235,547	332,010
Uruguay	—	—	75,000	154,760	218,971
Venezuela	50,000	62,000	—	160,000	201,760
Campesino Program C.A.	—	—	—	50,000	132,470
Total	$681,237	2,019,760	3,738,182	5,095,661	6,145,704

D. Memo to Attorney General Robert F. Kennedy: Prepared by Victor G. Reuther, Walter P. Reuther, and Joseph L. Rauh, Jr.

THE RADICAL RIGHT IN AMERICA TODAY

President Kennedy's addresses in Seattle and Los Angeles on November 16 and 18 evidenced both a deep concern with, and a profound understanding of, the serious problems injected into American life by the growing strength of the radical right. A spate of articles in responsible newspapers and periodicals reflect this same concern and understanding. Perhaps therefore this memorandum will prove but a repetition and restatement of suggestions already under consideration by the Administration. Since, however, the public discussion to date concerning the radical right has produced little in the line of suggested policies and programs for dealing with the serious problems raised, this memorandum may have some value in focusing attention upon possible Administration policies and programs to combat the radical right.

Initially, it needs to be said that far more is required in the struggle against the radical right than simply calling attention to present and potential dangers. If the Administration truly recognizes this as a serious problem, as it certainly appears to do, it is most important that President Kennedy's addresses in Seattle and Los Angeles be implemented. *Speeches without action may well only mobilize the radical right instead of mobilizing the democratic forces within our nation.* It is with this consideration in view that there is set forth below an estimate of the extent of the problem and suggested Administration policies and programs for dealing with the problem.

EXTENT OF PROBLEM

The radical right or extreme right-wing, or however it may be designated, includes an unknown number of millions of Americans of viewpoints bounded on the left by Senator Goldwater and on the right by Robert Welch. The active component of these radical right millions would, of course, be only a small fraction of the total. But, whatever may be the difficulty of ascertaining their numbers, these radical right groups are probably stronger and are almost certainly better organized than at any time in recent history. More significant yet, they are growing in strength and there is no reason to expect a turning of the tide in this regard during the foreseeable Cold War period ahead. And, possibly most significant of all, their relationship to and infiltration of the Armed Services adds a new dimension to the seriousness with which they must be viewed.

New radical right organizations have sprung up like weeds in the last few years; it is estimated by the Anti-Defamation League that almost a hundred such organizations have been organized in 1961 alone. Welch's Birch Society, Schwarz' Christian Anti-Communist Crusade, and Hargis's Christian Crusade are among the most powerful of the new groups. Benson's Harding College and National Education Program and H. L. Hunt's Life Line have earlier histories, but they have expanded along with the growth of the new groups. But all of these groups together are only part of an even larger and constantly growing movement which is well manned and even better financed. The Birch Society alone probably has a million dollars a year at its disposal; so does the Christian Crusade (which is just one of 3 Hargis ventures). The radical right as a whole — and estimating conservatively — must have twenty or more times this much on call. There are vast quantities of literature, films, and records emanating from the radical right and even such things as radical right bookshops are beginning to spring up. (General Walker gave one of these bookshops, The Bookmailer in New York, a big plug on national television December 3rd.)

The Birch Society may be the best known today. But others are equally strong and perhaps more influential. Take a look at Schwarz' Christian Anti-Communist Crusade, for example. In the Anti-Communist School he ran in St. Louis earlier this year he was backed by the St. Louis *Globe Democrat* and was sponsored by the Mayor and Chief of Police of St. Louis and both United States Senators. Governor John M. Dalton even officially proclaimed this "anti-Communism week in Missouri." The *New York Times* eye-witness report from St. Louis asserted that one of the most striking things there was "the large proportion of younger people." Schwarz' Hollywood rallies are even more disturbing than his St. Louis and other schools. His Crusade had a three-hour rally before some twelve to fifteen thousand persons in the Hollywood Bowl and an estimated four million more watched the program over television on 33 stations in six states. Actors John Wayne, James Stewart, Pat O'Brien, and George Murphy were there, as were such top "moviemakers" as Jack Warner of Warner Brothers and Y. Frank Freeman of Paramount. The gross take at the rally (plus the week's Hollywood Anti-Communist School) was $214,796. Even more significant was the presence of C. D. Jackson, a top executive of *Life* magazine. In early September *Life* had run a disparaging story about Schwarz. The kickback at *Life* was sufficient to induce Jackson to fly to Los Angeles to appear in the Hollywood Bowl and offer a public apology. Jackson told the audience, "I believe we were wrong and I am profoundly sorry. It's a great privilege to be here tonight and align Life Magazine with Senator Dodd, Representative Judd, Dr. Schwarz, and the rest of these implacable fighters against communism." Only recently the Los Angeles rallies were re-telecast in New York City for three full evening hours with the Schick Safety Razor Company picking up the tab. (Richfield Oil and Technicolor Corp., as well as Schick, appear to be regularly available to Schwarz as television sponsors.)

Take a look, too, at another one of these groups — Harding College and the National Education Program (both headed by Dr. George S. Benson). The propaganda operation, exclusive of the college, is budgeted at $200,000 a year. They produced some 30 movies of which "Communism on the Map" is the most famous and has been seen by 10 million persons. Dr. Benson's weekly column has wide distribution and one version is sent in bulk lots to a thousand business organizations. He has a monthly newsletter with 50 thousand subscribers; he has outlets in a great many Farm Bureau monthly state papers (the effect of which was seen at the recent Farm Bureau Convention). He has a series of high school study outlines in "American Citizenship Education" sent free to schools requesting them.

The Life Line Radio Program, now on about 200 radio stations (some run him twice), is planning to branch out into television. Businessmen all over the Nation are sponsoring this program. H. L. Hunt, one of the richest oil men in the country and owner of Life Line, boasts that "the Free World cannot be saved unless it is saved at a profit."

All of these radical right organizations have the same general line. The danger to America is *domestic* Communism. While their particular traitor will vary from Harry Hopkins to George Marshall, from President Truman to President Eisenhower, from Senator Fullbright to some labor leader, there is no question that anybody even slightly to the left of Senator Goldwater is suspect. They traffic in fear. Treason in high places is their slogan and slander is their weapon. They undermine loyal Americans' confidence in each other and in their government.

Their appeal is for "total victory" (note that Goldwater is with them all the way on this) and they thrive on every defeat, retreat, concession, or even negotiation. Americans feel they are "losing" for the first time in history. Since Americans intuitively tend not to believe they ever lose fairly, the radical right's charges that we are "losing" (itself a dubious assumption) because of treason in high places falls on fertile soil. In Schwarz's Southern California meetings, as shown in the New York re-telecast a couple of weeks ago, Senator Dodd's and Representative Judd's heavy-handed foreign policy polemics received little applause, but when W. Cleon Skouson (author of "The Naked Communist") charged treason in high places, the place went up in a roar of applause.

The suggestion is being made in some quarters (e.g., Reston in the *Times* of November 19, 1961) that the radical right is primarily a "Republican problem" because it utilizes money that might otherwise be available to Republican Party candidates. Former Vice President Nixon shares this view. Yet, on reflection, this would appear quite superficial. The growing strength of the radical right may indeed be an inconvenience to the Republican Party, but it is far worse than that for the Nation and the Democratic Party — for it threatens the President's program at home and abroad. By the use of the twin propaganda weapons of fear and slander, the radical right moves the national political spectrum away from the Administration's proposed liberal programs at home and abroad. By vicious local pressure campaigns against teachers or preachers or any one else who supports anything from negotiation in foreign affairs to governmental programs in domestic affairs, they frighten off support for much-needed Administration programs. Pressure tactics on already-timid Congressmen are reinforced with fanaticism and funds. The pressure campaign against the Katanga operation is only one example of what is ahead. Any hardboiled, realistic appraisal of the situation evokes this conclusion: The growing strength, organization and financial resources of the radical right is not something that can be wished away or that can be confidently ignored as a Republican problem.

ACTION ON THE PROBLEM

As the radical right cannot be wished away or ignored, likewise its demise is not something that can be readily accomplished. The struggle against the radical right is a long-term affair; total victory over the radical right is no more possible than total victory over the Communists. What are needed are deliberate Administration policies and programs to contain the radical right from further expansion and in the long run to reduce it to its historic role of the impotent lunatic fringe.*

As the radical right today feeds like a leech on the frustrations of the American people, so reducing these frustrations by accomplishments at home and abroad is the most important part of the long-range battle against the radical right. Indeed, in the long run, only democratic initiative in the world struggle against Communism will roll back the radical right to its traditional insignificance. But the Nation cannot look the other way and wait for this to happen. The radical right organizations threaten to render impossible the very steps (action *and* negotiation) that need to be taken by the Administration if our nation is to survive and succeed in the world struggle; they must never be permitted to become so strong as to obstruct action needed for democratic survival and success.

As we gird ourselves for a long struggle against world Communism, so we must gird ourselves for a long struggle against the radical right. But there are some steps which can and should be taken now to halt the growth of the radical right and possibly to turn the tide against it. There are other steps of a more long-range nature. Among the programs and policies of both types which the Administration might consider are the following:

1. *The radical right inside the Armed Services presents an immediate and special problem requiring immediate and special measures.*

The problem of radical right influences inside the Armed Services is an immediate one and made all the more so by the up-coming hearings of the Senate Armed Services Subcommittee. But even if there were no hearings, this challenge to the basic American concept of separating military personnel from partisan politics must be met now. Tolerance of such a challenge can only embolden those who do the challenging.

It has been widely reported that General Walker's radical right viewpoint is shared by a substantial number of his colleagues. One observer, Louis J. Halle, has reported that Walker's position "represents the publicly unexpressed but privately outspoken views of an important part of our American officer corps in all three services" (*New Republic*, November 20, 1961). Drew Pearson has twice reported without contradiction that a Lieutenant General has leaked secret information to Senator Thurmond in support of the Walker position. The "Americanism Seminars," espousing radical right doctrine and sponsored or co-sponsored by the Armed Services in various places, could only have been accomplished by radical right officer personnel

* Private agencies can do much, too, to identify and expose the radical right. Indeed, in the long-run the extent of participation by private agencies in this struggle is more likely to determine its outcome than anything the Government can do. The press, television, church, labor, civic, political and other groups whose constitutional freedom is directly involved must carry the prime burden in this struggle. But the purpose of this memorandum is to consider possible Administration policies and programs rather than those of private groups. Furthermore, affirmative Administration policies and programs can set the backdrop against which private activity is most likely to succeed.

within the armed forces; the spectacle of the U.S. Army sponsoring Skouson's reflection on the patriotism of Franklin Roosevelt and the loyalty of Harry Hopkins, could only have been achieved through the connivance of inside military personnel. Former top brass work with all the radical right groups. The recent experience in Algeria demonstrates that the soldiers of an army of a democratic nation may be tempted, out of frustration, to engage in anti-democratic operations; as reports from France make so abundantly clear, the radical right Generals and Admirals continue today to threaten the stability of France's democratic system.

What appears to support the position of widespread infiltration of the radical right into the Armed Services is the manner in which the Walker case was handled. Indeed, the shocking thing about the Walker case is not that his resignation was accepted in 1961, but that the Armed Services rejected his resignation in 1959 when he tried to resign because of "the fifth column conspiracy and influence in the United States" and the "conspiracy and its influences on the home front." Whether the resignation was rejected because Walker's superiors agreed with his views or simply were not shocked by them is not known; but in either event, the failure to accept his resignation constituted a dangerous tolerance of the radical right inside the Armed Services. Even worse was the action towards Walker in 1960 and early in 1961; the Army failed to act against Walker's obvious and illegal acts of "radical right politics" until public notice of Walker's offenses (brought about by a newspaper exposé) forced the Pentagon's hand. Again, it is not important why this happened; what is important is the degree of tolerance of the radical right inside the Armed Services.

It also appears to have been widespread pressure from right-wing Generals and Admirals in the Pentagon which brought about the recall to duty of General Van Fleet. It is common knowledge that General Van Fleet has himself been a member of the extreme right wing (board member of "For America"; endorser of the Florida Coalition of Patriotic Societies; Board of Advisors of H. L. Hunt's Life Line). Not only does the Pentagon pressure for the recall of General Van Fleet evidence radical right influence inside the military establishment, but it demonstrates the absolute unappeasability of this group. All that the recall has accomplished is to embarrass the Administration when Van Fleet irresponsibly attacked the Administration's Ambassador to the United Nations.

Once it is recognized that there is a serious problem of radical right infiltration of the military and that appeasement is not the answer, the indicated course of action becomes clear. The Administration must get off the defensive in the Walker case; it must shift the battleground from the defensive posture of justifying the "muzzling of Walker" to an offensive posture supporting the basic American concept of separation of military personnel from partisan politics. To shift the posture from defense to offense, consideration should be given to requesting Senator Russell to broaden the hearings to cover the problem of radical right infiltration of the Armed Services. As the Washington *Post* said on November 28th, the hearings "ought to be aimed not to determining whether General Walker and his imitators were improperly silenced by civilian authorities, but at determining how widely the infection they represent is spread in the armed services."

An alternative to getting Senator Russell to broaden the hearings would be for Secretary McNamara to start his own investigation of radical right

Generals and Admirals. Those Generals and Admirals who have lost confidence in democracy and who feel that the danger to our country is treason at home rather than the strength of the international Communist movement abroad, should be warned against political activity in any way, shape or form. This might have the effect of causing the resignation of some of these Generals and Admirals which would certainly be in the national interest. At any rate, political activity after such warning would be grounds for dismissal from the service. Above all, the suggested investigation would give courage to the officers, old and young, who believe in democracy and in a non-political democratic Army.

Then, too, Secretary McNamara should try to take the offensive at the forthcoming hearings.* Secretary McNamara certainly has the right to be the first witness at the hearings. Instead of being on the defensive concerning his muzzling of Walker, he should take the offensive by telling how action against Walker was too long delayed and how there is a serious problem in the Armed Services concerning persons who no longer believe in democracy. If, as suggested in the previous paragraph, Secretary McNamara has by that time instituted his own investigation of radical right Generals and Admirals, he should give a report of his plans in this regard. Whether or not he has instituted an investigation, he should make clear that the Defense Department's policy rejects these extreme right-wing organizations and rejects the views of those who participate in them. He should have those of the real top brass who share his views get right up behind him at the hearing and back him up. He should get the full support of the President. In this way, the hearings could be turned against those who presently plan to use them to help the right wing embarrass Secretary McNamara.

The strong posture against radical right Generals and Admirals suggested in this memorandum would go far to answer Soviet propaganda that American foreign policy is not in responsible hands and that there is a substantial "preventive war" group in the Pentagon which may ultimately get the upper hand. This strong posture would not only reassure our own allies, but might give support to factions within the Soviet Union that strive for a more flexible position on the Soviet's part.

2. *The radical right and the Attorney General's subversive list.*

The Attorney General's list of subversive organizations is lending aid and comfort to the radical right. Although the radical right poses a far greater danger to the success of this country in its battle against international Communism than does the domestic Communist movement, the latter have been branded subversive by the Government and the former have not. No one loses his job or is subjected to public obloquy because he joins one of these radical right groups; yet these groups can use the subversive list to get at liberals and moderates who twenty years earlier had joined some Communist "front" organization which looked patriotic and socially desirable. The list today is almost like a *Good Housekeeping* seal for the radical right. Whatever one's views may be toward the list, *as long as it exists* it should not remain one-sided and be permitted to work in favor of the radical right.

Under existing regulations, the Attorney General can only put an organization on the Attorney General's list if he finds, after notice and hearing,

---

* Possibly the public release at this time of the Army's interrogation of General Walker would be helpful in this regard.

that it meets the standards of the list — i.e., that the organization is "totalitarian, fascist, communist or subversive, or as having adopted a policy of advocating or approving the commission of acts of force or violence to deny others their rights under the Constitution . . . or as seeking to alter the form of government of the United States by unconstitutional means." Certain of the radical right organizations may well meet one or more of these criteria. For example, the Birch Society appears to advocate the denial of constitutional rights by force and openly seeks to substitute some other form of society for existing democratic forms; to it democracy is "merely a deceptive phrase, a weapon of demagoguery, and a perpetual fraud." Three of the best known radical right groups are predicated upon secrecy: the Birch Society keeps its members secret; Hargis, head of the Christian Crusade, has announced plans for a secret fraternity with Greek letters; and the Minutemen which conduct guerrilla warfare maneuvers also keeps its members secret. Then, too, Birch operates on a monolithic or totalitarian system within the organization and other radical right groups may also so operate. These organizations have succeeded in promoting disaffection and, as in the case of General Walker, outright rebellion in the Army. There would thus appear to be adequate grounds for holding a hearing on one or more of these organizations to determine whether they should be listed. It might therefore be advisable for the Attorney General to announce at this time that he is going to investigate one or more of these organizations with a view to determining whether charges will be filed and hearings held on the question of listing one or more of these organizations. The mere act of indicating that an investigation will be made will certainly bring home to many people something they have never considered — the subversive character of these organizations and their similarity to the listed groups on the left. To make this announcement before the hearings of the Armed Services Committee on the muzzling of General Walker might well be an additional way to take the offensives against Senator Thurmond and the radical right.

It is not known the extent to which the Federal Bureau of Investigation has planted undercover agents inside the radical right movement as it has inside the Communist Party and its allied organizations. If it has already done so, the information would be readily available upon which to draw up charges for a hearing against one or more of the radical right groups. If the Bureau has not as yet infiltrated these organizations, a longer time will of course be necessary to obtain the information for the charges, although much of the needed information is available through public sources. In any event, the announcement of the investigation would have an immediate salutary effect and the later announcement of the hearing or hearings might have an even greater one. It is not unlikely that these groups will refuse information and otherwise act towards the Attorney General's procedures just exactly as the Communists have acted in the past. Nothing could better reveal to the public the true nature of these groups than defiant resistance to their government.

3. *The flow of big money to the radical right should be dammed to the extent possible.*

The growing power of radical right propagandists and groups is directly related to their expanding ability to secure large sums of money. As funds are a source of power to the radical right, action to dam up these funds may be the quickest way to turn the tide now running in their favor.

Benson's National Education Program, Schwarz' Christian Anti-Communist Crusade, Hargis' Christian Crusade and William Volker Fund, Inc., are among the radical right groups which are reported to have federal tax exemptions. It would appear highly doubtful, to say the least, that any or all of these groups properly qualifies for a federal tax exemption. Prompt revocation in a few cases might scare off a substantial part of the big money now flowing into these tax exempt organizations.*

Then, too, corporate funds are used to put radical right views on the air for political rather than business reasons; propaganda is peddled far and wide under the guise of advertising. H. L. Hunt openly urges big business not to rely on contributions to finance the radical right but to use their advertising funds. The Internal Revenue Service some time ago banned certain propaganda ads by electrical utilities as deductible expenses. Consideration might be given to the question whether the broadcast and rebroadcast of Schwarz' Christian Anti-Communist Crusade rallies and similar rallies and propaganda of other groups is not in the same category.

A related question is that of free radio and television time for the radical right. Hargis' Christian Crusade has its messages reproduced by 70 radio stations across the country as public service features and Mutual Broadcasting System apparently gave him a special rate for network broadcasts. In Washington, D. C., radio station WEAM currently offers the "Know Your Enemy" program at 8:25 P.M., six days a week as a public service; in program No. 97 of this series the commentator advised listeners that Gus Hall of the Communist Party had evoked a plan for staffing the Kennedy Administration with his followers and that the plan was being carried out with success. Certainly the Federal Communications Commission might consider examining into the extent of the practice of giving free time to the radical right and could take measures to encourage stations to assign comparable time for an opposing point of view on a free basis. Incidentally, in the area of commercial (not free) broadcasting, there is now pending before the FCC, Cincinnati Station WLW's conduct in selling time to Life Line but refusing to sell time for the UAW program, "Eye Opener."

In addition to possible misuse of federal tax exemptions and the misuse of corporate funds for propaganda advertising, it seems not unlikely that corporation funds are flowing into the radical right in other and covert ways. The President of Schick Razor Company, for example, has made it clear that "Dr. Schwarz will not lack for money while I'm around." And, finally, there is the big question whether Schwarz, Hargis, etc., are themselves complying with tax laws.

Adequate information on the financing of the radical right can only come from the inside of these organizations. As already indicated, it is not known whether the Federal Bureau of Investigation has undercover agents inside these organizations in the same manner and to the same degree as the Bureau has inside the Communist Party and other left-wing groups. Similarly, it is not known what the Treasury Department has done in the way of undercover operations to get at tax violations in the financing of these organizations. Likewise, it is not known whether the Federal Communications

---

* An additional suggestion in this regard might be considered. This would be the feasibility of including in the publicly available files of these tax exempt organizations, their annual receipts and expenditures reports which can now be obtained only with great difficulty.

Commission has ever assembled information on the degree to which the radical right is getting free time without comparable expression of the opposing point of view. Certainly, there is sufficient public information indicating possible tax violations in this area and possible violations of FCC policies to justify the most complete check on these various means of financing the radical right.

4. *The Administration should take steps to end the Minutemen.*

Free speech is the essence of democracy, but armed bands are not the exercise of free speech. There is no warrant for permitting groups to organize into military cadres for the purpose of taking the law into their own hands.

It is not known whether the Minutemen will grow or whether they will fade out of the picture. They do, however, represent a dangerous precedent in our democracy. Consideration should be given to the question whether they are presently violating any Federal laws and, if not, to the Federal Government calling a conference of States where the Minutemen exist to see what action could be taken under state laws. There is, of course, the additional possibility, as indicated earlier, that the Minutemen might fall within the terms of the Attorney General's list of subversive organizations.

5. *The domestic Communist problem should be put in proper perspective for the American people, thus exposing the basic fallacy of the radical right.*

The radical right feeds upon charges of treason, traitors and treachery. It has its roots in a very real sense in the belief of the American people that domestic Communism has succeeded in betraying America and threatens its very survival. Putting the domestic Communist problem in proper perspective would do much to expose the basic fallacy of the radical right.

The Administration has inherited an extremely difficult problem and posture in this area. Executive and legislative speechwriters have automatically maximized the domestic Communist menace ever since World War II. The Director of the Federal Bureau of Investigation, Mr. Hoover, although he made an admirable recent statement concerning the radical right, exaggerates the domestic Communist menace at every turn and thus contributes to the public's frame of mind upon which the radical right feeds. Assistant Attorney General J. Walter Yeagley, who continues in charge of internal security matters, has always maximized the domestic Communist menace. There is grave danger that the upcoming legal battle between the Department of Justice and the Communist Party over registration (particularly if there are additional indictments of individuals) will itself fan these same flames.

Each Administration since World War II has maximized the Communist problem. It will therefore be no easy task for the Administration to turn the corner and take a different attitude. But action along this line is necessary to contain and in the long-run to roll back the radical right. Without minimizing the Communist Party strength or potential in the thirties and forties, it has no capacity today to endanger our national security or defeat our national policies. There is no need for a further effort to dramatize the domestic Communist issue; the need now is to rein in those who have created the unreasoned fear of the domestic Communist movement in the minds of the American people and slowly to develop a more rational attitude toward the strength of this movement: Without forbidding dissenting officials from expressing a contrary viewpoint (and thus evoking charges of muzzling

Hoover, etc.), an effort to take a more realistic view of domestic Communism by the leaders of the Administration would probably cause most of the Administration officials to fall into line and even some legislators might be affected thereby. Fifteen years of overstating a problem cannot be reversed overnight, but thoughtful handling can reduce tensions and misconceptions in this area, too.

It would be the easier course to look the other way and say that the radical right will disappear when we solve our problems at home and abroad. But the radical right may, if it is not contained, make it more difficult, if not impossible, to solve our problems at home and abroad.

Efforts to deal with radical right Generals and Admirals and Minutemen, investigation to determine whether to list radical right organizations, efforts to dam the illegal flow of money in their direction, efforts to set the domestic Communist problem in perspective — all will evoke immediate charges of softness on Communism. But this is not a problem that can be swept under the rug. The Administration can no more combat the radical right by being "tough on domestic Communism" or appeasing radical right Generals than the Republican Administration was able to fight McCarthyism by its own excesses in this area. It is very late in the day to start dealing with these problems, but it will never get earlier.

INDEX

Index